Planets in Astrology

The Ultimate Guide to Chiron, Pluto, Uranus, Saturn, Mercury, Venus, Jupiter, Neptune, the Moon, and Sun

Your Free Gift (only available for a limited time)

Thanks for getting this book! If you want to learn more about various spirituality topics, then join Mari Silva's community and get a free guided meditation MP3 for awakening your third eye. This guided meditation mp3 is designed to open and strengthen ones third eye so you can experience a higher state of consciousness. Simply visit the link below the image to get started.

https://spiritualityspot.com/meditation

Contents

Part 1: Chiron in Astrology

The Ultimate Guide to the Wounded Healer

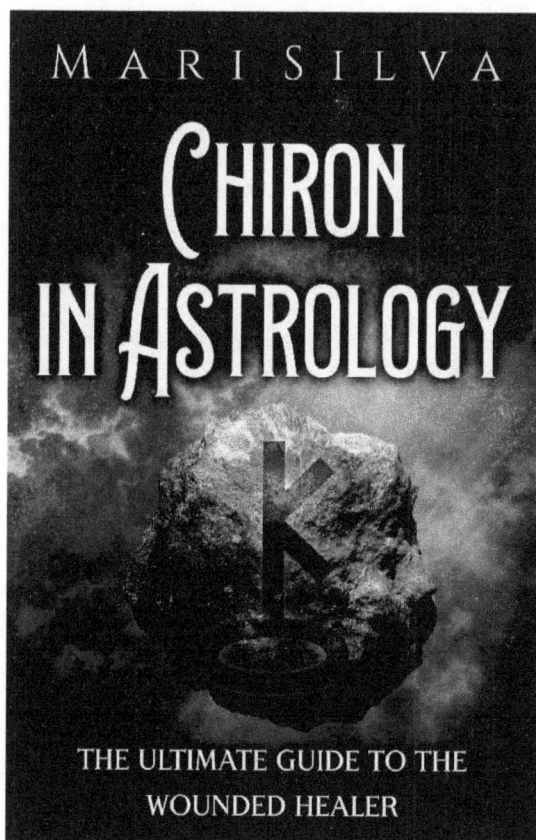

Introduction

Chiron is a fascinating heavenly body that shows us why we continue to experience painful patterns over and over, no matter what we do differently to address them. It reveals our core wounds that always keep us from feeling love and compassion for ourselves and make it terribly hard to forgive ourselves.

When you cannot feel compassion or empathy for yourself or others around you, it keeps you in a state of stagnancy, so no matter what you do, you can't create the life you desire. You can't live your dreams. You are merely stuck in the same place, day after day.

This book will teach you how to work with Chiron to discover your soul-level wounds and heal them so that you do not have to keep repeating the same patterns that bring you pain and suffering. Unlike other books on this subject, you will find that this is an easy read, even for beginners. You'll receive hands-on instructions on how to find and release your wounds so that you can forgive yourself. You'll also learn how to find it within you to not only forgive others but help them on their journey of discovering their wounds.

Within the pages of this book, you will discover the intricate connection between your personal psychology and your astrology. Working with Chiron, you will uncover how your deepest wounds are connected to the most significant challenges in your life. More than that, you'll bring your unconscious patterns of thought and action to light to effectively heal and send them through self-forgiveness and empathy. You'll discover why you keep sabotaging yourself in business, love, or other endeavors. You'll also learn how to set yourself free, so you can shoot for whatever heights you please.

As you discover your Chiron placement in this book, you will learn what you hide or edit because of your deep-rooted fear of rejection. We keep things from others because we worry about not being accepted by the people we hold dear. You'll now read about the potential and power Chiron has to heal you completely, so you no longer react to the world in negative and disempowering ways.

Have you ever felt like something is holding you back from success, keeping you from being your best self? Or have you wondered why you continue to throw a wrench in the works every time you draw close to your ideals in love, business, or relationships? You will find the answers within this book. They will show you the way to freedom, healing, power, and love.

Right now, self-forgiveness might seem impossible to you. Still, as you read and implement what you learn, you will experience undeniable transformation in your life.

Feel free to use this information to help yourself, a loved one, or a friend. In addition, refer to this book in your professional practice if you need a handy reference that could help your clients on their healing journeys.

Chapter 1: A Mythological Background of Chiron

Chiron's Story: From Wounded to Healer

The Greek mythology of Chiron, the wounded healer, holds essential lessons for us. These lessons help us make sense of why things happen the way they do and the value of pain and suffering.

Son of the sea nymph Philyra and the titan Cronus (Saturn), Chiron was the immortal god of healing and a centaur. Centaurs are creatures that have the lower bodies of horses and upper bodies of men. However, this god had the front legs of a human, which was one of the features that set him above the other centaurs.

Traditionally, centaurs were bloodthirsty and given to savagery. However, Chiron wasn't anything like that. He was very civilized, did not drink, and never gave in to lust. While other centaurs were born from the union of Nephele and Ixion, Chiron had a different lineage. Cultured and restrained, Zeus's half-brother was always depicted in clothes, whereas the other centaurs were naked.

His father, Cronus, knew he was going to be overthrown by one of his children. Thus, to avoid that, he made sure to devour all of them. Rhea, his wife, took their sixth son, Zeus, and hid him on the island of Crete. Cronus searched the heavens and Earth for him until he came upon Philyra, an Oceanid, and lusted after her.

To remain hidden from Rhea, he had taken on the form of a stallion, and in this form, he forced himself on Philyra. This rape led to Philyria giving birth in a lot of pain. The child was Chiron. When she saw that his upper body was a man's, and his lower body a horse's, she was overcome with disgust and shame at the sight of him. Of course, it did not help that she was raped. All of this caused her to abandon him in Thessaly, on Mound Pellion.

Fortunately, Apollo found Chiron and took him under his wing. He taught him everything about prophecy, music, and the healing arts. Chiron did excellently well in all fields, to the point where many began to seek him out as a teacher. His knowledge of health and medicine was unparalleled.

From Artemis (Apollo's twin sister), Chiron learned about hunting and archery and did marvelously. Some say this centaur is the inventor of medicine, surgery, and pharmacy. It makes sense to assume that, since etymologically, Chiron is from the Greek word kheir, which means "skilled with the hands" or "hand." This word also has connections to the English word "surgeon," originally from kheir *and* ergon, which, put together, means "hand worker."

With time, Chiron became the go-to guy to learn from. He had the perfect temperament for teaching and was very knowledgeable. Among his students are great heroes like Theseus, Perseus, Ajax the Great, Patroclus, Jason, and Achilles. He had a close bond with Achilles since he had given his father, Peleus, some sound advice for wooing his mother, Thetis.

Coronis, the Thessalian princess, was pregnant by Apollo. During her pregnancy, she let Ischys—a mortal—seduce her. So, Artemis murdered Coronis and her family by raining arrows on them. Somehow, Apollo performed the very first cesarean section on record and rescued their unborn child. He handed this child over to Chiron to raise. This child is the god of medicine, Asclepius, whom Chiron himself taught.

Hercules (also known as Herakles) was on a mission to capture the prized Erymanthian boar; this was his fourth labor. At this time, he visited Pholus, so Pholus opened some wine that had been gifted to him by Dionysus. Its aroma was so intense that it quickly drew the attention of other centaurs and sent them into a killing frenzy. Hercules did his best to defend the cave, firing arrows with tips dipped in the Lernaean hydra's blood from his second labor. Unfortunately, one of those arrows struck the refined centaur. It was an accident. Chiron and Hercules were friendly, but he was caught in the crossfire and got hit.

Chiron was immortal and beyond death. Thus, the poison moved through him, not killing him but creating indescribable pain. Though he was a master of healing, he could not heal himself. The pain became too much to bear, so he finally chose to trade his immortality for Prometheus's freedom. Prometheus had stolen fire and gifted it to humankind, and as punishment, he was bound to a rock. Each day, an eagle would peck out his liver. Since he was immortal, too, his liver would just grow back overnight, only to be pecked out again. So, Chiron chose to make something good out of his pain by setting Prometheus free. When he died, Zeus made good on his word to free Prometheus. He then set Chiron in the sky as the Centaurus, or Sagittarius constellation.

Chiron's Pain and Sacrifice

Chiron is the epitome of our most fatal flaws and deepest cuts. He represents that part of the human psyche that we lug around within our subconscious minds that weighs us down. He is whatever you carry within you that brings you a world of grief and misery because you do not allow yourself to heal by letting go.

What are these wounds? You know them all too well: insecurity, low self-esteem, self-hatred, the unwillingness or inability to forgive yourself for past wrongs. Our stories may differ, but we all share the same wounds in our core. We all have the same desire to understand where we fit in life precisely and how we are supposed to surmount all the obstacles that face us to reach the heights of success.

For some reason, many of us come into the world with these flaws. It is part of what makes us human. We have two options when it comes to dealing with these imperfections: We could let those deep gashes in our psyche act like an anchor around our neck and sink us in suffering or choose to rise above our doubts and base instincts to live a life full of joy. When you permit Chiron to move on, you will find that those same flaws and wounds within you will become your greatest strengths.

If you are born with Chiron at powerful positions on your natal chart, chances are you suffer more than others. You have many psychological wounds in your subconscious that affect you more than you might be willing to admit.

Chiron's Sufferings: A Mirror of Your Own

You take things personally. More than others do. Hercules's poisoned arrow was not even meant for Chiron, yet it not only struck him but caused him prolonged pain. You are reading this now, so you can probably relate to this. Someone says or does something insensitive, giving little thought to how you feel. They move on, but you're still hurting from the pain of their actions.

Some people can take a hit and keep moving. Any criticism they get is given about as much attention as a passing housefly. However, this is not who you are. You are not wired just to shrug off what people say. If you have low self-esteem and insecurity as your wounds, those harsh words spoken to you feel like death by a million cuts, and for a good reason.

Choosing to become introspective and practice mindfulness can teach you that there is no reason to allow people to have that sort of power over you. You can feel the sting, but you do not need to hold on to it. Instead, you can take back your power and be a great blessing to the people around you. Why? You know what it is like to be truly, deeply hurt. You know what it's like to have those hurtful words and memories of betrayal bouncing all over your head like a million ping-pong balls.

Thus, when you choose to heal yourself, you become very empathetic and compassionate to others. This, in turn, activates the godlike healing power within you, so you can help others treat their wounds. Having been through the wringer, you have the sensitivity most people lack, allowing you to understand precisely how others suffer.

Many people are in a never-ending tug of war with their psychological and emotional trauma that tinges everything they do. They have been betrayed and dismissed by family and friends emotionally stronger than they are. They've been disrespected their whole lives. They go through genuine pain. Maybe you can relate to this. The thing is, while the pain feels unmistakably present, its cause is not real. When you understand this, you are well on your way to setting yourself free, just like Chiron did.

The cause of the pain is only as real and powerful as you allow it to be. The beautiful thing about helping people come to this realization is that you will find your pain is not pointless. It showed you how to heal yourself, and with that knowledge, you can heal others. As you choose to make your sacrifice, you, like Chiron, will have played your part in teaching the lost and broken of humanity how to heal themselves.

Chiron's Major Symbols and What They Teach Us

We are the cause of our suffering. That is a terribly bitter pill to swallow, but accepting this is the first step to taking back your power. While it may appear that others are firing poisoned arrows at us, the truth is that we are the ones who let them. Healing begins with learning to be responsible for picking yourself up and cleaning your wounds. You can only blame everyone else for so long.

Chiron chose to give up being immortal. There is heavy symbolism in his decision. One of the hardest things anyone could do is let go of all illusions about being immortal and untouchable. However, it is okay to be honest with yourself and others around you. It's okay to say, "That really hurt me." When you speak up about your pain, you give others the chance to realize how much they are putting you through. Sometimes, they do not even know they have been hurting you. So, like Chiron, we must come to terms with the truth about how we feel; this is how to take charge of the recovery process.

Another thing we can glean from Chiron's story is that he had to give up something that was most precious to him. He had to let go of one of the things that he thought made up his entire self to end the pain. Now, ask yourself: What is it you need to give up for your suffering to heal? It is different for everyone. Maybe you think you need to be everyone's rock, and so you cannot afford to let yourself seem vulnerable, even though you badly want someone to hold your hand and tell you that you will be just fine. Or it could be that you consider the image of superiority and have worked so long and hard to build it, so it's too precious to let go. It could also be that all your life, you've just felt like you are constantly competing against everyone else.

The thing about competition is that someone has to lose so someone else can win. A better way of living would be to create a spirit of cooperation in all facets of our lives. Do this, and you will find that you are always on the winning side because there are only winners. It cannot be stressed enough how much you have to let go of the need to be better than the next person. There is nothing as liberating as not caring about the status quo, what others think about you, and the opinions you hold about yourself and everyone else. As you cut these anchors loose from your mind, you'll find it has room to see you for who you really are versus who you wish you were. The second you attain this level of self-awareness is when you will break free of the pain that haunts you.

Let us get back to Chiron. He was better than the other centaurs, who only engaged in sex, drugs, and Greek mythology "rock and roll." His interests lay with higher realms of existence and the art of healing. In a cruel twist of irony, Chiron was attacked by his own kind because they smelled the wine, a thing of pleasure for them that caused them to attack mindlessly. Their addictions led to needless deaths, and, in the same way, our mental attachments and addictions kill us softly each day.

Suppose we do not get rid of these toxic thoughts and attitudes toward ourselves. In that case, we risk being attacked unexpectedly by the people we hold near and dear to us. It is not because they want to, but because our assumptions about ourselves and others draw hurtful actions and words out of them.

The last thing a wounded healer needs is to be hurt by those who do not know what it is like to be wounded, to have to heal themselves, and stand in the gap for other souls in deep pain. Sadly, that is what tends to happen. The wounded healer is a spiritual teacher and is often made fun of by others, receiving cutting criticism. There is much persecution that comes with having Chiron's influence in your life. Still, if you allow yourself, you will see that other people's opinions and thoughts about you are theirs alone. Those opinions do not necessarily reflect the truth about who you are.

To be clear, the path you walk is not an easy one, but on it, you will find your greatest strengths and the blessings that lie hidden in every challenge you face along your journey. You would be hard pressed to find a stronger being than a wounded one who has learned to heal themselves.

Twice Wounded

Chiron was not just wounded in the cave. He was also emotionally wounded at the start of his life before he even had a chance. He was the product of rape, and both his parents rejected him. Through no fault of his own, he had a monstrous body and was orphaned.

Chiron is very symbolic of the human psyche, being part man and part animal. He is the epitome of the struggle within us between the profound and the profane, reason and animal instincts. The contrast between the savage Dionysian centaurs and the orderly Apollonian one also shows the conflict. Still, Chiron surpasses even the god of light. He mastered all he was taught and took things further in the sciences and arts—all to make up for being unwanted. He wanted to show himself and others that he deserved acceptance and love as much as anyone else.

His affinity for the art of healing was a way for him to heal himself and others around him. The thing he sought and needed the most, he gave to others. He did not let the first wound fester and turn into something worse; instead, he let it motivate him to achieve greatness. He let it give him purpose, a sense of duty and service that enriched his life so much it set him apart from the other centaurs. He was broken, but through the cracks, the light entered him and radiated from him.

When you choose to see the opportunities in your problems, you will empower yourself. You will attain heights of greatness you never thought possible, and you'll heal yourself. You'll welcome every experience, good, bad, or neutral, knowing that everything you go through is a chance to grow and become more than you ever thought you could. It is not so much a matter of becoming great; it's more that you discover just how much more there is to your life.

Chiron's final wound was caused by Hercules, who represents his superego, in the process of fighting the centaurs, which represent his identity. Rather than allow the darkness to swallow him, Hercules fights desperately. In the process, he hurts himself and others, as well as his dear friend

Chiron. In very much the same way, we battle each day to be the best versions of ourselves, whatever we think that looks like.

This immortal centaur chose to sacrifice his life for another god who was wounded, just like him. In the process, Prometheus got freedom and authentic, permanent healing. This is the purpose of pain and suffering, self-healing, and through that process, healing a world of wounded souls.

Chapter 2: From Mythology to Astrology

Astrological Meanings of Chiron's Symbols

In astrology today, Chiron represents the karmic wounds that lie deep within our subconscious. You do not carry these wounds for no reason; you have a purpose, and that is to heal all of them.

On November 1, 1977, American astronomer Charles T. Kowal discovered Chiron, a planetoid just like a comet. He spotted it in photos that were shot at the Palomar Observatory, San Diego, California. It was the first and largest object of its kind in the centaur class. Objects in this class have unstable orbits. At first, it was classed as a minor planet and an asteroid called 2060 Chiron. Now, it is a comet and a minor planet with the designation 95P/Chiron.

With a highly elliptical orbit spanning 51 years, Chiron moves through Uranus and Saturn. It moves quickly through some astrological signs like Libra but takes its sweet time through other signs like Aries. Astrologically, you can reveal your wounds that keep causing recurring problems, themes, and issues by pinpointing where Chiron is placed on your natal chart. Then, you can deal with the patterns and challenges to bring a permanent, lasting solution.

Chiron is in charge of relationships and healing and teaches us to reach our grandest potential. His emblem is a metaphor for holistic wisdom and understanding. When Chiron becomes active due to transits and progressions, you will experience things that force you to face what you need to heal in this world full of beauty and pain. All the sufferings and sorrows of your past lives become active and rise to the surface, not because the universe is a sadist but so that you can resolve them. There is no mistaking these experiences. They will shake you to your core and force you to wake up. The only way you'll remain asleep is if you stop the process with drugs or alcohol, bury yourself with work, or have sex compulsively.

Your character determines how Chiron affects you, and you can get a sense of this using your birth chart. For instance, if Chiron is in Mars for you, you tend to resort to violent and aggressive behavior to avoid dealing with the pain. If it is in Venus, you will use pleasure to dull it. If it's in the Moon, you'll probably give yourself to alcohol or drugs. Jupiter would lead you toward gambling, and Saturn would cause you to bury yourself in an avalanche of work.

Chiron and Saturn

Chiron was the result of a terrible thing Cronus or Saturn did. Yet, despite that, Chiron's birth turned out to be a blessing for one and all. Even in death, he did well, which shows that good can be found even in suffering. As Chiron brought meaning and purpose to Saturn's atrocious behavior, the wounded healer can bring meaning and purpose to others, even in the face of challenges and suffering.

You have a strong sense of empathy and are very sensitive to other people's limitations and wounds. These qualities will help others figure out how to begin their journey of growth and healing if you let them. For example, suppose Saturn had Chiron the respectable way; in that case, Chiron might never have felt the need to overcome anything because there would be little to no adversity, and he would have nothing to prove.

In the same way, these people you hold in contempt can teach you how to take responsibility for your life. You can use their undesirable behavior to help you discipline your mind, never to define yourself by their opinions. Also, a disciplined mind will allow you to heal yourself and learn how to let the poisoned arrows bounce off you like water off a duck's back. Begin now to put your struggles and hardships into the proper perspective, and you will come into your own. You'll discover the power that lies within you.

Chiron shows us that you can find deep meaning in the traumatic experiences of your past. It may not be immediately apparent because you are blinded by the pain you hold on to. However, the second you let it go, you'll see why things played out the way they did.

Astrologically, Chiron plays a significant role. He shows us our weakest points, or Achilles' heel if you will. While Chiron is usually linked to Saturn because they both involve suffering and pain, they are not the same.

Saturn is restrictive, keeping us in very tight binds that cause nothing but sorrow, despair, and misery. On the other hand, Chiron is delicate. Chiron is about transformation through pain and suffering, helping us bring light to our weaknesses and vulnerabilities and healing our wounds in the process. Chiron is a healer, a connector between Saturn and Uranus.

Where Saturn restricts us, Uranus works to destroy all forms, shocking us awake, setting us up for Saturn to begin its restrictive process all over again. Chiron works to mitigate the effects both planets have on our lives, ensuring we always get the gift from the pain and come out stronger and wiser than ever.

Chiron's Periodic Cycle

The Chiron Cycle is a critical astrological life cycle made up of a wounding and healing process over a series of stages. You can map out the cycle as it makes its journey around your horoscope. Along this journey, you have specific experiences that make you into the fullest, grandest version of yourself.

Chiron's orbit around our sun takes about 50 years. However, its orbit is elliptical, causing the planet to spend different durations across the signs. We all go through Chiron's Return when we hit 50, but the first sextile can happen anytime between ages three and sixteen. It all comes down to where Chiron lies on our natal chart. These are the ages for the Chiron Cycle's major transits:

1. The first square: 5 to 23.

2. The opposition: 13 to 37.

3. The second square: 27 to 44.

4. The return: 50 to 51.

Since there is so much variation in the ages for the earlier transits, it is a tough cookie trying to interpret what stage you are at. Still, some general guidelines can help. For instance, do not interpret Chiron the way you would the other planets, but based on your personal experience. Then you can observe your life to see how it all fits together. Chiron is all about the journey to your true self, so it only makes sense that the transits it makes would differ from person to person.

Also, recall that healing is not unique to Chiron, so you cannot pinpoint any one section of the horoscope since everything is connected. It helps if you understand the Chiron Cycle, but actual healing requires that you use your whole chart, focusing on what you glean from it through your Chiron placement.

Chiron's cycle shows you how to move toward being a whole individual by helping you see the gifts wrapped up by your wounds. Chiron transits and experiences will give you the golden opportunities to heal yourself, even though you experience them through the wounding of your ego. It might take a while before you are prepared to unwrap your gift, and that comes down to the way your Chiron Cycle connects with the rest of the major transits and changes in your life.

Let us talk about the process of becoming a mature grown-up, for instance. This process is handled by the Saturn Cycle. The first square of this cycle is at age seven. Say the first Chiron square takes place before age seven. It will very likely be a period of wounding and unhappiness that will cause you problems later. The earlier Chiron transits usually play out in the form of wounding at the hands of others. Whatever the case may be, these early wounds are likely to show up again throughout the cycle. They play out not in the sense that the same thing occurs, but you encounter the same archetypes, psychologically speaking, so you can be better at healing.

Just because you do not experience the first square of your Chiron's cycle until after the age range mentioned does not mean you will not experience it at all. Actually, the later it comes for you, the more wounded and alone you'll feel. This can happen because you have Chiron on your chart in a sign that is very far from the sun—the furthest point being in Aries. As a result, you are likely to feel completely abandoned by life, with no one to help you deal with your wounds. Still, do not despair. You will definitely find the motivation you need to pick yourself up again.

Each Chiron transit marks significant events in your life, turning points where everything you have ever known is different now. They give you many opportunities to connect with your true self and allow your most profound nature to manifest. They lead you to spiritual awakening (this depends on what age you have them). However, you might forget these experiences or repress them, no matter how transcendent they are, especially if you get no validation from people around you.

Since the Chiron Cycle maps out your personal awakening, you will notice patterns that run through the transits. Keep an eye out for the major ones that happen at hard angles, such as the conjunction, square, and opposition. Trines and sextiles matter, too. Now let us dive into each portion of the cycle.

The First Chiron Sextile: You experience this between ages three and sixteen, so all its effects are unconscious. You become aware of what is going on later in the cycle, close to the time of opposition. If you are old enough and have some autonomy over your life at this point, you might find your purpose in life or the chance to heal. This is when you get into new interests and hobbies critical to your future.

The First Chiron Square: This occurs anytime between ages five and twenty-three. Depending on how old you are, it could be the first time you are aware of your wounds. The experiences you have will serve as reinforcements to your first wound, though you might not quite grasp the hidden meaning yet. If you become aware of them, you will be powerfully driven to heal, even though you have no idea how.

At this time, you can have spiritual experiences or sudden awakenings, negative or positive, which show you that there is more to life than meets the eye. Unfortunately, you will most likely only make sense of them much later in the cycle. What happens in this square can be so shocking for most that they forget all about it. It is when you realize that there is more to you than just your physical body. Real-life seems fake, especially if your whole focus before now has been on the material. If you have had prior experience with the spiritual world before now, it might not be as shocking to you.

The level of shock can also depend on how connected you are to the transpersonal planets on your birth chart. For instance, you might already have the sensation of being "out of Eden," knowing you belong somewhere beyond the physical. This first square transit would then serve to push you to reestablish a conscious connection with your divinity.

The First Chiron Trine: This happens when you are between ages eight and twenty-nine. Just like the first sextile, it invites you to heal yourself. You might encounter people like mentors, friends, healers, and teachers who will give you bits and pieces of the puzzle to create the solutions you seek or help you find your actual purpose in life. You will start to realize why you're here and the true significance of your wound (depending on your age, of course).

The Chiron Opposition: Between ages thirteen and thirty-seven, you experience the Chiron opposition. Your experiences at this time depend on your awareness of your wounds before now. It is the peak of the Chiron's cycle and will give you insight into your life's meaning. It will reflect your experience in the first square and offer you a lovely chance to heal even more.

At this point, you can see your wounds better and even start to grasp the way they have helped with your awakening. Finally, you come face-to-face with your shadow self and accept it so that you can balance light and dark and become whole. If everything works out as it should, you will find the gift in your wound.

Chiron's opposition comes before Uranus's opposition in midlife. Thus, if you have not begun healing yet, and you are running from your wounds, Uranus will probably push you into crisis by your late 30s or early 40s. So, you must make the conscious decision right now to work with your wounds so that your experience of the Uranus opposition will gift you more healing and awakening.

The Second Chiron Trine: Expect this to come between ages twenty-one and forty-two. It is like the first and can come before, after, or while you are experiencing the Uranus opposition. It means time is of the essence, and what happens will depend on whether you have been mindful about working with your cycle. You could meet people who will accelerate your healing or experience circumstances that shift you closer to your purpose than ever before.

The Second Chiron Square: This square will happen between the ages of twenty-seven and forty-four. It could also be any time before, after, or during the Uranus opposition. Its outcome is entirely dependent on timing and how you have handled the previous transits, and your level of self-awareness.

Whatever is yet to be healed will definitely come up and demand your attention. If this occurs after the Uranus opposition, you will be able to hold your own well. If it comes before it, expect that you have much unfinished business to work with. If it happens simultaneously, you will have an intense experience. Still, the healing and insight you come away with will be equally profound.

This is the chance for you to get in touch with your soul again to manifest your authentic self. You are never more joyful than when you're who you were meant to be. When you try to match society's expectations of you, you lose that joy and your sense of purpose. This is the perfect time to recommit to being an individual, to walk the road less traveled. The rewards you will reap from carving out your path are worth it. If you have not done that at this point, you will become acutely aware of how you have betrayed yourself. Do not let this get you down. The fact is, you know now, and it is never too late to start your journey to your true self.

The Second Chiron Sextile: This transit is like the first sextile and offers you more healing opportunities. By this point, you are much more conscious of what you're doing. You might find your creative faculties taking on more profound, more vast qualities. You will definitely get to know more people who contribute to your growth and healing.

Chiron Return: The entire cycle ends with the return, which you should expect at age 50 or 51. You already know that the way this plays out depends on if you have been conscious about creating a whole, healed version of yourself. At this point, the levels of consciousness you can manifest are absolutely phenomenal.

The process largely depends on your individuation path and how far you are willing to walk down it. Some people want to be spiritual masters, and some do not. You don't have to—unless your soul demands it of you. Then, you will know what is right for you.

The essence of the entire Chiron cycle is healing, wholeness, and self-acceptance. The way to attain these three things will be different for each person. Fire is light and power. It is essential to all for life, you could say, as the sun is a great big glowing ball of fire, and that is how our food grows. The planets orbit around it, and we plan our lives around its rising and setting. Prometheus brought this fire to humankind and was wounded for daring to share this power. However, thanks to Chiron, he was set free and healed completely. This justified Prometheus's decision to share divinity with mortality, making his constant wounding a worthy, noble thing to have experienced.

For this reason, you should embrace Chiron's cycle. Learn to work with it, to look right at your wounds, to love yourself well enough to peel back the scabs and grab the gifts within. Do this, and you will set your soul free.

Chapter 3: Karmic Debts and Wounds of the Soul

What Are Karmic Debts?

The universe is a wondrous place that works in ways we do not fully understand yet. While we may not truly know its ways, we know that it is essentially energy in motion. Whether positive, negative, or neutral, we all have that energy swirling around and through us. We are a part of it, too. Sometimes, the most random things happen. We cannot figure out why, and they have no immediately discernible meaning—if any. Here is something to chew on, though: What if it all means something and there is no randomness to it? What if all the seemingly insignificant stuff you have never really looked at is by design?

There is so much more to life than what we do or who we are. Our past and future are very relevant to how things play out for us—and by past, this is not referring to this present incarnation of yours alone. Whether you know it or not, there's a plan for you. This plan has been in motion before you took your first breath, way before you were even conceived. To know where it leads, you need to hold yourself accountable for your present actions and all you have done in your past life.

This brings us to the subject of karmic debt. Karmic debt is a concentration of negative energy due to the wrong things you did in your previous lives. For example, you may have hurt someone or ruined many lives by making an unnecessary selfish choice. Thus, when you passed on, that negative energy or karma was attached to you, and you could pay your debts in the next incarnation.

It may seem weird, and it may feel unfair, especially if you think you have been doing your best to make good choices for one and all. However, it is how the universe maintains balance. On your return to Earth, you take all that negative karma with you. You may not be aware of it now, but not knowing does not mean you get a free pass from paying up. Suppose you decide to live consciously, do good, and follow your soul's calling moment by moment. In that case, you will accrue positive karma, which will make up for your wrongs.

How Do I Know I Have Karmic Debt?

Have you noticed that you have been struggling a lot in life? Do whole groups of people always victimize you? Maybe you are always stuck in one financial issue after another, not having enough to take care of yourself. It could be that you have the wrong friends and relationships, and they wind up destroying or betraying you. Or you might have a complete lack of excitement for life. If you are aware that these troubles are recurrent in your life, they could very well be on account of your karmic debt.

Reincarnation and Karma

Have you ever had the feeling of going through a moment before? Or déjà vu when you go someplace new? Or lifelong closeness to someone you have only known a few days? If you have, chances are you've reincarnated. This is not your first rodeo, you could say. Their previous incarnations so indelibly mark some people that they are obsessed with other countries and even dream in their old language. Reincarnation used to hold sway only in Eastern religions like

Buddhism and Hinduism. Now, even the West is embracing the idea, with psychologists offering past life regression therapy.

Reincarnation is the birth, death, and rebirth of a soul into a physical body. It is a cycle that goes on for thousands of years, with the soul gaining new experience and wisdom with each new life. Thus, reincarnation is what drives the evolution of the soul.

Think of karma as a form of checks and balances for the soul. Imagine a world where everyone knew they would reincarnate and there were no consequences for their actions in a previous life. It would be total chaos since there is no reason to choose to be good or to show any moral accountability. Also, the soul's goal of growth and evolution would not be accomplished since there are no wounds or sufferings to help its incarnations be better people. Therefore, when one soul does something irrevocably harmful to others, there's an imbalance of energy that must be evened out. The way balance is restored is through the assurance of karmic debt.

Repayment of karmic debts does not always involve punishment or suffering. Suppose you were a ruthless, bloodthirsty ruler in one life. In your next one, you could atone for that by being a surgeon who does surgeries pro bono, or you could save someone from getting hit by a car, and at that moment, the karmic debt is paid in full. Karma teaches you to be mindful of the choices you make because each one has its consequence.

Chiron in Karmic Astrology

You are an eternal soul constantly transforming yourself. With karmic law, you can get clues about your past lessons based on where the stars were at the time of your birth in this present life. It is called karmic astrology. It's a tool that lets you figure out the issues and problems you have, as well as things to be on the lookout for in the future.

With karmic astrology, you study the placement of the stars on your natal chart to figure out the burdens you piled up in your soul during previous incarnations. This way, you can sort out old conflicts, gain more insight into why your life is the way it is, and get a sneak peek of what the future might hold for you. You will also learn how to comport yourself in this life by connecting with your past ones to have better relationships with your present self and the people around you.

Chiron is one of the most relevant heavenly bodies. It is an asteroid that paints us an honest picture of the emotional wound we carry that never heals. It tries to show you that nestled in pain from that wound lies your gift, the gift of healing.

You can infer from the story of Chiron that our wounds are the best teachers we could have. Wounds are a necessary part of karmic debt repayment. For example, you might have become a heart surgeon because of a wound or situation you went through in a past life. Maybe a dear one had a specific condition, and no one could help them, so you lost them. This is just one of many ways that wounds come up to help us fulfill our karma. Knowing where Chiron lies on your chart will tell you what kind of wounds you are dealing with and the best way to heal them and grow. In the same way that Chiron's wound would not heal, aspects of our lives are locked into that pain and always in touch with it.

The Soul's Suffering

Suffering has always been and always will be. There will not be any incarnation where you won't find it. Even if you have the finest trappings of the era, you will suffer. That is just the way the cookie crumbles. However, you do have control over how you react to the sufferings that come your way. Your attitude toward suffering is what will either set you free from it or bind you even tighter.

If Chiron had insisted on remaining an immortal for whatever reason, he would most certainly have remained in immense suffering. Prometheus would also have continued to suffer as an indirect consequence of Chiron's refusal to trade his most precious immortality for his freedom. Hercules would forever have to suffer watching his friend suffer, knowing fully well it was his hand that fired the poisoned arrow. Are you beginning to understand the lesson here?

To make it clear, you can end suffering by choosing to let it go. This release is a feeling of acceptance as well, and this acceptance helps clean your eyes out so you can see the blessing in the suffering you had missed all along.

You may wonder, to what end do we suffer? What is the point of it? Remember, the soul desires to evolve, learn, and grow. Suffering is a great teacher. It teaches compassion and empathy, which helps your soul attain its desire. The role of suffering is to tear you down just enough for your soul to learn what it needs to and then build you back up to be stronger, better, more than you were before those experiences. It also shows you that things may change, they may be terrible, but no matter what, the essence of you remains.

The more you make a point to learn and grow from the sufferings of your karmic debts, the more you will build up positive karma for yourself, and the more evolved you will be. Eventually, you will become one of the wisest souls, having worked out most of your karma. Those souls are now in a place where the only thing keeping them coming back is a desire to be of service to those still finding their way.

Clearing Your Karmic Debts

When you clear your karmic debts, you set your soul free of all that binds it to Earth, allowing it to ascend and become one with the Source of All That Is. If you owe someone a karmic debt or someone owes you one, you are still under the law of karma, which is the law of action and consequence. You know how it goes, "For every action, there is an equal and opposite reaction." This same balance exists in life. Everything you do carries its consequence within it. Your current place in life is a reflection of your karmas put together. It may seem like you could never escape karma's grasp, but you can transcend the cycle.

Karmic debt is both good and bad karma that is yet to be realized, owed to you by others, or owed by others to you. Some relationships are based on karmic debts. For example, you may be in a relationship that's a continuation of one from a past life. Karma ensures that you will pay that debt if you owe someone, and vice versa, whether in this life or another to come. The debt could be on account of love, vengeance, anger, rendering help or service, or deception. It covers the entire range of human relations.

When your soul assumes a new identity on Earth, it takes along with it all past karma, recording it all as vasanas or impressions on your soul. Until all debts are paid in full, you will continue to come back. It is not like your soul is being compelled to do so. On the contrary, it actively seeks to return to fix things, pocking its life, circumstances, and family beforehand. It chooses the right combination of life's elements to allow it to resolve outstanding karma while learning soul-level lessons. Unfortunately, once you incarnate on Earth, you, like everyone else, forget what your soul intended. As a result, you may find yourself accruing more karma, which perpetuates the birth-death-rebirth process.

For this reason, you should want to clear your karmic debts so that you owe no one, and no one owes you. There are three kinds of karma:

1. Prarabdha

2. Sanchita

3. Agami

Prarabdha karma is the sort that is in motion already, waiting for you to experience it. You cannot avoid it, whatever it is. You do not get to opt out if you don't want to experience it. It is ready and waiting for you. However, having no control over this kind of karma doesn't mean you should automatically subject yourself to it mindlessly. As mentioned before, you can choose how to respond to it. You can experience it without identifying with it.

The trick here is to see yourself experiencing it as a distant, neutral observer. Suffering comes when you identify yourself with the experience. Liberation from suffering comes from knowing you are "in the world, but not of it." With this mindset, you can handle failure and success the same way, keeping a level head and not losing yourself. When you accept good and bad karma with the same attitude, unaffected by the results, you will set yourself free from that debt.

Sanchita karma is the sum of your past karmas, which you will not be able to fully experience in your lifetime on account of time and other human constraints. You will experience these in a different incarnation. That said, you can take over this karma and clear it in full in this life when you engage in the proper yogic practices with a sincere heart and seek the assistance of Source and those souls who have evolved and gone on to the next level.

Agami Karma is all karma created in the present incarnation. Thus, some of the new karma you create will become Prarabdha Karma, while others will be Sanchita. So, there is just one question now: How do you stop Agami Karma?

The process of living is all about choices and actions. There is no other way. Of course, your actions will have reactions, as noted before. However, should you understand that Source is acting through you and handing over both the action and consequence to Source, you would acquire no further karma. In other words, remaining conscious of your divinity at all times, regardless of what you are going through, will neutralize your karma.

Thus, just as the Bhagavad Gita suggests, detach yourself from the outcomes of your actions. See yourself as nothing more than an instrument of divinity or the universe. When you live your life with that awareness, you will be unbothered and untouched by karma.

Cause and effect are united, both of them being two sides of the same coin. If you linearly look at things, you can tell that the past creates the present, and the present creates the future. However, when you move beyond constraining concepts like time and space, you experience a paradigm shift where you realize the truth of all existence: There is no past, present, or future; there is only now. In this now, know that your present has crafted your history, and your future will craft the present. So, seeing your preferred future and choosing to act in line with it is all you need to create the present (and past) changes you wish to see.

With effort and awareness and a conscious decision to surrender all actions and consequences to the Divine while remaining detached from all outcomes, good or bad, we can effectively deal with all kinds of karma. You can, with focused awareness, distance yourself from the experience you are going through, acknowledging it is valid yet refusing to take it on as your identity. Doing this is how you reduce the severity of the suffering and stop further karma, which leads to you healing your soul.

Liberating your soul from the shackles of Earth means you no longer have to deal with the pain of wounds that inevitably accompany you on each incarnation. It means you can finally free yourself from the cosmic rat race. If your soul does decide to return to Earth for another round, this time, its only purpose will be to be of service to others still learning what you now know. As Apollo taught Chiron to heal, and Chiron shared that gift with others, you, too, can now be a healer, teacher, giver, transforming lives for the better.

Chapter 4: Power Disguised as Pain

When the poison arrow wounded Chiron, he lived on, being immortal. Thus, he lived his days in complete agony. However, this agony was not wasted, as, through it, he taught others about their pain. He found that the pain served as a connection between himself and other wounded souls and leveraged that to help them find their healing. In other words, he took that pain and turned it into power.

Pain can be incredibly motivational. The same thing applies to suffering. You must have experienced them in some way to understand either. They help the ones experiencing the grief and those looking on to heal, learn, and grow. You could say Chiron was a shaman in his own right. Having gone through pain and suffering and battled his own demons, he gained the power to transform other people's lives with his lessons on healing.

Ego death is a critical phase along the wounded healer's journey. On his way to enlightenment, you have no choice but to face your ego. It is your ego that keeps you striving continuously for material things. It drives you to jealousy and fear. It kills your self-esteem and steals your joy by compelling you to constantly compare yourself to everyone else, never to be satisfied and fully in the moment. When you lose your sense of self, you will come to see that you are not your ego. You are so much more than that. You are a soul, complete, possessing all things within you. The light of that knowledge is so powerful that the ego has no choice but to dissipate into nothing the moment you realize this.

Let go of the idea that we are all separate beings doing our own thing. Instead, realize that we're all the same Source Energy being expressed through various lives and paradigms. Then, you will naturally find your consciousness expanding. You will move into a state of unity and connection, where you are fully aware of other people's emotions. You'll see there's not much difference among us all if you look to find the threads that connect us in the beautiful tapestry of life.

There is nothing greater than setting aside your selfish desires and turning your energy toward helping others who struggle with what you once went through. You should appreciate the fact that it took a lot for you to get here. You had to die to yourself, wholly and willingly. That is something only the brave dare do because it is such a painful process, but that is where your true power resides.

Power of Perseverance

Chiron was unable to escape the pain of the poison or heal himself, but he did not let that keep him from sharing what he knew with others so that they, too, could overcome their pain. He ground on, through sheer perseverance, despite the pain. This attitude of persistence is a good one to have. It transmuted his pain into fuel to keep going until he was finally granted peace.

You must have heard inspirational stories of people who went to hell and back, and somehow every adversity they faced only propelled them to keep going. There are, of course, others whose stories we will never hear, not because they did not at some point give their best, but because they failed to keep going.

You see, there is power in being consistent with your efforts, no matter what you are doing. There is power in persistence and perseverance. You could have the fanciest mining tools to get diamonds out of the earth, but if you do not have the determination to keep looking until you find them, what good are your tools? Someone else with just a pickaxe and a wheelbarrow could do a lot better than you if they had perseverance.

Just take a few moments to think about where you are now and how much you want things to be better. Are you willing to keep going, regardless of what life throws your way? Can you find your inner Chiron and channel his energy? If you commit to yourself that, you will be glad you did.

Chiron shows up for all of us. In those moments, we must persist in facing our shadow, so we can heal ourselves and mine the precious diamonds that life has offered us through our pain. As we work with and through our shadow and wound, we will allow our healing and restorative powers to shine through.

Understanding Others Even in Your Darkness

No matter who or what we seek to blame for being where we are in life, we must be honest about the cause of our pain. It lies in the distance between our ideals and present reality and our inability to accept that humans are flawed. Sure, the temptation is there to rage against the universe. Still, in the end, the best way to not get swallowed up by bitterness, chewed up by corrosive hatred, and spat out into an abyss of meaninglessness, is to go past the rage and seek to be understanding.

You should do your best to understand yourself better because when you do, you find the self-loathing melts away, revealing your wound and the way to heal it. You should seek to understand others as well, so you can move beyond thinking of yourself as a victim or scapegoat and abandon the need to act as judge, jury, and executioner.

In other words, you need to realize that the darkness touches us one and all, but if everyone gives in to it, who will turn on the light? By choosing to understand, you will have a richer view of life and all your experiences. It calls for letting go of whatever convictions we hold so dearly. It calls for the death of your ego.

So how do you find it within you to look beyond your pain and darkness and understand others? How do you find the strength to truly forgive, with none of that holier-than-thou attitude that is a disguise for rage and resentment? The Sun can assist your inner Chiron with this. Where it is placed at your birth will show you what you need to become. If your Sun is in Aries in the fifth, chances are you devote your life to everyone but yourself. You are sacrificing yourself, and deep down, you know it; this adds more fuel to the fire of bitterness within you.

Turning Weakness into Strength

Wherever you find Chiron on the natal chart, you will find weakness there, a wound that you have a hard time healing. However, you do not have to allow this weakness to remain as it is. Know right away that all weaknesses can become strengths, and you have what it takes to do just that, no matter how dark things may seem to be right now. Chiron will give you the light you need to deal with these recurrent wounds that pop up in your life. You might not heal every wound right away or in full, but you can at least start the process and get to the point where they no longer cripple you as they once did. Thus, as you ponder Chiron on your birth chart, allow yourself to be open to enlightenment and healing. Tap into your inner resilience, and find the treasures that lie within your soul. Now, let us take a look at Chiron on the natal chart.

Chiron in Pisces

The Chiron in Pisces tends to have a victim mindset. They wallow and revel in their suffering. It is not that they have not suffered; it's just that they love it when everyone around them knows that they are going through a lot. They replay their suffering over and over in their minds to the point where it does them no good.

Natives of Chiron in Pisces also attract fellow "victims" who go out of their way to help. It would be good if they did not wear themselves down in the process and completely ignore their own needs. For the native of Chiron in Pisces, it would help if they could find the balance between mercy and pity in their lives. When they do this successfully, they will bless everyone else with the gift of genuine compassion, which is sorely needed in the world right now.

Chiron in Aries

With Chiron in Aries, identity takes a crushing blow. This person is constantly battling to find their authentic self in a world full of suffering. It is this way for the Chiron in Aries native because they have had a rough go of it, particularly in their early life, psychologically and physically. If this is you, you might constantly strive to know who you are. This placement is not one of the easiest, but the thing about having it is that you are the sort of person who has a grasp on the dynamics of pain like nobody else. You are the best fit for crisis counseling and the one friend everyone calls in an emergency. Your resilience did not just drop out of the sky; it was founded on hard times. You have wounds, but you know how to work with them in a way that helps you and those around you.

Chiron in Taurus

The Chiron in Taurus native equates their material possessions with their self-worth. The very last thing they want is to be behind the Joneses. They feel anything but complete if they do not have the best, latest, and most lavish things. Self-esteem is a challenging concept with this placement.

Natives of Chiron in Taurus can also take things to the other extreme. For example, they can altogether eschew materialism and take pride in not having any comforts. They do this just to prove a point to the world that it has nothing they need. It is hard to heal from this wound, but they can pass on the most effective tools for dealing with self-esteem issues to others around them when they do heal.

Chiron in Gemini

The wounds that this native struggles with are psychological. They pertain to communication. Growing up, their parents and others never listened to them, so they felt unheard and disregarded for their whole lives. Thus, they grow up speaking too many decibels above others around them, punishing everyone around them the same way they were punished. Or they clam up, keep their mouths shut, and are never heard from again.

If this is you, you need to find your voice—your authentic voice, not the one that overcompensates for feeling unloved. When you do, you will become one of the best teachers, showing people practical ways to communicate, having overcome that hurdle yourself. You will teach people how to be heard in a world that is not listening.

Chiron in Cancer

As a native of Chiron in Cancer, you have significant issues with your mother. This plays out either in the form of power struggles or as abandonment issues when you were much younger and still dependent on her. However, until now, something deep within you wants nothing more than to be nurtured. More than anyone else, you feel family issues on a profound level.

You struggle harder than most to gain your mother's love, but the pain eats away at you because you do not get it. However, this pain can become your greatest strength. You can show the world what it truly means to be nurturing. When you master your pain, you can give yourself to others, and you also give yourself the love you have always deserved, having realized you are worthy of it. Chiron in Cancer can teach the world what it means to love truly.

Chiron in Leo

The Chiron in a Leo person is all about being creative and wanting the world to see their work. However, they cannot stand it when their work is mocked or criticized, and it causes them so much pain. A cutting remark about their creative work cuts deeper than an actual cut with a sharp knife for them. It is like the child told that they should not draw anymore because they are awful at it or their dance is silly. This is the wounded artist who must do all they can to heal those wounds if they are going to overcome their creative block. Once they do, they will bless the world with fantastic insight through their art.

Chiron in Virgo

Chiron in Virgo is constantly dealing with health issues. Even when they are in perfect health, they worry about whether a little tickle in the throat is more than just a common cold or random sensation. Thus, they hop on WebMD and diagnose themselves to the point where they have anxiety, a health issue on its own.

When the native of this placement realizes and overcomes their weakness, they are very eager to share what they have learned about healing. They bless others with their healing skills, too. As with Virgo, Chiron is the sign of service, so this all fits together nicely.

Chiron in Libra

This wound involves relationships. The native of this placement is a little too skilled at being defensive, evasive, and non-committal, which is ironic because they crave union. They do not want to connect with others because they no longer want to deal with being hurt anymore. This native is healed when there is no further struggle for harmony and peace, no matter the cost. They are not afraid of commitment anymore and are ready to dedicate themselves to others. If this is you, give up the need to be defensive. Relax and be your honest self. No one is a better master of the saying, "If you love someone, let them go." Chiron in Libra, when healed, is a master of relationship skills.

Chiron in Scorpio

The idea of regeneration is common with the Chiron in Scorpio native. They might be in circumstances so terrible that even the Devil would not wish that on anyone, yet, they would pull through every time. They bear the weight of losing those near and dear to them each day, and they battle long and hard with grief. Yet, they rise and demonstrate to the rest of us that there is rebirth after each death and that life never ends. For them to come to the point of mastering this truth, they suffer far more than others. The road of the Chiron in Scorpio is paved with grief, and they move along it in humility. They make the best counselors due to their vast experiences with issues that most people run from.

Chiron in Sagittarius

Faith matters to this native more than anything else, not in the context of a mainstream religion (they could very well be atheists). Still, faith is a concept they live by, one they hold in their minds and souls, even if they will not admit to having it. If this native encounters deep wisdom, it won't matter if they do not feel connected to it. Still, they thirst for the true meaning of life and their experiences so that they can have wisdom and joy. When they realize that those things come from within, they will be more open to expressing their faith personally. In the process, they will grow in spiritual awareness. They usually teach others about faith and how it is a personal journey, stressing that true faith is not compelled. It just is. This is one lesson we need sorely.

Chiron in Capricorn

It is hard for you to find your place in the world if this is you. At least, that is how it seems to you. Even when you have accomplished so much and achieved heights of fame and success in your chosen field, you still feel like you do not fit in. You feel inadequate. You are haunted by impostor syndrome, day in and out. This will end when you know and acknowledge your true worth. It's not an easy thing to do, but you have to know you are worthy before you can give your best, which is even better than the amazing feats you have accomplished so far.

When you find this weakness in you, you will not stop until you have turned it into a strength. No one can turn negatives into positives better than you do. You would make a great consultant to captains of industry and business leaders, no matter the field they are in. You know what it is like to feel inadequate and then come out of that, helping others deal with their lack of confidence.

Chiron in Aquarius

This native displays incredible genius, coming up with ideas that are beyond the times. This is the great inventor who is unknown and working with limited resources in poverty, desperately trying to convince anyone that their invention will serve the world wonderfully. However, no one is listening to them; at best or worst, they are ridiculed. As a result, they isolate themselves, not because they want to be alone but because of the pain of ridicule. They want to help humankind, but they are sadly misunderstood by lesser minds and shunned on top of that. This native is a brilliant intellectual who may have significant issues seeing any point of view besides theirs. If this is you, know you are part of everyone else. Know that it is possible to remain connected with others even when in disagreement. Do this, and you will find peace. You will find ways to share your beautiful ideas without allowing rejection and ridicule to silence you.

Chapter 5: Chiron in the Natal Chart — I

A Quick Overview on Astrological Houses

Think of the twelve houses as various segments of a circle or points on a clock. Each part stands for an area of human life.

- The First House: Physical body, self, appearance.
- The Second House: Money, value, possessions, self-worth.
- The Third House: Early schooling, communication, siblings.
- The Fourth House: Family, home, ancestral patterns.
- The Fifth House: Play, romance, creativity.
- The Sixth House: Work, daily routine, health.
- The Seventh House: Partnerships, commitment.
- The Eight House: Intimacy, merging, transformation, death.
- The Ninth House: Spirituality, higher learning, media relations.
- The Tenth House: Public status, career, legacy.
- The Eleventh House: Hopes, dreams, friendships, community.
- The Twelfth House: Spirituality, endings.

Whatever houses the planets are in on your chart will show your destiny and are unique to the exact time you were born. You get more information from considering the entire natal chart rather than just your sun sign. Your natal chart begins with your ascendant sign, or rising sign, which oversees your first house. Observing the planets' present positions gives insight into why your life is as it is right now.

Chiron in the First House

The first house is ruled by Mars, which corresponds to Aries, the first Zodiac sign. When Chiron is in this house, your soul considers coming into this world as a wound of its own. The realization that you have had to cause pain to your mother (inadvertently) to come into this world is clear to your soul. This soul-level impression of your arrival on Earth can affect the way you perceive your reality. For example, you may assume that it is impossible to live without hurting others unintentionally. For this reason, you may be particularly sensitive to the idea of pain, especially as it relates to others. Also, you might find yourself in a position to help others in pain or need or provide comfort when misfortune hits them.

Vulnerability: If Chiron does not feel at home here, you might sense a bit of existential disgust or nausea when you are face-to-face with your imperfections. The wounded Chiron in this house feels psychologically powerless when taking on new things or decisions. For this very reason, you might swing the other way and become very impulsive about starting new things or making new decisions.

Other factors affect your impulsivity, and you might be worried about hurting others when you make decisions on your own. Dwell on this truth: You will unavoidably hurt someone unintentionally. That is life. Be at peace with this and become more at ease with acting on your own. A great way to heal is to help others make their decisions and take risks.

Evolution: You may feel pity for your shortcomings and extend this same empathy to others. You have an inexplicable attraction to the flawed and imperfect ones around you, particularly when it comes to physical appearance. You find it refreshing to see someone embody the same imperfection that troubles you on the inside.

Chiron in the Second House

This house is ruled by Venus and corresponds to Taurus. If you are this soul, you felt some awkwardness as you incarnated into a physical body with human needs. The idea of condescending to being human bothers your soul, and it hates having to lug around this flesh sack of blood and bones. This registers on your psyche and creates a feeling of never being comfortable in your skin, as well as utter disdain for having to deal with the dirty business of being human.

Vulnerability: When Chiron is not comfortable in this house, the body is looked upon with disdain. It causes you endless embarrassment. Without knowing it, you may constantly self-flagellate yourself metaphorically speaking, so you can purify your "unclean" body. You might choose to do this by avoiding sex or food. Alternatively, you may swing the other way engaging in both to the point of overindulgence, especially if you feel you have no hope of redeeming your body.

When Venus or Moon are stressed in this natal chart, this placement may reveal that being too close to others physically is disgusting to your soul. As such, you might act physically aloof or not be as willing to engage in sex as others would. The only exception to this is if Mars is strong in your chart.

Evolution: When you evolve, you can feel self-pity and pity for others. The fact that we all have to use the bathroom, have sex, eat, work for a living, or manage money is something that moves you so that you are more compassionate to others and yourself. You feel connected to human neediness, so you temper your idealism concerning lofty spiritual and intellectual pursuits.

On the flip side, your body is a sensitive topic in your psyche. You may choose a line of work that concerns body-related issues, like weight loss, eating disorders, etc. You may also work with money issues, like tax problems, debt consolidation, and so on. You can help people connect to their wallet or body healthily, so they can heal their physical and financial wounds and evolve, just like you have done.

Chiron in the Third House

The third house is ruled by Mercury and in the House of Communication. It corresponds with Gemini. If Chiron is in this house on your chart, your soul might have the idea that it is not possible to have intellectual rapport along with connection. In other words, it might have had trouble being understood by others in a past life, no matter how hard it tried to express itself.

That feeling of always being misunderstood can make you feel helpless, and you might never want to bother communicating your desires. Add in the fact that when you are born, the first and only thing you know to do is cry, and you can see how frustrating this is for the soul. This is the wound that plagues you. Therefore, you are very touchy on the subject of your intellectual capacity to understand others and your ability to communicate what you think clearly.

Vulnerability: If you are still dealing with your wound, you have issues expressing yourself. You are frustrated with people who do not know how to use language to get their message across effectively, and you might find profanity repulsive. Despite the difficulty with expressing ideas that comes with this placement, you are likely to be fluent in an impressive number of languages and pride yourself on speaking and writing politely and eloquently. More than a few poets, actors, and writers with this placement show that you can work constructively with your wound.

Evolution: If Chiron evolves in this house, in connection with Mercury or Gemini, you might find yourself drawn to situations that allow you to help others communicate better or help them in navigation or schoolwork. Importantly, you help them enhance the necessary skills for living. For example, you could become a tutor, driving instructor, speech therapist, or someone who helps kids with learning disabilities.

Chiron in the Fourth House

Cancer rules the fourth house, which corresponds with the Moon. A severe hypersensitivity on a soul level affects how you think about ideas like domicile, stability, a parental figure, or your origins. Your soul intensely perceives existence itself as a wound. It has given itself up to something that almost resembles predictability and safety on Earth and expects nothing more. It waits for the rug to be pulled out from under it (so when that happens, it is prepared and is not surprised or too hurt).

This placement shows much vulnerability in your relationship with your parents, especially one of them (usually your mother, but it could be your father). Your relationship with this parent is very problematic. In the best-case scenario, one of them is the safe haven, offering you support and protection, while the other is either absent or problematic in ways that affect every area of your life.

You are so connected to the problem parent that you almost put them on a pedestal. For you, their word is law, whether you adore them or despise them. Thus, you do your best to avoid seeming like that parent, and you look with disdain at any ideals that they hold and would like you to portray in your life.

Vulnerability: You tend to seek out and fall for emotionally unavailable people. Sometimes, it is so bad that you deify them—make them out to be more than they are. The wounded Chiron in the fourth house will become too attached to their romantic interests, often to the unhealthy degree that they lose themselves. Essentially, they unconsciously try to make that partner a stand-in for the parent figure they wish they had.

You might find you have a strong need to belong. You need to be needed. You are emotional, emphatic, compassionate, sensitive, and do a great job of absorbing other people's suffering. This can be a problem since you might cross the line all the time and not let people be independent. You want to be the sole nurturer and comforter, but life does not work that way. Unfortunately, things do not work out the way you would like. You feel like you're being manipulated and exploited with time, and your good intentions are used against you. Consequently, you become bitter, arrogant, and spiteful.

There is also a chance that you feel very vulnerable when people try to get you to open up, and you are not comfortable letting others protect you. When you're in a situation that requires you to open up, the pain is unbearable as it is precisely like opening your old, festering wounds.

Even though you hate opening up, you still feel like you are not getting enough attention and love from others. The Chiron in this placement might grow jealous of their kids because of the attention their partner shows them. That said, you're very intuitive and aware of what others are going through, even more than you are of your situation. You believe you should be admired for your ability to intuit what is wrong or needed.

When you do not feel appreciated, you get angry because a big part of your wound involves dissatisfied emotions and a lack of closure. It is usually because some violence was done to you as a child by your parent or experienced emotional manipulation and ridicule. Thus, you find it very hard to be emotionally satisfied. This issue is compounded because you are not quick to voice your wants and needs. So, your job is to learn to speak up about your needs and be more direct in asking for what you want. Also, allow others to be as they are, and let them have their independence.

Evolution: The evolved and healed Chiron has a profound level of empathy and care fueled by the soul. You offer emotional support and nurture others and might find yourself being the parent you wish you had but never got. Many therapists and psychologists have this placement on their birth charts. They are fantastic at assisting others emotionally and amazing at unraveling the twists and knots that lie in the human psyche.

Personalities in Each House

Celebrities with Chiron in the first house include Selena Gomez, Barack Obama, Oprah Winfrey, Heath Ledger, Shakira, James Dean, Whitney Houston, Bill Clinton, Gwyneth Paltrow, and J. K. Rowling.

Celebrities with Chiron in the second house include Sharon Tate, Emmanuel Macron, Donald Trump, Monica Bellucci, Robert Pattinson, Christina Aguilera, Ryan Gosling, Mother Teresa, Kristen Stewart, Elizabeth II, Timothee Chalamet, Audrey Hepburn, and Robin Williams.

Celebrities with Chiron in the third house include Jesus Christ, Ted Bundy, Rihanna, Vladimir Putin, Brad Pitt, Prince, Catherine Zeta-Jones, Jodie Foster, Khloe Kardashian, and Bjork.

Celebrities with Chiron in the fourth house include Nelson Mandela, Cher, Bruno Mars, Winona Ryder, Tom Cruise, Miley Cyrus, Jim Carey, Eminem, Mozart, Mick Jagger, Bradley Cooper, Jude Law, and Louis Tomlinson.

Chiron's Wounds and Gifts in Each Zodiac Sign

Aries Wound: Your wound affects your relationships, loving yourself, and trusting yourself to make the right move when it concerns others. You desire to love, and you are very aware of your issues with keeping positive relationships.

Healing Gifts: Other people come to you to help them with relationship issues because you intuitively know how to heal them. You can objectively point out what they need to do to bring balance and peace to their relationships. You help others break their patterns of self-destruction and understand their thoughts and emotions better.

Taurus Wound: The finality of death bothers you on a soul level. You have issues with endings and conclusions. You do not like to make concrete decisions or changes that would significantly affect your life because you fear the future. As a result, you struggle with stress and anxiety. Your fear of death leads you to live in the moment, even at the cost of your health.

Healing Gifts: You help people be in the now. You are the kind of person who makes others feel like they have all the attention in the world when they speak with you, making them feel validated. You are supportive of others' dreams, and your enthusiasm for their success encourages them. You help others see how beautiful life is and help them relax and accept where they are in life. You do not judge because you understand that everyone has their own journey. You offer them the gift of true freedom by showing them how to keep their awareness in the moment.

Gemini Wound: You overthink how you feel and struggle with being misunderstood. You are analytical to the point of putting labels on everything and everyone—including yourself. You wish you could be more open, but your mind will not allow it.

Healing Gifts: You are talented at sparking ideas in others. A conversation with you leads to feelings of empowerment and boldness, and deeper insight into one's situation in life. You lure people away from their negative thought patterns, inspiring them to be positive and greater heights. You help others with their spiritual awakening.

Cancer Wound: You want nothing more than to be nurturing, compassionate, and loving, but you either find ways to do this that are limiting, or you go to the extent of neglecting your needs. You deny your heart's desires and also have trouble finding ways to channel your emotional abundance. You might also be physically or creatively blocked.

Healing Gifts: You are amazing at healing others emotionally. You speak gently, with no judgment, and a heart full of love for one and all. You have a very soft spot for outcasts, people on the fringe. Others may have counted them out, but you give them the benefit of the doubt. You are also excellent at assisting others going through past trauma, familial or otherwise, showing them how to accept their past, find the lesson in it, and move on with their lives.

Leo Wound: There is a shadow over your ability and willingness to express yourself. You do not do very well accepting praise, and you would never be caught showing off. You are so humble that you dampen your creativity, but at the same time, you want nothing more than to be known for your achievements and creations.

Healing Gifts: You are great at helping others express their creativity. You bring out their ability to be decisive and their desire to express themselves in the most brilliant ways possible. You see the creativity that lies dormant in them, and you know how to wake it up. People often get positive feedback from you, and this encourages them to achieve more. They are invested in your opinions on what they have done. You can heal other people struggling to find their voice to know they are unique and have the confidence to do great things.

Virgo Wound: Your wound deals with inner strength and courage. You are usually working in the service of others and cannot find it in you to stand up for yourself even when you know you should. On the other hand, you're very efficient at work, and you're diligent, too. You go over every detail, obsessing to make sure the job is done to perfection. You put your soul into everything you do, and no drop of blood, sweat, or tears is spared. Thus, you do not do well with not taking constructive criticism personally.

Healing Gifts: You are an inspiration to others, driving them to speak up when there is injustice and take action. The energy you feed others in need of courage is incredible. You are the one behind the scenes giving all the help that activists and leaders need to get impossible tasks done. You give of yourself endlessly, without losing yourself in the process. So many could not possibly achieve any results without your help. You heal others by showing them that they are capable of whatever they set their minds to and that it is okay to seek help.

Libra Wound: The struggle here is with emotional and mental prisons you have created for yourself. You let everyone but yourself dictate what you should do, think, and how you should be, so you cage yourself with all these rules and labels, sacrificing your desires. Your intelligence and insight are remarkable, but you bottle all of that up because you are afraid of being judged. You have a desire to shake up the status quo. Still, you are apprehensive because you know what people expect of you, and you do not want to upset anyone in the process.

Healing Gifts: Your insight is objective and amazing. You can counsel others to recognize all the potential they have within them, as well as pitfalls they need to avoid. You are gentle about it, too, as you help others see how they hinder themselves. You have the strength to be very honest, to speak the truth without hurting others. People find just being around you very hopeful, as you give them hope that they can truly live the lives they desire. You help them realize that they can be who they are in every aspect of life.

Scorpio Wound: Your wound is intuitive and deeply emotional. You have a hard time rushing through things that need more patience so that you can get more out of the experience. You are scared of the emotional storm within you. You are an empath, but you deny it because you do not know how to deal with the depth of human emotions and experiences. You know there is much more to life than you are allowing yourself to experience. You seek definite answers, but instead, you keep finding a lot of duality and paradoxes that you cannot reconcile.

Healing Gifts: You know how to draw out another's truths. You help them to work with their innate abilities, to learn to accept them. Your presence allows others experience the depths of their soul. You are also great at leading people to realize their psychic nature and ability. Finally, you teach them the importance of slowing down when working with layers of trauma to find true healing to their psyche.

Sagittarius Wound: Your wound will drive you to be a healer or teacher, much like Chiron, if you let it. You find that you are caught up in so many belief systems, your dogma, and your view of how life should be. Your soul wants nothing more than to feel like you're giving back to the world in some way. You need to be cared for, and dealing with mental health issues or medical problems are usually seen as obstacles to success.

Healing Gifts: Your healing gifts are multifaceted. You can use them practically by taking care of kids, working in healthcare, or sharing helpful information with everyone. You are a teacher who is fantastic at communicating information to students, even more so than creating the work. Your down-to-earth nature is refreshing, and you help others heal spiritually.

Capricorn Wound: You feel alone in ways too deep to describe, and because of this, you want to connect with others and have them around you, but you do not know the right way to do this. You find yourself depressed when you cannot create meaningful relationships. You are tired of drifting as you make a habit of leaving before things fully play out because you're scared of the outcome, good or bad. You have a habit of avoiding your problems, something you're aware of and struggle with.

Healing Gifts: You are an advocate for other's needs. You have a knack for singling out the one person who needs some support in a crowd because you have fantastic intuition. You know how good it feels to be heard, and you give that gift to others. You are a matchmaker, bringing people together and connecting them. You know how to match people's energies so that the best outcome is inevitable.

Aquarius Wound: You want nothing more than to be your eccentric self freely, but you feel hindered. Your mindset is unique, but you do not express it, so you don't ruin other people's expectations of you. You have ideas you've buried in your soul, a deep desire to be your authentic self. You are loyal to what your group needs but struggle to balance that with your calling in life. You tend to re-examine your loyalties, philosophies, and ethics from time to time, seeking your life's purpose.

Healing Gifts: For the world's misfits, you give them a sense of solidarity. You are the patron saint for all the weird people under the sun, giving them a home, a sense of acceptance, and belonging. You heal those who do not "fit in" with their respective societies. Using the Internet and other means, you help them find their tribes so that they don't feel alone. This is healing for you and for those you help.

Pisces Wound: You are a natural healer, physically, spiritually, and mentally, yet you have an ailment that you cannot diagnose or overcome, which is a part of your journey. When you experience heartbreak, it affects your sensitivity and empathy profoundly. People with this Chiron placement are amazing at mediumship and channeling. Still, they usually struggle with accepting these gifts as they develop. They only find peace with the gifts when they finally understand what they are experiencing, thanks to a mentor or guide.

Healing Gifts: If you choose a career in astrology, medicine, or counseling, you are right on the money. Like Chiron was great working with medicinal plants, healing, teaching, and astrology, you, too, would do phenomenally well. Chiron's energy comes through Pisces strongly. This zodiac sign has spiritual tendencies and is very nurturing and loving at heart.

Chapter 6: Chiron in the Natal Chart — II

Chiron in the Fifth House

This house is ruled by the Sun and corresponds to Leo. There is a rupture in the psyche in this placement regarding creative outlets, ego structure, and self-consciousness. You may find it hard to figure out who you are or celebrate your authentic self. Chiron is connected with the real you. This means you feel embarrassed about being true to yourself instead of following the herd. This embarrassment can also be disguised by a drive to be yourself fully.

People with this placement will strive to be part of the collective. Many with fortune and fame have Chiron in the fifth house. They have embraced their weirdness, proving it can be an asset. Solar Chirons find healing through acting or creating, so they gravitate toward the media and entertainment industry.

Vulnerability: When Chiron finds the fifth house uncomfortable, they may have decided that they are not desirable and their presence is not needed. To combat this, they unconsciously might lean toward narcissism, becoming heavily preoccupied with themselves, making it very hard for them to connect with others around them.

One of the best ways to mitigate this narcissistic tendency is through creative expression. This often allows the Solar Chiron to connect with others, healing their wounds in the process. They need approval and attention and can only be soothed through self-expression and creativity.

If you choose to have kids, you might fixate on them because you see them as extensions of yourself when they are individuals.

Evolution: When you have evolved, you will find many outlets to express yourself creatively, which will help you discover your authentic self with the assistance of the collective. You will discover the unique abilities and talents you have and make an indelible mark on the world. Working with others, you'll heal the wound that starts in the center of your soul and find that, at last, you are proud of your existence and your role on life's stage.

Chiron in the Sixth House

This house is ruled by Mercury and correlates to Virgo. There is a deep, intense feeling of pity and a desperate compulsion on the soul level when it comes to matters of soberness and practicality. In other words, you might find you constantly disconnect from life's routines because you feel that despite your best efforts, perfection will always elude you.

Vulnerability: Usually, those who are natives of Chiron in the sixth house or connect with Mercury or Virgo always seek to escape from their lower, mercurial mind to their higher, Neptunian one, so that they do not feel the awkwardness of routine daily living.

This native escapes using anything from sleep medication, alcohol, and other drugs, to compulsively engaging in dance, music, and fantasy worlds. This person wastes no time engaging in activities that allow them to ignore the boring details of living in a physical world.

If this is you, you might find the biological processes of cleansing (sweating, urinating, defecating) are quite an embarrassment. You hate it when you are sick or in a position of need.

Thus, ironically, you might feel drawn to neediness and sickness in others because it gives you a sense of relief knowing that they have to deal with the same things you do. You find it soothing when you take care of animals (especially wounded ones or those with anomalies). You also enjoy caring for plants (the thornier or weirder, the better). Something about creatures that are in a very pathetic state draws you, and you seek to heal them as a way to scratch the itch your soul feels in striving for perfection.

Evolution: The evolved Chiron in this chart is okay with observing others' flaws and sins without feeling self-righteous or victimized in the process. In your evolution, you have learned the impracticality of your standards. You accept that everyone is imperfect and has limits. Your acceptance is not from a sense of superiority disguised as compassion but from authentic humility of recognizing that the same awkwardness in others exists within you and in all of life. You know that this is what it means to be human.

You can help heal others and yourself by moving your focus from what cannot be to what is possible. Simply pay attention to others, be of service to them, or just be a witness to their burdens. In turn, this blesses them with healing, as you show them that it is all right to be as they are and not strive for impossible, "perfect" standards.

Chiron in the Seventh House

This house is ruled by Venus and correlates to Libra. Relating with others allows you to share experiences you consider "pitiful," like the ephemeral nature of life and tenderness, which are involved in the idea of coexisting with others. As a native of this placement, you have to face the fact that your actions will somehow affect others no matter what you do. Your soul feels like it cannot escape this cause-and-effect nature of living. You can't be if there is no other person to be with, yet you find it hard to be *with* others. You see the other as a reflection of your wounded self and the wounded world around you.

Suppose Chiron is close to your descendant sign; in that case, you might encounter someone who will cause you to be aware of your wounds and blind spots, psychologically, as well as how those wounds affect your life. The experience could be a painful one where you find your way to healing by relating with others and seeing how all wounds are reflected in one another. This person or event will play a significant role in the shaping of your psyche. If it all plays out well, you will come to terms with the impossible, inevitable nature of coexistence, understanding that nothing is achieved in isolation.

Vulnerability: You might be thought of as pitiful or wounded by others, or you may think of others around you in this way. You tend to attract Chiron-like individuals who have wounds that are difficult to heal or who desire to heal others with wounds that have proven impervious to all healing. This wound can serve as the foundation for connection. So, there is a risk that you or the other person will unconsciously keep picking at the scabs to keep it open so that one does not have to lose the other person.

Evolution: You can see others in your life who act as agents of healing, no matter how much pain and hurt they might have inflicted on you. The very nature of coexistence implies that we will hurt each other. Yet, we can heal each other just the same, as long as we accept our part in hurting others. In isolation, there is only pleasure, not pain. However, pleasure and pain are concepts that are relative to each other. If you do not know what pain is, how can you appreciate pleasure? Also, without experiencing pleasure, how do you know you are in pain and need to heal? Therefore, pain and pleasure are unavoidable in our relationships. The evolved Chiron in this house comes to accept that as part of being human.

Chiron in the Eighth House

Ruled by Pluto in connection to Scorpio, you have some psychological and moral discomfort, awkwardness, or problem regarding your safety, mutual resources, shared experiences, and sexuality with others. You feel vulnerable as you protect yourself or others or bond with others psychologically and financially.

Vulnerability: When Chiron is not at home in this placement, you might be plagued by a constant feeling of dread when it comes to intimacy. This is diametrically opposed to your strong desire to be intimate with others, no matter what it costs you. You are unconsciously driven to share your body or resources in the most compulsive ways because you want to heal. Thus, you experience both extremes: The fear of intimacy and the obsessive drive to achieve it.

It is so easy to forget that intimacy in its purest form means you need to trust the other person counter-intuitively. You should trust them enough to lose your sense of self-control to them because you want to, not because you feel you must. Intimacy means allowing the other person to "trespass" freely on your sexual and psychic solitude or that which you hold as sacred to you. It implies you must turn off your survival instinct and instead allow the urge to merge to come through your soul so you can experience the beauty of togetherness.

With the wounded Chiron in this placement, the ability to experience true union and turn off the self-preservation instincts so that connection and communion with others are possible has been compromised. As a result, you find it hard to be open and let the other person in.

Evolution: Healed and evolved, you can heal others and yourself through the very act that you considered terrible, as you commune with others sexually, psychologically, and spiritually. You can instinctively tell how the other person has been wounded, and you just know what to do to heal that wound. You probably work as a bereavement counselor, sex therapist, or someone who helps victims of physical and sexual abuse. You know how to touch the scars of others in a way that heals them because those scars mirror yours.

The Tremendous Power of Chiron in the Eighth House

Chiron in this placement is one of the hardest to deal with. Do not let this scare you, though. Evolution and healing can lead to you becoming a mighty healer, transmuting pain to pleasure.

In your childhood, you might have experienced trauma surrounding the death of a good friend, pet, or close relative. This experience taught you about death's nature. However, no matter how you went through it, you understood it quickly and either got over your fear of death or grew even more afraid of it.

Healed, you become a powerful shaman. You can help others dive into the deepest recesses of their subconscious mind to grasp their darkest fears and heal them. If you can own the power of your fears and accept your shadow, you will make yourself whole, and this, in turn, will transform and heal others so they too can be complete.

Chiron in the eighth has incredible healing power. You just need to know that no matter how overwhelming your past trauma has been to your psyche, you can heal yourself by healing others. You can go beyond the subconscious mind, beyond the fourth dimension, to see the true nature of another's wound. There are times when you should simply focus on what appears in the now, on the surface, especially when you have fears of your future or past demanding your attention. Know that you are powerful, and you can create your reality. Those experiences from the past cannot hurt you now, and the future does not need to play out the way the past did.

Personalities in Each House

Dustin Hoffman starred as an autistic character in the 1988 hit *Rain Man*. He has Chiron in Gemini, in the fifth House. That role called out to him for so many reasons. For one thing, it allowed him to use the fifth house's chronic energy and his dominant Mercury. In addition, his character had issues with communication.

French filmmaker and writer Jean Cocteau also had his Chiron in this placement. *Les Enfants Terribles* (also titled *The Holy Terrors*) is one of his most-loved novels. It is about the isolation one experiences as a child and how inevitable it is to face anxieties and disappointments as an adolescent. This novel is a Chironic reflection of protection, sickness, abandonment, caring, and trauma—recurrent themes in Jean's later works. Other celebrities with Chiron in the fifth house include Steve Jobs, Kim Kardashian, Nicolas Sarkozy, Nicole Kidman, John Lennon, Megan Fox, Cristiano Ronaldo, Prince Harry, Paris Hilton, and Arnold Schwarzenegger.

Celebrities with Chiron in the sixth house include Carol Carpenter, Jessica Biel, Jennifer Lopez, and Ewan McGregor.

Celebrities with Chiron in the seventh house include Leonardo DiCaprio, Keanu Reeves, Grace Kelly, Jay Z, Ariana Grande, Kurt Cobain, Katy Perry, Bill Gates, Lana Del Rey, and Scarlett Johansson.

Celebrities with Chiron in the eighth house include Beyoncé Knowles, Taylor Swift, Johnny Depp, Jennifer Lawrence, David Bowie, Uma Thurman, Bruce Lee, Marion Cotillard, Charlize Theron, Robert Downey Jr., Jimi Hendrix, Marilyn Manson, and Ryan Reynolds.

Chapter 7: Chiron in the Natal Chart — III

Chiron in the Ninth House

This ninth house represents the concept of destiny. Ruled by Jupiter, in line with Sagittarius, this placement has some awkwardness when it comes to wisdom, spirituality, and faith. On the flip side, you may feel healed by engaging with these concepts. When Chiron is associated with Jupiter, you might find it hard to operate on blind faith alone. Or you might swing the other way by relying too much on theory because you are seeking meaning and purpose. You want reasons that justify what you do on an intellectual, moral, or religious level.

Vulnerability: When Chiron is not comfortable with this placement, you may refuse to take a good look at your life. Instead, you rationalize things using only your intellect. This winds up disguising your actual motives. However, it feels terrible when you choose to abandon self-reflection on your philosophies and constricting laws and decide instead to look for validation from outside yourself. Philosophical and religious ideologies may justify your behavior and thoughts, but you will not find the freedom your soul seeks. There is no more remarkable spiritual act than to choose to know yourself and guide yourself based on your self-awareness.

On the flip side, you might be keen on proving that faith is impossible. Your ability to have faith might have been ruined thanks to a traumatic experience or by coming to the wrong conclusions.

In the 1984 movie *Amadeus*, the protagonist Antonio Salieri was the most devout of Christians, who found joy in creating beautiful music for God. Much to his dismay, he learned that Mozart received much more talent from God. He could not quite fathom how or why, as to his thinking, Mozart cared nothing for religious rituals or morality. Enraged, Salieri burns his beloved crucifix and goes on a war against God. Curiously, the actual Antonio Salieri had Chiron in opposition to Jupiter. This configuration makes it difficult to accept one's limits, let alone confess them, so they keep on trucking the way they have been until the end justifies the means.

Evolution: The evolved Chiron in this placement feels the despair that ravages the human soul, and at the same time, finds joy in the limitless nature of choice, even within life's limits, because these limits allow the life to have more meaning, as we must make the right decisions and have some form of morality. There would be no such concepts as "meaning" or "right" in a life with no limits.

The healed Chiron can feel what it means to have a limited and personal reference point for all things. Yet, they find that this same limitation allows them to respect their inner morality and the morality of others.

Chiron in the Tenth House

The tenth house represents karma. It is ruled by Saturn and is connected to Capricorn. You may feel like you have disappointed a parental figure, someone you consider a superior, or your superego. This person is someone you think always expects you to be the very pinnacle of excellence in all you do. You feel odd when it comes to rising higher in life, be it socially or in your line of work. On the flip side, the drive for excellence can move you to connect with others and help them achieve their highest dreams and hopes as you allow yourself to be a means to their glorious end.

There could also be a rupture in how you relate with ideas of fatherhood, power, and divinity. Sometimes, this could happen with actual psychological problems with your father or a father figure. Also, you may have attempted to heal yourself and others around you your entire life.

The way we relate with the divine may begin with the ninth house, but it all comes to a head in the tenth one. Believing in a supernatural power or God is an illogical thing from a purely rational perspective. Thus, this is a ninth house issue. However, choosing to respect this power as logically as possible and feeling safe because it is like a surrogate parent is a matter for the tenth house. Chiron, in this placement, is a sign of how incapable or not you are of trusting this power. It's about your ability to "let go and let God" one hundred percent. Your ability to be fathered is compromised. This is the case, no matter how the father figure or power in your life may have acted toward you or how you have related to them in turn.

Vulnerability: It is not unusual for those with Chiron uncomfortable in this placement to be full of spite toward everything held dear by the intellect, culture, and society. You might feel equally drawn to and disgusted by everything that tradition honors, as well as those recognized by society as experts or champions of specific political ideologies, fields of knowledge, or popular causes. The trouble is that you tend to throw the baby out with the bathwater. So, you miss out on the usefulness of society's conventions, no matter how practical and common sense they are.

Evolution: As someone with their Chiron evolved in this placement, you seek to reconcile with society's power symbols, choosing to respect all who can offer wisdom, guidance, and admonishment. You also appreciate your own sovereignty. Your conscience speaks loud and clear. You have a genuinely moral outlook on life that is not the result of blindly following the herd or conforming to culture and religion with no questions asked.

When it comes to structure, you fully appreciate the importance of having figures who act as "guiding stars," so to speak, as they give direction to those sorely in need of it. You also are unswayed by sentiments, and because of this, you can achieve things beyond your wildest imaginations once you put your mind to it.

Chiron in the Eleventh House

This house correlates with Aquarius and is ruled by Uranus. This house has to do with gains. You might struggle with your ability to move past your ego so you can connect with others around you. On the other hand, you might feel a bit awkward about being part of humanity, and because of this, you might choose to look at others in a more forgiving light.

You feel a pervading sense of discomfort when it comes to being a part of a whole or tribe and playing your bit to contribute to the whole. On the other hand, your ability to listen and encourage others in their words and actions might have taken a hit. Sometimes, for just this reason, you might find yourself drawn to those who are good listeners, who genuinely encourage and support others' talents.

Vulnerability: When Chiron is wounded and uncomfortable in this placement, you may find it is hard to belong to anything larger than yourself. When this is the case, you start to feel like you are not moving anywhere, and nothing changes. As a result, your sense of self is static. You may, instead, find that it's boring to be someone defined by roles and labels. Thus, you are drawn to the thought of being nobody, which means the possibilities are endless for you. You might also carry a sense of awkwardness with you every day, which you use to mark yourself as separate and to define your place in the collective.

Evolution: You know how to heal the tribe through your strengths. You develop a unique identity as a healer, touching many lives by getting into their personal history while sharing your wounds to help them in the process. You come from a place of "one for all and all for one." In other words, you heal yourself through the collective and the collective through your divine presence. You are at peace with being somebody, and you can still transcend that on your terms so that you can be "nobody" through the process of allowing yourself to be part of the whole.

Chiron in the Twelfth House

This house is all about our exit from the world. It is ruled by Neptune and connected to Pisces. You have a deep desire to transcend the limits of being human and rise above your fears, doubts, and physical and spiritual deformities. You feel like your earthly experience is lacking in some way. It is like there is a spiritual or evolutionary drive within you to make peace with the fact that perfection and transcendence are impossible for you as a human.

Beethoven is an excellent example of one with Chiron in the twelfth house. He had a deep yearning for transcendence, and along with that, immense grief and pain. All through his life, he had passionately wanted nothing more than to create music that would be ahead of his time. In a twist reminiscent of Chiron, the god of healing who could not heal himself, Beethoven soon found that his hearing began to decline when he hit his late 20s. It was the one thing he needed to create music, and he was losing it. Somehow, he did not let that stop him. He kept on making music throughout the last decade of his life, never once hearing those compositions. Paradoxically, it turned out that when he lost his hearing, he composed the best of his pieces that millions around the world would come to love.

Vulnerability: You feel an insatiable hunger to escape the poverty, cruelty, viciousness, and ugliness that plagues humanity, refusing to understand or accept that these things cannot be helped, and you cannot escape from them. You cannot see how the things you run from are necessary to the human experience. Yet, these are the things that offer you a chance to transcend in spirit if you choose to do the little you can to help others or improve human conditions practically.

Evolution: The evolved Chiron in this placement will feel a yearning for perfection and beauty for as long as they live, but they now understand that the yearning is what connects us all. Even life's lowest forms have a strong desire to transcend their conditions until they reach completion or union with the Source.

You desire to find practical ways to achieve ascension beyond the present conditions of humanity. To achieve this, you rise above your primal drive to stick only with your tribe, culture, religion, gender, and other constructs you use to separate yourself from others.

You understand that boxing yourself up like that only polarizes and limits your life experience. You understand the awkwardness you feel because of your physicality. Still, you act divinely within the framework of earthly living, using all the resources available to you to do compassionate and kind acts, no matter how small.

You relinquish the grand ideals you had of spiritual superiority and humbly accept that you can still achieve much within your physical limits. Ironically, this will help you to rise above your earthly bonds and move into the realm of perfection and peace you have yearned for your whole life.

Personalities in Each House

Celebrities with Chiron in the ninth house include Marilyn Monroe, Justin Bieber, Adolf Hitler, Joe Biden, Justin Timberlake, Julia Roberts, Celine Dion, Mark Zuckerberg, Jessica Alba, Sylvester Stallone, Michelle Pfeiffer, Katie Holmes, Heidi Klum, and Adam Levine.

Celebrities with Chiron in the tenth house include Billie Eilish, Harry Styles, Cameron Diaz, Emma Watson, Kylie Jenner, Vanessa Redgrave, Francis Bacon, Jack Lemmon, Trisha Paytas, Ben Stiller, and Diana Ross.

Celebrities with Chiron in the eleventh house include Will Smith, Chris Brown, Albert Einstein, Paul McCartney, Pamela Anderson, Ashton Kutcher, Victoria Beckham, Halle Berry, Blake Lively, Jack Nicholson, Emma Stone, Matthew McConaughey, Helena Blavatsky, Drew Barrymore, and Gordon Ramsay.

Celebrities with Chiron in the twelfth house include Lady Gaga, Michael Jackson, Martin Luther King, George Clooney, Amy Winehouse, Hilary Clinton, Shane Dawson, Anne Sinclair, Virginia Woolf, John Krasinski, Whoopi Goldberg, Denise Richards, Charles Bukowski, Neil Armstrong, Immanuel Kant, Cyndi Lauper, and Armie Hammer.

Rising Above Destiny

Many have this erroneous idea that you are bound to what the stars say about you regarding astrology. That is not the case at all. The stars show you the basics about who you are. What you do with that information is entirely up to you.

Regardless of where Chiron is for you, know this: You can heal your wound. That is the point of Chiron's myth. He was in an impossible-seeming situation, full of so much pain that he wanted nothing more than to heal or to die but could not do either. Yet, he found a way by giving up his immortality. Prometheus was also in an impossible situation, destined to remain bound to that rock for all of eternity. Yet, that changed. He got freedom.

Regardless of where you find yourself in life, what you have been through to this point, or what your natal chart says, you can rise above your destiny. Destiny is not a fixed thing. It changes as you change. Thus, you need to decide right now to face your wounds with courage and love and seek how you can change them. It will not happen in a day. Still, with steady, consistent effort and loving patience with yourself and others around you, one day, you will look back and be amazed at how much progress you've made. In the meantime, you must keep a positive attitude and focus on one day at a time so you do not feel overwhelmed.

Good Deeds, Good Karma

When you consciously decide to do good and be that much better each day, you will create a ripple effect where your new life will be full of good karma that your next self will thank you for. You see, karma never ends, not even when you die. It goes on to affect your future lives. The only way to finally transcend humanity and the birth-death-rebirth cycle is to address and work out all your bad karma.

Understand that you alone are responsible for your choices. You are central to all the things you experience, good or bad. Know this, and you will stop blaming others for the bad stuff that happens to you—but this does not mean that you should wallow in guilt. It is about accepting responsibility and taking back the power that is yours instead of giving it away in the form of hatred or resentment.

It is so easy to blame the Hercules in your life for why you feel the way you do, but you must understand they are not the cause of your pain but the instrument of your karma, which had no choice but to play out. So, will you allow the poison of hatred and resentment to continue to run through you endlessly? Or will you accept your part in this, so you can begin to heal? The choice is yours.

Choose to do good. Listen to your conscience and follow its voice in all matters. Do not think you can avoid karma's effects by simply choosing to do nothing. Doing nothing is still doing something. It is a choice or decision you have come to. You are always deciding at every moment, so you might as well make it count.

Chapter 8: Self-Healing Through Chiron

Healing Your Soul

Now, let us put everything we have learned together so that you can heal your psychological and spiritual wounds. First, Chiron's placement on your natal chart clarifies what your soul has decided to spend this lifetime working on healing. Second, Chiron moves through all zodiac signs over fifty years, so you can expect your Chiron's return to happen when you are about fifty or fifty-one. At that point, you will either experience a healing crisis (which is a good thing) or a lightning bolt moment.

If you have chosen not to heal your old wounds or live up to your fullest potential, you experience a mid-life crisis. However, if you've been diligent about this, your life purpose will elevate you to new, unimaginable heights. You will find your life full of abundance, and you'll be in a place to help others along their journey.

Your Chiron placement shows you where your soul wound is, but more than that, it also shows you your natural talents for healing others. The wound you get is usually assigned to you before birth and lets you know about the state of the world when you came into it. It also gives you information on how you can evolve as a human in your present incarnation.

Your wounds may be physical, sexual, psychological, spiritual, or emotional. With time, you experience things that wound you over and over in the same way. Finally, however, you have to decide that you are done at some point and ready to be whole and healed of the wound at last. You also have to understand that there are some things you cannot change and ask for the strength to accept those things as they are. It will mean deliberately re-framing the problem, giving it a meaning that allows you to let go of the pain.

Putting It All to Use

This section will go over various affirmations to help you ground yourself in a new mental attitude to start your healing process. Take your time to meditate on them for just five minutes at the start of your day and five minutes when you retire to bed.

Please note that the affirmations are written to match the wound you specifically need to heal. The idea is to replace your current beliefs, which cause you continuous pain and wounding, with these affirmations until they take hold and become your new way of thinking.

Affirmations work best when you write them down and put them around your home, at work, in your car, or wallet. Thus, you can see them often, read them aloud or silently through the day, and reflect on what they mean to you. Stating them aloud is more potent than silently. With time, the more you repeat the words, they will form your core beliefs, which will drive your thoughts, words, and actions. So, read them with a smile and breathe them in. Declare them aloud every chance you get; this is how you get them to work powerfully for you. Then, after you have used them with success, you can go ahead and create affirmations that match your needs precisely.

First House: This is about your personality, body, and apparent traits, like your leadership style, temperament, ego, and ability to take the initiative.

Ask yourself: Have you ever put a limit on your self-expression, personality, or identity? If you have, you should work with the affirmations to come. Also, do you find it easy to set limits with others and yourself as needed? Do you know how to be clear with your boundaries? Do not be in a hurry to answer these questions. Be honest with yourself. It is how you let your true self shine forth.

Action: Do not be quick to respond to someone's request for your time, resources, or energy if you feel unsure about complying with their request. Take some time to figure out if committing to them will add to or remove your balance. Then, just say, "Maybe. I'll get back to you on that when I check my schedule." With time, you will get comfortable saying no.

Set limits when it comes to yourself, too. Make a point of carving out time each day to take care of your body, mind, and soul. If a commitment is no longer comfortable, be clear about it, and reschedule. People will respect you more for being upfront about it.

Encourage yourself the same way you would encourage others. Do not indulge in negative self-talk. When it crops up, stand up for yourself the same way you would if you saw someone speaking terribly to a loved one. Remind yourself that you are doing great.

Affirmations: I have a right to exist. My value comes from within me. I am worth it, and I am more than enough.

Second House: This deals with your values and valuables, as well as material wealth, personal finances, morals, and priorities.

Ask Yourself: Is your attitude and experience with money often all or nothing? Then you need to develop a secure and healthy mindset about money to attract and keep material resources. Also, can you find ways to live within your means while keeping an eye out for ways to grow your money? Finally, how can you balance your spending habits with your earnings?

Action: Get a financial planner to help you sort out your money issues. They can also help you with structuring your finances for a brighter, more secure future.

Adopt your personal code of ethics and morals that line up with your values and not someone else's.

If there are people you need to make amends with, get to it right away. But first, figure out a spiritual path that gives you guidance on what you should and should not do. You can start by following the golden rule, which says you should treat people how you would like them to treat you.

Always live from a place of kindness and genuine love, and you will find yourself doing well in your finances and other aspects of life.

Affirmations: I love myself. I approve of myself, exactly as I am. I let myself heal fully. I am very lovable and good enough as I am. I forgive myself, and I forgive everyone else.

Third House: This involves communication and the lessons you get from it, technology and devices, your years in grade school, and whether or not you have siblings.

Ask Yourself: Do you and your siblings have unresolved issues? First, it would be best to reflect on your role and genuinely seek to sort things out. Also, were you bullied in school, or were you the bully? Then, you can speak with a therapist or loved one to help you let go of the resentment or guilt you feel.

Action: Figure out how you may have wrongly communicated information, whether in tone or inaccuracy. Make a point of harmonizing your words in writing, speaking, and meaning so that you are always understood correctly.

Affirmation: I am genuinely heard and truly seen. I allow myself to be authentic. I always speak my truth. I am beautiful as my true self. I draw people who desire to be with me in my authenticity. I am always loved.

Fourth House: Emotional conditioning, nurturing, a sense of place, your family and childhood home, childhood emotional baseline, current family setup, and present physical home.

Ask Yourself: Did your home feel nurturing and full of love growing up? If it did not, understand that you can always create that for yourself and your loved ones right now. Was your home a violent, unpredictable space? Did you have to move around a lot? What was the emotional tone of your family in your childhood?

Action: Make your space beautiful, peaceful, safe, and joyful by de-cluttering. Anything you have not used in two years should go. Get rid of anything that brings up negative thoughts or emotions about painful experiences. Actively make your home feel like a proper home in any way you can. Give your space your personal touch.

Affirmation: I trust that wherever I am, I am at home. I am filling my home with love. I am home to my soul. I am of inestimable value. I am important, and I am safe.

Fifth House: Children, play, creativity, self-expression, romance, and pleasure.

Ask Yourself: What is a pleasure to you? How do you seek it out and experience it? What do you enjoy? What makes you burst into laughter?

Action: Speak with your friends and ask them what gives them pleasure, so you have ideas you could try and see what works for you. Speak with a healing practitioner if that helps you remove any blocks that stand in the way of you playing, creating, and being yourself. Meditation will serve you greatly.

Permit yourself to explore your dreams and desires, and have fun with as many as you can, so you feel more joy and flow in your life.

Affirmation: I am here to create. I create that which did not exist before I made it. I am powerful and unique. I prioritize myself. I always come first.

Sixth House: Daily routines, service, professional work, diet, fitness, exercise, physical health, and disease.

Ask Yourself: How can you boost your immune system? Are you taking medication and following the prescriptions correctly? Do you get yourself checked out each year and follow your doctor's orders? Are you regular with colonoscopies? If you are female, do you get a pap smear and a mammogram annually? If you're male, do you get your prostate examined? Do you eat healthily and work out regularly? Is your weight optimal for your height? Is there a balance between personal life and work? Do you have any outlet to be of service?

Action: Having answered all those questions, see what adjustments you must make. Treat your health as a priority, and make a point of taking time off work to relax and recharge.

Affirmation: I am flexible. I am whole and healthy. I have balance in all areas of life. I allow myself me-time. I set time for others and respect my boundaries. I am at peace with imperfection.

Seventh House: Business contracts and partnerships, personal relationships, divorce, and marriage.

Ask Yourself: Are you earning what you deserve, or do you need to negotiate to get pay commensurate to your efforts? Do you need to end or renegotiate your present contract? Is there an intimate relationship you need to fix? Are you and your partner happy together? If you are single, are you the sort of person you would love to be with? Do you need to forgive yourself for something?

Action: Consider what areas of your life need changes. Look over everything with a fine-tooth comb. Stop what your soul says it is done with, and start what you know it's calling you toward.

Affirmation: I love myself. I know myself. I trust my soul and inner voice. I share my preferences, and that brings me joy. I make my happiness myself. I express myself sexually, joyously, and without shame.

Eight House: Birth, sex, death, experiences that change you, intensely shared emotions, metaphysics, spirituality, mysticism, other people's property, and money.

Ask Yourself: What do you need to let go of in your life? How do you maintain your connection to spirit? Are there any practices you have that help you with this? Whom do you need to let go of? Are there people in your life with whom you enjoy intense, shared emotions? Are you following your bliss? Are you responsible for other people's money and possessions?

Action: Having asked yourself these questions makes the necessary lifestyle changes for more passion and joy in your life.

Affirmation: I am powerful, and I use my power for good. I am trusting and trusted. I am safe. All things work out for my good. I am kind and generous.

Ninth House: Religion, politics, news, law, higher education, international travel, world view, and philosophy.

Ask Yourself: Are there classes you would love to take, or is there a program you'd like to start to handle your other responsibilities? Are there outstanding legal issues you must resolve? Do you have any interest in helping disenfranchised people? Are there places you'd love to visit? Can you research your dream travel destination and plan it out thoroughly?

Action: Take steps toward making that class happen. Explore your life so you can live it to the fullest. Handle any looming issues so you can breathe easy and see if you are into giving back to those without voices.

Affirmation: I am connected to my divine, higher self. I am supported by my core beliefs. My core beliefs lead to my preferred experiences. I find and enjoy deep meaning in life. I enjoy a deep connection to all of life. I am truth in the flesh. I have clarity within me.

Tenth House: Social status, persona, public reputation, honor, achievement, fame, recognition, career.

Ask Yourself: Do you project your desired image in all aspects of your life to your detriment? Are you living way above your means to look like you are rich and feeling stressed out because of it? Are you given recognition for your accomplishments? Do you credit others their due, too? Do you follow your internal values? Do you only work to pay bills and do not care about your job?

Action: You have to clear up all the falsehood and misunderstanding surrounding your public persona. Do this, and you can finally breathe easy and set yourself free from the pressure of needing to meet other people's expectations of you.

Affirmations: I am more than good enough, just the way I am. I reach my goals always and with ease. I ask for help and always get it. I glow with success. I am dependable, and everyone knows it.

Eleventh House: Associations, groups, social justice, friends, and humanitarian causes.

Ask Yourself: Are your friendships meaningful, and do you nurture them? Do you engage with community events that call to your soul? Are you an active volunteer, or would you consider setting up an event for a worthy cause that means something to you? Is there a social issue you would like to tackle or a crowdfunding campaign you'd like to start?

Action: Make sure you let your voice be heard at every turn. If you feel the pull to start something for the greater good, now is the time. The resources you need will show up as soon as you commit and start taking action.

Affirmation: I let myself experience and enjoy connection. I move out of fear and into love. I make significant contributions in many ways. I am well connected. I am unconditionally loved.

Twelfth House: Shadow self, unconscious mind, addictions, fringes of society (psychiatric hospitals, jails, outliers), spirituality, imagination, and creativity in film, dance, arts, poetry, completions, and endings.

Ask Yourself: Are there things about you hidden and suppressed that you need to bring to your awareness? Is there a compulsion or addiction you can heal through music, dance, film, poetry, theater, or art? Do you have legal matters to resolve? Do you judge yourself because of things you did in the past and have trouble forgiving yourself? Do you have a dream journal? Do you connect with your intuition before taking action on things that matter to you?

Action: Keep a dream journal; it will serve you in ways you cannot begin to imagine, giving you insight into your life. Also, make a point of connecting to the arts and the mystical. Give of yourself in service, and you will see yourself heal.

Affirmation: I forgive myself fully. There is more than enough for one and all. I love myself as I am exactly. I am more than enough. Love opens every door for me.

Meaning in Suffering

All experiences in life have meaning, and suffering is no exception. Suffering is how we learn, grow, and evolve into better humans, and ultimately, better souls. Through suffering, we know not to treat others in any way that would cause them the pain we feel or felt in the past. It is suffering that shows us what is right and wrong, good or bad, selfless or selfish. We would not value life if it were all fun and games and no suffering.

Suffering or the avoidance and healing of it is what drives us all. Think about it. You get up and go to work because you know that if you do not, you will not get paid, and you and your loved ones might suffer for it in one way or another. Some group feels like they are the superior race. While that is not justifiable, the fact that other races exist causes their mental suffering, so they do terrible things to fix that. The child in her full diapers cries out because no one will know she is suffering in that condition if she does not. The point is that life is full of suffering, in one way or another.

You stand up to a bully on someone's behalf because you have suffered bullying yourself or suffered watching a loved one deal with that pain. Your friend is tender in their criticism because they have suffered being harshly criticized at some point and want to spare you that pain. Surely, you are starting to realize the inevitability of suffering. From birth to death, it follows us all. It elevates us when we allow it to, and when we do not, it beats us down to our lowest low, and we experience more pain and even more suffering for it.

Chiron tried to intervene in the battle with the savage centaurs, and for that, he was struck by Hercules's poison arrow. He then had to live with the suffering from the pain, unable to have the mortal gift of death. Zeus, moved by his grief, permitted him to make a deal to end it. In this case, we can see the mystery of unfair suffering. We want to believe the good should be rewarded, and the bad should be punished. We want to think that there is someone to be blamed for the condition we are in. The absolute truth is: there is no better way to deal with undeserved pain than to accept that life is suffering and make peace with the fact that being human has its limits.

Even Chiron's immortality could not keep him safe from life's pain and suffering, any more than we think we can do that for ourselves. However, unfortunately, this is the way of life. We either choose compassion and acceptance or give in to our base instincts. Life is sometimes unfair, but there is always meaning to be gleaned in suffering. Compassion is from a Latin root meaning "to suffer with." Grief transforms you, so this means that your deepest pain has a purpose, which you may not always be able to work out right away, but you will always find that it all comes down to compassion and love.

Stay Positive

Throughout your healing process, you have to stay positive. This is the best way to clean and dress your wound so that it can heal. Maintaining a positive outlook on life does wonders for the soul. It puts you in a frame of mind to see what you need to address in your life to allow healing energy to flow through you and to those around you.

Look at it this way: You already know what it is like to wallow in the depths of negative thinking. There is nothing new there. So, why not try being positive instead? Choosing a positive outlook on life as you work to heal your Chiron will give back to you, filling your life with joy and beauty. Does this mean you should completely ignore negative thoughts and emotions when they show up? Of course not. Acknowledge that they are there, and then gently remind yourself that you always have a choice. You can accept the negativity, welcome it back like a toxic old friend, and have it ruin your progress. Or you can remind yourself that just because you think a thought does not make it true. You do not have to own it if it does not give to you in good ways. Thank the negative thoughts for reminding you of your choice to see the good in everything and then release them lovingly.

Chapter 9: Finding Your Life Purpose

Knowing where Chiron is on your chart can help you discover your life's true purpose. That purpose is wrapped up in the bandages covering your wounds. Once you take a good look at your wound, you will know precisely what you should do. However, you cannot embark on your journey just yet without stitching yourself up so you can at least limp, if not walk properly. In other words, you can't give what you do not have. Thus, before you try to heal others with your wound, you must first heal yourself.

Your life's purpose is not something that exists in isolation, meant to serve only yourself and no one else. Instead, without fail, true purpose touches the lives of others around you. Your true purpose is service with love. It is when you give so much of yourself, and yet, paradoxically, you do not feel tapped out or drained because this is what you were meant to do.

To discover your purpose, deal with the pain so that it is no longer blinding you to what you are here to do. Your natal chart shows you your Dharma. Dharma is what you must do in life. It's what you need to learn and where you feel uncomfortable because you're unfamiliar with the terrain. As this book is about Chiron, we have looked at all of this already. It's now a simple two-step process: First, heal yourself, and then heal others. However, simple does not mean easy. You will need to put in the work, but it's worth it.

Suffering: The Key to A Greater Destiny Ahead

There is more to Chiron than just healing your pain and accepting your suffering. It is about the wisdom that it gives you, which you pass on to others. It's the key to a greater destiny for you and the people who will benefit from your decision to heal yourself and channel that healing to them as well. It's no coincidence that the symbol of Chiron is a key. This key unlocks a better, more rewarding end for all. It opens the door to a deep sense of security and peace within your soul.

Chiron invites you to go within yourself. When you come back out, you do so with deeper understanding, a healed sense of self, and true power. Unfortunately, most people have an aspect of life with patterns that repeat themselves endlessly, causing frustration each time, leaving one at a loss for how to end it.

Freud was the first to point out these painful cycles, which he called "repetition compulsion." They have been written about in so many ways since he created that term back in 1914. The creator of the stages of psychosocial development, Erik H. Erikson, a renowned psychoanalyst, had much to say about "destiny neurosis" in his 1950 book, *Childhood and Society*. Destiny neurosis was his way of talking about the mistakes that we repeat again and again. He wrote about how we unconsciously set things up to allow ourselves to experience different variations of the same theme, which we have not mastered or accepted.

Then there is the object relations theory, which suggests that we tend to repeat the relationships with our caregivers from childhood unconsciously. Patrick Casement, a British psychoanalyst, wrote about how these conflicts, left unresolved, continue to come up until you find a good solution. Finally, the attachment theory also suggests that patterns from our early development form the central theme of the relationships we engage in as adults.

Chiron helps us see these patterns more clearly. It shows us what we hide or try to change because we are afraid of being rejected. It also shows us what our triggers are. It has the potential and power to soothe the impulse to react negatively to the world within and without. If we allow it, we can change the narrative of our destiny so that we no longer have to be mired in our old ways, trying to wade through an ocean of glue. We can, with Chiron's help, unlock the door to a greater destiny ahead of us, one filled with joy, acceptance, and expansion.

Your Role in Society

It is incredibly vital that we pay attention to how we conduct ourselves in our day-to-day lives, whether at work or home. The goal each day should be to live in congruence, something that most people do not do. For instance, many compartmentalize their attitudes and behaviors, acting one way at home and another in a different setting. Worse still, we find reasons to justify why we are this way. We fight hard for the right to misrepresent who we really are in our lives. Instead, we should be looking at what we need to change; this leads to self-fragmentation. We are broken to pieces and add on things that are not true to our souls. Our broken pieces cry out for healing.

Your role in society is to be your authentic self. It means deciding to live congruently, discard whatever does not represent who you are, and reintegrate what you have tossed away, which makes up a core part of your being. Do you walk your talk? Not doing that can lead to more wounds, not just to your psyche but also to your society.

Chiron seeks to push us to increase our awareness of self-permissiveness and self-regulation to live in harmony in our professional and personal lives. A society full of people who can regulate themselves, and are at ease with allowing themselves to be who they are, is a healed and evolved world.

To make this practical, you should be attuned to what is happening between your ears and within your head. Be willing and ready to give yourself honest feedback to assess what you need to fix in your life. You owe it to society and yourself to be completely honest with your soul. Once you do that, you can look at your vulnerability, ego, and weakness, to release conservatism and rigidity. Having done this, you can create a space for yourself and others full of joy and spontaneity.

When you choose to be accountable for what you need to change, you take charge of your words and actions, knowing that you alone are responsible for them. You do this with understanding and compassion so that you do not go down the slippery slope of harsh judgments that spiral into self-loathing and shame, bringing on more pain.

This accountability to yourself and society will make it easier for you to sit with your wounds for longer, with compassion, so that you can heal them. It means learning to work with your guilt and shame and holding space for those parts of you that are deeply wounded and cause you to do the things you judge yourself for.

When you have empathy for your wounds, you can forgive the parts of yourself you resent, and this process will change your life. Do not engage in self-criticism as you do this. Instead, be compassionate and kind to yourself. Explore your habits thoroughly and gently deal with your wounds, and you will find true healing at last. Then you can bring that same gift of healing to a society that sorely needs it.

The Right Attitude to Others

Choose to see others through the eyes of love and compassion rather than through your ego. When you shift your perception this way, choosing to see the truth of whom you are dealing with, your behavior toward them will adjust accordingly.

Now, this is not an easy thing to do. However, the more intentional you are about this, the better you will get at doing it with time. You see, it might seem to you that we are all separate, and nothing is connecting us. Still, the truth is we're all one and the same spirit expressing ourselves in different forms.

Thus, when you choose to look lovingly at others, you get the same love beamed back at you. When you decide to heal yourself, you heal others, too, and as you help them heal, you find yourself healing. This is why the golden rule exists. What you do for others, you do for yourself.

Keep your eyes peeled for opportunities that will allow you to meet supportive wounded healers like yourself, regardless of what phase of healing they are in. You want to seek out the common thread between you and others so that you can find alignment in all your relationships.

Creating a Space of Solace for Others

You can create a safe space for others who are wounded, so they can find solace and the support they need to heal themselves. However, seeing the potential in others is a double-edged sword. You might find a propensity to criticize them when you know how much better they could be doing. Resist the urge to do that because it will only lead to unnecessary, avoidable wounding. Instead, learn to love others for their beautifully flawed selves, as they are only human.

Turn the same compassion you use on yourself when dealing with your wounds to help others work through their pain and suffering. We all have our individual paths to walk, but in the end, it is all with the same goal of fostering healing on a global scale. Understand those seeming others are a part of you and treat them with the same love you once longed for.

To give others the solace they need, you must respect their feelings and be patient and gentle with them as they discover themselves. Commit to trusting in their ability to heal and revel in every little step toward wholeness that they take. Believe with all your heart that they can move from living a life driven by fear to one fueled by love. Honor and respect them, no matter where they are on their journey, even if they are still wallowing in self-pity or denial.

Chiron's Beacons

Let us talk about **Marilyn Monroe,** with her Chiron-Venus connection. You are about to see how uncanny the Chironic themes are in her story. Like Chiron, Marilyn's first traumatic experience was being abandoned by her father and then later by her mother. This began the cycle of experiences with abandonment in her relationships, which affected her life's journey.

Her Chiron in the tenth house showed she struggled on the inside with the need to feel like everyone loves her while dealing with how intensely uncomfortable all that attention can be. First, of course, there is the thrill that comes with being adored as a sex symbol, which can be addictive. Then, there's the pressure of having to live up to everyone's expectations. Finally, she had to deal with the pressure of being over-sexualized and the shame that comes with only being appreciated for how you look (a Venusian struggle).

There is a fear of rejection that plagues people with this placement. Along with it comes a great mistrust of others, especially men, if it is a woman with this Chiron placement. Marilyn was afraid of love. This fear was reflected in her relationships, often with much older men, high profile and married, or overly possessive like Arthur Miller, John F. Kennedy, and Joe DiMaggio, respectively. She experienced being loved by men who would not or could not commit to her in each relationship. If they tried, they failed. They couldn't engage with her on any level besides physically.

Still, these relationships gave her the attention she needed to keep her sense of self—the fragile, beautiful blonde, which she also resented. It is hard to feel anything other than resentment when you are treasured just for your good looks because you're loved for just that one aspect of yourself and nothing else. Thus, Marilyn was forced to play the role of an object and nothing more. In this way, she was fragmented.

She had relationships with men who could not have a normal love life because of their circumstances. As a result, she set up a recurring theme where she was doomed to rejection, perpetuating the belief of the Venus-Chiron person that they are inherently unlovable. Her wound was clear, and perhaps if she had found someone who could help her figure it out and work through it, her story would have had a different ending.

Tony Robbins has his Chiron in the fifth house. He has written many best-selling self-help books. He also hosts seminars all over the world where he helps people work through their wounds. He does this by immersing himself in their personal history while at the same time sharing his wounds with everyone, right there on stage. Somehow, he has found a way to bring together the opposing archetypes of Aquarius and Leo, which is the collective versus the individual. Tony is an excellent example of a philanthropist healer who employs the "all for one and one for all" mindset in his professional and personal life. Furthermore, he remains in alignment with his true self in all his affairs.

Here is a list of other personalities who have made Chiron work well for them and have successfully healed their wounds: Jeff Bridges, Jon Bon Jovi, Queen Elizabeth II, Richard Dreyfuss, Hilary Clinton, Robert De Niro, Giovanni Casanova, Marlon Brando, Pat Boone, Marlene Dietrich, Hugh Hefner, Michael Douglas, Nat King Cole, Johannes Brahms, Prince Charles, Doris Day, Mae West, Juan Peron, Harry Houdini, Pierre Teilhard de Chardin, Coretta Scott King, Don Johnson, and Ringo Starr. All these people prove that you can indeed heal your wounds and move on to greatness.

Chapter 10: Spiritual Awakening with Chiron

Main Takeaways

As we come to the end of this book, let us go over the main takeaways you should keep in mind to guide you on your path to healing and self-actualization.

Chiron shows us the hero's path. He shows us how we can overcome our wounds and weaknesses while reminding us that the heroes, no matter how strong they are, also have their limits. It does not matter if you are far ahead of others in terms of consciousness. You still can only do so much.

The wounded healer is a reminder that the non-dual nature of the Spirit cannot express itself until you have chosen to work with your wounds. In other words, everyone is Superman until they are hit with kryptonite. Love and freedom are easy when things are great, but not when things go downhill.

When things are not looking up, we find ourselves face-to-face with the darkness, deceit, pain, betrayal, and wounds within us. This experience can be so intense that it makes you question if anything has meaning. You wonder if there is anyone at all behind the scenes who at least has a plan and will make everything make sense eventually.

Right now, the Earth is in a state of turmoil. We have overpopulated it to the point of draining it, playing out our wounds on a larger scale. Also, our wounds repeat themselves, coming back with a fury each time. We are in pain, but that pain lies in our misunderstanding of reality and our refusal to seek connection with our divinity. It is the major cosmic wound that we must heal within ourselves.

Chiron's consciousness is about knowing that life is pain, suffering, or a lack of satisfaction. It is Dukkha. It may feel negative, but Chiron's story is of existing in a life where Spirit is ignored because of our drive to live, no matter the cost. Still, there is a better way to approach the Chiron mythology: As our personal narrative. It is how we interpret life and how we face down our challenges.

We have to change the narrative of our suffering, but we must experience deep healing to do so. The energy of being diseased has to be released to allow ourselves to be whole again. Unfortunately, in our arrogance, we assume we can simply will our wounds away or ignore them until they disappear. Chiron shows us that we cannot pull an Icarus, trying to escape the prison of our wounds by flying a little too close to the sun. Instead, Chiron forces you to be grounded and face the reality of your situation.

Compassion is a virtue worth developing, so we can finally let go of pain and lighten our load. Chiron was well versed in compassion and was the perfect embodiment of acceptance, which set him and Prometheus free. One day, we will perfect the art of healing, but in the meantime, Chiron serves as a reminder that there is no magic pill and that healing is a process. We must learn to accept that there will most likely never be perfection on Earth, which is okay. The point is to learn to make peace with what is and do the best with what we have.

Nothing is Random; Life Is Full of Meaning

Everything has a purpose. Nothing is random. There is no senselessness to even the most mundane thing that happens, and there's no maniacal person in the sky making things happen just because they feel like it. There is meaning in everything if you are willing to seek it out and be open to what you get.

You must approach your search for meaning in your suffering and wounds with the right mindset. The universe is rich with meaning, yet it is paradoxically neutral. In other words, you will get the meaning you want to receive. If you are looking for definitions that imply that all is lost, your life is pointless, and there is no use in trying, you will get that. The universe is generous and loving to the point of impartiality, so you will get experiences that reflect the meaning you have chosen to pull from your wounds.

However, if you choose to receive empowering meaning from all you have been through, it will come through. You will begin to interpret everything from the standpoint of power, love, and compassion, and it will all begin to make sense to you. You will no longer indulge in disempowering thoughts and ideas about yourself and others. It only makes sense because you can see how that draws you back into those terrible cycles you were once desperate to be free from.

Why Spiritual Awakening Matters

Astrology tells stories using archetypes to help us make sense of why we are here. It is a great tool to allow us to experience a spiritual awakening. You are a miniature version of the cosmos— we all are. It means you have within you all of life, and your life is about how you express that wholeness through your "small" part. How well you express yourself depends on the archetypes on your natal chart and the level of spiritual awareness you have developed. Your willingness to be accountable for your experiences is just as vital, too.

When you are spiritually awake, you understand that all your choices and actions happen within a vast network of interactions, all of them connected. You never know what ripple effect your words and actions have had on others, and even if you did, chances are you would not be able to grasp them fully.

Chiron will show you how you and the world are connected in suffering and how you can interact with yourself and others to create a life full of purpose and meaning. When you understand the effects of Chiron on your life, the study of your placement will take on an entirely new dimension. Think of astrology as a form of astral or celestial language that helps you interpret the archetypal patterns that play out in your life and the lives of others.

All of the cosmos is in your chart as a seed that will grow and become you, but you must not feel that you are doomed to play out what the charts say about you. Remember this: People always transcend their stars. The spiritually awakened soul understands this and is also aware that there is neither good nor bad on their natal charts. You are not made of good and evil, and life is not black and white. Of course, those who have not spiritually awakened would argue differently, but you know better. You know that you contain all of it.

Knowing that you contain it makes it easier for you to work with your wounds and other wounded healers around you without judgment and criticism. Healing happens at a much more accelerated rate in an environment free of these things.

How to Spiritually Awaken with Chiron

Begin now to actively look for how Chiron's cycle is playing out in your life. There is no rushing this process. First, you must sit and take a good look at your life so far. Then, call up your most painful experiences, and try to find any similarities among them. Chances are, you will see the connection.

The next thing you must do is call up experiences where you are the one inflicting those same wounds on others. Now, this might be very tricky to do because your mind might want to forget those experiences. It does this because we all want to believe we are good people. We will fight tooth and nail to obscure anything that puts us in a bad light. Thus, take as much time as you need with this step.

Next, look for what it was that drove you to act the way you did when you wounded the others. Several answers will rush through your head, but do not be quick to settle on them. Dig deeper. You will know you have found it when you feel a deep, gnawing, indescribable pain within your soul. You'll have discovered your wound. When you have, don't be in a hurry to run from it. Just sit with it, not judging it. Allow yourself to feel what you feel. If you need to cry, that is fine. If you need to be held and there is someone you can go to, let them hold you. Take your time.

Now, it is time for you to feel love for yourself. Feel appreciation for having awakened spiritually to your true self and your core wound. Radiate loving energy to yourself. In your mind, visit every experience you have ever had where another wounded you or where you inflicted the wound on someone else. Keep your eyes shut through this. You may lie down if that feels better for you. Make a light fist with your dominant hand and place it over your chest. As each experience plays out in your mind, lightly beat your chest above your heart with love, as you say to yourself in each situation, "I love you." Let the beating be in time with the words. Do this over and over again, for all you can remember. Then take a moment to sit with your feelings and reassure yourself again with the words, "I love you."

This is how to awaken with Chiron fully. Now, you will move about your day conscious of this wound, not just in yourself, but in others, too. You'll feel healed. The scar will be there, but you'll be in a much better position. Then, when the cycle comes along again and tries to play out, you'll catch it, and with love and compassion for yourself, you will make different choices. Better ones.

Beyond Your Comfort Levels

The best things in life are way outside of your comfort zone. You did not come here to be comfortable; you came here to live—and the business of living can be pretty messy. Keep this in mind. Just because you have healed your wound does not make you immortal. You can still be wounded. The difference is that now, you are spiritually awake. You can deal with the wounds consciously. You can look at the people hurting you and understand that they do so only because they are in pain and desperate for healing. You can look at them with compassion, not with a better-than-thou attitude, but with solidarity.

Compassion is not a comfortable thing. Imagine being Jesus and having to look at the people piercing you, spitting on you, calling you names while knowing you are going through all of that for their sakes. It is not an easy thing to do, but that is part of life. It does not mean you should not establish firm boundaries. It merely means you shouldn't waste your time and energy being resentful or wallowing in the pain. Instead, seek ways to help those who want assistance and bless those who will not have it as you let them go their way.

The Choice of Forgiveness

Every day, we must make choices about being empathetic or withholding kindness in our thoughts, words, and actions. When you open up to healing, you will find yourself willing to forgive everyone, including those who have hurt you the most. This experience is a form of enlightenment.

Your eyes open up, and you see that these people have given you a gift. They have offered you a clear view of your soul's wound so that you can heal it. They also caused the wounded healer within you to wake up. Your experiences, you will find, drive you to look into the power of healing and then take care of yourself the way you have always desired.

You will experience radical transformation when you realize that you are here on Earth to love and be loved. With your mind full of love, you have the power to make the impossible happen. Your thought pattern shifts so that you begin to attract all the love the world has to offer. This shift in thought is the epitome of enlightenment. It is not something you have to work hard for; it's something that hits you in a moment if you are open to it.

Most people lean too heavily on their intellect to resolve their problems. Maybe you can relate to this. Perhaps you have spent the bulk of your life using your intelligence to deal with betrayal, grief, loss, and other challenges that are hard to push through. However, you must realize by now that thinking your way through them is not enough. You could never understand why something happened enough to heal it. Healing isn't a mind thing; it is a heart matter. In its truest form, healing means you must have compassion, and you must forgive and let go of past hurts.

Forgiveness is a word people use too often yet understand too little. The process of forgiveness is talked about a lot but not practiced nearly enough. It is not something you do just once, and you are done with it. It's something that you do time and time again. Forgiveness is a progressive action. We will always be in the process of forgiving.

Asking you to forgive the people that hurt you in one fell swoop or at a moment's notice is not only unkind but impossible. It is something you must do in stages. Eventually, you will get to a place where you can look at them and know in your heart that the old familiar feeling of resentment is no longer there. All you feel is love and appreciation for them.

The concept can be very abstract until you have an experience where you must practice it. Usually, that experience will begin with learning to forgive yourself, right along with another person. You do your best to move along, to forget about the pain, but you find you cannot. No matter how hard you try, you are stuck. You feel disempowered, like there are at least a dozen heavy, wet blankets over your head.

Perhaps you know what it is like to be mired in detrimental emotions, sometimes even to the point of causing physical illness. You know what experience you are reminded of right now, and it probably feels almost as fresh as when it happened, no matter how long ago that was. However, if you take the time to look closely, you will find that the person who hurt you is a catalyst for your wounds to reveal themselves. It allowed you to sit and stare your deepest fears in the face.

Maybe you fear that you are unworthy, unlovable, disposable. Perhaps it is that you will never amount to anything in life. Whatever it is, that sensation is jarring and can be paralyzing, but if you keep looking at them, you will find your wound coming to light, ready to heal.

We must handle ourselves with compassion and care as we heal. When possible and needed, enlist the help of a professional so you can work through the pain. You are not weak or stupid for wanting to reach out to others in your darkest moments.

When you feel lost, uncertain, and hopeless, beneath that swirling madness is a chance for you to begin anew. You must first acknowledge that there is deep work you must do, especially when loving yourself. You must find a way to forgive yourself for not showing up when you needed you the most. With a shift in perspective, you will realize that your heart was broken to allow you to love even deeper than you have ever done.

The Vessel for Change

You can transform your suffering into a strength by willingly changing your mind about what you experienced and growing in love, understanding, and self-forgiveness. You can also choose to see your painful moments through new eyes to feel more peace and joy in the present moment. Finally, you should take charge of your life by being more deliberate about how you create your life from here on out. Make it a point of duty to give yourself the love and acceptance you seek. This way, if someone hurts you by rejecting you, you know you have infinite pools of love within your soul for yourself, and you will find it easier to heal and move on.

Rather than create your life based on your former mindset (affected by the old, undesired experiences), move forward in power. Set clear intentions about what you want for yourself. In other words, the best way to live is not by focusing on avoiding what you do not want but by actively moving toward what you prefer. This mindset is what draws you to the places, people, and things you would love to make a part of your life. At the root of all this is the vital work of forgiveness. You already know how much easier it is to blame others, hold grudges, or blame ourselves. Thus, the real work is in learning to forgive.

When you decide to hold on to your old perspectives, which draw life from your belief of being wronged by someone else, you cut the cord that would have empowered you to create the change you seek. So, you have the option of leaving your comfort zone, where nothing changes and everything sucks. You can take that risk by opening up your mind to new ways of looking at your life so far. It allows you many opportunities to manifest your chosen outcomes. The more you can live from your heart, fueling every action and word with kindness and empathy, the faster you will change your life. Thus, every chance you get, make this shift within you. Keep it at the forefront of your mind as you interact with others, and watch the magic unfold.

Transformation

You can use your wounds to live a happier life, but to do that, you need to expose them to the harsh daylight so you can see them clearly. You want to hear them out and understand them. Only then can you transform and integrate them. Thus, take everything you have learned in this book to heart, and put it all into practice. Reading alone does you no good. Break down every thought system rooted in fear, and decide to think from love instead.

As you consciously practice empathy and self-forgiveness, your consciousness will shift for the better. This shift is what transforms your soul wound. You will get flashes of insight, and your love for others and yourself will blossom and grow more than you ever imagined possible. You will start to see problems and situations in a whole new light.

In psychology and traditional psychotherapy, this process is known as reframing. It is you shifting your paradigm to line up with your preferred experiences. It will move you into a world where you feel happy, content, joyful, and at peace. It's a skill you can master, and it will help you move through past hurts and get the meaning out of those experiences.

You see, life is all about discovering yourself. As Louise Hay puts it, enlightenment involves going within yourself to know who you are. It is about knowing that you can change yourself for the better by choosing to love and take care of the person you see in the mirror. In other words, you need to develop a deep, passionate appreciation for all that you are. Accept the bits you are proud of and those you are not. Accept what you're great at and what you fail at. Accept your quirks and your weirdness and all the beautiful things about you. Stop putting conditions on your love for yourself. Love you, as you are, right now.

Enlist Your Mind

Most people go around reacting to things. A more conscious and powerful way to live would be to respond, not react. To do that, you need to work on the skills that let you interrupt the unhelpful thought patterns that have led you to act in ways you do not want to. One powerful way to accomplish this is to use somatic screening skills. These skills help you interpret and intervene before your brain escalates things to the point where you react in ways that do not serve you.

Your brain and central nervous system can gather and decode all memories similar to what you are experiencing at the present moment in an instant. This process is over in a matter of nanoseconds.

We consider the inner meanings we have, which are founded on our sensory awareness. Know that the world outside is just a reflection of what you think within you. In other words, what you perceive is what you project, or "As within, so without." So, if there is an outcome you want to see out there, you should look to change yourself and not the world outside of you.

To develop your somatic screening skill, one thing you can do is breathe. You can slow down that emotional reactivity by breathing. Before you respond, shut your eyes and breathe in slowly and deeply, keeping your attention on your breath. This way, you will buy time to decode the information you are receiving and give it a meaning that will lead to you acting in a way that works for everyone. This skill is so vital when dealing with heated situations with our loved ones. Developing it will save you and your friends or family from needless wounding through harsh words and actions.

Did you know your mind can also trigger you when you are all by yourself? For example, how often have you thought about a conversation with someone on a matter that angers you both? Also, have you noticed that you begin to get all worked up even when they are not there? You might even get to the point of imagining conversations that would not happen in real life. You do this just so you can feel justified in your anger and have the last word—at least, in your mind.

You might also have remembered a conversation that took place many years ago. As you recall it, you find that you are starting to itch and sweat, your breathing is shallow, your mannerisms are agitated, and your palms are sweaty. There you are, huffing in anger, pacing back and forth across the room, when the only opponent you're engaged in a heated battle with is in your head and nowhere near you!

It is funny how one can go from being calm and at ease to raging in just a few seconds, simply by running an experience through their head that caused them deep anger or sadness. It does not matter how long ago it happened; it feels like it was just a few seconds ago. Funnier still how we can get worked up over things that have not happened and likely never will.

Thus, if your mind can make you react this way to nonexistent threats and triggers, you can reverse engineer the process and make your mind work to give you the opposite outcome. You can think of something that happened and deliberately reframe it in a way that empowers you. This is another helpful hack in addition to breathing to collect your thoughts.

Practice generating emotions without context. For example, sit down, and feel anger for a bit. Then, when you have that down, feel elated. Practice feeling different emotions, and you will notice a curious thing: The way you perceive things changes with the way you feel. So, the next time you think about a terrible event, try to do so while holding on to your unconditional happiness and peace, and you'll find you are no longer triggered. You might discover valuable lessons from those trigger events that you had not thought about until just then.

Self-Actualization

The house Chiron is placed in on your chart is the means of transformation through your life's journey, from where you have been to where you are at and where you're headed. You can move through these stages with your words, thoughts, emotions, or through illness, parenthood, or the simple realization of your wounds to turn the pain into wisdom. We are all on our unique paths to self-actualization.

It can feel like a terrible world of chaos as you move through your life. You may feel like you are always stuck in place at best or, in reverse, at worst. However, you can empower yourself to be grounded in the now and remain very aware moment to moment. The journey of life and its purpose is where we receive healing to our psyche. It lets us redefine ourselves however we choose, however often we must. Chiron shows us that all the choices and their attendant responsibilities are in our hands.

With this knowledge driving us, we can become the grandest versions of ourselves that we hold in our minds. We can use our pain, suffering, and wounds to propel us to heights of self-actualization. There is no wound deep enough to hold you back from your grandest ideas. Know this, and you will have transcended your pain.

Conclusion

Turn on the TV, pick up a newspaper, eavesdrop on a conversation two tables away, and you will hear the same thing repeatedly: The world is in dire straits right now. From political and economic issues to troubles with relationships and mental health, it is evident that most of us are hurting very badly.

The reason we are in this situation seems pretty straightforward: People suck. People are terrible. That is just it . . . Or is it? It goes much deeper than that. When we act out of hatred, vengeance, anger, and spite, what is really going on is that we are at war within ourselves. Every day, we wrestle our pain to the ground. We slap Band-Aid after Band-Aid on our wounds. We pretend like it is something outside of us causing our discomfort because it's a lot easier than looking within.

This is why now more than ever, it is vital that we all sit down and come face-to-face with the things that hurt us the most. It seems a grueling task. That hurt is compounded by the fact that none of us asked for this! You did not ask to be born, but here you are. You didn't ask to be betrayed, hurt, laughed at, or mocked, but it happened, and now those experiences tinge everything you do. You didn't ask to come into a world where you would invariably hurt someone, but it is what it is. Thus, why should you have to be the one to heal yourself? It would be so much easier to take it out on everyone else and let the world burn, right?

The thing is, though, that there is only one way to become whole again—or at least begin your journey to complete healing. There's only one person with the power to draw out the poison of self-loathing within you. That is the person through whose eyes you are reading this. It does not seem fair, but when you accept this truth, you will reclaim your power. The pain will no longer control you. You will finally come to realize that in every moment, you have options, and you can choose to respond with love and understanding each time.

There is a saying that goes, "Your dog never remembers where it pooped, so you've got to scoop it up." In other words, people hurt us, and they forget all about it sometimes. What can you do? Rage against them in your mind while they walk around clueless and free? Or would you like to make a list of everyone who has ever hurt you, round them up and demand an apology? What happens when it is someone who refuses to give you that? Or when the one who cut you the deepest is long gone from this world? How then will you heal?

This is why we owe it to ourselves to let go of the outside, dig deep within, and finally pay attention to what ails us. This is the lesson that Chiron teaches everyone. Imagine for a moment a world where everyone chose to face their inner demons, recognize their flaws and hurts, and chose healing regardless. So many of the horrendous things that we hear about constantly in the news would simply stop because we would come to realize that our enemy is not outside of us but within us. It is an incredibly liberating experience to give yourself the healing the world seems desperate to hold back or take away from you.

Here is a further incentive to get started fixing yourself up: This is the only way to true success and joy in life. When you are hurting and angry at those who caused you pain, that bitterness seeps into everything you do, whether you know it or not. It puts a glass ceiling over the heights that you could reach in life. Worse still, it does not allow you to see how worthy you are, and when you do not see it, no one else can. This is why you find yourself being taken advantage of in relationships, at work, and in every other way possible. This is what is really holding you back from the bounty that life has to offer.

Worse still, your refusal to treat your wound makes it impossible for you to give the best of yourself to the people nearest and dearest to your heart. It causes needless friction at best and more pain for them at worst. Even the most bitter people would not want to hurt their loved ones, but they do that anyway. They allow their souls to be a breeding ground for more pain. It gets to the point where even when they do not consciously want to hurt anyone, they inadvertently do so.

Maybe you can relate to that experience. You hurt someone else so terribly, and you cannot for the life of you figure out why. They have been nothing but good to you, but you find it hard to accept their love. They could bring you the sun and the moon, and yet you would find yourself crushing their spirits, unable to stop yourself from saying or doing the things you know in your heart you should not. Chances are, you have some wounds that you need to tend to. If you will not heal yourself for your own sake, maybe you could make an effort to do so for theirs. Just like Chiron's choice to relinquish his immortality (and therefore his pain) led to Prometheus's freedom, your choice to release the hurt will definitely benefit those around you.

Chiron shows us that we have no reason to keep the pain going or the wound fresh. There is nothing in this world that is worth going through mental torture day after day. There's no justifiable reason for trying to act like you are okay or doling out the poison from the arrow in your soul, so everyone else feels your heartbreak. You do not have to bear that burden any longer when you can set yourself free. This is how the world gets better, one person at a time.

Part 2: Pluto in Astrology

The Ultimate Guide to the Planet of Transformation, Regeneration, and Rebirth

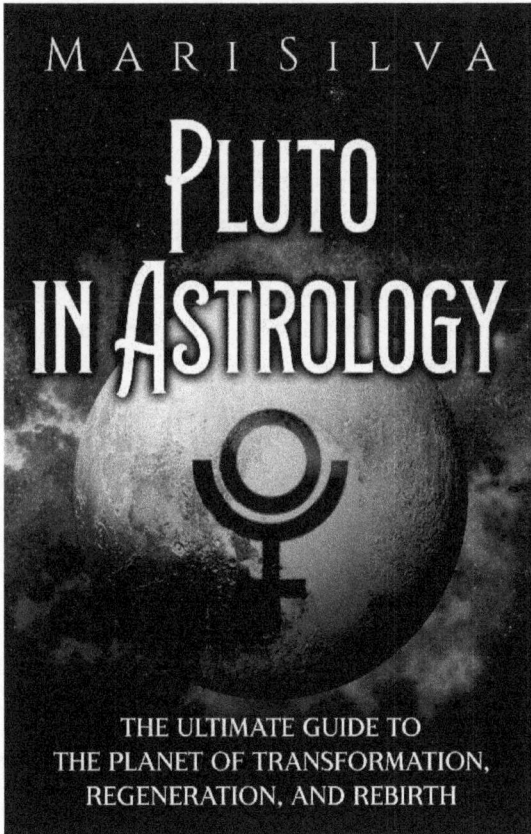

MARI SILVA

PLUTO IN ASTROLOGY

THE ULTIMATE GUIDE TO
THE PLANET OF TRANSFORMATION,
REGENERATION, AND REBIRTH

Introduction

The planet Pluto is one of the most influential planets in the science of astrology. Even though Pluto is minuscule compared to other planets, its influence on our lives is far more than most people think. Understanding how Pluto influences your signs and personality helps to uncover your true potential, as this planet is responsible for all the hidden things inside us.

Pluto is considered the key to discovering the different phases of our lives as the planet responsible for regeneration and new beginnings. The influence of Pluto determines when a drastic change is about to come and in what manner it will change our lives. A person's natal chart can easily point to the times in their life when they will face new beginnings and have to leave the past behind.

Pluto is also responsible for other negatively perceived aspects like death, destruction, kidnappings, coercion, and obsession. However, these areas are equally essential as the new beginnings since destruction and rebirth are an endless cycle. After going through these chapters, which are divided into various subsections, you will be able to gain a deeper understanding of all the transformational events that have happened in your life.

Knowing one's Pluto placements can help to determine what lies beneath the surface appearances. Pluto's depth and hidden aspects can identify the subconscious motivations and emotions within all of us. This book will help you discover the hidden truths inside your mind and provide insight into the changes that might be due.

Pluto influences a person's love life, informing us more about the nature of the love we find. The passionate and darker side of love is under the heavy influence of the tiny planet since it emphasizes exploring and honoring the darker sentiments existing inside all of us. With the proper knowledge of how Pluto influences your love life, you will gain deeper insights into your past and present relationships. This planet is one of the few that encourages us to embrace our dark side rather than hiding it. This is a highly influential factor that changes our love life.

The power struggles that people experience because of the desire for fame and renown can be understood by exploring Pluto. These power struggles can also exist inside our relationships. With the proper understanding of Pluto gained from the contents of this book, you will uncover how to overcome and balance out these struggles that exist in your life.

All the desires that the other planets do not explore and the obsessions of the human mind are explored fearlessly by Pluto. The desire for limitless power, the thirst for fame, raw sexual desire, and any other hidden facets of life can be much better understood with the influence of Pluto in mind. This book will help you gain a new perspective on all the different issues we usually repress.

The study of Pluto is extremely important in astrology since it lays a considerable emphasis on the hidden and darker side of things. After going through this book, you will find yourself coming back to the contents presented here to gain deeper insight into the events transpiring in your life.

Chapter 1: Pluto: The God of the Underworld

The dwarf planet Pluto is one of the outermost planets in our solar system. According to NASA's report in 2019, a NASA spacecraft traveling at a speed of more than 45,000 km/h confirmed that Pluto is much larger than previously thought. While the size of Pluto is only as large as half the width of the entire United States, it has a greater impact than most planets in astrology. Pluto is the smallest and slowest planet to revolve around the sun, taking around 248 years to complete a circuit around the blazing star. This is exactly the number of years that Pluto takes to move through the whole zodiac. That said, Pluto takes around twelve to thirty years to move through a single zodiac sign. This is why Pluto is often called a generational planet because an entire generation can have the same Pluto sign.

Discovered in 1930, the dwarf planet Pluto is also the last planet of our solar system. American astronomer Clyde Tombaugh first discovered Pluto residing at the edge of our solar system in the Kuiper belt beyond the planet Neptune. The name Pluto was suggested by an eleven-year-old girl named Venetia Burney to the board members of the Lowell observatory. The board members of the observatory selected the name Pluto out of options that included Cronus and Minerva.

In modern astrology, Pluto plays a subtle yet significant role. Since Pluto takes a lot of time to move from one zodiac sign to another, its movements are associated with the bigger picture rather than day-to-day effects. All the people born between 1983 and 1995 have their Pluto in the zodiac sign Scorpio. The last time Pluto was in Capricorn was in the year 1778. To understand it better, let us compare the effects of Pluto with Mercury. The planet Mercury may affect the details of your daily life, such as how confident or unsure you feel on a given day. Unlike Mercury, Pluto may affect an entire generation, influencing events such as a worldwide pandemic. Yes, astrologers believe that the conjunction between Saturn and Pluto in January 2020 was a sign that something world-changing was about to happen.

Also known as the god of the underworld, Pluto has great significance in Roman mythology and is revered in astrology. In this chapter, you will understand the importance of the planet Pluto concerning mythology and why Pluto is known as the last transcendental planet in astrology. You will also learn how Pluto affects all the other inner planets in our solar system.

Pluto in Mythology

Preserved in the Heraklion Archaeological Museum of Crete, Greece, the statue of the wizened god Pluto from the second century CE shows him leaning on his staff with his three-headed hound, also known as Cerberus, keeping watch. Pluto is believed to be one of the foremost deities of Roman subterranean mythology. He is worshiped as the god of the dead and the lord of the underworld. Dreaded by many, Pluto possesses terrible might. It is believed that Pluto controls the fates of all people and is responsible for dispensing luck. Pluto is celebrated as the bringer of wealth because he is the commander of the subterranean realms and master of the metals, ores, and other precious stones found in these realms. Pluto is often compared to Hades, a deity in Greek mythology who ruled the underworld.

Etymology

Pluto has a complex history in Roman mythology and is identified as the god of the underworld, wealth, and the dead. It is often thought that Pluto's identity was developed through the compositing of elements from two distinct deities. In Greek mythology, Hades is believed to be the ruler of the underworld, while Plouton is said to be the lord of wealth. The name Plouton has its roots in the ancient Greek noun "ploutus," which means riches or wealth. Pluto's name was derived from the Greek name Plouton, crystallizing Pluto as "the wealthy one." Pluto is often referred to as "Dīs Pater," a name derived from the Proto Indo-European words "Dīs" and "Pater" that translate to "god" and "father," respectively. Evidence suggests that, in ancient Roman culture, the names Pluto and Dīs Pater were often used interchangeably to denote the god of the underworld.

Pluto's Attributes

According to Roman mythology, Pluto, the lord of the subterranean underworld, had little to no interest in the world of the mortals and resided in a gloomy palace underground. The underworld was thought to serve as a resting place for all souls that depart from the mortal world. And just as he had no interest in the world of men, Pluto refrained from involving himself in the affairs of the gods. Pluto is depicted wearing a warrior's helmet in Roman mythology, carrying a mighty staff, and riding his chariot. Cerberus, the three-headed beast that often accompanied Pluto, served as the guardian of the underworld and a beloved pet of the god of the underworld.

Pluto's Family

In Roman mythology, Saturn, the ruler of the cosmos, and Ops, the goddess of the earth, were Pluto's parents. According to popular belief, Jupiter was said to be Pluto's brother. It was also believed that Jupiter freed Pluto and his other siblings from the wrath of Saturn. One of those siblings, Ceres, was worshiped as a fertility goddess and often associated with agriculture. Saturn's other children included Vesta, the guardian of home and hearth, Neptune, the lord of all waters, and Juno, the matron goddess. Jupiter and Ceres's daughter, Proserpina, married Pluto and lived with him in his realm under the earth for much of their lives. Both Roman and Greek mythology hint that Pluto had many children with Proserpina. Eumenides, the deity of vengeance who lived in the chthonic darkness of the underworld, is one of the most popular children of Pluto.

The Most Famous Myth about Pluto

The abduction of Proserpina is probably the most famous myth associated with Pluto. The god of the underworld was known to be a lonely deity who rarely encountered others. The tale starts with Venus asking her son Cupid to fire a love arrow at Pluto to make him fall in love with the next maiden he laid eyes upon. This act of pity on Pluto by Venus turned into a nightmare for Proserpina. She was the woman that Pluto first saw after being hit by Cupid's arrow. Pluto seized Proserpina from the fields of Nysa and flew off with her in his chariot to the underworld. However, this act unleashed intense grief on Proserpina's mother, Ceres, the goddess of the harvest.

According to Roman mythology, anyone who eats a meal in the underworld will never be able to leave again. In the hope that someone would come to rescue her, Proserpina held out as long as she could without eating for almost a week. However, when she could no longer bear starvation, she ate six pomegranate seeds. In the meantime, back on earth, Jupiter grew increasingly worried about Ceres and the crops. Thus, Jupiter sent his youngest son Mercury, an excellent negotiator, to make a deal with Pluto. The threat of Jupiter's wrath compelled Pluto to allow Proserpina to return to earth. However, since Proserpina had already eaten the seeds of the underworld, Pluto laid the terms that Proserpina was to stay with him for six months every year. After much discourse, Proserpina, and her mother Ceres, agreed to these terms.

According to the legend, Ceres welcomes her beloved daughter with bloom every spring. When Proserpina returns to the underworld each autumn, Ceres weeps and lets all the crops die until the cycle begins once again. This is believed to be the reason why we have seasons.

Pluto in Astrology

As the farthest planet from the sun, Pluto has very subtle energy. However, it can play a significant role in influencing the zodiac signs. In astrology, Pluto rules the zodiac sign Scorpio and the eighth house. It is believed to be a higher octave of the planet Mars. Standing last among the transcendental planets, Pluto essentially symbolizes transformation, rebirth, and regeneration. The dwarf planet Pluto is known to help people transform, evolve, or change their perspectives and establish new outlooks toward life. However, death and destruction come before birth and regeneration. Pluto is also associated with coercion, darkness, death, kidnapping, obsession, virus, and waste.

Known to be a great revealer, Pluto releases core truths and buried power. Often referred to as a creative destroyer, Pluto's transit can feel like extended ordeals, like a long night before the sun shines again. Pluto represents the underbelly of emotions, and its energy is extremely potent and powerful. Pluto is often associated with things that lie beneath the surface, such as the subconscious mind. This may include things or parts of ourselves that we are not comfortable sharing with the outside world. The creative destroyer is known to demolish weak foundations and rebuild more resilient and stronger foundations than before. Known to be a natural investigator, nothing can get past the intense Pluto.

Pluto is believed to be the master of transformation. It is believed to find great pleasure in pain, which often borders on masochism. Just like Scorpio, Pluto is associated with sexual exploration. Apart from this, Pluto honors and loves to explore the more profound sentiment within. Pluto is associated with the urge to normalize and embrace the fetish within us. The reasoning behind this is that Pluto wants us all to live genuinely and stop hiding this part of ourselves.

Pluto in Birth Chart

Due to its slow transition, the position of Pluto in your birth chart will be shared with other people of your generation. Pluto can stay in each sign for up to thirty years, which means it rules a generation more than a person. Pluto rules control, intensity, obsession, and power. If you were born between 1983 and 1995, your Pluto would be in Scorpio, which means that your generation's psyche is intense, private, passionate, self-obsessed, perceptive, and serious compared to other generations. However, the house position in which Pluto resides is key to understanding the area of your life that will undergo the most dramatic transformation. For example, if Pluto is in your tenth house, it means you are personally transforming outdated definitions of responsibility and success.

Through its house position, Pluto shows the area that you most long for. It is often the area that is very difficult or often impossible for you to attain your ideal vision. Pluto's position in the houses shows you the area where you search for deeper meaning and truths. This section of your life may be associated with issues of control, dramatic changes, power struggles, and even upheaval.

Pluto is consistent in most of our birth charts, and it often points to a lifelong meditation on a particular issue. For example, our generation faces climate change, depletion of fossil fuels, and a global pandemic. The potent energy of Pluto burns away everything unnecessary through both changes from external circumstances and our initiatives. Pluto can often make you undergo an agonizing process of letting things go and building faith in life itself. This is to create space for something new and for miracles to occur. Pluto emphasizes energies that display obsessive qualities, willingness to examine, the urge to explore, the need to find deeper meanings, and power struggles regarding the other planets in your birth chart. The placement of Pluto in your birth chart can help you recognize the part of your life where you seek transformation and change. If you refuse to accept your deepest needs, you may have them thrust upon you. Fearing Pluto's energies or your "dark" side can even lead you to destructiveness. Accepting life in its true essence is what Pluto is all about.

Pluto in the Twelve Zodiac Signs

In the natal chart, Pluto rules over the power you have within yourself, power you might not be utilizing correctly. It rules over self-empowerment, the power that helps you evolve in life. Currently, Pluto is placed in the house of Capricorn, the sign of structure, and will continue to be there until 2024. This section will discuss Pluto's transit from one zodiac sign to another and its various effects on a generation based on the different zodiac signs it is placed in.

• Aries

Pluto was placed in the house of Aries between 1822 and 1853. It will return to Aries in 2068. People born with Pluto and Aries are highly optimistic, impulsive, and quick to take advantage of favorable situations. Although often lacking patience, these people can do great things in life through sheer will and power.

• Taurus

Pluto was placed in the house of Taurus between 1853 and 1884. Pluto will return to Taurus in 2098. People with a Taurus Pluto can be highly persistent and stubborn. They are attracted by materialism and orderliness and hate frequent changes. Although they are smart in handling resources, they cannot be satisfied easily. These people can excel in financial and personal progress.

• Gemini

Pluto was placed in the house of Gemini between 1882 and 1914. It will return to the house of Gemini in 2132. People born with Gemini Pluto are known to be versatile, highly inquisitive, and thirsty for knowledge. These people are born with innovative ideas and are inclined intellectually. They can bring about major changes in innovation and technology.

• Cancer

Pluto was in Cancer between 1914 and 1939. People born with Pluto in the zodiac sign of Cancer are known to derive their power through their emotional and sensitive nature. These people value relationships and possessions very dearly. They make good parents and friends due to their innate nurturing nature. These people are also known to stick to traditions and age-old customs.

• Leo

Pluto was placed in the zodiac sign of Leo between 1937 and 1958. People born with Leo crave recognition and being in the limelight. They grow in life through challenging situations. With great leadership skills, these people like to lead teams. However, they may face the challenge of needing constant appreciation for their actions.

• Virgo

Pluto was in the zodiac sign Virgo between 1956 and 1972. People born under this sign are known to be highly obsessive with whatever they like or do. Known to have great perceptive skills and analytical power, they can often be highly critical of themselves. They can be highly emotional in life and love perfection in everything they do.

• Libra

Pluto was in the sign of Libra between 1971 and 1984. People born with Libra Pluto tend to be very compulsive. Known to be hard workers, they like to help themselves and those around them. However, they may face the challenge of being impulsive in their acts, and hasty decisions may lead them to disappointment. These people always aim for harmony and peace in life.

• Scorpio

Pluto was in the sign of Scorpio between 1735 and 1747. It was also in the house of Scorpio between 1983 and 1995. People born with Pluto in the house of Scorpio are highly sensitive, extremely intense, and might be ruled by their emotional side. It is easy for them to understand the feelings and emotions of other people. These people like to unearth unexplored secrets and are more attracted to unconventional ways in life.

- Sagittarius

Pluto was in the house of Sagittarius between 1746 and 1762. It returned to the house of Sagittarius between 1995 and 2008. People with Sagittarius Pluto like adventures, exploring, freedom, and independence. To gain a lot of experience, they love traveling to different places. Many people who have Sagittarius Pluto are willing to question traditional ways and customs.

- Capricorn

Pluto is currently in the zodiac sign of Capricorn and will continue to stay there until 2024. People born with Pluto in the house of Capricorn are known to be very cautious in life. Slow yet steady steps make them feel secure. Ambitious but patient simultaneously, they take calculated steps that would not bring any drastic change in life.

- Aquarius

Pluto was in the zodiac sign of Aquarius between 1778 and 1798. It will be in the house of Aquarius again between 2024 and 2044. People born with Aquarius Pluto are known to be very erratic in life. Following their ideals and ideas, they would easily rebel against established rules and norms in society. They do not stick to conventional ideas or thoughts.

- Pisces

Pluto was in the zodiac house of Pisces between 1797 and 1823. It will again be in Pisces between 2044 and 2068. People born under Pisces Pluto are believed to be highly emotional and sensitive. Satisfying others and acting to please them may make these people miss out a lot in life. Attracted by social works and spirituality, these people possess inherent artistic talent that can inspire others around them.

Since January 24, 2008, Pluto has been in the house of Capricorn. Pluto will transition into the house of Aquarius in 2024. However, for a few months in 2023, it will exit Capricorn and return during its retrograde. During this period, Pluto will help expose abuses of power, encourage equal pay for equal work, and build better business models. It will help us move forward with a deeper understanding of our passions and, most importantly, our deepest needs. The last retrograde period of Pluto began on April 27, 2021. For now, you can enjoy the moment of calm, look back and appreciate your growth, and wait for another retrograde to begin.

Chapter 2: Destruction: The First Step to Cleansing

Pluto as a planet represents the endless and inevitable cycle of death and rebirth. It is closely associated with destruction and poses a threat to the ego. While Neptune and Uranus neglect ego, Pluto thrives on destroying it. Most of us have and are still struggling to combat our egos, making it challenging to avoid Pluto altogether. Even though Pluto is associated with ego and destruction, it contextualizes the power of unconditional love that can make or break someone's universe. Since unconditional love is often confused with destruction, all individuals are unable to let go. This enumerates Pluto's energy in detail.

Pluto — the Greek God Hades

Poseidon and Zeus's younger brother, and the son of Rhea and Cronus, Hades, is also referred to as Pluto in Greek mythology. Myths say that the attributes shared by Pluto and the Greek god Hades are conflated, which makes it an interesting comparison. In other words, Hades' "Roman version" and Latinization was Pluto or Pluton.

Hades governed the underworld and Erebus, a subterranean region. The underworld and Erebus were filled with negative energies and evil deities who were banished from earth and exiled to this place by Zeus and his comrades. Due to the nature of the underworld, Hades was often found sulking and gloomy, which made him the "grim" ruler of this dreadful place. Erebus also hosted dead spirits and heinous shades that were supervised under Hades' governance.

Other gods highly detested Hades due to his evil demeanor. He possessed great wealth, which is an etymological connection to his name. Since the underworld carried resources and riches upon mining, Pluto became the primary ruler of the world beneath the earth. Interestingly, his moniker was not adapted from his evil nature but his positive traits. In a way, the name "Hades" evokes fear due to its translation to "aeides," which means invisible or unseen. This led people to call him Pluto. A similar tale to Pluto and Proserpina is found in Greek mythology, involving Hades and Persephone, Proserpina's Greek counterpart. Hades kidnapped Persephone, Zeus and Demeter's daughter, and kept her in the underworld as her wife. Upon knowing this, Demeter caused havoc on earth and searched for her daughter endlessly. She even blocked the crops from growing and let the inhabitants starve. She went to all lengths to get her daughter back. Eventually, Hades and Demeter agreed to let Persephone stay with both of them throughout the year. According to this agreement, she stayed with Hades for one-third of the entire year, served Zeus during the second quarter, and visited her mother for the rest of the year.

With time, he ruled the underworld with the assistance of Persephone, his queen, and Cerberus, his three-headed dog. Even though Pluto was responsible as a supervisor of the underworld, he was personally not inclined toward judging or torturing the ones sent down. Sacrifices and prayers hardly moved Pluto, as he was pitiless. In Greek Mythology, despite being Zeus's brother, Hades was barely recognized as one of the main Olympian gods—mainly because gods were bright and represented celestial powers. This might have stemmed from Zeus's dark side and his roots with the underworld.

Even though he was perceived as a grim god, Hades' complementary traits of positivity and nobility gave him the titles Eubouleus ("Good Counsellor") and Clymenus ("the Renowned"). He was also perceived as Aidoneus in some legends, holding a specter with a bird tip. Hades' deceptive and impulsive characteristics enhanced his wrath and anger. However, he was weak due to his undying passion and love for Persephone. He was also believed to own other black pets apart from Cerberus, mainly black hounds and black horses.

Pluto and the Hindu God Shiva

The Hindu God Shiva is often associated with destruction and rebirth, much like Pluto. This enunciates a discreet amalgamation between the two entities, which is also why they are often compared in the astrological domain. Some Hindus also link Pluto with Lord Rudra and consider their destructive power essential to regenerate life and begin a new phase. Any planet touched by Pluto is magnified, just like Rahu. As stated, the ultimate motive of this destruction is resurrection. Hindus and believers of Shiva do not deem the god as the ultimate force of destruction. In Hindu mythology, Shiva is a significant part of creation that binds the whole scheme together. This entails reverence and affirmation among believers.

In a way, Shiva is worshipped for this energy and force that turns the wheel and commences a new cycle. Worshipping Lord Shiva is believed to bring blessings to believers. They are blessed with abundant ground and energy that helps them begin a new change in their life. With heavy degeneration follows creative regeneration—a quality that both Pluto and Lord Shiva are known for. This energy is necessary to sustain life and keep things in motion. In essence, this is how the universe is supposed to function.

The Goddess of Death, Kali, is Lord Shiva's feminine counterpart who symbolizes the destruction of evil. The word "Kali" comes from "Kala," a Sanskrit word meaning time. This also explains Pluto's association with Kali—the process of destruction, rebirth, growth, and decay takes place in time. The position of Pluto in one's life determines one's sense of control. For instance, if Pluto is well placed in a person's life, they may control others and exercise power. On the other hand, if the planet is acting up, the person may be doomed and suffer from poverty or misery.

Furthermore, qualities like death, dissolution, ego, and a multifaceted nature are shared attributes in Lord Shiva and Pluto. These traits are also deemed masculine and highlighted among both entities. On the contrary, Lord Shiva also exhibits feminine energy through his demeanor, such as his wild locks, the coiled serpent on his neck, and the portrayal of Mother Ganges on his hair. One can say that Lord Shiva is an amalgamation of both masculine and feminine energies, which dictates the term "Shiva and Shakti" or "Shiva and Kali." We can also draw this comparison between Pluto and Proserpina, who ruled the underworld as a couple.

This states that Pluto is ingrained with deeper forces and primal depths instead of the masculine energy that is frequently discussed. If the charts spot Pluto's explosive energy, it is often related to Shiva's tantric exploration. The trinity in Hindu mythology—Brahma, Vishnu, and Shiva—are counterparts of the celestial bodies Uranus, Neptune, and Pluto, respectively. Both Shiva and Pluto are the accumulators of the rejected items that establish a system in the universe. Astronomers also draw parallels between Pluto and its main moon, Charon. Just like Shiv and Shakti are the eternal pair representing masculine and feminine energies, Pluto and Charon also form a binary pair in the sky.

Destruction — An Active Force

This active force is needed in the universe for regeneration and cleansing. Without destruction, one may not be able to dig deeper and touch their subconscious self. You are much more than you think you are, and you possess incredible power and skills. However, not everyone is blessed with the ability to decipher this hidden potential, which is where Pluto steps in. While other planets help stabilize one's life and keep the framework in place, Pluto directs an individual to tear their system down to make room for new structures to be built from scratch.

To peek into the bigger picture, take your daily life as an example. All the garbage and gunk you collect after going through an average day needs to be recycled or discarded to keep your house clean, hygienic, and spotless. All the dirt and deposits accumulated in the sewage pipes must be removed to ensure a steady flow of water. Such actions keep things in order and push daily life into a conventional drill, as it is supposed to be. Consider this the physical manifestation of removing toxicity and making way for new and positive entities to restore the universe's system.

This manifestation is, in a way, governed by Pluto and Lord Shiva in their distinct ways. Your physical, emotional, mental, and spiritual energies need to be cleansed as well because it will bring inner joy and peace.

This also explains that the Plutonian crusade should be acknowledged instead of shunned or put away. It simply implies that your life is ready to take a new turn and unfold in its own peculiar way. Learn that the power of Pluto insists on turning on a new life. However, to do that, one must stay positive and focus on the brighter side instead of diverting their attention solely to destructive power. Needless to say, no one takes pleasure in suffering. Who likes the idea of striking rock bottom and journeying into the deepest crevices that portray nothing but horror and dismay? This feeling can only be combatted by contemplating the idea of rebirth and the tingling temptation it brings.

We all would like to transmute our old and tired selves and be reborn as energetic and fresh souls. This is what Pluto thrives for. The planet's profound energy is telling you to improve and elucidates a new path for you. It packs its energies and learnings in a golden bowl and presents it to you. It is up to you whether you use it for your benefit. Contemplate its symbolic energy and take time to reexamine the parcel before throwing it away. It will surely help you develop a new perception and way of living. Let us not narrate hate speeches toward Pluto (like "Die Pluto" or "Hate Pluto") before fully envisaging its presence in your life.

Be conscious of this planet if you actually want to apprehend "a new you." Pluto's incredible powers will help you get through the destructive phase and give you the strength to embark on a new, fresh, and fruitful journey.

The Conservation Principle

The conservation principle states that the universe's order depends on the phenomenon where one form of energy can mutate into another form. During this process, energy is neither created nor destroyed—it stays as it is. This fundamental law also states that an isolated system's energy will also remain constant.

Let us understand this principle from a scientific angle. When an asteroid travels through space, it picks up a definite speed (say 6.2 miles per second). If a planet comes in its way, the kinetic energy possessed by the asteroid may clash with its gravitational energy. However, since the latter is much smaller than the former, the asteroid will accumulate more kinetic energy on its way before it hits the planet. Once it touches the planet's surface, its higher amount of kinetic energy and the small amount of gravitational energy is transformed into heat. The way the energy is transformed also depends on the asteroid's size. While large asteroids break into smaller pieces and become rocks, the smaller ones emit extra heat. In both cases, the energy is neither created nor destroyed but transformed into another form.

Let's take it down a notch and understand the principle by taking an example of our daily lives. The food we eat is consumed in the form of macronutrients and calories. With time, our body converts it into energy to sustain its functions. We need ample energy to perform basic activities, such as standing, cooking, walking, and even sleeping. This energy is either used by the body or expelled as heat when exercising or burning extra calories when performing physical activities. Furthermore, the electric energy supplied to our homes is converted into light energy when passed through light bulbs.

Similarly, the energy used for the creation process in the universe is carried forward and used for destruction. This energy is transformed into some other entity that stays in the void until the regeneration process begins. When we die, our body's chemical energy is used in decomposition, and our brain's electrical energy breaks down into heat.

Pluto's Role in the Stability of Society

Pluto plays a significant role in bringing stability to society and encouraging youths and adults alike to make a change. In general, it influences a particular age group that is triggered by a falling system. Even though it was labeled as a "dwarf planet" in the year 2006, one cannot deny the powerful force and energy it possesses. Whether you want to use Pluto's influence on an individual or collectively enforce it on a group, the results are always awe-inspiring.

Power and Resources

The way you handle money and make use of available resources is also dictated by Pluto. Pluto ensures wise use and sharing of resources among a group of people that will help better the community. Objects and topics concerning power also fall under Pluto's governance. For example, politics, weapons, energy preservation, corporations, success, etc., are widely discussed among individuals with a favorable Pluto placement. Characteristics of oppression and dictatorship are also part and parcel of this planet's influence.

Influence on an Age Group

Pluto's influence on generational trends stems from its ability to hover among a group of individuals that share the same sign. This is why some people complain of being under the radar of Pluto for at least a decade. Pluto can maintain a prominent stance in an individual's life for ten to twenty years. Due to this, the Baby Boomers and Millennials possess different abilities passed down by Pluto during its rule over each generation. Furthermore, the traits are also distinct due to the difference in the zodiac signs.

For instance, while the Virgos may show the true potential of becoming activists and raising their opinions due to Pluto's influence, the Libras may become more marriage-minded. Here are some examples of a deciphered pattern based on Pluto's influence on different generations:

- *Virgos (1958 to 1971)*: This group was noted to be more ethical and possessed traits of activists. Some of them even displayed "hippie" vibes. In general, they were eco-conscious.

- *Libras (1971 to 1984)*: These individuals were more marriage-minded but somehow trapped in an era of divorces. Some of them were forced to witness their parents separating and taking charge of their lives from an early age. Due to this, the eldest siblings of the broken families had to reinvent the rules and establish a new family system.

- *Scorpios (1984 to 1995)*: This group of individuals was exposed to difficult subjects at a tender age. Worldwide calamities and repercussions forced them to deal with topics such as teenage pregnancy, AIDS, and gun violence. However, this generation had the guts to address these topics and raise awareness about gender inequality and sexual orientation, which helped bring about more inclusivity today.

- *Sagittarius (1995 to 2008)*: This group has been rebelling about the inequality and unacceptability of taboos in society. This rebellion is steadily opening eyes and helping everyone understand inclusiveness.

- *Capricorn (2008 to 2024)*: It is believed that Pluto's influence on this generation will mingle with Capricorn's leadership skills and help them change the world. Topics such as climate change and revising hierarchy will be talked about and implemented.

Pluto's Role in Our Lives

Pluto is often compared to a phoenix, which poses a symbolic significance in legends. Just like the phoenix dies and rises from the ashes as a more powerful and tenacious creature, Pluto brings intensity and passion into people's lives. With this energy, everyone can live life to their fullest. If you feel helpless or need to find a new direction in life, take help from Pluto. Even though this planet will not provide the ultimate solution or do the heavy lifting to pave your path, you will definitely gain a new perspective to take things forward.

Wealth

Money, wealth, power, and financial security are other strong attributes that fall under the umbrella of Pluto. With a well-placed Pluto on your natal chart, you can attract abundant wealth and finances. Investments, payments, lending money, clearing debts, etc., are some riches displayed by individuals blessed with wealth from Pluto. However, if these individuals take the wrong direction, they may get addicted to betting and gambling.

Sexuality

Pluto is closely associated with sexuality, obsessive desires, and lust. Since Mars is also associated with physical attraction, astrologers often find a connection between these two planets. Sexual and emotional obsessions are difficult to overrule, however, and Pluto's influence can become burdensome. Unlike Venus's attributes of seduction and lovemaking, Pluto represents the actual act of sex.

Relationships

If the birth charts of two individuals note a coinciding presence of Pluto, they may face issues in their relationship. The individuals can be possessed by jealousy, compulsion, possession, obsession, and other toxic traits that can ruin healthy relationships. If you are not careful, you may end up fighting over petty issues with your partner, which can eventually bring an end to your relationship. Manipulation, control, and pointing out weaknesses in your partner are other common traits. However, if you are aware of this influence and show some maturity throughout the relationship, you can handle such situations and save yourself.

Shame

While this word may initially shock you, it will actually help you in the long run. Since Pluto helps an individual reveal their addictions and vices, they can transform this feeling of shame and guilt into a positive emotion. Pluto will guide you in turning your lead and raw metals into gold.

Soul Growth

As mentioned, if your natal chart displays Pluto's placement in your life, know that you are meant to sacrifice and give up in the near future. If you rebel, things may not turn out in your favor. Let go and welcome change for your soul to breathe and grow. You may experience minor to major devastating experiences in your life, but you will eventually come out stronger and braver. This planet will guide you on the right path instead of making one for you. It will enable you to dig deeper and unravel your most creative regenerative powers.

Pluto is often misunderstood and feared by individuals who are unaware of its true powers and significance. It is high time you acknowledge this planet's presence in your natal chart (if that is your case) and make room for better things.

Chapter 3: The Mantra: Make Way for the New You

In the context of astrology, Pluto is all about transformation. Therefore, it is somewhat ironic that its status as a planet has changed in recent years. When the classification of what constituted a "planet" was redefined in 2006, Pluto was declared a "dwarf planet" instead. You only have to look at its peculiar orbit to understand how change is a fundamental part of its astrological power. One of the eccentricities of Pluto's orbit around the Sun is that, at times, it moves closer to the Sun than Neptune does. Since it takes 248 years before Pluto has passed through the entire zodiac, it can take anywhere between twelve and thirty-one years to move through a single sign.

Pluto also tends to be associated with extremes, such as a major economic boom or depression. It often influences the masses just as much as the individual, forcing you to look inside yourself to accept aspects of your subconscious that you may not want to face. The power of Pluto is that it helps you discard old aspects of your life to allow for new things to replace them. The mantra of "out with the old, in with the new" is a key part of Pluto's influence over your life.

Destruction and Rebirth

Pluto governs the domains of both destruction and rebirth. These two forces are intrinsically linked as parts of the natural cycle that all living things experience. This can be equally terrifying and encouraging. While you must accept that everything will come to an end, including the universe itself, something is comforting in knowing that everything will also begin anew. When looking at these forces individually, we can uncover many aspects that will help you better understand how Pluto's energy enacts transformation in your life and the world.

Pluto as a Force of Destruction

As a force of destruction, Pluto holds sway over things like death, waste, viruses, kidnapping, coercion, obsession, crime, terrorism, and despotic authority. These are undoubtedly negative forces that can cause great harm to yourself and those around you. The power of Pluto should not be taken lightly, as its influence in the world is dangerous. Being aware of this fact and understanding how Pluto's energy can affect thoughts, emotions, and events can help you safeguard yourself from the consequences that come from these things.

Destruction is a form of transformation as it changes the fundamental nature of something from alive to dead, positive to negative, or existence to emptiness. There is nothing in this universe that can remain in one particular state for all eternity. Everything will transform at some point in time, and everything eventually meets its end. You must be cognizant of this reality and learn to accept it; otherwise, you will always be fighting a losing battle as you attempt in vain to cling to something that cannot remain in its current state. This is true for relationships, events, possessions, societal status, and cultural norms.

Pluto as a Force of Rebirth

On the opposite side of destruction is Pluto's power over rebirth, rejuvenation, and regeneration. Just as everything ends, everything must also begin and sometimes begin again. Like the mythological Phoenix that dies in flames, is reduced to ashes, and is reborn again from those ashes, Pluto controls the cyclical nature of death and rebirth. It is another form of transformation, but one that has a positive connotation. Every time you start a new journey or relationship, you participate in this cycle on some level.

When a new star is born, it is created by pulling matter toward its core, building up mass until it transforms into a burning celestial body. Upon the collapse and death of a star, a supernova occurs, and much of the star's matter is expelled outward. Some of this matter can then become part of a new star or other celestial body. This cycle of birth, death, and rebirth can be seen everywhere in the natural world, and it often encompasses the more esoteric aspects of your life as well. Even on a microscale, you can view going to sleep and reawakening as another part of this cycle.

The Power of Time

Time is ultimately a force of destruction, as decay and death occur due to the passage of time. Time governs everything in the universe. You move from one moment to the next, building upon each prior moment until you can look back at the procession of these moments and understand that time has passed for you. Without time's unrelenting march forward, everything would exist in a state of stagnation, never changing and preventing any conscious beings from experiencing being alive.

Looking at Pluto's influence over destruction and rebirth, time is simply another aspect of those forces. It is a conduit to facilitate the transformation from one state of existence to another. Transformation is only possible because of the passage of time, and it is important to understand that this fundamental force is beyond your control. You cannot stop time from passing any more than you can reach into the ocean and hold the water in your hands. Embracing the reality that time will go on regardless of what you desire is something you must do if you want to find inner peace and live harmoniously with the rest of the world.

Pluto and the Inner Self

One of Pluto's powers is that it gives you the ability to look inside yourself and unlock aspects of your personality that you have resisted or attempted to hide. Instead of keeping the undesirable parts of yourself locked away in the deepest recesses of your mind, you can face your negative traits and either embrace them or purge them from your psyche. Everyone has fears, bad habits, prejudices, and damaging behaviors. You can expend your energy trying to deny these things exist, or you can acknowledge these negative aspects of yourself and find a way to overcome them. Your greatest weaknesses can be transformed into strengths if you allow yourself to follow the path set forth by Pluto.

When you can recognize and eliminate the parts of yourself that have been holding you back, you will find you've been transformed into a healthier and happier person. Your emotional, psychological, and physical well-being can be significantly improved when you stop holding on to things that need to change. It is essential to let go of anything you have no control over, learn to adapt to new situations, and find the best way to engage with them, even if these situations were not something you would ideally desire. The only way to thrive in an ever-changing world is to be willing to adjust your thoughts and behaviors to better interact with the new realities in your life.

Pluto and Society

A significant aspect of Pluto's influence is the way it affects society as a whole. The power of Pluto can determine extreme positive or negative events. As time marches on, there will always be massive upheavals in the status quo of society, which are often looked back on as important benchmarks in the progression of human history. Following these extreme events, society is usually transformed into something new due to what had occurred. These changes can be challenging to accept, and people will resist them for as long as they can manage. However, in the end, everyone must either adapt to the new normal or perish as a casualty of progression.

After the tragedy of the September 11, 2001 terrorist attacks on the World Trade Center in New York City, much of the United States experienced a massive transformation. There was a huge crackdown on the freedoms of its citizens through the passage of the "Patriot Act." This greatly increased the government's ability to track and monitor the activities of individuals, regardless of intrusion upon their privacy. Electronic communication began being recorded and inspected by the government, while visual monitoring became increasingly prevalent.

At the time, many people sought a return to the way things were before the terrorist attacks. However, once the change had started, it was impossible to stop. Nowadays, most people understand that anything they say or do can be documented and recorded for later reference if necessary. Every email you write, post you make, or text message you send may eventually be used against you. There are cameras in nearly every public space now, and smartphones are so ubiquitous that you are likely to be recorded every time you step outside your home. Those who have tried to fight these changes are engaged in a losing battle. People who accept this change and adapt their behaviors to suit the reality they have been given can better navigate the constant invasion of privacy by refraining from saying or doing anything that could harm them at some point in the future.

Accepting the Power of Pluto

You must accept the power of Pluto to bring about change in your life. Transformation occurs with or without you, so the only way to thrive is to embrace these changes. If you try to fight the things in your life to prevent them from changing, you will be swept away as it pushes right past you. The world around you will never again be the same as it is at this very moment, just as it is vastly different today than it was 100 years ago. Throughout your lifetime, you will see this transformation occur bit by bit on a macro and microscale, along with changes to your personal life and society as a whole.

Out With the Old, In With the New

The transformational process induced by the energy from Pluto includes ridding yourself of some things in your life and allowing new things to take their place. This can be anything from friends and lovers to a job, hobby, or habit. You might have been a procrastinator for a long time, but through the power of Pluto, you can transform into someone who gets things done early and on time. Maybe you have been stagnating in a toxic relationship—getting out of that situation and finding a new means of empowering yourself without a significant other is a transformation that Pluto can bring forth.

It needs to be said that not all these transformations will be positive. The mantra of "out with the old, in with the new" applies to many upsetting or bittersweet things. Think about your extended family—someone may have recently given birth to a new baby, which is a positive change, but another member of your family may have also died. New life has joined your community of family and friends, but older lives have also been removed from it. Sometimes these changes are not as drastic as life and death; they can be as simple as meeting a new friend while you drift away from another. Change is constantly happening all around you, and there is no way to prevent it from occurring.

The Dangers of Resisting Pluto's Power

Change can be challenging to accept. Many people will fight against it with all their will. However, resisting the transformation brought about by Pluto can be severely detrimental to your well-being.

When you try to prevent change from occurring, you interfere with a natural, organic cycle that needs to happen. Clinging to the past and struggling against change in your life can quickly spiral out of control. Eventually, you will feel like the world has passed you by while you fall into a state of negativity.

Becoming bitter and resentful is often a result of a person's inability to accept and embrace the changes in their life. You might hear such a person say things like, "I hate x nowadays. The way things used to be was so much better." This typically happens when society advances in ways that certain people deem as undesirable. Instead of moving on with the times, they try to force things to regress to a previous state of existence. This never works and can make you into an incredibly unhappy person once your attempts prove unsuccessful.

Using the Mantra in Your Life

Using the mantra of "out with the old, in with the new" in your everyday life can help you overcome many obstacles to happiness that you may not be able to conquer if you are resisting change. Many people struggle with this concept, but it is never too late to begin using this mantra to accept the transformation brought about by Pluto's energy. To understand what this means in practice, let us examine the story of a young man named David.

David hated change. Whenever something in his life began to transform, he did everything he could to prevent it from happening. When his friends got married and started having children, he refused to accept that his relationship with them would, by necessity, become fundamentally different from how it was when they were in college and young singles living in the city. He would constantly berate them when they said they could not join him for their regular bar meetups or weekend gatherings where they watched sports together. As more and more of his friends embraced their newfound responsibilities as spouses and parents, David became increasingly frustrated and unhappy that this meant his life was changing as well.

In an effort to resist accepting that his relationship with his friends needed to transform to survive, David demanded that either they hang out with him as they used to, or he would cut them out of his life. One by one, he eventually lost contact with his friends, until finally, he realized he was all alone. David was bitter and unhappy and probably would have remained that way if he had not taken a good, hard look inside himself. He realized that maintaining a relationship with his friends, even if it was in an altered state from what it had once been, was preferable to being completely alone. "Out with the old, in with the new" became his mantra.

David reconnected with his friends and embraced the new form that their relationships took on. Instead of meeting up for drinks at the bar, he accompanied them when they took their children fishing or attended the birthday parties thrown for their kids. He came to understand that his friends' time needed to be devoted to the responsibilities in their lives, so he learned to work around their busy schedules to talk to them or go out for a coffee and catch up for an hour. His day-to-day life changed as well, especially once he married a woman whom he met at one of his friend's son's birthday parties. She was a single mother, and he soon found himself transformed from a single man into a husband and stepfather.

Once David accepted that these changes would continue to occur and that things would again become very different in five or ten years, he could find inner peace and true happiness. You cannot stop the world from changing, but if you choose to step aboard the boat and let it carry you forward down the river instead of leaping into the water and trying to swim upstream, you will find that the problems in your life become much easier to handle. Even when things are not going your way, understanding that your bad luck will eventually change can help you get through those tough times.

Chapter 4: Pluto in Society

Pluto's role and effect on society are not far off from its nature. Pluto is a slow orbiter, taking 248 years to complete one rotation around the sun, and in turn, the whole zodiac. Its motion is subtle but powerful, nonetheless.

It is not surprising that Pluto's nature is quite a double-edged sword. As cold and lifeless as this planet is, it becomes warmer when its orbit brings it closer to the sun, at times coming closer than Neptune even. In 2015, NASA's spacecraft "New Horizons" flew past Pluto, taking pictures and accumulating data. From this data, NASA found significant evidence of a water ocean and a geological heart under the planet's frozen solid surface that is thought to be responsible for reorientating the planet's spin axis. They also discovered that Charon's north pole, one of Pluto's moons, possessed certain organic compounds and molecules that make it a potential candidate for extraterrestrial life.

The planet's motion circles the sun in an oval shape, yet it orbits the sun in the same direction as the rest. It rotates around its own axis in the opposite direction of most planets as well. In other words, it has a retrograde rotation, similar to Venus and Uranus. Thus, as you can see, Pluto is a mysterious and powerful planet with a heavily contradicting nature. It is a cold, dead planet on the surface, yet a lively one deep within. The transformations it brings about with its every move echo throughout the world on a universal level and individual and collective levels. Pluto is a significant player in ideological, societal, political, and economic changes and developments.

Pluto and the Darkness

Pluto's power of transformation is neither a bad thing nor a good thing. It is merely an effect. Transformation can be for the better or worse. However, you should keep in mind that Pluto's natural dark energy always plays a part, whether in strengthening the righteous against darkness or pushing the corrupt deeper into their corruption. Various reasons explain Pluto's dark energy. For starters, it has a similar energy to Lord Shiva, the father of destruction. Secondly, rebirth cannot take place without destruction. Lastly, each conjunction between Pluto and other planets brings with it some form of drastic change, from world wars to explosions, and most recently, the coronavirus pandemic.

In 1914, the Pluto-Saturn conjunction in Cancer indicated impending destruction. Later that year, near the end of June, Europe witnessed an assassination of the heir to the Austro-Hungarian throne, followed by military escalations, rising tensions, and the division of the major powers in Europe. In August, Germany officially declared war on Russia. The war claimed millions of lives and destroyed many lands but did not stop there. One young soldier in this particular war was none other than Adolf Hitler. It was during the war and after the German defeat that his anti-Semitic ideology started to take shape. Bear in mind that Hitler was an artist before the war. Like many artists, he could have channeled the transformation and destruction he witnessed into his art by joining the surrealist, anti-war art movements that erupted after the war. Yet, he succumbed to Pluto's dark energy and eventually transformed from a traumatized artist into a dictator.

Another example of Pluto's influence on society is the infamous cult leader Charles Manson, known for convincing his followers to murder actress Sharon Tate and four other people. While Manson cited his ideology as his core influence, Manson's natal chart shows more subtle powers at work that affected his destructive and domineering tendencies. Manson was born with Pluto in his fourth house, indicating a turbulent life at home. Pluto was also in Cancer for Manson, suggesting powerful emotional transformation and a tendency to seek out strong bonds.

An examination of Manson's childhood reveals that his biological father abandoned his sixteen-year-old mother when he found out she was pregnant. His mother was then arrested and sent to jail for five years. After serving her sentence, she took up drinking, leaving young Manson without love, guidance, or support. Like Hitler, Manson was an artist (a musician, to be specific). His emotions already fueled him, yet under the influence of Pluto, this proved to be a dangerous thing. He fulfilled his hunger for strong bonds by forming a cult and channeled his anger into ordering his people to commit gruesome murders.

Lastly, before the COVID-19 pandemic hit, many astrologers anticipated such an event for no small reason. Early in January 2020, the Pluto-Saturn conjunction took place in Capricorn. It did not take long for the amplified energies resulting from this conjunction to take effect. In March, the World Health Organization officially declared COVID-19 a pandemic. In addition to causing over three million deaths, the coronavirus pandemic ultimately toppled the global economy. From mandatory curfews, quarantines, and contingency policies implemented worldwide to world trade regulations and forced layoffs by businesses that could not adapt to consumer spending changes, the impact of the pandemic was drastic.

The aftermath of the Pluto-Saturn conjunction was not just limited to a virus, either. In the middle of this pandemic, the world's eyes shifted toward the U.S. after the murder of George Floyd. The event caused a deep state of unrest as many became aware of the systemic racism that was taking place around them.

Darkness before Dawn

When Pluto approaches, it brings with it strong forces of destruction, as you have seen in the examples above. Whether it is the destruction of human lives or systems, governments, economies, and ideologies, this destruction is usually nothing but one frame in a long film or a step in a journey. For a deep cut to properly heal, you need to remove the old dressing, disinfect the cut, then re-dress it. The destruction that Pluto brings is the equivalent of alcohol on a wound, often making way for the proper healing of internal wounds and radical social, political, and economic reform. In this way, Pluto is also a planet of rebirth that embodies the saying, "Night is darkest before dawn." Suppose you trace the events mentioned above and the many more where Pluto acted as the primary influence. In that case, you will notice that with every period of destruction comes a period of renewal and heightened awareness.

Amidst the destruction brought by the First World War, women had a chance to make their voices heard and claim their place in a patriarchal society. Through their war effort, they proved that women were no less than men, earning their right to vote in 1918 when the British Parliament issued the Representation of the People Act. The war also highlighted the role of education in molding younger generations. Thus, Britain made school attendance mandatory until the age of fourteen. Last but not least, the abnormally elevated mortality rates due to the war and the Spanish flu pandemic managed to shed light on the need for suitable healthcare systems in all the countries involved in the war. All in all, the war forced the world's governments to reconsider their policies and rearrange their priorities. What testifies to that is the overall improvement in the quality of life for the working classes.

Pluto's transformative power can also be seen in its effect on Mahatma Gandhi's life. While in conjunction with Jupiter at the beginning of Gandhi's protesting journey, Pluto gave Gandhi an unparalleled driving force to make a change. Gandhi created disorder by putting pressure on Britain through non-violent civil protests. However, he laid the groundwork for and eventually negotiated India's independence by challenging the British occupation. Needless to say, Gandhi went on to become an idol for many leaders and advocates for freedom.

Nelson Mandela, the former South African president and anti-apartheid revolutionary, was born during the Jupiter-Pluto conjunction in Cancer. However, this conjunction caused tension between the rest of the planets and their energies. On the one hand, the energies of Pluto and Jupiter gave Mandela a powerful love for those around him and a heightened sense of empathy. On the other hand, the tension between Pluto and the other planets in their respective houses gave him the anger and the drive he needed to affect change. That exact Pluto-Jupiter conjunction was there during the 1994 elections, where he emerged victorious as the first black president of South Africa.

Above, you read about the negative impacts of the pandemic and systemic racism. How did such darkness bring about light? How did Pluto's energy drive political, social, and economic change? As humanity suffered the pandemic as one, new bonds formed, uniting countries against the one foe, a virus. Whether it was through the collective search for a cure, or medical supply donations, monetary reliefs, and research efforts, several countries banded together. Similarly, people worldwide were suffering from the same virus, facing the same losses and pressures. What better to shake the irrational boundaries segregating religions, races, and ethnicities other than a global tragedy? Granted, one could argue that nothing much has changed, at least globally, but mentalities are slowly changing. Perhaps more time is still needed until humanity overcomes its differences, but it all starts with a seed.

Politically and economically, the pandemic presented the ultimate test for all countries impacted, allowing each country to see its strengths and weaknesses. While one can only reflect on the pandemic's outcomes when it has been contained, common sense dictates that reform is the step that comes after awareness, similar to the aftermath of World War I.

The events after the January 2020 Pluto-Saturn conjunction, which highlighted systemic racism, resulted in nationwide protests across the United States. The Black Lives Matter movement had rejuvenated, attracting eyes from all over the world, and educating people on the struggles of people of color. As the Washington Post wrote soon after the event, "Whether these events will move the country closer to its long-cherished ideal of equality may be years in the answering, but the past days have suggested that something is changing." This indicates that, once again, the death and destruction from Pluto's energies are always making way for new laws and healthier environments, be they social or political.

Pluto's Motion and Its Effect on Generations

Pluto has the largest orbit out of all the planets, which means that it takes longer than any of the other nine planets to complete a full rotation around the zodiacs. On average, it spends about twenty-one years in each house. This can only be put into context when you compare Pluto with Venus, a planet that spends two months and a few days in each house at most. What does this mean for those living with Pluto in any of their houses? To understand that, you need to understand the impact of a sign in a house.

Every sign/planet possesses a certain type of energy, be it Pluto's destruction and transformation, Mars's aggression and passion, or Venus's love and attraction. These signs/planets are in constant motion, making their way around the zodiac (the twelve houses). The twelve houses of each individual represent aspects of their personality, existence, and experience. Aries represents one's ego and consciousness, Cancer represents family and home, and Capricorn represents achievements, ambitions, and authority. When a sign passes through a house, it exerts its energy on that specific aspect of one's life. This definition splits planets into two main groups: personal planets and generational planets.

The personal planets govern an individual or a group of individuals because they only stay in a house for a month or two. These include the Sun, the Moon, Mercury, Venus, and Mars. No matter what happens, you will never find an entire generation extremely like-minded on account of one of those signs. At most, you can find some common traits between all those born in the same month of that same year. On the other hand, generational planets affect entire generations because they stay in a house for a year or more. These include Jupiter, Saturn, Uranus, Neptune, and Pluto. When one of those planets passes, it exerts its energy on that particular house for years, affecting millions and millions of people. That is why it is easy to call out a particular generation for a specific set of traits. It is also why people find it easy to classify humans into Silent Generation, Baby Boomers, Generation X, Y, and Z. However, this does not mean that generations affected by these planets are all the same; it only means that they carry similar core traits.

Going back to the example of young Hitler (born 1889) turning to politics and anti-Semitism instead of art, let us look at Pluto's position. Between the years 1884 and 1914, Pluto was in the house of Gemini (communication, intelligence, and development). This suggests that Adolf Hitler's astrological generation was all going through a period of intensive ideological transformation. However, not all individuals changed in the same way.

Many of that same generation went on to adopt anti-Semitism and eventually fight a second world war. Others, like Max Ernst, completely rejected violence and all rational thought along with it and then turned to art, giving birth to several art movements, including Dadaism and surrealism. Following Picasso, many artists went in the opposite direction and pursued comfort in past works, trying to retrieve the calmness they lost by bringing to life the art movements of the pre-war past. During this period, minds were changing, and revolutionary ideas were being born. As a collective, humanity was being remodeled not just on an individual level but a geopolitical level.

To see this contrast, look at the period from 1995 to 2008, also known as "Generation Z," when Pluto passed through Sagittarius. Sagittarius represents religion, belief systems, and systemic organizations overall, including education, politics, and law. As the bringer of destruction and transformation, Pluto pushed this generation to question the ideals it grew up with. If you are a part of this generation, like many of your peers, you desire to break free from social constructs and seek out what you want rather than what you have been told to want by the previous generation. This is no surprise, given that this generation was parented by the Pluto in Libra/Virgo generation (Generation X/early millennials), two generations coming from a much more rigid background and a desire for conventionality, stability, and safety after two world wars, the Vietnam war, and the cold war. Although many members of Generation Z have seen their fair share of global trauma—from the events of September 11 to the Gulf War, civil war in Afghanistan, the Taliban insurgency, and more—Pluto's transformational energy pushed them to seek radical change. If you stop to take note of today's loudest activists and advocates for social justice, you will notice that most of them are quite young. They lead the fight against outdated beliefs, laws, intolerant language, and neglected rights.

Even on an individual level, this generation seems to be the one seeking out ways to heal past trauma, rewire their minds, and let loose from what controls them. It is important to note that each person has their way of healing, coping, and evolving. The more personal signs (Sun, Moon, Mercury, etc.) can help give more insight regarding how each individual may change. Generally speaking, one can confidently say that Generation Z shares the common trait of questioning their pre-programmed beliefs and challenging the status quo in all its shapes and forms.

We exist together in this world. Each generation plays a part in shaping the one that comes after it. In turn, each new generation pulls the ones that came before it into the future. While both scenarios are examples of change, perhaps someone with a keen eye would be able to see the subtle difference. One type of change is conscious, and the other is unconscious. Generational trauma, ideas, norms, archetypes, and embedded patterns are considered items in our collective unconscious. Meanwhile, a new idea, behavior, or law (official or social) consciously introduced and adopted is an example of collective consciousness.

Pluto mainly operates on the collective unconscious. Its slow-motion through each house allows it to affect change on such a deep level. For a minimum of nine years, the planet exerts its transformational energy on specific aspects of society, thus changing its very fabric. This energy creates a sense of hyper-awareness within the collective unconscious, highlighting societal flaws. From there, people start to affect change, rejecting the outdated unconscious and adopting a better alternative. As you have seen, this process of building a better society is never pretty, often preceded by destruction. Once a better mode of thinking/behaving has been adopted into the collective consciousness, it spends some time there before seeping into the world's collective unconscious, only to be stripped down 248 years later during Pluto's next cycle.

Chapter 5: Pluto in Our Life

Pluto is the ultimate discloser of the zodiac, revealing all the lies and fundamental truths that we work tenaciously to conceal. Pluto is the epitome of change, constantly urging us to give up our egotism and relinquish all that stands in the way of our progression. Although it is quite small in size—about half the United States width—it is loaded with more vigor than the majority of the other astrological planets. Pluto's movements in the zodiac have far more impact than you may have previously thought.

As discussed in the previous chapter, Pluto signifies how every generation or age group discovers its ability to change society significantly. Since each generation typically shares the same Pluto sign, Pluto's influence over a group provides layers of meaning to the stamp they leave on the world.

While it signifies transformation, Pluto comes with a great ordeal of darkness before it makes way for rebirth. It accompanies the culminating cleansing and purification of the mind. Pluto releases all the concealed power of fundamental truths. Where there is Pluto, there is prolific destruction, and as Pluto transits, the process can be tormenting.

Pluto and Individuals

Pluto pinpoints the aspects of life in your birth chart where you will come into contact with fervent destructive and creative powers. Along with our personal efforts, the external world triggers the release of all the fragile, suppressed, and masked core, self, and spiritual energies. Pluto's energy cannot be vanquished, and its power is usually feared. This leaves you conflicted between pursuing your deepest desires and the substantial fear of destruction. Your ego will fight to keep its guard up. However, Pluto will persuade you to let go of all that is holding you back. It urges you to embrace personal evolution.

Pluto is the ruler of Scorpio that mandates death and rebirth. Pluto causes you to perish, hypothetically, multiple times before you die. The lessons that the dwarf planet teaches you will force you to rejuvenate yourself over and over into a new person. Notice the changes you experience, at the very deep and fundamental levels of your being, whenever you experience something catastrophic. These changes are inherently the product of Pluto's workings. By nature, we humans are led to believe that our existence relies on our physical surroundings and sense of self. However, those who are brave enough eventually realize that there is life even after ego extermination.

Power, as an entire concept, is also governed by Pluto. Everything power-related, from the power struggles of nations to personal power, is regulated by Pluto. Pluto's potency comes into play when competent people fall under someone else's total control. Pluto's energy emerges whenever we are subject to the manipulation and control of others and changes us once again.

Pluto and Zodiac Houses

Knowing the house positioning of Pluto will reveal the areas of your life that are subject to the most sizeable transformation. Often, you will find that these areas are the ones of utmost yearning. They are where the achievement of your perfect intuition becomes extremely challenging or even impossible. As explained above, Pluto plays a huge role in the renewal and growth of your zodiac sign. It also shows where you will experience these types of changes. Your sign or house placement in your natal chart is what determines death, power, and other types of transportation, as indicated by Pluto's position. The presence of Pluto in a specific zodiac house could be associated with good self-control. It could signify that you have a strong sense of strength and resilience regarding life events and the general surroundings.

If someone feels the strong urge to undergo a physical and/or emotional change, for example, their Pluto may be transiting their sixth or eighth house. Since everything has its pros and cons, and Pluto is already known for being notoriously destructive, there are, of course, negative elements of having Pluto occupy a certain house. It could be an indicator of the rise of either internal or external power struggles of some sort. This is usually most eminent whenever a person plays on their manipulative side to get what they want.

Pluto in Different Houses

Pluto's position in each house affects where we search for deeper meanings and hidden truths. These meanings and truths can be associated with turbulences, changes, power struggles, and control problems. The themes that encompass these aspects of life are intensity, passion, paranoia, self-preservation, protection, fear of loss, obsession, and betrayal. We are usually propelled in the events of the house that Pluto inhabits in our natal charts.

Pluto in the First House

If your Pluto is in the first house, then you may give off feelings of intensity. People usually get very strong first impressions from you. Perhaps you even throw off many people with your behavior, even when it is unintentional. Even when you remain very reserved when it comes to your privacy, your fierce presence may cause people to find you intriguing. Your struggles may include constant fears of rejection and feeling belittled or overpowered. However, luckily for you, most people cannot tell if you lack an ounce of confidence. When it comes to unfamiliar situations, your gut feeling is that of determination. You also never accept things as they really are. You always try to find more information on deeper or concealed levels of the matter at hand. Your challenge in life is to try to go through life without thinking of it as a battlefield.

Pluto in the Second House

You have great instincts when it is time to gather strong resources. You tend to find sentimental value in each of your possessions, making it very hard to let anything go. You may also do so due to a fear of poverty or because you always feel needy and helpless. Many people who have Pluto in their second house feel a powerful urge to take complete control over their money and belongings. They may even be compelled to make more money. If your Pluto is in the second house, your biggest pet peeve might be someone who takes something of yours without asking. This does not necessarily mean that you are ungenerous; instead, it simply means that your sense of ownership is heightened. Pluto may eventually have you experience some type of loss in life. This will teach you several life-changing lessons. You may come out of this situation aware that worth, wealth, strength, and value are all products of your being. You may also be an excellent strategist and planner in terms of handling your finances. You have a good eye for valuable objects or great deals, and you can spot them right away. The advice that you offer to others on these subjects can prove to be invaluable.

Pluto in the Third House

Those with Pluto in the third house are always searching for hidden meanings. You find it challenging to accept words that you stumble across or anything you hear at face value. Instead, you are propelled to dig deeper into the matter yourself. Not only do you have a powerful analytical mind, but you are also naturally eloquent in expressing yourself. You can be quite convincing in your ability to communicate with power, influence, strength, certainty, and decisiveness, whether in writing or the spoken word. Although you tend to dig deep in matters, you genuinely learn by observing instead of asking questions. In many or most situations, you will find yourself holding out against learning from others. You prefer to teach yourself on all issues of interest. This may extend to academic learning and expanding your knowledge in the workplace. When expressing yourself, you often fear losing your sense of self. This is why you carefully consider what you share about yourself, and you are very selective of the word choice you employ. In essence, you do not like others to know too much about who you are.

Pluto in the Fourth House

You may feel the extra need to be secretive or reserved with who you are due to early experiences. Your self-protectiveness may result from a shameful or secretive parent, for instance. As a result, this pattern of thought may have become deeply ingrained in your subconscious mind. Even if you find pride in where you come from and deeply appreciate your roots, you may still experience the contradictory emotion of guilt. This could be because a parent, an authority figure, or someone else who plays an important role in your life has encouraged you to search far beyond the facade of varying issues. This may have even triggered a love for psychology. The person who urged you to become this way may have always been extremely protective of you. They may have always tried their best to keep you away from negative situations and experiences. This, consequently, has led you to fear any life changes. Your fear of change may also result from intense experiences that left a traumatic mark on you. It could also have sprung from something as simple as soaking up the obsessions and fears that your parents projected onto you.

Pluto in the Fifth House

If your Pluto is in the fifth house, you may often experience innovative solid impulses. You find yourself investing a lot of your passion, time, and energy in anything related to the arts. You may also be very devoted to the things that bring out your inner child or even romance. You attach much of your ego to the things you create, and you take pride in them. When it comes to romance, you go all in—it is all or nothing for you. You shy away from light emotions and love that may be deemed as superficial, searching for fervent romance and deep, intense emotions. You want something very intimate and passionate. If you lack the attitude that most of those with Pluto in the fifth house possess, you may find this type of energy in your romantic partners. This is why you may be attracting controlling, extremely passionate, or intense lovers. Whether romance-related or associated with creative activities, any controlling or obsessive behavior can result from deep-rooted fears of betrayal or loss. Even in areas of entertainment and play, your approach may be rather intense. You might feel the urge to just go with the flow, especially with creative ventures. However, your fears may ultimately hold you back at times.

Pluto in the Sixth House

You are a very hard worker who exhibits a strong sense of protection or privacy regarding your work achievements. You can become highly obsessed with finding answers to all your issues, even though you are a great analyst. You may even be consumed by the search for problems that others may not even notice. Your senses are heightened whenever you come into contact with a problem that needs much analysis and research. You can easily turn into a workaholic. In addition to being overly private with your work, you may be extremely attached to what you do—to the point of paranoia. You can be terrified of criticism when it comes to your work. This is why it is best to manage your own work or direct a business, as you can find it troublesome to have someone else manage your work and schedule. You are possibly interested in areas of self-development and health. You may also feel intrigued by the strong connection that lies between the mind and body. You may also actively search for alternative healing therapies. Many of those with Pluto in the sixth house can be great researchers in these specific areas.

Pluto in the Seventh House

If Pluto is in the seventh house, you may notice a recurrent theme of power struggles in your relationships. This can render itself in multiple ways. You can be in a constant conflicting state of both fearing and wanting a single engrossing relationship, or you can find yourself highly resistant to close relationships and in fear of losing control over your personal life. You are highly attracted to jealous, obsessive, intense, or possessive people. In retrospect, your partner can display control issues resulting from your resistance and out of a fear of losing you or being betrayed by you. Your behavior in relationships can bring out the worst in your partner. You can lead people to find more about their intrinsic fears and instincts. Your powers may be discovered through relationships as well. This may often feel uncomfortable. The outcome, however, primarily depends on how you deal with the process. In relationships, you might feel trapped or unable to obtain the deep connections that you desire. You will find yourself constantly obsessing over your connections in relationships. Ensure you do not project your desire for control on your partner, as this can be severely detrimental for both of you. Instead, work hard to accept the intense, deep-rooted fears of betrayal and loss in your close relationships. Facing these transformative relationships can be hard. However, you will be able to make it through self-awareness and care.

Pluto in the Eighth House

With your Pluto in the Eighth house, you may feel naturally drawn to whatever is dark and mysterious. This fascination with the hidden can cause you to live through more peculiar experiences than anyone else. You are something of a psychologist at heart, very skilled at pushing through appearances to get to what truly matters. Your sexual relationships can be quite complex and intense. You and your partner may be allured by profound, fearful intimacy. You may both desire to share passionate, intense, and extensive experiences. This desire will ultimately bring you and your partner closer and cause you to become fascinated with unconventional sexual experiences. Attracting controlling individuals can make you feel very uncomfortable. If that is the case, you should explore and understand all the fears tied to your issues with power and sharing. Some people with Pluto in the eighth house might experience financial power struggles—usually ones that involve a partner. You can also be very skilled as a healing expert, especially when helping others cope with trauma and crises.

Pluto in the Ninth House

You are very attached to your beliefs and opinions, which may easily turn any debate into a full-blown argument if you are not cautious enough. You're likely very intelligent and convincing, with a highly determined mind. You have well-supported, structured, and strong opinions. You find joy in backing your claims, making them challenging to falsify. However, your toxic trait is becoming very consumed by the desire to convince others of your beliefs. You are usually skeptical of new ideas at first glance, though you might become intrigued if you give them more thought. You dislike hypocrites and anyone who blindly follows certain beliefs. Those with Pluto in the ninth house often come up with peculiar ideas just to impress others. This can make others think of you as a perceptive intellect. You have a deep longing for adventure that takes you on atypical journeys. You would make an inspiring and charming lecturer, teacher, or instructor. You are not someone who constantly prattles on about their beliefs and ideas. When you speak up, though, you can be very innovative and persuasive.

Pluto in the Tenth House

You are a unique person, typically possessing a particular trait that makes you different from those around you. You have well-structured ambitions, and you know how to approach your goals with commitment. You are interested in finding out how different things work, and you like to research. You make use of these traits professionally and in a public setting. These traits may have been passed down to you by a driven parental figure or one who was involved in research or healing professions. Because of your powerful presence, you may evoke several love-hate responses from others. Either way, you can become persuasive when needed. You are highly responsible, committed, and detail-oriented.

Pluto in the Eleventh House

Whenever you are in group settings and friendships, you usually go all in. However, you may face some issues with power and control, and your social life may undergo many significant changes. You value loyalty in your friendships the most. You would make a great leader who is interested in changing the world and spreading your influence. Most of your power struggles can arise in your social circle, especially when dealing with topics of interest or political issues. Keep in mind that if you have not developed your own set of strong opinions and beliefs yet, you may fall under the control of others. This can be troublesome since you naturally find it hard to accept being a follower.

Pluto in the Twelfth House

You feel compelled to explore your personal psychology, make sense of your dreams, and understand their hidden meanings. This also makes you very understanding of other people's motives. You may even discover that you hold great healing powers, allowing you to tap into other people's vulnerabilities and challenges quickly. You can easily become so consumed in helping others with their problems that you put your well-being at risk. You keep too many things to yourself and put an unnecessary load on your mind. You can be your own enemy, as certain parts of you can act impulsively and irrationally. This can result in various problems if not managed.

Your birth chart essentially signals a lifetime of deliberation on a certain topic at hand. Unfortunately, Pluto criticizes and troubles us persistently like no other astrological planet. Pluto's inner workings strip us away from all the unnecessary aspects of self-initiated and externally provoked changes. In this case, we only need to take a leap of faith. We have to experience the torture of letting go so that we can allow miracles to take place.

Chapter 6: The Stages of Transformation

Pluto reigns over your subconscious mind and everything that dwells beneath the surface when it comes to astrology. Like the underworld that the God Pluto ruled over, these parts of yourself often remain hidden from the outside world. However, they are integral to who you are as a person. Learning to reconcile the darker aspects of your personality with more positive aspects is essential to becoming a well-rounded human being. Nobody wants to operate at only half their total capacity. It is important not to repress the things about you that might be difficult to handle.

Our society typically tries to shun anything considered "problematic" about a person, but you cut off a significant part of what makes you unique when you deny these traits within yourself. You cannot have light without darkness, and you can't have good without evil. Everyone experiences negative thoughts and emotions—it is never wise to suppress them and pretend they do not exist inside you. Instead, try to embrace them, understand why you have them, and find a productive way to integrate them into your personality. You can do this with the transformative energy offered by Pluto.

Pluto and the First Four Houses

Pluto's placement in the first four houses of the natal chart represents the stages of transformation. Based on where Pluto is positioned within each of these houses, the traits ascribed to you can cause great difficulty in your life. However, while Pluto embodies destruction, it is also a force of rebirth, so there are positive aspects to its power over your personality. There are always good and bad things related to change and transformation, so it's necessary to use the insight you gain from Pluto's place in your natal chart to find a way to balance them out.

House One

This house is the "House of Self" and is related to the sign of Aries. It is the natal house that governs your physical characteristics as well as your personality traits. Your attitudes and the attitudes of the world toward you are dictated by the first house. If you have a natal Pluto here, you are a very intense and passionate person. Your presence is quite powerful, and others often defer to you based on the aura of authority you emit. You also have a very strong physical body that can withstand significant challenges. While you may enjoy exercise, sports, and other physical activities, you can sometimes become too focused on keeping your body in peak condition.

You have a magnetic personality that is only intensified by the memorable first impression you make on others. This can result in them either immediately being drawn to you or becoming repelled by your powerful aura. People may even discover they are irrationally attracted to you, claiming, "There's just something about you..." This power you seem to hold over them can be wielded for good or for ill. The choice is entirely up to you.

Unfortunately, Pluto in the first house is also indicative that you suffered deep emotional, psychological, and/or physical trauma early on in your life. This has had a serious effect on your development as a person. The charisma you exude can also contain a dark, mysterious aspect that may cause others to fear you. With your passion and intensity comes a capability for violence.

Despite how easily you can influence people, you can also be a very private individual, making you come off as secretive and reserved.

Since Pluto is related to power, having a strong Pluto influence in your natal chart can indicate that you are obsessive or a control freak. You may be the type of person who seeks out the opportunity to wield power over others. When you do not have a tight handle on a situation, you feel distressed. You feel a need to ensure everything in your environment is exactly how you want it. While this is a positive trait when organization and structure are necessary, it can become detrimental if you focus too much on every tiny detail. You need to temper the more negative aspects of your intense personality with the positive ones, preventing you from falling into the trap of obsession.

By tapping into the power of Pluto, you can uncover deep reserves of inner strength that can help you survive any crisis. The trauma from your past has taught you how to protect yourself and become a resilient person. Part of protecting yourself includes hiding the fact that you can be somewhat insecure. You fear rejection, which can make you work harder to gain the affection of other people. There are ways you can work on this, such as using your natural strength to remind yourself that you are worthy of love and respect.

Another aspect of Pluto's influence over you is your powerful ego. This can manifest negatively when it comes to your relationship with others. You do not forgive, and you don't forget. You can hold a grudge for a long time, and you become very hostile when you feel that someone has wronged you. You can also be uncooperative and seek revenge, going out of your way to get back at others. The pain you felt in your youth can fester over time, and when augmented by your intense passions, may result in you becoming involved in criminal activity, particularly of a violent nature.

When you use the power derived from Pluto positively, you can affect great change in other people's lives. If you can find a way to heal your own wounds, you will be capable of helping others to heal. As someone people look to as a leader, you can inspire them to get past their trauma. There are always ways to take something negative and transform it into something positive, and you have the power to do so.

House Two

This house is the "House of Value" and is related to the sign of Taurus. It is the natal house that controls your connection to money and material possessions. This can also extend to control over other people. You highly value financial power and have the ability to gain it. The obsessive aspects of Pluto's influence can cause you to become too heavily focused on this, though. To avoid becoming consumed by this, you must engage in a precarious balancing act.

One of the negative sides of the second house is that it may provide you with a fear of letting go. You hold onto things like money, possessions, relationships, and power, even when it would be better to give them up. You worry about losing your wealth and becoming impoverished, possibly due to having gone through a financial crisis in your youth. Pluto's power causes you to have self-destructive tendencies and will put you through painful learning experiences before you can get a handle on these issues.

Self-esteem troubles can also plague those placed within the second house. You can often feel that others are overlooking you and that your efforts are not always properly recognized. This subconscious insecurity will make you constantly strive to prove your worth to other people and fear that you will not be accepted and your contributions won't be valued, even when this is clearly not the case. Again, this can stem from an obsessive nature and being ever consumed by the desire to show that you are deserving of praise and affection.

Part of the transformative aspect of Pluto in the second house is your talent for turning debt into great wealth. You are willing to do anything to achieve success and build your fortune, which can sometimes come at a price. You have no problem using others to help you gain money and power and can even obtain these things through marriage or inheritance. Your personality is suited for a career in banking, financial management, stock brokerage, or capital investments. However, the negative energy of Pluto can also lead you to a life as a criminal and to building your wealth through illicit means. Regardless of how you acquire your money, you will often be loath to part with any of it and may appear to others as greedy and stringy.

The traits of the second house support those of the first house. While the latter describes the self, the former determines your self-worth. This is partly because of your self-esteem issues, as you strive to overcome this weakness by using material things as tangible proof that you are truly valuable as a human being. You view your possessions as intrinsically linked to who you are as a person. You desire comfort in your life, and you see having money as the way to achieve that goal.

House Three

This house is the "House of Sharing" and is related to the sign of Gemini. It influences the way you think, communicate, and learn. Through Pluto's power, you seek to uncover profound truths about yourself and the world around you, and you have a very strong mind. You ruminate on matters and consider many different options before coming to a decision. However, your intelligence can be both an asset and a drawback. You do not believe in sugarcoating things, causing you too often to be very blunt with others, resulting in problems with interpersonal relationships.

Pluto's transformative aspect means you tend to replace your old thinking patterns with new ones that support your ideas and goals. This is not always an easy process and requires a significant amount of self-reflection and open-mindedness. When you look back on your life, you will find that you held very different views in the past than you do in the present. Sometimes, this change can appear to turn you into an entirely new person, especially when compared to the way you were in your youth. Part of this is due to the trauma you suffered in your younger years, which caused you to develop a more fluid psychological character, and you are now willing to alter your views as you uncover new truths and gain more life experience.

The third house correlates to the journey of self-discovery you underwent during your formative years. This was when you established many of your habits and the mindset you now hold. Pluto's extreme and intense nature influenced the way you interact with others and the environment around you. You may have trouble fitting in with a community or peer group, as you prefer not to conform to societal norms. You may have been bullied or felt ignored by people in your youth, and you had difficulty making your voice heard. This was very isolating, and you often felt misunderstood and overlooked by the people around you.

When you are positioned within the third house, you will be constantly vigilant regarding your relationships. You may have experienced much abuse, betrayal, and violence when you were younger, causing you to mistrust people and believe they will harm you in some way. In a group setting, you may engage in power struggles and an inability to get along with certain people you view as possible threats. The intensity of your passions can be off-putting to others, especially when combined with your bluntness and tendencies to show off your material possessions to impress them.

As someone placed in the third house, you have a wide variety of unique hobbies and interests that those around you may not understand, causing friction between you and them. You are also susceptible to dangers in this world and are prone to accidents and hazards that can cause you severe pain. It is important to be aware of any perilous situation you might find yourself in so that you can avoid danger by exercising great caution. You have a natural curiosity, but as the saying goes, "Curiosity killed the cat." You need to find a balance between learning the truth and preventing yourself from bringing trouble upon yourself.

House Four

This house is the "House of Home and Family" and is related to the sign of Cancer. It influences your home life and your relationship with friends and family members. You may have experienced a troubled childhood, as the families of those placed in the fourth house are typically dysfunctional. Unfortunately, this pattern can repeat itself when you grow older and start a family of your own. You need to understand the power that Pluto exerts over your home life so you can make an effort to avoid passing on these negative traits to your offspring.

Your family may often deal with internal power struggles, and you are likely to have friction with one or both of your parents or guardians. When parents and children fight with one another, it can create deep psychological wounds that fester in the back of your mind and affect your behavior. You carry these wounds throughout your life, and subconsciously, you are influenced by them, especially when it comes to other relationships. You always carry the fear that everyone you know will act similarly, making it difficult for you to trust others and get along with them.

Due to your childhood lacking the comfort and safety it should have provided, you seek to fill this lack through material possessions and wealth. You may become controlling to prevent chaos and uncertainty in your life. You may attempt to keep the problems that afflicted you as a child from recurring in adulthood by taking on a dictatorial and manipulative manner. There is a significant potential for susceptibility to violence and abuse among those in the fourth house. These things are often cyclical and a result of experiencing the same sort of trauma while growing up. However, you can overcome this and put your power to good use by attempting to live harmoniously with other people.

Those positioned in the fourth house are very private and secretive, even from their close ones. The outside world is often completely unaware of what is happening behind the scenes, causing you to come off as a mysterious and standoffish person. Part of this is also rooted in your lack of self-esteem and insecurities, as you fear that if people know what you think and do in private, they will view you as unworthy of their attention and affection. These traits can even manifest themselves in bullying since bullies often project their insecurities outward in an attempt to conceal these parts of themselves from others.

Pluto's power in the fourth house can influence your sense of belonging within a family, peer group, or community. You have trouble accepting yourself, making it feel as if others do not accept you, either. You may not like your heritage and believe that where you came from is a detriment to you personally. You feel a sense of isolation stemming from a lack of connection to your roots. Sometimes, those placed in the fourth house will try to make up for their lack of compatibility with their heritage by integrating themselves with a broader cultural or political structure. With Pluto's energy filling you with passion and obsession, you may become extremely patriotic or zealous in your support of whatever you have chosen to identify with.

Pluto and You

Pluto has a potent effect on your internal processes, and you must be careful not to let your passions and obsessions consume you. There are many harmful and destructive aspects to your personality, but you also have the power to transform these into more positive ones. By overcoming your trauma, you can be reborn as a much healthier individual. You can improve your relationships with other people and the environment around you so long as you recognize the darker parts of your subconscious and learn to control them. You have the strength to face the things you fear and discover truths about yourself and the world you inhabit. This change in how you think feel and can lead to a regeneration of your soul.

Chapter 7: The Stages of Regeneration

Pluto is the Roman god of the underworld, and his Greek counterpart is Hades. These different adaptations of the same god are always symbolic of that which lies underneath the surface. The tiny planet that astronomers demoted to dwarf planet characterizes our personality's hidden aspects. However, in astrology, Pluto still remains a planet.

The correlation of the planet to Hades is suitable, considering that astrologers have long associated feelings of lust and envy with Pluto. Hades is a symbol of lust since he forcefully kidnapped Persephone to make her his wife. The reign of Hades over the underworld is symbolic of the deep-rooted and hidden darkness in our subconscious and unconscious minds.

The positioning of Pluto in the natal chart signifies how a person reacts to power and how they seize it to manipulate others. The darkest desires and the deepest secrets of the human mind, including envy, lust, resentment, and greed, are revealed by this dark planet. Reading Pluto in the natal charts reveals how people can transform themselves through the various phases of life. The primary effect of Pluto on our lives is that it brings massive changes to our lives, and these changes can be long-lasting and have a transformative effect on an individual's life.

Pluto in Brief

The positive effects of Pluto include the renewal, regeneration, evolution, rebirth, and transformation of an individual's life positively. The secretive aspects that Pluto exhibits can be understood positively as well since they can provide many hidden gifts and resources to an individual.

There are as many problematic aspects of Pluto as there are positive ones, if not more. Feelings of jealousy and resentment, obsession with power, hidden dark secrets, the desire for destruction and violence, and the ability to manipulate others are some of the problems that this planet can instill in a person if they are not careful.

The zodiac sign that Pluto rules is Scorpio since this sign is an expression of the sheer energies of Pluto in the best way possible. Pluto is exalted in the sign of Aries, meaning that its qualities are amplified when it influences the fiery Aries.

However, Pluto is debilitated in the sign of Taurus, meaning that the planet's energies are quite weak when in this zodiac sign. Libra is not particularly compatible with Pluto, either, because Pluto's energy is usually in decline when in the rational and balanced Libra.

Pluto in the Zodiac

The orbit of Pluto is not exactly like some other planets. How long Pluto spends in each zodiac sign varies greatly, as it can spend as many as thirty-two years through Taurus, for instance, but only eleven years through Scorpio. The long duration of Pluto in any zodiac sign is responsible for generational effects. Entire generations of people are influenced similarly by Pluto, which leads to the entire world going through similar phases simultaneously. This is why Pluto's position in varying houses is essential in determining its effects on an individual rather than a generation.

The zodiac sign of Scorpio is where Pluto shines the most. The last time Pluto was in Scorpio was between 1984–1995, and the influence of Pluto on this generation was connected to the emergence of untethered sexuality and the rise of HIV. The generation influenced by Pluto in Scorpio had an increased interest in the darker aspect of human existence, like the occult. It was tasked with handling a society that was on the brink of collapse.

The Scorpios under the influence of Pluto are usually the most contradictory ones in the entire zodiac. The mindset of these Scorpios is shaped and influenced by the different perspectives they have. However, these people are usually very gullible. They can be easily influenced by others since their logical abilities are not as keen as some other zodiac signs.

The Scorpios influenced by Pluto are often free-spirited, not particularly rule-abiding, and enjoy bending societal standards. For them, authority figures are nothing more than shackles restricting their freedom. These Scorpios are very passionate, driven by their emotions, and operate on their instincts.

Since Scorpios operate under the influence of their emotions alone, they can be very disposed toward helping others while under the influence of Pluto. These people like to maintain a harmonious environment wherever they go and want to break society's stereotypes and taboos.

Contrary to their raw and instinctual nature, these Scorpios are not very giddy about the idea of love. Instead, they would rather dedicate their time to more serious pursuits in life, including their professional life, position in society, and dealing with inner demons. The pursuit of money is very important for these people since Pluto's greed and envy influence them. Love is not one of their top priorities by a long shot.

However, if a Scorpio falls in love, they like to dive in and give their all to the relationship. It is not in their nature to take things for granted. Loyalty in this kind of love is their strong suit, leading to deepening the bond between them and their partner.

The sexual desires of Scorpios influenced by Pluto are relatively strong, and they are known to be passionate lovers. Sexuality for them is very natural, and they do not associate any taboos along with it. These people are generally very open about their desires and don't like to keep them hidden under a false pretense. Instead, they see desire as something that should be celebrated due to its pleasure.

Pluto in the Houses

The impact of Pluto in the natal chart is usually clearly visible in a person's daily life. The house occupied by Pluto is typically a place of power struggles and revolutionary events. The person who can control the whims and fantasies of his plutonic mind can utilize the power of this planet to direct their life in the desired direction and avoid any harmful effects altogether.

The house that Pluto presides over in your natal chart will be somewhat sensitive to control issues, and the desire for power will dictate the characteristics of that house. These tensions are usually caused due to the feeling that something or someone is trying to control you in the house where Pluto resides. This can lead to feelings of stress and can manifest itself physically as well.

This struggle for control is not usually expressed in the form of aggression. Until Pluto is present in association with the fiery Aries or Mars, the person involved in the power struggle will not be prone to showing anger or aggression. This is because anger is not a trait of a person in control, and Pluto thrives when controlling and manipulating everything.

Let us now look into the different effects Pluto can have on an individual depending on the house over which the planet presides.

Fifth House

When Pluto is found in the fifth house, creative pursuits are taken very seriously, often to an overly heightened degree. The chart holder is likely to choose their medium of expression very carefully and avoid showing any of their imperfections to the world. Often, this hampers the person's creative spirits, and they end up placing an excessive amount of focus on perfection.

These chart holders are also gifted with determination and perseverance, which gives them the ability to create marvelous works of art, to say the least. Suppose your Pluto is in the fifth house. In that case, it is in your best interest to adopt a lighthearted attitude toward life since your seriousness can turn even a form of entertainment into something very stressful for you.

In romance, these people are either blatantly cold or excessively warm. They do not do a very good job of maintaining balance in their love life and are inclined toward excesses. If you fall into this category, you will want a passionate and intense relationship since anything superficial will not be able to satisfy your desire for all-consuming love.

If these people wish to express their interest in the other person, they will make it abundantly clear, and the person on the receiving end will realize it almost immediately. However, if the chart holder is not very interested, they will evidently be cold and come across as stand-offish.

This intensity of Pluto chart holders in this house is also abundantly clear when having offspring. These people will either delay having children until they are ready or face problems with having kids and completing the pregnancy. Their children will be very appreciated once they're born, and these people make excellent parents by taking the job of parenthood very seriously. Their children become their topmost priority, and these parents wish to do a perfect job raising them.

Sixth House

The sixth house inspires a person to serve the others around them, but Pluto's nature is the exact opposite of servitude. Pluto is an independent planet that does not like following orders or working for others. The chart holder in this house can become very vengeful and harbor negative emotions if forced to serve others. Power struggles are very common when Pluto is in the sixth house and can lead to the deteriorating health of the chart holder if these issues are not resolved quickly.

Pluto is an emotional planet. As already discussed, since emotions are an unconscious and intangible thing, the presence of Pluto in the sixth house can lead to physical manifestations of these unconscious struggles. The chart holder will try to repress their feelings, which can lead to them developing multiple ailments. This is why this chart holder needs to express their emotions freely. Expressing how one feels will prevent the emotions from festering inside, and as a result, the person's physical health will not be harmed.

The sixth house can make you very insecure about your work, and if this is your chart placement, you will want to avoid criticism at all costs. Your attachment to whatever you are doing can quickly turn into an obsession, which might even turn into paranoia. This is why you're best suited to working for yourself by starting a business or an independent career where you do not constantly have to worry about being supervised or criticized by higher authorities.

However, the sixth house has its merits, and not all is dark and gloomy for this chart holder. With Pluto in this house, you will have the gift of intense focus and be able to dedicate yourself to whatever you choose to do. The 100 percent effort invested by these people in all their endeavors can bring them immense growth as long as they do not engage in a power struggle that could slow their progress.

Seventh House

When Pluto is in the seventh house, a distrustful and intense nature is relatively common. These chart holders often try to observe their partner's actions acutely and decipher the meaning behind every small move their partner makes. Chart holders with Pluto in the seventh house are often very good judges of human dynamics, and they often patiently probe to gather more details before making their move.

These people do not readily associate with anyone, whether in romantic relationships, business partnerships, or even friendships. They exercise caution until they can be sure that the other party is worth trusting. These people are very sensitive to the power dynamic in any situation and often try to seize power for themselves.

Their power struggles in intimate relationships can cause undue stress and damage their bonds with others. These chart holders generally fear the attachment and vulnerability that comes with opening up to someone, which is a prerequisite for any romantic relationship—yet, at the same time, they also desire and long for a close and personal connection. The kind of people that attract you if you are someone with Pluto in the seventh house are often jealous, obsessed, overpossessive, or simply toxic.

These people consider everyone a threat until proven otherwise and tread cautiously. They are more likely to be attracted to others who exhibit similar characteristics, like a Scorpio, which can lead to great partnerships in the future.

Eighth House

Pluto is a natural ruler in the eighth house, and this house is also associated with Scorpio. The biggest challenge faced by Pluto in this house is the ability to let go. The chart holder with their Pluto in this house takes things like relationships very seriously and experiences much uneasiness and difficulty when discussing the hidden aspects of a relationship.

This chart holder might feel that they need to express their dissatisfaction and disappointment through outbursts of screaming and fits of rage. These people can turn a relationship into a power struggle by trying to seize power at every opportunity that presents itself. This power struggle usually has one of two possible outcomes: either the other person submits and accepts Pluto's dominance, or they are driven so far away that it becomes impossible for the relationship to return to normal.

Even after the end of the relationship, these chart holders do not end their power struggle with their former lover. If they divorce, the process is often dragged on for years in courts, and things will not end peacefully.

Facing deep losses during childhood and being tugged in a power struggle inside the family is a common feature for the person whose house Pluto falls in. The losses and the emotional wounds are never entirely healed, leading to a festering inability to ever let go. If these people find the courage to move on and let go of their bitter past without trying to seize power or manipulate others, they will only find happiness in their lives.

Pluto's Energy

The energy of Pluto varies between extremes. The incredible power that Pluto holds is to influence events on a global scale. Pluto's energy is known to amplify the energy and powers of other planets when it interacts with them.

Pluto's energy is so varied in its effects that it can push people deep into darker situations with debt, frustration, anger, and envy. On the other hand, it can positively affect the chart holder and make them an overnight success. The destructive energy of Pluto is no doubt a cause of chaos and catastrophe, but it is important to keep in mind that this destruction always leads to a new beginning.

If we consider the destruction and reconstruction caused by Pluto as a cycle, we can easily understand the grand plan and be less cautious about Pluto negatively affecting our lives. The change brought by Pluto is not usually a simple one, either. The massive energy of Pluto generally leads to a change of astronomical levels, completely altering the life and perspective of the person affected by it.

Chapter 8: The Stages of Rebirth

Despite circling far from the Sun, Pluto can have an immense influence on your Sun zodiac sign. While residing in the different houses of the natal chart, Pluto determines your life in different ways. Consequently, it can be useful to consult the dwarf planet when you feel stuck in your life and are looking for spiritual guidance. Thus far, this book has covered how Pluto affects death, destruction, and transformation, which are all the necessary steps before rebirth. However, since the whole purpose of leaving your past behind is to create a new, better you, this last stage is vital to your rejuvenation journey. It is essential to mention that aside from symbolizing destruction and transformation, Pluto also signifies rebirth. Pluto has the most significant impact on your emotional regeneration when it is in one of the last houses of the zodiac. Although Pluto's influence on rebirth is often overshadowed by destruction, it can have the opposite effect when housed in the ninth, tenth, eleventh, or twelfth house of your natal chart. Instead of causing destruction, the last houses of the zodiac will help create. And as each of these houses represents the beginning of something new or the drive to achieve something, you can use them as indispensable building blocks of a new, better life.

Ninth House

The house of expansion and philosophy plays a crucial role in reforming your life. If Pluto is the ninth house of your natal chart, your main goal in life is to sharpen your mind by expanding your knowledge. Your biggest passions are philosophy and religion, and you spend a great deal of time devoted to them. By questioning everything you hear, read, and believe, you can gain extensive knowledge about anything you wish. Learning only superficial data is never enough, as you always yearn for more. Despite this, if you happen to uncover anything unusual under the surface, you can accept even the most controversial finding as long as proven facts support it. Part of this stems from the fact that you are naturally inclined to uncover the truth. You feel the need to understand how the different parts of knowledge are connected to each other. When you succeed in this, you will be able to understand far more than most people do. Some would say that this drive is only your fondness for philosophy at work. And although this might be true, if doing this makes you happy, there is absolutely no reason not to continue with it.

Your willingness to uncover hidden truths suggests that your biggest strength is your intelligence. Consequently, if you are looking for a change, you should begin your journey with a mental rebirth. As mental changes can be much more arduous to achieve than physical ones, you might find this process quite overwhelming at first. However, you should never let your fears get in the way of achieving your dreams. Furthermore, because you are not ready to accept anything on blind faith, you are a good candidate for a leader. You also do not like sugarcoating facts, which, again, often separates you from the masses. While this could make you feel unappreciated, the solution is to find people who are willing to follow you. And frankly, with your capabilities, you should not settle for anything less than being an authority in your field, as only this could make you truly happy. While you might find some level of joy in other things, you will never feel complete until you can be devoted to your true calling. A career in higher education or something that equally stimulates your mind is probably one of the best choices for you.

When it comes to Pluto in the ninth house, there are several things you should be aware of that can hinder your emotional rebirth. For one, due to Pluto's strong influence, your insatiable hunger for knowledge can very well turn into a full-blown obsession. Focusing on a single subject can make you lose objectivity. Instead of helping you get unstuck from an unfavorable position in life, this quality can push you further down into a path of mental self-destruction. Additionally, having strong beliefs about something could make you want to force your convictions on others, in turn disregarding their belief system. If you are not careful enough, you can easily find yourself trying to convince others that you are right about something, whether it is true or not. With your fanatic beliefs, you are being conditioned to think that your knowledge is superior, and at the same time, you may fail to recognize an even higher form of consciousness. This very same characteristic can make you vulnerable to emotional and mental manipulation. Those who have a strong affinity toward religion are especially in danger of this. It is good to be passionate about something, but you should never let yourself be manipulated, nor should you manipulate others.

Tenth House

The tenth house of the zodiac is reserved for karma and finding your voice among the masses. If Pluto resides here in your natal chart, you can use this house to continue your rebirth. After gaining knowledge about its importance in the previous stage, now you can proceed to the regeneration of your social self. With your powerful personality, you can influence people around you, making it easier to forge connections that contribute to your mental rejuvenation. Here, Pluto supports your ambitions and can help you achieve your dream results. This is particularly important because sometimes Pluto's influence in this house is the only thing that makes it possible for you to forge these powerful connections. No matter how ambitious you are, only the dwarf planet will be able to help you establish yourself as an authority figure. The secret to your success lies in the way you approach your career. While it is crucial to gain knowledge and do your job efficiently, you should also focus on your interactions and mentally dealing with them. You want the public to know how good you are at your job and show them how you obtained your position. As this is something Pluto in the tenth house promotes, it's easy to see how greatly it affects your professional rebirth.

One of the best things about this house is that it can give you strength even in the most trying times and help you triumph over them by exerting your power. When you feel all your dreams going down the drain, you can build new ones with a renewed sense of strength. The lesson to learn here is clearly that of patience, something we should all practice more. Although you might find it tedious to go slower initially, you will soon learn that building a successful career takes time. After your mental regeneration is complete, you can begin changing people's perceptions of you. If they perceive you as an emotionally stable and trustworthy person, they will be more inclined to interact with you. When this happens, be prepared to find yourself following a new and exciting career path, and be careful not to underestimate your capabilities. Even if Pluto does not take you to a favorable route initially, try to work harder on your karma to achieve your goals. Avoid descending into despair like you are prone to do, as this was what got you stuck in the first place.

Because of your strong personality, you tend to get into confrontations with authorities. Due to the negative influence of older relatives, you often find yourself rebelling against their decisions, especially when you feel these decisions were not justified. Unfortunately, nowadays, it is not uncommon for a parent to lose perspective when raising a child. If you experienced something like this, you might require Pluto's help from the tenth house to help you rise above parental issues. Besides parents, the person you look up to can be your boss or mentor and most likely works in the field of science, whether natural or political. However, you will also need to make sure you do not become an overly authoritative person yourself, either. Just as you fear someone else's strong personality, those in positions below you may begin to perceive you the same way. On the other hand, if an authority figure positively influenced you in the past, they can serve as a good example for you in the future. Understanding the importance of harmony in your professional life will make you become a better leader. It can also prepare you to cope with difficulties and teach you how to handle any mishap, regardless of its size.

Eleventh House

This is the house where true friends are the most decisive factor in your journey of personal rebirth. With Pluto in the eleventh house, your natal chart promises you extensive lessons about friendship. This does not mean that it will make it easier for you to make friends. On the contrary, Pluto will probably decrease your ability to relate and compromise, which can actually reduce your number of friends. However, this is exactly the point of this stage. With less compromise comes less advantage for the people around you, and if they cannot accept that, they were never your friends in the first place. Those who stay will be worthy of sharing confidential information, which is a rarity for this house. However, even though close friends don't belong in this house, Pluto can help recognize them in time. Being forced to rely only on yourself instead of a large group of friends can make you a much stronger person, as can helping others through volunteer work, social work, or any other kind of assistance. Sharing is vital in every aspect of your life, and as soon as you learn this on your journey, your rejuvenation will be more successful.

Under Pluto's guidance and with the ability to recognize true friends, you can build an exceptional social circle based on harmony, and most importantly, mutual support. The people in this circle will be the people you can always count on, and the closer they are to you, the more benefits they bring. Should something bad happen that drags you down, these friends will be able to lift your spirits. With a positive outlook, your mental strength will replenish and enable you to take on any challenge. Plus, having reliable people in your life can be a great advantage in realizing your dreams.

On the other hand, friends who react with jealousy when you achieve success can only hinder your journey. Their envious nature can make them manipulate things in their favor and against yours. Perhaps, you are better off without them. It is one thing if your friends do not always share your point of view—differences in opinions are bound to happen even between the closest friends—but no one should prevent others from deciding anything on their own. Pluto in the eleventh house can help you remember this important lesson. This concept might be hard to grasp, as it involves spending some time alone and resisting peer pressure.

Interestingly enough, the eleventh house associates social interactions with material wealth as well. This means that by choosing your social circle carefully, you can have a successful career and all the commodities you require. What is more, the messages of Pluto from this house even suggest that doing charity work and helping those in need can also be rewarding in the monetary sense. Do not let the dwarf planet fool you, though, as it can make anything larger than it seems, including your courage to take on new challenges in the future. However, you should be careful not to become too focused on your future goals, as this can make your present less significant, and you can end up living in the future in your mind while dealing with present unresolved issues. If you don't get your priorities straight, you will not see your goals clearly anymore. Sometimes it is beneficial to cut back your intensity slightly, even if it takes longer to reach a certain goal. If you listen to Pluto's warning about your goals during rebirth, your life will become much more harmonious.

Twelfth House

Although commonly associated with emotional rebirth after a traumatic event, the twelfth house could also be interpreted as a form of escape from this world. For those with Pluto in the last house of their natal chart, this could mean a regression to one's subconscious and examining your thoughts. If you could not move on after a destructive event or break out from your current position, this house can resolve that. By delving into your unconscious, you can become part of something much bigger than your problems. The twelfth house of the zodiac encourages isolation, both physically and emotionally. This has the purpose of teaching you about the importance of self-evaluation and can help you resolve many of your problems. Finding a time to examine our subconscious has become somewhat difficult in these modern times. Since this process requires a great deal of imagination, it often comes hard if you are used to relying on facts. However, it is necessary to move on from the past and break the chains that hold you back from achieving more in life.

You might have grown up thinking that you cannot do more in life, or something may have happened to you later to make you believe this. For whatever reason, you have concluded that you deserve to be at the place where you are, no matter how unsatisfying it is. As long as you maintain this belief, you will not be able to achieve a full rebirth. Eventually, you will have to relinquish control, which terrifies you. What is even scarier for you is realizing, while you can actually reach your full potential someday, this might hurt other people along the way. Even if that were true, you could still positively work on yourself without beating yourself up, or even worse, using your role as a martyr to gain more power and manipulate others into taking your side. As you will soon come to realize, that kind of dark power does not last long. Sooner or later, people will leave your side, and you will be left to your own devices again. This, again, will only fuel your feelings of incompetence and will completely deplete your self-esteem levels. Instead of resorting to these kinds of tactics, you should learn how to use Pluto's power to achieve your goals. They are readily available for you in the twelfth house—you just have to reach out to them.

Unfortunately, with Pluto in your twelfth house, you are often very reserved and tend to keep everything to yourself. Bottled-up emotions fester within you, poisoning your mind and body. To move on, you may need to find an outlet for all these emotions. Even if you do not want to talk about your negative thoughts, you will need to work on them on a subconscious level—otherwise, you will become an overly sensitive person with an emotional imbalance, which can escalate and bring you great unhappiness. Without a proper outlet, eventually, you will no longer be able to find your place anywhere in the world, mentally or physically. Pluto in this house can also point out unconscious guilt about something you perhaps are not even responsible for. You can hinder your own self-improvement by denying yourself certain comforts in more ways than one. Although physical comfort is beneficial for your rebirth, emotional well-being has even more power when trying to move forward. Whether you surround yourself with people who only have a negative effect on your life or block your path of self-fulfillment, you will need to find a way to eradicate these problems.

Chapter 9: The Process of Self-Cleansing

We humans take care of our physical selves extensively. Wearing clean clothes, washing our hands, taking a bath, and feeding ourselves are all a part of our daily routine. We wear masks and maintain social distance to prevent any harmful bacteria from coming our way. Shouldn't we do the same to keep our mental and emotional sides healthy? Shouldn't you filter out the negative thoughts that emerge in your mind? Shouldn't you maintain distance from things that drain energy from your soul? The dirt and negativity that builds up within you need as much attention as your outer self. If you let it build up, the intensity of the darkness within you can overpower your life in drastic ways. To avoid that, you must understand and implement the important process of self-cleansing in your life.

In astrology, the position of the planet Pluto can assist individuals in confronting the areas of their lives where they search for deeper meaning and truths. Astrologers believe that the area marked by Pluto is associated with control issues, power struggles, possible change, and often upheaval. These areas of life are marked with passion, obsession, intensity, paranoia, fear of betrayal or loss, and self-protection. The house position of Pluto drives you toward the affairs related to that particular house in your natal charts. In this chapter, we will discuss interpretations of Pluto in the different houses of your chart and guide you to accept and implement positive changes in your lifestyle and behavior to overcome the effect of Pluto in your life.

Pluto in the First House

In your natal chart, if the planet Pluto is present in the first house of the chart, you might radiate intense energy, and the first impressions you leave on people tend to be strong in one way or the other. Your personality might often intimidate others whether or not you intend to do that. You may be very protective of your privacy, and your strong presence can generate much interest and intrigue others.

With Pluto in this house, you might struggle with rejection, or the fear of being overpowered, or feeling unrecognized. However, very few people can guess that you might be anything but less than confident. In most situations, your first instinct is to be defensive, determined, gutsy, and intense. You tend to analyze situations by reading between the lines and finding any hidden information that might be present. It is a rare occurrence for you to accept the surface of matters or obvious things easily. You might face the challenges of viewing life as a battlefield and being defensive more than necessary. You can easily conquer these traits by being a little laid-back whenever it is possible. If you take things easy, you can find great joy and security in life.

Pluto in the Second House

If Pluto is found in the second house of your natal chart, you have a powerful instinct when it comes to building and managing your resources. You tend to attach sentimental value to your possessions, making it difficult for you to let go of things. You might have to face the fear of feeling helpless or the fear of poverty, which can make you hold onto things much longer than is necessary. Some people who have Pluto in the second house of the natal chart might feel a powerful need to have complete control over their money and possessions. This aspect of your personality can drive you to make a lot of money in your life.

If someone borrows or takes something from you without your permission, you could easily be irritated by it. You have a strong sense of ownership, and you feel annoyed when people do not ask for permission. You prefer that people ask you before they take something from you. In your life, some experiences of loss can teach you lessons of change. However, you need to understand that wealth, strength, value, and worth come from within yourself. With that being said, you are excellent at strategizing and planning your finances. It is very easy for you to spot valuable objects and good deals instantly. Your instincts and advice on such matters can be helpful to others.

Pluto in the Third House

If you have the planet Pluto in the third house of your natal chart, you might not expect what you hear or read to be truthful until you completely analyze it. Since your mind is extremely instinctive and analytical, you search for hidden meanings in everything. In your self-expression, you can be extremely persuasive. Be it through written text or spoken words, you can communicate with conviction, decisiveness, strength, and authority.

People who have Pluto in the third house of their natal chart tend to learn things through observation and detailed analysis. You prefer to teach yourself rather than learning directly from others or by asking questions. You might face a deep-seated fear related to the loss of self via self-expression. This fear can make you choose your words carefully to avoid letting others know too much about your life. To overcome these fears, you need to be confident and rely on the genuine advice of the people closest to you. Those who love you will always want the best for you—this is something that you must believe in the core of your heart to overcome the challenges that Pluto thrusts upon you.

Pluto in the Fourth House

If you have Pluto in the fourth house of your natal chart, it is possible that the experiences you had early in your life compel you to be self-protective and secretive about personal matters. Perhaps you dealt with an authoritative figure who was secretive or ashamed. That said, this quality is ingrained very deeply in your consciousness. You may feel a sense of shame or guilt about where you belong, even if you feel proud of your background.

You might have absorbed the obsessions or strong fears of a parent or authoritative figure in your life. This figure could have been very protective of you and shielded you from negative experiences. This could be the reason why you grew to fear change in your life. It is also possible that the experiences you had very early in your life included a tragedy, scary event, shock, or intense situations. To overcome this challenge in your life, you will have to stop fearing change and stimulate your psychology's attraction.

Pluto in the Fifth House

If the planet Pluto resides in the fifth house of your natal chart, your passion and much of your energy are invested in creativity, romance, or taking care of children. You possess very powerful and creative impulses. You invest much of your ego into and take great pride in whatever you create or produce. You may need your romantic life to be deeply intimate, intense, and passionate. If your romances are light or superficial, you will cut yourself off from them. People with Pluto in the fifth house of their natal charts usually have an "all or nothing" kind of attitude regarding romance. This attitude or energy is deeply ingrained in your psyche, and if you choose not to own or acknowledge it, you may meet the energies of Pluto through your lover. Thus, you will attract impassioned, intense, or controlling romantic partners.

Any feelings of obsessiveness, jealousy, or controlling behavior can be attributed to a deep-seated fear of betrayal or loss. This can encompass your creative endeavors, child-rearing, and romantic relationships. Apart from an intense romantic experience, you prefer to have equally intense experiences in recreation, entertainment, and play. Although you try to invest your soul completely into your creative endeavors, the fear of losing or failure can prevent you from completely indulging in those activities. To overcome and conquer this fear, you need to understand that failure is the first step to success, and it is all right to lose in some things.

Pluto in the Sixth House

If you have Pluto in the sixth house of your natal chart, you can be quite private or protective when it comes to your work. However, you are a hard worker and excellent at everything that you do. Due to your highly analytical mind, you can easily become obsessed with finding solutions to difficult problems. That said, quite often, you may find problems that are missed or overlooked by others.

Researching and analyzing problems are food for your soul. You tend to feel more alive and valuable when you have a problem that needs to be solved. Due to this attitude, you might become a workaholic and work almost tirelessly without even realizing that you are missing the true joys of life. You may even find yourself becoming overly attached to your work, so much so that you insulate yourself and feel paranoid. You may also face the fear of criticism when it comes to your work, and you may resent others who control your work or schedule. To overcome these challenges in your life, you must take an interest in self-improvement and explore the mystical connection between the mind and the body. Alternatively, you can try seeking healing therapies.

Pluto in the Seventh House

Relationship power struggles can be very prominent in your life. If your natal chart has Pluto in the seventh house, you may find yourself struggling with close relationships. You may feel a loss of control over your life and find yourself resisting close partnerships or relationships. That said, you may even desire complete absorption by people who are possessive, obsessive, jealous, intense, or powerful.

On the other hand, you might bring out the worst behavior in your partners who fear losing you or being betrayed. You may have to face uncomfortable situations once you eventually discover your power in your partnerships or relationships. The way you deal with these circumstances will undoubtedly shape the outcomes. You may obsess over your partners. Pluto may challenge you by making you feel trapped in an unwanted or difficult relationship. To overcome this challenge, you must remember not to project your expectations onto others and tame your urge to control your partner. If you fail to acknowledge and accept your deep-seated fear of losing someone you love, you might have to face these situations repeatedly in your life. The best way to experience loving and rewarding relationships is through care and self-awareness. Instilling this attitude will lead you to a powerful transformation in life.

Pluto in the Eighth House

People with Pluto in their native chart's eighth house tend to be naturally attracted to things that are hidden, dark, or considered taboo. Your fascination with these things can lead you to experience uncommon situations and unusual events that others rarely experience. You are an expert at getting to the core of matters and cutting through the outer appearances. You are a natural psychologist who is extremely fascinated with motivation, occult sciences, hypnosis, healing therapies, mysteries, and the darker side of life.

You are deeply fascinated by and simultaneously fearful of intimacy, and as a result, you crave passionate, intense, and deep experiences with others. Your sexual relationships may perhaps be complicated in addition to being extremely intense. This fascination with deep intimacy may attract non-traditional sexual experiences with others that may involve control, possession, submission, and domination. Because of Pluto's presence in the eighth house of your natal chart, the challenges you face include deep-seated fears about sharing and power issues. You may even experience power struggles with finances, especially with your partner. To overcome the challenges put forward by the planet Pluto, you may benefit from helping others deal with trauma and crisis. You have an innate talent for healing, and you must utilize it for your benefit and help others.

Pluto in the Ninth House

If you have Pluto in the ninth house of your natal chart, you may be very attached to your belief system and opinions. This attachment can easily lead you into unwanted arguments if you are not mindful. Your intelligent and analytical mind complements your intelligence and persuasive skills. Most of your opinions tend to be well-researched and based on strong points. You enjoy backing up your arguments with viable reasons. Pluto challenges you by giving you an obsession with thrusting your beliefs upon others and a desire to convert others to your ideas. You may be naturally suspicious of new experiences and ideas until you have thoroughly examined and analyzed them. You may be irritated by blind followers of belief systems and hypocrites. Your natural talent for persuasive language may lead you to become an inspiring and captivating speaker, lecturer, or teacher. While you may not be very open to sharing your ideas, you can be persuasive and creative when expressing your thoughts. To overcome the challenges in your life, you must travel, share, publish, and connect with other people to gain intense and life-altering experiences.

Pluto in the Tenth House

If Pluto is in the tenth house of your natal chart, you are unique and stand out from the general crowd. You are very goal-oriented, ambitious, and tend to pursue your targets with great determination and focus. With a strong interest in researching various things, you improve your life by understanding how things work and transforming yourself based on your research. These qualities are best utilized in your career or when you are dealing with other people. It is common for those with Pluto in the tenth house to have an authoritative figure or parent who is highly driven in healing or professions that require research.

With a strong personal presence, you may inspire love as well as hateful reactions in your professional field. However, you can also be persuasive when you want to. With that being said, you have a strong sense of responsibility and commitment. You may find yourself going against the grain or denying traditions that you feel are out of date. Often, you may face emotional issues that revolve around your relationship with a parent, mainly a father responsible for instilling the intensity in you regarding your status or profession. You must confront these issues to live a light-hearted life. You can be especially detail-oriented, on the verge of being a perfectionist, particularly in your profession. Being in a position of subordination does not suit you, and you naturally tend to enjoy taking the lead.

Pluto in the Eleventh House

If you have Pluto in the eleventh house of your natal chart, your social life might go through drastic changes, and your friendships often begin with an intense experience. When it comes to group associations or friendships, you can have an all-or-nothing approach. Even in casual relationships, you value and expect loyalty very intensely. If interested in leadership, you can be influential. You believe that to make necessary changes, you require the power of a group. This is why you do not take any association lightly and always value it to the core. You may be easily compelled to make a difference and might feel moved by the problems of humankind, particularly later in your life. You are born to be a natural leader and don't want to be a follower.

The challenges posed by this position of Pluto may compel you to change whether you are ready or not. You may have to address power issues in your social circles, especially when dealing with political processes. You often feel that you must listen to what other people want and follow the same things. To overcome these obstacles, you must listen to your inner voice and recognize your desires. If you do not develop beliefs and ideals, you can easily be wrongly influenced by other people. However, once you have decided what drives and motivates you, you can instigate change in your social circles and become a highly influential leader.

Pluto in the Twelfth House

If Pluto is in the twelfth house of your natal chart, you can easily identify and comprehend other people's motives. You may find yourself inclined to explore the world within yourself on a deep psychological level. You may also find it extremely easy to connect with others and understand the struggles that they go through. You have healing powers that can make you deeply involved when you try to help others, sometimes at the cost of your peace of mind. You can be very empathetic and understanding. However, you may find yourself being secretive or keeping things to yourself that could harm your health. You need to understand that some things are better solved when they are shared with someone.

The challenges put forward by Pluto in your life revolve around your impulsiveness and unconscious reactions. You may become your enemy by challenging yourself to push boundaries. You need to understand that repressing emotions and doubting your abilities can cause you extreme sadness. You must use your time and energy to hone your skills and examine the root of your problems. Utilize your private time and moments of peace to build your power and conquer the demons within. Once you have gained control over your feelings and thoughts, you can become a healer and leader who guides others through their issues and problems. You will find great joy in sharing your grief and helping out others to live a happy life.

Chapter 10: Starting a New Chapter

Astrology is connected to our actions and how we behave during different situations in life, whether good or bad. This is because our feelings are linked to astrological sources. Pluto encompasses both sides of human nature, the good and the evil.

As discussed, Pluto is all about change and rebirth. It explains the Yin and Yang in human nature, with all its good and bad sides—this is the polarity of Higher and Lower Pluto. Higher Pluto contains positivity, bringing people together and calling for peace and harmony, while Lower Pluto manifests in evil ways through crime, wars, and corruption. These two extreme traits belong to one dwarf planet, making up the complex and multi-layered Pluto.

In this chapter, we will talk about the positive sides of Pluto concerning regeneration and rebirth and embodying new beginnings and spiritual development. No matter how hard your life has been, the difficulties you have faced, and the traumas that left scars in you, you can always start a new chapter in your life, a new beginning that brings hope for better days to come. This section will introduce you to some life lessons Pluto has provided us before we dig deeper into how you can plan and start a new life and let go of tough past experiences.

1. *It is completely fine if no one notices you the first time around.* Scientists did not notice Pluto until 1930 because of its small size and extreme distance. However, it has been orbiting in space and crossing our night sky for ages. Eventually, it was noticed and classified as the ninth planet from the sun until 2006, when it was reclassified as a dwarf planet. According to scientists, it failed to fulfill one of the criteria that identifies a planet, as it does not consume or propel away smaller objects around its orbit.

2. *Be yourself and accept that just because people might have higher expectations of you, their expectations are not your fault, which does not mean that you are not enough.* Astronomers believed that Pluto was a large planet simply because they needed an explanation for Uranus's orbiting manner. However, Pluto is an equally important dwarf planet that never tried to act or seem beyond its size.

3. *Do not worry too much about today's problems—you might find out that there are actually no problems at all, just mere misunderstandings.* Scientists tried to find the planet behind the irregular orbiting manner of Neptune and started to perceive Pluto as the mysterious force causing these irregularities. However, it emerged that the real reason behind these orbital irregularities was a miscalculation of Neptune's estimated mass. Once adjustments were made, everything fell into place, and Pluto was no longer perceived as the force causing Neptune's orbital irregularities.

4. *Even if the world underestimates you, you are still magnificent the way you are.* After being demoted to a dwarf planet in 2006, Pluto returned to shock the world when new discoveries about this amazing dwarf planet were revealed. It was even called the most fascinating and scientifically important planet at the border of the solar system!

Moreover, the astrology keywords of Pluto are transformation, power, death, rebirth, and evolution. Hence, people associated with this dwarf planet can transform, change, and always reconstruct themselves. If they fall, they get back on their feet again and create a new beginning. This is how influential Planet Pluto is on people's ability to change and start a new life.

As mentioned before, this chapter is all about starting over and new beginnings. Therefore, here are some tips about how to start a peaceful new life.

- *A new life requires new experiences.* Thus, you need to try new things. It does not have to be something major. Try new foods, new places to hang out, and new movie genres you have never seen before. If you seek greater changes, move to a new city and experience new streets and neighbors. Experiencing new things and feelings will broaden your perspective in life.

- *Accept change, even if that change is inside of you.* Do not be afraid to let go of useless habits, toxic relationships, and a fixed mindset. Embrace a growth mindset and open up for a new understanding of life. Perhaps the new perspectives will make you a happier person.

- *Allow yourself to fail and learn from your mistakes.* Failure is necessary for the process of personal growth and learning. We learn from our mistakes. Therefore, do not be scared of failure—accept, embrace it, and learn from it.

- *Stand out and never try to fit in.* Accept yourself the way you are, and be proud of yourself. Your tribe will be attracted to you, and people who are different will respect the differences between you.

- *Focus on small victories and celebrate them.* Do not get sucked into the pursuit of long-term goals and spend all your time running after them. Celebrate every milestone and every step that brings you closer to your goals.

- *Focus on your needs without being selfish.* You cannot make others happy or contribute to society without being happy yourself. Focus on your needs and try to fulfill them. "Me-time" is very important for healthy mental and emotional well-being.

- *Distance yourself from negative people and negative thoughts.* Hold on to the good things in life instead. Let go of what you cannot control or is out of your reach. When you stop dwelling on your past failures and hurtful experiences, you make way for positive thoughts and better future opportunities.

Our mindset is what controls the way we perceive life events, both the stressful and joyful ones. There is nothing innately wrong or bad about change. However, the impact of changes in your life depends on how you perceive the different factors reflected by this change. Here are some ways that can help you manage transitions in your life.

- Perceive stress as a challenge, not a threat. Try to change how you look at stressful events and turn them into a challenge that you can win instead of thinking of these events as overwhelming situations that might cause you any kind of discomfort. Moreover, remind yourself that it is completely fine to get scared and fail to rise above the situation. You can always do better next time.

- Keep in mind that transitions in our lives become memories and that most of the time, we remember how strong we were at that time. Try to respect these transitions and remember that after a while, they will become memories.

- Remind yourself that as a rule in life, change is good and needed for personal growth. Moreover, change creates new neural pathways in stagnant nervous systems. That is how significant and beneficial change can be.

- This, too, shall pass. Always remind yourself of how you dealt with and got over previous transitions in your life.

- There is always a positive side to any stressful situation. Clear your mind of negative thoughts and feelings so you can find them, and when you do, focus on them.

- If there is a planned transition in your life or a change that you already know will occur, like retirement, for example, or having to leave a country when your fixed-term contract ends, plan and prepare for this transition. This will make for a much easier and smoother transition than one where you deal with everything in a short period.

- Use a transition to reflect on where you stand in life right now and where your life is going.

- A life without change is a stagnant and boring journey. Keep reminding yourself that change is what stimulates and gives meaning and joy to life. If nothing changes in your life, you are not developing or growing. Instead, you are standing still, and even if it feels good at the moment, it will start to backfire later on.

- There are many inspiring real-life stories about people who rose above transitions and challenging times in their lives. Whenever you feel scared and helpless, search for inspiring stories and use those people as role models.

Now that you are ready to start a new chapter in your life and have a good idea of managing this phase in your life, you need to balance yourself through this transitional stage. However, to find equilibrium, you need physical and mental energy. Some exercises can help you learn more about yourself. With this knowledge, you will manage new life transitions and cope with the change in your life without being thrown off balance. Healthy transitions should not be an exhausting experience. On the contrary, they should be fun experiences that lead to a healthier and balanced life.

Here are a few exercises that can help you manage transitions in your life:

Create a Vision Board

Many successful people around the world use vision boards to achieve their goals. A vision board is a collage of images and words that should be placed somewhere visible to you to remind you of your goals, dreams, and why you do what you do in life. It allows you to see and visualize your goals and motivate you to achieve them. The first thing you need to do is self-reflect. Find out what you value most in life and the two things that you want to change about your life. Then ask yourself, "Do I want my vision board to represent long or short-term change?" Get photos or any form of visual representation of your goals and stick them on your vision board. Of course, if you prefer digital methods, you can find many online programs that will help you create a free digital vision board. Write down your goals next to the photos in bold fonts or use colors. Attach anything that catches your eye and hang the vision board somewhere you can see it. You can constantly update your vision board. However, the main idea behind vision boards is to put goals in a visual format to motivate you and help you visualize your dreams so they can manifest later on. It is a tool to help you achieve your goal. Therefore, you need to pursue your dreams and work hard to achieve these goals.

Document Your History of Transitions

Get a paper or a notebook (of course, you can go digital if you want) and draw a horizontal line. Write the date you were born at the start of the line, and write today's date at the other end. Highlight all of the transitions you have been through since you were born up until today. Write down how you felt during each transition and how you managed to control your feelings and frustrations—if any. Document the impact these transitions had on you back then. When you are done documenting all of your feelings and transitions, write a message to your younger self. Make a note of how you can learn from the history of your transitions.

Gratitude Journal

To appreciate your current circumstances, appreciate people and things in your life, and train your brain to focus on the positive things in life during hard times, create a gratitude journal. Every day, write what you are grateful for in the journal. Write down all the positive aspects of your day. This way, you will make a habit of noticing the good things in life, and your brain will eventually focus on the positive side of life instead of negative thoughts.

Create a Life Map

To keep track of the critical moments in your life, whether they were happy or sad, you need to create a life map. This allows you to store all the beautiful and challenging moments in your life on paper and look at your journey in life from different angles. This way, you can gain insight, improve, and grow.

Give yourself enough time to think about all the critical moments in your life. Then, using different colors to document different feelings and emotions, write them down in order. You can use symbols if you want—whatever works for you. When you are done, you will find yourself able to assemble the pieces of emotions and memories in your life into a new narrative and gain a new understanding of your journey in life.

Mindfulness

Mindfulness practices are much needed when you are about to start a new chapter in your life. Mindfulness is a method of meditation where you direct all your focus and sensations to the present moment. Mindfulness practices can transform your life and change the way you perceive things in it for the better. In the busy digital age, many people have resorted to mindfulness practices to manage their stress levels and add peace of mind to their hectic lives.

Tune in with yourself daily by meditating. This way, you will get in touch with your true self and become more centered. Moreover, you will clear your mind and make way for negative thoughts to enter your body and mind. Connecting to your real self will help you achieve more in life than you have dreamed of.

Find a physical activity that you enjoy, and connect with your body. Take dance classes, for example, or practice yoga. The more you connect with your body, the better you will feel about yourself.

Learn how to say no! Do not force yourself to do something that does not resonate with your true self or body. This is very important when you start a new chapter in your life, and it becomes much easier when you have a healthy connection with your inner self.

The virtue of patience is crucial in your new chapter in life. Everything will unfold in its own time, which is the right time, and there is nothing that you can do about it but observe and learn. Learn how to be patient, as this will save you many stressful moments, frustrations, and disappointments.

Any yoga and meditation will surely help you balance your emotions and stand your ground during difficult times. Find the practice that resonates with you and start right away. You do not have to spend hours meditating and practicing yoga. Take your time, and you will notice that over time you will continue to get better and better until you reach the state of mind and awareness you desire.

All of these tips and exercises will help you apply the teachings of Pluto in your life, as they allow you to get back on your feet even stronger than before (rebirth) and grow after episodes of frustrations or uncertainty.

While Pluto is linked to a lack of harmony and destruction, it is also linked to rebirth and new beginnings. After all, it is the planet of extremes. Therefore, Pluto's life lessons and teachings will come in handy when starting a new chapter in your life. A deep understanding of Pluto's lessons combined with the tips and exercises mentioned above will help you cope with transitions in your life in a balanced manner and start a new chapter while rising above all previous disappointments and failures. These failures will become your teachers in planning a better future full of hope and joy.

Once regarded as the god of the underworld in Roman mythology, with the power of change and transformation, and located in a distant part of the solar system while slowly moving in it, this dwarf planet never ceases to amaze astronomers and scientists. Pluto has a lot in store to teach those who seek its guidance in transforming and starting a new chapter in their lives.

Conclusion

Pluto has an immense significance in astrology, and after paging through the various carefully crafted chapters of this book, you undoubtedly have grasped the importance of the tiny planet. This book reviews each essential aspect of Pluto that you must be familiar with to fully understand the implications and the consequences of having Pluto in your natal chart.

The book is designed so that even amateur astrologers can understand how Pluto affects the various areas of our daily lives. You can refer to this book repeatedly if you wish to refresh your understanding of the meaning of Pluto in your life.

Pluto has a hugely significant role in regeneration, rebirth, and destruction—all critical parts of one's life. You will go through various phases in your life where you are given a fresh start, and understanding the role of Pluto can help you better comprehend the significance of those phases.

The cycle of destruction and regeneration has been highlighted so that you can understand when a drastic change in your life is forthcoming. Pluto also governs the changes in our lives that affect our perceptions of the world.

All of the lessons you learn from Pluto can be easily implemented in every area of your life. The little planet is a great guide, as its presence serves as a road map for the path you need to pursue in life. The book has thoroughly explained the concepts of change and transformation, which are inherent parts of our lives. Pluto is all about coming to terms with these changes, and hopefully, you now understand the path you need to take to embrace that change.

Pluto has vastly different effects on a person's life depending on its position and the different houses that it rules. The chapters in this book dedicated to understanding these houses covered how Pluto's influence can bring changes in your life. Pluto has unique connections to lesser touched issues, such as next life and rebirth, which stem from its mysterious nature. The study of Pluto is essential if you wish to understand how these aspects of your life have been influenced in the past and how they will continue to be influenced.

The book also explored how the presence of Pluto in different houses can affect intimate relationships, competition, sexual desires, enmities, frauds, and even death that might manifest in your life. This book has provided you with adequate tools to explore these aspects further so that you can have a greater degree of control over them.

Pluto greatly influences our darker sides, and in-depth knowledge of this planet helps us understand our regrets, desire for destruction, feelings of vengeance, obsessions, and other suppressed parts of our personalities. With the help of this book, you should have discovered how to identify these repressed emotions in your personality, and an understanding of these can help you deal with your inner demons in a better way.

This book explored the interesting effects of Pluto on entire generations that emerge from the planet's rate of traversal across the zodiac. Adept astrologists have been able to predict catastrophic events or generation-defining changes by studying Pluto. This planet, associated with the Hindu god of destruction and rebirth, Shiva, is a critical component of Western and Vedic astrology due to its vastly different nature from the other planets.

After reading this book, you should clearly understand the correlation between the various negative and positive attributes associated with Pluto. In the future, you will can utilize this knowledge to read into your natal charts and bring transformation for the better.

Part 3: Uranus in Astrology

The Ultimate Guide to the Planet of Change

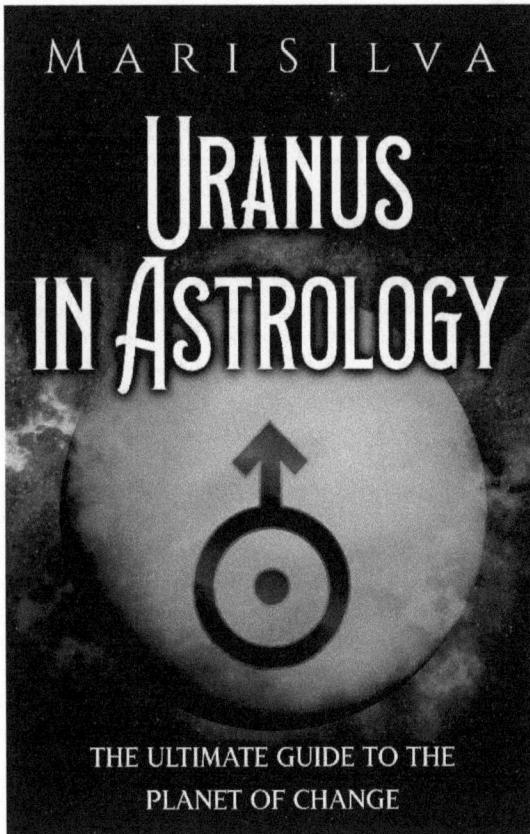

Introduction

Uranus is an ancient Greek deity who played a significant role in determining the course of the universe. Uranus is still revered today, though not in a temple or on an altar. Uranus is one of the modern era's newly discovered planets, and its relevance in astrology is undeniable.

Studying Uranus and its attributes can be incredibly beneficial to you since you will better understand the greater significance it plays in the events that occur throughout the world. This book seeks to explain in detail how and why Uranus acts the way it does. Once you are done reading through the guidebook, you'll have a deeper understanding of how Uranus works.

Uranus is said to be a generational planet, more so than anything else. While this is valid, you may not understand why, and this book seeks to clarify this topic for you. Understanding how Uranus influences the entire world is crucial for assessing the current citation and potential future concerns that the entire world may experience.

Once you begin reading, you will become engrossed in the backstory of Uranus and its connections with other planets. Uranus' interactions with other planets are directly tied to Greek mythology stories, and these have been smoothly integrated into the various chapters of this book. The readability of the book has been prioritized. Thus, each chapter is subdivided into bite-sized sections to make it easier to assimilate the content. Every chapter focuses on a different element of Uranus, such as its impact on societal transformation, its position in the natal chart, interactions with other planets, and much more.

This book tries not only to endlessly drone on about how Uranus does this or does that; instead, it is written with an eye and goal of helping you with the practical application of this knowledge. Each positive or negative aspect of this ever-changing planet is illustrated with a real-world example to make it easier for you to implement these ideas in your own life.

You'll be provided with insight into various topics that are not directly related to Uranus but have a hidden connection to the planet, making them worthy of investigation. No other book would attempt to delve as deep as the American Revolution and its astrological correlation. However, this book scratches beneath the surface to reveal astounding facts about Uranus that you may not have considered previously.

If you set out the time to divulge this book with focus, you can complete it in a few hours. The information provided is organized elegantly and precisely to make the reading experience pleasant. This straightforward and concise presentation of information also guarantees that navigation is simple at all times. If you ever have a question about Uranus, you may easily flip through the pages and quickly find what you are looking for!

To know more about astrology, this book is a must-read. The information and insight you gain about Uranus will help you better understand the topic. Since Uranus is such an important and distinct planet in astrology, it's the best one to start with. We'll help you grasp how different astrological concepts such as zodiac signs, houses, and exaltations/debilitations work from a broader perspective of Uranus.

Chapter 1: Uranus: The Primordial God of the Sky

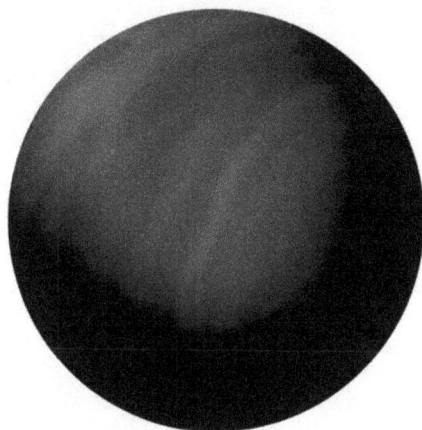

Uranus protogenos
God of the sky
and the heavens

The electric energy of Uranus makes it an intriguing addition to the astrological domain. The planet rules Aquarius and brings about tremendous changes in a person's life. The planet represents exploration, invention, creativity, uniqueness, and authenticity. It allows you to look ahead and reminds you that change is inevitable and constant. While it has positive characteristics such as novelty, illumination, and ingenuity, it may also make one irresponsible and rebellious.

The Legend Behind the Name

Uranus (or Ouranos in Greek), popularly known as the Father Sky or the Primordial God of the Sky, was deemed a popular god in Ancient Greek. Uranus, the brother of Pontus and Ourea, was regarded as the supreme god and the ruler of all. His association with the term "primordial" indicated his existence and governance from the beginning of time. Various myths narrate the story of Uranus' birth from a different viewpoint. While some say he was the son of a distinct couple, others claim he was the sole offspring of his mother, Gaia.

The ancient Greeks were unaware of the existence of other planets and acknowledged the presence of just five celestial bodies of the solar system. The planets were given the name "wandering stars." Unlike the other planets named after Roman gods, Uranus was the only celestial body named after a Greek god. We can draw parallels between the Greek and Roman Gods since Ouranos' Romanized version is Uranus. In the year 1781, astronomer William Herschel used a telescope to discover the celestial body.

Herschel discovered this planet by chance while sitting in his backyard, viewing the sky and examining comets with his telescope. This planet's peculiar innovation and perplexing stance make its name appropriate. Experts say people have been noticing and monitoring the movement of Uranus since the 12th century, but they mistook it for a star. Furthermore, it is situated far away from the Sun and the Earth, making it nearly undetectable. It would have been virtually impossible to detect this planet without using a telescope to observe and identify it.

It took time and effort to come up with a name for this celestial body. "Georgium Sidus" (from King George III, his patron), "George's star," and "Herschel" (as suggested by others who wanted to name the body after its discoverer) were among his options. Some even proposed the name "Neptune."

A German astronomer named Johann Elert Bode assisted Herschel in describing the characteristics of this newly discovered planet. He was also tasked with coming up with a suitable name for the planet. He made comparisons between the names of the planets and their Roman god counterparts. Saturn's father should be attributed in some way since Jupiter's father was Saturn. Bode concluded that the best name for this new planet would be "Uranus," the name of the primordial Sky God. Even though the new planet's name was derived from a Greek God rather than a Roman God (like the names of the other planets), it was given the name "Uranus."

His Connection to Gaia

Legends say that Gaia gave birth to Uranus without a partner to make him her equivalent. She desired a powerful character who could dominate the universe both for her and alongside her. Gaia, the Earth Mother, raised Uranus to equal stature and elevated him to the ultimate ruler of the universe. Gaia represents the Earth, whereas Uranus represents the sky. With time, Gaia and Uranus evolved into the universe's first or primordial couple. The legends about Uranus' father have always been obscure. Early accounts identify Akmon as his father. However, newer versions of the tale claim Aether could be his father. Since Aether symbolizes light and the bright blue ether of the sky, his relationship with Uranus appears more convincing.

Initially, ancient Greeks thought the Earth was a flat disc with a dome on top. This dome, which also served as the sky, was made of brass and had dazzling, twinkling stars and celestial bodies on its surface. The sky was said to have three layers of air: upper air (or dazzling blue air), middle air, and lower air. Due to his demeanor and association with the sky, Aether was considered to represent the upper air. The upper air filled the layer above the middle air and the sky dome. Legend has it that Uranus' father could have been Aether.

With time, Gaia and Uranus became a couple and collectively ruled the universe. They also birthed 18 children, who were -

- the three Hecatoncheires: Briareos, Cottus, and Gyges;
- the three Cyclopes: Steropes, Brontes, and Arges; and,
- the twelve Titans: Cronus, Crius, Oceanus, Hyperion, Coeus, and Lapetus were the gods, and Rhea, Theia, Mnemosyne, Tethys, Phoebe, and Themis were the goddesses.

The Titans were the pre-Olympian gods, while the Hecatoncheires and Cyclopes were giants. Uranus was dissatisfied even though he was a father to numerous children at the same time. He was continually concerned that one of his children would overthrow him and become the ultimate ruler. Instead of loving his children, Uranus detested them and made multiple attempts to get rid of them. He also couldn't stand the sight of the Hecatoncheires and frequently likened their demeanor to that of the Titans, who were said to be magnificent. Once, Uranus saw the Hecatoncheires, and he was so enraged that he tried to thrust them into Gaia's womb. Gaia was in excruciating pain and agony because of this.

Fearing this change, Uranus locked up all the Hecatoncheires and the Cyclopes in Tartarus (a place below Earth ruled by Hades). Gaia was furious and heartbroken when she saw this. Her anguish and pain were turning into resentment, and she was determined to free her children at any cost. She devised a plan with the Titans to kill Uranus using a weapon (a flint sickle) she created. However, the plan was likely to fail because Uranus was immortal. Gaia and the Titans agreed that one of the more powerful Titans should overthrow Uranus. Cronus (the youngest son) was the hungriest and most determined Titan to seize the throne, which is why he decided to assist his mother immediately.

When Uranus approached Gaia to lay with her one night, the Titans pounced on him from behind and got his grip. Cronus appeared in front of Uranus with Gaia's flint sickle and castrated him. Cronus chopped out Uranus' genitals and flung them into the sea, along with the sickle. Uranus, filled with anger, pain, and agony, felt betrayed and renamed his children "Titanes"- the straining ones. He cursed Cronus, saying he, too, would be overthrown by his children and betrayed. The Olympian gods quickly overthrew the Titans, as predicted.

Uranus' genitals that were thrown into the sea produced more offspring from his spilled blood. His new offspring included the ash-tree nymph (the Meliai), the Giants, and the Furies. His genitals also formed a white foamy layer over the sea, from which Aphrodite (the Goddess of Beauty and Love) was born. The Giants, or Gigantes, engaged in battle with the Olympian Gods. Despite their medium stature, they fought valiantly and furiously.

Zeus, Poseidon, Hera, Hades, Demeter, and Hestia were born to Rhea and Cronus. However, just as Uranus believed his children would usurp his throne, Cronus, too, made a similar assumption and loathed his children. He swallowed all of his children but could not capture Zeus because Rhea, his mother, assisted him in hiding. The Furies, the Goddesses of Vengeance, aided Rhea by raising Zeus and preparing him to assume the throne. The Furies had the appearance of old women, with fiery red eyes and a frightening demeanor. Their bat wings and snake-like hair accentuated their hideous appearance and drove the victims insane.

Uranus, who lacked genitals and could not impregnate Gaia, eventually took the position of the sky's bowl, which Atlas, his grandson, held.

The sky constantly changes due to the shifting positions of the stars and the irregular movement of the clouds. Soft showers can bring comfort and restore the Earth's balance at one time, while thunderstorms can wreak havoc. Uranus is personified in this way - while he creates and gives life, he can also wreak havoc and destruction on the planet.

Uranus and Other Gods

Since all planets were named after Roman and Greek gods, myths can draw connections between Uranus and other gods. As previously stated, the ancient Greeks labeled the planets "wandering stars," and each one was given a name inspired by a Greek or Roman god. Each god's attributes, characteristics, and appearances were matched with all planets, giving rise to their distinct names.

Mercury and Uranus

Mercury/Hermes
God of wealth and
good fortune

Mercury, the fast messenger, was also known as Hermes. Mercury is connected with Hermes since it is also a rapidly moving planet. The winged sandals of this god allowed him to walk steadily between two worlds (the worlds of the divine and the mortals). Hermes was Uranus' great-grandson and the son of Maia and Zeus. Hermes protected all travelers on Earth and beyond. Merchants, thieves, gypsies, orators, and other travelers were all shielded by this god. Hermes was also well-known for the tricks he performed on commoners and other gods.

Venus and Uranus

Venus/Aphrodite
Goddess of love,
beauty and pleasure.

Venus was named after the Goddess of Beauty and Light, Aphrodite. The connection makes sense, given that Venus is also one of the brightest celestial bodies in the sky. Venus, the Roman goddess, was well-known and desired by other gods owing to her beauty and charm. Since no other planet shines as bright as Venus, the name of this god seems appropriate. Venus was a Titan since she was the daughter of Uranus and Gaia. According to some myths, Aphrodite was Zeus's daughter who transformed into a person from the sea's white foam, which was said to be Uranus's sperm and blood in other tales.

Earth and Uranus

Earth/Gaea/Ge
Goddess of immortality
and mother nature

Mother Earth, or Gaia, gave birth to Uranus and later had 18 offspring with him, as previously stated. Their connection brought balance and order to the universe until Uranus became greedy and worried about losing his position to his children. Uranus and Gaia had an intimate relationship that deteriorated into bloodlust and murder due to Uranus' greed. The Gods and Titans then went to war at a point, destroying the generational bond.

Mars and Uranus

Mars/Ares
God of war and
agricultural guardian

Ares, the god with a short temper and a furious disposition, was associated with the planet Mars. Ares was identified with Mars since it is considered red and flaming. As one of the Twelve Olympians, Ares was Uranus's grandchild and was closely identified with him. Ares, the son of Hera and Zeus, was known as the God of War and Courage. Ares was frequently compared to his sister, Athena, who signified intelligence and companionship. Ares can be compared to his grandfather, who possessed similar characteristics because this god was considered to embody bloodlust and brutality.

Jupiter and Uranus

Jupiter/Zeus
God of sky and thunder

Jupiter was named after Zeus because of his power and authority. Jupiter is the largest planet, which justifies this correlation. According to certain legends, Uranus was supposed to be stronger than Zeus because he was Zeus' grandfather. Although he sat on Uranus' throne and continued his bloodline, his grandfather was said to be more powerful. Some claim that Zeus was the sole ruler of the Earth and remained on the throne, making him more powerful than Uranus and Cronus. According to legend, each generation becomes weaker, implying that Uranus is the strongest of all.

Saturn and Uranus

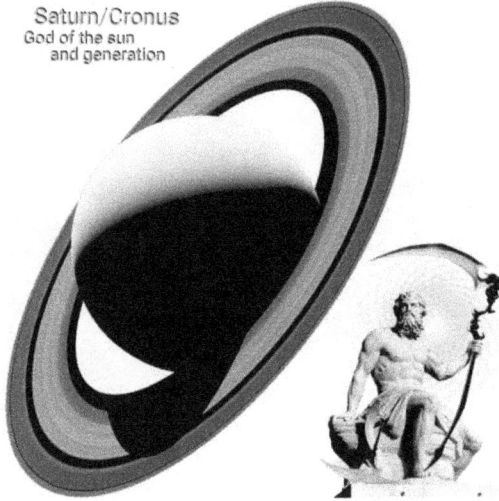

Saturn/Cronus
God of the sun
and generation

Cronus, Zeus' father and Uranus' son, provides the inspiration for Saturn's existence. Saturn and Jupiter constantly fight to establish their supremacy in the sky, just as Zeus and Cronus fought to seize the throne. In Roman mythology, Saturn was also believed to be influenced by the God of Harvest and Agriculture. Cronus, as previously stated, was Uranus' son, and he castrated him to ascend to the throne. Cronus persuaded the other Titans to join his protest and revolt against their father because he wanted to sit on the throne and overthrow his father. Cronus was overthrown by his son, Zeus, just as his father predicted.

Neptune and Uranus

Neptune/Poseidon
God of fresh water
and the sea

Neptune is also known as Poseidon due to the bright-blue hues it represents. Since Poseidon was known as the God of the Sea and symbolized luscious blue waves, this connection appears legitimate. Poseidon was an Olympian, and hence Uranus' grandson. Following Cronus' downfall, each of his three sons was granted a portion of the world to command. Poseidon was given command of the sea while Zeus and Hades ruled over the Earth and the underworld. If the other gods ignored Poseidon, he would strike the ground with his trident, causing earthquakes. Typically, he was in charge of establishing calm seas and new islands.

Pluto and Uranus

Pluto/Hades
God of the underground

Pluto, also known as the Greek God Hades, was sent to the underworld to reign over evil spirits and gods exiled from the skies. Just as Pluto was pushed to the outermost reaches of the solar system, Hades remained isolated and separated from the other gods. Hades was Zeus and Poseidon's brother, making him Uranus' grandchild. Hades was tasked with ruling over the underworld, where the guilty gods and evil spirits had been abandoned. While there is no direct relationship between Hades and Uranus, we can connect them through the occurrence in which Uranus ambushed his sons and led them to the underworld, where Hades assumed command.

Uranus and Varuna

Varuna is the Hindu deity of the sky and ocean, which explains his connection to Uranus. The celestial ocean governed by Varuna is believed to be connected to the Milky Way. Experts linked the two gods further through the concept of "binding": while Uranus bound his children into the underworld, Varuna bound the wicked. We shall study Varuna's attributes and significance in Hindu mythology to draw comparisons between the two gods.

Varuna fights with a Pasha (rope loop) and travels from heaven to Earth on a Makara (crocodile). He rules over the western direction and resides in Jal Loka (the ocean). To honor the God Varuna, Hindus chant the mantras "Om Varunaaya Namah," "Om Jala bimbhaya," "Purushaya Dheemahe," "Vidhmahe Nila," and "Thanno Varuna Prachodayath." The god, known as the governor of moral law, occupies a significant portion of the Rigveda. Under Varuna's reign, sinners are punished, while the innocent are protected.

Mitra and Varuna are commonly called "Mitra-Varuna" because they both represent "oath" and other societal issues. While some records call them Asuras (demons or wicked gods), others call them Devas (the noble gods). This reveals another link between Uranus and Varuna, as they both possess both evil and noble qualities. Varuna was the Asuras' king initially, but he later became a Deva. The event of the primordial cosmos that occurred after Indra's victory triggered this transformation. Varuna, as a result, ordered the restructuring.

Uranus and Ahura Mazda

The Zoroastrian god, Ahura Mazda, worshiped by Parsis, is usually associated with Uranus. While some see connections between Ahura Mazda and Zeus, the linkage between the Zoroastrian god and Uranus is more evident. One of the signs is their relationship with their spouses, both of whom were chthonic goddesses. While Uranus was Gaia's companion, Ahura Mazda's wife was the Iranic Spenta Armaiti, who represents Earth and Mother Nature. Spenta Armaiti, like Gaia, ensured fertility and supervised agriculture.

Furthermore, both gods were considered the primordial deities of their mythologies, who had multiple children with their spouses. With the arrival of the deities of the new generation, both gods continued their legacy.

While some of these associations help solidify the myths and bring different cultures together, they are still loosely linked and do not offer a complete picture from which we can draw a conclusion. We can infer from these assumptions that gods with similar characteristics similarly influenced their cultures.

Traits of Uranus as a Planet

When this planet shadows one's Natal chart in an incomplete or underdeveloped state, it reacts and confuses the individual. However, when Uranus is fully attuned, one becomes extraordinarily intuitive and innovative.

This intuition enhances a person's investigation and digging deeper into a subject for better comprehension. Since Uranus moves slower than other planets, it may appear in many people's horoscopes and Natal charts at the same time. Not surprisingly, to have multiple persons of the same generation sharing this planet in their reading. Locate Uranus' position when reading your house to find solutions and stir things up. If you already have a strategy in place, but it isn't working, this planet will advise you to alter the sequence or take a different approach.

Uranus, in general, has big plans for you that will arrive as major surprises or shocks. You may be living happily and orderly, which is when Uranus may intervene and provide unexpected triggering circumstances. The planet indicates a brilliant mind and innovative ideas and hence corresponds to Mercury on a higher octave. Uranus, often known as the "Awakener" in astrology, assists people in confronting reality and accepting change that comes in big parcels. As previously stated, it can affect a cohort's lifespan due to its gradual movement, which can span a few decades.

Finally, check for Uranus's points of interaction with other celestial bodies in your chart. If it comes in contact with the Moon or Sun sign, the associated characteristics are bound to intensify. While Uranus takes over 80 years to traverse a zodiac, it is expected to dwell in a sign for about seven years. However, if it retrogrades, it may persist for a longer period. Overall, with Uranus, be prepared for the unexpected.

Chapter 2: Uranus: The Great Awakener

Uranus, like a planet in our solar system, is a unique subject to explore. This planet is unlike any other regarding how it behaves, how it is built, and its attributes. Other planets have rings and moons, but not as many as Uranus and are not as interestingly positioned. You can see why Uranus stands out like a sore thumb if you look at how it is tilted, how its electromagnetic waves are out of sync and the effect this has on its surroundings, and how Uranus goes east to west as it orbits the sun rather than west to east like other planets.

Uranus's surface temperatures are exceedingly cold, whereas the heart of this largely gaseous planet is tremendously hot, reaching almost 5000 degrees Celsius. Seasons on this planet can be exceptionally long. For example, Uranus' winter blankets half the planet in utter darkness and lasts more than two decades (Earth-time decades). With these distinct peculiarities and traits of Uranus, it's easy to see why this planet has captivated both astronomers and astrologists.

A History of Uranus: Fitting to its Character

Of course, astronomers of the early days had no idea about the physical characteristics of Uranus, but they could observe its movement and, to some degree, get a vague picture of the planet when it was visible.

In European astrology, Uranus was regarded as the husband/son of Gaia, Earth, who was portrayed as the mother/wife and played the female role. In Egyptian astrology, on the other hand, Earth was represented as the male, Geb, and Nut as the goddess of the sky. Furthermore, astronomers only recently discovered Uranus. William Herschel discovered Uranus in 1781, initially mistaking it for a comet or a star. Upon closer inspection, he realized that it was, in fact, a planet in our solar system. It just so happened that Mr. Herschel was using a homemade telescope in his backyard when he discovered this unusual planet.

Considering the nature of Uranus and how it influences human life and events on Earth, the way it was discovered and how it was perceived in the past couldn't be more perfect.

Uranus is associated with drastic changes, and this couldn't play out more beautifully than the fact that the discovery of Uranus coincides with the industrial revolution that was taking place in Europe and America. Everything from the classical perception of Uranus to its discovery and integration into modern astronomy and astrology works congruently with the nature of this planet and its effects on people who have it in their natal chart. People may feel the effects of Uranus to varying degrees depending on how this planet is influencing their natal chart and to what degree it is playing a role in their generation.

Astrological Role of Uranus

Uranus derives its name from Ouranos, who was the Greek God of Heaven. He was the son and husband of Gaia, Mother Earth, and together they had several children. All other characters in Greek mythology are considered offspring of this power couple. Some of the lesser-known Gods who haven't made it to the modern-day spotlight carried some of the negative traits associated with Uranus, whereas those who we still know today were reflections of Ouranos's positive traits. The word Ouranos literally translates to "rainmaker," and it is associated with thunder, lightning, electromagnetic waves, and the transition of an environment from dry and barren to wet and fertile.

Similarly, Ouranos' ability to generate thunder and lightning relates to the idea of him being responsible for the "first spark" that set things in motion and spurred the evolution of life. This is closely related to Uranus' association with new beginnings and its highlighted trait of being "The Great Awakener."

The Nature of Uranus and Its Influence on Mythology

Ouranos is one of the lesser-known characters in Greek mythology, and many aspects of his life have not been properly documented. However, the things about him that are documented, and the information we have about his influence on other characters and events in mythology as a whole, are very congruent with how Uranus affects us today.

Uranus is the first planet in our solar system that lies outside the visible sphere of which Saturn is the last point. This is partly why it took so long to notice Uranus was even there since it's difficult to see. When it was discovered, it revolutionized our perspective of our solar system. This is exactly the effect that Uranus has on people, communities, and entire generations. Some say it facilitates, while others say it forces change. Uranus is also the first of what astrologers describe as the "outer planets," those planets that have more of an effect on our external lives and society at large rather than affecting us as individuals. This is not to say that Uranus's effects can't be felt at a personal level. Generally, these outer planets are used to study the environment we are in and the changes we can expect to see around us. As we will see in the life of Ouranos, the change can be positive or negative, but essentially it acts as a catalyst and sets things on a path that leads them to a very different destination.

Uranus is also associated with creativity and bringing ideas to the material world due to its ability to transform and initiate change by altering perspectives and thoughts. However, this is not always a fruitful endeavor, and the result is frequently far from what we had in mind. This is due, in part, to the fact that the process of transforming an idea or thought into a tangible product alters the mental image. Just the process of bringing it to life changes the concept, and when it finally materializes, we aren't always happy with it, or it doesn't please us as much as we had thought it would. In this very manner, when Ouranos had children, some were titans, some were giants, while others were purely evil and did no good at all. He was quick to take care of those he felt were not beneficial to society overall. Even with many children, he only left a few to live on because the majority of the others were evil and caused harm. However, the ones that did do good were good, and their legend lives till today.

In Greek tradition, Ouranos was also known as Aion, the god of eternal time and the god who held the zodiac wheel firmly in place around the Earth. This could be why even modern astrologers see Uranus as the ruler of the zodiac and one with a unique ability over it. The concept of a planet having influence and control over all other members of the zodiac can be difficult to grasp. The whole point of Uranus is to bring to our lives a thought, an inspiration we would not have received otherwise from our environment. It truly is a thought from a different world. The manifestation of this is seen through various examples in our world. This includes the transition to industrialization, the drastic change in racism and class differences, and the change in the status of many minorities across the world. And the process of change hasn't stopped. It's still happening, every day, everywhere. Moreover, it is very difficult to understand something of this nature from the perspective of a person who lives in a material world. Uranus is all about influencing things that are not visible or tangible, so trying to make sense of it all from our perspective will be a futile effort.

Time

Uranus is one of three planets we classify as generational planets. Neptune, Pluto, and Uranus all spend several years in each sign, and for this reason, the effect they have is often very widespread and can influence the behavior of entire generations. The effect these planets have is also very slow-moving, with a high impact. The big changes we have seen throughout history, whether it is a physical development or a change in mentality, has taken time, had a great impact, and can be associated with the movement of one of these three planets.

The changes caused by these planets can be viewed as those that assist us in aligning ourselves with the flow of universal energy transmuted into our lives by these cosmic actors. Being the natural ruler of Aquarius gives us fluidity, expression, freedom, and rhythm. However, these traits can manifest themselves in the form of dictatorships, anarchy, rebellion, and destruction. The influence of Aquarius in relation to Uranus is a complicated one to understand as we have both Uranus and Saturn competing to rule the same zodiac sign. This is reflected in how the Greek god Ouranos had conflicting relations with his different children, sometimes being amazing, sometimes resulting in the father killing the son.

Influence on Other Planets

Like how Uranus's physical characteristics are completely contradictory to those of other planets, the effect Uranus has on other planets in a house can be difficult to comprehend. Often throwing the behavior of other planets completely, and their influence on an individual's life is drastically altered.

In some cases, this is all that is required. If one planet is having a negative impact on you, Uranus can help turn things around and make them work in your favor. On the other hand, Uranus's arrival can completely derail something that was going perfectly well and distort any harmony you may have been developing in your life.

While Uranus has an archetypal relationship with Saturn as they both battle for Aquarius, Uranus' primary adversary in the zodiac is the Sun, ruler of Leo.

Ruling Sign and House

Uranus is the natural ruler of Aquarius though it does have a troubled relationship with this sign as it shares ownership of Aquarius with Saturn. Both these planets naturally rule Aquarius, and due to their significantly different characteristics, they can magnify the effects of Aquarius very differently in your life. Uranus has a feminine Element - Air.

Uranus in the 1st House

In the first house, this will cause a person with a strong sense of self, who can be a bit stubborn. They have copious amounts of creativity, they are independent, and they also display a sharp intuition. These people usually have a friendly demeanor that attracts other people. On the negative side, this person may be feeling a lot of nervousness, anxiety, and stress. Uranus in the first house also causes people to feel lonely and uneasy. If you are enjoying the positives, keep it up. If you are on the downward trend, trust your instincts and go for it.

Uranus in the 2nd House

This is an excellent time to start a new business or invest in a venture you've always wanted to be a part of. With Uranus in the second house, people can come up with brilliant money-making ideas, seize the right deal at the right time, and break free from financial constraints. On the other hand, it may lead to you making extreme business or career decisions that appear to be a good idea at the time but turn out to be costly mistakes in the future. You could be in a place to make money, and you need to pursue those dreams of yours. However, don't get too carried away. Make a calculated decision on anything you do.

Uranus in the 3rd House

When the ice giant is in the third house, you become more creative, inquisitive, and spontaneous. You may have an urge to go against the tide and do something you believe will be a great idea. However, the desire to do something may cause you to seek knowledge and become stressed if you cannot locate the resources you require. Even if you are processing information and learning as you have never done before, you may be becoming stressed due to all the work you are doing. Every new thing you read and every new person you interact with is either convincing you extremely well to pursue what you are thinking off or being so critical that you are losing all hope. In either case, you are still confused and unable to decide which direction you want to go.

In this house, Uranus can greatly improve your relationships with family and friends, as well as your social life. You may also find yourself frequently traveling for work.

Uranus in the 4th House

As the planet moves out to areas of your social relationships and overall interacting and networking capabilities, it may motivate you to reach out to new people and expand your network. Moreover, it could also mean a big change in your family relations is about to happen. If you have many friends, then it might be some change coming regarding your friends and people you hang out with casually. Whatever the result is, you need to keep yourself calm and continue to be who you are.

Uranus in the 5th house

Uranus provokes creativity, independence, and inquisitive nature in this house, resulting in a diverse range of interests and some peculiar hobbies in such individuals. As a free thinker and highly independent individual, this person may experience difficulties in love and marriage. This person may feel a strong disconnect with children, while children may feel as if they will never understand their Uranial mother or father.

Uranus in the 6th House

These people love unusual jobs - they can be rescue workers, medical staff, and people who work in extreme conditions. They don't mind the dangerous nature of their job and enjoy these challenging environments. Getting injured on their job is not a problem for them and something to which they are accustomed. However, being the passionate worker you are, don't overwork and burn out. Nervousness, stress, and tension-related problems are things you should keep an eye out for.

Uranus in the 7th House

This is someone who either has fantastic relations with a person or simply does not get along with them. You enjoy connecting with people, however, you will still want to maintain a high degree of independence, and you may even specifically seek out relationships that require very little commitment. Whether it is work or personal relationships, you want to be able to alter them to your requirements, and if they are getting out of your control, it can be a source of stress and worry for you to the point where you attempt to flee.

Uranus in the 8th House

Your understanding of concepts such as life, marriage, love, children, and work is not only unusual; it is out of this world. Your unique perception and unique approach to life radiate into these key areas, and they can be a source of great pleasure or great pain. Your intuition is strong, but you need to learn to rely on it and not let your critical mind get in the way. Resource management will depend on how you perform your duties and how you can attain and maintain different resources in your life.

Uranus in the 9th House

Travel is something you enjoy, but only if it is for work or a task that needs to be completed. Going to a place just to explore is not your type of travel, even if you would be happy to travel for many days and nights to see specific things or have a particular experience. Dreams, thoughts, and visions are something you do see well but something you need to develop trust in. You are naturally a great long-term planner, but your ability to plan extensively and in detail can leave you mentally exhausted and overwhelmed about the task.

Uranus in the 10th House

Business is a great option for these people because it provides them with the flexibility and diversity they crave while also making use of their high energy and providing them with a place to exert as much of it as possible. It's also a work environment where they need not work for anyone else and allows their rebellious side to stay at bay. Don't be surprised if you see yourself moving around a few different jobs and occupations.

Uranus in the 11th House

You are the type of person interested in everyone and everything, which has led you to form some very unusual relationships and become friends with people with whom others would not easily connect. This may not seem unusual to you, but your social circle is anything but normal. This does not imply that you know many people. You prefer your intimate inner circle, but meeting new people and making new acquaintances is not a problem for you.

Uranus in the 12th House

Being the wild thinker you are, you may have extreme views about life, death, luck, and the purpose of being. You are always in a state of learning about the higher things in life and trying to discover the answers to the big life question. However, you tend to keep your views and thoughts to yourself so as not to attract negativity from other people. In your mind, you also have your own thought process to battle, and you need to manage the way negative thoughts cycle through your mind. Many problems you see are only in your head, and if you can get control over this, you can enjoy a much more fulfilling life. Everything you dream of can easily be achieved if you can get over the problems you present yourself with.

Chapter 3: How Uranus Transforms Society

Uranus took a long time to be discovered by astrologers around the world due to a lack of proper equipment and its low visibility in the sky. If you try to spot it with your naked eye in the evening sky, you might mistake it for a very faint star in the distance. William Herschel discovered it in 1781 after using a more powerful telescope.

This discovery was made nine years before the French Revolution, and it was a time of great tumult and revolutionary ideas. It's said that we only discover a planet when we, as humankind, are ready to experience its complete influence. Uranus is a planet characterized by rebellion, change, and disruption, which is evident in the later sections of this chapter when we study how the various revolutions and world-changing incidents occurred in the time of Uranus traveling to a different zodiac sign.

Herschel initially believed he had seen a comet and reported his findings to the other astronomers of the Royal Society. However, it was discovered that the object was not bright enough to be a comet and was also moving much slower without a tail. The newly discovered object appeared to move in a circular orbit, and it was determined that it is, in fact, a planet.

Before the discovery of Uranus, the astrological relationship of the planets with the zodiac signs was pretty symmetrical. The sun and the moon used to rule one sign each, and all the planets ruled two different zodiac signs. In Vedic astrology, there were two planets called Rahu and Ketu. The Rahu and Ketu aren't planets, but they are the points of intersection of the orbits of the moon and the Earth. However, as Neptune and Pluto were discovered after the discovery of Uranus due to greater technological advancements, this symmetry was permanently changed.

Uranus was the first planet discovered as one of the three transpersonal outer planets in the modern age. It has a unique orbit around the sun because its axis is at a 90-degree angle, and it has four moons called Ariel, Umbriel, Oberon, and Titania.

Uranus takes roughly 76-84 years to complete its orbit through all the zodiacs, and it stays in each zodiac sign for a considerable amount of time. This extended duration of Uranus in every zodiac is why Uranus is considered to have a generational influence on not just one person but on the entire generation of people on the planet who were born in the same period.

In mythology, Uranus is the god of the open skies and rules the various elements like earthquakes and electrical storms. Uranus is said to have emerged from the womb of Gaia, the titan goddess symbolizing the Earth. Uranus united with Gaia to give birth to the various lifeforms on Earth, and he also gave birth to the Titan Saturn, also known as Kronos/Cronus in Greek mythology. Uranus was castrated by Saturn and cast away due to his irrational behavior and poor temperament. The direct contradictions of these two planets' characteristics relate to this myth, depicting how Kronos and Uranus were at odds due to their history.

Uranus is a symbol of the spirit of revolution, unlike its more austere and composed counterpart Saturn. Uranus has some unusual characteristics, and even its discovery was highly disruptive in the world of astronomy and astrology. What had previously been thought to be a well-understood solar system had suddenly changed, and an new planet was added to the list, resulting in the metamorphosis of astrology into the form we are all familiar with.

Uranus generally dictates how an individual's relationships with friends and family are shaped. It's a sociable planet as the individuals affected by it are usually not shy, and they handle social interactions pretty, which is important for their proper development in life. The social impact of this planet can also be seen in how it affects cooperation, community involvement, and social transformations. This planet has a generational effect on all the people born under its influence, and it shapes the experience for humankind.

Uranus is a symbol of spiritual principles that extend to the cosmic levels, and it also serves as a societal guide. Uranus is responsible for advancing humanity as a whole and is credited with the evolution of a greater consciousness in which humanity is prioritized over selfish interests. The major disadvantage of Uranus is its overly optimistic attitude, which can be harnessed to inspire confidence if used appropriately.

Traits of Uranians

If Uranus is on your side in your natal chart, it is more likely to show the positive aspects of itself. It can bestow adaptability, high intellect, originality in ideas, highly individualistic personality, independence, leadership skills, and even spiritual gifts upon you. The knowledge gotten from Uranus is usually deep and insightful because it is more profound and emerges from a cosmic level. The Uranians are very innovative and have a thirst for knowledge since they're naturally more inclined towards scientific pursuits, leading to great leaps in human development.

The people who are blessed by this planet are highly unconventional, and they are more adept at the skills required to lead the entire world to a path of progress and betterment. Uranus influences the mind such that the person affected by it usually develops a deep interest in scientific endeavors and leading the waves of change. The Uranians are often revolutionaries who know how to bring in a change without resorting to aggression. The Uranians are always in sync with the current state of the world and can create long-lasting reforms in society.

Another effect of Uranus on a person is that it makes them have strong opinions about matters of global importance. The influence of this planet gifts people with courage and a very high level of intellect. The zodiac sign and the house greatly influence these qualities, and different combinations produce different results for every person.

Uranians are exceptionally adventurous and enjoy experimenting with various things in life. This is because they already have a strong desire to explore and innovate, and the more experiences they have, the better their ability to innovate. These people make exceptional leaders because they have a sense of adventure, exploration, intellect, and courage.

Uranus is also the coldest planet in our solar system and is suitably the ruler of Aquarius, a sign that occupies the mid-winter in the Northern Hemisphere. As the co-ruler of Aquarius, it influences the behavior of this zodiac sign as well. Most Aquarians are very revolutionary in their ideas and like to forge their path instead of following what society expects from them. The Aquarians are highly self-sufficient, and they aspire to improve the status of society. Many Uranians have been at the forefront of discovering and implementing new technologies that have transformed how our systems operate.

As a transpersonal planet, Uranus inspires its subjects differently from planets such as Saturn. While Saturn's influence is one of hard work, Uranians are more prone to being dynamic and breaking down mental barriers. The ideas provided by Uranus can be compared to eureka moments in one's life, and the source of that idea is often divine. The people under the influence of Uranus are usually very exceptional in some respects, and the presence of this planet in your chart denotes the areas of your life that'll be filled with upheaval and rebellion.

The negative side of Uranus can create people who're often misunderstood due to them being ahead of their time. Uranians are prone to moodiness and bitterness because they are hypersensitive people who can feel a wide range of emotions, and a few insulting experiences can leave them disgruntled. If these people are in a negative state of mind, then anyone who comes into contact with them will be negatively affected. The influence of Uranus extends to the person's entire nervous system and can harm their health if they harbor negative emotions.

Uranus is associated with virtues like freedom, liberty, and justice, just like the revolutions that it inspired in France and the Americas. Those strongly influenced by Uranus generally exhibit these attributes and serve as a beacon of these traits. Uranus also stands for advancements in technology and society since it also played a critical role during the Industrial Revolution by inspiring new ideas.

Technological Innovations

These aspects are reflected similarly in people with the presence of a revolutionary mindset and capacity for innovation. The people with the influence of Uranus are usually very free-spirited, and their thought process can't be just restricted to follow a straight and established line of thought. These people will often branch out of society as they're not happy when their freedom is restricted in any manner whatsoever.

To make things clearer, it's worth noting that Einstein was a Uranian as well, and his ideas were beyond anything seen in his time. The ideas put forward by him in the fields of quantum mechanics and the theory of relativity revolutionized science and the way physicists think about energy and mass to this day.

Not only was Einstein a Uranian, but so was Thomas Edison, the inventor of the light bulb. Edison's inventions were revolutionary at the time, and they set the stage for all subsequent technological advancements. Edison also invented the Dictaphone, the electric lamp, the autographic printer, and numerous other devices in the fields of electric power generation, sound recording, mass communication, and even motion pictures.

The negative influence of Uranus on the technological field was also observed in 2008. Uranus was in Pisces and was in opposition to Saturn, who was in Virgo at the time. This resulted in widespread layoffs in the IT sector and had a negative impact on all technology-related fields. However, this did not last long, and the effects were greatly mitigated over the next few years.

The willingness to explore the world around them is why Uranians are so good at coming up with new and ingenious solutions that can revolutionize existing processes. The innate sense of adventure that drives these people to seek new experiences and knowledge makes them ideal for coming up with unique ideas. The Uranians are rather sociable, and they don't mind asking for help. This helps them greatly increase their learning because they don't shy away from seeking proper guidance.

The empathetic nature of the people influenced by Uranus makes them desirous of improving the lives of those around them. Their humanitarian goals motivate them to develop solutions to the problems no one else thought of solving before.

Generational Impact

Uranus heavily influences the course of global events, and its effects vary depending on which zodiac sign it is traversing. Some of the most disastrous events in recent history occurred when Uranus traversed Aries. Hitler came to power the first time and wreaked havoc on the world by drowning the entire planet in turmoil. ISIS rose to power the second time around, threatening the world order with their conquest of blood and war. This is due to the inherent nature of Aries, which is full of aggression and strife. Uranus simply brought in a huge change that reflected this zodiac sign.

However, Uranus's influence has not always been negative. Since Uranus is unbiased and simply amplifies the characteristics of the zodiac sign it is traversing, there have been instances of this planet having a positive impact. Uranus entered Aquarius when the world was witnessing the meteoric rise of advanced technology such as smartphones and the internet. The advancements were implemented at a rapid pace, and the world moved toward a better future.

The current situation is a perfect example of the generational impact of Uranus. With Uranus entering Taurus in 2019, it was predicted there would be widespread famine, and the world as we know it will fall apart. Since Taurus is an earth sign and Uranus represents the open sky, the two don't get along very well. This prediction came true as we can all see the rapidly changing world amid the global pandemic when even our personal lives have been greatly influenced. These changes swept in and affected entire generations worldwide at the same time, as Uranus is known for.

For those who find it difficult to believe that Uranus has had such a profound impact on the world, it's worth noting that the last time Uranus entered Taurus, the United States of America was engulfed in civil war. Many generations were involved in the war and perished due to the horrors. These events weren't isolated to the USA either. The entire global economy had been affected at that time by the civil war.

The universal impact of Uranus just doesn't end here either. The planet has been a symbol of platonic love, and the sense of universal connection and oneness can be inspired in our minds under this planet's influence. Uranus can remind us that we're all one, and the differences of color, race, caste, creed, or nationality are just superficial ones. The humanitarian side of Uranus is really strong, and modern innovations like crowd-funding, carpooling, co-working spaces, and humanitarian relief efforts are all just another facet of Uranus.

Revolutionary Tendencies

The rebellious nature of Uranus is directly opposed to the austere attitude of Saturn. While Saturn relishes in an environment where rules are imposed, Uranus thrives by breaking these rules and challenging the status quo. While Saturn is a very cautious and sensible planet in its influence, Uranus is more of a rowdy and wild influence on the people affected by it. Uranians love to break the boundaries imposed by the planet Saturn by being innovative, explosive, dynamic, and unpredictable.

The period that Uranus was discovered in coincides with perhaps two of the most famous and paradigm-shifting revolutions in the history of mankind. The American Revolution of 1776 and the French Revolution of 1789 occurred near the period when Uranus was discovered. This points towards the basic characteristics of the planet, which include rebellion, chaos, and change.

The American Revolution stood for justice and equality, which are the cornerstones of Uranus. These ideals can be found in those Uranus has heavily influenced, and they were a major cause of conflict between colonists and imperialists. The colonists felt that they were taxed but not represented, which was unjustified and a blow to the concept of equality. Another reason for the revolution was justice, as the crown took resources from the colonies without providing any substantial representation to the various colonies. This was seen as a gross injustice to the people of the colonies, sparking a full-fledged war for independence.

Even the French Revolution erupted due to the same issues. The monarchy and the clergy of France were disproportionately powerful and had access to unjustified resources, while the lower echelons of the city were starving to death. Due to this injustice, people came together to protest their severe exploitation, which resulted in the establishment of an order that promised equality to all social classes. The entire French Revolution was founded on the core values of liberty, equality, and fraternity. These are also the characteristics that Uranus bestows on people. Since the effects of Uranus are generational, it affected this era strongly and led to an upheaval that toppled the existing world order to establish new and just systems.

It's said that Uranus was discovered during that period as the world was ready to discover it then. This was the first time in history that such large-scale rebellions were happening in such a short time, and this was the perfect time for Uranus to show itself. This period in human history was perhaps the first time that mankind was ready to influence Uranus and its highly eccentric and earth-shattering effects.

Even in recent years, we've seen people take a stand for various social causes that affect the entire world. The rise of the LGBTQ movement is one such example in which various groups worldwide came together to advocate for social justice. This is a significant shift in the social structure because homosexuality and transgender have long been marginalized and considered taboo by society.

Uranus' influence is responsible for such a significant change in which the world is becoming more compassionate toward these groups and adopting a more humanitarian approach. Since Uranus specializes in causing drastic changes, this is a perfectly valid example of Uranus' capabilities.

If these examples aren't enough, another example would be the rise of feminism and the MeToo movement. The entire world was shaken when women started coming out with their experiences and stories. It was perhaps for the first time that so many women decided to launch an attack on sexual misconduct. Uranus is responsible for such large-scale events due to its very nature of bringing in enormous changes to the entire world simultaneously.

Chapter 4: Uranus in Your Natal Chart – Part I

Knowing how the planet's energy affects your houses will help you to work with this planet better. It will give you the knowledge and confidence to create change and transformation in these areas of your life.

Knowing the planetary influences in your natal chart allows you to gain a better understanding of yourself. In this chapter, we'll look at how Uranus affects your 1ˢᵗ through 4th houses. Uranus' electrifying, awakening, and unpredictable genius has a different impact on each house.

1st House

Your first house is concerned with your identity. This is the way you present yourself and the way others perceive you. If you have Uranus in this house, you likely have unique qualities. As the 1st house is related to our external appearance and characteristics, there could be a sense of rebellion and non-conformity regarding behavior or dress.

Individuals born with this planet in their first house are frequently perceived as reformists or unique in their personality and appearance. They may take pride in this aspect of themselves and enjoy being unique. Due to the planetary energy in this house, they prefer to do whatever they want without regard for social norms.

These individuals will often spend their lifetimes on a journey of self-discovery and introspection. Things can often happen suddenly or unexpectedly. Life-changing events can pop up and turn everything on its head. It's a good thing these individuals lean towards unpredictability and adventure as opposed to a more secure or mundane life. Strange or seemingly bizarre events may occur, often quite suddenly. If the planet has difficult aspects in the chart, this could mean abrupt deprecation and the cutting off of social connections.

The planet's placement points to where the person is most innovative, creative, and unconventional. It is in this area that they seek the most liberation and freedom. These individuals may be prone to changing their minds and positions quickly and radically. They tend to oppose the more traditional thinking and routes and opt for the path less trodden.

These individuals are said to be prone to danger from electricity, lighting, and gadgets if the planet is badly afflicted. This planet brings the influence of risk-taking, scientific and occult exploration, and new ways of thinking and doing. These people make great leaders and have a great vision for the future. They can express old ideas in new ways.

In true Uranus fashion, they have a fantastic ability to be inventive and cause immense change and transformation. Since this planet influences us to break free and do things our own way, these people are often considered trailblazers of their time.

These individuals often feel they have an important and unique purpose, but it can be difficult for them to put their finger on this, especially during their younger years. They may have the experience of going through life feeling different from others and their surroundings. But the planet is trying to push them to make a real difference and do things differently.

It is worth mentioning that in this house, this planet can cause trouble. Because these individuals like to be rebellious or shocking, they can cause other's expectations of them to be destroyed. They can also be unreasonable, stubborn, and disruptive. They do, however, live a lively and interesting life.

As the planet of awakening, these individuals are often ahead of their time. However, this introduces unique challenges. To best work with this planet, they must learn to cooperate and live in harmony in a more conservative society. This must be done to develop a balance between themselves and their external world.

2nd House

The second house is associated with money and education. Those with Uranus in their second house have a unique relationship with money. Many will not care for it and will often keep their material needs to a minimum. They value freedom above else, so they avoid being attached to material possessions. This detachment to money could mean they dislike owning material objects such as a house or car. This is because it makes them feel restricted or stressed out. Similarly, they also dislike borrowing money even when in an extremely difficult position.

This doesn't mean they won't make good money. In fact, they will often prioritize saving. Typically, their financial circumstances can swing between two extremes. Uranus in the second house indicates that individuals may have a career in technology. They are also prone to carving a career from their uniqueness, work in a team, or be supported by friends in their business ventures.

Typically, these individuals will make their living from being innovative and unique. Whatever path they go down financially, it will be different to others. Being assisted by friends could be a key to their success. The eccentric influences of this planet mean these will bleed into their career choices.

These individuals may experience being fired more than others. Maybe strange occurrences happen during the job, which tends not to be tolerated in place of work. This is why many of these people choose self-employment, but this does mean they may have to juggle between having lots of money one day and next to nothing the next day.

Fortunately, they can make enough to make up for the bad days. This is why they should commit to saving and not spend too recklessly when their money is up. Most will have unique experiences when it comes to work due to the unusual things that happen.

They often have a strong desire for solitude, which they use to self-soothe. They also tend to be detached during sexual activities. This isn't a hard and fast rule, but it can be the case for many people with Uranus in the 2nd house. Due to this level of detachment, they often make good butchers or coroners.

As the planet of awakening, in the second house, Uranus could cause values and beliefs to change throughout life. They are prone to letting go of outdated ways of thinking as they want to head towards all that is innovative and transformative. They are efficient and will use their unique and creative ways to complete projects promptly. Others will appreciate this aspect of getting things done efficiently.

These individuals are more likely to take financial risks. To mitigate the risks, they should focus on their innovativeness and focus on the future to ensure they make enough money to support themselves. During their 30s, they will often focus more on matters of spirituality and let go of money.

In this house, Uranus brings in the influence of great taste. They tend to orient towards unique art pieces and are sentimental. They relish cultivating these art pieces. Despite their different ways of doing and thinking, their own way will lead them to great fortune and success as long as they work hard. If Uranus is comfortably placed in this house, they may be prone to owning and physically taking part in various activities.

Individuals with Uranus in the second house may become irritated and stubborn if others pressure them to get things done. If this occurs, they may become cold and shut out what others are saying. To break through this barrier, these individuals should cultivate spontaneity and work on providing solutions quicker, even if their natural state is slower. Since the world does not operate at this pace, they should try to find answers faster to cultivate greater harmony and avoid challenges. The more they practice this, the more logical and decision-making skills they develop.

Humility is also needed for greater evolution. Despite their unique logic, it won't always be the right thing, so they need to work on allowing in and accepting other people's viewpoints. Stubbornness will pop up here, especially for those who disagree with them, so this needs to be worked with to overcome these egotistical challenges. Transcending this will bring in more success and growth. By being open to others creates a forum for collaboration and acceptance. It calls in better opportunities and experiences.

If this planet has a bad aspect with a difficult planet, this can cause these people to have subconscious negative thoughts about their physical bodies. Engage in therapy such as hypnosis or talk therapy to figure out what makes them dislike their bodies so much to heal this. This will give them more mental freedom and keep them from engaging in potentially harmful physical activities.

3rd House

Uranus in the third house is linked to intelligence. Individuals with this planet in their third house are great communicators. They are attracted to innovation as their thinking is original and unique. They hate boredom and prefer to do unique or unusual things. There is an air of eccentricity around them, but they are loved by most as they are friendly and inviting.

They are free-thinkers and are constantly pursuing new ideas and thoughts on their journey of evolution. They prioritize studying and have a thirst for knowledge. Their curiosity is a driving force and seeks different and unusual philosophical wisdom. All that is new and different causes them to thrive. They communicate and express themselves through the mediums of writing and public speaking.

They will regularly alter their lives to avoid mundane routines. These people should feel at ease and free to express themselves in the presence of their loved ones, giving them a sense of happiness. They tend to avoid drama by avoiding exaggeration. It is best for their evolution if they occasionally step outside of their comfort zone.

Their excellent communication and expression will take the form of originality, innovation, and uniqueness, and they will be academically oriented. They are notoriously inquisitive about what others think and say, making some friendships difficult, especially when those friends lack an opinion. They were probably perceived as an outsider as a child, but they are incredibly open and sincere. Some people admire these traits, while others despise them. They commonly have strained or difficult relationships with their siblings.

They are inclined towards spirituality, the New Age, and mystic topics. They are very intrigued and curious by it and will delve deep into these topics. Because they seek to reform, they will often use these ways of thinking to try to enact change. If they feel a sudden urge, they are likely to act on it. They may have experiences of encounters with the paranormal throughout their lifetime.

The most important thing for them is independence and objectivity. They seek to understand more and satisfy their curiosities as much as they can. Their desire for objectivity is linked to their free-thinking. They want to have as much information available to them, and they want the same for others. They advocate for individual thinking and despite any kind of censorship. They want to be able to express and communicate from a place of truth. This is why they avoid anyone who stops them from the independent, free-thinkers that they are.

They can often express themselves vaguely or even in confusing ways. These people are often excellent writers and poets, and they will achieve success if they pursue a career in this field. Due to their freedom-oriented thinking can be chaotic, but this allows them to be creative and expressive. If Uranus makes contact with Mercury in this house, they may find it easy to come up with solutions and ideas for everyday problems. They will frequently encounter bizarre events and adventures while traveling and will always have a good story to tell others.

Their creativity can be cultivated through journaling or keeping a record of their thoughts. They can be controversial and shocking with their thoughts and writing. Despite the tendencies for others to see them as a little crazy, they can, in fact, be geniuses. Their ability to tell the truth can cause others to become more grounded as they grapple with their chaos. Their incredible sense of humor keeps others entertained.

Their talent for free-thinking means they can often come up with the solution for difficult situations. They dislike outdated or more traditional viewpoints. Many activities or politics have Uranus in their third house, likely due to their great communication and ability to spread the messages they deeply care about.

Some challenges they may face include unnecessarily interrupting conversations. Because they are constantly thinking, they rarely miss an opportunity to converse. However, this will not always be appreciated by others, so they must learn when and when not to speak. They can learn a lot by learning how to lean back and listen to others.

4th House

The 4th house is related to your personal life and mother. If Uranus is found in the 4th house, these people tend to have unusual childhoods. Most likely, the family was different or unconventional. The planet in this house often indicates some kind of internal conflict. The fourth house deals with safety and stability. As these planetary influences bring about sudden changes, this is often experienced during early life and within the home.

Maybe these individuals did not have emotionally intelligent families that could not provide the emotional support and stability they needed. This could lead to feelings of misunderstanding. The parents of this individual are usually eccentric. Often these individuals are seen as the black sheep of the family.

These people often prefer intellectual bonds to emotional ones. This links back to their childhood experiences of extreme emotional independence, creating a desire to be loved and to belong. Their preference for an intellectual bond is often misaligned with their deep inner desire to form emotional connections. They can often live with a sense of feeling displaced as they may have moved often, which prevented them from laying down roots. This can lead to feelings of in settlement or never quite belonging.

Since they value freedom, they may relocate frequently. They may be forced to do so. Feeling stuffy or overwhelmed could be a sign they need to move due to their love and desire to be free. This is also why these people dislike those who try to impose their thoughts and ideas on them. Both freedom and independence are important to them, and they prioritize them in their daily lives and decisions.

Their chaotic domestic life means they can struggle to take care of themselves and their family. They often need to be helped out when it comes to domestic chores. When they receive assistance and help, they feel an immense release of stress. They feel a great sense of appreciation and care for those who help them out.

These individuals often seek solitude to gain mental clarity. They need this to decide what they want and their life plans. They tend to avoid chaotic or noisy places like bars. Their chaotic early life often means they despite the chaos in their own lives, which is why they cling to their alone time.

However, their desire to not let others down can cause guilt if they spend too much time alone. They love and appreciate their loved ones and try to avoid doing anything to hurt them.

They should look to the past to heal from their childhood wounds, many of which they will deny and insist are part of their natural character. This will allow them to heal and keep them from making the same mistakes with their children in the future. Typically, they will discover that their parents could not be emotionally present with them. Due to their childhood influences, they often have conflicts in their romantic lives and find themselves disagreeing on the same topics.

They can find a lot of positive energy in staying flexible and moving around when they need to. This can, of course, cause issues with their partner; however, stability is not their natural course. They resent the feeling of being tied down. Despite this, they have good intentions. Due to their childhood experiences, they can be emotionally unstable and even cold. They are this way because their upbringing did not teach them to nurture and form emotional connections. They should invest in therapy or some form of self-development work to heal this, develop deeper emotional bonds, and gain the ability to be nurturing.

They may even struggle to understand other people's emotions due to their emotional neglect. By becoming aware of this, they can seek to heal and overcome this. They seek this detachment because being emotional could often mean losing control, especially over their future. They tend to lean towards solitude and not getting too close to the depth of a true emotional connection. To heal further, they should focus on finding ways to illustrate that they care, although it is unnatural for them. With enough introspection, reflection, and work, they overcome this block. Their love of solitude can be used to allow themselves true reflection.

By learning how to understand Uranus' influence in your natal chart, you can better understand the challenges and blessings it brings you. This can help you see where you can expand and ascend on your path of transformation and evolution. Uranus is the planet of awakening, and by allowing yourself to see the good, bad, and ugly within yourself, you can evolve much faster. It can also provide a deeper understanding of others and how they act and think. We can guide and love them in the best way possible if we understand this.

Chapter 5: Uranus in Your Natal Chart – Part II

In astrology, the planet Uranus is believed to be the higher octave of Mercury. It is often associated with surprises and big shocks. Uranus is known as the planet of breakthroughs and the one that triggers unexpected events. Also known as the cosmic alarm clock, Uranus is known to be the bringer of sudden changes that often cause upheavals in life. These upheavals are sometimes necessary to break away from the bond of restrictions towards a more liberated life. Just like the planet Mercury, Uranus is related to the genius streak of the human mind. Uranus is often called the "Awakener" because its transits are connected to dramatic changes in one's life.

Since Uranus stays in a sign for around seven years, it is known as a generational planet, and it makes the same impression on all the people born under this sign. To discover which area of your life is likely to be affected by the presence of Uranus, you need to know its placement in the astrological houses of your natal chart. This allows you to understand which aspects of your life are in focus, what you should work on, and better understand the effects Uranus has on your life. In this chapter, we'll look at the different implications that Uranus has on your life if it is in the fifth, sixth, seventh, or eighth house of your natal chart.

5th House

Pleasure, joy, fun, and creativity are associated with the fifth house in your natal chart. If Uranus is in your fifth house, it indicates that you have a unique approach to your career, social groups, romantic relationships, and the pleasures of life. The fifth house, also known as the "house of pleasures," is associated with imagination, emotions, and children. This house in your natal chart is an indicator of the things you find the most enjoyable and pleasurable in life. It helps you find the things that make you happy and the kind of pleasures you search for in your life. However, this house is connected with creativity as well as growth. Both of these aspects affect your experience, perception, and sense of pleasure.

The fifth house is connected with your skills, imagination, and talents linked to your interests, education, versatility, and intellectual growth. It is believed that your creativity leads you to the greatest pleasures in your life. The fifth house is also associated with children, offspring, and procreation. However, it can be applied to a wide range of things, not only to biological parenthood. Your followers, students, or fellows can also be considered as your children in a figurative sense. The fifth house of your natal chart is associated with instructing, guiding, teaching, upbringing, pregnancy, and childcare. Furthermore, the fifth house is believed to be an emotional house. This house is often referred to as the house of passion and is associated with emotional fulfillment and satisfaction.

If Uranus is in the fifth house of your natal chart, it indicates that you enjoy the things in life in a unique way. You are an artist of life, with your uniqueness entwined with innovation and knowledge. People with the planet Uranus in the fifth house of the natal chart have an original attitude towards life and can develop extraordinary approaches and ideas. You have a fantastic approach towards your career, romantic relationships, and social connections. You can find pleasure in things that others would never think of. Your intelligence and knack for innovation make you interested in various subjects. You can find your unique way into everything. This aspect of your life brings you the greatest satisfaction of mind and heart. However, you may be subject to instability when it comes to your emotional side.

While at times you may feel guided and instructed by divine forces and higher power, you may find yourself falling into despair or a bottomless pit at other times. Often, you may feel like everyone has forgotten about you. Due to their incredible imagination, intelligence, and creativity, people with Uranus in the fifth house face these common challenges. You are unique, and others may not appreciate or comprehend your unconventional ideas. Although it may make you feel hopeless and doubtful you are capable of regaining your composure and discovering new ways to make your dreams come true. However, it is highly likely that you will experience some level of fame and popularity in your life.

6th House

In astrology, the sixth house in the natal chart is associated with routine jobs, hygiene, health, service, and responsibilities. This house is ruled by the planet mercury and corresponds to the zodiac sign of Virgo. It is believed that Uranus is not comfortable in the sixth house. The planet Uranus feels trapped if it is in the sixth house and will constantly find ways to break free from the petty concerns of this house. It constantly yearns to invent new techniques to make the work more efficient. But it will simply ignore, separate, or detach from the issues of service and work.

The sixth house in your natal chart reveals your attitude towards health, work, hygiene, physical condition, and responsibilities. In astrology, by analyzing the sixth house, you can determine your sleeping patterns, eating habits, and the kind of animals you prefer to keep as your pets. However, it can also give you additional details about your physical condition and possible health issues you could experience in your life. It can also help reveal your attitude towards work, whether you are uninterested in your work, lazy, or tend to exhaust yourself by overworking. The sixth house of your natal chart also helps to discover your attitude towards diet, health, and hygiene. It can also help you reveal the kind of relationship you have with your coworkers and the atmosphere you are usually surrounded with at work.

In astrology, it is believed that the people with the planet Uranus in the sixth house of their natal chart prefer to remain as separate as possible and tend to find new ways of navigating the day-to-day chores that offer the most freedom. Although this approach is very efficient and productive, it often backfires, making you aggressive and reactive, leading to stress-related illnesses. If you have no outlet for your aggression in a work environment, you may often feel trapped. The presence of Uranus in the sixth house of the natal chart usually indicates unpredictable and unprecedented issues concerning the things associated with the sixth house. Often, when Uranus is present in the sixth house, the people may suffer from sudden and unexpected illnesses or accidents that can even be life-threatening in some situations. However, if Uranus is well-placed, you can avoid threatening situations and disasters in an unexplained way or even experience sudden recovery from illnesses.

The presence of Uranus in the sixth house often indicates tension between coworkers or partners at work. You might face problems when working with a team and may usually prefer working independently and individually. Due to your unconventional approach towards work, you are highly likely to be criticized by your bosses and coworkers for doing things differently from everyone else, no matter the cost. However, this criticism is often short-lived since, with time, the colleagues and the bosses accept these improvisations as great solutions. In the end, people with Uranus in the sixth house are often considered reliable workers who produce great results at work.

If Uranus is in the sixth house of your natal chart, you might have an unusual diet routine and unique habits regarding your hygiene. You are prone to extremities in your attitude regarding your hygiene. You can be overly concerned with your hygiene or completely unconcerned about it. Due to your love for animals and humanitarian nature, you often eat healthy food, mostly vegetarian or vegan.

7th House

In astrology, the seventh house of the natal chart is associated with partnerships, marriage, and long-term relationships. The ruling planet of this house is Venus, and the house corresponds to the zodiac sign of Libra. This house can help give you an accurate description of your ideal life partner. It can also help you gain insight into your partnerships and long-term relationships, indicating whether they'll be harmonious and long-lasting or not. When someone has the planet Uranus occupying the seventh house, it is a sign of a sudden relationship where both people can help understand and change things related to their relationship or partnership. The presence of Uranus in the seventh house of your natal chart may mean you enter a marriage or relationship based on an impulse. However, once you realize you've made a mistake, the relationship or marriage will end abruptly. Uranus in the seventh house is usually associated with an inability to maintain a marriage or long-term relationship. It also indicates the possibility of multiple marriages and divorces.

In your natal chart, the seventh house rules your romantic relations, business partnerships, marriage, divorce, and relationships with the public. The seventh house can help reveal whether you are likely to experience a satisfying love life or face disappointments in your love experiences. Depending on the planet that occupies the seventh house in your natal chart, you can gain insight into the possible issues you could experience in your partnerships. If you have a benefic planet in your seventh house, it is a really good sign. On the other hand, if you have a malefic planet occupying the seventh house of your natal chart, it indicates the potential issues you might be forced to deal with in your life. Besides your relations with your romantic partners, the seventh house can also describe your enemies.

Should Uranus be in the seventh house of your natal chart, it is usually a warning sign for the types of partnerships and relationships you have in your life, especially long-term relationships and marriage. It is believed that if you have Uranus in the seventh house, you will be drawn to people who have a strong Uranus presence in their lives. That said, you may have "Uranus" types of experiences in your relationships and marriage which means that you may be subject to a sudden commitment and marriage. However, there is also a possibility of sudden ending of your relationships and divorce. Your constant need for change makes you unable to establish a commitment.

The planet Uranus in the seventh house may make you feel attracted to eccentric partners who stand out from the crowd and are different from others. You may find yourself drawn to people who prefer open relationships and are not fond of traditional commitments. Due to divorces and frequent breakups, people with Uranus in the seventh house have an unconventional approach to marriage and relationships. You must choose a partner who understands your need for freedom and who isn't possessive or jealous of you. Your partners must understand and accept you the way you are and your need to keep a part of your life private. If your partners cannot accept this part of you, they won't stay in your life for long.

The presence of Uranus in the seventh house is often a sign of multiple relationships, cheating, and selfishness. People with the planet Uranus in the seventh house often find it hard to decide whom to share the time with. They don't like being pressured into commitment, and others can't make them commit to something if they don't want to do that. That said, if they feel pressured in some way or if their partner is demanding, they can often leave the relationship without an explanation. If you have Uranus in the seventh house, partners who inspire and make it possible for you to have a life outside the relationship are the ones that you'll find the most attractive. You'll get along well with someone whose entire life doesn't revolve around you but instead seems to have their own interests to keep them busy. Your partners must tolerate and understand your various interests and activities even if you do not wish to share them with them. If you find such a partner or spouse who understands and supports your need, you will be truly and loyally committed to them.

8th House

The eighth house of the natal chart is associated with deep emotions, transformation, birth, death, and financials. It also indicates the type of bond you have with people and the deep emotional experiences that can transform your life and your soul. If you have the planet Uranus in your 8th house, it indicates that you may experience a powerful transformation. The eighth house is also associated with others' money, and it could indicate sudden losses or profit from other people. However, the eighth house also rules property, inheritance, alimony, loans, and property.

The eighth house of the natal chart is associated with the matters of death and situations related to it. However, this can also be a symbol representing the death of a part of the person's soul, which is then reborn in a new form. The eighth house is also associated with secrets and matters that are kept hidden. The eighth house rules changes and transformations that can happen in the areas associated with it. This house can help you determine whether you will be obsessed with someone or something in your life.

If you have the planet Uranus in the eighth house of your natal chart, it can be a sign of a great emotional shock that can transform you completely. This position of Uranus in the natal chart is often an indication of the sudden death of someone close to you. This traumatic experience can be a lesson for you to learn to detach from people and stressful situations to easily deal with the unpredictability of life. You need to learn that change in life is constant and that people will not always remain in your life. However, you may also experience the unexpected and sudden revealing of the secrets you tried hard to remain hidden. This experience can come as a shock to you, but you will need to confront the situation to deal with it properly.

If you have the planet Uranus in the eighth house, likely, a person with a strong presence of Uranus in their life may make a sudden appearance that will mark the beginning of a transformation in your life. This person may trigger some emotions that you have buried deep inside of you for a long time. These emotions may be preventing you from moving on with your life, and therefore it will be a good thing. The presence of Uranus in the eighth house is usually to make you aware and confront the emotions you constantly try to suppress. An individual who is heavily influenced by Uranus and enters your life unexpectedly will assist you in this process of letting go. This person will play a significant role in your life. Should Uranus be in the eighth house of your natal chart, you should expect significant transformational events during your lifetime. These events or situations will cause a complete and beneficial evolution of your personality and your perception of and approach to life.

Chapter 6: Uranus in Your Natal Chart – Part III

As shown by Uranus's physical structure and cosmic behavior, it is a very distinctive planet with some very unique effects on the people it influences. Considering that it is a very distant planet from the sun and the first planet in what we call the outer solar system, it takes many years for it to orbit the sun, and as a result, it affects people for a long time as it spends several years in each house and sign. Depending on how Uranus influences your natal chart and your life, this long-staying guest could be a welcome influence or an uncomfortably long ride to bear.

Uranus has always been considered the "Awakener" or the "Disruptor," bringing significant change and causing things to take a completely new direction. Whether we talk about individuals or entire generations, Uranus has played a pivotal role and changed the course of nature with its presence. Its unique traits also give the people it influences a uniqueness in every aspect of their being. Its distinct characteristics endow the people it affects with individuality in every aspect of their being. For some, Uranus is integral to their being. They are more cognizant of its effects than those who stand near the edge of its shade and are only vaguely affected by its aura. The energy Uranus resonates with illuminates each house of the natal chart in a unique way that no other planet does. In this section, we will look specifically at Uranus' effect in the last four houses of the natal chart.

The Last Four Houses

9th House

This house is concerned with travel, specifically the longer routes and journeys one takes in contrast to the short journeys in the third house. This is the house you need to be looking at if you are interested in understanding the kind of expansion that your life will undergo, whether that is financial and professional, intellectual and personal, intimate and emotional, or metaphysical and philosophical. This is the house of purpose.

10th House

This house delves deeper into the philosophical realm, addressing issues such as achievement, authority, goals, and societal influence. This section discusses how socially valuable your work will be, how significant your contributions to your personal circle and society at large will be, and what kind of advantages or disadvantages you might experience. This is important for people looking to head towards business and entrepreneurship, your social ties are a big player in that line of work, and this house goes to great lengths to understand your position in this area.

11th House

This house discusses technology and innovation, its impact on you, and the impact you will have on it as the houses begin their descent. It's called the House of Blessings, and it talks about how fruitful your efforts will be in any direction. You can see the worth of your social connections and the relationships you form throughout your life in this house. It discusses love, how successful you will be with it, and the quality of your relationships with your loved ones. It discusses how useful your wealth will be to you and how useful your wealth and monetary assets will be to society.

12th House

On a physical level, the last house corresponds to the house that was descending and exiting the zodiac wheel at the time of your birth, just as the first house is home to your ascendant, which was the planet that was entering the horizon at the time of your birth. This is the house hidden behind the shadows - it is not visible, but it exists. Similarly, it deals with all those things without a physical form but are very real, and we can feel their existence just as much, if not more, than other physical entities in our lives. Some of the intangible things that reside in this house are dreams, emotions, fears, hopes, and secrets. As the House of Sacrifice summarizes your existence, it discusses luck and miracles and their roles in your life in relation to the cosmic forces that influence you. If you are looking for healing, forgiveness, or a resolution, this is the place to be.

How will Uranus affect these houses?

Uranus in the 9th House

For this person, nothing is unbelievable; nothing is too extreme, and nothing is impossible. Innovation is the only way they can work, and even things that already have a clearly defined path have room for improvement and have enough given to accommodate a new perspective. You won't find these people at the same table with those who firmly grasp long-standing traditions and take pride in doing things as they have always been done. This doesn't mean they don't respect culture and norms, but this is the thinker who likes to take a different route.

Positives

A love of travel, not to get away from a hectic work life but to put more hours into learning about new people, new places, and gathering new experiences. They not only like to see these new things, but they also implement them into their lives and live what they learn. They never know where they might end up. They may start in a direction opposite to traditions, only to circle the world to come to settle down back into the same traditions, done their way.

Whether it is religion or politics, they enjoy looking towards tomorrow rather than focusing on current beliefs and keeping an ear open to new ideas, something exciting. It's not their fault. When Uranus is influencing their mind, they can't help but think in ways that seem absurd to others but completely rational to themselves. These are people who are very open-minded and have flexible perspectives, and they are always looking to learn something new and refine their outlook on life. The fact that they hold a mindset not widely accepted by others adds to their delight in meeting other freethinkers.

However, even with their unusual approach and near-bizarre views of the world, they are far from silly or dumb. They have a phenomenal mental capacity to learn, process, and implement information, and they are very innovative thinkers. Although their solutions may appear too extreme, there is no denying that they might just work.

Negatives

While there are advantages to their free spirit, they also face problems with love, personal relationships, and friendships. It is hard for this person to balance work, play, and personal time as all of these things are intertwined for them. If they can find the right kind of work and the right kind of people to spend time with, you will find them enjoying work incredibly and discussing all their unusual thoughts with the people close to them. They are so infatuated with their own thoughts and so confident in their ideas that it can make other people feel like their input doesn't matter to this person. While they love socializing and meeting people, coming across people with a mindset similar to theirs is often rare.

Their perception of right and wrong can differ greatly from those who adhere to social norms and what is socially defined as good and bad. This can lead to them getting into trouble and having a difficult relationship with those close to them. These are the people who will question things for which people do not always have an answer. They can be stingy in life because they want to spend their money on travel, experiences, and education. With their diverse range of interests, they will come up with clever ways to achieve everything they desire but can be quite bitter if they fail to accomplish even a few things on that list.

Uranus in the 10th House

Building on their unique perspectives and out-of-the-world world views, these folks are very confident in how they see the world and choose to do things their way. For this reason, they excel in professions that grant them room to incorporate their creative abilities and unique approach to problems. The last thing on their mind would be climbing up the corporate ladder. As long as they get to do what they want to do, the way they want to do it, they are happy workers. This house is concerned with a person's professional life, career development, and concerned domains and is something that can be tricky for Uranians.

Positives

The way they approach work creates a big probability for these people to be well known for their work. Even though fame does not attract them, nor is it something that they actively work towards, their use of unconventional techniques and often achieving fantastic results naturally draws people to them. They are difficult to put into a box, and if they are placed under the administration of monotone management, their abilities and personalities suffer. Their creative streak is displayed differently, and even though it is unusual for some people, it is easily sensed and appreciated by those with a creative disposition. Fields of technology, science, and digital work appeal to these people and are things that they naturally excel in.

Since they love to travel, they are always interested in work that gives them physical freedom. In the modern era, this comes in the form of digital work. In the past, it was entrepreneurship and business life that facilitated travel and trade in various areas.

Due to this right-brained instinct, these people are also very in tune with their spiritual side and have great regard for the soul and everything holy. Even if they are not avid practitioners of any faith, they have a deep respect for cultures and religions.

As parents, they are strong anchors for the children and the family as a whole; however, they can be difficult family members to deal with because they have mixed views and can often have a drastic change in perception and think everyone can adapt as they do.

Negative

However creative and ingenious they are in their work, they tend to get bored quickly, and their spontaneous mind always seeks new things. This can often limit their professional lives as they bounce around different jobs saying yes to new employers because the job role attracts them. This makes it difficult for them to develop a strong career path and reach a height in any one field.

They do not acknowledge authority well and prefer to do things at their own pace. Even in creative roles, there is always some sense of direction and management to keep things in order. If they don't like how things are managed, they will be the first to leave.

As parents, they can be tough on children because of their unusual mentalities. Even though they mean no harm and only want the best for their child, it can be difficult for them to communicate with their children. These people often have difficult family lives, and if their spouse is flexible and understanding, they could make it work. Otherwise, it will be a bumpy ride for everyone. With time, they can learn to accommodate others, but that may require more than one lifetime.

Uranus in the 11th House

These people have a deep and pure connection with like-minded friends and family members with whom they resonate, and the attachments they form are lifelong. They are genuinely interested in the ups and downs in the lives of people to whom they feel connected, even if the other person does not always understand the Uranian's feelings for them. Moreover, they are attracted to people from whom they believe they can learn. They are interested in learning about anything and everything, whether professional, spiritual, materialistic, or intangible. For this reason, they resonate with people who are generous with words, thoughts, and ideas. However, being under the influence of a planet that spins on its side, they are not the easiest people to socialize with. Their complex thought processes, unusual wit, and fast analysis make them a double-edged social sword. While they are quick to form bonds, they are even quicker to sever them if they feel the person is not responding well.

Positives

When part of a group they have good chemistry with, this person will be the center of attention. Not because they enjoy the attention but because they have so much to give out. They are very strong friends who care immensely about the people they love. They are brutally honest with a bright sense of humor and captivating style of conversation, which brings together their unique personalities and incredible intelligence.

Their difficult shells hide a soft underbelly. You will often see them volunteering for work, helping out those in need, and going out of their way to accommodate a stranger. Their creative streaks also transfer to entertainment and artistic talents, and they make wonderful musicians, actors, and artists. So good that you might find some doing it professionally.

Negatives

They can be a bit harsh in their mindset and the mental systems they have in place, often being quick to nullify someone else's opinion and hurt people with their adherence to their own views. They don't like to compromise on their ideals and goals. They will step out of a relationship, job, or situation so they can stick to what they believe and do things their way. They will take on the job of a team just so they can do everything their own way, regardless of how grueling it may be. Individuality is so essential to this person that it may cost them in life. When combined with the fact that they are constantly changing, they might be beating themselves up and regretting something they have done shortly after deciding to do it. Being an outer lying planet, they might have a hard time letting go of things, and this is the type of friend who remembers that you took their seat at that movie in high school 15 years ago.

Uranus in the 12th House

In line with their strong social circles, they are not just happy being part of a circle. They want to be an active contributor who is constantly helping people out in the most unusual ways. They genuinely want nothing in return, but they can't help but try and help in intangible ways. It's in the structure of their planet to collaborate and generate something bigger than themselves, and they will lend a helping hand in anything you ask them to.

Positives

They are naturally very interested in and very good at understanding metaphysical things and concepts that make no sense to more streamlined thinkers. Abstract ideas and incomputable concepts are their preferred food for thought, and they like it served buffet style.

As a result, they are very introspective, constantly returning to and analyzing past events in their lives and frequently floating into the future and hypothesizing potential situations. They enjoy dreaming and discussing it with others who love dreaming as well. They are big-hearted people, always up for a challenge and willing to help anyone in any way.

Negatives

While they love company, there are some things that they always keep to themselves. Much like the long, long winter on their planet, some things of their lives always stay in the dark, and no matter how close someone is, they just won't ever let them into that secret. They aren't very good at hiding the fact that they are hiding something, which is even worse for the person they are hiding it from. It's a sense of shyness and insecurity that they have trouble managing—a flip side to their loud social self.

While being excellent observers, some may also tend to be uncomfortably quiet. Leaving others to wonder what's going on when they're actually just enjoying some comfortable silence, although it's not comfortable for anyone other than the Uranians.

If they feel they don't fit in or the people around them do not understand them, they can turtle up and suppress their original emotions and thoughts. Just riding the wave, carrying on surface-level interactions looking for an exit. If they feel they are not welcome, when they exit, they won't be coming back for a long time, if ever. These are not the kind of people who give you a chance to hurt them again and again. In fact, if they sense some negativity coming their way, they take proactive steps to get out of their way permanently.

Chapter 7: When Uranus Meets Other Planets

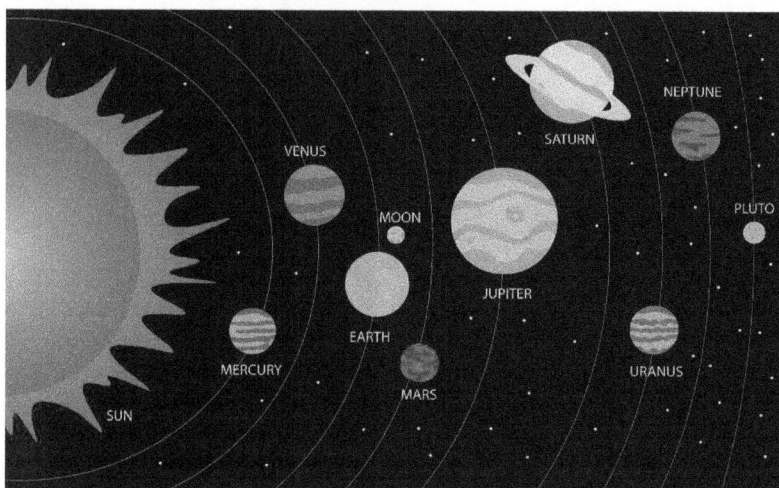

Uranus is associated with intelligence and plays an important role in research. Similarly, Uranus the planet comes in proximity to other planets at some point, which can have various effects on other planets in the solar system. This chapter will look at the changes that occur when Uranus is around other planets. The chapter will be divided into sections that will attempt to explain the various relations. It also describes what happens when Uranus interacts with other planets. Astrologers believe that the interactions of the planets affect human affairs.

Definition of Terms

There are six degrees of tolerance for all the relations that exist between Uranus and other planets. The relations are highlighted below:

1. Trine or Naypancham- Trine refers to triple or threefold, and in astrology, it refers to a favorable astrological aspect involving two celestial bodies. Trine refers to the flow of the planets at a harmonious angle on the chart.

2. Sextile or Labhyog- Individuals born with the sextile planetary elements may discover hidden talents and set certain goals related to the planets. The energies can make a relationship more enjoyable. The disadvantage of the sextile aspect is that the person involved may be quite unmotivated to take appropriate action to pursue ideas that may never be realized.

However, the good thing about sextile is that it is not disruptive, and it is viewed as positive since it is a pleasant force in your life.

3. Conjunction or Yativog- The conjunction aspect in astrology involves a scenario when energies of two planets are shared. The conjunction aspects play an essential role in reading the chart as they determine how the energy will manifest. Two planets often get nearby and occupy the same zodiac sign on a horoscope wheel. They are said to be conjunct and combine energies that bring a greater sum of their parts.

4. Opposition or Pratiyog- This is a planetary aspect that involves a 180-degree angle when divided by two and is called opposition. Simply put, these planets are opposite to each other on the chart, and they create a lot of tension. The energy can be used for better purposes if the planets can find a compromise.

In life, the planetary element of opposition can cause frustration and a great deal of tension. While this tension can be resolved, sometimes you may need to push harder to achieve a balance between the conflicting scenarios. There is a lot of work to be done to grow as a person.

5. Square or Kendrayog- If you divide the natal chart by 4, you will get a 90-degree angle. The square planetary aspect reveals the conflicts and challenges between the planets involved. There is no easy win over each planet.

With the square aspect, there is a tendency to avoid major decisions concerning those planets unless you have no choice. However, there will come a certain period where the energy of the square will push you to a situation where change becomes inevitable. To achieve the best outcome, assess both the good and bad things about a particular situation. You can also use the square aspect to self-introspect to regain your balance in different elements of your life.

6. Sesquiquadrate or Shadashtakyog- A Sesquiquadrate reveals an area of disappointment and frustration where you try to make a mountain out of a mole-hill. This can result from blowing the facts out of proportion.

However, you need to develop patience, persistence, and endurance to avoid the feelings of resentment and impatience that can be overwhelming. This aspect requires you to relax to achieve positive goals.

What Are the Effects of Uranus When It Meets Other Planets?

As you are now aware, Uranus is the solar system's seventh planet, and it also suggests intelligence. This planet plays a crucial role in research work. This section discusses the effects of Uranus on the other planets. Six degrees of tolerance outlined above are involved in the discussions of the relations.

Uranus revolves around the sun horizontally, yet all other planets revolve in a vertical way around the polar axis. Since Uranus is an outsider physically, not surprisingly, its impacts on our lives are the most unpredictable of all the other planets. Uranus can be anything from producing social misfits, eccentrics, or sociopaths. But it also produces geniuses. Foremost, you need to know the things offered by Uranus.

1. Heightens intuition- When Uranus awakens you, you can perceive the quality of the inner energy of life in its various forms. When you look at another person, you are not only attracted to or repelled by their personality. You can see the human inside the physical body. In the same vein, when you look at a painting, you think beyond the subject matter and color scheme that appears on the canvas. With true intuition, you can experience the state of mind and the painter's consciousness concerning what they wanted to portray.

2. Uranus also helps to quicken the desire to improve the environment's established order. In other words, the planet plays a role in stimulating your energies to allow you to experience the reality of the relationship that exists between the inner order and outer order of society. It helps you to perceive and act in a particular way relative to what you see.

3. Uranus also fosters individualism within a group context where self-centeredness precedes other social aspirations. Uranus can lead individuals to pursue occult ways or the path of divine knowledge. It also utilizes ancient wisdom teachings in our daily lives. When Uranus is in contact with other planets, it produces different variables.

There is a general trend in the relations between the various aspects highlighted from the degrees of tolerance outlined above. For example, the first two relations show that Trine and Sextile provide positive results, whereas the last two relations, Square and Sesquiquadrate, provide negative results. The remaining two relations produce either negative or positive results. The following are three sets of results indicating Uranus in contact with trine or sextile, conjunction, and square or opposition:

Results of Trine / Sextile of Uranus in Contact With

Sun: This combination offers several opportunities in life and also produces a good leader in social life. It also offers a highly willful and individualistic nature that mainly depends on the degree of consciousness of the individual and the geometric aspect. The main driver, in this case, is to be oneself and aspire to achieve great things.

Moon: The combination allows individuals to perceive nature in all its different forms through which our lives take place. This is perfect for an intelligent person with a keen interest in science and modern art. It is also excellent for a social worker or an astrologer. It is concerned with nurturing talent and group consciousness. The combination suggests a successful life that may, however, be characterized by hidden or secret affairs.

Mars: The contact of Uranus and Mars produces courage and determination to see justice no matter what kind of risk may be involved to someone. You have to work in unfavorable and often difficult conditions in life to achieve success. Mars also rules the degree of sexual process from the personality level, while Uranus will hold the rulership from the degree of the soul. When they are harmoniously linked, they also lead to the promotion of reproduction of different forms in life that represent the soul's intent in its present state.

Another notable aspect about this combination is that it presents with the person involved ambition and many opportunities in life. One of the siblings may get a chance to go abroad if Uranus is in the third position from Mars.

Mercury: This combination blends well with mental energy and the intuitive. The individual involved is highly perceptive, and they can also interpret different perceptions through a spoken word or written language. Such people can access different sources of information that help them to perceive a lot of things. The person may also be very intelligent and have a sharp memory. It is good for research work since it is premised on intelligence.

Jupiter: Contact between these two planets can have amazing results. Jupiter, the esoteric ruler of Aquarius, brings the second wave of love and wisdom to various human relationships. People with strong connections to these two planets are eager to learn and are highly philosophical in their spiritual development. It also represents a good financial situation, which can help you gain assistance from different friends.

Venus: The combination of Uranus and Venus leads one to be experimental, and this is often expressed through unconventional behavior and relationships. Both Uranus and Venus can free someone from racism and prejudice. It is also good for companionship and marriage. The person becomes more sensitive and sexier, leading to the growth of a strong bond between the parties involved.

Saturn: The combination between Saturn and Uranus offers the person involved the capability to bridge generations and unite people with different social and political views. There is a possibility of flexibility in adapting to the changing rules and regulations in law, business, and other forms of social structures. It also connotes good administrative power, an intelligent quotient, and is ideal for research. It also gets support from Jupiter or the sun.

Results of Conjunction/Opposition of Uranus and Others

Sun: There is a chance that the house where the sun is the Lord will experience a negative result. In the 7th house, marital life can be disrupted, leading to divorce. The other issue is that it is bad for the father's health and, more broadly, for marital relationships. Sometimes, the personality may form connections with others to demonstrate inclusivity and universality.

Moon: You can feel that your source of emotional nurturing has suddenly shifted or somehow been removed. This can cause challenges to the relationship with one's mother. And the combination is not ideal for the mother's health, and it can lead to mental problems. It can lead to disturbances in the marital life of the female.

Mars: This Uranus-Mars combination can promote a harmful sexual orientation. These are also known to appear in the charts of individuals who are victims or perpetrators of general violence and sexual abuse. The individuals involved are prone to unfortunate incidents. The female in a marriage is more likely to be disturbed on the 2nd, 3rd, 4th, 7th, 8th, or 12th. There is also a possibility of your vehicle or house catching fire. However, on a positive note, Uranus and Mars can also create social justice. They can also advance a fruitful social agenda against the background of serious opposition.

Mercury: The combination of Uranus and Mercury can produce an overly active mind. However, this does not diminish your genius and natural talents. The goal is to be busy, but it can also contribute to a generally nervous disposition. It gives a good IQ if not placed on the 6th, 8th, or 12th and is ideal for an astrologer so long as the conditions mentioned above are met.

Jupiter: This combination can give rise to concerns about the children. With females, they may have the problem of conceiving, and a combination of the 7th may lead to a handicapped partner as well.

Venus: The combination will contribute to someone's desire to know people from different national or ethnic backgrounds. It also produces people with eclectic or unusual artistic tastes. The conjunction also provides an intense need for diverse friendships and social interactions. A combination involving Scorpio, Aries, Taurus, and Gemini makes a person sexy. However, there can also be sexual problems that can be encountered.

Saturn: When it is in C, chances of the invention of regulations and new rules for one's conduct are likely to be high. These can change because of different life circumstances being experienced by the person in different situations. On a different note, it gives a good IQ if a combination includes Scorpio, Libra, Aquarius, and Capricorn. It also gives positive results. However, conjunction in Taurus, Aries, Cancer, and Leo provides negative results.

If Uranus is in conjunction with the Lord of the 7th House, there is likely to be a possibility of riots, tremors, fire, accidents, or death, especially at a time of marriage. In the same vein, these aspects cannot be ruled out when it is time for the baby's birth if the sub lord of the 5th is in conjunction with Uranus.

Results of Square / Sesquiquadrate of Uranus and Other Planets

Sun: The conjunction of Uranus and the Sun can lead to serious problems in business, challenges in married life if it comes on the female's chart, and losses caused by accidents. And these aspects may produce individuals that only obey their laws, and they can break them depending on their mood swings and other circumstances in life. The individual is primarily concerned with attaining freedom at all costs. However, the only difference is when the person is attracted to a radical political group or separatist cult where liberty is sacrificed unknowingly.

Moon: When combined with the aspects, this conjunction creates a strong desire to rebel against past behavioral patterns ingrained in society or family. The aspects are difficult on the emotional nature because there is a tendency for one to be unavailable or with people who are not emotionally available. Sudden and erratic emotional shifts are common. Conversely, the combination also demonstrates intelligence and smartness at work. However, the individuals involved are not good at maintaining relationships.

If Uranus is in 4th, the individual may change places of work or business. It also gives negative aspects in different types of comfort when Uranus is 4th from the Moon. It can force someone to change jobs or business when Uranus is 10th from the Moon.

Mars: Chances of heavy financial losses will be very high if any combinations are in the 1st, 4th, or 8th. Kidnapping may not be ruled out in the case of a female chart. Other issues like social oppression may also be great.

Mercury: It creates a confusing condition that can lead to applying the knowledge for criminal purposes. On top of that, you can be right for the wrong reasons.

Jupiter: The tendency to be too experimental may be too high in the quest to gain higher knowledge. This can be more like jumping from what you are to the same position as your current state. Unsuccessful life, children-related issues, and losses in different court cases are some of the challenges likely to be encountered.

Venus: The conjunction can bring complications into your relationships. It is possible to be attracted to inappropriate people who are potentially harmful. Other complications may arise due to unhappiness in a marriage in which a partner is cheated on. Sexual relationships can bring sadness rather than joy.

Saturn: The aspects often lead to the creation of a feeling of being oppressed. Sometimes, you may be limited by collective regulations. The individuals may view themselves as a law unto themselves.

Uranus and Neptune

Naturally, the combination is generational and not usually personal unless the two planets are connected to the Moon, Sun, Mercury, Mars, or Venus. Whenever Neptune and Uranus touch the chart, there is a likelihood of raising energies involved in the collective or the universal level. The other aspect of Neptune and Uranus to the Sun can offer an individual who is liberal and also has good communication talents healing to help others. This also allows us to be in contact with various transcendental forces that usually flood the earth. However, not everyone can respond to such positive and evolutionary impulses.

Uranus and Pluto

The Uranus and Pluto combination offers color generations, which serve to break down structures and social patterns, allowing for integrated contact on the consciousness level. People born in the mid-1960s with Pluto in conjunction with Uranus and Virgo are considered the computer age generation. They invented those technologies, such as the internet and the World Wide Web. Technology played a crucial role in bringing people from different parts of the globe together. The Uranus links have also transformed Pluto society forever. If you experience Uranus/Pluto contacts in the horoscope, you will be consciously playing a role as an agent for transformation. Other people with close Uranus/Pluto contacts with the Moon and Sun are often uncomfortable with their social stings, and they tend to be restless and nervous.

Uranus is the seventh planet in the solar system, and it plays a crucial role in research work. It also connotes intelligence and offers a variety of personalities when it meets with other planets. In this chapter, we outlined different combinations created when Uranus meets with other planets. There is a general trend in different relations created from the six degrees of tolerance. Trine and sextile provide positive results, Square and Sesquiquadrate offer negative results, while Conjunction can offer either positive or negative results.

Chapter 8: Uranus Returns with a Midlife Crisis

Experiencing a midlife crisis is an almost universal concept that everyone can understand. Upon reaching a particular age, namely around age 40, people tend to begin looking back and reevaluating their lives. They are also concerned that they have not accomplished all of their goals and that time is running out for them. This can manifest as a denial of aging and an attempt to relive the feelings and experiences of their youth. Other times, there may be a significant shift in their personality and values because of their desire to get more out of life. Regardless of how someone expresses their dissatisfaction with their lives, it is usually extreme, which is related to the planet Uranus and how it works in astrology.

A midlife crisis coincides with a transiting Uranus that is in opposition to a natal Uranus. This causes an awakening in people as they become consumed by restless energy they feel a strong need to express. This can take many different forms, such as purchasing frivolous material things like a new sports car or attempting to enrich themselves by going back to college. It can also affect interpersonal relationships, where a former lifelong bachelor suddenly gets married, or a couple who had once seemed to be solid end up getting divorced. These are major upheavals in a person's life that can fundamentally change who they are and how they present themselves to the rest of the world.

The Awakener

In astrology, Uranus is known as "The Awakener." This is due to the sudden changes it initiates in people when it's transiting. Uranus controls the transitions that occur in your life, as it embodies progressiveness, individuality, discovery, and innovation. An association with Uranus results in having a desire to buck tradition and forge your path. You may not have previously known that you had these needs, as they remained buried deep within your subconscious mind for many years. Rebellion is a common outcome of association with Uranus, whether it's rebelling against your family, job, society, or even yourself. Sometimes, seeking things that go against social norms can be disastrous, so it's necessary to learn how to deal with these feelings and urges productively.

Experiencing an awakening can be scary, especially if it compels you to uncover aspects of your personality you consider undesirable. However, you mustn't suppress the truth you discover about yourself. It's difficult ever to be truly happy and satisfied with your life if you are constantly denying a part of yourself from ever being expressed. An awakening brought on by the transiting Uranus can also bring a better understanding of the world. You might realize that certain things you'd always considered to be true differ from your long-held beliefs. If you will explore these things, you can develop new ideas and grow emotionally and psychologically.

Transiting Uranus

When Uranus transits, it means it moves across the various signs and houses. It will spend about seven years in each sign and be in retrograde for roughly five months each year. Every sign it passes through impacts various aspects of your thoughts, emotions, and personality. Uranus, as the planet of change and innovation, can usher in transitional periods in your life. You can sometimes feel the energy it emits, causing what appears to be an electrical charge throughout your body.

A transiting Uranus will reach significant positions in the zodiac, which correspond to times in your life when you are at a crossroads. During this time, you will need to decide what path you want to take and what options are available to you; assuming the average human lives about 84 years, Uranus will complete one entire cycle through the zodiac in the same amount of time. Thus, when you are about 40-42 years old, Uranus will be positioned in direct opposition to where it was at the time of your birth.

Uranus in Opposition

Upon reaching the opposite position of where it was when you were born, Uranus reflects the tension between where your life is going and where it has already been. You are essentially looking in the mirror and being forced to confront aspects of yourself that you may not have noticed previously. There is a confrontation with your inner self, and you gain knowledge about hidden truths. Your life can be cast in a new light by viewing yourself from a different perspective. Following this, you are left with the desire to explore what this means for you as a person and what changes you will make because of it.

Dealing with the Uranus opposition can be challenging. You will experience turmoil in your life, and the many ways that conflict is expressed can have a serious effect on those around you. Once you've begun reevaluating your goals and priorities, there are people and things you will decide to either keep in your life or cast aside. This might be friends, family members, a job, a hobby, or material possessions. In addition, there will be new people and things you bring into your life, and this can be a difficult adjustment for you and those around you to make.

A midlife crisis is often accompanied by feelings of failure or regret for the choices made in your life. You dwell more on things left undone or unspoken, wishing for a chance to go back and do it over again. To avoid accruing additional regrets, you might start taking more risks or behaving in a rebellious manner. This results from that tension between Uranus being in opposition to your natal Uranus. The energy radiated from it fills you with anxiety you have too many unfulfilled goals and desires because Uranus is connected to change. In a midlife crisis, your thoughts, feelings, and behaviors boil down to a need to change something about your life.

Extreme Reactions

It is no secret that Uranus provokes significant shifts in your life. These can be major positive changes that give you a sense of liberation from the stagnation in your life, or they can be overwhelmingly negative changes that leave your world in utter chaos. The power of Uranus magnifies everything you think, feel, and do, causing minor issues to become major ones. Mild frustrations with your significant other or job can result in you hating your partner and wanting to leave them or becoming so disillusioned at work that you decide to quit. The extreme reactions you have to things in your life become more potent when Uranus is in opposition to where it's located in your natal chart. This is often identified as being symptoms of a midlife crisis.

Chasing Your Dreams

During a midlife crisis, you may have the urge to start or pick back up a desire to chase your dreams. Many people who once sought to achieve some lofty goal end up having to give it up for more practical pursuits. You may have wanted to be a world-famous musician or open up a five-star restaurant, but various obstacles and responsibilities ended up getting in the way. In the time since that happened, you may have resigned yourself to the fact that you could never make your dreams come true. However, when you find yourself in a midlife crisis, you might decide you want to give that pursuit a second chance.

The power of Uranus encourages you to take risks and make changes in your life. With its connection to so many aspects of transitioning to new phases of your life, you can use its power to help you finally achieve your goals. As much as Uranus causes you to face challenges, it also gives you the strength to overcome these problems and succeed. While you may want to chase your dreams, don't let the pursuit consume you. It's easy to fall into the trap of spending large amounts of time, energy, and money going after something that you may never attain. Instead, focus more on the journey, as the experiences you have in the process of seeking a way to reach your goals can be just as fulfilling as attaining your dreams.

Coping with a Midlife Crisis

The opposition of Uranus and the ensuing midlife crisis is often a turning point in people's lives. While there is a transformation that occurs within you, there are ways you can cope with the extreme changes that you experience. One way is to simply achieve as many of your goals as possible before you reach your 40s. Of course, this is easier said than done, but people who have experienced success in their lives often remain unaffected by the Uranus opposition. If you have lived life to the fullest, there won't be nearly as strong a desire to pivot what you are doing to gain the experience of living without regrets. There still might be some subtle alterations that you undergo, but for the most part, you'll pass through your midlife stage with little trouble.

For anyone who does go through a midlife crisis, tempering your restlessness and drive to experience new things is an important part of managing any issues that come along with the conflict between your old life and the new one you want to have. It's fine to find a new job, take up new hobbies, or attempt to go through new experiences to sate these desires. However, you don't want to allow yourself to abandon everything that was once important to you completely. If you need an outlet to express your frustration with where you are in your life, there are plenty of constructive ways to do so that don't involve overhauling it entirely.

You can prepare for the transformative period brought on by Uranus by making little changes in your everyday life to help release some of the tension that comes with the opposing position of the planet. Try placing your keys in a different pocket than you usually do, or learn something new outside your usual interests. By altering your routine, you can express your need to change something about your life without going to the extreme. These are good outlets for that built-up energy being drawn from Uranus, and it can help you avoid any issues that might arise from making more significant changes that will affect others around you.

If you are currently in a relationship, you might feel like it's become stagnant when you are in the midst of a midlife crisis. Instead of breaking off the relationship because you think you will find a new one more satisfying, you can instead try taking on different roles with your partner than you typically do. If you are the one who initiates conversations or makes decisions about where to go or what activities to participate in, sit back and let your partner do these things. If the opposite is true, take on the responsibility of initiating communication and the activities you do together. This will allow you to view your relationship from a new perspective and possibly give you a renewed appreciation for your partner.

With your career choices, the opposition of Uranus could influence you to seek a new job. Rather than looking for a similar position in a different company to the one you are already doing, you can try to strike out on your own. Uranus governs innovation and entrepreneurship. This would be a good time to explore opportunities to become your own boss, as many people find this to be far more satisfying than having to work for someone else. The key to succeeding in this endeavor is not to take on more than you can handle. If you overreach to achieve your goals sooner than normal, you can quickly become overwhelmed, causing you to stumble and create more problems for yourself. Patience is important when you try out anything new. While you might fear you are running out of time, you must have faith that good things will come in their own due time.

By undergoing such an extreme and intense transformation during a midlife crisis, you risk alienating others in your life. While change isn't always a bad thing, you don't want to make changes that will negatively affect you. It's easy to go out and buy a flashy new sports car, but if you have a family, this can be detrimental to them. It can be an unnecessary financial burden, and inconvenient to use as a vehicle for transporting your children. If you believe it is time to change your vehicle, look for something different from what you currently have but is still practical enough to meet your family's needs. There are always ways to express your desire for change without causing problems for the people in your life.

Bringing Out the Best in You

The opposition of Uranus offers you an opportunity to improve yourself. During this period of transition and transformation, you can direct your energy toward becoming an exceptional person. It's never too late to learn something new, and you can take steps to change your thought patterns and behavior positively. If you have certain unhelpful traits or habits, this is a good time to fix those things and learn to deal with them productively. A midlife crisis can be a turning point where you work to become a better person instead of making selfish decisions that could harm people you care about.

At some point in life, everyone wishes to change the way they do things. This is difficult to achieve at most points in their lives, but a transiting Uranus makes it easier to initiate this change. You can change your approach to relationships by spending more time listening to and understanding your loved ones' thoughts and feelings. You can also use this time to remove toxic people from your life, helping you to improve your mental health. In addition, you can eliminate toxic thoughts and behaviors of your own, learning to engage with others more positively. This will leave you a better version of yourself than you were before.

The End of a Midlife Crisis

Most of the time, a midlife crisis lasts only a few years. The feelings of restlessness and urgency to make changes in your life will dissipate as Uranus moves beyond the opposite position from your natal Uranus. While your experiences during this period will forever change you, you may have a desire to return to certain things you abandoned during your midlife crisis. Other aspects of your life will also be things you want to keep doing, especially if they have made you feel fulfilled in ways you haven't felt before. You will soon settle into a new status quo, so I hope you can successfully navigate this transition phase.

Uranus' influence on you during a midlife crisis is undeniable. The sudden urge to make changes in your life stems directly from the power it wields when positioned in opposition to your natal Uranus. While any sort of change or transition can be scary, there are also great opportunities to acquire more knowledge about the world around you and gain an appreciation for the people and things in your life. It's an experience that many people will go through, so you are not alone if you have a midlife crisis. The real measure of a person isn't whether they have one — it's how they decide to handle a midlife crisis when they go through it. Any change can be positive or negative, so the decision about which you want it to be is entirely up to you.

Chapter 9: How to Ride the Winds of Change

Uranus is a planet that encourages and values individuality. It is associated with change, but the kind of change Uranus is associated with is the good kind of change, the kind that pushes you to take risks, explore new frontiers, and progress in life. Furthermore, it is associated with innovation and technology, as its discovery opened up a new understanding and opportunities to learn more about the universe, of which we are a tiny part.

Progress means growth, and growth doesn't occur in still and stagnant environments. Since Uranus is linked to progress, it is all about changing routines and shaking things up. When this special planet is in transit, you have to prepare yourself and expect the unexpected! However, this transit and changes that occur because of it can teach some valuable life lessons, and if you pay attention to these messages and learn these lessons, you will start to make changes in your life that would set you free and expand your awareness about the universe.

Uranus's Transits across the Houses

Uranus and its transits affect all of us. Uranus takes eighty-four (84) years to complete its orbit around the zodiac! However, you will feel the effects of this transit at various stages of your life. Before discussing how you can deal with the changes that may occur when Uranus transits each of the twelve houses of astrology, let's look closely at each transit.

The First House (Aries)

When Uranus is transiting Aries, you will feel that your life is changing in a way or another. A need for more freedom and independence will rise, and you will be ready to explore new ways of life and new ideas. Unexpected incidents might take place that would call for change.

The Second House (Taurus)

Transit Uranus in Taurus will cause a change in your value system. You will start to seek progressive values that cope with the present and the future.

The Third House (Gemini)

While transiting your third house, you will feel you need change and mental stimulation. Becoming mentally restless, you might end up taking new courses to gain knowledge in new fields. However, most probably, you won't finish any of them.

The Fourth House (Cancer)

When in your fourth house, which is Cancer, the changes that may occur will be linked to your home and family. You may feel the urge to make some home improvements, and again most probably, you will not finish what you have started. Problems that rarely occurred in your house may start occurring, like problems with family members, for example.

The Fifth House (Leo)

When Uranus is in your fifth house, you may notice changes in yourself related to your interests and hobbies. You may begin to venture outside of your comfort zone and explore usual hobbies. You may find yourself falling in and out of love fast with people you usually wouldn't be interested in. Moreover, your relationship with your children, if you have any, might change.

The Sixth House (Virgo)

When in your sixth house, Uranus will encourage you to break your daily routines and shake things up a little. You would start going for freelancing and more flexible working hours. You may work hard and then let go of what you are doing.

The Seventh House (Libra)

The change here is linked to your close relationships. During that time, you may feel that you need more freedom in these relationships. You may experience some instability in your relationships as you might fall for people fast and break up with them fast. However, these relationships will be exciting for you.

The Eighth House (Scorpio)

When transit Uranus is in Scorpio, your finances may get affected. You may become unable to rely on other people in your life who used to help you financially. Therefore, you must learn how to be financially independent.

The Ninth House (Sagittarius)

When Uranus is in Sagittarius, you may experience changes that would expand your awareness and knowledge about life. You may get introduced to new cultures and people who walk different paths of life than yours and learn about and from them. Studying new things may interest you; however, you may lose interest after a while.

The Tenth House (Capricorn)

When in your tenth house, Uranus will affect your career and the decisions you make related to it. You may suddenly find yourself drawn to unusual jobs. You may become anxious and agitated, and this state might result in you changing the direction of your career.

The Eleventh House (Aquarius)

When in Aquarius, Uranus's influence on you would be related to friendships as you won't be interested in committing to any kind of friendship. However, you may become interested in meeting new, unique people and make friends with them. The way you perceive your future may change too.

The Twelfth House (Pisces)

Transiting your twelfth house, Uranus will affect your old habits. You may realize that you need to let go of the past in order to progress in life. Moreover, you may take an unusual approach to do good things and helping others.

As you can see, all of the changes mentioned in every house are linked to progress and freedom in one way or another, and that is how Uranus teaches you valuable lessons in life through sudden changes and unexpected turns of events. If you focus on the positive aspects of these changes, you will manage these transitions and changes in your life to make you a better person with a better understanding of how things work in the universe. However, the most significant impact of these changes will be felt in the future. If you view these changes as opportunities for growth and learning, you will progress in life and broaden your awareness of new aspects of life, leading to a better future.

The Winds of Change

It is difficult to take advantage of new circumstances and life changes. It is easier said than done, but some strategies can help you manage this phase and make the most of the new changes in your life.

Here are some tips and tricks to help you learn how to accept change and improve the quality of your life:

Embrace your Feelings

When faced with any kind of change in your life, you start feeling alarmed and confused, and some people get unnerved. The key to managing those negative and overwhelming emotions is to embrace all of these feelings, no matter how unsettling they are. Ignoring and avoiding those feelings will get you nowhere. You need to work your way through them to accept change and move on with your life. Talk to your friends and express your fears and disappointments or whatever negative emotions are lingering inside of you - let them all out in a decent way. If you are experiencing grief, let yourself grieve and let it all out. If your negative thoughts and feelings didn't get out of your system, they will stay there no matter how good you are at tricking yourself and ignoring them, as one day they will come out in the most unexpected manner, which most probably would cause some damage and till then you will stay stuck where you are. What is worse than an explosion of stored negative feelings is that they will keep affecting different aspects of your life without you even noticing if ignored.

Understand that Change is Inevitable

Our whole existence depends on change. This is a fact that you need to fully understand before life puts you through unexpected situations and transitions. This way, accepting change will be much easier for you. Look around you and read history - you will realize that change is key for evolution and progress. If old habits and ways of life didn't change, we would have perished a long time ago. Change means new chances and opportunities in life. To move on and become a successful person, you need to learn from transitions in your life, the good and the bad ones alike. Remember that anger is blind, so don't let it control you when faced with life changes. Get angry, but then calm down and process and absorb the new facts and situation you've found yourself in. Reading success stories will help you understand that change is inevitable and that you can turn negative life experiences and difficult times into steppingstones to a better future.

Put Matters into Perspective

Putting things into perspective will help you control your emotions and think positively.

Calm down and evaluate your situation by asking yourself questions that will help you reframe the current situation, like "Why am I anxious about the new changes in my life?" and "What's the worst that could happen?" Then think about your expectations and fears to see if you are being realistic or if you've exaggerated things. After all, you might discover that things aren't as bad as you think.

Practice gratitude by writing down all of the positive things and blessings in your life and those things for which you have and are. Make it a daily habit. List ten things you are grateful for having every day. Start by the obvious things like food, family, friends, and shelter, for example, and then start noticing the small things in life like the first sip of your favorite cup of coffee in the morning or the smell of fresh air at dawn.

Focus on the Bright Side

Often, change can have a negative impact on our lives, but often there is a positive side to change. Breaking up with your partner, for example, can be devastating, especially if you have been together for a long time. However, if you take your time to feel sad and hurt, then think things through, you might discover that you will be happier this way and that you were just too much in love to think straight and realize this relationship has a negative effect on your life. Losing a job is another good example, as you can perceive it as an opportunity to explore a new work environment you might enjoy more or help you grow and progress in your career.

Figure Out Why you are Worried

When you consider why a particular change in your life caused you anxiety, you will better understand yourself and the way you perceive things. When you figure out why you are worried, you will be relieved. Sit down and ask yourself what it is about this change that is causing you to worry and triggering your anxiety. Take your time until you figure out the real reasons for your anxiety, and when you do, try to assess them because you may discover that you are worrying too much, and the situation is not that bad.

Remind Yourself of your Dynamic Nature

Remind yourself that if you accept new challenges in life, you will come out of these experiences stronger than before. We are dynamic, and it is up to us to enforce and develop it or step back and lose it. Take up new challenges life has offered you and take it as an opportunity to grow and learn new things about life. Change can motivate or stress you, and it is all about the way you will perceive it.

Take Action

Several physical activities can alleviate and reduce stress and anxiety. Yoga, running, swimming, working out, or any form of physical exercise can boost your mood and make you a happier person even though you are going through transitions in life. You can practice meditation as a mental exercise to clear your mind and control your emotions and inner thoughts. Physical activity is crucial for a stable state of mind and positive emotions. Many studies have proven that being physically active makes you a happier person.

Stay Busy

If you are experiencing a transition or a change in your life affecting you negatively, keep yourself busy and productive. However, that doesn't mean you should ignore your feelings and drown them by getting busy. Embrace your feelings, and find something that would keep you occupied. You can find a new hobby, for example, and other than giving you pleasure, a hobby allows you to create beautiful things like music or paintings. When you see your own little creations or hear them, your mood will get boosted, and you will discover new aspects of your life and things you are capable of doing.

Communicate your Feelings

Talking about and communicating your concerns to people you trust will make you feel a lot better once you've gotten those feelings out of your system. Furthermore, they may assist you in seeing things from different perspectives and shine a new light on the situation, which may change your mind and reduce the negative thoughts and fears haunting you. When you talk to others about your distress, you may find they had a similar experience. Knowing that you are not alone and that others have gone through the same thing or are still going through will push you to keep going and accept the changes occurring in your life.

List your Goals

Accepting change means you are on your way to moving forward in your life, as it is the first step in progressing and advancing in life. After you have embraced your feelings and accepted the new changes in your life, it is time to look ahead of you and think about your future. Create a list with all the things you want to achieve in life after the changes that occurred in it. You can aspire to find a better job, eat healthily, and meet new people, for example.

Do Good

Transform all of the unsettling feelings and thoughts caused by changes in your life into a moving force that can build a better community. Volunteer for a good cause that you believe in, helping others, whether they are your friends, family members, or strangers in need. Another way you can contribute to making the world a better and kinder place is by adopting a homeless pet and giving it a home and a loving family, which can be very rewarding and fulfilling. Moreover, pets add joy and color to life. However, you have to be sure that you are up to it.

Set Reasonable Expectations in Life

Dreaming big is important. However, to embrace new changes in life and uncertainties, you need to set reasonable expectations and realize that nothing stays the same way forever. Change is a fact in life we have to learn how to deal with. That doesn't mean you need to limit your dreams or underestimate your potential. It means you shouldn't expect relationships and people in your life to stay the same forever. Accept there will be ups and downs and turbulences in all of your relationships.

Uranus influences generations as it is a slow-moving planet. It spends about seven years in each house. However, it brings unexpected and sudden changes that result in awakenings and new challenges in life that promote progress and new inventions.

Change can become your greatest teacher if you allow yourself to learn from it and see beyond all the frustrations and disappointments that come with it. Accepting change will solidify and strengthen you to stand your ground when faced with new challenges in life. Thus, all of these exercises and tips are related to Uranus and its teachings because they all lead to progress in life and understanding it, which is what Uranus is all about. Furthermore, Uranus encourages freedom, individuality, and standing out from the crowd. Listen to Uranus's energy that encourages people to accept every aspect of life and all the changes and transitions in it. By doing so, the world will grow and evolve, allowing a brighter future for humanity.

Chapter 10: Change the World with Uranus

Uranus is the planet of transformation. It is provocative and seeks freedom and innovation. Using the energies of this planet can allow you to embrace your role as an agent of change in your society. Allow the planet to transform you internally so you can go out into the world and transform the world at a larger scale.

Society has evolved to the point where many of us now have a stronger voice than we did previously. Social media has enabled us to connect, engage, and enrage the entire world. We've been introduced to a whole new community of people. New worlds, cultures, and beliefs from which we can learn and teach. This coming together and collective awareness allows us to bring about change from a place of deep integrity and authenticity.

This chapter is titled change the world with Uranus. But first, we must address the first and hardest thing to change: ourselves. It may seem that changing the world and making our mark in society towards good is an almost impossible project. Compared to facing and changing our internal self, it is almost a piece of cake.

Look at it like this, our internal self creates and molds the external. How we see society, life, the collective influences and shapes everything. We are all part of the fabric of society, and thus who we are and the role we play in this world is huge. There has been a numbing and dumbing down of society from mass information and nervous system overload. We are struggling to deal with the amount of information headed away almost every minute. The ease of information distortion and "fake news" has caused many of us to become disillusioned and confused. We are losing touch with the core of ourselves - with our intuition and sensitivity.

This happens partially because we allow it to. We see everyone else living their lives in a specific way, and our ego selves seek to please others and fall in with the herd. Sometimes this is okay. In fact, it is even encouraged. Sometimes we need to do things as others do because it's the right way or it's the easy way based on trial and error. More often than not, however, the societal conditioning we receive dampens our true spirits.

It's easy to go through life unaware of this as we get swept up in the daily commotion of life. But when you notice that spark inside of you. That little voice that tells you that you are meant for something greater, something different. Sometimes it's a big catastrophic event that happens— forcing us to reexamine ourselves and our future. It is the events that are catalysts for great transformation. Despite the pain they bring, they are necessary to bring us immense evolution and healing. In this space, you can step into your true power.

How to Create Change in Yourself

A starting point to creating change within yourself is to take stock of yourself. Here, you need to be as honest as possible. If the idea of it seems daunting to you, that's okay. It would be weird if it weren't - and can even suggest a level of denial. You can start slow with this. Separate the areas of your life, for example, money, love, friendships, career, education, etc. Whatever categories of your life seem important, relevant, or resonate with you should be looked at. Even one of these categories is very broad - let's make love. With this, you can consider your previous and (if relevant) current relationships. What was the cause of any breakups? How do you show up in your relationships? What are your predominant thoughts about love and relationships? What were your caregivers' relationships like? What about all the relationships you witnessed growing up?

It's important to notice any common threads or reoccurring theses. This could point to your belief system and view of the world, possibly where many of your behaviors and thoughts stem from. This then influences how you show up in the world and, more specifically, in your relationships. To get deeper, and there's a lot of room to do that here (we've only scratched the surface), look up books or podcasts surrounding this topic or anything specific you feel you want to work on or understand more.

This journey of self-discovery is vital to change. We cannot truly change unless we understand ourselves on a deep and intimate level. We can progress to acceptance once we have reached a level of understanding. We begin to shift and change in this space of acceptance. Acceptance is a big part of your journey to change, and there's a lot to say about it. Its importance cannot be overemphasized.

Acceptance

Radical self-acceptance is key. Before we go further, it must be said that this doesn't mean we accept the parts of ourselves that are harmful or painful to others. When we come across these characteristics within ourselves, it can be difficult to deal with. Most of us just shut down and ignore this aspect and try to focus on more positive thoughts. But it is looking at and dealing with these parts of ourselves that bring us epic transformation. When we come across these more difficult parts, it is important to shower ourselves with love and move towards healing. Then we can integrate this part of ourselves and move towards acceptance. Self-acceptance is not deciding to accept everything about yourself and move on.

Rather it is to reflect and inspect yourself and choose to accept the parts that feel different or wonky. Acceptance means to look at your past and accept all that has happened. Even if you made mistakes or did something that wasn't aligned with your values or belief system, accept that it happened, and allow yourself to be comforted by the knowledge that you know better now. Allow yourself to deeply acknowledge the fact that you were operating from a different level of consciousness. It does more harm than good when you continuously berate yourself for not making a different choice.

Acceptance brings healing. It brings comfort and joy and allows you to move forward with the understanding that you are taking accountability for yourself. Acceptance is not easy, however. It will take work, and it is not a linear path of progression. There may be days where you feel happy and relish in the joy of accepting yourself, and other days it can feel difficult. Know that this is normal and that you can't expect yourself to move smoothly on this path. Be comforted by knowing that when things don't feel so good, your higher self tells you that you need to become aware of and integrate things. Take these moments as further healing. This mindset will help you to navigate these harder moments.

Mistakes and errors are normal. They are part of the human experience. Let yourself see that and know that it does not make you a terrible person. It does not affect your self-worth, instead of seeing your mistakes as failings and falling into a negative thought spiral. Choose empowerment. Choose differently. Choose to see that a mistake is a mistake; it has no bearing on who you are at a soul level. It does not change your essence. Forgive yourself. Accept yourself. Radically and unconditionally.

It can be difficult to accept yourself in a society with certain standards for beauty, intelligence, or behavior when you contradict all of these. And that's fine. Acceptance is still the best option. It's also fine if your personality aligns with societal norms. Accept yourself for who you are. To choose radical self-acceptance, you don't have to fit into a certain mold or look a certain way.

Different doesn't always mean authentic. Different just means different. If you know yourself deeply, no one can ever take that from you. Bask in the glory of who you are. There is, literally ,no one like you, no matter what.

Embodiment

Embodiment is a key to feeling into your authentic self and embracing the fullest expression of yourself. Embodiment means to feel present in your body at this moment. In this day and age, it can be hard to do this. We are surrounded by so many distractions that make it almost impossible to be present. Being present and being relaxed enough to just be in the moment without getting stuck in your mind is key to change and transformation. Being present is the key to your creativity and authenticity. It is in the present that you find the truth. The past has gone, and the future doesn't exist. The only time that exists is now. When we spend our lives in our heads, we are missing out on life. We miss out on the joy and exquisiteness of being here, right now.

Our brains and bodies have been conditioned over the years to concentrate on everything except ourselves. Unless you have grown up with meditative teachings or religious practice, it is difficult to bring a practice of just being with yourself into your life. Even if you have been around these teachings, they can be difficult to implement. Some ways to deal with this are reducing your distractions, which means less social media time, less Netflix, less consumption of external information. Introduce a few moments of mediation or reflection every day. One or two minutes before bed each day is enough to start. If this feels challenging at first, that's okay – that's normal.

As time goes on, you can increase the time and see how your brain quietens down. Finding silent moments in the day will become more delicious and easier to enjoy. You might even start looking forward to these moments when you notice the discrepancy between how you feel outside of this time. Most of us thrive in environments of less stimulation and relaxation. It allows us to recalibrate and get back in touch with ourselves. It is from this place of intuition and authenticity we should be living our lives.

You can create these moments of peace in your daily life. It might need some commitment, but eventually, your brain will adapt and create new neural pathways. This will gear your brain towards different thoughts and feelings. There are other ways to head towards embodiment, one of the most important being movement. This could be any type of movement. A type of movement that resonates is key here as it will allow you to connect deeply with your body. Some options are yoga, exercise, walking, and dancing. An easy embodiment exercise is to quieten your mind and slowly feel into each part of your body. Do this as often as you can, ground yourself and notice how your relationship with your body and inner self transforms.

Commitment

Change cannot happen without commitment. Change does not happen by relying on bursts of motivation. Instead, it comes when we are committed and disciplined. That does not mean we should cast aside our random bursts of energy or motivation. Often this could be our intuition nudging us in the path of our dreams. Take note of these. But don't rely on these times to get you through the path of transformation. Commit to yourself, and keep working towards whatever goal you have envisioned. The smaller, the better. This enriches your self-esteem and self-care, which makes the path easier. It creates discipline within you that is unmatched. This discipline can get you through even the darkest days. This discipline shapes warriors and creates winning mindsets.

The World

Uranus' influence of transformation within a society happens because it encourages individuals to change. Individual healing heals the collective. When you are clear, aligned, and acting from a place of authenticity, your presence in the world is that much more impactful. Your words land differently, your actions are more powerful, your energy changes every room you walk into. From this place, your desire to change the world does not come from the go. It comes from a place of integrity. It stems from understanding that we are all one - when one of us is hurting, we all hurt.

This selfless drive motivates us to see the wrongs of the world - *and make them right.* It may be easier than ever to do that in this day and age. Technological advancement has made our voices louder, and now, we can reach a wider audience. The benefit of social media and technological advancements is that we are now much more informed. We should stay as conscious and intentional as we can when it comes to the information we consume. But we are much more informed and have so much more knowledge and wisdom at our fingertips than even 50 years ago. Use this for good. Use this to advance society and the world.

Become an advocate for the injustices that touch your heart—the injustices you see around you, on the news, on social media. Don't allow yourself to become desensitized. It is easy to scroll past another article or tweet, and sometimes that's just how we cope with the hurt the world is going through. Slow down and allow yourself to empathize. If there is something in the world that you do not understand, do your due diligence. Do your research and ignore any ploys of manipulation or propaganda that may be around. It's all too easy to make a pretty intro graphic and have you believing something that isn't true.

Be an advocate for the truth and ascend the ego. You need not know everything all the time or always be right. Commit to the truth, and that will bring you closer to being an advocate for justice. If you don't know where to start, look up any organizations or charities related to a cause close to your heart. Most places will be happy to take on volunteers and are usually on the lookout for some. Volunteering will help you to make strides in society and use yourself for true action and change.

Watch your Money

In today's world, your attention is currency, as is your actual money. Place your attention in places that will help you and others. Use your money wisely. As they say, "vote with the dollar." When we choose to buy from certain corporations, we cast a vote their way, even if these corporations are causing harm somehow. Staying informed is key here, so you are aware of where you are using your money.

Another way to use your coins wisely is to give to your favorite causes and charity. You can do this easily by setting up a standing order to give monthly to support the causes close to your heart. This is an easy way to "put your money where your mouth is."

Politics

Politicians don't have the best rep, but many are genuinely interested in making change happen. Writing letters to the parliament of your local MP can have a bigger impact than you may think. It allows you to put forward your voice democratically and have the chance to voice your concerns to a member of the government. If this intimidates you a little, many organizations have a ready-made template you can use to contact your local MP. It's sometimes just a matter of entering your name and email address, and voila!

Petitions are another way to get involved in making change. They increase publicity of certain issues and get people talking. They are a way to get your voice heard and ensure that injustices are given the attention they deserve.

Talents

If you have a talent or skill, consider putting it forward to further causes close to your heart. Maybe you are good at writing or art, or you are a great public speaker. Putting your passions and talents to good use can help further a cause massively as you are acting in alignment with yourself. That which comes naturally and easily to you is often where you should be heading. The path of least resistance is often the path to your success and fulfillment.

Spark Conversation

One of the greatest ways to spark change is to begin speaking about important things with those close to you. These conversations can be difficult, especially when they challenge someone's long-held beliefs and assumptions, but they allow us to progress as a society. Knowledge is power. By educating others lovingly and kindly, we can encourage each other to learn and move forward.

Sparking important conversations has a domino effect. Where we can open up the conversation for new ways of thinking and new information, we spark within others a similar desire. Truth is catchy. All humans seek the path to perfection, which they see in the call to truth and justice. Regardless of the conditioning we all have to deal with, each of us can want more, do more, and be more. Don't be afraid to use your voice to do good. You never know what kind of impact it will have.

Prometheus, the God of Fire

Prometheus, the God of fire, is known in legend for stealing fire for the benefit of mankind. It is this spark of fire that Uranus lights within all of us. Uranus comes to seek change. It pushes us into ourselves, for that is where the change comes. That drive is similar to that of Prometheus. Will we cultivate fire within us to hand out to mankind? Will we transform ourselves so we are operating from a place of authenticity and alignment? Ready to give our gifts over to assist mankind?

Will Prometheus' fire be lit in our stomachs as we journey on the path of truth? Will cries of justice be heard from our lungs? Our voices are ours. Take back your sovereignty. Take back your power.

Conclusion

After going through the various chapters that carefully detail the role this planet plays in astrology, the significance of Uranus in astrology should be abundantly clear. The icy giant is one of the most significant planets in determining how global events are affected.

The book has been written with the needs of the budding astrologer in mind. It thoroughly covers every aspect of Uranus, from its influence in our personal lives to its effects on entire generations at a time.

A very significant part of Greek mythology, Uranus assumes similar importance with astrology. The planet stands for constant change and rebellion due to the Greek god's powers relating to the open skies. Uranus is a forward-looking planet responsible for global events due to its long time in each zodiac sign. We have explored all these correlations between the different planets, with Saturn having a head-to-head comparison with Uranus.

Uranus has been portrayed as the great awakener because of inherent traits like freedom, reform, innovation, eccentricity, upheaval, and rebellion. Uranus brings about unexpected changes, similar to how the open sky cannot be predicted or tamed. We have delved deep into Uranus' fundamental elements, such as its ruling house, the exalted and debilitated zodiac signs, and even its opponents. These basics serve as the foundation for gaining a deeper understanding of this strange planet.

The impact of Uranus on all of society has been explored, and it was seen that Uranus could influence entire generations. The interesting turn of events that took place due to the influence of Uranus, like the American and French Revolutions, have been analyzed from an astrologer's perspective. Even the current era is attributed to Uranus's traits because of its transit through Taurus. The book detailed past experiences of mankind when Uranus was passing through Aries and how this caused strife all over the world.

The interactions of Uranus with a person's natal chart were touched upon in detail; the different houses are affected differently due to Uranus. Knowing which house in your natal chart is affected can help you better understand the challenges and opportunities in your life. The book explores every house, and the positive or negative impacts of each are studied in-depth to provide you a better understanding of the interactions of Uranus with your chart.

The interactions of a planet with other planets are just as important as its interactions with zodiac signs. The book delves deeply into the implications of the positioning of Uranus in relation to the other planets. Uranus' enemies and allies should give you a general idea of how Uranus will act in different circumstances.

The natal Uranus is the most misunderstood aspect of the journey of Uranus, and we've attempted clarify it in a concise manner. After reading through these chapters, there should be no doubt left in your mind about how Uranus affects an individual and mankind as a whole.

Uranus is widely recognized for bringing about change, and the emphasis on these changes in the last chapters will assist the reader in dealing with the changes that Uranus brings. If you wish to learn everything there is to know about Uranus and improve your understanding of astrology, this book will come in handy more than you can imagine!

Thanks for reading, and best of luck in your astrological studies.

Part 4: Saturn in Astrology

The Ultimate Guide to the Planet of Karma

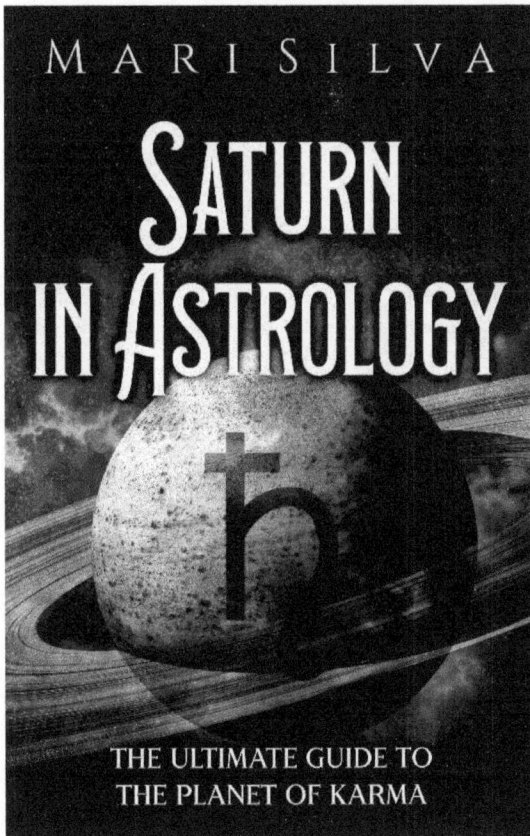

Introduction

Perhaps you are fascinated by karma, and you want to find a way to reduce its burden on you so you can live your life to the fullest. You may have even browsed the internet or books, only to be frustrated by what you found. There are so many articles by "experts" who are enthusiastic in their "take" on the subject – but these go on and on about minute details you don't care about or espouse a very narrow perspective that turns you off. Often, these experts don't even know the subject about which they are talking. Many articles are short; you have to spend hours in frustration looking through them all to find relevant information. Or perhaps you've checked out Wikipedia, only to find it heavily sanitized and all too brief, leaving you wanting more.

Not here!

We have taken care to lay out the basics in very simple but profound terms, quenching your thirst for karma and what it means to you.

Are you interested in astrology and want to know more about Saturn's importance? We can't get enough on the topic. In fact, check out the other books on astrology in our series—Venus (check out what it means for your love life!), Uranus (how to manage change and the stress in your life), Pluto (handy for transforming yourself into the person you want to be), Mercury (how to communicate and link to your loved ones), and Chiron, the "wounded healer" asteroid (how to stay in terrific physical health).

How does a ringed, faraway giant like Saturn relate to karma? The answers will fascinate you. You'll learn how its origins as a Greek God found its way into Roman legend, which in turn was borrowed by Hindu mythology, ending with Vedic astrology! Which special groups of houses does Saturn prefer? With all the zodiac signs, ruling planets, and the Twelve Houses, Vedic Astrology can seem incomprehensible to the uninitiated because of its hundreds of possible permutations. A beginner's guide will not turn you into an expert, just as a medical book like Gray's Anatomy can't make you a doctor. But we will explain the opening concepts clearly and concisely, so the knowledge you gain is valuable and applicable to your life. For fans of Western astrology, we'll discuss the similarities and differences so you can enjoy the best of both worlds. Vedic astrology is steeped in myths and folklore you will find fascinating and useful.

Dive in, and enjoy!

Chapter 1: Saturn: The Manifestation of Our Karma

Saturn is known as a Roman God as well as a plant. In fact, the second biggest planet in our solar system is named after Saturn, and he is revered in many cultures. In Greece, he was worshipped as the Greek God Cronus, and when the Romans invaded Greece, they renamed him Saturn. In Hinduism, he (both the god and the planet) is named Shani.

Did you know that Vedic mythology in Hinduism considers Saturn to be the son of the Sun? While ancient cultures each see Saturn a little differently, many interesting threads connect to make Saturn the inevitable manifestation of our karma.

In Greek mythology, Cronus was the God of Time, often shown with a sickle—but why? In all ancient civilizations, agriculture was vital for survival. The sickle symbolizes harvest, turning crops into food for hungry families. And what does agriculture represent? This fundamental industry marks the passing of seasons, which in turn reflects the passage of time.

The Sun controls the seasons. When the Sun pulled away from the crops during fall, it was time for harvest. When winter ended, and the Sun drew closer to give more warmth, it was time to plant crops. In a sense, the Sun both marked time and gave a call to action, for it was time to plant or harvest.

While the Sun sets out time, his son, Saturn—according to Vedic mythology—judges your actions in the different timeframes that determine karma. "*Karm*" is the Sanskrit word for "action" (Sanskrit is the oldest language in India and gave birth to its modern and most popular language, Hindi). There are three types of karma—sanchita, prarabdha, and agami. Sanchita means accumulated actions (the past), prarabdha means ripe or fructifying actions (the past that affects the present), and agami means future actions. All those definitions relate to time. Which planet better than Saturn to be the planet of karma?

Simply put, karma is a matter of cause and effect. Our perception of time is important in determining the consequences of our actions through cause and effect. Saturn is a very strict judge of our actions. But, if you embrace Saturn as a strict but wise teacher, you can discipline your actions to reap the maximum benefit from your choices. If you make decisions with the intent of bringing happiness and justice to yourself and others, you will be rewarded with Saturn's blessing.

Roman mythology explains that Saturn seeks power to maintain the cyclic course of time and seasons. Interestingly (and sometimes confusingly), the slow passage of time transformed Cronus into Saturn. When the Romans invaded Greece, they renamed him, giving him the Roman name Saturn. However, it is likely the Romans mixed up the Greek spelling of Cronus versus Chronos, because in Greek, "Chrono" (Χρόνος) means time. That's why "Father Time," a popular symbol or character in Western civilization, is shown with a scythe—because of the conflation of the God of Harvest (Cronus) and the God of Time (Chronos). Eventually, the scythe, an agricultural tool, came to represent time. In some fables, the Grim Reaper, a dreadful figure representing death, also carries a scythe. You would be forgiven for thinking the scythe symbolizes the end and death, and over time it has come to symbolize death, but it originally represents harvest time and the reaping of crops (life-force or the soul) to leave lands vacant for another season. In essence, it is about rebirth.

This God Saturn may have been granted his name because he was sate (satisfied) with time. Having overthrown his father, he heard a prophecy that his sons would, in turn, overthrow him. According to myth, Saturn devoured each son as he was born to prevent that prophecy from happening. Pretty gruesome to imagine, right? Let's move on to Hindu mythology, where the story of Saturn undergoes many drastic changes, as often happens when legends are transmitted from one culture to another through oral history. We already talked about Shani being the Hindu equivalent of Saturn. Shani is strongly linked to karma because he is the son of Surya (the Sun) and the shadow of Surya's wife, Saranyu. As myth explains, Saranyu often left the house because she could not bear the fire of Surya—the Sun. To make sure her presence was still felt, she left her shadow behind her. And the Sun God Surya made her shadow—named Chhaya—his mistress, and she bore his son, Shani. Because he was born of a black shadow, Shani is depicted in illustrations as very dark-skinned.

Due to this affair, Shani left his father when he came of age and harbored resentment against him. This may explain why Shani—Saturn—is a harsh teacher. He was born of bad karma, but he knows that bad karma can always be supplemented by good karma if one works hard enough to lead a good life. This background helps you understand more about Saturn's difficult start to life and why you may be apprehensive about his exacting standards, but you can also see he is fair and will reward hard work.

Just as Saturn led to the naming of Saturday in the Roman calendar, Shani led to the name of the same day in the Hindu calendar, Shanivara.

Saturn is considered the planet of democracy. Thus, leaders who earn their positions through votes tend to do well with a strong Saturn in their astrological charts. Jupiter was once a factor in leadership because it represented kings, queens, and royalty. As democracy took hold in recent eras, Saturn, in astrology, has taken on an even greater significance in world affairs. Even today, Indian astrologers unearth birth charts to predict the fortunes of national politicians and the outcomes of elections.

The Influence of Ancient Greek Astrology on Vedic Astrology

Ancient Greek astrology influenced Vedic astrology, which is probably why Roman influence made its way into designating Shani as the near-replica of the Saturn God. According to Japanese researcher Michio Yano, the first evidence of Greek astrology introduced into India was in the early centuries after 1 CE. This was discovered in the ancient Sanskrit astrology text Yavanajataka, literally "Sayings of the Greeks." It was translated from Greek to Sanskrit. It was one of the earliest works referencing Western astrology and followed other ancient Western texts.

For example, Yavanajataka contained this excerpt, which experts have identified as clearly arising from Greek astrology: The seventh place from the ascendant, the descendent, is called jamitra (diametros) in the language of the Greeks, the tenth from the ascendant, the mid-heaven, they say, is the mesurana (mesouranema). (Chapter 1/49, The Yavanajataka of Sphujidhvaja)

Subsequent works on Roman astrology arrived within the next few centuries, namely the Paulisa Siddhanta (Doctrine of Pau) and the Romaka Siddhanta (Doctrine of the Roman). One ancient Indian astrologer who praised these Western texts was Varahamihira, who learned the Greek language and praised the Greeks for being "well trained in the sciences." You could say, at its historical juncture, Vedic astrology was influenced by other cultures and not wholly developed within the Indian subcontinent.

It would be impossible to pinpoint exactly how the Cronus of Greek mythology and astrology (God of Harvest) transmuted into Saturn (also the God of Harvest) and, in turn, became personified by the Hindu God Shani (God of Karma, Justice, and Retribution). However, we can see how shared learning between ancient civilizations gave rise to this fascinating development.

Saturn: The Taskmaster

So far, we've seen how mythology created the power and aura of Saturn. Yes, Saturn can be difficult, but he can ultimately be rewarding, just as all hard life lessons seem to be. Saturn's reliance on the discipline of time requires you to make choices. Now that you're here, what do you do today? Tomorrow? To us, time can seem unlimited, yet there are consequences when we prioritize. When you take a hard look at your goals and make tough decisions, it may be painful, but the choices you make today will align well with Saturn's discerning eye. Think of it as tough love, which sets you on a better path.

The key is commitment and discipline. You need to train your brain and thought processes, just as you would train your body. And, similar to going to the gym, you may not see the fruition of your efforts at first, but this is a journey and not a change in mindset. Are you willing to set aside your daily distractions and stick to the bigger goal? That's what Saturn will demand from you. Once you have satisfied Saturn and have done the best you can, it can become a most benevolent planet. Push aside the doubts spread by those naysayers who claim Saturn is a dreaded planet in astrology. Saturn doesn't deserve that reputation. Saturn is often misunderstood, but you will find it an important part of your life's journey if you continue to explore your karma.

In Greek mythology, Sisyphus was a doomed man harshly punished by the Gods, doomed to eternally roll a huge boulder up the side of a mountain, only to see it roll back to the bottom. He repeated this futile labor day after day with no end in sight. One solution suggested by a present-day German author was for Sisyphus to break off a chunk off the mountain each time he reached the top. According to this thinking, Sisyphus would level the mountain over an eternity, and the boulder would no longer roll down. Thus, Sisyphus would prove his worth by literally "moving a mountain" to accomplish his goal. Are you willing to put in such effort to "move a mountain"?

If you have had many bad habits in your past or present, they can lead to bad karma. But there is hope! If you embrace Saturn and slowly adopt good habits, you will attain a fruitful life and benefit from positive returns. Saturn will push you to your limits and help you remember that life's lessons are not punishments but, rather, valuable gems of knowledge for you to learn and use.

How to Worship Saturn (Shani)

Many Indians seeking to balance their karma follow the underlying theoretical principles of karma and worship Shani as a deity, hoping that Shani will be appeased. Remember that Shani the God represents Saturn the planet, so when you worship Shani, you worship both the god and his planet.

One way to honor Lord Shani is to offer mustard oil and sesame seeds on a copper spoon to an idol at a place of worship dedicated to this God. (Shani loves taking baths in mustard oil). When you do this, the appropriate chant is Om Praam Preem Proum Sah Shanaischaraya Namah (Ode to Lord Shani to be in my favor and calm my senses). Another mantra for Saturn translates in English as—I bow down to slow-moving Saturn, whose complexion is dark blue like nilanjana ointment. The elder brother of Lord Yamaraj is born from the Sun god and his wife, Chhay. In Sanskrit, it is worded as *Nilañjana-samabhasam ravi-putram yamagrajam; chaya-martanda-sambhutam tam namami shaishcharam.*

Lord Shani disavows superficiality and therefore seeks cunning. Although unpopular among the general populace, this means crows have a special place in his heart because those birds are intelligent. If you feed a crow on the day of the week set aside for his worship, Saturday, you may earn some positive karma. It's been said crows are your ancestors in spirit, and they volunteer to take away your negative karma when you feed them. To end your day, you could pour mustard oil on a few leaves of Shani's favorite tree, the sacred fig, and worship this type of tree before sunrise. And wear rings with brilliant blue sapphires—which combines Shani's favorite gem and color!

Lord Hanuman once saved Shani from misfortune. Thus, Shani smiles upon any effort to honor his savior. If you devote yourself to Lord Hanuman and Lord Shani, this will help to balance your karma. Shani also approves the worship of Lord Ganesha, the elephant-headed God.

Being the Lord of Justice and Karma, Shani approves of any means of donating to the poor and disadvantaged. Donating to those in need seeking nothing in return is one way to increase your positive karma energy, which will meet his favor. He's also strict about order, which extends to the tidiness of your living quarters. Therefore, if you clean up your clutter, he will be favorably predisposed to award you relief from bad karma. This can apply to negative thoughts too, which should be purged from your mind as they cause unnecessary distraction and can lead to unhappiness. Simplicity is good—try to focus on what remains after you take out the trivial, and you'll discover what is important.

How Does Astrology Affect Our Karma?

By now, you may be asking, Saturn aside, why do the stars and planets affect our karma? That is a very good question and is answered by the cosmic law of synchronicity. The planets revolve around the sun, so do the electrons around the nucleus in the atom. The universe follows this fundamental law, setting out cosmic patterns. And so do we. When you were born, the planetary paths determined your karma (destiny). What is macrocosmic is also reflected at the microcosmic level.

However, astrology cannot see everything. It is only a guide. For example, if you get your time of birth wrong, then your predictions will be wrong, too. The best astrologer can only see the patterns, and they must be humble enough not to claim they know everything. Astrology is an art form, not a science. If you practice it repeatedly, each subsequent attempt at a deeper level, you will appreciate its nuances and its patterns and be able to benefit from it more immensely over time to bring about a happier life for yourself and those around you. The best Vedic astrologers are those who practice its principles deeply by meditating and believing in karma. The mandate is to help you achieve your spiritual path and nothing more. Also, we must respect the basic human principle of "free will." If astrologists could predict our life paths down to the minute, we are no better than automatons. The task of an astrologist is to set the goals, not the path through life, and warn us of obstacles to be overcome and opportunities to be seized.

In the book "Astrology of the Seers," the author states the planets are no more than points of light in a vast energy network. Intricately connected by unseen lines of force, the astrological planets link the entire solar system into a single, vital organism. To us, in the night sky, planets appear like small points of light. Yet, there is much we can't see. Their energy fields surge over the earth's crust, forming life everywhere and shaping destiny. The planets are like referees in a soccer match, keeping an eye on both actions on the playing field and watching the clock as the game progresses. The planets also monitor order, like referees enforce the rules of soccer.

Saturn is the last of the planets seen with the naked eye. Back when Vedic astrology started, they didn't have telescopes. Saturn takes close to thirty years to orbit the Sun and is easily distinguished from the other planets by its striking rings. That's why Saturn is one of the astrological planets in Vedic astrology, not Neptune, Uranus, or Pluto, which cannot be seen with the naked eye.

Eastern vs. Western Astrology

You know those "Daily Horoscope" features found in newspapers in Europe and the United States? Those have nothing at all to do with Vedic astrology. It should be remembered that Western astrology and Vedic astrology have very different bases, and the Vedic model is far more accurate. For example, both Vedic astrology and Western astrology, for the past 2,000 years, have monitored the ecliptic paths of the planets but diverged when Vedic astrology started accounting for the Earth's wobble in its spin on its axis; Western astrology does not incorporate this adjustment. The Earth's wobble takes 26,000 years to complete, resulting in a shift in the Earth's ecliptic plane by about one degree every 72 years. Over thousands of years, the ecliptic plane has shifted enough to render the old ecliptic plane no longer a true cosmic model. Vedic astrology did well in recognizing this gradual but fundamental shift, so its forecasts are far more accurate.

Vedic astrology uses a complex set of inputs, all measurable:

• The nine heavenly bodies: Sun, Moon, Mars, Mercury, Jupiter, Venus, Saturn, and the two nodes of the moon, Rahu and Ketu.

• Twelve signs of the zodiac.

• Twenty-seven lunar constellations, each spanning 13 degrees and 20 minutes (the nakshatras, which we will explore later).

In comparison, Western astrology is not nearly as detailed. Western astrology is focused on the Sun, which changes its sign once a month, while Vedic astrology uses the Moon, which changes its sign every 2.25 days, leading to more accuracy.

Chapter 2: Karmic Debts: The Principle of Karma

The Various Types of Karma

Many of us in Western civilization have a passing familiarity with karma. You've probably seen popular movies or shows with the spoken line, "It was karma." Other similar sayings (said in passing without the deep appreciation of the true meaning of karma) are "what goes around, comes around," "he had it coming," or "it's payback time." However, karma is a lot more complex than that.

As previously mentioned, there are three main types of karma, loosely categorized as past, present, and future: sanchita, prarabdha, and agami. Sanchita is stored karma from the past and will take effect in the future. Prarabdha is karma that arises from the actions we take today and also carries forward in the future, eventually becoming part of our sanchita as time marches on. In understanding prarabdha, we look back at the sanchita we have carried forward, whether it is good karma or bad karma. If we practice good karma today, it will deplete the bad karma that is part of our sanchita and lighten the burden each of us carries. Lastly, agami is the karma that manifests in the future. Thus, we must carefully choose our present actions to control our destiny better.

Interestingly, only sanchita karma and agami karma can be eliminated because prarabdha is our present, which yields results yet to be experienced and is hence labeled "unavoidable karma."

Esteemed spiritual leader Sri Swami Sivananda quoted, "Prarabdha is that portion of the past karma responsible for the present body. That portion of the sanchita karma that influences human life in the present incarnation is called prarabdha. It is ripe for reaping. It cannot be avoided or changed. It is only exhausted by being experienced. You pay your past debts. Prarabdha karma is that which has begun and is actually bearing fruit. It is selected out of the mass of the sanchita karma."

Western science has already formulated a physics treatise that recognizes the essence of karma but as mass and energy. For example, Sir Isaac Newton postulated there is an opposite and equal reaction for every action. Push against a wall, and the wall pushes back with an equal force so it does not collapse. In Hinduism, karma is the law that states every mental, physical, and emotional act is projected out into the Divine and eventually returns to the individual with equal impact. Similarly, physics stands on the first law of thermodynamics: Energy can be changed from one form to another, but it cannot be created or destroyed. The total amount of energy and matter in the Universe remains constant, merely changing from one form to another. This sounds very much like karma, suggesting that different civilizations abide by the same truths, just that they are expressed differently.

How Karmic Debt Arises

Karma outlives the body. Your karma is not the sum of everything you've done in your life but also in previous lives. When one dies, the physical body may no longer exist, but karma continues. Karma cannot be freed until all the karmic debt is discharged. Hence it is important to make choices that positively empower you and others. Karmic debt consists of unresolved issues in your life you carry forward because they must be dealt with. Otherwise, you cannot transcend into the afterlife.

Karmic debt can arise due to interactions between you and your loved ones. This is called runanubandha. "Runa" means debt arising from karma, and "anubandha" means relationship. In a relationship, whether it be with a friend, child, parent, co-worker, or lover, there is a karmic debt between the two of you. The ideal is to have each loved one reciprocate until the karmic debt is balanced. One good deed deserves another. Similarly, bad deeds should be rectified as soon as possible, or if it's impossible to remedy them directly, compensate the karmic debt by doing another deed with a benefit to the other person. For example, a boy who steals and eats his mother's freshly baked cookies could do hours of work in her vegetable garden, restoring the balance of karma.

Another common example is between a mother and daughter. When the daughter is born, the mother cares and nurtures the girl, ensuring she receives all the necessities of life plus all the motherly love that can be given. When the daughter reaches adulthood and the mother ages and cannot function as she once did, the adult daughter will reverse roles and care for the mother.

Examples are not limited to family only and can encompass any relationship.

Living through the Divine

One way to deal with all three karmas (sanchita, prarabdha, and agami) is to offer yourself freely to the Divine, the Supreme Universal Consciousness. Once you clear your karmic debt, you are situated to transcend this seemingly never-ending cycle of karma. As we've explained, you cannot choose to avoid present karma (prarabdha) since it's transitory. All you can do for this type of karma is to control your reactions and your consequences.

As for past karma, sanchita, it is very rare that one eliminates all the baggage from the past, usually carried forward from another incarnation of the soul. However, by undertaking deep Yogic practices, it is possible to exhaust it fully by setting aside your mind and doing the deed in the name of the Divine. This way, you are not the perpetrator of your actions, but instead, you are offering yourself up for the Supreme Universal Consciousness. This deep cleansing also removes future karma (agami) since you personally do not acquire that karma. Instead, you are acting as an instrument for a higher power to do positive good.

If you have not exhausted all your karmic debt, you will be reincarnated in another body. However, if you cleanse all your karmic debt, you have attained moksha (also called liberation). There are two schools of thought about what moksha means, but essentially in either scenario, you have attained unity with the Divine, and you are freed from the cycle of death and rebirth. One outcome is like you are a drop of water that has joined the ocean (the Supreme Universal Consciousness), and you become one. The other outcome is similar to you becoming a beautiful, green-colored parrot that lands in a dazzling green tree and blends in so you are no longer seen distinctly. However, you retain your own identity in servitude to the Divine.

Destiny vs. Free Will

We've already pointed out that while we can't do much to manage present karma (prarabdha), we definitely have a lot of leeway to make choices that affect our lives. One school of thought is that our free will determines our destiny. Our destiny is the sum of choices chosen to lessen our karma and achieve happiness.

Vedic astrology recognizes and validates life's four aims: dharma, artha, kama, and moksha. Moksha, as we've already explored above, is the end result of life. What then are the other three? Moksha is the anchor for the first three goals. Without moksha, there is no justification and no framework for dharma, artha, and kama, which all must lead to liberation, the essential accomplishment for humans.

The first aim, dharma, relates to our moral compass. When living your life, you must strive to be ethical and to accomplish achievements, so it respects your peers. For example, if you rob a bank and steal money, that certainly accomplishes the goal of having a fortune, but the underhanded way you go about this will undoubtedly lead to bad karma. Instead, let's say you founded a company, employed several people, and sold enough products or services to earn a fortune. This is good karma—passed on to many others through gainful employment, tax revenue to the government to pay for social services, pride in results, and model corporate citizenship. In short, dharma brings meaning and honor to a person's life.

The second, artha, is about achievement, mainly in wealth and income that not only maintains your standard of living, but also allows you to give to others, such as gifts to loved ones to make them happy, or to charity to help people in need. This ability to earn money spreads good karma because money is a reward for hard work and wise choices. Moreover, money is a way of spreading good fortune (and karma) without you having to be present everywhere. For example, a generous donation toward cancer research could lead to lives saved, even if you were not the one making the discoveries.

Kama, the third goal, is more intangible but no less important. It relates to desire, to the need for happiness and love. It is a well-known saying that "love makes the world go round." If you please people, the chances are favorable that those happy people will meet others in a good mood and spread positivity—enhancing your karma.

It is interesting how those three balance each other out to arrive at the final congruence—moksha. This framework recognizes that all three initial factors are important. What good is money if one is not happy? What good are money and pleasure if those are taken from others through immoral means, causing sadness in the world? Although Bill Gates is probably not a practicing follower of Vedic astrology, his post-retirement goals are equally laudable—he has devoted billions of dollars to improving lives worldwide.

The Five Debts of Dharma

A Hindu worshipper is taught that every person is born with five spiritual debts. The three main debts are to sages, Gods, and ancestors. An ancient Hindu scripture added two more, making a total of five: debts to humanity and nature. Let's go through them in turn because not repaying those debts will increase karma. At the same time, those spiritual debts should not be dreaded but welcomed as appreciation for being born into the richness of our civilization and as a way to thank our ancestors for the world they have built for us.

Sages are the wise people who have advanced our civilization through their research and discoveries. In historic times, those sages were spiritual leaders and gurus. However, you are permitted to celebrate the incredible advancements made by scientists and leaders of peace, whatever their beliefs or background. To repay this debt, you are encouraged to study their body of knowledge and familiarize yourself with their teachings so you can carry on the progress and spread knowledge among your peers.

Hindu deities are of vital importance to us, for they sustain our existence from birth to death through the air we breathe, the food we eat, and the water that nourishes us. We are indebted to them for the sustenance they give us and the belief that makes life rich and fulfilling. To show our gratitude, regular prayer and understanding of sacred Hindu texts are a must.

It goes without saying that our ancestors are the past generations of our family who made us who we are. Our ancestors have struggled, worked, and cared for one another, enabling our family line to survive and thrive. We owe them a great deal. We can acknowledge them every day by continuing their traditions and, in the long term, by procreating to continue the family lineage. We must instill in our children the positive values and principles of our family and inspire them to greatness and humility.

In a broad sense, humanity can be acknowledged by treating people with respect, not just our family. We can donate money or volunteer for a charity to help the less fortunate. If we have talents to contribute, we can enrich civilization through the arts, the sciences, and philosophy. If we leave a better world than the one we found, we have done our job.

Nature is sacrosanct and must be respected. The Earth has nourished us with its riches, and we must co-exist with our environment and ecology, whether it be terrain, water reservoirs, plants, or animals.

If we positively honor the five debts, we can incorporate this positive way of thinking into our everyday lives, so much so that benefiting others becomes natural and an effective means of reducing karmic debt.

In the zodiac chart, Capricorn (the 10th house in the base Vedic chart) rules karma, which makes sense, as Saturn is the Lord of Capricorn. Later on, we'll discover that in terms of astrological houses, the 10th house is the house of business relationships and hard work, and hence is the house of karma.

How Does Vedic Astrology Help Me with My Karma?

In Vedic astrology, your birth chart is determined by the exact position of planets, viewed from your birthplace at the time of your birth, which is why it is essential to know the exact time at which you were born. As we will explore later, your birth chart is found by using a sidereal (fixed star) system, which converges 23 degrees from the western tropical (fixed season) system. Also, we consider dashas (planetary periods) that analyze events and attempt to decipher and predict the beneficial and problematic periods of life. The Vedic system breaks down those dashas further into lunar periods, called nakshatras. When you discover the nakshatra that bears your rising sign (the zodiac sign over the horizon just as you are born), this helps map out the grand scheme the stars have to tell us, broken down into smaller periods that are more convenient to manage.

When you see your Vedic birth chart (also called a natal chart), you will see the various locations and combinations of planets that convey a sense of the collective karma from previous incarnations in many aspects of life. This birth chart breaks down life's stages and experiences into twelve "houses," which are concepts that pay particular attention to certain life goals, responsibilities, and potential obstacles such as marriage, children, career, charity, personal health, education, and even wealth. From birth to death, just about everything in life is accounted for in this chart.

If bad karma is found, let's say in your career, in your birth chart, and you find it is consistent from house to house within the chart, you may face the undesired outcome that this karma will follow you throughout your life. However, not all is lost. Even if such bad karma is persistent (for example, being born with a birth defect such as a learning disability), it is possible to manage your abilities and network to remove obstacles that face you. Or you could focus on other means of enjoying a high quality of life, for example, choosing a lucrative career that does not require skills or abilities that your birth chart warns you are lacking. It can be sometimes daunting to gaze at your birth chart, seeing such a depressing pattern, and wondering how you can overcome karma that has befallen you from before birth.

If bad karma occurs in some patterns in the birth chart and not in others that are relevant, then this karma may not be so profound. This may be unfinished business from a previous life (incarnation), and it falls to you to deal with a burden that someone else in the past had to deal with but could not. People who have gone on to become world leaders or entrepreneurs have successfully overcome past karma to create their own positive accomplishments. For example, Albert Einstein; he overcame the inability to speak until he was five years old, and he performed poorly in math at school. When we take on bad karma, we learn for ourselves about what may have happened in the past so we can fix it.

Vedic astrology predicts, among broad guidelines, the timing of important life events such as choosing higher education, getting married, or embarking on a new career or entrepreneurial business. At any moment of your life, you are going through a planetary period that will persist for several years (as we will explore below), along with sub-periods coordinated with other planets working in tandem. For example, if you are going through a Saturn period, it will persist for a long but important period of your life. If Saturn is a good planet for you and does well in your birth chart, then you will reap the benefits of a beneficial Saturn and do well. However, if Saturn is not a good planet for you and doesn't do well in your birth chart, you may struggle throughout this period. You may attempt to invent wisely and use fundamental approaches to work with this bad karma, like delaying marriage and putting your career first so, when you finish your work goals and make more money, you are better situated to attract a suitable partner.

If this feels like despair, you may ask yourself, what is the point of knowing all this? Why put up with this bad news? But we must heed the Boy Scouts motto, "Be prepared." Using your ingenuity, bad karma can be overcome by knowing the stakes and working with your birth chart to find your strengths or choosing not to engage in battle with the unknown. You can leave the battlefield for greener pastures, prosper elsewhere, and return to the battle when you have far greater strength. Aided by Vedic astrology, you can anticipate the difficult years ahead, and you can marshal your dedication and hope into overcoming your bad karma.

Chapter 3: Saturn: An Astrological Profile

Astronomy 101: An Intro to Astrology Terms

Great, you've made it this far! Before we reveal all the fascinating astrological secrets of Saturn, let's go over some terms that may bewilder the layman but are extensively used in astrology, especially Vedic astrology. Fear not. Once you master them, it becomes a lot easier to understand horoscopes.

One such revelation is if a planet is *malefic* or *benefic*. Think of malefic as malevolent and benefic as benevolent. Word association, right? Unfortunately, Saturn is considered malefic, which may explain the general impression given in an earlier chapter about its "difficult" nature. A malefic planet is thought to bring bad luck and misfortune to those born within its radius. However, as explained earlier, this is just a perception that can be overcome. We need to appreciate Saturn's wisdom and stern guidance to bring about some much-needed direction in our lives.

Of the planets, Mars and Saturn are thought to be the malefic planets, with Saturn bearing the worst reputation. Meanwhile, Jupiter and Venus are said to be benefic planets, bringing good fortune.

Saturn the Planet: A Basic Astronomy

The second-largest planet in our solar system (only Jupiter is bigger), Saturn is sixth from the Sun, after Mercury, Venus, Earth, Mars, and Jupiter. (By the way, Jupiter is so big that all the other planets in our solar system could fit onto it). In turn, Saturn can fit 760 Earths. Saturn is the second most *massive* planet in our solar system - it is 95 times Earth's mass. While Jupiter, Neptune, and Uranus also have rings, Saturn's stand out the most.

As of the time of discovery by the Cassini spacecraft, eighty-two known moons surround Saturn, and they are very diverse. For example, one important moon, Titan, is the only other place in our solar system to have clouds, an atmosphere, and liquid lakes. Titan also has possible volcanic and tectonic activity. On this moon, water sculpts the topography, raining from clouds into methane lakes and seas, which then evaporate back into the sky. One other moon, Enceladus, has a surface that is almost pure ice. Through geysers, Enceladus shoots sprays of water and icy particles into its atmosphere. Imagine visiting there in a spacecraft.

Our ancient ancestors have long known of Saturn, the farthest planet from Earth that can be seen by the naked eye.

Saturn has an average radius of 36,183 miles (58,232 kilometers) and is nine times wider than Earth. To compare, if Earth were the size of a Ping-Pong ball, Saturn would be about as big as a volleyball. People may be surprised to learn that Saturn is like a flattened ball because of its very fast rotation, squished at the poles, and bulging at the equator. Actually, the distance from its center (the core within the planet) to its equator is over 10% longer than the distance from its center to the South or North Poles.

Saturn's distance from the Sun (no planetary orbit around the Sun is a perfect circle) averages around 886 million miles (1.4 billion kilometers). Light from the Sun takes about 80 minutes to reach Saturn (compare that to eight minutes and 20 seconds for sunlight to reach the Earth).

Interestingly, for a planet that big, Saturn can certainly spin fast. It has the second-shortest day in the solar system—only Jupiter is faster but only by several minutes. One day on Saturn takes only 10.7 hours, while Jupiter takes almost exactly ten hours. Saturn revolves around the Sun (a year in Saturn's time) in about 29.4 Earth years (10,756 Earth days). Imagine living for a year on Saturn—you would only live about three Saturn years at the most.

Saturn's axis tilts by 26.7 degrees with respect to its orbit around the Sun. By comparison, Earth tilts by 23.5 degrees. Saturn goes through seasons, just like Earth does.

Saturn's outer surface is mostly hydrogen. However, it has a dense core of iron-nickel. Saturn is enveloped by liquid hydrogen on its outer layer, which gradually turns into metallic hydrogen the deeper it goes into the core. Jupiter has a similar core, but Saturn's is considerably smaller. Overall, this planet is so light that its average density is 30% less than that of water. You could not stand on Saturn's surface—you would not only sink through but also be crushed by the immense pressure.

Adding to its allure in the night sky, several bands of yellow and gold crisscross Saturn's surface. Those consist of jet streams and clouds swirling across its surface at extraordinary speeds of 1,800 kilometers per hour (1,100 miles per hour).

Saturn has a weather feature not found anywhere else in our solar system. A six-sided jet stream hovers over its north pole, a phenomenon that scientists think is a standing wave pattern. While the Voyager I deep space probe first detected this strange hexagonal-shaped pattern, the more recent Cassini deep space probe confirmed this discovery. Saturn is so large that the sides of the hexagon are at least 10,800 kilometers across (8,600 miles), which is wider than the Earth's diameter.

Now for the question on everyone's minds when we think of Saturn. Where did the rings come from? Thanks to new information passed along from the recent Saturn probe, Cassini, scientists now think the rings formed less than 100 million years ago—which would put them on par in galactic history with that of the Earth's dinosaurs. Therefore, the rings are much, much younger than Saturn. The rings probably appeared because several of Saturn's moons collided while in orbit or were torn apart by Saturn's immense gravity. The debris inside the rings could also have come from comets that were smashed up. All taken together, the mass of the rings is much smaller than that of the Earth's moon.

While we tend to think of the universe as unchanging, the fact remains that Saturn's rings could be changing temporarily. In a few million years, Saturn's rings could completely disappear. Another interesting observation is that the tilts of Saturn and Earth are different. When Saturn and Earth take their respective orbits around the Sun, Saturn's rings will sometimes appear perpendicular to us, so they look like they have "disappeared"—like looking at a vinyl record from the edge. Many people do not know that each ring orbits around the planet at a different speed.

Saturn's rings are labeled alphabetically, from A to G, but that's not in the order as seen when we look at the planet. Rather, the rings were labeled based upon the timing of discovery, so actually, the E ring is the farthest out, and the D ring is the closest to Saturn. A, B, and C were the first rings to be discovered, then the rest were observed. A wide gap separates the A and B rings, called the Cassini Division. One of Saturn's moons, Enceladus, supplies much of the ice particles that form the E ring. But the rings are quite thin.

Saturn hosts a bewildering array of incredible micro-worlds in its orbit. We've already discussed Titan and Enceladus, but there's also Phoebe with its crater-marked surface, just like Earth's moon, but Phoebe has an irregular shape like it was a fragment of a planet. Phoebe's average radius is only about 66.2 miles (106.5 kilometers). So far, scientists have confirmed Saturn has 53 moons, but 29 additional provisional moons await official sanction.

Clearing up the Confusion: The Sun Sign, The Moon Sign, and the Rising Sign

The Sun Sign

The Sun sign is what people mostly talk about, as it's the time of year you were born. If you gaze up in the sky at an angle away from the Sun (to protect your eyes), there will be a constellation you can't see, a zodiac is behind it. So if you are facing the sun and, for example, Cancer is behind it, the Sun sign at the time of your observation will be Cancer. The Sun transits across a zodiac sign every thirty to thirty-one days, which we know as one month.

The Moon Sign

What many non-astrologers do not realize is there is also a Moon sign. Just as the Earth orbits the Sun, the Moon also orbits the Earth (and unlike the Sun, the Moon is safe to look directly at). When the Moon transits a zodiac, it is called the Moon sign. Daily horoscopes in the Western world, the kind popular in newspapers and on horoscope websites, typically speak of the Sun sign. However, as we all know, the Moon orbits a lot faster around the Earth than the Earth does around the Sun. It also orbits a lot faster than the other astrological planets orbit around the Sun. The Sun sign shifts every thirty days. The Moon shifts its zodiac sign about every 2.5 days! It makes sense: if the Moon orbits the Earth every thirty days, it revolves through the twelve zodiac signs in our constellations as seen from Earth. The math says 30 days divided by 12 zodiacs is 2.5 days per zodiac. Thus, the Moon sign is in a happy place between the Sun sign and the rising sign. It is much more accurate than the Sun sign (from thirty days per zodiac to only 2.5 days per zodiac), but not as exacting as the rising sign (which transits the eastern horizon only every two hours). Not everyone (especially us in the Western world) knows their exact time of birth, which can make it hard to know our rising sign.

Two people with the same Sun sign can have very different Moon signs, especially people who weren't born at the beginning or end of the Sun's zodiac cycles. Somebody born on March 3 will have a different Moon sign than a person born on March 7.

What Is the Difference Between a Sun Sign and Moon Sign?

The Sun represents ego and your soul, while the Moon represents your perception, reasoning, and emotions and conveys how you react to events. Most Vedic astrologers believe the Moon sign is more important than the Sun sign, which is one very significant difference from Western astrology.

The Rising Sign

The rising sign, which we will explain very shortly, also called the ascendant, can only be extracted from a specific time and place. To Vedic astrologers, it brings about the aspect of individuality by noting the place, date, and hour of birth. It also brings out aspects of childhood. As I'll note in a later chapter, the rising sign is the one ascending upon the eastern horizon when you were born and only lasts two hours at a time from one zodiac to the next.

The Moon sign is considered the most important of the three, and the Sun sign is the second most essential; the rising sign comes third. However, Vedic astrologers like to use it because of how an individual relates themself to their world, which is often explored in the rising sign, even giving some ability to see past any layer of insecurity that person may choose to guard.

Basic Astrological Properties of Saturn

Saturn takes about two-and-a-half years to cross a zodiac sign.

Saturn's astrological symbol is shown below. If you stare at it long enough, you might just make out its scythe symbol, representing its initial connection to Cronus, the God of Harvest.

What then is the zodiac? It's the view of the night sky, divided into twelve 30° zodiac sections (recall a full circle is 360°, so 360° ÷ twelve zodiacs = 30°).

I mentioned that Saturn takes two-and-a-half years to cross a zodiac sign. Imagine Saturn, so far away on a circle very big, outside this chart, and taking its slow time to pass by one zodiac at a time. That's why it can take two-and-a-half years to pass by one zodiac, a 30° arc. Now, to make a complete revolution, to return to the same zodiac sign, this planet would need to orbit the Sun past twelve zodiacs, so let's multiply the average per zodiac, 2.5 years, by 12 zodiacs. The answer is thirty years, which is how long you have to wait for Saturn to re-connect to your zodiac. This is why we all have to be patient.

Everyone is familiar with the zodiac signs, such as Cancer, Pisces, Taurus, etc. Astrology states that certain planets rule different zodiac signs. While all planets pass through every zodiac as they complete their revolution around the Sun, it's said that due to this matching, the planet's influence is "strongest" when it orbits through its zodiac pair. For Saturn, its zodiac signs are Capricorn and Aquarius. So, when Saturn aligns (for two-and-a-half years at a time every thirty years) with either Capricorn or Aquarius, watch out! Pay heed to Saturn, for its powers will be most strongly experienced, and plan your decisions to fit within Saturn's signals. It signifies a new cycle in your life, and be prepared. In addition, if you are a Capricorn or Aquarius, then this is the purest moment you can face, provided that no other destabilizing astrological events exist.

Another term given to each zodiac sign is "house," used to represent the feel of comfort of fitting in with something that is yours. Since there are twelve zodiac signs, there are twelve houses. However, each house is identified by its ranking, i.e., the first to twelfth house, allocated among the zodiac signs in the same order as found along the zodiac. It starts with Aries, the first house, and ends with Pisces, the twelfth house, following the zodiac counter-clockwise (and following the calendar in sync).

Since Capricorn has been designated as the tenth house, and Aquarius the eleventh house, you would say Saturn rules the tenth and eleventh houses.

Is each house different? For sure! The 10th house represents your reputation and professional life, so it is important for ambitious people. In contrast, the 11th house signifies community, a banding together of selfless interests, like charity, to help others.

The Earth's Morning Sun: What It Means to Astrology

The term ascendant is important in Vedic astrology, but what does it mean? When you're referring to a specific event, like the day you were born, it had to happen at a specific time (hour and minute), and astrology will tie that into the zodiac sign at the time of the morning sun. That's why Vedic astrologers ask for your time of birth, something we're not used to thinking of in Western civilization. And if you don't know your birth time, and can't get it from your parents or other close relatives, then a skilled astrologer will do their best to remedy your need.

As the Earth revolves, you can imagine being on any point of the Earth and visualizing an imaginary line from yourself across to the horizon just as the Sun rises. At the moment you see this horizon (the eastern horizon, since the Sun rises in the East), you can imagine seeing far, far ahead in the sky to the zodiac that surely lies ahead by millions and millions of kilometers in space. If it's daytime, you, of course, won't be able to see the stars. Since there are twelve zodiacs and twenty-four hours in a day, the eastern horizon will align with each zodiac for two hours at a time. That's why it's called a rising sign, or ascendant, because if it were possible to see the zodiac with your eyes at sunrise, this zodiac would look like it's rising up in the sky.

For Saturn, if its zodiac sign (Capricorn or Aquarius) was ascendant at the time in the place where you were born, that means Saturn is your planet.

More Tips: Exalted and Debilitated

Hang in there. I am about to load you up with more information. Each planet in Vedic astrology is said to be exalted at one period of the year, which is a specific marker of the path of the zodiac. Origins as to why and how those exaltations arose are obscure, but the importance to Vedic astrology persists and is still revered. For Saturn, the assigned position of being exalted is the 21st degree of Libra (remember, each zodiac sign possesses exactly 30 degrees and no more). Since the next zodiac sign after Libra is Scorpio, Saturn would be nearing the end of the Libra zodiac and nearing the Scorpio zodiac. In the same manner, Saturn is debilitated at the 21st degree of Aries.

It is useful to look at the chart below to see the periods of exaltation and debilitation as total opposites. You'll see that the exaltation (21° Libra) and fall (21° Aries) are polar opposites! (Saturn is marked by symbol ♄).

So what does this mean for you? Followers of astrology argue that a planet is stronger in its own exaltation than it is in its own paired zodiac sign. Therefore, Saturn is at its strongest when it is in the 21st degree of Libra.

Is Saturn Friendly or Hostile?

According to Vedic astrology, planets are friendly, neutral, or hostile to one another. Saturn is friendly with the two planets closest to the Sun, Mercury, and Venus. It is neutral toward its similarly large neighbor, Jupiter, and hostile toward the Sun, the Moon, and Mars.

Again, Hindu mythology creates those relationships, so enjoy the rich folklore. But some reasoning applies. We've already heard about the estranged relationship between Surya and Shani, respectively, the Sun God and the God of Saturn. Thus, it's natural that Saturn is hostile to the Sun.

The Moon represents the mother in Hinduism, so perhaps Saturn is also feeling estranged from a celestial object that represents motherhood (being born of a mistress). That's why Saturn's signs and the Moon's signs are opposite on the zodiac chart.

Mars is hot and fast as it orbits around the Sun, compared to Saturn, which is cold and slow. Thus, those planets being very much opposites, perhaps it's inevitable they would be hostile to one another.

This conflict (or co-operation) between planets is important when orbiting around the Sun and pass through the twelve zodiacs. When one planet passes through a zodiac, when Saturn passes through the Leo zodiac, for example, it will be marked with Leo inside the house assigned to Leo, the 5th house, by the natal chart (astrological chart). Now suppose at the same time Saturn and Mars are closely aligned in their orbits, within a few degrees of each other as seen from Earth, they will both be marked in the same house. If Mars is also passing through the Leo zodiac at the same time as Saturn, it will be placed beside Saturn in the 5th house. And when that happens—it is said to be planetary conflict. Who would win more influence out of Leo, Saturn, or Mars? Since Saturn is hostile to Mars, both will be debilitated by the "war," and Leo will have to be careful to avoid bad luck.

All the Astrological Details on Saturn

In Vedic astrology, the planets are personalized as much as possible—each has a favorite color or cherished metal. Again, this detail has been passed down from eons ago with no information as to how those results were derived.

Saturn's assigned color is blue. Its metal is iron, and its precious stone is blue sapphire (naturally, due to its chosen color).

In accordance with Vastu Shastra's overlap with Vedic astrology, Saturn is granted dominance in the western direction. Vastu Shastra is the ancient Indian theory of architecture that gives spiritual energy to the cardinal directions, i.e., north, south, east, and west.

Of the five Vedic elements, fire, earth, air, water, and space, Saturn rules the element of air (or wind). Interestingly, Saturn's two zodiac signs also abide by the elements. Capricorn's sign is earth. Thus, his main concern is success. As for Aquarius, his airy sign signifies his desire to uplift humanity.

As mentioned in an earlier chapter, Saturn's day of the week is Saturday. Of all the parts of the body, Saturn is most closely identified with teeth, bones, and joints.

Chapter 4: How Does Saturn Work?

Saturn's Place in Vedic Astrology

In event-oriented Vedic astrology, Saturn is the most dreaded. It is the most malevolent and, unless other offsetting factors are present, harms the house it occupies or aspects, and spoils any planet it conjoins or aspects. With Saturn as an unforgiving planet, it uses a rather direct, fateful approach—"karmic," in keeping with its reputation as a planet of karma. However, a follower may use some offsetting advantages in their arsenal to compensate, a house happy to welcome a malefic planet—for example, the upachaya ("growth") 3rd, 6th, 10th, and 11th houses. Although Saturn's nature is to be a little cold, distant, and disapproving, as one of the two outer planets in Vedic astrology, it can effect fundamental, meaningful change that the worshipper will remember as a life-altering event.

Saturn is masculine. It is cold, dry, and earthy. By popular myth, Saturn is an elderly planet. When placed to influence a follower in a significant way in a house, the follower may look older than his peers. For example, when Saturn aspects the 7th house, the house of marriage, some say that you will be well paired with a spouse older than you to better help you handle life's challenges in a harmonious marriage. Saturn in the 7th house is terrible for married life, but when you become aware through understanding the challenges of your astrological chart, you can handle Saturn's challenge, and your marriage will be even stronger.

However, not all is lost. If aspected positively and well-placed, Saturn will confer on his follower's wisdom, truth, and a sense of self-discipline and accomplishment. If you are spiritual and do not seek materialistic pleasures, and you seek hard work for its own sake, Saturn will approve and install a sense of dignity, humility, and inner peace that will serve you well. Another excellent lesson from Saturn is its tendency to bestow leadership ability, as we'll see later on from the Vedic birth charts of famous and wealthy leaders. Such devoted seekers almost always have Saturn aspecting the Sun, Moon, planet present in the ascendant, or another planet that rules the zodiac sign present in the ascendant. Indeed, in ancient Vedic scriptures, Saturn is said sometimes to make a person leader of his village. This may be because of the life journey chosen to earn wisdom, enjoying the experience day to day rather than experience artificially set out goals or arrogant assumptions.

Another important benefit attributed to Saturn is longevity. A powerful and well-placed Saturn indicates a long life, although one must look closely at the 8th house, which also rules longevity. In ancient Vedic texts, the term "ayush karaka" denotes longevity, and scholars have determined this claim had Saturn in mind.

Saturn receives digbala, or directional strength, in the 7th house. Marriage is a very important event for everyone who wants a family or to celebrate a loving relationship, and marriage is centered in the 7th house. Thanks to digbala, Saturn acquires power, strengthening all its other associations with the planets and zodiacs. While a malefic planet like Saturn in its digbala position can cause great destruction to the house it occupies, moderating counter-effects from beneficial planets and approving houses can offset this to some degree. The benefit of Saturn's power in the digbala scheme is that it makes the houses it rules, Capricorn and Aquarius, very strong, converting negatives into positives. Activities involving construction or real estate are enhanced, as are the technical occupations like engineering, computer science, and mathematics, as we'll soon see when examining accomplished leaders later on. When considering Saturn's transits through the zodiac, this planet functions best in Libra, where it is exalted, and the worst in Aries, its fallen sign.

Why does Saturn get assigned the 7th house to be strong? Vedic mythology states that since the 7th house represents sunset, Saturn finds his strength at the time of day's end (seeking to escape his estranged father, the Sun, according to ancient folklore).

Though it is not written in most textbooks, Vedic astrologers like to remind everyone that Saturn may not be as bad as commonly feared. When exalted or present in its own zodiac signs (Libra, Capricorn, or Aquarius), Saturn rarely produces the extreme benefit as other exalted or afflicted planets. Occasionally, an exalted Saturn can give tremendous gain, but more often than not, its malefic tendency reduces the immense positivity and benefit that one would ordinarily expect from a well-disposed Saturn.

The Cycles of Life

The Earth revolves around the Sun every 365 days (roughly). The seasons pass through the same cycle year after year: summer, autumn, winter, and spring. The world's oceans have the same major currents that go into cycles, carrying warm water before heading to colder depths and returning to warm depths to start the cycle anew. Astrology, too, follows certain cycles just like the ones above.

One important cycle in Vedic astrology is the mahadasha (main dasha). It starts at a different point for each person, but the order and the lengths of "seasons" (the matadashas) are the same. The life as defined by the entire baseline is called the vimshottari dasha (vim = 20, shottari = 100, add them together to get 120). Conceptually, this is every person's entire life. Since it must have a fixed number of years, it has been set at 120 years—an age very few people attain. Within these 120 years, each planet (as defined in Vedic astrology, including the Sun and the Moon, and two imaginary planets, Rahu and Ketu) rule with its own mahadasha, giving way to the next planet in the exact same order.

Here is a table showing the lengths of each mahadasha in terms of years and the order. The table showing Ketu to start off the vimshottari dasha, 120 years, is entirely arbitrary and is just an example. Instead, it could be Mars or Jupiter that starts the vimshottari dasha, or any planet. As you can see, there are 9 "planets."

Planet	Years
Ketu	7
Venus	20
Sun	6
Moon	10
Mars	7
Rahu	18
Jupiter	16

Saturn	19	
Mercury	17	
Total	120 years	

As you can see from this table, Saturn has one of the longer mahadasha at 19 years, second to Venus, which dominates for 20 years. Thus, no matter where Saturn's mahadasha starts in a person's life unless it's after the age of the current average life expectancy, this planet is bound to have a major impact on everyone. At a reign of 19 years, Saturn is automatically a governor for 19 years out of 120, or 15.8% of this theoretical lifespan. And if a person lived instead for 80 years, and if they had completed all of those 19 years in Saturn's cycle, Saturn would have dominated 23.8% of their experiences—nearly one-quarter!

Dividing Up Each Mahadasha—the Antardasha

Like a foot is divided into twelve inches, and each inch is further subdivided into eighths of an inch, so is each planet's mahadasha. Each mahadasha is further subdivided into "mini-mahadashas," repeating the cycle in the table, except on a much smaller scale. (The smaller, faster wheel within the wheel of time!) This "mini-mahadasha" is called an antardasha (also called an inner dasha). For example, when it's Saturn's turn to dominate for 19 years, all those planets (including Saturn helping itself!) would take their turns as "understudy" to Saturn on a pro-rated basis.

And how long is each antardasha? It's calculated with a simple mathematical premise: you take the mahadasha of the planet currently ruling, divide it by its proportion of 120 years, and that becomes the proportion you apply to get the antardasha. Suppose it's Saturn, which will rule for 19 years. Suppose the current antardasha period you're in is the Moon, which has its usual mahadasha period of 10 years. So the calculation for weighing Moon's antardasha is Moon mahadasha ÷ 120 years = 8.3%.

Then you go to the mahadasha you're in (as mentioned, we took the Saturn example), which is 19 years that now becomes the base. You apply the Moon's weighing proportion of 8.3% and apply to 19 years and get 1.58 years - one year and seven months. Thus when you're in the Saturn mahadasha Moon antardasha (which is how astrologers specify the periods), your current antardasha would be one year and seven months as both Saturn and the Moon work together to influence your life's issues.

How Do You Know Which Stage You're In?

The 120-year cycle, the vimshottari dasha, starts differently for every person. The start at a certain spot in its timeline is determined by the Moon's position in your birth chart. The Moon will be orbiting the Earth to a certain degree in its nakshatra. You use your astrological birth chart (called a natal chart), and you discover the degree of the nakshatra

They share the same chart as the zodiac signs, and you'll recall from earlier chapters that the planets and their assigned "houses" also form part of the zodiac chart. Most charts show 27 nakshatras. Since a circle is 360°, you divide as follows, 360° ÷ 27, to get 13 1/3 ° per nakshatra. Each nakshatra has its own name, too many to list here, but you can read them inside the chart.

Remember the nine planets in the vimshottari? The chart tells you which planet is associated with each nakshatra, and then you can find the paired mahadasha. Furthermore, the number of degrees left to go on the nakshatra (lots of mathematics here) will tell you the number of years left to go for that planet's mahadasha (Remember, the direction to trace the nakshatras, ruling planets, and zodiac signs are always counter-clockwise).

Once you've determined your mahadasha, figuring out the sequence of the antardashas is simple. The same planet that rules the mahadasha will also start the antardasha. Then the rest of the sequence will follow in the same order as the table above (remember to "wrap around" when you reach the bottom of the list, so you start at the top of the list after it's exhausted). For example, suppose your mahadasha is Saturn. When you start the Saturn mahadasha, you automatically start the Saturn antardasha as well (which is why astrologer followers experience a sudden intensity when a brand new mahadasha starts since it's double the energy).

As seen in any chart, Saturn rules the Pushpa, Anuradha, and Uttarbhadrapada Nakshatras. You'll see that Ketu starts the very first nakshatra, named asvini. Ketu represents our past karma. When one life ends, and the next life begins, transferring this unspent karma, Ketu is there because it represents moksha, which we've reviewed as enlightenment. Similarly, in this chart, Ketu takes on starting the new cycle, much like a new birth.

Saturn's Crossing of a Zodiac Sign: The Dhaiya

Since Saturn takes about 30 years to orbit the sun, it takes about 2.5 years to cross (or transit) each zodiac sign. However, there are two transits of Saturn that, according to mythology, greatly trouble Vedic astrologers. This is when Saturn enters a certain zodiac, a certain number of astrological houses away from your birth zodiac (but it is the Moon sign, not the Sun sign or ascendant/rising sign). As mentioned, there are two; the zodiac that is three spaces away from your Moon sign (i.e., 4th away from 1st is three spaces), and the one seven spaces away from yours (i.e., 8th away from 1st is seven spaces). Note we are not talking about the traditional "house" numbers, like 1st house for Aries. Rather, we are talking about shifting positional numbers that are relative according to your birth sign.

Examples would work well here. Let's suppose you are of the Moon sign Cancer because you were born under a time when the Moon transited the Cancer zodiac. Now we'll temporarily designate Cancer as the first zodiac in terms of position. Following the usual calendar sequence of zodiac signs, the fourth zodiac (three spaces away from the first) in sequence from Cancer would be Libra. The eighth sign from Cancer (seven spaces away from the first) would be Aquarius.

Therefore, a Cancerian would dread the 2.5 years Saturn enters Libra, and the 2.5 years Saturn enters Aquarius. However, with careful planning and confidence, the Cancerian can negate the adverse effects of the dhaiya.

The "Difficult Period" — Saturn's Sade Sati

Sade sati is a dreaded 7.5-year period in Vedic astrology. It's the transit of Saturn across the three "home" zodiac signs—your own Moon sign and the two adjoining signs. For example, if your sign is Aries, then your neighboring signs are Pisces (right before Aries) and Taurus (immediately after Aries). Thus, in this specific example, if a person were born with their Moon sign as Aries, their sade sati would start when Saturn enters Pisces in its orbit around the Sun and end when it departs the Taurus zodiac. Since Saturn takes 2.5 years to transit through a zodiac sign, those three zodiac signs during a sade sati would be 3 x 2.5 = 7.5 years (in Sanskrit, "sade" means half, and "sati" means seven, which we add together to get 7.5). Saturn would have entered Pisces, then Aries, finished off with Taurus, and then continued on to the next nine zodiac signs in sequence. Please note, the sade sati is always based on the Moon sign, not the Sun sign or rising sign. Thus, even if you don't know your exact time of birth, you can still calculate the sade sati because as long as you know your date of birth, you will know your Moon sign.

Vedic astrologers advise not to fear this sade sati. It may be challenging, but as a real-world experience, like entering a brand-new university program or opening a business, the strong and disciplined will emerge victoriously (sounds like Saturn's personality). Astrologers do offer suggestions on how to manage the sade sati better. Worship to Lord Shani, God of Saturn, for example, can really help (stock up on mustard oil, honor the ancient fig tree, and keep up the prayers to the Lord). Since Saturn is the planet of karma, if you work hard, you will reap the rewards.

Chapter 5: Saturn in Angular: The Early Life

What Are the Angular Houses?

One of the best ways to know how the houses fit together and affect each other is through a Vedic house chart. You can find dozens online. But what are the angular houses (also called kendra houses)? As hinted earlier, these form the core houses that support life.

Let me explain.

The 1st house represents yourself as a person, including the way you look. This is about your personality, your opinions, and your outlook on life. What could be more centered than that? The 4th house portrays your domestic life, like the house you have and your valued possessions. It includes your childhood memories and your relationship with your mother. This, too, is at the center of your life.

Now on to the last two angular houses. The 7th house is about your loved ones, such as your spouse, relatives, and friends. It also incorporates business partners, who you have to trust and collaborate with. Without love and camaraderie, life is less fulfilling, so this house is vitally important.

Finally, the 10th house is karma—your reputation and hard work, crucial to your prosperity and ability to sustain a vibrant livelihood. It is also the house that represents the relationship with your father.

If you use a different chart, such as a circular one, you'll see that the four houses make up two opposite pairs. For example, the 1st house and the 7th house. The 4th house and the 10th house. They co-exist in balance, like a seesaw. Keeping both sides level is key to a well-adjusted life.

This balance makes sense. The 1st house represents yourself in a marriage, and the 7th house your spouse. Meanwhile, the 4th house portrays your private life, and the 10th house your public life.

"Aspects" of Saturn on Astrological Houses

In Vedic astrology, Saturn has a special influence ("aspect," in astrological terms) on other astrological houses in a shifting positional pattern. However, that depends on where it sits in the birth chart. What's important to remember is that you count Saturn's currently occupied house as the 1st positional house, whichever house that might be (Saturn moves around according to its current position in the night sky, so you must get astronomical information as to Saturn's current orbit). Remember, according to the North Indian model, houses do not change on the chart, and all attributes of that house, such as feelings, relationships, and finances, stay where they exist on the traditional chart. When discussing aspects of a planet like Saturn, we are merely identifying the target houses.

Saturn, and only Saturn, has aspects upon the 3rd, 7th, and 10th houses from where it sits in the Vedic astrology chart. The meaning of the 3rd, 7th, and 10th relate to an ever-changing positional pattern depending upon where Saturn is found at a certain time.

It's a little tricky because if the first position is designated as 1st (i.e., not as zero, which is the way we mathematically start counting), then the 3rd, 7th, and 10th would all have one taken off each when jumping the spaces in the Vedic chart. So to get to the 3rd position from the 1st position, you jump by two. For the 7th, you advance by 6. And finally, for the 10th, you move ahead 9 spaces.

We've figured out how to find the houses that Saturn aspects. But what does it mean?

It means that the malefic (stressful) traits of Saturn can affect the traits in that house. For example, if Saturn aspects upon the 4th house (or is positioned in the night sky in the 4th house), it could mean a strict mother (Saturn is a disciplinarian planet). As we recall, the 4th house is the house of the mother. However, like all strategies to deal with Saturn's influence, the best approach is to focus on the beneficial qualities of Saturn, like rewarding him with hard work. So, if the mother is strict, the child could learn to follow the rules of the house and still have fun while working hard.

Just What Are the Stages of Life in the Zodiac Chart, Anyhow?

We've examined the angular houses above, but before we proceed further, perhaps we should step back a bit with the direction we're taking. The angular houses represent youth, but what set of astrological houses represent middle age and old age? The answer is:

Angular: Youth (Sanskrit: kendra)

Succedent: Middle Age (Sanskrit: panaphara)

Cadent: Old Age (Sanskrit: apoklima)

Using a zodiac circle chart, we can see that, like in life, youth comes first, succeeded by middle age, and then old age, all in a counter-clockwise direction. Since there are twelve zodiacs and three stages of life, there are four astrological houses in each life stage.

In the same way that childhood and youth have so much energy, the angular houses are considered in Vedic astrology to be much more significant than the next life stage, the succedent houses. The final life stage that portrays decline and loss of energy has cadent houses much weaker than the succedent houses.

Which Houses Represent the Four Goals of Life?

Remember we discussed the four aims of life—dharma, artha, kama, and moksha? Here's news for you...the horoscope houses incorporate those too. Amazing how everything lines up, right? Here is the list of the dharma, artha, kama, and moksha houses:

- 1st, 5th, and 9th houses correspond to the dharma houses (purpose and truth)

- 2nd, 6th, and 10th houses refer to artha (money)

- 3rd, 7th, and 11th houses are kama (love and desires)

- 4th, 8th, and 12th houses represent death and final liberation

Therefore, while you cascade through the houses to find where your strengths and weaknesses lie in a horoscope, remember the broad themes, which will help you remember the general purpose of each of the three houses that are bundled together. For example, when you know the 1st house is the house of self, the 5th house is for your children, and the 9th house represents worship, you can start to find a common theme of "purpose and truth" among them all.

Saturn's Unique Approach in the Angular Houses—Sasa Yoga

The Hindu spiritual exercise of yoga orients the body into stretching positions that worship deities. Its secular version has become a thriving sport among those who seek calming exercise and not worship. Yoga has a different meaning in astrology. It means the relationship between planets, zodiac signs, and astrological houses. While there are thousands of possible combinations, yogas are specifically selected for their importance and are named accordingly. The great yogas can be either beneficial or detrimental. One such beneficial yoga is sasa yoga, which only occurs through Saturn.

Sasa yoga occurs when Saturn is present or exalted when it passes through one of the four angular houses: the 1st, 4th, 7th, and 10th. Because of the placement of the zodiac sign that is ascendant (and therefore placed in the 1st house), then Capricorn, Aquarius, or Libra have to be in one of those houses, as mentioned. The 1st, 4th, 7th, and 10th and Saturn also have to be present physically (in the same house according to its constellation presence...looks for the "Sa" which is Saturn) for Saturn to give its blessing. A person born under a sasa yoga is said to someday become a leader and command good servants.

When a person is born under sasa yoga, Saturn is said to test them early on, giving his followers a chance to make mistakes, improve, and progress, so they become strong managers and leaders later on. The translation for sasa from Sanskrit is "rabbit"—this association makes us think of an agile person, ready to sprint at the first sign of trouble and someone who is wise and proactive.

Such people born under a sasa yoga are excellent candidates to serve in the judiciary system, politics, real estate, and bureaucracy. For example, Bill Gates, born at 8:58 p.m. on October 28, 1955, was born in Seattle, Washington State, with a Mercury ascendant (meaning Gemini was in his 1st house). That day, Saturn was placed in the 5th house, and since Libra was slotted into his 5th house as well, Saturn was exalted, meeting one of the conditions for sasa yoga. The other condition, being in the angular houses, was also met because Saturn was physically present in Bill Gates' 5th house. It aspected the 7th house, which is part of the angular houses (Saturn aspects upon the 3rd, 7th, and 10th houses away from its location).

Effect of Saturn on the Angular Houses

Let us go through the astrological houses one by one to see Saturn's impact since the concept is very important. Also, it is what most people seek when they request a horoscope.

1st House. This house is the most important since it is how the world will see you. This house rules your personality, temperament, and disposition. For example, if you were born a Capricorn, Saturn will rule this house since Saturn rules Capricorn. Thus, you will somewhat take on Saturn's personality, and you could be of serious temperament, ready to transact business. However, since Saturn is a malefic (difficult) planet, this house will suffer by having you as a malefic person unless you can mitigate these inborn traits. Astrologers prefer benefic (pleasant) planets to be placed in the 1st house, but they also stress that Saturn brings you humility and the ability to meditate.

When Saturn is in the first house, you will have probably regretted your past lives and reap the karma. Since you may have been born unhappy, you may have had a difficult childhood, mature beyond your years, as the 1st house also relates to childhood. However, you could work harder to overcome your lack of confidence instead of being shy and introverted. In terms of health, you are more likely to be jittery and stressed and need to take care by giving yourself "time out." Rest, eat well, and exercise regularly to overcome your lack of confidence. Fortunately, Saturn is the planet responsible for longevity, and you should have a long, fulfilling life.

Recall that Saturn is stronger when passing through Capricorn and Aquarius since it rules those two zodiac signs. Also, Saturn is stronger when it passes through Libra, since it is exalted in Libra. When that happens, and Saturn is already in the 1st house, all of Saturn's positive characteristics, such as discipline and hard work, will be enhanced. In contrast, when Saturn passes through Aries (which debilitates Saturn), it is "fallen," and you may have been born into a weak or poor family because of this.

4th House. This house portrays the mother and is full of happiness and contentment at home. As such, this house is one of the most important in Vedic astrology, particularly in ancient times when life was more difficult without modern conveniences. Since the 4th house is the house of the heart, whatever affects the heart (both physically and emotionally) tends to have an outsized effect on the other astrological houses, even if not apparently visible.

As a negative influence, Saturn's presence in the 4th house might signify a difficult relationship with the mother and less happiness at home with family life. Physically, you may have to seek regular heart checkups since this house rules the heart.

When Saturn transits Capricorn or Aquarius, where it rules, this means additional significance for the 4th house if Saturn already resides there. This also happens if Saturn transits Libra, where it is exalted. Since the 4th house is real estate, you will do well owning property and profit from investment in the real estate industry. With Saturn present, your mother may have endured a hard life, but she is very strong, strengthening her relationship with you.

7th House. This is the house of marriage and business interests. Unfortunately, if Saturn dominated this house when you were born, this could mean difficulty securing marriage. Or, if married, it could mean a short marriage. With Saturn's reliance on karma, this could mean your past lives involved matrimonial difficulty, and you may be reaping the karma of failed marriages that occurred before your time.

In overcoming this inherent burden, it is recommended to find a partner to marry who is older and more experienced, so it satisfies Saturn's proclivity for discipline and endurance. Such a partner may be more compatible and hence assure a long-lasting and happy marriage. Also, since Saturn aspects the 3rd, 7th, and 10th houses away from the house it currently occupies, this means Saturn already influences the 1st, 4th, and 9th houses, and perhaps not in a good way. The 1st and 4th houses are already the central houses, the angular ones, which are very important. Therefore, you must be very strong to overcome Saturn's adverse impact upon the central houses. When you have persevered, so you succeed beyond those barriers, Saturn will reward you mightily.

10th House. Career and profession dominate this house, as does the relationship with your father. Thus, this is another important house. As the house of karma, it ensures that you receive acknowledgment for all the good deeds and preparation you've achieved since birth.

When Saturn is strong in this house, due to the enhancing influence by Capricorn, Aquarius, or Libra, you are likely to do very well in this house, possessing great organizational and administrative skills. Your approach to your career is highly disciplined, just as Saturn desires. You must honor your commitment to a successful career by putting aside any lack of confidence.

When Saturn is strong, it also adversely affects your relationship with your father. But if your father is strong and well-versed, you will enjoy a solid relationship with him. However, let's say Saturn is debilitated by transiting through Aries. Maybe your father was emotionally distant or preoccupied with health problems, so you must persevere in maintaining your gains and supporting him from a position of strength.

Chapter 6: Saturn in Succedent: The Middle Life

What Are the Succedent Houses?

In archaic English, the word "succedent" means succeeding (as in coming after). So it makes sense that this word fits the next life stage after childhood, the angular houses. Put simply, the succedent houses (also named panaphara in Sanskrit) are the 2nd, 5th, 8th, and 11th houses.

The succedent houses represent stability and maturity, consolidation of gains from mistakes, and rectifications of youth. Succedent houses are happy and content with the resources earned to date. You are likely married, have built a business, or have acquired a career, and you enjoy certain hobbies such as gardening or golf.

The 2nd house deals with wealth and possessions, including the salary you earn from work or profits from your business. The 5th house is the house of creativity, joy, and playfulness. It also relates to having children (and training them to become well-earning and independent adults when they come of age).

The 8th house portrays surprise, such as sudden gains, like a lottery win or an inheritance, but can also portend to losses, so one has to be careful. The 11th house is the house of prosperity, reputation, and community where you form strong relationships outside your home. These four houses have a strong inclination toward money and finances, which is expected to be a preoccupation among those in middle age so they can save for retirement and live the life they have envisioned.

The Effect of Saturn in Succedent Houses

As a strict and harsh judge, Saturn casts a stern eye on any astrological house it enters, and since the succedent houses focus heavily on money and earnings, you have to be careful and aware of Saturn's influence. He will shake your confidence and perhaps give you valuable life lessons in how you can lose money. This could come from things such as bad investments. However, if you persist and accept the life lesson, learning from it and improving yourself, you will see that Saturn is doing you a favor by preparing you for the everyday reality of an unforgiving world. Should you master this trepidation and go on to be assured in your decisions and your networks, Saturn will reward you handsomely.

2nd House. As the planet of karma, Saturn (as a malefic planet) in the 2nd house may mean the person has cheated others financially in the past (or a past life) and must now account for the past bad karma. In some extraordinary situations, especially if Saturn in the 2nd house is aspected by beneficial planets, there could be a windfall from past lives, and you will gain an inheritance.

I mentioned how Saturn aspects the 3rd, 7th, and 10th houses away from its present position. Without going through the details again, that means Saturn positively aspects the 8th house, which is the house of longevity. Combined with Saturn's proclivity for long life, this really benefits you. If Saturn is in Libra (its exalted zodiac sign) or in Capricorn or Aquarius (its ruled zodiac signs) while in the 2nd house, the benefits of the 2nd house are accentuated. Since it is the house of earning income, you will become wealthy, working slow and steadily towards your goals.

Saturn is debilitated in Aries, so if Saturn is in Aries while in the 2nd house, you may become one of the working poor and earn your money through repetitive, tedious jobs.

5th House. This house deals with your own children and playfulness, such as sports or the arts. It is also the house of the mind and intelligence. Being the house of ethics and morality, this house is vital in a well-disciplined life so you can become highly respected in your profession, and accordingly, be able to use your good standing to move forward. Due to Saturn's serious reputation, this house of fun rarely welcomes Saturn. When this house is in harmony, people celebrate this fun through hosting parties, gatherings, and dances.

Since this is the house of a future with children, beneficial planets appearing in this house usually lead to bearing children if children are wanted in the family. However, if malefic planets rule this house, there might be a child unless a beneficial planet also presents in the same house.

When Saturn is present in this house, few children may be born to you, and relationships with your children may be difficult. However, when Saturn transits Capricorn or Aquarius or becomes exalted in Libra, you can make the best of a difficult situation. While you may have fewer children, your relationships with them could be strong and disciplined, and they will become more mature and better able to handle their own responsibilities.

8th House. The 8th house is considered the house of death and is often dreaded. However, if Saturn is prominent in the 8th house, being the planet that controls longevity, it can counteract the morbidity of this house and ensure you live a long life. A strong Saturn will enhance the odds of a surprise windfall, such as an inheritance or winnings from a lottery. People strong in this house are said to have a strong interest in the metaphysical, such as the occult and mystery. You could also have an alluring physical appeal and magnetism.

In the ancient past, the 8th house was especially dreaded. Today, astrologists have an enhanced understanding, and they claim that the 8th house could symbolize resurrections through transformation and change, which is Saturn's strength. So the concept of "death" in this house is far more benign. Here, the prediction is for the end of self-defeating habits and a toxic personality as you transform into a more caring and wiser person. Take the time to embrace change, understand why this change is happening, and struggle through the inevitable soul-searching that accompanies this change. In the end, you will be a much better person, equipped to handle life's challenges.

11th House. This is the house of community, where you form relationships outside of your family, such as with friends or volunteers for a charity. If you are strong in the 11th house, you give your time to good causes like helping the poor. Since Saturn people like to form strong relationships with others, you may find the effort put into making friends tiresome. You have to resist this temptation and encourage yourself to go out and mingle and to give everyone your equal attention, even if it is tiring.

As the house of prosperity, this is of immense value to the hardworking Saturnian. In the strength of this house, you will consolidate the energy you invested into your career and be financially well off. If you have an elder brother or sister, he or she will be successful, but you may still have a difficult relationship with them.

When you learn to pinpoint your fear of failure, you'll discover that was the key thing holding you back from making commitments to making new close friends and volunteering with the community. As a Saturnian, you will be sought out by community groups who seek hardworking volunteers with good hearts.

How the South Indian Chart Works

So far, we've relied heavily on the North Indian astrological chart. The South Indian astrological chart looks different. Instead of a pattern of diamonds, it looks more like a checkerboard. For the

North Indian chart, I explained that the astrological houses always remain fixed, and the 1st house always starts in the top diamond of the center. The South Indian chart is similarly always fixed, but with a different method. Instead of house numbers, the zodiacs are always fixed in place. Pisces is <u>always</u> in the top left corner, for example. Sagittarius is always in the left bottom corner. So, it's the house numbers that actually move around the chart, following the fixed zodiac template, depending on the night sky at a certain point in time, like the time and date of your birth.

Here is a quick and concise table of the similarities and differences between the North and South Indian charts:

	North Indian	South Indian
Appearance	Diamonds	Squares
Direction	Counter-Clockwise	Clockwise
What Stays Fixed in Position	The houses (#'s) i.e., 4th House	The zodiacs i.e., Capricorn ♑
What Moves According to Night Sky Position	The zodiacs and the planets	The houses and the planets

Which is better? Neither. They are both just two ways of showing the same thing, and the results from both charts are the same.

How to Start Mapping Your Zodiac Chart?

It all starts with the ascendant or rising sign. That's why your date of birth is important because that will make it your "1st House." There is often some confusion for newcomers to Vedic astrology, as we commonly think of our "signs" with the common assumption we're born under them. We may mix up the "rising sign" (which is the ascendant) and the "Sun sign," the zodiac geared to our calendar. Anyone can look up Cancer and see it covers the dates June 21 to July 22, just as Virgo will cover August 23 to September 22, but this is not the information you need.

The "typical" zodiac we're thinking of in the Western world is actually the Sun signs, which change every month or so; this is what you discover when you use your birthday and trace the zodiac calendar to see which sign you fall under. That's when our Sun transits the zodiac, when it crosses the constellation in our line of view from Earth. However, the rising sign, which is very important in Vedic astrology (the ascendant), changes every two hours, so that's why it's important to nail down the *time* of your birth. Since there are twelve zodiac signs and 24 hours a day, it works out that the rising sign changes every two hours.

Zodiac Sign	Symbol	Zodiac Sign	Symbol
1. Aries	♈	7. Libra	♎
2. Taurus	♉	8. Scorpio	♏
3. Gemini	♊	9. Sagittarius	♐
4. Cancer	♋	10. Capricorn	♑
5. Leo	♌	11. Aquarius	♒
6. Virgo	♍	12. Pisces	♓

When you find your rising sign (ascendant) based on your birth time on your birth day, you need to put it into your zodiac chart. It will take over the 1st house, and the rest of the zodiac signs will then automatically follow in sequence. If you use the astrological sign based on your *day* of birth, your chart will most likely be wrong.

Chapter 7: Saturn in Cadent: The Final Portion of Life

What Are the Cadent Houses?

The cadent houses relate to the final period of someone's life—old age and the preparation for their eventual departure from this world. This comprises the 3rd, 6th, 9th, and 12th houses.

The 3rd house signifies learning, perception, and communication, including broadcast media such as television and newspapers. It also covers brothers and sisters, especially younger ones.

The 6th house demonstrates concern for your personal health and the everyday decisions you make to keep yourself healthy.

The 9th house contains all the lofty abstract but vitally important concepts such as truth, principles, dreams, and intuition. You also show your ethics and commitment to charity in this house.

Finally, the 12th house, being the last house, represents the end of your astrological journey and can, at times, be considered an unfortunate house to be in. However, Saturn reigns strongly there (because it controls longevity) and will reward hard workers with dignity and accomplishments earned by the end of your life.

How can Saturn disrupt those cadent houses? In the 3rd house, the house of communication, Saturn can be mischievous and encourage gossip among your friends and neighbors, and that rarely turns out well. To resist Saturn's influence, stay away from gossip and either say nothing or tell the truth. As for the 6th house, the house of personal health, it's easy to fall into bad health habits, like overeating or smoking. When Saturn is present, we have to resist temptation and stick to healthy daily habits like good nutrition and good exercise. If we keep a good regimen, Saturn will reward us with a healthy body and a healthy mind, ready to take on new challenges.

For the 9th house, it's about spirituality, and Saturn may challenge your faith, but try to understand that enlightenment is actually helpful for your relationships and your moral fiber. The 12th house is the last house in the astrological chart, so it's tempting to spend away from the fortune you've accumulated over the years. Cherish the fruits of your labor slowly, and preserve your fortune instead.

The Effect of Saturn in Cadent Houses

3rd House. The third house is one of adventure and daring, and also advocates for brothers and sisters during childhood. It is a house of life energy, radiating excitement and motivation. This house has a somewhat split personality for choice of profession since it covers technicians, computer programmers, and lawyers, but also speaks for artists such as musicians, dancers, singers, and actors. There's a saying that if the ruling planet in that house at the time of birth is beneficial, the person will take the artist's career path. However, if a malefic planet, like Saturn, is the ruling planet, then the person will take the technical career path. Therefore, for Saturn, the person born in that astrological house will likely be an engineer, architect, or have some other similar profession.

Because Saturn is malefic, if it rules the 3rd house, you will likely work hard alone, not receiving much support from others. You must be self-sufficient because you will have a hard life ahead and have to achieve your rewards on your own. If Saturn is governing, you may have had estranged relationships with your brother and sisters since this is the house for siblings during childhood. This is why astrological forecasts are helpful, as you will know what obstacles you will need to overcome. This foreknowledge will greatly assist you in identifying what will be difficult and help to redouble your efforts, so you end up with lots of achievement in life, like in the 3rd house having excellent relations with your siblings and in accomplishing your work.

Remember Saturn will aspect the 3rd, 7th, and 10th houses in shifting position wherever it occupies, so when Saturn is in the 3rd house, it will affect the house two houses away, the 5th house (and the 9th and 12th houses). The 5th house, which Saturn will negatively affect, concerns the mind, so you may feel lonely and isolated.

When Saturn is ruling or exalted (with any of the usual trio of Capricorn, Aquarius, and Libra), then you are likely to be confident and self-assured, and if Saturn is debilitated (because it's crossing through Aries), you may be disillusioned and lack an appetite for hard work.

6th House. The 6th house speaks for your daily health regimen and working hard and networking in a way to out-maneuver competitors so you will be considered the best person for the job. If you are strong in the 6th house, you will find leadership positions easier to attain, having outwitted possible competitors.

When Saturn dominates the 6th house, you are often very healthy because you take good care of your daily fitness and grooming. You have an uncanny ability to outsmart your colleagues during your career, which is excellent for your income-producing ability. However, if Saturn is debilitated because it is passing through Aries, you may find the opposite has occurred. You could have poor relations with your bosses and co-workers and not be able to capitalize on any ability that will allow you to rise to the top of your profession. Also, you may be in poor health.

9th House. This house governs spiritual guidance and higher education, such as university and college. It is also the house for the legal system and covers lawyers, judges, and magistrates. I mentioned dharma earlier as being your moral compass and sense of what is right or wrong. Dharma is very strong in the 9th house. In fact, the 9th house is considered an important and coveted house for someone striving to be ethical.

If Saturn was in this house at the time of your birth and was also in transit through its ruled zodiacs, Capricorn and Aquarius, or it transits Libra, where it is exalted, you may end up having great spiritual belief. Normally, Saturn's malefic effect on this house will mean a lack of interest in religion and worship. But under those favorable conditions, your faith will be enhanced.

Also, the 9th house signals willingness to embrace new ideas, philosophy, and perspectives. If you are strong with Saturn, you may need to go further beyond your very practical instinct and let your mind consider new possibilities.

12th House. This is the last house, so there is a sense of finality, which suits Saturn because it takes the longest to go around the Sun and hence can be thought of as the last to arrive. Saturn is the house of moksha, as we've discussed in an earlier chapter—final liberation. If you organize your life just right, you will be on your way to higher consciousness and enlightenment. Hindu scriptures state that in a beneficial 12th house, the afterlife will be pleasant and heavenly.

Astrologers do well not to fear the ancient Vedic texts, which strongly dread the 12th house. Without the 12th house, there would be no path to higher spirituality, paving the way for moksha. Since this is the house of expenditures, Saturnians, with their usual solid careers and high earnings, will be tempted to spend in the last stage of life. This is a caution where you would be wise to refrain from spending away from your legacy. Preserve your fortune for future generations, and pass on your good deeds to lessen your karma.

While many fear isolation in the 12th house before death, this house can teach us about the benefit of "aloneness" rather than labeling it loneliness. This house also has many opportunities for people to practice meditation, yoga, and worship. It houses the subconscious, and one goal of astrology is to allow us to process our thoughts to realize exactly what we are thinking, whether we know it or not. The traditional karaka for this house is Saturn. Also, the shadow planet Ketu can be considered the second karaka because it is the planet of enlightenment and liberation. For example, Mother Teresa had Ketu in her 12th house.

Fear of the unknown (especially since the 12th house represents the afterlife) may be holding you back. Rather than retreat into yourself, it is a good idea to allow others to help you as Mother Teresa did.

The Dusthana (Grief-Producing) Houses

Now that we have reviewed the cadent houses, we should look at all the dusthana (grief-producing) houses—6th, 8th, and 12th. Those are often the dreaded houses in astrology—the houses very few want to be in. In the 6th house, we face a lot of challenges in life, such as disease, debts, legal issues, and adversaries at work. This is the phase in life in which we need to learn to cooperate with people and pay heed to our physical health to stave off misfortune later on. Otherwise, karma will accrue and return to worsen our lives.

As for the 8th house, it is traditionally the most dreaded house in astrology. As mentioned, it is considered the house of death. Death, loss of loved ones, transformations of character, and spiritual rebirth take place in this house. This means it is a difficult transitional house for you to pass through, but it is necessary to appreciate the good things in life.

We've explained before that the 12th house is the last phase before moksha—spiritual liberation. The most mystical house, it's where the planet Saturn provides the essential connection to the next world. It is difficult to let go. The most important thing is to cherish what you have earned, the family and friends you have gained, and realize that it is the journey, not the end, which counts. With that positive frame of mind, you can manage passage through the final house and let go of your karma.

The Upachaya (Growth) Houses

In contrast to the dreaded dusthana houses, the upachaya (growth-producing) houses are most welcome in Vedic astrology. They are the houses where beneficial growth can occur in life, giving rise to character development and material gains. They are the 3rd, 6th, 10th, and 11th houses. Strangely enough, those houses welcome the malefic (troublesome) planets where the other houses would dread them. Thus, the malefic planets such as Mars, Saturn, Rahu, Ketu, and the Sun will enhance these houses. Mercury could be malefic depending upon the astrological zodiac sign it occupies. The Moon can be malefic in its waning phase since its shadow is lengthening.

Of the upachayas, the 3rd house is the weakest, and the 11th house is the strongest. The 3rd house is where you take chances to learn and grow. This signifies learning, perception, and communication. The 6th house is interesting because it is both a dusthana and upachaya house. This sounds contradictory, but some people point out that much development comes from overcoming suffering and hardship. Both the 10th and 11th houses relate to community and professional development. You consolidate the career development and hard work in the 10th house. By the time you reach the 11th house, you reach out to the community to fortify your social standing and networks.

The Dharma Trikona Houses

The dharma trikona houses are the 1st, 5th, and 9th houses and are most welcome since they bring spirituality, goodness, and knowledge if the planets are well-placed. They show karma from past lives and signify the past, present, and future. The 1st house is also an angular house, which is highly desired. As you recall, dharma is moral righteousness and judgment, which blesses those who benefit from the 1st, 5th, and 9th houses.

The first house is the house of self, which is essential to get right early, so you can take the initial step toward a prosperous and humble life. The 5th house is about emotion, memory, and education, which is essential for dharma. The 9th house, meanwhile, represents the highest principles we can uphold, enabling good luck and fortune.

The Karaka Houses

All the astrological planets significantly affect certain houses because they have a special "fit" with the characteristics of those astrological houses. For example, the beneficial Jupiter promotes luck and fortune. Since the 2nd house rules wealth, astrologers consider Jupiter an excellent fit and declare it as a karaka of the 2nd house. From this limited perspective, it matters not where the planets are in the constellations at a given moment for this chart. It matters not where the zodiac signs are at the moment for this chart. All that matters is the standard house number, like 1st house, 2nd house, and so on, because, as we've seen, they all have their own distinctive characteristics. They all have a certain "feel," much like how you know how different Albert Einstein and Elton John are. In that way, we distinguish their "natural" affiliation to certain planets.

The 8th and 12th houses are cadent houses—meaning the end of the cycle. As the slowest astrological planet and the one that takes the longest to orbit the Sun—remember we are talking only about astrological planets, which only go out as far as Saturn—Saturn is considered the oldest planet. Here we are not considering its actual age as a planet, which is billions of years, but rather how we characterize it emotionally. The 8th house is, of course, the house of death. Again, this is a natural fit for Saturn, given its reputation as a planet of karma.

Why is Saturn the karaka for the 6th house? The 6th house covers disease, and so does Saturn (remember this planet's association with old age and health). So, Saturn is a natural fit for the 6th house. As for the 10th house, it is the house of career, and Saturn, as the stern and disciplined taskmaster, is also a natural fit as one of its three karakas.

The Maraka Houses

Morbidly, the maraka houses are the "death-inflicting" houses, and thankfully, they are few; the 2nd and 7th houses. Why those two houses? The houses of life are the 3rd house and the 8th house, so the transition from death to life (reflecting the karma burden) makes a lot of sense as the houses immediately before each life-giving house, the 2nd and 7th houses. While a lot of observers fear those maraka houses, astrologers caution they should be considered but not dreaded since certain beneficial planets placed in the right positions on the birth chart can alleviate the effects of those maraka houses. Also, remember that there can be several interpretations of the meaning of "maraka." For example, it could mean the end of a career or a relationship rather than a drastic and sudden death.

Summing up Saturn's Relationships with Zodiacs

The table below sums up Saturn's effect on each zodiac should the sign be ascendant (a zodiac sign is ascendant at a specific place and time if it rises on the eastern horizon).

	Best	Good	Bad
Aries ♈			Saturn ♄
Taurus ♉	Saturn ♄		
Gemini ♊			Saturn ♄
Cancer ♋			Saturn ♄
Leo ♌			
Virgo ♍			
Libra ♎	Saturn ♄		
Scorpio ♏			
Sagittarius ♐			Saturn ♄
Capricorn ♑		Saturn ♄	
Aquarius ♒		Saturn ♄	
Pisces ♓			Saturn ♄

Chapter 8: When Saturn Smiles Upon You

What Are Yogas?

As explained in an earlier chapter, yoga in astrology means the relationship between planets, zodiac signs, and astrological houses. The word "yoga" means union, and a union is a relationship, a bringing together. While there are thousands of possible yogas, astrologers focus on the several that are important. Several distinctive yogas include Saturn as one of the principal planets. Yogas can be either good or bad. They are not always beneficial, unlike the physical yoga that a Hindu worshipper performs.

We already explained the powerful sasa yoga, which can only occur with Saturn. However, one dreaded yoga is the shrapit dosh, when Saturn and Rahu are present together in any astrological house in the birth chart. Potential problems include obstacles in pursuing education, finances, happy marriage, and prosperous business.

There are, indeed, hundreds of possible yogas, and it would be difficult to go through them all and still be familiar with them. Rather than name them all, let us go through a list of horoscope conditions of interest to Saturn followers:

• Venus and Saturn present in the same house, or even when Saturn is in a house adjacent to one which Venus occupies, means talent or career in the arts.

• Saturn aspecting the Sun leads to more spiritual life, even religious devotion. Since Saturn is the son of the Sun in Vedic astrology, other qualities such as integrity, responsibility, and humility are also enhanced in such a relationship.

• If Mars or Saturn aspects each other, the person ruled by either planet will excel in building and all mechanical or technical fields.

• Jupiter aspected by Saturn will indicate one who is a "perpetual student," one who finds it hard to kick themselves out of college or university.

Raja Yoga: The "Royal Yoga"

One highly sought yoga is the raja yoga, which implies royalty and exalted status. Raja means king in Sanskrit. Raja yoga occurs under certain combinations highly desired by Vedic astrologers. Let us focus on Saturn.

It's interesting to note that only five of the nine astrological planets can each produce a yoga karaka because each such planet already rules two zodiac signs. Those five planets are Mercury, Venus, Mars, Saturn, and Jupiter. The Sun and the Moon only rule one zodiac sign each. Rahu and Ketu rule no zodiac signs. Thus, Saturn is a powerful planet in that it rules two zodiac signs, Capricorn and Aquarius.

What is a yoga karaka? We've talked about karakas already, but this is a yoga karaka—meaning a combination of relationship (yoga) and action (karaka). Yoga karaka is a powerful raja yoga where two zodiac signs ruled simultaneously by one planet are captured in a powerful pattern on the birth chart. That would be a moment, like a time of birth, with the right ascendant in the

1st house. When those two special zodiac signs are present in the right places, that alone produces a yoga karaka without the need for planets to be physically present in optimal placements. For Saturn, which rules Capricorn and Aquarius, that only possible combination happens when Libra becomes the ascendant, the 1st house, and Capricorn shows up in the 4th house, with Aquarius in the 5th house. Why is that pattern significant?

It's significant because Saturn rules both Capricorn and Aquarius. Remember our discussion on trikona houses? As you'll recall, the trikona houses are the 1st, 5th, and 9th houses. These three houses are considered a powerful trio of houses.

Aquarius is in the 5th house, which makes it part of the trikona. And there's another powerful pattern ahead, the angular houses, which we've also discussed. Capricorn is in the 4th house, which makes it part of the angular houses (also called Kendra houses). The combination of having a ruling planet in both the trikona houses and angular houses is considered very fortunate. So, look out for this yoga karaka!

There is one other yoga karaka, similar to having Libra as the ascendant, and that is Taurus. If Taurus is ascendant and is in the 1st house, then Capricorn moves to the 9th house, which is part of the trikona houses, and Aquarius moves to the 10th house, which is part of the angular houses. Again, a magic combination of trikona and angular houses! Therefore, for Saturn's yoga karakas, only Libra or Taurus can be the ascendant (and therefore automatically slotted into the 1st house).

Dhana Yoga: Another Yoga of Great Wealth

More planetary relationships can bring wealth if you have the right birth chart. One of them is dhana yoga, as dhan in Sanskrit means wealth.

Let's say Saturn is present as a planet in the celestial constellations in the 5th house, and also Capricorn or Aquarius (both ruled by Saturn) are in the 5th house, and a final condition is met—that the Sun and the Moon (together) are in the 11th house. That specific combination is a dhana yoga. In fact, the 1st, 2nd, 5th, 9th, and 11th houses are the key houses in a dhana yoga; any two of them paired up with the right planets or zodiac signs can create a dhana yoga.

Another pattern is if the Moon is physically present in the 5th house and its only sign, Cancer, is also in the 5th house, with Saturn physically present in the 11th house, which also has the zodiac sign Aquarius (one of the two zodiacs ruled by Saturn). This is another strong pattern that should be investigated in any chart.

Two more dhana yogas for Saturn are possible if the person is born at the time of Capricorn or Aquarius ascendant (when it rose on the eastern horizon). For a Capricorn ascendant, if the Moon and Mars—together but not necessarily in the same house—are observed in the trikona or angular houses, a dhana yoga is formed. For an Aquarius ascendant, if the Moon and Saturn are together in the 10th house, the lucky person has every chance of becoming rich.

Famous Wealthy People Born under Dhana Yoga

If you are new to Vedic astrology, you may be saying, "Yeah, right. Show me the money!" All right, how about three of the richest people in the world—Bill Gates, Jeff Bezos, and Warren Buffet? All were born under a dhana yoga.

Jeff Bezos

Jeff Bezos, the founder of Amazon.com, Inc., was born on January 12, 1964, at noon in Albuquerque, New Mexico. In the Moon birth chart, his ascendant (rising sign) is Pisces. On January 12, 1964, the Moon sign was Sagittarius, and the Sun sign was Capricorn—a sign ruled by Saturn.

Jupiter is powerful as the planet is placed in the ascendant sign (automatically the first house). At the moment of Jeff Bezos' birth, the Pisces sign was present in the first house in the constellation, and Jupiter rules Pisces. It rules the 1st house, which is the fundamental house of self. The first house is also powerful as being part of the trikona and the angular houses. Jeff Bezos has a powerful gaja kesari yoga which is formed when Jupiter is in the ascendant (i.e., the 1st house) and is four houses away from the Moon. The Moon being in the 10th house (one of the auspicious angular houses) aspects upon Jupiter, which is four houses away in the 1st house. The "home" house starts in the counting position of being 1st, so the 4th house away is actually three houses counter-clockwise as counted—i.e., 10th, 11th, 12th, getting us to 1st as we rolled over to the beginning.

As previously explained, Saturn has a powerful influence on wealth, and Jeff Bezos is lucky enough to have a Saturn dhana yoga. Remember I mentioned that the key houses are the 1st, 2nd, 5th, 9th, and 11th—any paired combination between those houses creates an incredible dhana yoga. You have Jupiter and its sign Pisces in the 1st house and then Saturn and its sign Capricorn in the 11th house. With this fortuitous combination, Jeff Bezos also has a dhana yoga thanks to Saturn, in addition to the gaja kesari yoga thanks to Jupiter. It's interesting that Jeff Bezos earned a degree in electrical engineering and computer science from Princeton University, one of the technical fields blessed by Saturn.

To top it off, he also has a raja yoga, thanks to Mercury combined with the Moon. Mercury rules two signs: Gemini and Virgo. Gemini is number 3, and Virgo is number 6-you'll see those two numbers on Jeff Bezos' chart. They are in the 4th and 7th houses, respectively—the angular houses. Now we need a partner in the trikona houses, any of the 1st, 5th, or 9th houses, as we explored previously. Mercury rules Cancer, which is in the 5th house as number 4 on the default zodiac chart. Both the Moon and Mercury as planets are physically present in the 10th house, the house of career, so they are powerful when together in the same house.

Bill Gates

We've briefly discussed Bill Gates in this book when examining his sasa yoga, but let's go into more detail here. Bill Gates, the founder of Microsoft Corporation, was born on October 28, 1955, at 8:58 a.m., in Seattle, Washington. In his Moon chart, he was born with Gemini as his ascendant, so it is slotted in the 1st house. However, unlike Jeff Bezos, there is no planet physically present in the constellation in his Moon chart, so there is no lord of the ascendant in the same house. We know the Moon rules the Gemini zodiac sign, so we look to the Moon's location, which is in the 10th house. Just like Jeff Bezos, the presence of a strong planet in the 10th house, the house of career, is a great indicator of stamina and drive.

As mentioned previously, Bill Gates has sasa yoga, which is only possible under Saturn. He gets this because Saturn is present in his 5th house, and while the 5th house is not part of the angular houses, Saturn does impact the 3rd, 7th, and 10th houses that lie ahead of where this planet appears. The 7th house is two houses away (the 3rd house count) from the 5th house, so Bill Gates has a sasa yoga, which is favorable toward wealth and privilege.

Let me bring up another yoga. You can see in his birth chart that Saturn and Venus rule two dusthana (grief-producing) houses. We discussed dusthana houses in a previous chapter. How can you find them? The dusthana houses are the 6th, 8th, and 12th houses. Saturn rules the zodiac sign of the 8th house, and this zodiac sign is 10, or Capricorn. As for the 12th house, the zodiac sign is 2, which is Taurus, and Venus rules this sign. By themselves, those two facts don't bring forward yoga. But Saturn and Venus transit together in the 5th house, so their planetary combination has a powerful effect on those grief-producing houses, turning their typical dreaded influence into a powerful gain for Bill Gates.

Steve Jobs

On February 25, 1955, Steve Jobs was born in San Francisco, California, at 7:15 p.m. Steve Jobs has a powerful raja yoga since Saturn is exalted in Libra—Saturn is located as a planet in the 3rd house since it was passing through Libra at the time Steve Jobs was born. Libra is in the 3rd house because Leo was ascendant (rising on the eastern horizon in San Francisco) at the time of Steve Jobs' birth. Mars is located in the 9th house, where its ruled sign, Aries, was passing through at the time. Therefore, you combine powerful symmetrical pairs of planets in their own signs since their houses are exactly six houses away.

Another raja yoga is created when a house with both its planet and that planet's sign is in the angular houses and another auspicious house in the trikona houses. The 9th house is a trikona house, and as mentioned, Mars is in it, and so is its sign Aries. (Aries = 1 in the default zodiac chart). Actually, if Mars wasn't there, Venus is just as good because it is in the 5th house, a trikona house. The angular house drawn into this particular raja yoga is the 7th house, thanks to Jupiter's 9th aspect—which counts down from the 11th house and then starts anew, all the way to the 7th house.

Another raja yoga is where the ruling planet (also called lord) of the 12th house is present in the 6th or 8th house—as the 6th, 8th, and 12th houses are considered the evil houses as we've previously reviewed under the topic of dusthana houses. Here, the Moon is physically present in the 6th house, but it rules the zodiac sign of the 12th house, which is Cancer. So you could say the lord of the 12th house is in the 8th house.

An interesting loop is observed when four planets have exclusively occupied each other's signs. Here is the loop:

	In this house...	This planet occupies...	This zodiac number...	Which is named...	Which is ruled by...
1	3rd House	Saturn	7	Libra	Venus
2	5th House	Venus	9	Sagittarius	Jupiter
3	11th House	Jupiter	3	Gemini	Mercury
4	6th House	Mercury	10	Capricorn	Saturn

You see the cycle go from Saturn to Venus, Jupiter, Mercury, and back again to Saturn. Interesting! This is a very rare yoga.

One similarity with the birth chart of Bill Gates is that Saturn ("Sa") is physically present in the number 7 sign, which is Libra. This is good because Libra is the only planet that is not a ruling planet (Capricorn and Aquarius, in Saturn's case) that exalts Saturn.

Mark Zuckerberg

Mark Zuckerberg's birth chart is very powerful. He is a Saturn ascendant! When he was born in White Plains, New York, around midnight (his real birth time seems unknown) on May 14, 1984, Capricorn was rising on the eastern horizon. And since Saturn rules Capricorn, this makes Saturn his dominant planet. Also, at this time, Saturn was in transit through the Libra constellation, noted by the "Sa" in the 10th house, where Libra was. This means Saturn was exalted and had an outsized influence on Mark Zuckerberg's career, particularly because the 10th house is the house of career. Saturn favors those in technical fields like computer science, so Saturn was smiling upon him.

We've discussed sasa yogas. Mark Zuckerberg has a powerful one since Saturn is already in the 10th house, which is aspected through the 10th house away from the 1st house and is also in the angular (kendra) houses.

Chapter 9: Freeing Your Chakras: The Yogic Aspect of Saturn

The Planets and the Chakras

Those of us in the Western world find the Hindu-inspired chakras very beguiling and fascinating, as we have no cultural or historical equivalent. We may vaguely know that the chakras are energy centers within the body that channel life forces. Let's learn more about the concept of chakras before we match them to the planets.

There are seven chakras, and these are numbered one through seven, starting with the chakra at the bottom of the body as number one. The seventh chakra ends at the top of the head, at the crown. Also, each chakra is associated with a function. For example, the chakra located at the throat governs communication (makes sense). Each chakra has a Sanskrit name, for they are derived from ancient India in a time when Sanskrit was spoken by everyone. The root chakra (located at the base of the spine) originated in Sanskrit as muladhara and is symbolized by the red lotus, a beautiful flower. The root chakra represents the strength of safety and security, which is fitting since the root chakra is the very basis of the chakras and the original starting point. Tellingly, all the chakras are very near the body's major organs, which are centralized in the chest and the head.

Chakras are not physical components of the human body. Rather, they are nodes of spiritual energy that convey vitality. If any of them are blocked, you may experience symptoms such as lack of energy or depression, and depending on the chakra that is blocked, even more severe health problems like migraines, extreme pain, and heart problems. We'll explore some techniques later for relieving chakras later, but one common approach to unblocking chakras is through yoga, the exercise.

What do the planets have to do with the chakras? Since there are seven astrological planets (Rahu and Ketu are shadow planets and do not exist in the celestial sky), each chakra has been assigned to a planet. Interestingly, there is no general agreement about which planets are assigned to which chakras.

The chakras align directly with the actual orbits of the planets around the sun. The crown of the head is taken to be the starting point, as the most enlightened chakra, dealing with spirituality and dynamic thought. You can consider this as an analogy of the Sun, as the center of the flow (although this chakra is sometimes portrayed as the Moon, which governs conscious thought). Following the order of distance from the Sun, you move to the next chakra down from the crown of the head, and you move through Mercury, Venus, Mars, Jupiter, and finally Saturn. So Saturn is taken to be the root chakra, governing safety and security (which does match its reputation in Vedic astrology—being the arbiter of judgment.)

First Chakra Represents Stability and Security

There are differences of opinion as to which planet controls which chakra. Let's start again with the premise that Saturn rules the root chakra, the muladhara in Sanskrit. Saturn is known as the planet of discipline and structure, demonstrating how the chakras and the planets can intertwine. This chakra is located at the base of the spine, encompassing the first three vertebrae, the colon, and the bladder. It reinforces the fight or flight instinct, and when this chakra is blocked, you may feel a sense of insecurity and anxiety.

You can counteract this troubling sense of anxiety by being grounded; walk barefoot on fresh soft grass or on a sandy beach. You can distract your mind by daydreaming and visualizing your desires—a vacation to a tropical resort, skiing in the great mountains, relaxing in a hot tub, and so on. A healthy routine that targets the root chakra focuses on the basics—healthy sleeping, eating, exercising, and avoiding toxic people.

For those people who do not regard Saturn as the first chakra, what planet takes up that mantle? According to those who place Saturn as the first chakra, Mars represents the root chakra. They point out that its color red also symbolizes Mars.

Fifth Chakra Represents Truth and Judgment

The fifth chakra (chakras are numbered starting from the bottom and moving up the body) is the throat chakra, which originated with the Sanskrit name vishuddha. According to some believers, the throat governs the sense of right and wrong within a person, so Saturn is a natural fit for this as well. When you use this chakra, you are speaking your most authentic truth. In Hindu mythology, this chakra is represented by a blue lotus with sixteen petals.

If this chakra is blocked, that may cause poor judgment and an inability to communicate effectively. This is why some other believers state that Mercury is the planet that governs the fifth chakra since Mercury is the lord of communication and the mind. People with an effective vishuddha are great orators and storytellers, and they can speak with passion and conviction. They are great problem-solvers with an eye for detail, and they tend to be optimistic and forthcoming.

When this chakra is blocked, you may feel a lack of confidence and restrain yourself from speaking your true beliefs. You may feel you will say something foolish because your mind is cluttered. Meditation is an effective way to clear up this chakra, to clear your thoughts.

Sometimes you may feel your throat tighten, but you are not sick. It could be because of some deep-rooted anger or sadness, something we may not be aware of right away. You can often feel that your throat is constricting, even choking. The throat chakra gives rise to the voice of your body like a pressure valve that releases your thoughts. To release all that pent-up energy inside your throat, there are many things you can try. You can write down your thoughts in a journal, talk to someone about what's bothering you, or write songs or poetry that reveal how you feel. You don't have to show your private writings to anyone; they will still help to unblock your chakra.

Before we end our section about chakras, let's talk a little more about where the chakras fall. Some thinkers consider Saturn to be the governor for the sixth chakra, the third eye chakra, or the Ajna. However, since most seem to place Saturn in the first or fifth chakras, and we're focused on Saturn, we will not explore this option further in this book.

Where Does Yoga Come In?

It is a little confusing to speak of the word "yoga," which has two meanings in this book. We've already extensively explored astrological yoga, the relationship between the planets. This chapter will only focus on yoga as a spiritual exercise, which involves stretching and meditation. Yoga involves physical postures, breathing exercises, and concentration to enhance mental and physical harmony. It's very telling, though, that just as in astrology, "yoga" in Sanskrit means "union." It's the convergence of the mind and the body in its physical and mental form, which is why, among worshippers, it is not merely considered exercise and flexibility.

One large benefit of yoga to Vedic astrology followers is the blending of the philosophies of yoga with the deep tradition of astrology. Energy healers will ask questions about your health and advise if your chakras are off-balance, over-active, or blocked. Chakras can indicate unresolved health issues and pinpoint specific troubles.

Vedic astrology is unique because it works with planetary energy rather than standalone energy as a hermetically sealed discipline. Yoga works directly with the energy of the chakras. Thus, an understanding of the planetary influence is essential to perform effective yoga that will release the pent-up energy of the chakras. When done correctly, you can work off the malefic influence of Saturn's presence. Saturn actually endorses the practice of meditation, an essential part of yoga, since it is essential to its belief in discipline and patience.

Essentially, there exist four primary types of yoga: karma, bhakti, jnana, and raja.

As we've already explored, karma promotes bringing good to the world through selfless actions done for the good of others. Many instructors teaching yoga programs require students to practice karma yoga through cooking and cleaning or volunteering for others. Karma is the yoga of action.

Bhakti yoga stresses rituals and ceremonies to express love for the Divine, such as praying, chanting, singing, and dancing. Bhakti is the yoga of devotion.

Jnana yoga emphasizes spiritual study, such as using sacred texts and philosophical discussions. Jnana is the yoga of knowledge.

Raja means the "royal path," and this type of yoga aspires to attain enlightenment. Besides studying the three other forms of yoga as above, it also integrates the eight limbs (stages) of yoga. One of its sub-disciplines, hatha yoga, combines asana and pranayama. Asana in Sanskrit literally means "body posture," which is the yoga we see on television screens and in community exercise centers. Pranayama in Sanskrit means "extension of the life force," or as we commonly know it, breath control. That's why you see so many breathing exercises in regular yoga classes.

Yoga Techniques for First Chakra

Any good hatha yoga instructor will offer suggestions about how the integrated physical, meditative, and spiritual practices can deal with any blockage in the first chakra, the root chakra. This is assuming Saturn governs the root chakra, as many yoga practitioners believe. Hatha yoga is probably the most widely available yoga philosophy and practice in the Western world that incorporates the essentials of Vedic yoga that began thousands of years ago. If you believe that Saturn is responsible for the throat chakra instead of the root chakra, you may skip ahead to the next paragraph, which will cover the fifth chakra.

The mantra for the first chakra is a simple sound you can chant lightly; it is pronounced "lam." The word has a short "ah" sound, but you may wish to draw out the ending m a little more to emphasize your dedication and to help you to get into the right frame of mind. As the color red corresponds to the first chakra, you may wish to have a red object in your line of vision to calm you, like flowers or an inspirational print.

Each chakra has its own hand gesture, originally called a mudra.

These yoga poses are specifically for the root chakra. For each one, take five deep breaths.

Warrior II (Virabhadrasana II)

Grounded in our primal instincts, the root chakra helps us face our fears, so we feel strong and confident. To do this yoga, step back and lower your hips, your feet slightly wider than shoulder-width apart. Raise your arms to shoulder level and spread out your hands, so your palms face the floor. Once done, bend both knees, so they are directly over the ankle with your thighs parallel to the floor.

This pose has a storied origin. The term "vira" means warrior or hero, and "bhadra" means friend in Sanskrit. This asana (yoga pose) was named after the God of Destruction, Virabhadra.

Standing Forward Fold (Uttanasana)

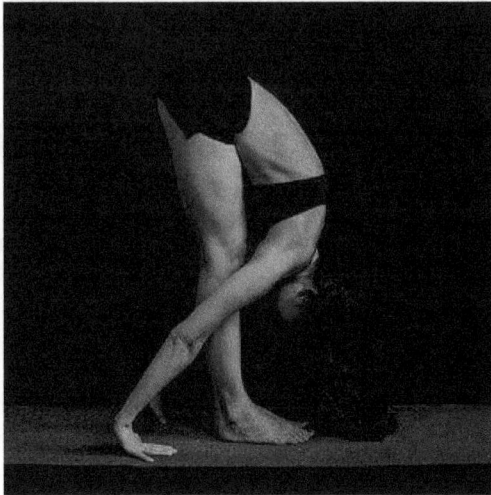

Stand with your feet shoulder-width apart. With your arms reaching upwards, bend over gradually and allow your arms to sweep down either side of the body. It's important to bend your pelvis rather than your back. Otherwise, you can put your back under too much strain. This position can bring a sense of peace and calm, but often the sensation of having tight hamstrings can have you feeling like you need to stop. To lessen this discomfort, stretch your hamstring muscles before doing this pose. Take it easy at first by bending down loosely and testing your limit of flexibility first rather than pushing yourself too hard. Only bend as far as feels comfortable, and work on your flexibility over time.

The Sanskrit words "ut" mean intense, and "tan" means to stretch, so it's considered an intense stretch.

Garland Pose (Malasana)

"Mala" means garland, rosary, or necklace, while "asana" refers to a yoga position. This pose draws us closer to the earth, strengthening the bond of energy. Also, it firms up the lower back, ankles, and calves while fortifying our sense of balance. In the Western world, we often spend so much time sitting in our chairs, so this deep squat may be uncomfortable for us at first. It makes sense to prop up our position by using mats underneath until we become stronger and more proficient.

To get into position, stand with your knees slightly wider than shoulder-width and slowly squat toward the floor. Move your arms and hands into a praying position with your upper arms close to your thighs. Keep your spine straight and your shoulders relaxed.

Head to Knee Forward Bend (Janu Sirsasana)

This seated pose allows you to feel grounded and secure and develops flexibility in your back, hamstrings, and hips. It is an excellent pose to stretch your hamstring muscles. If you find it hard to stretch with both legs, you can start with one and tuck the other under yourself.

- Sit on the floor, and stretch both legs out in front of you, sitting with your spine straight. Be careful with your back, and only stretch as far as you are comfortable.

- Bend with your pelvis, not your lower back.

- Let your fingers "walk" along your outstretched legs until you reach an angle that is comfortable. If your hands reach your feet, grasp them and hold on, leaning into the stretch, but if you can't reach that far quite yet, that's okay too.

In Sanskrit, "janu" means knee, and "sirsh" translates to head. Hence, head to forward knee bend.

Easy Pose (Sukhasana)

While it looks easy at first, the challenge is staying comfortable in this pose and holding it in a relaxing position without losing balance. Like the other yoga positions we've discussed, remember they date back to when chairs weren't as common, and our ancients were more comfortable sitting or squatting on the ground. Some people find crossing their legs as they sit to be uncomfortable, but unlike another classic yoga position, you need not tuck your feet underneath your thighs for this one. This is why it's called the "Easy Pose." You do not have to force your feet into specific positions. "Shukh" in Sanskrit means pleasure, and "asana" refers to a yoga pose.

- The knees are bent in order for slightly more blood to be diverted into your organs, which increases their activity. It removes tension and improves positive energy by focusing on the mind.

- Sit on the floor, and cross your legs under yourself. With your spine straight, place each hand on a knee.

- Imagine drawing energy up from the ground up into your body. Breathe in and out slowly, imagining the energy flowing up your torso into the crown of your head to the seventh chakra.

Yoga Techniques for Fifth Chakra

We have explored some yoga positions and techniques with the belief that Saturn is responsible for the root or first chakra. What about those who believe that Saturn governs the fifth chakra, the throat? Not to worry, we have yoga poses for that too.

We need to balance our vishuddha chakra to express ourselves and to summon confidence for when what we have to say is important and appreciated. The throat is essential to communication, so these exercises ahead will focus on the chest and throat region. The larynx is thought to be wired directly into the human brain, so that's why we often feel a lump in our throat when we feel emotional distress.

During yoga for the throat chakra, chant "ham," letting your vocalization draw out to clear your airway. Visualize the color blue, or bring a blue object such as a beautiful flower or hang up a print of something solidly blue.

Baby Cobra Pose (Bhujangasana)

To achieve this gentle pose, lie on your stomach flat on the floor and gently push up into a backbend so that your chest and shoulders are off the floor. You should feel the abdominal muscles tighten—it's a great way to tone your abdominal muscles. The idea is to bend your head upwards a little to allow as much air as possible to enter your chest and open up your airway to maximize the flow through the throat chakra.

Remember, be careful with your back—you don't want to cause an injury. And yes, it's okay to bend your elbows a little to ease up if your back feels uncomfortable. "bhujang" means cobra or snake, and "asana" means yoga posture.

Camel Pose (Ustrasana)

Begin with a high kneeling position. Plant your knees on the floor, and align your spine and thighs, so you are tall in the position. Place the heels of your hands on your lower back, and keep your fingers pointed downwards. Move your shoulders and upper arms gently back and inhale deeply. In Sanskrit, "ustra" means camel, and "asana" means yoga posture.

Slowly, ease your shoulder blades together as you bend backward, keeping your eyes on the ceiling. Rest your hands on your heels and tip your neck back to keep your airway open.

Supported Shoulder Stand (Salamba Sarvangasana)

This name is a mouthful! "Sarvang" in Sanskrit means the "whole person." By standing on one foot, you get as much of your body away from the floor as possible. The shoulders do support you, though, and "salamba" in Sanskrit means to support.

To accomplish this pose, start by lying on your back with arms by your sides, palms down, and legs stretched out. Now, slowly bend your knees, placing the soles of the feet on the floor.

After taking a deep breath, use your abdominal muscles to lift your hips slowly, bringing your knees toward your chest and your feet off the floor. Ground your elbows onto the mat, place both hands on your lower back, and slowly lift the thighs. Gradually straighten the legs to lift them straight up in the air, but let your feet move as they need to make it easier to balance. With a burst of energy, transfer more of your body weight onto your shoulders, keep your body straight up, and balance well so you can stay in position. If you have difficulty with the supported shoulder pose, you could use a yoga block (a cork or foam large brick-shaped material) and use it on your upper back to keep your balance in place.

Plow Pose (Halasana)

This pose can be pursued as a variation to the shoulder stand, which we explored above. Instead of straight-up, the legs move over your head in an arc until (hopefully) the toes touch the floor behind you. If it's difficult, you could always place a yoga block behind your head to rest your feet higher above the floor or use a wall instead.

This has the opposite effect of most yoga poses designed for the throat chakra. Instead of opening up your throat, it compresses it. This back-and-forth stretching allows your throat to be more flexible.

"Hal" means plow, and this pose looks like a plow of old times, a simple metal apparatus intended to be hauled by oxen and dragged through a field of soil. The tool was effective in helping to sow seeds for the harvest, so connect your mind to this fertility, and feel the new life in your chakra as you are performing this pose.

Fish Pose (Matsyasana)

"Matsya" means fish in Sanskrit. This yoga position targets your neck, effectively stretching it to open your airway to let the energy flow unobstructed.

When starting this exercise, it is best to allow your elbows and arms to support your back rather than the back of your head, making this pose safer. You can still tilt your head back to assist your throat chakra. Another technique to help lessen the discomfort is to use small support under your back, such as another yoga mat but rolled up.

Lay flat on your back, your arms on the mat. Lift your abdomen, chest, and shoulders from the mat while keeping your head touching it. Balance yourself with your hands, forearms, and elbows. If you cannot lift your torso far from the mat, let your head lift too, or support it with a yoga block until you gain more flexibility.

Feel the power of self-expression by exposing your throat. Imagine yourself in a situation where the truth is powerful, and your need to articulate your feelings.

Chapter 10: Saturn: The Ultimate Teacher

How to Reconcile Western and Vedic Astrology

We each grow attached to our principles and values, and it is the same with our adopted astrological system. We've briefly touched upon the differences between Western and Vedic astrology, but let's explore them a bit more here to wrap up how we can talk to each other as dedicated astrologers.

Sometimes, Western astrologers find Vedic astrology to be cluttered with religious and spiritual beliefs, while Vedic astrologers perceive the Western version to be lacking, needing more context such as planetary periods and karmic debts. Here, I will put together some common observations on adjusting our frame of mind as we go back and forth between those two fascinating but equally valid viewpoints.

For convenience, let's temporarily categorize followers of Western astrology as "W's" and the adherents of Vedic astrology as "V's."

The Chosen Zodiac Sign. If asked for their sign, W's would always say the Sun sign, whereas V's would reveal their Moon sign. The Moon has far more frequent adjustments than the Sun in astrology. This is because the Moon sign changes every 2.5 days—12 zodiac signs go through 30 days of the Moon cycle, which is the time it takes the Moon to revolve around the Earth—while the Sun sign changes every 30 days (12 zodiac signs go through 365 days of the Earth's rotation around the Sun). We've already explored how we read the Vedic astrological charts and how at a specific moment in time, we capture the zodiacs and the planets based upon the Moon's position in the constellation, not the Sun's.

Also, with three additional planets, W's assign Aquarius to Uranus, Pisces to Neptune, and Scorpio to Pluto (an asteroid, Ceres, rules Taurus). Thus, in modern Western astrology, no planet rules more than one sign each. However, some traditional W's keep the original pairings that originated in Vedic astrology or blend the two.

The Zodiac Itself. Remember, the zodiac is nothing more complicated than what we see when we look at the stars. W's define the zodiac as the Sun's movement around the Earth (its path is called the elliptical). The Earth tilts away from its poles when orbiting the Sun, so when you imagine a plane that bisects the Earth, you can imagine an angle between the one that forms when the sun hits the Earth and one that shows the equator.

Thus, the W's define their astrological system as "tropical," and the V's define theirs as "sidereal" (the Latin "sidereus" means "star"). That's because in the Western system when the Sun crosses the equator going north, the zodiac becomes Aries. When the Sun crosses the equator going south, the zodiac becomes Taurus. In other words, the Sun sign is based upon the Sun as referenced against the Earth's horizon at a specific location on the Earth's surface.

However, in Vedic astrology, the zodiac signs are based on the constellations, not on the Earth's horizon.

The four points that form the highs and lows of every season that most people are familiar with: the autumnal equinox, the winter solstice, the vernal equinox, and the summer solstice are perfectly aligned with the tropical zodiac. Western astrology is based on the seasons and line up perfectly with them.

But for the sidereal model (Vedic), the 0° Aries is actually 23°36 counterclockwise from the Aries point in the tropical model. This is the amount of "slippage" that has occurred for the past 2,000 years: 1 degree every 72 years, so this is very slow.

The Planets. W's consider all the planets in our solar system to be astrological planets, even Pluto, which is no longer classified as a true astronomical planet. W's reason that Pluto still exists as a considerable mass, orbiting the Sun, so its changing scientific status shouldn't affect astrology. However, Vedic astrology started in ancient India, which could view no planet beyond Saturn without telescopes, which were not invented until after the Middle Ages. Also, V's include two shadow planets, which don't exist in space but are based on Vedic folklore. Ketu and Rahu are derived lunar nodes. Rahu is the northern node, and Ketu is the southern node.

Since the Moon moves counterclockwise around the Earth, it sinks below the Sun's elliptical when it crosses Ketu, which is why Ketu is called the southern node. When it's "south" of the Sun's elliptical, it will continue spinning until it emerges at Rahu, to pop up in the north for yet another cycle. This is why Rahu is called the northern node.

In contrast, Western astrology does not consider lunar nodes. Rather, W's accept the eight standard planets as astrological planets and add Pluto as a former planet. That's nine planets, and W's add three more astrological bodies: The Sun, the Moon (the same as in Vedic astrology), and Ceres (which Vedic astrology has never acknowledged). Ceres is the only dwarf planet inside the inner solar system, which includes Mercury, Venus, Earth, Mars, and the asteroid belt that orbits the Sun between Mars and Jupiter. Therefore, Ceres is closer to the Sun than Jupiter. Ceres, an asteroid, is the largest celestial object within the inner solar system.

The Houses. W's and V's both use the ascendant as the starting point in the birth chart (or any other astrological chart picking another point), so they do share that similarity. However, V's use lunar mansions (the nakshatras), but W's do not. The way the houses are portrayed is quite different. Western astrology uses a compass-looking symbol to show the horoscope. As a contrast, you've seen often on the Vedic astrological charts the North Indian style (diamonds and triangle shapes for the houses) and the South Indian style (squares along the edges surrounding a rectangle in the middle).

Methods of Prediction. Here W's and V's differ significantly in techniques. As we've explored, V's divide up a lifetime of planetary influences by using a vimshottari dasha of 120 years and allocate a pre-determined number of years to each planet, then further divide each planet's path into antardashas. W's do not use this technique.

In Western astrology, planets use different aspects, such as a square, trine, sextile, or opposition, based upon the concept of geometrical symmetry within an astrological chart. Those are based upon angles formed inside the circular chart. All planets use such aspects equally—none is stronger than the other. However, V's use special aspects, and each planet has more strength or weakness than another according to an oral tradition recorded in texts. While V's classify planets and houses as either "malefic" or "benefic," W's prefer to consider them neutral and only look at developing patterns from the charts using placements of planets.

W's don't use *directional strength*, which is integral to Vedic astrology. In the V's view, each planet performs at its best at a certain number of houses away from the ascendant house. For Saturn, the most strength is derived from the 7th house away from the ascendant, or six spaces away.

Houses in Western astrology are rarely classified beyond their angles, forming many symbolic shapes and elemental affiliation (i.e., fire, air, water, and earth). In contrast, in Vedic astrology, houses are awarded additional factors including good or bad (i.e., the "grief-producing" houses), upachaya ("growth"), kendras, trikonas (special patterns in the chart, like the points of an imaginary superimposed triangle or a diamond), marakas ("death-inflicting"), and so on. Those Vedic terms have been passed on over thousands of years through oral tradition, and they have no equivalent in modern Western astrology.

While the rulership of houses is used by some W's, V's extensively analyze and interpret charts figuring out which planets rule which signs, giving rise to the hundreds of yogas, a few of which we have reviewed. Those planetary yogas rely upon many factors, including the houses ruled by individual planets and pairs of planets. The rich contextual history of such yogas does not have similar origins in Western astrology. Also, Vedic astrology is extensively multi-dimensional, tying into legends, myths, worship, deities, and even physical demonstrations of devotion (the "asanas" that gave rise to the physical yoga we know today).

Overall Attitude. In general, V's take a "realist" approach to human life, possibly because life was harsh in ancient times, as evidenced by the historic scripts, the Vedas. The V's assert a more sober appraisal of life, exploring risks and weaknesses deeply rather than take the risk of not confronting things they don't want to see. However, W's prefer positive messages and outcomes, working with a person's strengths and not pointing out possible weaknesses. In that sense, W's are more neutral and see astrology from a more modern perspective, which places reliance on the individual and self-affirmation.

For Students: General Principles

Nominally, MERCURY rules the conscious mind, senses, and communication, but in astrology, it's always been a balanced approach between several factors, including multiple planets.

SATURN, when used wisely, confers discipline, self-control, and structure as to your studies, enabling you to accomplish your tasks.

MARS, on the other hand, provides the energy and passion for pursuing your studies. If you don't have the zeal, then it's hard to do well at school.

VENUS is more in the background when it comes to formal education, but it can shape your character as a dedicated student as it rules love, pleasures, and values.

Finally, JUPITER governs over your higher intellect and your curiosity to discover all the answers that school (or life) has to offer.

As you can see, you must consider much more than one single planet to weigh which ones and in which astrological houses you need to focus on to better your studies.

The planets that rule the 3rd house (children's and teenagers' education) and the 9th house (college or university education) in your chart will also be considered when determining your ability to study well and hard.

Conclusion

As we have discussed, among all the astrological planets, Saturn, "Shani" in Sanskrit, is often considered as the most dreadful. As we will see below, Saturn's effect can be felt in almost all the astrological houses. As previously explored, it is the most significant planet of karma affecting our past, present, and future.

Lordships: Saturn rules two zodiacs, Capricorn and Aquarius, which naturally will occupy any two houses in the astrological chart since there can be only one zodiac sign per house in sequence. As the houses with Saturn's strongest influence, those two will start the count.

Location of Saturn, the Planet: The house where Saturn sits (as observed among the constellations in which the zodiacs are clearly seen) becomes its own house. Due to its dominant presence, Saturn will aspect upon the other lord ruling the zodiac in that house. This brings Saturn's influence up to three astrological houses. Of course, we always acknowledge that overlapping is possible. For example, Saturn the planet could sit in one of its own zodiacs in a house, i.e., Capricorn or Aquarius. If Saturn sits in its own house, its power is even stronger.

Aspect: Saturn aspects three houses, which is a lot for an astrological planet. It aspects the 3rd house, 7th house, and the 10th house from where it sits. As explained before, since the house in which Saturn is currently sitting is taken as the 1st (similar to point zero), take off one numerically for every advance from Saturn's current house to find the next house aspected. (i.e., move six spaces to find the 7th house away). Add three houses to the current tally of three, and you have six total so far.

Karaka: Saturn is the karaka (enabler) of four houses, and those are the 6th, 8th, 10th, and 12th houses. Since Saturn's personality and agenda is a natural fit for the characteristics of those four houses, we say that Saturn is a karaka for each. Since we're at a running total of six houses affected by Saturn, let's add those four, and now we have ten potential houses under the influence of Saturn.

There may be duplicate houses. For example, Capricorn, which is Saturn's ruling house, could also be aspected by Saturn in the 7th house from where the planet sits. So depending on the particular combination of patterns, the number of astrological houses under Saturn's influence could be ten, at the most, but could be as few as seven or eight. Plus, throw in all the other astrological planets and zodiac signs as they appear in the chart. Saturn's influence soon adds up!

Along with its influence on every aspect of human life, karmic results are also influenced by Saturn's transit through the constellation not just daily but also on its long cycles. Remember we discussed Saturn's longer orbits, the dhaiya, and the sade sati? That affects the houses, too. As we'll recall from earlier discussions, under the dhaiya, if it is happening currently, it will affect the astrological houses 4th and 8th away from the person's Moon sign (the zodiac sign at his birth in which the Moon was orbiting through at the time). And the sade sati, if it is currently occurring, will affect the astrological houses immediately before and succeeding his Moon sign, which is two additional houses affected. So, many layers besides the regular birth chart.

As we recall, the dasha or period of Saturn is very long at nineteen years (it is a number chosen by astrologers based upon tradition). Astrologers consider this number to be true because Saturn moves slowly to render judgments on our actions, good or bad. Saturn is the planet of truth and judgment, and as a wise heavenly body, he takes his time and patience to orbit the Sun.

There are certain periods important to Saturn because the time of the dasha is set at nineteen years. Let's see how the nineteen years repeat as cycles in a person's life (note: it matters not in this reasoning at what point of the dasha the person was born, as astrologers are just applying here the concept of the dasha to the long stages of every person's life. Think of it as our "generations" in the Western world, which we set at thirty years (more or less)).

- 1st Phase (19 Years): During the first nineteen years, the person grows up and experiences the first three houses (1st to 3rd) that concern their upbringing and education and defines their courage and conviction needed to meet a wider world.

- 2nd Phase (20 to 38 Years): The 4th to 6th houses succeed in turn as the next three houses, which decide many crucial decisions as a young adult - namely, their career, marriage (or not), having children, and their network of connections, both business and family.

- 3rd Phase (39 to 57 Years): The 7th to 9th houses take their place as the next three houses, as they consolidate their place in life, enjoying the peak of their career and perhaps anticipating grandchildren. Their fortune should be consolidated, and they should enjoy foreign travel and some leisure to reap the benefits of years of hard work.

- 4th Phase (58 to 75 Years): The last three houses, the 10th to the 12th, cap off an extraordinary life as they start volunteering in their community, doing charity work, and perhaps is recognized as a leader or wise person to whom everyone looks to. They must also contemplate the end of their life (even if they are very healthy and expected to live for decades more) and prepare to achieve moksha.

Therefore, we should understand the effect of Saturn in each stage of life, using clues gleaned from our astrological charts to help us make wise decisions.

The Ultimate Teacher

You need Saturn to balance your karma. Whether it's during Saturn's dasha or antardasha, or its dhaiya or sade sati, or a combination of any of those, these are good times to let go of your karma, to work hard, and to care for others so bad karma will melt away, helping to unburden you and your past. Many people fearful of Saturn's malefic reputation will blame Saturn if they get into trouble, but the truth is that it's not Saturn's doing. Saturn is a tough teacher, but it only sets the example. It does not tell you to take on wrongful acts or to choose not to persevere. Only you can decide that. When you make good decisions to enhance your judgment, your stamina, and your health, and to ensure that you spread goodness and generosity among your world, then you will find that Saturn can be most forgiving and gentle.

Part 5: Mercury in Astrology

The Ultimate Guide to the Planet of Communication, Intellect, Memory, and Transportation

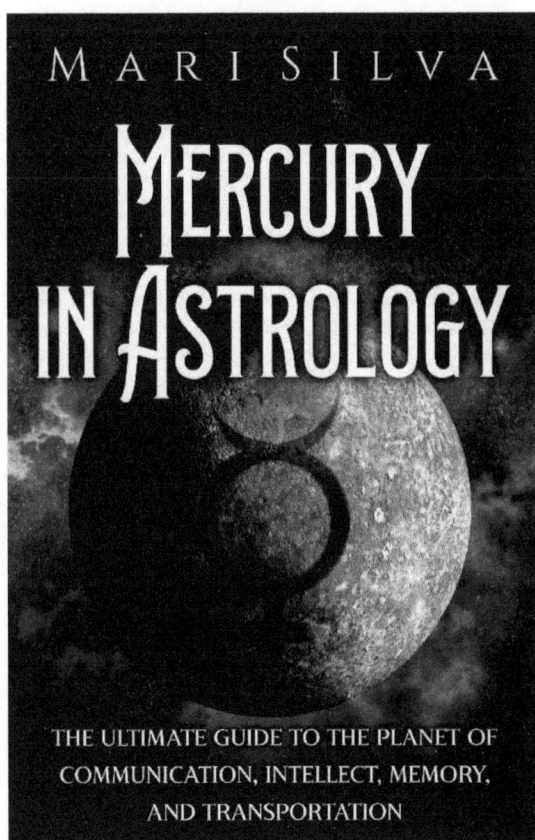

Introduction

If you have decided to take a deeper look into astrology to understand how cosmology plays a significant role in every aspect of your life, studying the planets in our solar system will be very helpful.

You've probably heard of Mercury as being this tiny little red planet that buzzes around the sun much quicker than Earth does. You may have heard that when ancient Romans noticed how quick Mercury was in orbiting the sun, they named it after their messenger god. You may also have heard that while Mercury is much smaller than Earth and orbits the Sun much faster than Earth does, it has incredibly long days. One day on Mercury is equivalent to nearly two months here on Earth.

While all of these things are true, what's more important is how Mercury as a planet influences us as individuals and our existence at large as a species.

This book is designed to help you understand the astrological importance of Mercury and how it plays a role, to varying degrees, in the lives of people that it comes in contact with. Mercury has its own unique set of features, traits, and energies that are broadcasted to individuals who come under the influence of this fascinating planet, whether they like it or not. As recipients of cosmic energy, we have little control over how this force influences us, but with a better understanding of this energy, we can channel it and modify our behavior in a way that propels our lives toward success.

In the discussions that follow, we will dive into the finer details of Mercury as a planet and its astrological value. We'll also talk about the implications it has when we understand astrological analysis at a deeper level. Finally, by employing natal charts and understanding the features of various houses, we will build the groundwork upon which the performance of various actors can be evaluated.

Within these houses, we will look at how Mercury plays a role and its effect on each house's properties. In essence, we are all affected by the natal chart elements, with the only variable being the extent to which we are affected.

While Mercury is one of the oldest known planets and has been a part of astrological study for centuries, we have taken a broader perspective. We have incorporated long-standing beliefs together with modern-day research to compile a book that yields a well-informed and up-to-date analysis. Most books are either superficial and surface or too technically advanced for the average person to gain insight into. This book delivers a balanced approach that enlightens you on the technical aspect of astrology and conveys this information in an easy-to-understand manner you can relate to.

Whether you are a complete beginner or have some understanding and familiarity with astrology, this book will help clarify existing perspectives.

With easy-to-follow instructions, relatable examples, and hands-on methods, this book aims to be just as entertaining as it is informative. Without going into too much detail, the aim is to familiarize the reader with the astrological landscape focusing on Mercury. If you wish to explore some of the topics discussed in this book separately, you can easily supplement your learning with external resources.

If you are ready to gain a more in-depth perspective of astrology and how Mercury influences your stars, let's begin.

Chapter 1: Mercury: The Messenger of the Gods

Mercury is one of only five planets in our Solar System that we can see with the naked eye. The smallest planet among the eight planets that revolve around the Sun, Mercury has been known to humans for thousands of years.

The earliest known observations of the planet are found in Babylonian tablets that have been dated back to about the 14th century B.C. - nearly 3500 years ago! The first confirmed observation is credited to the ancient Greek astronomer, Timocharis, who mentioned the planet in 265 B.C.

The earliest Greeks believed that the planet Mercury was two distinct objects - the Morning Star, Apollo, and the Evening Star, Hermes. The Romans gave the planet its modern name, Mercury, thought to be the equivalent of the Greek God, Hermes.

The ancient Egyptians knew the planet as Sabkou and were the first people to discover that it orbited the Sun. In ancient China, on the other hand, the planet was given the name the "Hour Star" and was linked to the cardinal direction north, as well as the water phase based on the traditional Chinese scheme of the Five Phases. This led the planet to become known as the water star by modern Chinese, Japanese, Korean, and Vietnamese cultures.

Hindu mythology and Germanic paganism both associated the planet with Wednesday. Mercury is given the name Buddha by Hindus and Woden by the Teutonic people. The Maya of Mesoamerica represented Mercury as an owl (or four owls) that also served as a messenger to their Underworld.

Other observations include those by medieval Islamic astronomers Abū Ishāq Ibrāhīm al-Zarqālīr, Ibn Bajjah, and Qotb al-Din Shirazi between the 11th and 13th centuries, by Kerala school astronomer, Nilakantha Somayaji, in the 15th century, and by noted Danish astronomer, Tycho Brahe, in the 16th century.

Galileo's first telescopic observation was made in the 17th century, with Italian astronomer, Zupus first observing the phases of Mercury as early as 1639. These observations noted the start of modern astronomical research and exploration of the planet.

Mercury in Ancient Babylon

Nabu

Ancient Babylonian astrologers associated the planet we know today as Mercury with the Mesopotamian god Nabu. Nabu was one of the most important deities in the pantheon and was the son of Marduk, the king of the gods and the head of the Mesopotamian pantheon.

Nabu was the patron god of rational arts and literacy, including wisdom, scribes, and writing. Additionally, he was also identified as a divine messenger. Nabu gained prominence as a deity in the 1st millennium BC, following the rise in prominence of his father Marduk in the early second and late first millenniums B.C.

Their rise coincided with the observation of the planet Mercury by ancient Mesopotamian astronomers. This overlap undoubtedly helped the ancient Mesopotamians link the planet with Nabu, the prince of the gods.

Nabu is not the only messenger deity linked to the planet Mercury - other similar deities linked to the planet include the Greek Hermes and the Roman Mercury. Even the Maya believed the planet to represent the owl as a divine messenger to the Underworld.

However, Nabu's relationship with Hermes and Mercury - all three being messenger gods, and Nabu and Hermes serving as wisdom deities - served as a key factor in the evolution of the way people viewed the closest planet to the Sun. Even contemporary astrologers still respect the planet's history. After all, it is known today by the name of Nabu's brother-god, Mercury.

Hermes, the Herald of the Gods

Hermes

When later Greeks realized that Mercury was, in fact, a single astronomical object instead of two separate ones, they knew it as Hermes due to its speed as it traveled across the sky. Indeed, Hermes is also identified as the god of speed and travel, equipped with winged sandals that granted him the power of flight and helped him complete his role as messenger of the gods.

But the Green God Hermes was identified as far more than just that.

The Birth of Hermes

Hermes was one of the divine sons of Zeus, king of the gods, by the Pleiad Maia, one of the daughters of the Titan Atlas. Maia gave birth to the newborn god in a sacred cave on Kyllene or Mount Kyllini.

When Maia fell asleep, the rapidly maturing infant snuck out of the cave, making his way to Pieria (Thessaly), where he stole some cattle from Apollo. Hiding his tracks, he led them to Pylos, where he hid them – save for two, which he sacrificed. He then invented a plectrum and a lyre using a nearby tortoise, stringing it with the guts of the cattle he had just sacrificed.

Meanwhile, Apollo discovered the theft of his cattle and soon learned that Hermes was the thief. When he confronted Maia with this, she would not believe him, saying that Hermes was still a newborn in his swaddling clothes. So the sun god brought his claims to their shared father, Zeus, who sided with him.

Under his father's command, Hermes led his half-brother to where he had hidden the cattle. There, Apollo first heard the sound of the lyre and was immediately enchanted – so enchanted that he exchanged his cattle for it. The lyre would then forever be associated with Apollo as one of his sacred symbols and identifying attributes.

Still, the exchange between Apollo and Hermes was not yet complete. As Hermes tended to the cattle that were now his, he invented another instrument, the shepherd's pipe. As with the lyre, when Apollo heard their music, he was enchanted, and in exchange, he offered him a golden staff.

Hermes, however, craved both the staff and the knowledge of the art of prophecy, over which Apollo had dominion. So he exchanged the pipe only after Apollo had committed to giving him the staff and teaching him prophecy by using pebbles.

Following this adventure, Zeus confirmed Hermes as the messenger of the gods and his own personal herald. The staff that Hermes won from his half-brother would become the caduceus, one of his sacred symbols.

Hermes, the "Divine Trickster"

In addition to gaining status as a messenger to the gods, Hermes' theft of Apollo's cattle also cemented his place as the god of thieves and trickery. He stole Poseidon's trident, Aphrodite's girdle, and Artemis's arrows at different times in mythology.

Hermes served as Zeus's primary agent when he needed something stolen or needed to orchestrate a trick. In one of the best-known examples, he was the one who was noted as having gifted Pandora, the first woman, with the gifts of lies and seductive words.

At the same time, however, this trickster nature also meant that he was extremely quick-witted and able to talk himself out of the most challenging situations. This extended to dealings with other gods.

In one story, the giant twin sons of Poseidon, Otus, and Ephialtes (also known as the Aloadae), once kidnapped Ares. They held the war god captive in a bronze jar for thirteen months until he became weak and near death. At this point, Hermes was told of the kidnapping by Eriboea, the giant's stepmother. He then rescued his half-brother by stealing him away from the Aloadae.

Hermes as Mercury

As Rome became the most important kingdom in the Western world, Roman beliefs started to take precedence over Greek ones. The ancient Romans syncretized existing religious beliefs with Green beliefs to make Roman religion more palatable to the citizens of other states.

One major aspect of this syncretization was associating Roman deities with existing Greek ones. Zeus became linked to Jupiter, Hera to Juno, Demeter to Ceres, and Hermes to Mercury.

Like his Greek counterpart, Mercury was known as the god of commerce, messages, luck, thieves, merchants, and communication, among other things. Like Mercury, he was also one of the Dii Consentes, one of the twelve major deities in the Roman pantheon, just as he was one of the Twelve Olympian Gods in the Greek pantheons.

In his role as god of thieves, Mercury was the father of Autolycus, also known as the prince of thieves. By his wife Amphithea, Autolycus was the father to Anticlea, granddaughter of Mercury.

Anticlea would marry Laërtes, King of Ithaca, and become the mother of Odysseus, making Hermes/Mercury the great-grandfather the renowned hero. Indeed, it was Autolycus who gave Odysseus his name.

Hermes/Mercury and Odysseus

Odysseus

Hermes/Mercury is intrinsically linked to his great-grandson. Both the god and hero experienced similar experiences in their respective myths. For example, both were trickster figures (Odysseus's trick of the Trojan Horse was one of the most famous in history). Both slain giants (Argos for Mercury, Polyphemus for Odysseus) traveled – and rose – from the Underworld.

Yet, their relationship went beyond the symbolic. Hermes/Mercury also played a key role during the Odyssey, Odysseus's ten-year journey to return to Ithaca following the ten years he spent fighting the Trojan War.

During the Odyssey, Odysseus and his crew found themselves led to an island-ruled enchantress and minor goddess, Circe. Circe welcomed the men and fed them cheese and wine before turning half of the crew into pigs.

Before Odysseus could be caught in her trap, Hermes/Mercury visited his great-grandson to warn him about the fate that lay in front of him. He also gifted him a magical herb known as moly, which helped Odysseus trick Circe and resisted the effects of her magic.

This, one of the hero's most famous adventures, led to the goddess falling in love with him and releasing his sailors. Odysseus and his men proceeded to stay on her island for a year, with Odysseus as Circe's lover, before finally departing and resuming their journey back to Ithaca.

Later, he was enchanted by the nymph Calypso, who held him, prisoner on her island Ogygia, where he served as her consort for seven years. Though Calypso imprisoned him by enchanting him with her singing, at the end of the seven years, Odysseus could no longer bear his longing for his wife, Penelope.

For his sake, his patron goddess Athena begged her father, Zeus, to order him released from the island. It was Hermes/Mercury that Zeus sent to fulfill this task, acting in his role as the messenger of the gods. The messenger god ordered Calypso to free his great-grandson, for

Odysseus was destined to have a greater destiny than living with her forever. Once again, Odysseus was able to escape an enchanted island through the actions of his godly ancestor, resuming his journey home.

Hermes/Mercury, Helper of Heroes

Aside from Odysseus, Hermes/Mercury also played a significant role in stories of other mythological heroes. One of the most significant of these is the role he played in the story Perseus.

Polydectes, the ruler of the island of Seriphos, had demanded from Perseus, son of Zeus, the head of the Gorgon Medusa, as a gift. Athena, who bore a grudge against the Gorgon, served as Perseus's patron goddess during this quest, guiding him to kill Medusa.

To aid in his quest, the gods offered Perseus a host of divine gifts. From Zeus, he received a sword and Hades's helm of darkness and from Athena a polished shield. Hermes/Mercury, however, gifted Perseus a pair of winged sandals, allowing him to fly and complete his task quicker.

Roman mythographers noted that Mercury bore a special love for Perseus, and some considered the two to have been lovers. Some Roman traditions bore that Mercury also gifted the hero a winged cap and that it was he who gifted Perseus a helmet of invisibility rather than Zeus.

Mercury's sandals would come in useful for more than simply the slaying of the Gorgon. On Perseus's journey home, he encountered Princess Andromeda, chained to a rock in the middle of the ocean and left as a sacrifice to the sea monster Cetus. There, he used the sandals to free the princess, whom he would later marry.

Hermes/Mercury the Psychopomp

Beyond his role as messenger to the gods, Hermes/Mercury was a guide to the souls of the dead. His task was to guide them to the domain of Hades/Pluto in the Underworld, where their actions in life would be judged.

In his role as the guide of the dead, Hermes/Mercury served as a guide to Hercules, the greatest of all heroes, during the Twelfth and final task of his famous Labors. He was the one who helped direct Hercules as he traveled to Hades and captured the three-headed dog Cerberus, who guarded the gates of the Underworld.

Guided by the divine messenger, the hero was able to carry Cerberus back to the world of the living. Once above, he brought him to Eurystheus, the king under whose command Hercules had completed his labors.

In another story that shows his role as guide of the dead, Mercury intervened in the grief of the mortal queen Laodameia. Laodameia was a queen of Phylake, whose husband, Protesilaos, had been the first Greek killed in Troy. Yet, even after his death, she continued to love him and grieved his loss.

Her devotion moved the gods that Jupiter commanded Mercury to guide her husband's ghost out of the Underworld. Mercury brought the ghost of Protesilaos to his wife, where they spoke for three hours before the god returned the man to the Underworld once again.

In addition to being the Psychopompus and guide of the dead, Hermes/Mercury was the yearly guide to the goddess of springtime, Persephone.

Hades had taken Persephone to serve as his bride in the Underworld. Yet her mother, Demeter, was so grieved at the loss of her daughter that she neglected her divine duties. As Demeter was the goddess of agriculture and grain, her grief meant the earth grew cold, and no crops grew.

Eventually, Zeus was forced to intervene. He forced Hades to return Persephone to her mother. Unfortunately, however, the goddess of spring had consumed a handful of pomegranate seeds during her stay in the Underworld. Thus, she was compelled to return to the realm of the dead for part of the year.

This episode was the reason the seasons changed from winter to summer. As god of trade and thieves and in his role as Psyhopompus, Hermes/Mercury was the only Olympian god who could cross the boundary between life and death whenever he wished. Thus, Zeus commanded him to accompany his half-sister each year as she returned to the world of the living from the Underworld. So, Hermes/Mercury also served as the herald of spring and the god of fertility and animal husbandry.

Hermes/Mercury, the Agent of Zeus/Jupiter

Zeus

As herald to the king of the gods, Hermes/Mercury was closely linked to his father, Zeus/Jupiter. Nowhere is this more visible than in the story of Io and Argus.

Io was an Argive princess and one of the most beautiful mortal women of her time. She caught the eye of Zeus/Jupiter, who made her his lover. By the king of the gods, Io would bear their daughter, Ceroessa, and son, Epaphus. Through these children, she would be the ancestor to some of the best-known heroes of old, including Hercules and Perseus.

Yet, in her role as mortal lover to Zeus/Jupiter, Io also drew the jealous wrath of his wife, Hera/Juno, who she had served as a priestess before gaining the attention of her husband. To protect her from the queen of the gods, Jupiter transformed her into a white cow.

However, Hera/Juno discovered this deception and begged for the cow as a gift from her husband. With no obvious reason to refuse his wife, Zeus/Jupiter was forced to acquiesce.

Now possessing Io, Hera/Juno then sent her agent, Argus Panoptes, to watch over her and prevent Zeus/Jupiter from visiting. A giant with 100 eyes, Argus always slept with at least a few of his many eyes open.

Zeus/Jupiter could no longer bear the distress of Io, and so he devised a plan to free her. To this end, he commanded Hermes/Mercury to go to Argus and kill him.

Hermes/Mercury was aware that as long as even one of his eyes was open, Argus could not be killed. So, he visited the giant in the guise of a shepherd, playing the pipes he had invented when he did so.

Charmed by Hermes/Mercury's music, Argus invited him to sit and rest. So Hermes/Mercury joined him, and to entertain his host, started telling him tales of the gods. These included the competition between Apollo and the wind god Zephyrus for the love of the mortal youth Hyacinthus and how Zephyrus killed the youth when he chose the love of Apollo.

He told the story of Asclepius, the god of medicine and son of Apollo, who Zeus/Jupiter killed for resurrecting the dead before he (Asclepius) was made a god. Hermes/Mercury continued to tell Argus stories of the gods and lovers before he finally started the tale of his son Pan and his chase of the nymph Syrinx.

However, by this tale, Argus had fallen into a deep sleep, and all his eyes had closed. Seeing his chance, Hermes/Mercury drew his sword, killing the giant. In her grief, Hera/Juno used the giant's eyes to decorate the peacock's tail feathers, her sacred bird, so that he would be remembered for years to come.

So, through Hermes/Mercury's quick wit and skilled tongue, Io was freed from her imprisonment. Hera/Juno, however, had not forgiven her and sent a gadfly to chase her until she finally reached Egypt. There, Zeus/Jupiter restored her to human form, and it was there that she bore the king of the gods two children.

Hermes/Mercury and the Divine Skies

More than simply the name of the planet, the myths of Hermes/Mercury still play a role in the way the planet known as Mercury is viewed today.

Mercury was known for his quick-wit and skill at communication and being the god of travel. Similarly, the planet rules over human wit and their ability to interact with other people and cover transportation and other forms of travel. Indeed, the astronomical symbol for Mercury draws from the head and winged cap of the messenger god and the caduceus that is his sacred symbol.

Chapter 2: Mercury in Astrology

Mercury, also known as Hermes in Greek mythology and Budh in Vedic astrology, is the winged messenger of the gods. Hermes is considered the chatty god of speed who excels at being witty with his sharp tongue. In the Roman mythos, he's depicted as a trickster god who outwits monsters, humans, demigods, and even the other gods with his cunning and silver tongue. The astrological importance of Mercury is very similar to the mythological aspects we'll be discussing.

Mercury is the tiniest planet in our solar system. Mercury's speed is very fast, traveling around the Sun in just 88 days, mirroring the reputation of Hermes as being the fastest god. Mercury stays in each zodiac sign for three weeks on average.

Mercury even passes the Earth and sometimes causes the Mercury retrograde, which can last for up to nine weeks. This retrograde will be discussed further in detail, but it happens around three to four times per year and causes a disruption in communication systems. This disturbance to communications systems is relatable to the mythos as Mercury is the messenger of the gods and governs all forms of communication.

Language and Communication

Whenever we meet new people, we're always experiencing their Mercury counterpart since it's the planet that commands a person's communication skills. This applies even when the interactions aren't in the real world and exist in the online sphere. The words that we use to type our e-mails and messages fall under the purview of Mercury as well.

As the translator and messenger, Mercury also governs the various aspects of language, including verbal and written words. The transfer and synthesis of all our data, including mobile communication, transportation, logistics, and multiple other factors, are governed by the tiny planet. Since Mercury is the messenger of the gods and has a sharp tongue, it's also very much responsible for the speech articulation skills in people. It can drastically affect the oratory abilities of those influenced by it.

The reputation of Mercury as a trickster is demonstrated in the astrological context as well. The sharp wit, sense of humor, and quick-thinking skills are what Mercury brings into the signs it influences.

Perception of the World

Mercury lords over two different astrological signs, as would be expected of the dual-natured god who handles so many divine duties at once. The signs governed by this planet are Gemini and Virgo, which we'll be studying later in this chapter.

Perhaps the most interesting feature of Mercury is its influence on our perception of the world around us. The dual-natured planet works in mysterious ways and determines how we perceive the different elements of our surroundings. For example, Hermes in Greek mythology is present in both the spiritual realm of the gods and the material world of humans, representing the transcending qualities of the mind.

The way a person shares the ideas in their minds, how the various senses work together to make sense of the various stimuli, and the attitude toward all this feedback is what Mercury governs in a person.

The influence of this planet also goes as far as our understanding of the different ideas we have. Mercury operates from both the conscious and the unconscious planes since it has a dual nature. The way we process and analyze things is affected by how this planet impacts us, and it also helps us handle our pent-up energies.

Mercury truly has a profound impact on our understanding. It affects how we approach various facets of our life and helps us rearrange our thoughts to make them easier to convey. These qualities imparted by Mercury due to the conversational and critical nature it has to us play a greater role in our lives than we can initially comprehend.

Influence on the Signs

Even recent research by psychologists and cognitive scientists has also determined that multiple types of intelligence exist in every person. This was known to the ancient astrologers long before today's researchers, and they attributed these different types of intelligence to the planet Mercury. So it is very influential in determining if you're leaning more toward the logical and rational side or the inspired and creative side.

When Mercury is lord of the 7th, 8th, and 12th houses, it doesn't bode well and creates many hindrances. However, the Virgo and the Gemini greatly benefit from the presence of Mercury due to Mercury being their governing planet. Virgos especially benefit a lot more than any other signs since Mercury is exalted when it's present in the house of Virgo. We'll be looking at exaltation and debilitation in detail in the upcoming sections, but they can be understood as the amplification or diminishing of the benefits of Mercury depending on the house it's present in.

Since Mercury itself belongs to the air signs, it leans more toward unemotional, practical, and logical thinking. If Mercury is present in the water signs, that makes the person more inclined toward the intuitive and emotional side. However, in the fire signs it is biased toward instinct and inspiration. Mercury is also present in the earth signs, but in this case, it tends to be pragmatic and very stable, just like the Earth.

Influence on Personal Life

Even in an individual's personal life, Mercury is highly influential as it determines the motivation behind each action that the person takes. The impact of Mercury in the life of a person is so strong that it dictates where the mental energy is directed. The effect of Mercury on the thinking of a person greatly influences the career path that they choose, and this decides the direction that their life takes.

Even in the various relationships in your life, the clashing Mercury can cause a lot of damage. There can be strife, lack of clarity, and conflict if Mercury isn't at the right place. The earth sign Mercury and the air sign Mercury may face issues with compatibility, and the air signs may get along pretty well due to the inherent nature of the planet. The air signs will get along due to the similar speed of communication and peace of mind whereas, the Mercury in other signs may lead to conflict.

The Mercury in your chart can point toward how an individual uses the information to convey their message and their unique method of communication. The strongest effect that Mercury has on other planets is the desire for effective communication. Even the way that other planets affect Mercury influences communication as well. This shows how much of an emphasis this planet places on proper and effective communication.

Often, the people with dominant Mercury are also very well-behaved, and others find it easy to like them due to their demeanor. People under the influence of this planet are also liked by almost everyone because they are very generous and have a great sense of humor. Moreover, they make great orators because of their perfect articulation skills, their charm, their unflawed reasoning, and their natural gift of diction.

Since Mercury is known to be a planet that blesses those under its influence with wit, the people with a favorable Mercury position are also very intelligent and intellectually capable. They have a good intelligence factor and are generally very wise when making decisions in life. This, combined with their social appeal, makes them more inclined toward widespread fame and recognition as well.

In life, everything has its own positive and negative effects, which is why Mercury has a few negative sides to it as well. The nervousness or indecisiveness in a personality is usually one of the drawbacks of Mercury. This makes it extremely difficult for people who Mercury dominates to stick to a repetitive and boring job. Mercury dominance shapes a person's attitude, so they'll have a constant hunger for new and adventurous experiences, which is why a challenging job is best suited for them.

More often than not, the people who are dominated by this planet are born with an innate sense of anxiety. This anxiety can get too much at times to be handled properly and will lead to poor decisions. Even though people influenced by Mercury are known for their communication and oratory skills, crippling anxiety can negatively affect these positive qualities.

If Mercury is unfavorable, then it can cause harm to a person's health or even life. People heavily influenced by Mercury are more prone to disease and serious health-related conditions. This can be one of the biggest drawbacks of having Mercury as your dominant planet.

There are other negative effects of Mercury too, which include being excessively picky and overly technical. The positives of Mercury are often more than enough to offset the few negative qualities, but they were pointed out nonetheless so that you have a better understanding of the effects that this small planet has on people.

Suitable Professions

The people with a dominant Mercury are often very good at jobs like editing, teaching, training, and other similar professions. Mercury is suitable for these jobs since these jobs require a personality that can make mundane tasks into something much more interesting. His students will likely not like a teacher who simply keeps teaching on the same boring concepts, but likeability plays a huge role in a teacher's success. The people influenced by Mercury can infuse their sense of humor and great communication skills into their work, making it sound much more interesting and appealing.

A lot of writers are dominated by Mercury as well. This is especially applicable to those writers who have to write short-form content like poems, guides, white papers, short stories, or lyrics. This is because they are very practical. After all, their indecisiveness makes them less suitable for work that may require long and concentrated efforts.

This isn't only applicable to the people, but it applies to the different companies as well. A company with a lot of influence from Mercury in its charts will more likely be successful at sales, telecommunications, advertising, or other similar tasks. This is because Mercury favors great communication skills, and this company type exactly matches the characteristics required of a Mercurial personality.

The qualities imparted by Mercury are very analytical and logical. This planet doesn't depend a lot on the emotional spectrum but rather utilizes reasoning. This is why mercurial people can make excellent mathematicians, scientists, doctors, and engineers. Likewise, their logical thinking and unemotional attitude are why they make very good teachers, as they know what to focus on to deliver the most comprehensive and logical explanation of new concepts.

Sales and advertisement are the professions where people who have Mercury in their charts dominate. However, promoting them to senior positions often results in the opposite effect since they're not very competent at managing and delegating responsibilities. A Mercurial personality should be kept where they can utilize all of their communication skills, charm, and humor to the fullest, and then they can be much more productive than others.

The same can be said for telecommunications personnel since they will effortlessly communicate with their clients and turn even the cold calls into sales. The dominant feature of Mercury is communication ability, and this is where these skills are utilized to their fullest. The conversational skills and humor help here a lot as mercurial people know how to rope in someone by keeping them entertained throughout the conversation. They can also utilize their gift of articulation to speak out just the right combination of words which can resuscitate even a deal that's doomed.

The Mercury is especially favorable to people to wish to start their own business since a business involves a lot of pitching and selling of ideas. Mercurial people are naturally good at pitching their ideas and convincing others with their smooth talking skills. The other important factor is their intellectual ability, which helps them come up with new and innovative ideas that can easily be sold to investors and consumers. The speed at which they can gather information and then analyze it to gain maximum insight is astronomical and helps a lot while doing business.

If a job involves traveling, Mercury-dominated people will absolutely love it since Hermes is considered the gods' messenger. Traveling throughout the material world and the divine worlds were his task. Mercurials also love traveling and visiting new places, making them ideal international executives, photographers, or traveling salespeople.

Mercury Retrograde

A fascinating aspect of Mercury is retrograde, which has many effects on your overall personality. These effects are vastly different from the effects that Mercury would otherwise have if it weren't retrograde. A retrograde is usually a negative event in astrology, and it leads to multiple complications that can nullify many of the positive effects of Mercury. Not only can the retrograde diminish the positive, but it can also lead to a complete inversion by displaying opposite signs to what should be displayed by a mercurial person.

During a retrograde, Mercury appears to go backward in its orbit. This usually happens due to the slowing speed of Mercury. It's an optical illusion that can be attributed to the different speeds of movement of the planets. It's just like an illusion you might experience while you're in a car that's traveling faster than another car on the road. While both the cars are going forward, you'll feel like the other car is going backward.

The Mercury retrograde happens three to four times a year and is signified by an "R" in your charts, and has some interesting effects. Almost 25% of people with a dominant Mercury are born with a retrograde that causes them to develop more reflective and introverted personalities. During a retrograde, communications on Earth can act up, contrary to Mercury's communicative nature. Similarly, retrograde Mercurials develop qualities opposite to the usual nature of Mercury in people.

A Mercury retrograde is often a time for contemplation, and it's advised that people don't sign any new agreements or contracts during this time since it isn't auspicious to do so. The retrograde is highly dependent on the zodiac sign it's interacting with, as different signs can have different effects.

Effects on Gemini and Virgo

Every planet in astrology rules over a zodiac sign, but Mercury is special. Since Mercury has a dual nature, it lords over two different zodiac signs: Gemini and Virgo. Both the signs are associated with entirely different characteristics of Mercury which we'll be discussing in this section.

Virgo represents the feminine side of the planet, and it focuses more on the analytical and tactile part of Mercury. Virgos have a talent for organizing and processing information. Virgos depend on their analytical ability to navigate through life, and it's a strong suit for them. Another interesting thing that works in favor of Virgos is that Mercury is exalted in the house of Virgo. This means that Mercury is the only planet that is exalted in the house which it lords over. The people with exalted Mercury have even greater skills in communication and persuasion and many other traits compared to standard Mercurial people.

While on the other side of the spectrum, the Gemini is the masculine aspect of Mercury. Geminis represent the chatty aspects and have a mastery over the art of oration and convincing people. Geminis who are under the influence of Mercury can easily convince anyone about their point of view and make excellent salespeople. However, Geminis are prone to making overstatements and promises they can't keep due to their extravagance and overconfidence in their own abilities.

Mercury and Pisces

Pisces is the house where Mercury is debilitated, which means that the traits of Mercury will not meld well together with the traits of Pisces. This is because Mercury is rational, practical, unemotional, and logical in nature, whereas Pisces is a creative and artistic sign.

A person with a debilitated Mercury will most likely harness the traits of Mercury in the wrong direction, and it'll lead to great difficulties in their life. It will cause failed marriages, lost business ventures, failure to achieve fame, being prone to committing fraud, and even having a wicked mind.

Mercury will repress Pisces' positive traits, and it'll lead them to fare poorly in life. However, there are a few combinations with other planets like Jupiter where it can be a wonderful combination if the alignments are just right, but that won't be discussed here due to its vast length.

Tabular Summary

- Orbit Time in One Zodiac Sign: 25 days (approximately)
- Orbit Time of the Entire Zodiac: 10 months (approximately)
- Zodiac Signs Ruled: Virgo and Gemini
- Exalted In: Virgo
- Debilitated In: Pisces
- Lucky Day: Wednesday
- Lucky Color: Green
- Lucky Gemstone: Emerald
- Lucky Metal: Silver
- Favorite Metal: Brass
- Favorite Direction: North
- Friendly Planets: Sun, Venus, and Ascended Moon
- Enemy Planets: Moon
- Neutral Planets: Mars, Saturn, and Jupiter
- Body Parts Ruled: Skin and Nervous System

Chapter 3: What's Your Communication Style?

In Astrology, Mercury, the smallest planet of our solar system, is often associated with communication and the overall thinking process. The same way Mercury conveys messages around the Sun, your Mercury sign allows you to share your thoughts with other people. Since Mercury is the planet closest to the Sun, its sign also has a bearing on your main zodiac sign, the Sun sign, defining your overall personality. Consequently, your Mercury sign will determine how you make connections with people based on your ability to relate to their emotions and engage in conversations. People use different methods to communicate, and it's no secret that for some, being a great conversationalist comes more naturally than for others. Some people are better at expressing themselves and are glad to delve into meaningful topics, while others prefer to chat about trivialities. According to your Mercury sign, understanding your communication style can help you learn to convey your message more efficiently. It can also teach you how to be a better listener, the part of a conversation people often struggle with. As you will learn from this chapter, your willingness to talk about anything will often be enough to have a meaningful conversation. And if you are one of those people who prefers to let others lead a discussion, you can also learn why it's vital to express yourself from time to time.

Capricorn	Aquarius	Pisces	Aries
♑	♒	♓	♈
22 Dec - 20 Jan	21 Jan -19 Feb	20 Feb - 20 Mar	21 Mar- 19 Apr
Taurus	Gemini	Cancer	Leo
♉	♊	♋	♌
20 Apr - 20 May	21 May - 21 Jun	22 Jun - 23 Jul	24 Jul - 23 Aug
Virgo	Libra	Scorpio	Sagitarius
♍	♎	♏	♐
24 Aug - 22 Sept	23 Sept - 22 Oct	23 Oct - 22 Nov	23 Nov - 20 Dec

Aries

As an Aries Mercury, you tend to speak from your heart and love to engage in passionate discussions. Even though you are a straight shooter, this will not prevent you from giving longer speeches if you need to. You are not afraid of speaking up for anything you consider a worthy cause, which can be a wonderful trait. Your energy can inspire others to speak up as well, whether they know you personally or not. And if you have a friend who cannot do so, they can always count on you to fight for their cause. However, your emotional communication style will often mean that you don't think things through. You won't choose your words either, which can get you into a lot of trouble if they are directed toward the wrong person. Plus, you tend to raise your voice in the heat of the moment, which can be off-putting if someone is just trying to hold a civil conversation with you. If you want to share your passion with others, you will need to learn to leave your immature tantrums behind and raise your voice only when you absolutely need to. Next time, when something evokes strong emotions in you, take a deep breath first, and take your time to think before voicing your opinion about it.

Taurus

Mercury makes Taurus one of the most tenacious signs of the zodiac. You can argue your point for hours at a time, and there will be nothing that will change your mind. Although you only speak when you absolutely need to, when you do, you are usually very passionate about the topic, and you make sure everyone knows that. Because of your rare shining moments, you often feel misunderstood, which will further fuel your need to prove your point in a discussion. Unfortunately, when it comes to having a meaningful conversation, you sometimes neglect actually listening to the other person talking. You can be so bent on proving your point that you won't even consider whether they are right or wrong, so you just keep talking about what you think. This can be quite an irritating trait and can even make significant people in your life turn away from you. If you aren't careful about what you are arguing about, you can come off as offensive and selfish. Remember, a conversation consists of two equal components: speaking and listening. You should aim to alternate between these two parts in an equal measure instead of having a one-sided conversation. You will be surprised how much you can learn by listening to others.

Gemini

Gemini in Mercury usually have an active social life and are very accomplished conversationalists. Whether you are having a long discussion in real life or putting short messages on social media, you like to be up to date with everything and everyone around you. This can come in handy if you have a work position that requires you to make small talk with clients, followed by more meaningful professional discussions. Although you can never run out of conversation topics or people to talk to, you are not always interested in hearing what other people have to say. You will focus your mind on a certain part of the conversation and try to persuade your partner to accept your point of view. If you fail to do so at first, you will keep returning to that part and be even more passionate about it. As this can give you an air of aggression, don't be surprised if you are left alone in the middle of the conversation. You will need to learn that you cannot control every conversation you have and that everyone has the same right to speak their mind as you do. Sometimes, you will just need to let go and concede victory to the other person.

Cancer

Instead of engaging in a conversation with someone, Cancers in Mercury often prefer to express their thoughts in other forms. Even if you take part in a discussion, you rarely initiate it, and you never do much actual talking. You prefer to observe your partner and listen to them, carefully analyzing their every word. Because you want to avoid misunderstanding, the answers you provide to their questions or point of view are always thought through. The problem is, all that thinking can make it seem you are disinterested in a conversation, and the people you are talking to will probably wonder why. They can erroneously conclude that you have nothing meaningful to add to any discussion. If you are a typical representative of your sign, you will be anything but an uninformed and slow conversationalist. To make sure everyone is aware of your true colors, you will need to learn to speak up from time to time. There is nothing wrong with staying calm during heated arguments but try not to look like you are bored either. Additionally, you will win more debates by talking more often, which can be a great confidence booster.

Leo

There is no other sign that possesses more talent for grabbing attention than a Leo. If you are born under this sign, Mercury will always guide you in the direction of individuals you can share your thoughts with. You will find it easy to talk to them about literally anything, and you won't have to worry about keeping their attention either. By carefully choosing your words and always aiming to avoid offending anyone, you can charm the most powerful opponents. This characteristic can make it seem like you are a trustworthy individual with whom almost anyone can relax and have a meaningful chat. While it's vital to emphasize your words to prove your point, you can also go too far with this. Your opponents will find your use of dramatic expression quite annoying, leading to some unsavory opinions about your personality. Others often confront constant attention seekers about their need to be in the spotlight. And let's face it, some people will only be by your side as long as you have the attention of the masses. On the other hand, if you learn to act like an average person and tone your style down a bit, you can forge far more lasting friendships.

Virgo

Having the annoying habit of internalizing thoughts a little too often, a Virgo will often find themselves in some awkward situations. Instead of speaking your mind about things you are passionate about at the right moment, you regularly delay this, causing an emotional imbalance within you. And when you have had enough of keeping things to yourself, you may have an explosion of temper at the wrong moment and over a seemingly insignificant issue. When this happens, you will find flaws in everyone else's reasoning, choosing to disregard every opinion but your own. Yet another personality trait of yours that may lead you to some impediments is your prejudice towards deceit. While this is a decidedly positive quality to possess, you may take it to the extreme by frowning upon any form of falsehood. Whether someone is telling a good-natured lie or deliberately deceiving someone, it won't make any difference in your mind. If you want to avoid offending people, you should learn the importance of diplomacy. You may also want to consider revealing your emotions more often. Whether it's through spoken words or in any other form, openly expressed feelings can lose their significance or at least be seen in a more positive light.

Libra

True to their name, Libras can weigh in the options from both sides of a dispute and find a solution to any problem presented to them. Due to Mercury's influence, staying impartial is an essential part of your thinking process, and you often try to find a solution that pleases everyone. And you do all this without even a minimal sign of aggression by using your powers of persuasion. For you, forging lasting relationships is important but no more than the way you build them. In your eyes, the only valid relationships are the ones based on mutual acceptance and honesty. Besides choosing sides in an argument, there is one thing your sign hates the most, and that is being deceived. However, try as you might two avoid them in life, both of these things are inevitable, so you will just have to learn how to cope with them. Expressing your own opinions is far healthier than voicing opinions others want to hear. Bringing peace to anyone else will only be enjoyable if you can find your own inner peace as well. For this reason, it's a practice highly recommended to everyone struggling to balance others' beliefs with their own.

Scorpio

Scorpio is definitely a sign that can prove their point the easiest way possible. Unfortunately, this also means you tend to disregard other people's opinions and feelings, making you seem cruel and detached from your own emotions. You enjoy having long-winded debates about anything and everything, especially with someone of a similar disposition. The fascinating way you express yourself often draws attention to your intellectual capabilities, and for a good reason. Scorpios can be strong leaders if only they apply the right approach to certain things in life and make sure others are heard as well. This also comes easy to you, and it shouldn't be a problem to leave things unresolved although, you will need to learn not to take advantage of the feelings of your conversation partners. No matter how tempting it might be to simply try to turn your emotions against them to convey your message, it's best to dissuade yourself from this notion. If for nothing else, it can make you more trusting, something you often struggle with, fearing someone may use your own technique against you. Free will exists for a reason and is much more appreciated than manipulation, after all.

Sagittarius

Gifted with an incredible imagination, a Sagittarius in Mercury can be quite charismatic and inspiring to others. Coupled with the yearning to gain knowledge from numerous different topics in life, this makes this sign the perfect teacher material. Even people who you just met can listen to you debate everything from mundane topics to an entirely fictional alternative. Despite this, you are most verbal about your ever-changing plans and prefer to talk about things on a more general level. Unfortunately, your true feelings are rarely included in your fantastic stories, as they are something you like to keep private. While people enjoy your tales and are happy to contribute to your ambitions, keeping yourself closed is not always a good thing. To the people close to you, understanding your feelings is far more important than what you plan to do in the next year or so. Even if you can't voice your emotions, you should try to make them evident to your loved ones in how you conduct yourself. Instead of passionately arguing with them about the things you have learned, you can concede their point as they may know a thing or two about the subject too.

Capricorn

The ever-practical Capricorn never speaks before thinking things through a couple of times and then once more for good measure. Born under this sign, you probably won't talk much at all, and when you do, you will get to the point fast. Although this makes you communicate slower than any other sign, it also ensures you never say things you may regret later. Because this a highly respectable and somewhat feared quality, being clear in what you want can make you the perfect authority figure in any field. On the other hand, this can turn into an issue if you take it to a level where you barely speak to people at all. What you fail to realize is that being social creatures, your loved ones will often crave social interactions even if you don't. You are also extremely distrustful and are unwilling to open up to strangers or even to people close to you. If you feel that it's something they will never understand, you won't talk about it, no matter how hard someone tries to persuade you to do so. Opening up more can resolve many of your communication issues and build more connections. You may even want to rethink the manner you choose your friends as well, as this can help you appreciate the differences between all of you.

Aquarius

Not one to avoid arguments, the Aquarius loves to air their opinion with everyone, whether someone is interested in it or not. What's more, being an Aquarius will make you seem like a rigid person who doesn't really care about others. This mostly happens because, during an argument, you tend to disregard every opinion except your own. Your unwillingness to talk about yourself and only keeping to neutral subjects doesn't put you in a better light either. However, you can easily turn all this around if you try to persuade more people about a certain subject, but with a more relatable approach. Offering a fact or two about yourself occasionally can help you a lot, should you decide to try this approach. Although for you, having a personal conversation with someone close can be a lot harder than any public debate, you can work on improving that. Since it's easier to concentrate on their feelings instead of yours, you should do exactly that, and you will be able to connect with them on a more personal level. This will make it much easier for you to see if their personality matches yours and if things with them will work out.

Pisces

While many zodiac signs struggle to open up, Mercury Pisces seem to be in an opposite predicament because they can talk about themselves relentlessly. Not only that, but your sign isn't always the clearest when it comes to expressing your thoughts, making your debates confusing and frustrating to listen to. This stems from the fact that your mind is often very active, taking you in all kinds of directions. Your mind tends to wander off during conversations and stop listening to others altogether. Needless to say, this is something people aren't happy to see, and if it happens more than once, they won't hold you in the highest regard afterward. When it comes to expressing your feelings, you should try to find a way to channel them in one direction and present them in a more organized way so that you won't jumble things up.

Similarly, reigning in your imagination will enable you to focus more on handling your conversations. This will not only make people willing to engage you in meaningful debates, but they will begin to trust you more too. And because trustworthy people make for better leaders, improving your communication style can be a crucial step toward a better future.

Chapter 4: What Type of Learner Are You?

Mercury is the ruler of communication as it represents communication and perception. Learning what Mercury sign you are will help you understand what type of learner you are. Moreover, you will learn how to express your ideas and inner thoughts to others, especially if you know your Mercury sign.

Your natal chart will help you learn which zodiac sign planet Mercury traveled through when you were born. Usually, it takes Mercury from three to four weeks to travel through each zodiac sign unless it is retrograde.

You may think that it is too late to learn what type of learner you are, but that is not true. Your learning style has a strong effect on your life and the decisions you make in life, even if you have finished school and have finished all of your studies. It affects almost all aspects of your life, like relationships, work, and parenting. In any kind of relationship, communication is key to its success. Understanding how you learn new information will help you better communicate with others. Moreover, knowing how others learn and express their thoughts will help you understand them and deal with them in much better ways.

If you are a parent, you need to find out what type of learner your child is. That way, you will avoid any confusion, disappointments, or stressing yourself and your child while studying. In a work environment, it is very beneficial to know the different learning styles of your employees or team. As you can see, there are many benefits to knowing what type of learner you and others around you are.

This chapter will help you figure out what type of learner you are by providing you with information about how each zodiac sign, occupied by Mercury in the natal chart, learns and communicates. Remember the information below is not about your zodiac sign. The zodiac signs below refer to the zodiac sign Mercury occupies on your natal chart. You can find many websites that will ask you to provide them with some information to create your natal chart.

Mercury in Aries

Aries is a fire sign, which means it is full of energy. If Aries is your Mercury sign, you need to look out for when the subjects you are learning are interesting and stimulating. You are a sharp learner who can easily grasp new topics when they are action-oriented and challenging. Teachers will make things much easier for you if they start introducing new ideas in a way that makes them appear interesting. Moreover, you do better when given short instructions without going through a lot of details. While learning, you need to feel safe to fail and try again. You are a "big picture first and details later" kind of learner who needs visuals to grasp new information. Finally, to fully comprehend new ideas and information you have learned, you need to implement what you have learned right away.

Tips for You

- As much as possible, avoid doing things out of obligation. You are highly focused when the topic inspires you.

- When working on a project, work in short sprints, and you will become more productive.
- Always challenge yourself.

Mercury in Taurus

Taurus is an earth sign, so your learning style is thorough and logical. Hands-on learning is the best method for you. You need to touch things to digest new information, like tracing letters while reading. Reading is never enough for you, as you need to do things with your hands and use your sense of touch to learn. Those whose Mercury sign is Taurus best learn in a self-paced learning environment, as they take their time to process new information. You need proof and use your common sense to believe in new ideas. Step-by-step instructions and solid evidence are how you learn and believe in things. Abstract concepts are hard for you to comprehend, and that is why sometimes you need to figure out a link between abstract and concrete worlds.

Tips for You

- To become more productive at work or in life in general, always write down step-by-step instructions to help you operate things and perform tasks.
- Always break your goals down into smaller ones and take them one step at a time.

Mercury in Gemini

As for Gemini, it is an air sign. Therefore, you tend to be a free thinker who learns better in social and interactive learning environments. Listening to lectures is not the best way for you to learn as you need to ask questions and engage in a discussion to grasp new information as you always need to learn why things happen. You are a natural communicator, a quick thinker, and a fast learner. However, you are easily bored. Therefore, you can't give it your 100% focus when learning abstract and overly philosophical concepts.

Tips for You

- To become more productive, keep taking new courses and participate in discussion groups.
- When learning new things or taking new courses, try to turn your learning environment into a social and interactive one. One way to achieve this is to invite your classmates over to study together.

Mercury in Cancer

The element related to Cancer is water. Thus, you have a very high sense of intuition, and that is why you learn more by perceiving things rather than just hearing facts. Being emotionally connected to the subject you are learning is key for you and helps you understand and take in new ideas and concepts. Having a high emotional intelligence, you learn best when new information is gently introduced to you, and you are in a safe environment where you feel that you can ask whatever you want and express yourself freely.

Tips for You

- Add any form of art like music or pictures to the subject you are learning to get an emotional connection. This way, it will be much easier for you to comprehend new material and reach your full potential.
- While you are studying or working on a project, keep everything that makes you feel comfortable and in a good mood next to you, like snacks, tea, coffee, and music. Moreover, make sure that you are wearing comfortable clothes.

Mercury in Leo

Leo's element is fire. Therefore, the same as all fire signs, they are action-oriented. You learn best through adventure and trial and error. People who were born while Mercury was in Leo are into bold ideas and get really excited when learning new things at first. You learn better when new information is presented to you in a fun way, like a game, for example, or an experiment. Moreover, you will process new information introduced to you through storytelling easily, especially if you can relate to the story. However, you need to be careful where you are directing your attention to avoid getting sucked into futile experiences and adventures.

Tips for You

- After learning a new subject, you need to cement what you have learned by putting it into action. For example, doing a presentation is a good idea to learn new information and memorize it.
- While you are learning, if you need to memorize information, figure out a way to make it fun, like turning it into a challenging game to play with your study mates. This way, the information will stick in your mind.

Mercury in Virgo

If Mercury was in Virgo when you were born, you learn by doing. Virgo's element is earth. Add Mercury to an earth element, and you get a kinesthetic learner. If you want to learn something new, you better take it slow and take your time in processing new information and topics. You need structure first to learn a new subject. If you think that what you are learning is useless or you can't see a reason to do it, you lose interest as you need information that has value and use. Moreover, you need to be shown how to apply this information in real life. Being a systematic thinker, you tend to plan everything.

Tips for You

- To learn better, ask for simplified and to-the-point information.
- You need data and facts to be convinced, so always have your books and tools around you to help you understand the topic at hand better while studying.

Mercury in Libra

Libra's element is air, and unlike earth elements, you tend to get interested in new ideas more than applying them. In other words, you fall in love with ideas regardless of their implementation in real life. You are a fast learner and tend to skim over subjects rather than digging deep into them. You learn better from listening to lectures even without taking notes, as air learns better through hearing. Love for reading books and gaining more knowledge is innate in you.

Tips for You

- When learning a new subject, try to engage in many discussions as your brain processes information best through dialogues and discussions.
- You are more productive when you work with others.

Mercury in Scorpio

You are an emotive learner. In other words, you learn by feeling your way through. How you feel has a great impact on how you process information. If you are upset or angry, you might not understand what is being taught to you that day. Incredibly sensitive and intuitive, to the point that you pick up on the vibes of your teachers, and your comprehension depends on it. If you do not like a teacher, or you sense a negative vibe from them, you may not be able to process the information they are providing you with. You are not a quitter, as you never give up until you get the job done! You are so much into learning how things work and problem-solving games and puzzles.

Tips for You

- You learn best when you are alone and understand and process new information when alone without any interruptions.
- You tend to get sucked into your work. Therefore, you need to remind yourself that you need a break.

Mercury in Sagittarius

Sagittarius's element is fire, and when you add Mercury, you get a visual learner who is dynamic and needs a stimulating and challenging learning environment that matches their energetic nature and love of adventure. You are into learning ideas that have a big impact on others. Moreover, you are a multitasker. However, you have trouble concentrating and sitting still. You learn best when you do things your way and on your own terms.

Tips for You

- You can make the best of any learning experience when you combine traveling and learning together.
- You will reach your full potential when you fully understand the purpose behind what you are doing. Therefore, set your goal before learning anything new to connect to and excel in it.

Mercury in Capricorn

You are a kinesthetic learner who learns by doing. You enjoy learning new skills and things that will actually serve you in real life, louche as helping you get a salary raise or a promotion. You are not into learning abstract ideas or skills that do not directly impact your career. When given enough time, you can learn new subjects and process new information efficiently as you are a steady learner who takes things slow to ensure that you absorb new information and topics. You don't learn a lot by memorization as you need to get involved and do practical things to learn new material. You love to learn about history and tradition. You need facts and solid evidence to be able to comprehend and believe. Moreover, you learn and work better alone, not in a group.

Tips for You

- When working on a project, set your goal first, then plan your steps.
- To avoid burning out as you tend to when working on something, reward yourself whenever you succeed in taking a step forward.

Mercury in Aquarius

You are a quick and flexible thinker who is a natural communicator. You learn best in interactive learning environments, and you can absorb several pieces of information at once. Rather than lectures, you learn best through arguments and discussions. When learning new subjects, you seek untraditional explanations to facts. Moreover, you need to understand the bigger picture first, then work your way through the details. Being told what to do and how things work is not enough for you, as you need to explore things your own way. To learn and process new information, you need to experience things rather than get instructed by others, no matter how professional they are. You do not let your emotions get in the way of your learning process, as you are completely unbiased. You are into subjects like science and foreign languages. Incorporating technology into the learning process is definitely your thing!

Tips for You

- You learn and work best in a group. However, the members of this group should be open-minded and flexible thinkers.
- You get really motivated and process new information faster and better when learning about things that positively impact the world. You reach your full potential when you know that what you are doing will somehow benefit the environment and humanity.

Mercury in Pisces

Pisces's element is water. Mercury and water result in creative abstract thinkers. You need your time to think things through before you conclude. While learning new things, you need to use your emotions and intuition alongside your intellect. Mundane subjects do not really interest you.

On the other hand, you love learning about music, poetry, and art. However, sometimes, you can't avoid learning mundane and concrete subjects. Therefore, you need to find a way and come up with creative incentives to motivate yourself. Being emotionally connected to the topic you are learning new information about is crucial for you to process this new information. Memorizing instructions and information won't work for you. You need to feel your way through and use your emotions to learn why things are the way they are instead of being instructed about how things work. Your brain digests new information when at rest, and that is why you need to have enough sleep and sleep on problems before coming up with a solution for them.

Tips for You

- Since you are a dreamer and a creative thinker, you tend to get absorbed in your inner thoughts and lose track of time while working on a project or studying. Therefore, you need to redirect your focus constantly to the task at hand.

- When you are studying or working, you'd better do it outdoors surrounded by nature and listening to music.
- When you want to express your thoughts to others, you should draw charts or pictures or show them what you mean rather than telling them verbally.

People are different, and as you can see, the way we perceive and process information varies from one person to another. However, learning what Mercury sign you are will help you grasp new information and learn new concepts that will suit your learning style. Moreover, parents and teachers will benefit from learning Mercury's placement on their children's and students' natal charts. By learning how their children are motivated and how their brains process new information, they will be able to accommodate the needs of each child, pushing them to reach their full potential.

Of course, other factors influence your learning style. However, the position of Mercury in your placement chart and the element and zodiac sign it inhabited at the time you were born has a great influence on how you communicate and perceive the world, thus affecting your learning style. Finding out what type of learner you are will help you achieve your goals in life without disappointments or frustrations. Knowing how your brain works and the best ways to express your thoughts will facilitate your journey and make your life much easier.

Chapter 5: Mercury in Your Natal Chart I

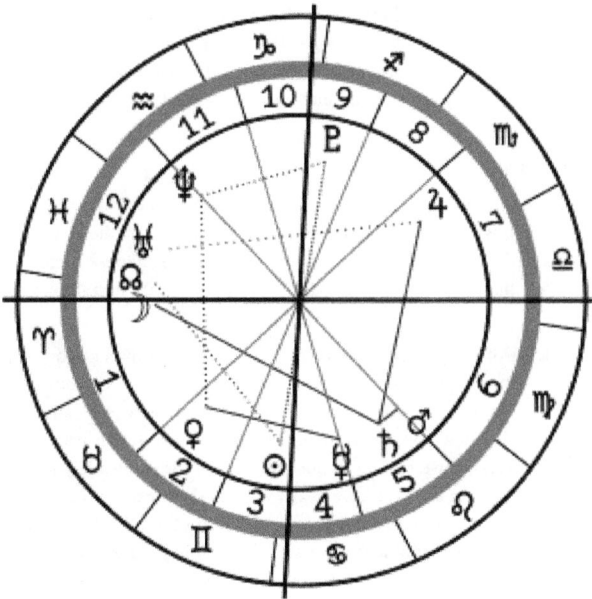

Do you want to better understand your communication style, how easy or difficult it is for you to deliver ideas to other people, how you learn, and how you process ideas and thoughts? Then you need to understand Mercury and how its position in the natal chart affects various aspects of your life.

Mercury is considered the planet of the mind. Being the closest planet to the Sun, it has an intricate relationship with the self. Moreover, retrogrades in Mercury can also be very intense and seriously impact communication and transportation in our lives. Mercury is placed in different astrology systems, which is used as a reference to gauge when would be the best time to travel, invest, or make a big commitment.

The impact of Mercury on a person's life can often be difficult to understand and complex to explain, even for a seasoned astrologist. While Mercury is the planet of communication and intellect, as previously stated, it's also the planet that governs the Zodiac signs Gemini and Virgo.

Mercury is named after the Roman deity who served as a messenger of the Gods, and this is why it is generally associated with communication and the ability to sort, interpret and deliver information. The two signs that it rules can be seen as taking in and giving out information. For this reason, Mercury is also associated with duality. Gemini, being an air sign, and Virgo, being an earth sign, depict two different sides to Mercury, and we can see their impact when Mercury enters a new house. In terms of communication, Virgo can be seen as input while Gemini is output.

The positioning of Mercury in different houses across your natal chart will tell you where you communicate the best. It will also show you where you may be particularly good at analyzing, processing, and internalizing information or ideas.

Mercury in Your First House

First House Features

The first house is all about 'firsts' and basic, fundamental things that relate to you as a person. Things such as first impressions, beginnings, ego, traits, characteristics, and even physical appearances all come under the first house. Moreover, the first house is also the ascendant and is the house from which you derive your rising sign. Having Mercury in your first house significantly amplifies its effects on your personality and personal traits. The fact that Mercury is a planet with a duality also means that it can significantly be influenced by aspects and will absorb the traits of the sign that it is placed under.

Mercurial Ascending

Intelligence, critical thinking, in-depth analysis, and eloquent communication of complex thought highlight people with Mercury in the first house. Moreover, these are highly inquisitive people always looking to learn the whys of everything. This intense urge to have a deep understanding of everything around them makes them spontaneous, and they can even come off as impatient.

These are the kind of people who would love to debate and discuss complex ideas. While they are firm believers in their own ideas and are confident in their viewpoints, they are flexible individuals who are always open to considering new perspectives and modifying their understanding if something new appeals to them. Having a conversation with this person can be challenging since they already have two more questions ready for you while you are still starting to answer the first one. If they feel like you have nearly answered their question or they have received enough information on a topic, they are quick to bring up another. They will always keep you in the hot seat since they are so genuinely interested in learning. They love mental stimulation, particularly if it's through a verbal or communicative format. Even when these individuals are quiet, their minds are still buzzing away and internalizing any information they are processing.

Mercury is all about communication, and whether this is communicating externally with people around you or communicating with yourself at an internal level, people with Mercury in the first house demonstrate this characteristic to the maximum.

These individuals are born with a love of communication, but they are also very talented at it and can word their thoughts so that it is easy for everyone to understand. They make excellent speakers, commentators, and even salespeople. Their spontaneous nature results from their thought processes as they enjoy thinking laterally and drawing comparisons to broadly unrelated fields. They are continually in the process of refining thoughts and ideas in their minds and love sharing their most recent developments with people who have the stamina to withstand their verbal firepower.

Positives

One of the best things about people with this planet in the first house is their flexibility. In terms of learning new things and listening to new ideas, they are welcoming and love to improve their own understanding of things. However, they are not easily convinced and will go to great lengths to ensure that what they are learning really is better than what they already know.

Subjects such as philosophy, literature, linguistics in general, and more discussion-heavy fields of study such as psychology are things that they have a natural tendency toward.

Some are more disposed to learning through video or other interactive mediums as they can find reading to be slow and cumbersome. The way they learn will greatly depend on the kind of experiences they have had and what they have become accustomed to.

In terms of physical appearance, these individuals are usually fit and in good physical condition most of the time.

Negatives

Not giving the other person a chance to talk and being overly quick to respond to someone are things Mercurial risers tend to do. Due to their viciously fast communicative abilities, they may come off to some people as being rude, abrupt, and disrespectful.

When faced with competition just as skilled and knowledgeable as they are, they can find themselves stumbling and appearing less sharp than they otherwise are. That shiny coat of confidence gets a little dim, and even though they have the skills and abilities necessary to face the competition, they can struggle to keep up.

Mercury in Your Second House

Second House Features

In the second house, the focus pivots to things connected to you rather than things that intrinsically influence who you are as a person. The second house is what you can study to better understand how astrology will play a role in your financial position, material possessions, self-image, money management skills, and even the kind of relationships you develop in this lifetime.

Positives

People with Mercury in their second house have a natural instinct for money management, resourcefulness, and economic understanding. Managing finances and efficiently using resources is something they don't have to put much effort into. Rather the way they are as people naturally enhances these capabilities. Roles such as financial analysts, economists, banking, and portfolio management, align with this person's natural abilities and thought patterns.

When this skill set is combined with this person's ability to talk convincingly and communicate fluently, they make terrific entrepreneurs and C-suite administration. Their blunt and pragmatic approach to life makes them very grounded and very aware of potential risks. They have a very balanced mindset with the right amount of positivity and caution. Not only do they love knowledge, but they have a thirst specifically for that knowledge which will drive them closer to their goals and ambitions.

Negatives

Where their deep thinking and structured approach to life make them incredible people to work with, they suffer in fast-moving environments and can't work well in a timeframe that requires instant delivery. Lines of work that require the person to change and constantly adapt in a short period of time are not something they will enjoy being a part of. This is the kind of person who can't even hurry up their morning routine, they have a way of doing things, and that's how they do it.

Their focus on the minute details can also make them come off as perfectionists and people who are incredibly difficult to satisfy. They just can't understand why people can't deliver work to the quality that they want and the standard that they set for themselves.

They love reliability, durability, and consistency in life and don't mind going the tougher route to ensure that they don't have to face constant change, indecisiveness, and suspense. For this reason, they may appear to be hard-headed or arrogant, but in reality, they are just trying to maintain consistency and succeed at what they are doing with tunnel vision.

Mercury in Your Third House

Third House Features

The third house is also known as the house of sharing, and its natural ruler is Gemini. With Mercury in this house, you can find out a lot about your ability to share knowledge through communication, how generous you are, and how well or poorly you share with people around you. It also talks about movement and transportation, especially short trips and day-to-day transport. Moreover, you can also learn what this house has to say about your fate with siblings and other close relatives, and it also talks about your intelligence and mental development.

Positives

People with Mercury in their third house are the crème de la crème of communicative social beings. Gemini's are naturally gifted with advanced social abilities, eloquent speech, and a fantastic ability to weave wonders through words. When this is combined with a passion for knowledge and a Mercurial communication-based thinking pattern, the results are truly astounding. These guys are the kind of people who aren't necessarily experts or very knowledgeable about a subject, but they can make industry veterans feel insecure when they talk about it. They talk with unusual energy and charm. But they can also blend together things they know really well with ideas they aren't too familiar with and deliver a talk in a league of its own.

Like other Mercurials, they have a passion for knowledge and learning. When combined with their social skills, they have no problem communicating with new people and becoming part of a conversation. Their love for knowledge is so profound that others may see them as nerdy, completely absorbed in their reading or learning. For people with Mercury in their third house, it's almost like the whole purpose of their existence is just to learn. Regardless of what the subject is, they just want to know. Their mental capacity in memory, analysis, critical thinking, and logic is unparalleled.

They have different personalities when they are with people they don't know and nearly opposite personalities when they are with close friends.

Their intense capacity to learn and continually grow their knowledge means they are always seeking new things to read about, experience, and be a part of. This diverse set of interests and their ability to socialize helps them increase their social outreach. They usually have many friends from a very diverse range of industries with very different interests.

People with Mercury in their third house tend to travel a lot, mostly a lot of short trips, usually for their work and related to their profession. In terms of their profession, they can be quite successful because of their diverse range of interests. They also do exceptionally well in any field that requires knowledge and a creative approach. However, due to their sporadic lifestyle, they are best suited to jobs with a fixed work schedule, or else they risk losing track of work and getting distracted.

Being a people person, they thrive in situations where they can get plenty of support from their peers, family, and social circle. Their playful and fun-loving nature makes them a great company to have in any setting. However, they can get a bit carried away, and this can hurt their relationships as well.

Negatives

Being a quick learner and someone with very varied interests, it can be easy for this person to get bored and switch to something else. For this reason, they are known to be a jack-of-all-trades with no real specialization. This is also a problem for academic or professional achievements, as even though they are very talented, they find it tough to put in dedicated effort to reach a high level of competence and achieve proficiency in one area. Moreover, because they are interested in so many things, they are at risk of burning out very quickly since they are invested in many different things.

They find it difficult to stick to one thing and keep working at it over an extended period of time. This tendency also causes people around them to sometimes feel ignored or sidelined. People with Mercury in the third house can quickly switch social circles and make people feel very awkward. This is because they socialize to a very deep level and then vanish all of a sudden.

They also tend to make decisions hastily, without weighing up the pros and cons and often suffer from this rash behavior.

Mercury in Your Fourth House

Fourth House Features

The fourth house in the natal chart pertains to ancestry, roots, and an individual's heritage. It also gives vital information about a person's household, family life, and family relationships. Things such as your neighborhood ties, the environment you are in, both social and physical, the security of your physical environment can all be studied in this house.

Positives

People with Mercury in their fourth house tend to be amazing parents, very focused on family life, and with a strong urge to create the best environment at home for their spouse and children. Their Mercurial elements make them very intelligent parents. They love educating their children, doing learning activities with them, and placing significant importance on education, knowledge, and mental exercises.

However, even in the home environment, their knack for learning is hard to curb. Being an intensely focused and highly intellectual being, you will find them coming up with incredible ideas for the home even while being stay-at-home parents. They don't enjoy monotonous routines and create a very lively environment wherever they are.

Whether it is at home or at work, they are always looking to do something new and to being part of something adventurous. However, they have a more refined sense of study. Their education and knowledge are reflected in their complex speech, which they deliver naturally without trying to appear sophisticated. This person is a deep thinker who won't accept any knowledge until it is crystal clear to them and can prove it. They are the kind of people who won't shy away from an extreme adventure or lifestyle as their minds are not at peace just by knowing something. They have to go out and experience it for themselves.

Negatives

With their unique approach to life and Mercurial communicative skills, they can be manipulative. This may not be with a bad intention, but it's just easy for them to get people to do what they want. Combined with the fact that they are difficult to convince to see things differently, they can be argumentative and quite difficult to deal with. Sometimes even when they want to change, they find it very difficult to convince themselves.

They rely on themselves far more than any other Mercurial and often see themselves as their own best friend, causing people around them to feel like they don't matter as much. Even at home with people they love the most, it is difficult for them to prevent others from feeling bad as they continue to do things their own way. They can also reform themselves over time and be drastically different people at different time periods in their life, causing other people in their life to feel like they don't care for anyone else except themselves, even though this is not the case.

Chapter 6: Mercury in Your Natal Chart II

Mercury in the Fifth House

The fifth house is the house of pleasure. It's the house of creativity and fun. It is mainly concerned with the "release of one's energies," as the astrologist Dane Rudhyar wrote. In the fifth house, releasing energy means several things. It stands for how we relax and enjoy ourselves to release tension/negative energy. It also stands for how we create by putting our own energy into our own unique creations. This release can refer to your inner child, the child within who delights in exploration and play. It can even refer to your existent (or potential) biological children as, in a way, they are a form of creation. The good news is, despite the one negative aspect, having Mercury in the fifth house is a good sign.

Positive Traits

Named after the Roman messenger god, Mercury symbolizes communication and quick-wittedness. In the fifth house, the nature of Mercury manifests itself in one's ability to communicate with themselves and with the people around them. Your quick wit and curiosity allow you to understand and analyze the person in front of you to tailor your message toward them. This is a key characteristic possessed by any successful artist or marketer. Meanwhile, your ability to communicate can help you understand, and in turn, express yourself in a creative form. In other words, Mercury in the fifth house means you can creatively express yourself in a way that people not only understand but also empathize with. And in some cases, relate to.

Mercury also symbolizes curiosity. When combined with creativity and energy release, this thirst for knowledge is guaranteed to show some interesting results as it fuels your creative drive. Don't forget that acting on your curiosity is, in itself, a release of energy. A person with Mercury in their fifth house is almost always looking for new adventures, which makes them far from boring to be around. Other than fueling their creativity, this hunger for new experiences is a characteristic that makes them appealing as a partner, and it's not the only one.

Mercury in the fifth house romantically makes you a playful partner and a good, if not great, flirter. When paired with a high sexual drive, creativity and playfulness take up their fair share of space in the bedroom. However, most individuals with Mercury in their fifth house tend to be a tad picky when it comes to their partners. They prefer people with matching intellectual abilities and open-mindedness to those with empty-headed beauty. As they are considered to be wanderers and adventurers, they are constantly evolving and expanding, which can make being with a stagnant, devolving partner difficult.

Negative Traits

There are two sides to every coin, and this remains true for the traits mentioned above. You already know that Mercury in the fifth house means that you're gifted with a silver tongue. It means you can get people to empathize and connect with almost anything you say. That's all well and good when you're talking about a personal experience or when creating art. The danger lies in how this silver tongue can blur the lines between communication and manipulation. For example, you may tend to exaggerate certain aspects of your stories. You may also be exceptionally gifted in convincing people, getting what you want, and talking your way out of trouble. These traits can be a source of trouble when it comes to romantic relationships and friendships. Keep in mind this doesn't mean that you are or are going to be a liar or a serial manipulator. It only means that you can do such a thing, but it is up to you whether to exercise it or not. You may be tempted to use your silver tongue to get what you want in a tough situation where a decision has to be made. In fact, you may already be doing that subconsciously. It only takes a small amount of self-awareness to rearrange your priorities.

All in all, Mercury in the fifth house stands for a highly creative drive and an especially unique ability to create and communicate, especially when it comes to artistic forms of expression. The house and planet pairing also signify playfulness, curiosity, and flirtatiousness. The one downside is that you have a natural tendency to bend the facts a little to get a desirable outcome. Especially because you can already understand and connect with people all too well.

Mercury in the Sixth House

The sixth house is concerned with the more practical side of life; in other words, everyday duties include one's professional life, routine, and overall lifestyle. The life a person leads undoubtedly affects their health, so analyzing this house and planet pair can help you better understand and manage what influences your health. The sixth house explains your approach to the more serious side of life, your decision-making process, your learning process, and how you choose to care for yourself.

Positive Traits

Mercury, the messenger god, was not exactly known for his prudence, given that he stole Apollo's cows when he was a little boy. However, he was known for being exceptionally clever. Similarly, Mercury, the planet, is a sign known to represent rational ability, as opposed to the moon, which mainly reflects emotions. Having Mercury in your sixth house means that you are a critical thinker, able to dissect and analyze your input to make a decision. You're most likely very pragmatic and rational, carefully weighing your variables before taking action. These qualities are found in great leaders and entrepreneurs.

Mercury in the sixth house also means that you are a natural-born perfectionist with an eye for detail. If you are involved in a group project, you may have already noticed your tendency to excessively worry about an insignificant imperfection rather than focus on the bigger picture. It's a double-edged sword, but for now, consider its positive effect on your professional life and learn how to utilize that.

People with this planet-house combination are also known to take an interest in how the human mind works. They are already curious, and so, the pursuit of knowledge isn't all that foreign. Learning how the human mind works are only a way for them to improve their own learning, decision-making, and thinking abilities. If they are struggling with an excessive workload, they're more likely to figure out how to increase their efficiency and minimize time loss rather than stop replenishing their energy. They are also very organized, adopting a systematic approach to every problem and a keen eye for the intricacies that others often overlook. When combined with ambition and perfection, this approach creates a triple threat that bodes well for your professional life. It also means better life decisions when it comes to pragmatics.

Health-wise, a Mercury in the sixth house pays a great deal of attention to personal hygiene and rarely overlooks physical irregularities.

If feeling unusually tired, they will more likely sift through their mind for a potential cause and solution rather than take a few pills. This can especially come in handy when tackling mental health problems. The process requires a great deal of reflection, analysis, and making the subtlest of connections which are all part of the Mercury in the sixth house native's skillset.

Negative Traits

In the same way, they are skilled at rational thinking. People with Mercury in their sixth house are at risk of being overly rational, often neglecting their emotions in the process. Not just that, but they are most likely to use adopted rationalization as a defense mechanism. If not careful, they can also be at risk of being perceived as apathetic by more emotional people, leading to relational tension. Here it is important to balance the rational and the emotional to achieve a deeper level of fulfillment.

The house-planet pair is also prone to neglecting their own needs in favor of a project or a task, often pushing themselves until they burn out. While this discipline and dedication is a good characteristic, it is the negligence of needs that has negative effects. When needs such as sleep, food, and maintaining self-connection are neglected, one develops an unhealthy internal environment, with dissatisfaction, lack of fulfillment, and loss of motivation. In many cases, it leads to depression, weakened immune system, and impacts other areas of one's life. As dedicated as you are, don't forget to take some time off and tend to your own physical and emotional needs.

The last negative trait is a downside of deep analysis and excessively thorough thinking. This type of person is often at risk of developing anxiety due to their awareness of what can/may happen and their desire to control the outcome.

Mercury in the Seventh House

The seventh house is all about relationships, not specifically romantic ones, although it does talk about romantic relationships. The house is concerned with one's relationship with others. The traits they are attracted to, the traits that repulse them, how they are in a relationship/friendship, and their strong points and fatal flaws. By analyzing Mercury's effects in the seventh house, you can better understand who you are and what you need to do to have a more fulfilling social life and healthier relationships.

Positive Traits

People with this planet and house combination are gifted with the key to healthy relationships. Being such good communicators and open-minded debaters, they feel somewhat comfortable discussing things openly with whoever they are with. Their ability to analyze and reflect also helps them a great deal when working through problems.

Their ability to analyze also plays a great role when it comes to giving out advice. They are always ready for any problem with interesting takes, apt analyses, and thought-provoking questions.

Due to their natural tendency to be rationally driven, they can greatly benefit from a life partner who is naturally more emotionally driven. If both are determined to grow, the pair can balance and challenge each other enough to regulate their modes of thinking. People with Mercury in the seventh house are predominantly attracted to minds rather than other characteristics. They are intrigued by individual thinkers and independent and ever-evolving people. While physical appearance may be a valued factor for some, it is far from a deciding factor.

Their curiosity and drive are integral parts of their being. So, being in a restraining relationship that does not foster these traits can cause them great unhappiness. Because of how important their freedom and independence are, they should take their time choosing a partner. They should make sure that they are not sacrificing their identity for a relationship.

While they may seem cold and logical to a fault, when they fall in love, they are as affectionate and loyal as a person can be. Generally, Mercury in the seventh house indicates that the person prefers deeper connections in a one-on-one setting. While they may be extremely comfortable in a group setting, it is during a one-on-one sit-down when they can truly show their depth and develop meaningful connections. In other words, they do not take their bonds and relationships lightly.

Negative Traits

In the same way, you may dig deeper to analyze the possible consequences of a decision that you and a partner make together. This thinking ability can easily turn into a self-destructive habit. If you find it difficult to trust people, anxiety - manifesting in over-analysis and poking holes - will keep you from developing deep connections in an attempt to protect you from potential pain. In friendships and partnerships, Mercury in the seventh house natives can sometimes become too critical, often focusing on one's flaws rather than them as a whole.

Another thing you might need to watch out for if this is where Mercury lies for you is your tendency to resist opposing opinions. While you may be curious and often intrigued by opposing opinions, it can be challenging to accept them from those close to you. Especially if you already have relationship anxiety. It's important to learn to accept and respect different points of view to foster intellectual intimacy. Remember that it takes vulnerability to share thoughts and opinions.

The Mercury in the seventh house native makes a great partner, romantically and otherwise. While they may have some flaws, nothing is out of control, as it only takes self-awareness and patience to work through any barriers. Remember, you already have the gift of being a great communicator; use it to know yourself first.

Mercury in the Eighth House

This is one of the most interesting houses, known for being concerned with death, transformation, and everything unspoken, unknown, and unseen. These matters also include the inner workings of human beings, their most primal drives, their non-verbal cues, and their intentions. Overall, the eighth house is a deeper territory, and Mercury takes to the unknown quite well, not just tolerating it but actively pursuing it, which can be both a positive and a negative trait.

Positive Traits

Natives here are highly likely to develop an interest in the spiritual realm and other mysterious subjects like death, souls, consciousness, and enlightenment. However, their critical, rational approach often keeps them grounded, preventing them from mindlessly believing whatever they are told without putting it to the test first. For them, there is no subject beyond questioning.

When it comes to relationships with others, a Mercury in the eighth house native is often highly intuitive, able to detect the slightest changes in the atmosphere around them. They're highly sensitive to power dynamics, relationship dynamics, and the different energies in a room. If you are a native, you may have noticed that you sometimes feel uncomfortable around certain people without any obvious reason. If they have eventually turned out to be bad news, take the time to show gratitude to your intuition/gut. The next time around, make sure you listen to your instinct as you have been gifted with a strong intuition.

In the same way, as a native can read the people in front of them like a book by analyzing their verbal and non-verbal cues, they also know how to lie low. They are aware of what they want to communicate and what they would rather keep private for the time being. While it can seem like a negative trait, this ability to maintain privacy keeps them from opening up to those who are unworthy.

Negative Traits

Manipulation has been mentioned repeatedly, but that is only because it comes easy to a Mercury in the eighth house native. While persuasion has its perks when it comes to professional life, it is never a good basis to build a relationship on. Even if it may seem safer to have control over those close to you, manipulation robs a bond of its authenticity. Love and connection aren't about control, after all.

When it comes to supernatural matters, a native's critical approach can easily turn to a cynicism that robs them of genuine experiences and life-transforming journeys. It can keep them heavily rooted in pragmatism without the willingness to entertain any of the world's vast possibilities.

Some natives manage to develop a deep interest in the occult, successfully contacting forces they can neither control nor fully comprehend. Releasing this dark energy can gravely impact a Mercury in the eighth house native. For example, a native's ability to see through their peers on a psychological level can leap into action when they're aggravated. A native affected by the eighth house's dark energy won't hesitate to use all sorts of psychological ammo to shred their enemies. This may even include information they have been told in a moment of vulnerability.

As you see, the eighth house is a powerful one. It isn't one to be messed with, nor taken lightly. Through studying the house's effect on you, you can understand how you relate to the immaterial world around you.

Chapter 7: Mercury in Your Natal Chart III

Mercury is a planet that symbolizes excellent communication, oratory skills, the pursuit of knowledge, and spirituality. Since Mercury is the messenger of the gods, communication and being witty are skills that come naturally to those positively influenced by this planet.

People under the positive influence of Mercury are more inclined towards higher learning in life, and education forms an important part of their lives. They are generally very intelligent, and spirituality is something where this intelligence shines through.

The various houses greatly influence how Mercury will influence a person's pursuits in life. Studying these houses can help you determine the exact influence of this speedy planet on your life. We'll be looking at the last four houses in this chapter and how they shape the personality and the overall experience in life.

So, let's get to it and find out how Mercury interacts with the ninth, tenth, eleventh, and twelfth houses so that you can determine how this planet affects you at a personal level.

Ninth House

This is the house responsible for luck, religion, and fate in a person's life. This house greatly relates to a person's spirituality, and the presence of different planets affects how a person will react to the spiritual side of life. It also represents the materialistic side of a person's life and significantly impacts a person's wealth and prosperity.

The dual nature of Mercury ensures that the person affected by this house will be inclined towards both spirituality and materialistic pursuits in life. This should come as no surprise as Mercury is a planet that, much like the Greek god Hermes, travels in between the realm of gods and men. This means that Mercury has an important role in the cosmic realm and the material realm of men.

A person who has Mercury in the ninth house can become a great spiritual teacher in life due to their exceptional oratory skills. The ability to communicate their ideas clearly and the talent of influencing a large group of people make these individuals extremely successful at being a spiritual guru who everyone likes to listen to.

However, they can sometimes overreact or overthink in response to even the slightest provocations. They have huge reserves of knowledge and are great at influencing others, but these skills can only be properly channeled if they learn to control their impulsive and fickle behavior.

These individuals tend to focus on the materialistic side of things, and money is an important factor for them to work for. The highly talented individuals in this position are very adept at utilizing their skills to earn money, and they'll rarely work without any expectations of a financial reward. These money-minded people excel at juggling many things and can undertake many endeavors to earn money simultaneously. These chart holders often monetize even the oratory skills they are renowned for, which grants them a massive amount of wealth.

Their love for life is often very rosy and blooming with passion. They find their soulmates at an early point in their lives, and the failure to do so can leave them jaded and disgruntled towards the world. The satisfaction and success that they find in their love lives are often of textbook quality and seem too good to be true.

They derive immense pleasure and satisfaction from their love life, and their partners are usually very reciprocating as well. Their are usually very loyal, helpful, caring, and honest, which are the essential qualities needed to lead a happy love life. Love marriage is written in the cards, and they often find this love from a very young age.

Their married life is also similarly very harmonious and leads to a happy and prosperous household. Their spouse is usually good at taking care of the children and handling a job at the same time. Even their children are bright, and usually this leads to a peaceful family life.

Even though the marriage will be long-lasting and very successful, they urge to flirt with others casually. This will not lead to any major problems, but it'll make their spouses feel uncomfortable and annoyed at times. If they can control these impulses, then their love life is nothing short of being ideal.

Their skills make them ideal for a profession as writers, editors, journalists, bloggers, content creators, and orators. They are often very comfortable from a financial standpoint in their lives, even though they like to spend lavishly on themselves and those around them.

Even their health is usually good, and they don't suffer from any major ailments other than a few complications in joints and bones. However, none of these problems will be permanent, and they'll recover soon enough. They suffer from minor seasonal diseases, but other than that, they are usually in very good shape.

Tenth House

The tenth house is the house that correlates to an individual's success in the professional side of life. This house is directly influential on the career of a person and what's their attitude towards it. This house assumes great importance in our current modern-day society due to its focus on the professional side of things. It can offer us insights into how a person is likely to achieve professional success.

A novice astrologer who's not very experienced will often misunderstand this correlation of the tenth house to the profession or the degree of success, but that's not the case at all. An individual's success depends on many other factors, and the tenth house simply offers us an insight into the potential for professional success. This doesn't mean that it's useless to study this house if you wish to achieve success. A deep understanding of this house means that you'll identify the patterns and develop a strategy to maximize your success in life.

Due to Mercury's proximity to both the sun and the Earth, we associate it with the earthly success that a person encounters in their life. The tenth house has some interesting characteristics when it's affected by Mercury.

The people under the influence of this planet in the tenth house are usually very sharp-minded and career-oriented. This doesn't mean that they are obsessed with their careers, but it simply means that they enjoy putting their energy into their jobs. They love to work in a challenging environment where they can stimulate their sharp minds.

Unlike most other intellectuals, the people in this category are very optimistic, making it an added advantage over their already quick wit. They are also quite efficient and precise with applying their knowledge and can utilize it in a practical way rather than just being book-smart.

They wish to attain higher professional and social status rather than growth in their careers. This aspiration for achieving fame stems from the events that mostly transpire in their childhood. They see their career in a fresh light, which doesn't make them feel very tense about it.

They also reach emotional maturity sooner than others around them, so their focus in life becomes crystal clear, and they know exactly what they want to achieve. They like to utilize their high levels of intelligence constructively and are often suited for careers that involve writing, researching, and learning.

The people who Mercury influences in their tenth house are very adept at handling responsibilities and have a knack for making big decisions. This makes them perfect for landing top-level jobs, but it should be in their area of interest for them to be actually productive.

They choose their career based on how well it works in their brains, and once they're invested in a career, they see it as a challenge to be overcome rather than a constant struggle. Any mundane and routine jobs will bore them, and they'll quickly get tired of it due to the lack of any mental stimulation.

However, their optimism kicks in whenever they're in such an undesirable situation, and they adjust to make the best of it. They are dominant in the workplace, and this trait crosses over into their personal lives as well. They like to be in charge and can take the leading role in any relationship as well.

Eleventh House

Also known as the house of profits and gains, this house determines how individuals obtain wealth in their lives and how they'll handle it. It's also known as the "kama house" in Vedic astrology, which means that it's responsible for desire, passion, and lust as well.

The mind of a person influenced by Mercury in this house is quite sharp, as is expected of Mercury. They are burdened with many responsibilities like family, career, wealth, and much more. However, these responsibilities don't make the person risk-averse, and they are always willing to experiment with doing new things, which often leads to success in life.

They are quite assertive and have a knack for earning money as well. Their romantic relationships are usually smooth-sailing and harmonious, but their dedication toward their work is very strong, and they become serious when in work mode.

A person influenced by this house will often be well-off from a financial standpoint as they'll find overwhelming success in their business endeavors. They believe in gathering material gains and will have a lot of liquid assets and property. They can even become quite famous and may even attain widespread renown just like a celebrity.

They are also very punctual, and this trait, combined with a little hard work, can take them to astronomical success in a professional setting. The career choices suitable for their personality are marketing, media, consultancy, advertising, and businesses. The effect of Mercury in this house is that they are blessed with an unmatched level of intelligence and business acumen.

Not only are these subjects prosperous, but their overall health and happiness levels are generally high as well. They usually lead very happy and satisfying lives with much renown and fame as the cherry on the top.

They will also find a lot of success in love, although it'll take a little bit of time and effort. The long-lasting love affair will come after a few breakups or separations, which cause heartache. However, the love affair that'll be cemented into marriage will come around soon enough, and it'll be the talk of the town.

Although the person under the influence of Mercury in the ninth house will be loyal for the most part, there will be a few secret affairs that'll come and go. For the most part, their marriages are harmonious and full of love. The marriage will usher in a period of relaxation and calm for this person as the spouse is highly likely to be very devoted, loyal, and affectionate.

They are usually self-made people who build themselves up from the ground even if their family has a lot of pre-existing wealth. They will face some hardships and losses at a certain point in their adult lives, but they will rebound and remain undisputedly more successful than any family member or peer group.

Twelfth House

This house is called the unseen realm of astrology due to its ability to govern dreams, emotions, secrets, and other things deep inside our consciousness. The people born into this house are usually very spiritual, and they have a very intuitive understanding of the others around them. They often border on being psychics due to their natural inclinations.

The people who have Mercury in their twelfth house are usually very reserved and introverted kind of people. They cannot express their thoughts and feelings very clearly, which is quite the opposite of Mercury's famous chatty nature.

However, this provides them with another advantage that the other houses influenced by Mercury don't have. They have an exceptionally sensitive mind, and can understand the various situations and their surroundings very well. They compensate for their lack of expression by this abundance of understanding.

They spend most of their time studying, contemplating, writing, and thinking about the higher-order problems in life. They are very well suited to artistic pursuits due to the combination of their creative mind with a very high intellect seen in Mercury-influenced people.

Even though they don't like to communicate all that much themselves, they are very good at helping others to do so. They can excel at psychology, dream interpretations, and any other skills where a person needs to help bring out what's going on in the minds of others. Sometimes this can pose a problem as they may not be able to tune out the thoughts of others, and that greatly interferes with their own abilities to think.

Often, others may misunderstand them, leading to unnecessary miscommunications, making life more difficult for them. They are more susceptible to mental issues like anxiety and stress due to their more intuitive mindset. Not only mentally, but these problems can also manifest in physical forms with issues like learning disability, hearing issues, impaired speech, or anything else that can prevent them from being properly understood.

The love life of these individuals might not be very successful either. They will most likely suffer from multiple heartbreaks, which lead to short-term clandestine affairs. The spark that's felt when first meeting someone will be very intense, but it will fade as quickly as it was ignited, and the relationships will often meet a tragic and painful end.

The person will feel sadness, sorrow, and loneliness in their life from a young age, and the romantic life will be of no help either. Problems like divorce and separation are pretty common among the holders of the twelfth house, and they often end up marrying more than once. There can also be sexual issues in a marriage with problems conceiving a child.

The career paths are vastly different than others. They may choose to be actors, psychologists, astrologers, martial artists, sailors, writers, and some may even gravitate towards the occult.

Their lifestyle will be very lavish and full of luxuries, but there will always be a cash crunch due to the shortage of liquid assets. They often start their journey with a relatively low income but manage to reach the upper echelons of society by stabilizing their finances during the later stages of their lives.

They will not be very healthy, and their immune system will be weak too. They are more prone to suffering from anemia, obesity, tooth decay, leprosy, high/low blood pressure, and many other serious ailments.

We saw that different houses can greatly affect how a person's life is lived even if Mercury is present in their charts. The placement of Mercury usually determines a person's intelligence, communication skills, and spirituality according to the house it's in.

It's important to know which house your Mercury falls in. This will help you better understand how the planet affects you and how you can take steps to improve the issues you discover along the way. It can also help you determine what strengths you possess to formulate a strategy and utilize your strong points to work in your favor.

Mercury is the fastest and the most multifaceted planet in our solar system and knowing how it works in astrology is critical if you wish to better understand it.

Chapter 8: Aspects with Other Planets

The aspects between planets are an important part of astrology. As the planets move around the sun, they begin forming angular relationships with each other. They use the Sun and the Earth as the center, and these are called aspects.

When your chart shows numbers like 0 degrees, this means the aspect is in conjunction. When it shows 180 degrees, it means it is in opposition. It is a trine at 120 degrees and a square at 90 degrees. These are the most common aspects, but there are more, and you will probably come across them by just looking at your own chart. These aspects come from dividing the circle by numbers like 1, 2, 3, or 4 resulting in the aspects.

If two planets are in the same sign, this is when they are in conjunction. A set tile aspect is when the two planets are two signs away from each other. An example would be when Mars is in Aries and Venus is in Gemini. A square aspect is one when planets are three signs away from each other; an example is when Mars is in Aries and Venus in Gemini.

A Trine aspect is when a planet is four signs away from each other, like when Mars is in Aries and Venus in Leo. In an Opposition aspect, this is when planets are six signs away from each other. As two planets form an aspect with each other, their nature and energies come together. The principle behind aspects is that planets must be able to connect to influence each other. However, planets can only connect under particular conditions. Planets connect when they are in the same sign or when they are 2, 3, 4, or 6 signs away from one another.

Hard and Soft Aspects

Aspects are split into hard and soft: the square and opposition and hard aspects. This means the aspects are rough and jarring in comparison to the soft aspects. These aspects are harder to handle. They are more intense and tend to signify the areas you find more challenging or difficult to work with.

The soft aspects are the sextile and trine aspects. They are much smoother and harmonious and are much easier to handle compared to the hard aspects. They are less intense and signify the areas you find easier, which may come naturally to you. These are usually the areas that you might even take for granted.

Conjunctions are an anomaly because they are neither hard nor soft. You can judge conjunctions based on the closeness of the planets. Planets in conjunctions are united in their energy, and because of this, they act in partnership. The closer the conjunction is, the more subjective these energies are. Conjunctions can, in fact, be blind spots.

Now let's consider the aspects and what they mean for Mercury and the rest of the planets.

Mercury and the Moon

The hard aspects of these two planets mean that you will be forced to constantly cultivate self-awareness around your emotional reactions from a detached mental view. Almost like an outsider to the self. It is important that if these two planets are in a hard aspect in your chart that you don't act spontaneously. You must first take a look at your mental reactions. You must constantly be reviewing what you think about your feelings.

Typically, you will waste money on unnecessary household items. If this describes you, you need to concentrate on learning how to compromise and become aware of and control your ego. Ego work would be a good undertaking in this instance.

If these planets are in the soft aspects, you could be shrewd, intuitive and honest, and logical. You can have a decent amount of common sense and will very likely be in good health. When you feel like it, your feelings are most likely thought out, or your thoughts can be quite emotional. However, it can also be that you feel independent of your mental reactivity, or you think independently of your emotions. Typically, you will be a good teacher, writer, or reporter. You will also likely be a good conversationalist. Men with these soft aspects will usually have a good marriage and/or an intelligent wife.

Mercury and the Sun

Because Mercury is only ever 28 degrees behind or in front of the Sun, the only relevant aspect is close conjunction. Mercury tends to be better when it has no aspect to the Sun. This provides the individual with objectivity in their thinking. It provides greater communication skills due to the integrity and harmony with the thoughts and sense of self. It gives the mind a clear and objective focus.

With Mercury and the Sun in a soft aspect, the ego may have some issues expressing its true self. It may be that there is a lot more thinking from the ego, which can cause conflict between what the person thinks and what they actually do. The conflict here is because the person can be both introspective and reflective but also egocentric and stubborn. If the conjunction is less than five degrees, this leads to some inflexibility in the mind.

It can be difficult for there to be truly objective self-analysis as the mind and ego are closely intertwined. Selfishness may be a natural instinct since the majority of their thoughts are concentrated on themselves. Their communication skills makes them great teachers.

Mercury and Venus

Venus is the planet of love. It has been given the name of the goddess of love and beauty. It was thus named as the planet shares similar characteristics to passion, love, and inspiration. This planet is the hottest in the solar system and does its own thing as it turns in a different direction to the other planets. Venus is a physically mysterious planet as clouds of sulphuric acid cover it. It manifests beauty as it shines bright and is visible for many with the naked eye.

If a person's Mercury and Venus are in a hard aspect, they will probably have to learn how to communicate more pleasantly. It may be that they have experienced speaking and then had to retract their statement and rephrase it more succinctly and pleasantly. What this person thinks and the way they express it needs to be cultivated pleasantly.

When these two planets are in the soft aspects, the person is usually sweet and pleasant in speech. Their thoughts and expressions are also sweet. However, they are most likely forgotten soon after. This person may be a great writer, thinker, and speaker and can make friends easily. These friendships may be quite superficial, however. This person can persuade people easily to their point of view. There tends to be a personality of calmness.

Mercury and Mars

Mars gets its name from the god of war, a god who is stubborn and fearless. The planet manifests these similar qualities even in its physical appearance. It is a brutish red color and has the most in common with the Earth. Due to how useful it is, this planet strengthens Mercury's positive influence but can cause people to become angry and impulsive on the more unfavorable side.

These planets provide good mental energy and a clear, decisive mind to make and act upon instinctual decisions in the hard aspects. They are known to express themselves explosively, which can shock others and make them react quite defensively. This individual will often be harsh in achieving their objectives. However, this route can be important sometimes and is usually revealed as an important purpose. The explosions and the fights that may ensue can cultivate a strong mental attitude. They have the energy and mindset to succeed. However, they may work themselves to the point of a breakdown.

These planets give a person brave, trustworthy, worthy, and practical qualities in the soft aspects. If the Aries is strong here, there may also be some recklessness. Compared to the hard aspects of these planets, there may be some diplomacy here. It can still have the shock factor, but this person may use it cleverly when they want to or feel that the situation warrants it. They have common sense, great sight, and hearing. They may also be fond of children but are often childless.

Mercury and Jupiter

This planet was named after the Roman god, the lord of the sky and thunderstorms. It's not surprising this planet is named after this god as the planet's thunderstorms are incredibly powerful. Jupiter has a large red spot on the side of the planet, which is a giant storm. This spot has been seen by astrologers from as early as the 17th century.

Jupiter is just, and as long as you've been good, you should not be scared of this planet and its influences. If you've been on your best behavior, Jupiter has a lot of gifts to give.

In the hard aspects, this person may find it hard to think expansively. When their thoughts get out of control, they may lose their sense of composure and balance and just start shooting aimlessly. Through a series of learning and compromise, this person will begin establishing their position. This conjunction tends to be quite harmonious.

In their soft aspects, these planets provide a person with a good-natured temperament. They are generous and easy-going with their friends. They may enjoy hosting guests and entertaining in their own homes. Similar to the hard aspects, this person's thoughts can easily go haywire. However, their thinking can sound fairly impressive. This means the person is not reminded enough that their thinking has spiraled a little. They may, however, see for themselves that their thinking is flighty or illogical. Their style can impress others, sometimes very easily. They tend to be fond of travel and very optimistic in their thinking.

Mercury and Saturn

This plant was named after Saturn, an ancient Roman god. This god was cruel and known to devour his children. He was once a great god. However, after being overthrown, this god began to reside in the darkness.

The planet is located just behind Jupiter in the solar system. Astrologically, it is almost as paradoxical as the god it is named after. If your behavior is in line with this planet, Saturn encourages this more.

In the hard aspects, they are logical, careful, and systematic. They are ambitious and very responsible. They can be very serious and have great mental depth. Despite their mental ambition, they may not receive the recognition they want and usually deserve. Their thinking tends to be limited to practical situations surrounding serious topics. Whenever their thinking veers away from this pattern, issues can occur. This person can have jealous tendencies and fear change. This fear and their expectations of failure can mean they have few meaningful friendships. If this person is in a position of authority, they can be known to belittle other people's ideas.

In a soft aspect, this person has a disciplined mind. There is great depth to their mind, and they are direct and concise with their speech. They tend to be moral and honest and hold these qualities in high regard. They have great health, physically and mentally. They are often geared toward serious topics and can very easily discipline themselves to the point where they approach things in a very scientific manner. They often prefer to think about frustrating scenarios, which often leads to hindrances in their lives. By releasing this, they can allow themselves to concentrate on lighter issues.

Mercury and Uranus

In the hard aspects, these planets give an individual a very alert mind. They need constant stimulation. Otherwise, they find themselves twiddling their thumbs. They often start projects but don't see them through to the end. Because they tend to waste energy, they can create a lot of conditions or tension within themselves. Their thinking can be all over the place and out of the box. Because this person is so wild and independent in their thinking, they may find themselves in difficult situations facing internal conflicts about whether they did the right thing. This person has a unique way of thinking that can lead to great success, as long as they allow themselves to think freely. If this person has evolved, they can be dedicated to teaching the truth to others in a prophetic manner.

In a soft aspect, their thinking and communication can also be all over the place. Contrary to the hard aspects, however, this person does not affect others. They do not learn how to cultivate this and may have to learn just how different their thinking really is. They may also figure out how to work with this to produce some mentally ingenious results. The reaction that comes with these planets being in a hard aspect allows them to see themselves as their behavior profoundly affects others due to its harshness. Because the soft aspects allow the thinking to flow much more easily, there is less chance of it being shown the truth and given the ability to evolve. They have a great memory and the ability to communicate effectively. They are, however, quite impatient with people who aren't as sharp as they are. The solution to an issue comes to them in the form of a flash of inspiration. If this aspect exists in a chart, it points to a soul that is pretty advanced in its evolution.

Mercury and Neptune

This planet is similar to Uranus astrologically in that they provide a stormy fantasy and creativity. Neptune is, however, much more sensitive. Interestingly, Neptune was the first planet to be found purely from calculations. This suits the nature of this planet as it allows us to find subtle and intangible things.

In hard aspects, this person tends to learn the ability to combine the inspirational influence of Neptune through pleasant expression and communication. This person will have to learn this through trial and error as their communications may be seen as bogus. This is just because many people aren't tuned into the planet Neptune. Despite potentially hostile reactions, they should be ignored, and this person should go ahead with their own style and avoid vagueness. Issues can arise from this person associating with the wrong crowd. This person should also be careful of too much emotional distress as it can have a profound effect on the nervous system, and they can also have breathing issues.

In a soft aspect, this person's thoughts follow a pattern that is unlike others. Their thought patterns are also not easily understood by others because they are so different. They are known to be drawn to mystic ideas and thoughts and are not likely to ground this into reality. This is because they tend to indulge themselves in this fantastical thinking for their own benefit. Unlike the hard aspects, this person is not forced to face reality and the bogus side of Neptune.

Mercury and Pluto

Pluto is no longer considered a planet in the world of astronomy. In the world of astrology, it is still very influential. This planet is very far away from the Sun and resides in darkness. Named after the god of the Dead world, the god was feared in ancient times, and people were often afraid even to utter his name. This planet has the strongest orbit and, due to its shape, can come very close to the Sun. At other times it runs very far away. This manifests as a sort of polarity and demonstrates the planets leaning toward extremes. This planet can empower people with this polarity and provide independence and unpredictability.

In its hard aspects, this planet makes a person a die-hard pursuer of their own thinking. At the same time, they are guided to reflect on matters around them, leading to complete overhauls. This way of being is often at the expense of other people's ways of thinking or belief systems. This aspect manifests positively as a new way of thinking or doing in almost any industry or field. This planet makes way for innovation. They are almost always thinking progressively and have a psychic understanding of the new potential. However, this person can be quite harsh in their speaking and expression and accept being spoken to in this manner. At the same time, they can be quite diplomatic in their expression.

In soft aspects, their thoughts can run wild. This leads to innovation and revolution. When these thoughts make their way into the outside world, they do not cause a negative effect due to this influence being in a soft aspect. Interestingly, this person may not use this wild thinking to get behind a good cause and use their thoughts as a force for change. This is because they will only really go after these thoughts when they feel inclined to do so or when they can do so without any potential backfiring. This person can get away with saying whatever they like, even if it is outrageous or controversial.

Although the hard aspects can often be perceived as unfavorable, it may be more helpful to view these aspects as the ability to reach evolution much quicker. It is this fiction that allows for movement in a specific direction. When everything is in constant harmony or balance, this doesn't allow for much room for growth.

Greater self-awareness will allow these hard aspects to lead to more understanding of the self. Because the influence of the planets provides a harsh and sharp landing, this can cause negative ripples. However, with awareness, these ripples can lead to great evolution and growth.

Chapter 9: When Mercury Goes Retrograde

Every 88 days, the planet of Mercury presents us with an unusual phenomenon called apparent retrograde motion. This is the exact amount of time it takes for this planet to circle the Sun, which indicates that Mercury moves a lot faster than Earth. Due to its speed, Mercury can pass us four times per year. And each time it moves past our planet, it changes its primary, prograde direction. Of course, this is purely an optical illusion, caused by the fast movement we notice going by us (like when you are driving, and someone drives by your car at a much higher speed). However, according to astrology, this phenomenon causes quite a disturbance in the life of each zodiac sign. And while contrary to popular belief, the motion won't cause everything in your life to go wrong, but it will likely cause some disturbances.

Mercury in retrograde disrupts your professional and personal life in equal measures, often making it impossible for you to live your life the way you used to. Because of their inability to cope with changes, zodiac signs comfortable living an orderly life will be bound to suffer a great deal from this. From this chapter, you will learn why this disruptive motion influences our lives in general and how each sign is affected by it. You will also understand how to recognize some of the warning signs that may signify an incoming retrograde, which will help you prepare yourself and plan accordingly. Having a sound plan for a scenario you want to avoid will make the whole period seem less stressful. You may end up being grateful for this otherwise disruptive motion, as it will give you a chance to stop and reflect on some of the choices you have made in your life. After all, we can only grow as human beings if we learn from our mistakes and gain the ability to do better in the future.

Why Does Mercury Retrograde Affect Us?

Since Mercury is considered the messenger of the solar system, from an astrological point of view, this planet has an enormous bearing on our communication style. Mercury affects how we relate to others and our environment, often determining the entire course of our lives. Going retrograde interrupts the path of information carried by this planet, causing a disturbance in the solar system. Translated into zodiac terms, this means that any effect Mercury previously had on each zodiac sign will change, at least until the planet returns to its prograde motion. Unfortunately, most of these changes will have a negative influence on each sign's ability to communicate. The full effect of each retrograde is determined by the Zodiac house where Mercury is found during this period. As some of these houses govern our social lives, while others interfere with our professional capacity, we may experience different consequences after each motion.

Now, you may be wondering, how can this apparent retrograde motion of Mercury cause so much trouble? And why do you have to pay attention to it in the first place? The answer to these crucial questions may be found in the way we live our lives, especially in recent times. Namely, we built ourselves a world intertwined with digital technology, which influences our everyday actions. And because this world is based on our need to interact, our technology will be governed by Mercury as well. One would think, living in this mercurial world, that we would be used to sudden changes. After all, all the change happening to the world in leaps and bounds is the consequence of the incredible technological advancements being made constantly. Ideally, technology should be beneficial for our interactions and make our lives easier in general. However, as recent

Mercury retrogrades have proven, this is certainly not the case. It appears that all these technological advancements are only making us depend on them even more. Because of that, even the tiniest glitch in the system can wreak major havoc in our lives. When something goes wrong, we are suddenly confronted with the disadvantages of our digital dependency. This, unfortunately, reflects not only in the lack of our communication ability but we can fail to conduct commerce and actualize travel plans as well.

Albeit modern technology is often a useful tool to facilitate communication, being overly dependent on it can cost you a lot. With digital communication lacking any personal touch, you can easily forget about the importance of having personal interactions with your loved ones. Without these, your bond will become fragile, and you may lose each other. Failing to communicate appropriately will also cause your anxiety and anger levels to rise. Digital communication is often happening too fast for our minds to comprehend and leaves room for misunderstandings. While pretty inconvenient, Mercury retrograde can actually be a good reminder for you to replace some of these digital interactions with live conversations. This will straighten up your bond with your loved ones. It doesn't even have to be a meaningful conversation, as having the person sitting across from you will already feel a thousand times more personal than any message would. Reflecting on your past relationships is also a good idea, and not just to reevaluate your bond. Because the retrograde motion disrupts the way you interact with others physically, it may teach you something about yourself. By providing you with time to reflect on what you are doing wrong, retrograde will help you improve your communication style in the future.

Besides using them for convenient communication, we rely heavily on our numerous gadgets to perform some of the most mundane tasks. From having drinking water and clean air in our homes to keeping us safe online and offline, we use technology for everything. When was the last time you did anything for fun without using one of your gadgets? Just being relaxed and enjoying life as it is? It may sound like a simple thing to do, but many people struggle to let go of digital comfort, even for a day. However, when Mercury retrograde happens, you might find yourself getting robbed of some of these comforts. No matter how incredible it sounds, sometimes going back to basics is one of the best things that can happen to you. Plus, it can give you ample time to consider any opportunities you may have overlooked, whether from your past or present. You certainly should not buy any new devices, no matter how small it is. If they don't work, you can just end up throwing them out along with your money.

We are also used to coming and going as we please, using the fastest mode of transportation available. Living in a city, if you don't use your car every day for work, you probably use it for running errands. Taking a vacation has never been easier than in these modern times either. Whether you want to take a trip to the nearest city or continent, you will find plenty of options to do so. Because this has also been made possible through technology, Mercury in retrograde can also foil your travel plans pretty easily. Whether a flight cancellation or bad weather, something is bound to happen to make you give up your dreams. As with any other loss, this also happens for a reason. You can always spend your vacation with the people close to you and learn to appreciate them more.

Signs of Mercury Retrograde

Fortunately, the retrograde motion usually happens in several stages and does not cause all the mayhem at once. If you learn how to recognize the signs of each phase, you can prepare yourself even for the worst-case scenario. For example, Zodiac signs housing Mercury when the planet retrogrades will be more sensitive to its ill effects. So they are more likely to notice the earliest manifestations. Although the other signs will be affected, they may fail to heed the warning signs of a possible incoming retrograde. However, unless you are one of those people who are really good at going with the flow, you will probably feel the changes and won't like them at all.

Pre-Retroshade Phase

This is the phase of a pre retrograde shade, in which Mercury prepares to move into retrograde. Using your intuition, you may be able to sense that something will happen soon, and it probably won't be a good thing. This can be a confusing time, and if you aren't sure what exactly is wrong, watch out for everything and everyone around you. Should any of those appear in the next stage, you will know from which direction the blow comes.

Stationing Retrograde

As Mercury is about to launch into the apparent retrograde motion, you may experience a sudden feeling that stops you in your tracks and makes you look out for danger. Deep down, you will know for sure that something is about to happen, even if you have no clue what that may be. Although if you are careful enough, you may even perceive the first signs of a communication stopping or something else beginning to go wrong.

True Mercury Retrograde

Here, Mercury appears to be moving actively backward, so the effects of retrograde will be in full swing. For over 21 days, you can expect everything from technological issues to old acquaintances popping up, causing you headaches. Plus, you will probably experience some level of hindrance in your interaction with others, as retrograde causes your mind to slow down, making relating to others a lot harder. Depending on which zodiac house Mercury currently resides in, this can span from minor personal squabbles to more notable misunderstandings in professional venues.

Conjunction with the Sun

About halfway through the retrograde process, Mercury will be in close conjunction with the Sun. This can shine new light on your problem in the form of a sudden revelation. You will be able to see the way out even from the darkest of tunnels. It's particularly recommended to watch out for this, as this new hope can make the rest of the motion a lot more bearable.

Stationing Mercury

Mercury comes to a halt again, and you will be able to relax because you realize the worst is already over. This phase will show you where the retrograde will take you and reveal almost everything you can expect until the end. Whatever the end result will be, you won't be surprised by it anymore.

Post-Retrograde Shade

This is when Mercury begins moving in a prograde motion again, and things slowly return to normal. Similar to the pre-shade phase, the end of the retrograde cycle is also a gradual process. Nevertheless, it will still be visible both in the sky and in your actions. Although still a bit dazed, you will slowly be able to relax and take full stock of what happened. Now that it's over, you will get the chance to analyze everything and draw possible conclusions as well.

How Retrograde Mercury Affects Each Sign

Aries

Expect lots of confusion in the field of communication, complete with drama and deliberate misunderstandings. On top of your own inability to interact efficiently, some people will make it particularly hard for you to get along with them. And because they can come from any of your social cycles, you will have to be vigilant around everyone, from coworkers to neighbors. You may want to be extra careful with your interactions with your closest circle of friends. Real friends are a rarity, and you may discover that some of them aren't who you thought they were.

Taurus

If you are born under the zodiac sign of Taurus, financial difficulties and work-related issues may both be on the horizon for you during a mercurial retrograde. Whether it happens due to your own fault or not, you may fail to complete some crucial work assignments, resulting in a lot of stress and a possible loss of income. On top of that, you may realize you have spent way too much money on something as well. You really don't want to lose your Romney. Otherwise, you may get stuck with items you will never have a use for.

Gemini

As your sign happens to be housing Mercury each year when it retrogrades, you will often feel its full effects. You will have trouble expressing yourself, which is something that otherwise comes naturally to you. However, with your thoughts scattered, you will probably make a mockery of some serious conversations. This will not bode well in your relationships, especially the personal ones. Conflicting beliefs can also cause trouble when you interact with people because you will lose your ability to listen and relate emotionally. What's more, you may even begin to question your own beliefs in the process.

Cancer

During this trying time, a Cancer will most likely lose touch with their inner self, which will be a hard pill to swallow as they rely on it so much. And as if that wasn't enough, the lack of your usual intuition can lead to memory problems as well. You can easily forget about some important tasks, like paying bills or buying a present for a loved one, something that would never happen to you otherwise. Speaking of which, you will probably find the need to evaluate some of your acquaintances, as some of them may have ulterior motives. Be careful not to trust the wrong people, especially when you can't even trust yourself.

Leo

While it usually serves you well, your organizational skill is not something you want to rely on as a Leo during a retrograde. Because of the confusing backward motion of Mercury, your thoughts are likely to be jumbled, and almost none of your ideas will be coherent enough. Regardless of how many beneficial contributions you have otherwise made in your workplace, teamwork leaves much room for misunderstandings. This can easily result in financial loss too, so be prepared for that. Your personal relationship will suffer as well, as you will often struggle to express yourself properly.

Virgo

This is definitely not the optimal time for a Virgo to form any new relationship. Whether it's personal or professional, any connection you forge during a retrograde is bound to go downhill very quickly. Technological glitches are also making annoying appearances, causing everything from lost emails to deleting important work-related data. Instead of planning ahead, you should look back to your past, as there may be a few unwelcome surprises ready to jump out at you. It may be a work deal gone wrong or a loose end from a past relationship, but it definitely won't be pleasant.

Libra

Unfortunately, traveling will not be on the books for you during this period, and you will have difficulty accepting that. If you planned anything, expect it to be canceled for one reason or another. Even if you can travel, you will probably experience several delays, which will ruin the whole trip. Since the trip won't be worth all the unnecessary drama, you can avoid everything by canceling it beforehand. During Mercury retrograde, Libras may get an unwelcome visit from some old acquaintances as well, bringing some unpleasant memories a little too close to the surface.

Scorpio

If you want to avoid being scammed, you may want to leave making significant investments for another time. Due to not being able to think clearly under the influence of the retrograde motion, you will not recognize false information or shady people, for that matter. If you fall victim to a scam, you may feel unjust resentment toward people who had little to do with anything. Similarly, as a Scorpio, you should also avoid moving at all costs unless you want to risk losing money and valuable personal property.

Sagittarius

Ironically, when Mercury goes retrograde, the least romantic zodiac sign can have the most relationship issues. Unfortunately, most of your problems stem from the fact that you won't hold yourself back even a little bit and may end up hurting people around you. Besides speaking harshly to your partner, you might cause a couple of misunderstandings by sending the wrong text messages as well. When in a hurry, you will probably forget to check some of the messages you sent and may end up sending confusing messages.

Capricorn

A retrograde is never a beneficial period for a Capricorn who thrives on flawlessly functioning schedules. During the retrograde, your sign can expect anything from unusual traffic delays to disastrous appointment mix-ups. So essentially, everything that can go backward and ruin a perfect day will happen unquestionably. Even if you check everything you do or say multiple times, it will still be hard to keep everything on track, not to mention how much time you will lose spent checking.

Aquarius

Because Mercury retrogrades in their astrological house every year, Aquarius may experience the motion on a deeper level than many other signs. As the retrograde affects their basic communication levels, this will make it almost impossible for you not to get into confusing situations. Getting into any new relationship is ill-advised because you won't see things clearly enough to make rational decisions. And if one thing will not happen during retrograde, it's you obtaining an authority position in your professional life.

Pisces

A retrograde is a stressful period for any Pisces, even if you don't have much going on. And if you add some major change, like moving or reconnecting with someone into the mixture, something is bound to go terribly wrong. No matter how appealing the idea of moving to a new apartment seems initially, it won't be worth the extra hassle brought on by Mercury retrograde. So instead of looking outside, try to pay attention to self-care and introspection, as you may experience some issue with either your mental or physical health.

Chapter 10: Mercury Retrograde-Proof Hack

We've all come across the frenzy that happens when mercury is in retrograde. The memes come flying out. Communication and travel seem to grind to a halt. Ex's jump out of the woodwork. But what exactly is mercury retrograde?

Mercury is the planet that is associated with travel, tech, communication, and clear thoughts. When the planet goes retrograde, these things can start to get messy, hence the warning signs of not texting your ex or avoiding travel.

One reason Mercury can have such a big impact in this day and age is the sheer amount of daily technology usage. Combine that with the fact that a lot of our communication happens over technology, and you can see the disaster we might be in for.

Mercury has a big job, and technology has a huge influence on the way we live our lives. In fact, nowadays, it's very difficult to get much done without it. The word 'retrograde' can be a little misleading. The planet isn't going backward. In fact, a retrograde is an optical illusion. During a retrograde, the planet seems to be moving backward from our vantage point on Earth.

All planets are going through a retrograde period. During this time, the things associated with the planet appear to get a bit messy despite seeming like we all need to take cover and hide during the Mercury retrograde. That's simply not the case. The things that can happen as a result of this shake-up can actually be for the better. It can be difficult to see the areas you need to grow in or evolve when everything goes smoothly. It's easy to get comfortable. But a retrograde is here to shake us out of our comfort and apathy and get us to look at things differently.

Most things that feel like they are "going wrong" are actually blessings in disguise. It's the universe's way of nudging us toward our evolution. Get out of your own way, it tells us. You may have been able to tell, but Mercury retrograde is not the time to start something new, in fact. Instead, it is a time to go inwards. It is a time to relax, recalibrate, and see where you care to evolve and grow in your life. The retrograde will give you this information by shaking up the areas of your life that can do with some pruning.

How to Survive

Now that you know that this time can be a blessing instead of a curse, it's time to learn how to work with it instead of letting it work against you. It can feel like a major inconvenience at the time, but if you're prepared, you can come out of this period a much better person than when you went in.

This time can be a period of creativity and connection. That is if you let yourself be open-hearted and ignore the details. Despite the earlier warnings, the more prepared you are, the easier it will be for you to navigate situations like making big financial decisions or starting a new job. You can simultaneously make this a period of reflection and rest while also making big life-changing decisions. It's about your level of preparation and willingness to allow this time to work through you and for you.

What Not to Do

Let's first sink our teeth into what you should avoid doing during this time. This will ensure that you avoid making any rookie mistakes that can make this time more frustrating than it needs to be.

Negativity

First things first. Your negative thinking needs to go. It can be easy to get sucked into the mentality that a retrograde is a terrible time, and you need to avoid everything until it is over. However, this kind of thinking will make this period worse and can, in fact, cause things to deteriorate as a result of your negative thinking. Where attention goes, energy flows. And a negative mindset will herald more retrograde troubles.

Instead, focus your thoughts and energy on making this a time of introspection and evolution. Allow it to show you where you need to grow. Of course, this process is painful in and of itself, so brace yourself. But the braver you are, the quicker you can ascend. Often, it just takes a greater level of self-awareness and willingness to evolve that allows us to transcend the behaviors and thoughts we no longer align with.

Loneliness

Avoid being a lone wolf. If something does go wrong during this time, allow a professional to waltz in and fix it instead of trying to do it yourself. This will allow you to have greater peace of mind, teach you to surrender, and ensure that you don't make a bigger mess of it.

Rely on Tech

Of course, technology runs through almost every facet of our lives. It's difficult to avoid. Instead, try to avoid it during this time. Take some precautions instead, back up your phone, tablet, or laptop. Carry your charger with you. If you have an important meeting, write it down. Ensure your connection is good on the day. Make sure your device is juiced up.

Take some extra precautions during this time, so technology doesn't get the better of you. If something does go wrong, breathe deeply, allow the annoyance and frustration to come up and wash over you. Once a few moments have passed, give yourself a pat on the back for not giving in to it. If you do give in to it, breathe in again, know that you are only human and that these reactions are normal and inevitable. Make a little promise to yourself that next time you'll take a little longer before you react.

Rush

Taking the time to slow down and get into the moment can help you avoid making any major mistakes. Use this time to nourish yourself and get into the routine of prioritizing your rest. In this busy age, it can be hard to make time for this. The focus tends to be on the hustle and bustle and grind so much that it can seem like a difficult and unnatural feeling to truly relax and be present despite our human nature.

Take some time each day to sit with yourself. This can be in the form of guided meditation, taking a few breaths focusing deeply on yourself, or taking a walk by yourself. Try and do these things without the distraction of music or your phone. At first, this can be difficult to do, so work your way up to it. Start with a few minutes each day and watch how you find it much easier to be with yourself for a longer time by the end of this period.

If you can, try to have a couple of rest and introspection moments throughout the day. This helps keep you grounded and connected, and you can avoid making decisions when you are rushed or stressed.

You don't need to try and meditate every day to slow down. You can choose anything that gives you a sense of relaxation as long as it resonates with you. That's the most important thing. This can be prayer, yoga, reading, having a bath, etc.

Expect Too Much

During this time, things can go wrong. Don't expect them to go wrong, but rather don't have unrealistic expectations. Misunderstandings, confusions, and mix-ups are very likely to happen, so be open to anything happening. Have some contingency plans in place if necessary. If not, be mentally prepared for things not to go your way. This will help you avoid feeling disappointed or overwhelmed.

What You Should Do

Now that you know what to avoid, it's time to discuss what you should be doing during this time to maximize the potential of the retrograde.

Brainstorm

Stay open-minded and flexible. It's key to remember that just because your first or second attempt at something didn't work out, it doesn't mean nothing will. Keep your mind to possible solutions, and eventually, something will work out. Don't give up too easily and blame it on the planets. Instead, this can be the planets pushing you to discover something that will work better for you.

Get Out of Your Comfort Zone

To get through this period without a scratch, you need to get out of your comfort zone. Specifically, you need to be flexible, patient, and adaptable. If things do go wrong, exercise patience and try to see things from a different perspective. This period is forcing you to think and act differently, so start doing that. You never know what can transpire as a result. Remember that retrograde is here to help you. The best way to allow the help to happen is to stay open-minded and easy-going.

Car

Because mercury can cause vehicle issues, make sure that you are taking care of your car. Schedule a maintenance appointment during this time, and take care of any issues you may have noticed or anything you've put off related to your car. It doesn't hurt to be safe rather than sorry.

Timeline

Mercury retrograde is a great time to finish off projects that have already been started. If you've found that there are things you've begun, but you've lost the motivation, time, or energy to complete them. This period can be the perfect time for you to finish them as opposed to starting new projects. However, the energy isn't super aligned with starting new things, so try to avoid doing that. Instead, you may want to make a timeline to complete your project. This will give you something to focus your energy on and ensure you use that energy in the right places.

Ensure the timeline isn't too strict, though, but allow yourself to be generous with your time.

Time Management

Because this period can cause travel mix-ups and confusion, make sure you keep tabs on time. If you aren't great at time management already, you need to be extra careful about it during this time.

Maybe plan to be at places earlier than you need to be and ensure you have plenty of time and space in your schedule to maneuver around.

Single-Tasking

Multi-tasking is hailed as a skill, but it's not the most optimum skill for your brain even outside of Mercury retrograde. This is because your brain will be giving away less energy to each task than when you concentrate on one task. When you're single-tasking, your brain can place all the necessary energy and brainpower into doing that, and you will probably find that you are much more productive and effective that way.

The Past

This is a good time to revisit the past since much wisdom and growth can be garnered from reflection. Looking at the past allows you to notice the threads of common behavior that can help you see where your wounds are. Once you know, they exist it is so much easier to work with them and heal.

Mercury retrograde is the perfect time to address old wounds. If something about yourself has been on your mind for a long time, this is the best time to try and resolve it.

Vacation and Travel

Despite the warning signs against traveling during this time, it may not always be a choice. Perhaps you booked a holiday a while before realizing it was retrograde, or it was the only time you had off. Whatever the reason, it's not always practical to plan your travels around planetary movements. However, it can certainly bring some alignment into your life.

If you are going to travel during this time, there are some things you can do to make the trip as smooth as possible.

Leave Early

Mercury governs transportation which means getting ahead of things and leaving for the airport or any other destination early will help prevent any mishaps. As trains can be delayed, make it easier for yourself and opt for a cab, especially if you're off to somewhere important. Arrange for your transportation to pick you up earlier than you would usually arrange.

If you're on a road trip, ensure you fill up your tank and have all the necessary gear should you run into any issues. Make sure you have a spare tire in the vehicle and the appropriate numbers for any emergencies.

Triple-Confirm Everything

You want to triple-confirm everything, especially your reservations. Follow up with any hotel, restaurant, or sight-seeking bookings just to make sure everything is all set. Mercury retrograde has a history of wiping out data, and this is Mercury's way of communicating that it's time to upgrade.

You will want to check all the details, such as whether the time is AM or PM, and ensure the names are spelled correctly. These small details, if missed, can put a huge spanner in the works. This is vital for other aspects of your life during the retrograde, which means keeping an eye out for the details.

If you are booking something during this time, make sure you read the fine print and t+c's because the planet rules contracts. So, you must take your time with signing any.

Share the Itinerary

Communication can go a little haywire during this time, so make sure you are open and vocal about any plans. On your trip, share your itinerary with your travel buddies. This will help prevent any miscommunications or confusion and ensure you are all on the same page. Make sure you are all in agreement before the trip even begins. Once again, allow yourself to be flexible and adaptable so that you welcome any changes in the plan from your travel buddies.

If one of you fancy a beach day and another a slight-seeing day, allow the group to split up. There's no need to force anything. In fact, this can further hinder communication. Let things flow as they happen.

Peppermint Oil

This is a great little hack as herbalists believe this plant is great to get on Mercury's good side. Add some drops of peppermint essential oil to the bath or rub it into your pulse points. You can even spray it on your sheets before you sleep or rub some on your temples.

The cooling effect of this oil can help induce feelings of calm and relaxation and bring you back into the moment. If you want to bring some peppermint goodness into your life, opt for some peppermint tea as your drink of choice whenever you can.

Relationships

During Mercury retrograde, you may feel that your relationship isn't quite working out. If your relationship before the retrograde was fine, don't allow this time to interfere with this. This time has the effect of bringing up issues from the past, so you may find that your relationship can worsen during this period as old wounds are brought up.

To deal with this and get through the period with your relationship intact, make sure that you are aware of this. Openly communicate with your partner and allow them to safely bring up any issues, even if they are from the past. You can use this period to put them to bed for the final time instead of letting it affect your relationship.

Retrograde offers a rehashing of the past, but it also offers solutions. Allow yourself to be solution-focused during this time so that you bring healing and growth into your relationship as opposed to creating more upset.

This is why we tend to see many ex's pops out of nowhere. The rehashing of the past means many people feel inclined to reach out. This doesn't necessarily mean that you need to find a solution and work on getting back with them. If you broke up with them for a good reason, stay objective and keep your head above the chaotic Mercury retrograde waters. Reaching out to an ex or having an ex reach out can be the closure you need to step into your next upgrade. Often we need to shut one door firmly for another to open.

Beware that this period won't just affect your romantic relationships. But it can affect other relationships in your life.

To ensure you stay aware and adjust your behavior and mindset to make the most of this period, here are upcoming retrogrades for 2021-2022:

- May 29 – June 22, 2021, in air-sign Gemini
- September 27 – October 18, 2021, in air-sign Libra
- January 14 – February 3, 2022, starts in air sign Aquarius, ends in earth-sign Capricorn
- May 10 – June 2, 2022, starts in air sign Gemini, ends in earth-sign Taurus
- September 9 – October 2, 2022, starts in air sign Libra, ends in earth-sign
- December 29 – January 18, 2022, in earth-sign Capricorn

The key to dealing with this transformative time is to be aware. Awareness will allow you to notice when the planet forces you to see something you need to ascend or evolve. It will give you the objectivity to know when something is out of your hands and surrender to the universe. This will cause you to become in alignment very quickly with yourself, and you will watch yourself go from strength to strength.

You need a very healthy dose of patience, ensuring you are resting and recuperating. You can view this as a time to gather your energy to gain energy from this period and use it to be ready to tackle the next stage in your life.

Allow your spirit to realign by spending quality time with yourself and witness who you are. Retrograde is the perfect time to practice and reflect, and the tips above will help you make the most of it and ensure you come out of it a little more evolved than when you went in.

Conclusion

Now is the time to get your natal chart ready and use the information in this book to better analyze how Mercury influences your astrology.

When it comes to natal charts, you have many options:

- Get a free reading from online sources
- Hire a professional online to more accurately calculate your natal readings and develop a chart
- Consult with a professional astrologer in your area. They will be able to develop a natal chart for you and discuss its implications with you.

When you go out to get a natal chart reading, make sure you have your birth date, month and year, location of birth, and time of birth. For the best possible results, you need to make this information as precise and accurate as possible. If you don't have this information with you already, don't rely on the memory of your parents or other relatives. Even a difference of a few minutes in your time of birth can have a huge impact on your natal chart.

Suppose you have a regular ID like a driver's license or national ID that will most likely only mention your date, month, and year of birth. Next, you should try to get hold of your birth certificate, issued by the hospital where you were born. In many states and countries worldwide, the birth certificate does not mention the time of birth. If you still have no luck, you can contact local authorities such as the hospital or citizen registration center to request a detailed birth certificate. This is your best chance of finding out your time of birth. If you still have no luck, there are some other online resources that you can use to find out exactly what time you were born. It will be a lengthy process, but it is worth every second.

Your birth chart is basically a way to understand the position of planets at the exact time of your birth. The way they were positioned in the sky will be reflected in their placement on the natal chart, which will influence the behavior of each house in the natal chart. Moreover, the four critical aspects of the natal chart, the Ascendant, the Midheaven, the Descendant, and the Nadir, can only be found accurately if you have the right time of birth. Like the minutes of the day, the natal chart is continuously changing. The previously mentioned critical points rotate through the natal chart every twenty-four hours.

There are 1440 minutes in a day, and 360 degrees in the circular natal chart, which means that the chart changes by one degree for every minute of the day. This means that two people born 4 minutes apart will be affected by the same zodiac sign with a difference of 1 degree. Each degree in the 12 zodiac signs across the natal chart significantly influences how that person is affected by that zodiac sign. Keep in mind that with the zodiac signs and degrees of influence of each sign, the position of the planets and transits they are in also change. Apart from all of this, location is also important. In some very large cities and countries, being born at one end of the country can have a different effect than being born in a different corner of the same city or country.

In this way, precise birth data is critical if you want to derive accurate information from your natal chart that will actually be relevant to you. Without the right information to start with, everything you have studied in this book will still hold true, but it won't be specifically relevant to your situation. Even though you will understand the influences of Mercury, you won't be able to understand how it's influencing you specifically.

Part 6: Venus in Astrology

The Ultimate Guide to the Planet of Love and Romance

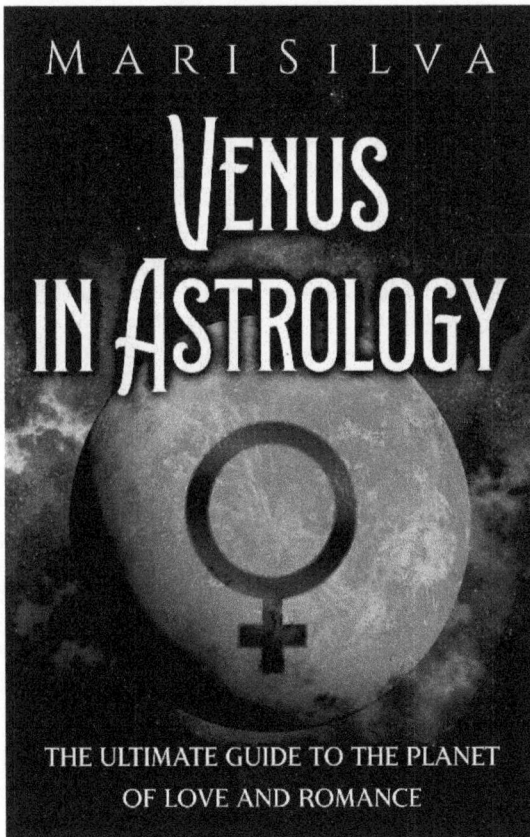

Introduction

So, you found the person of your dreams. Everything started so beautifully. Your stomach had butterflies when you met them, and every time you touched—the standard requisite for falling in love, according to every romance novel out there. You had a beautiful period of romance, and you were sure that while things wouldn't be Disney-perfect, you would have a lifetime of happiness and wholeness with this person.

Until they changed, that is. Right now, you are probably thinking about your college lover or ex-partner. Maybe wondering how you could have missed the fact that it had been a frog you were kissing all along. Or perhaps things aren't that bad, but you just wonder how you two got into the rough patch you are in and if there is any way to claw your way back out.

This is where astrology - specifically Venus - can help you.

If you want to understand what you and your partner think about love, loving, and being loved, then you have picked the perfect book. You will learn how and why you choose the kind of partners you do and how your partner is likely to relate with you throughout your union. If you are not already partnered up and you want to be, this book will show you what you must do to bring the love you seek into your life.

Other books and blogs might talk about sun signs and their compatibilities, but rest assured, this book is so much more than that. You will understand how everything on your natal chart dovetails nicely (or doesn't) with your partner's. This way, you will know what you must do to fix your relationship or avoid having it end in shambles.

When you know how to work with Venus' energy and discover how it affects you and your partner, you will have found the key to a life of happiness and bliss. In addition, you will also know the truth about how to attract love to your life, critical information that most of the world is sadly ignorant of. But not you. At least, not anymore, since you made the right call by deciding to read this book.

You are about to discover the fantastic world of Venus and how this planet - the goddess of love, pleasure, and all things luxury - affects your love life. Other books might try to convince you that you are doomed to a loveless life, but not this one. When you know how to work with your Venus, you will find yourself effortlessly attracting **and** maintaining love. Not only that, your relationships and friendships will be a lot healthier, and they will give to you and reciprocate with you in ways you've never imagined.

Love doesn't always have to lead to heartache, and heartache need not be forever. So, get ready to discover your Venusian side and work with it, so you can finally get the happiness and permanence you desire in your love life.

Chapter 1: Venus in Mythology

Venus was the Roman goddess of sex, love, fertility, and beauty. As it were, the Romans took over a lot of Greek deities. For instance, Hephaestus became Vulcan, Zeus became Jupiter, and Aphrodite was renamed *Venus*. The main difference between Venus and Aphrodite is that the former has more abilities than the latter. She was also the goddess of prostitution and victory. Hesiod's Theogony states that after Uranus was castrated by his son Saturn (Cronus) with a sickle, his blood and semen fell to the sea, and Venus was born from the sea foam as a result.

Venus and Her Lovers

Venus had two lovers: Vulcan, also called Hephaistos, and Mars, also called Ares. She was trapped in a loveless marriage with Vulcan, and they had no children. Vulcan had children with four other women (that we know of), and Venus was fine with his extramarital activities. The longest dalliance she had was with the god of war, Ares/Mars, the son of Juno and Jupiter. While Mars was brutal and aggressive, Vulcan was more sweet-tempered. Still, Venus had become enamored with the former.

Helios (or Sol, the sun god in Roman and Greek mythology) discovered the affair between Venus and Mars and informed Vulcan. In revenge, Vulcan created an invisible net and set it around his lover's bed. When Venus brought Mars back home again, they were both caught in the net, which was highly embarrassing and humiliating for the lovers. Vulcan then called on all the gods to come into the bedroom and watch the trapped duo. Gods, ever seeking amusement, came in to look. Vulcan relished this because, as a child, he was mocked and laughed at for being ugly, and now he was the one laughing instead.

Venus and Her Offspring

She had many children from various gods. With Mars, she had Timor (Phobos), who was fear personified; Metus (Deimos), who represented terror; Concordia (Harmonia), who embodied concord and harmony; and Cupid (Eros), a group of winged deities who personified various aspects of love. How Venus could keep five pregnancies away from Vulcan is something we must chalk up to the absurdity of myths.

According to Ovid, the Greek goddess Aphrodite had Hermaphroditos with Hermes. This child was androgyny and effeminacy personified. Also, with Hermes (Zeus), she had Fortuna (Tyche), who represented fate and luck in Roman philosophy and religion.

Venus also had a child with Bacchus named Priapus, a minor deity and fertility god often depicted with a disproportionately large phallus. The Graces (personifications of charm, beauty, and grace) are also thought of as being children of Bacchus and Venus, but you are more likely to hear of them being the children of Euynome and Jupiter. However, they did belong to Venus' retinue, as did Suadela, the goddess of persuasion in love, romance, and seduction. Some say Venus' ability to love so many and bear many children might have something to do with it being the power in Uranus' genitals, that Saturn had cut off, and that the blood, testicles, and penis mixed with the seafoam to create this love goddess.

The love goddess romantically entangled with mortals. A Sicilian king was also her lover, and they had a son named Eryx. With Phaethon, she had Sandocus as well. The most famous of her mortal lovers were Adonis and Anchises. Venus fell in love with the former for his beauty or an error by Cupid's bow. She asked Proserpina (Persephone) to take care of him until she was ready to come for him, but the other goddess also became enamored with Adonis, and they fought over him. For this reason, Zeus deemed it fit that Adonis spend a third of the year with each goddess and a third wherever he wanted to be. In the end, he spent his time with Venus until their love was cut short when a boar killed him.

The Jealous Goddess

One of the most recounted myths of Aphrodite/Venus is the start of the famous Trojan War. Along with Athena and Hera (also goddesses), Aphrodite had been invited to King Peleus' wedding to Thetis, the sea nymph. It infuriated Eris, the goddess of discord, that she wasn't given an invitation, and so she threw down a golden apple with a label on it however, "To the fairest," that landed in the middle of the floor. The trouble was, Venus, Athena, and Hera all considered themselves "the fairest," and so they fought over the apple.

When Zeus refused to pick the fairest of them all, the goddesses then sought out Paris, the Prince of Troy, to decide. They all offered him bribes so he could pick them. He had a hard time turning down Aphrodite's bribe because she told him Helen of Troy, the world's most beautiful woman, would be his if he chose her. The trouble with this (besides giving away people like trophies) was that Helen was married to King Menelaus of Greece. When Paris abducted the king's wife with Aphrodite's help (she made Helen fall in love with Paris), this sparked the Trojan War. Aphrodite also swayed Ares into supporting the Trojans, ironically. At first, he had been indifferent, promising both his sister Athena and mother Hera that he would side with the Greeks until Aphrodite worked her magic on him.

Anchises was a Dardanian prince on Troy's side during the war, was seduced by Venus. She made herself up to look like a Phrygian princess to win his affection, keeping her divinity secret until nine months later. She then presented Aenaeas to Anchises as their son. Venus warned her lover not to go around bragging about their affair, or Jupiter would strike him. But of course, he boasted, and for that, Jupiter's bolt crippled him.

Nevertheless, Aeneas the Trojan had the destiny to found Rome under Venus' guidance. His son, Iulus (Ascanius), king of Alba Longa, was the ancestor of Romulus and Remus, Rome's founders. He was also the ancestor of Gen Julia, the family that spawned Augustus (Octavian) Caesar, Julius Caesar, and many others.

Venus in Other Cultures

There are other deities besides Venus in Roman culture that embody the essence of this goddess. For example, in ancient Mesopotamia (now Iraq), Ishtar, the Queen of Heaven, was one of the most revered female deities in the land. She and the Sumerian goddess Inana (or Inanna) share a lot of traits.

"Ishtar" is from the Akkadian Semitic language. That name was ascribed to the Mesopotamian goddess around 23000 BCE. There are many aspects to her, but she takes on three primary forms. First, she is the goddess of sexuality and love, and as a result, fertility. It then follows that she's responsible for all of life, yet she isn't considered a Mother Goddess. Second, she is usually depicted with wings, bearing arms, for she is also known as the goddess of war. Her final aspect is celestial is nature, where she represents the morning and the evening star, also known as Venus.

One of the most recounted myths of Inana or Ishtar talks about how she fell in love with a shepherd named Dumuzi (or Tammuz) and became one with him through the Sacred Marriage ritual, effectively claiming him as her lover. Soon after, the shepherd died. One version of the myth says raiders murdered him and that his mother, wife, and sister mourned him. In another version, Inana traveled to the underworld, and the only way for her to have left was to offer Dumuzi as a sacrificial replacement. So, for six months each year, he comes back to Earth to be replaced by his sister in the underworld, which was how Dumuzi became the dying reborn god over land fertility, the one that farmers would pray to or thank in a drought or a bountiful harvest.

Love, Sex, Inana

Like Venus, Inana had a lot of lovers. In the *Epic of Gilgamesh*, the story's hero refuses Inana's advances, pointing out that all her lovers often end up with terrible fates. Other myths say Ishtar wields the power of rain and thunderstorms. In the divine world, she wages war and steals Sumerian offices or "me" from Enki, another god. *Me* are divine principles and powers that allow institutions and order to continue, and as a result, they lead to civilization as we know it. That Ishtar/Inana owns them all makes her a very prodigious goddess indeed.

Naturally, the Sacred Marriage is one ritual connected to Inana worship. In this ritual, a male ruler represents Dumuzi. Since the only reference we have for this practice is in literature, it's not clear if this was an actual reenactment of Dumuzi and Ishtar's own ceremony or if it's only symbolic. If you look up most texts and art on Ishtar, and you'll find she usually supports her favorite rulers in times of war. Quite possibly, ancient kings showed their dedication to her so they could prove their regime was a legitimate one. Locally, the people worshiped Inana as the goddess connected to certain cities. Still, most references to this goddess come from epics, ancient literature, myths, and hymns. Unfortunately, there isn't enough documentation on the practices of the Ishtar cult.

Being the goddess of sex, Inana might have had connections with the sexual rituals practiced by cults, though it isn't clear exactly how that is. Some texts say she is also associated with prostitution. Starting with Herodotus, more recent Greek accounts speak of a practice where women must have sex with a stranger within Inana's temple, at least once in their lives. While prostitution was a normal thing in Mesopotamia, this was a different practice. This was "sacred prostitution" in service to the goddess. You will find many sexual references and explicit eroticism in texts about the goddess of sexuality.

With her many powers and aspects, Inana/Ishtar is a complex goddess, a confusing one for modern scholars, who suggest that she embodies contradictory forces. Within this great goddess are divine paradoxes of sex and violence, death and fertility, terror and beauty, marginality and centrality, chaos and order.

Venus as a Man ... In India

According to Jyotish, Indian Vedic astrology, Venus is the most refined of all the bodies in heaven. It is called Sucra, which means "sugar" in English. This female planet represents reproductive fluids and semen, so it depicts fertility in a natal chart. It's also the planet for enjoyment, romance, and love. In Vedic tradition, this planet or goddess had many hats to wear, from advising demons on connecting with their lost souls to being one of the most outstanding spiritual teachers.

According to Indian mythology, there once was a time when Venus took on a man's role, seeking to make his daughter's dream come true. Venus's daughter was in love with a king and wanted nothing more than to be his wife, his first and last. Venus did as Venus does, and the marriage was successfully arranged. Unfortunately, the king was in love with someone else, so the union wasn't happy. It stayed unfulfilling and loveless for the couple.

A Lesson on Happiness

This myth aims to show us that with Venus, we can reach our sensory and material goals, but this doesn't necessarily mean we will have true happiness that lasts.

Also, Venus simply can't prevent Karma that is destined to happen no matter what. While we can make our desires come to life, we have no idea once we have them what that implies. We don't know what needs to happen or what will change when that desire is a reality. There is no sorrow more profound than finally getting what you want and finding it disappointing.

When Venus' positives shine through, you receive guidance on how to manifest real joy in your life, as she helps you change the way you think about life so you can see how things are perfect as they are and stop with the constant struggle of comparing what *is* to what you think should or could be.

Venus can guide us through learning that sensual and material gratification only offer brief moments of enjoyment no longer than a flash in the pan. These things cannot bring us pure happiness. People often think, "Well, when I get this, or that thing or person changes, then I'll be happy." They believe happiness is contingent on what happens on the outside. The trouble with thinking this way is that even if you finally get your way, you'll quickly find another thing to be unhappy about. That's because you've made the terms of your happiness conditional, based on external situations and other people, all outside of your control.

Venus can show you that true happiness comes from within. True happiness is a decision, not a feeling that "just happens" without your say. You can decide right now to be happy. Choose joy regardless of what you've gone through or what you are dealing with now. Also, it is unfair and wrong to place the responsibility of your happiness on another person, as this can cause resentment to build between you two. You must learn to be responsible for your happiness, and there is no better teacher than Venus herself to teach you this.

A Lesson on Romance

Vedic astrology has it that Venus rules romance and love. This force could bring you a loving partner, but to keep that partner and to remain joyous in a relationship with them, each of you will have to be responsible for your happiness and needs. So many say, "Oh, you complete me." Venus says, "Complete yourself." When two people understand that they alone can choose to be happy and that each of them is complete on their own, then you have a relationship built to last a lifetime.

It's a sad state of affairs that many look for someone to rescue them from their depression, loneliness, or unhappiness and to make the clouds in the sky turn to colorful rainbows for them. Sure, your partner can help. They can take care of your sensual, material, and physical needs, but only for a moment. The enjoyment you glean from that is very brief. If you don't understand the idea of self-love and the wholeness of your soul, then you will be back at square one, feeling empty, wondering what's missing, looking over at the neighbors, and admiring how much greener their grass seems.

Instant relationships are the norm these days. Don't feel happy with your partner? No worries! Get a new one. Did you just realize after a few weeks or months that this new partner isn't *doing it* for you? Well, get another one! On and on this goes, leaving a world full of lonely, broken hearts. So, what's the best approach? At the end of a relationship, or before starting a new one, look at yourself. Critically examine your expectations. Look at the real you, the thoughts that zip through the space between your ears. Be honest about who you are and learn that all you seek outside is within you. Of course, this is easier said than done, but you can accomplish it.

Many will have more than one relationship in their lives. There is nothing wrong with this, as long as you take the time to learn more about who you are, what you want out of life, and how you can give it to yourself before you hop on to the next relationship. Besides, Venus might have set things up for us to kiss a few frogs before finding our prince or princess, but you must play your part by receiving the gift and lesson each relationship brings you.

In the end, Venus is a beacon, guiding us to develop richer, more meaningful inner lives and to choose spiritual connection with our true, higher self. We will have inner peace beyond compare when we do this, and an infinite pool of happiness will come well up from within and washes over us. Then from that state, we may enjoy the relationships in our lives and continue to ride the waves of pleasure and love from each one, and this further feeds the self-love we have developed so the happiness continues to blossom.

Chapter 2: The Planet of Love

Fun fact, Venus is the solar system's warmest planet, even though it's not the closest one to the sun. It's warm because it has a thick, heavy atmosphere, which gives the term "greenhouse effect" a whole new meaning. Also, it has the most volcanoes of all the planets, which only lends further weight to Pluto's astrological symbolism.

Because of how close it is to Earth, Venus is one of the brightest planets in the night sky. Also, it's the only planet that represents a female deity, which implies that its feminine role is influential. The only other celestial body with feminine energy is the moon, and on the natal chart, you don't see many heavenly bodies that are feminine as opposed to masculine. Of all the stars, Venus is a true lady. She opposes them all and is enshrouded in thick clouds, making it almost impossible for whatever is on its surface to see anything outside itself.

The Astrological Significance of Venus

As Venus the planet, Venus in astrology is full of warmth. Its influence will keep you preoccupied with enjoying yourself. You'll be drunk on feelings, in love with food, people, and hallucinogens if you allow her to seduce you this way. However, when we go too far with indulgence, we lose balance. Mood swings rule along with impulsively changing your mind about everything. While this is behavior mostly assigned to the Moon, Venus is very involved in this. This planet is supposed to help us balance our whole lives physically, mentally, and spiritually. It helps us be aware of what we need to do to remain a whole, healthy individual.

Venus oversees Libra and Taurus. These signs have always had issues coexisting and accepting one another. Tauris is a fixed Earth sign, while Libra is a mutable air sign. One character would rather be physical and practical in all they do, while the other is more concerned with beauty in all its expressions, people, and situations.

Nestled within Venus is the conflict of outer beauty and pose versus practicality and use. So, it's good practice to check in with ourselves now and then to see which part of that equation needs to be balanced. The goddess of romance is all about love in all forms, be it platonic, physical, and even the unreachable, unrequited ideal of this emotion. She is Venus, the sacred prostitute, and the sleeping beauty. She teaches us that obligation and morals have no connection with creation, passion, or love.

Venus is the polar opposite of Mercury, so any sign where one planet is exalted, the other will be debilitated. For example, Mercury is exalted in Virgo, the 6th sign, while Venus is debilitated to 27 degrees. In Pisces (the 12th sign), Venus is exalted to 27 degrees, while Mercury isn't. At no point will you find Venus beyond 48 degrees from the sun. Those with Venus exalted in their natal charts tend to have a smooth face, beautiful round eyes, and dimples in their cheeks.

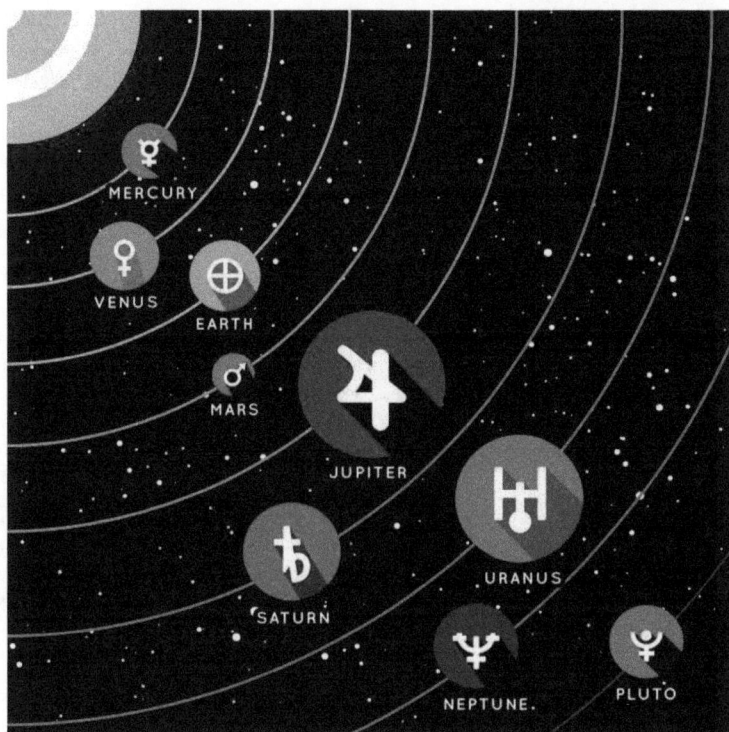

Venus Energy

Venus is the sign of destiny and is all about pleasure and attraction. This planet draws us to the finer things in life and to the people who make us feel love intensely, or love's first cousin, lust. Her energy causes us to lust for life's pleasures and to seek them out. She rules on an emotional level, but she also has things to say about our idea of self-worth, jewelry, money, sweet things, banks, and so on. Taurus Venus might want a practical meal of lasagna, while Libra Venus will go on and on about chocolates and wine. When we bring these two together, we get pleasure on many levels, experiencing them through every sense of the body and the soul. Particularly, Venus is associated primarily with touch, smell, and taste and will cause us to fall in love with things unique to us. Where Venus is placed in house and sign will let you know what inspires and moves you, what you relate to, and what you feel strongly about in matters of devotion and love.

Venus embodies our ability to feel, move with grace, and love freely. She affects our ability to make money, appreciate ourselves and others, and our energies. When Venus is challenged, we become highly critical of others and ourselves. We become dissatisfied and don't see all the good around us for which we should be thankful. Venus affects the laziness in us all, whether we can just lounge on a couch eating ice cream, or singing, dancing, and playing. This planet is all about diplomacy, tact, and food.

To discover the planet ruling your marriage or find your "missing rib," you should look at where Venus is on your chart. Many astrologers say that when your Venus is badly wounded, you can't find it in you to let yourself be loved, let alone believe you can be cherished at all. However, astrology doesn't mean your destiny is firmly fixed. It only shows you where you are relative to where you want to be and what you need to do to get there. If you sense that you have issues accepting love or believing you deserve it, you can fix it.

You can buy someone you love something you know they will appreciate, without expecting them to give you something in return. Do that for yourself. Buy yourself something nice, like your favorite flower or perfume. You can seek self-expression in art or fashion. Make time each day to indulge your inner hedonist. Decide you will be a flexible person every moment when it comes to interpersonal dealings and your body. Right now, burn this in your brain: There is nothing that could stand in the way of you receiving satisfaction, love, desire, beauty, and artistic expression in whatever form you desire. So, dance, sing, live a little, and watch your life become magical.

Harmonious Emotional Attachment

A strong Venus can affect your relationships and friendships significantly. Your Venus sign lets you know the integral parts of your personality. On the one hand, it represents your idea of what is esthetically pleasing. On the other, it paints a picture of your relationship style. Psychologically, Venus on your natal chart determines how you experience enjoyment and pleasure and how you relate to others. Your Venus profile is also very enlightening when it comes to how you attract other people.

In astrology, houses are the areas on your natal chart where planets are located. When you know your Venus sign and house, you know what it is that gives you the most pleasure in life, what delights you, and how you connect with others. Understanding what your Venus placement says about you will help you find satisfaction and happiness in life. In addition, you'll have a finger on the pulse of the patterns hidden in your psyche that affect how you live your life.

When your Venus energy is channeled positively, you'll find you usually have the most harmonious relationships with one and all. You could charm a cactus in the middle of a desert enough to get it to shed all its spines. That will be your thing.

Venusian Traits

When Venus is strong on your chart, you probably draw many stares because of your beauty. You have grace, charm, a certain *je ne sais quoi* about you. You have creativity in spades, and no one has a keener, appreciative eye for the fine things in life. You are an intensely sensual person. In addition, you ooze charm, and you often play peacekeeper very well. But you might also be a little lazy, preferring to be comfortable than disciplining yourself or go through unnecessary hardship. Usually, those who have conventional beauty and those who work in creative fields or jobs that require relationship-building abilities are affected by a strong Venus.

Venus can also show you lean towards greed and indulgence, depending on where it is on your chart. Another thing is you might also be seductive or flirtatious and have an uncanny ability to manipulate others using your charm. The following are Venusian themes that affect both your emotions and psychology:

- Attraction power

- Self-worth

- Social interaction

- Sexuality

- Sensuality

- Balance, proportion, and harmony

- Protocol and manners

- Materialism

- Relationships

Venus Debilitation in Virgo

Venus' debilitation happens at 27 degrees of Virgo. The latter is governed by Mercury, which makes Venus and Virgo buddies. This begs the question, why is Venus debilitated here?

Venus is about physical pleasure and beauty, but when it comes to Vedic astrology, Venus is Daitya Guru Shukracharya; beyond enlightened, having rare healing knowledge thanks to Mrit Sanjeevani Mantra (the mantra for bringing people back to life). So, underneath the glitz and the glam of Venusian materialism, this planet is about spirituality on a deep level. If you don't have Venus fueling you with its energy, you can't spiritually progress.

Virgo is the sign of the analytical, calculating mind of the perfectionist. With Venus here, the planet is no longer soft, no longer about beauty and pure love. Instead, it becomes differing, finding faults with the expression of its attributes. If you have a debilitated Venus, you feel insecure about your looks, peace, general happiness, and lovability. Your overly critical mind constantly looks for ways to make you "better" and criticizes how others choose to present themselves. As a result, you are never satisfied with the good things you've managed to create for yourself.

Women with their Venus debilitated often look the most stunning, yet their insecurities cripple them, so they never feel confident about themselves. There is always one spot to touch up, one barely noticeable stretchmark to cover up, one pudgy feature to hide. Virgo belongs to the 6th house of humanity's six sins, so it's hard for the spirituality of Venus to come through in this sign. The goddess can only express herself through this person in terms of materialism and the superficial things of life. Therefore, people with this Venus placement are very materialistic in outlook.

According to Vedic astrology, Pisces is the most spiritual sign, and therefore Venus is exalted here. Expressed positively, Venus is not about passion. Passion is Mars' scene. Venus is about expressing universal love in the purest form possible. So, when it's not expressed purely, it expresses itself in a tainted way, coming across as passion and a never-ending search for pleasure.

The effect of a debilitated Venus on your life depends on the houses it occupies on your natal chart. When you overindulge, seeking to satisfy your sensual desires, you probably have a debilitated Venus. Usually, this debilitation makes Venus overcompensate for all its natural attributes, physically and sensually. So, this means you need to put in more effort when it comes to money, love, comfort, relationships, and luxuries than someone with a strong Venus.

Now, I know all of this sounds terrible, but again, this doesn't mean you cannot overcome this, or won't ever get married or become rich, or that your relationships will end. Furthermore, the stars simply show you things to look out for and are not the arbiter of your destiny. Also, you need to check the influences of other planets on your natal chart to get the full story of your life's trajectory to determine the outcome. The following is what happens with a debilitated Venus in each house. Again, do not jump to conclusions without holistically looking at your birth chart for other influences.

- In the first house, you are insecure about how you look and act. As a result, you have low self-esteem and don't consider spiritual matters important.

- In the second house, you need to work harder than most to earn even a bit of money. As a result, you might be a bit too materialistic, placing stuff over people and rich experiences.

- In the third house, there is a lack of comfort. You want to attain peace and happiness, but you are trying to do that from a very materialistic perspective, which causes you deep dissatisfaction on the inside.

- In the fourth house, you are afraid of isolation, and this affects your romantic life. You don't prioritize romance much, mainly to avoid the pain of being left alone again. As a result, you don't get a lot of action with your lover.

- In the fifth house, your earning power and love life take a hit. You don't have as many obstacles to deal with as others—still, you are neither tact nor moral.

- In the sixth house, you are always finding fault with your significant other. Your spiritual life is still dormant.

- In the seventh house, you have trouble with your partnerships and your spouse as well. This is because you are full of lust. People would also describe you as lazy.

- In the eighth house, you have a lot of problems in your domestic life. You aren't content with your lot in life. Spirituality doesn't matter all that much to you, and your laziness does you more harm than good.

- In the ninth house, you have issues with your children. Your relationship also is in trouble because you can't help but be critical, and you are all about attaining stuff and more stuff.

- In the tenth house, you have no ambition. Your coworkers will cause you problems - especially female ones.

- In the twelfth house, your health yoyos. There is no warmth in your physical relations.

Now let's talk about Pisces, where Venus is exalted at the 27th degree. Pisces is a sign of Jupiter, who is Venus' enemy. So why the exaltation? It's because beneath the razzle-dazzle of materialism and luxury, Venus is about spiritual resurrection and a connection with the Source of all life. This is what Pisces is about as well. So, when the two come together, those energies merge, along with Jupiter and Venus, causing self-realization and liberation of the soul from the shackles of materialism.

Again, you need to check to see how the other planets conjunct with your Venus to know the precise effects of having an exalted Venus. Remember that while Venus is exalted, it is combust because of the Sun, so Venus might find it hard to manifest its energy, depending on your chart and your willingness to work on yourself. When Venus is in Pisces, it also must deal with being *aspected* by the planet Saturn, which means even more difficulty with manifesting the positives of Venus, making the goddess both debilitated and exalted.

More on Venus

Venus is the Lady of Friday. You might find you get better results in your endeavors when you plan things for Fridays. The diamond is the gemstone of this planet. Copper, brass, silver, beryl, alabaster, jade, and coral are the lucky gemstones and metals for the love goddess. Ivory, cream, and white are its lucky colors. The shrouded planet rules over our generative system, eyes, chin, throat, kidneys, and cheeks.

With physical appearance, those strongly influenced by Venus are usually of average height, with a lovely round or oval face and a plump body. They might have kind, bright, warm eyes, a sweet voice, curly hair, and an endearing smile. If their Venus is poorly affected, then they will not be that attractive. Usually, they always win competitions.

With diseases, they deal with inflammation, anemia, gout, goiter, skin diseases, and diseases affecting reproductive health. These diseases are usually caused by indulging too much in food, drink, sex, and drugs.

Venusians usually work in entertainment and the arts in general. They also make great politicians and diplomats.

Chapter 3: What Is Love?

Have you ever thought about what love really means? It's one thing to try to describe it, and another thing entirely to feel it. Dictionaries do their best, and cultures worldwide have been attempting to describe it, but somehow nothing comes close to encapsulating the emotion that is love. Still, there is no harm in trying.

Hindus on Love

According to Hinduism, love has six forms. First, you have **Kama**, which is sexual craving and desire (you may already know this one from the famous phrase Kama Sutra). Then, there is **Shringara**, which involves the romantic intimacy shared between lovers. This is reflected in the mythology of Krishna and Radha. **Maitri** is the third form of love, which you could interpret as "mother's love." Still, it is about having compassion for all living things and doing simple acts of kindness for one and all, regardless of the differences between us.

Bhakti means devotion to a higher cause or ideal, or the world, or to the divine Source of all life. Hanuman is the epitome of this in Hindu mythology. **Karuna**, the fifth form of love, means "sadness." It's about the compassion that stirs within us because we understand what the other person or creature is going through. This isn't pity at all, which comes from a place of condescension. This is empathy, walking in the other's shoes and knowing how it hurts.

Finally, there is **Atma-Prema**, which is love for the one thing that connects all of us. It is pure love directed at the soul, or in simpler terms, self-love. It's the realization that the thing that makes you who you are is shared by everyone and everything else. It's love without condition because you realize that we all come from the Source.

The Ancient Greeks on Love

Ancient Greeks recognized eight kinds of love. First, there is **Eros**, which is sexual desire, just like Kama. The Greeks did not think too highly of this form of love because they thought it was a sign of a lack of control and irrationality. This word is also the Greek name of the god Cupid and the root of the word **erotic**.

Then comes **Ludus,** a playful love, the kind you find between children. It's what you share with your friends as you tease one another. It is also the love shared by those flirting with each other or in the process of falling in love. It's the root of the word **ludicrous**, which infers something amusing and absurd.

Mania is obsessive love. The stuff of romantic psychological thrillers, or Billie Eilish music videos, if you prefer. The fourth is **Philia,** the root of the word filial and the suffix that implies one is a lover of something (audiophile, bibliophile, etc.). It's love shared by friends loyal to each other, where you are both willing to make sacrifices for the other person. It's shared by people who have been in the trenches together, whether on a battlefield or metaphorically.

Pragma is love that endures. It is built on patience, compromise, and tolerance, often shared by couples whose relationship has lasted a long time or between friends who have known each other for ages. This is also the root of the word **pragmatic**, which means "practical."

Then comes Storge, the love shared by family members. *Philautia* is the love of self. This isn't the same thing as narcissism but is expressed positively, like choosing to feel good about who you are, having good self-esteem, and respecting yourself. This love allows you to be good to others in the same way you are good to yourself.

Finally, there is *Agape,* the selfless, unconditional love. This is genuine empathy and charity, the purest form of love. It is also love for the Divine and the love that Divine has for us as well. There are no conditions here, just like with Karuna.

Venus in All Forms of Love

People who dabble in astrology might assume that all there is to Venus is just money and love, but there is so much more depth to this planet in matters of the heart. Our books, shows, movies, and magazines like to paint love as this wild thing that just grips you and makes you do crazy things. However, there is more to life than simply romance and family, and Venus is goddess over love in all its forms.

Love isn't just a feeling. It's also a decision you make each moment. You are only ever acting out of love or fear. Those two decisions drive you. When you choose to eat the grapes instead of the cheesy garlic bread, that decision comes from a place of self-love. When you decide to use your headphones to listen to music instead of being a rhymes-with-ash-hole and playing it out loud, you do that out of love for the people around you (and it's only proper etiquette, anyway). These are just a few mundane ways in which love affects our decisions.

Venus teaches us about our pleasures, inclinations, tastes, and the things that bring us joy. Want to know how you deal with your romantic relationships and what inspires you? Check out Venus on your birth chart. If Venus is in Libra, then you enjoy equality in your relationships. You love it when both sides of the equation of giving and taking are balanced. If you love the feeling of security that comes with being in a relationship, then your Venus might be in Cancer. If what drives you is the thrill of the chase, then Venus might be in Aries for you.

The placement of this planet in various houses shows you what aspects of your life you choose to refine and balance to get maximum pleasure. For instance, those with Venus in the 4th house love to take care of their home. The person who loves to travel and study probably has Venus in the 9th house. Venus in the 6th house means you might really enjoy your routines.

So, whether it's love for yourself, for another, a hobby, art, your habits, or whatever else, Venus rules them all. She oversees all our values and sentiments. She ultimately shows us how we spend money (you mostly spend money on what you value). Venus is what drives the need to appreciate and be appreciated in turn.

Love, Karma, Relationships

Karma is the sum of your choices from your previous life and their outcome. It is the choices that must be accounted for in this present one or the one to come. Put differently, "What goes around comes around." You can't live life without having a ripple effect. For example, this morning, you complimented someone on his outfit. He then had such a good day that he, in turn, helped someone else in need before they did something that would have had terrible consequences. Every action has a reaction, and all of this adds up, for better or worse, to form your Karma.

Karma affects everything, including relationships. Your past relationships from your previous lives shape your present one, and the present one will shape the ones to come. That's just the way the cookie crumbles. You can't avoid it because we all come to each life with it.

Just because you've got Karma doesn't mean you are doomed. It just means we all have some things to work on to create and have fulfilling and empowering relationships. Think of it as garbage. The trashcan may be full, but that doesn't mean it's the end of the world. You can just take out the trash. The way to do this is through meditation, aura cleansing, chakra healing, or any energy healing modality that works best for you.

When you work through all your relationship blocks, you'll find it easier to bond with others around you. The love you and your partner have for each other will strengthen and deepen, growing in spirit as well. This is the purpose of love Karma, to begin with. If you don't open your eyes to it or run away from it, you will have problem after problem. But when you decide to look your demons in the eye and tell them you've had enough, you own your power. You get to experience the richness of love and happiness that has eluded you for so long.

Understanding the influence Karma has on your love life will help to personify love for you. First, give it the attributes of a human you have a relationship with. Next, ask yourself this: "How do I relate with Love?" You'll find the answer very enlightening indeed, revealing a lot of sweetness and sadness. From now on, assume that being in a relationship with someone else or regular friendships with others around you means that you are in a relationship with love as well. Since Karma states you reap what you sow, what seeds have you planted in your relationship to reap love?

Think about how you relate to people who matter the most to you in life. Reflect on these relationships, understanding you also have a relationship with an invisible, mysterious being called love in each one. Each time you do something that isn't very loving, you sow undesirable seeds of bad Karma. Conversely, when you do well, you generate good Karma.

The Ripple Effect of Karma

Some assume that when they do something terrible in a relationship, the consequences remain within the confines of the affected relationship. But what's really going on is you are going to experience the outcome of your actions elsewhere. So, we must never assume we can be horrible to people and not get the just reward for our poor choices.

In the same way, if you are good to your partner, your friends, your relatives, then you can expect that you will receive a reward that matches your energy and actions, not just in the relationships you have right now, but in the ones to come. There is no way to tell for sure when, where, how, and with whom we will get the effects of our actions but be sure that it will happen.

Harmonize Karma through Love

Knowing your Venus placement can help you work out what you need to fix about how you relate to people. Venus will show you your flaws and your strengths. When you know these things, you can turn them to your advantage and determine in your heart you will be better to your partner and others in general. This is how Venus helps us achieve Karmic harmony in love through love.

The changes you make about loving and allowing yourself to be loved are rooted in love itself. If you couldn't care for others and yourself, then you wouldn't even bother reading this book, nor would you bother with trying to treat people better. So, if you realize you haven't been doing right by your partner and the loved ones in your life, don't beat yourself up. You can fix things, and you will. You can make Karma work in your favor when it comes to love. Besides looking at what Venus on your natal chart recommends for you, here are a few things you should start doing right away:

Use the Dalai Lama's 3 Rs. They are respect for yourself, respect for others, and responsibility for all your choices. Self-respect is very difficult for many, sadly. However, it's worth learning to do because when you respect yourself, it becomes easier to respect others, and you become better at holding yourself accountable for what you do and say. Choose to love and respect yourself, and your heart chakra will open so you can finally experience unconditional love and share that with others as well.

Concentrate on Growth. If you keep your mind on everything you've done or are doing wrong, things will only get worse. Attention and focus grow things, so pay attention to what you want to experience more of. This means you should pay attention to your growth. Notice the little ways in which you've improved. Pat yourself on the back when you choose to show a little more kindness. I'm in no way suggesting you act like the bad stuff doesn't exist. Instead, I recommend that you look at them only long enough to work out that you need to change those things, and no longer than required. If you hold on to negative energy, it sucks the life out of you, seeps into your relationships, and ruins your experiences.

Get Chummy with Failure. We live in a world that glamorizes success and treats loss like its taboo. Einstein failed no less than two thousand times before he discovered the Relativity Theory. Stephen King was rejected 217 times before he sold Carrie, his first novel. If you work at something and stop just because you do not see success, then you are not going to make any progress. Failure by no means implies that you should stop what you are doing. It just means you haven't found the key to your success yet.

So, let's bring this concept back to Karma. Failure is mandatory. That's how you get the lessons you need that help you grow into the grandest version of yourself. So often, we get into relationships trying to mask our damaged bits. We shove our garbage underneath the bed with a foot, hoping no one notices the strange smell coming from there. However, that's not healthy, and it's dishonest. Ideally, we should come into relationships as our authentic selves, warts and all. But unfortunately, everyone's failed at stuff. Everyone's got baggage.

To attract your soulmate or true love, you must be the most authentic version of yourself. This means you don't act perfect or act in any way. In other words, simply be. If your love life isn't going as well as you'd like it, try being yourself, no sugarcoating, no hiding your failures and struggles. You'll find this empowering and liberating.

Make Peace with your Feelings. There is a saying that goes, "The three hardest things to say in life are 'I need help,' 'I love you,' and 'I'm sorry.'" Now ask yourself if you struggle with these phrases. If you do, you need to change how you look at things, which means doing some deep soul searching. Should you tell your loved ones you love them more often? Should you let your guard down and reach out for help? Do you sense you should apologize more than you do? It's okay to feel remorseful, to need help, to love. You are not hurting anyone when you communicate your emotions. When you embrace your feelings, you allow yourself to be karmically rewarded, especially in matters of love.

Be Open in your Communication. Communicate with your lover often. If you are not with anyone right now, you should decide right now that you will be honest with them when you meet the one. Decide that you will always be transparent, no matter what. This will draw them to you.

Another great way to draw good Karma in love (and possibly a soulmate) is to be proactive about sharing the things you know matter to you. You can get on forums or join meetups and share your advice on whatever you are most knowledgeable about with people who have similar interests. You could start a vlog or a blog, volunteer for things, and so on. It doesn't matter what you are sharing or how you do it. It just matters that you are giving of yourself. You see, sharing what you've learned along your life's journey is an act of kindness because someone will learn something from you and better their life in the process. Do this, and you will harmonize your Karma and pull in more love.

Be Okay with Letting Go. A crucial Buddhist principle is letting go, especially when it comes to soulmates and experiencing unconditional love. The law of Karma affects those who have parted from their true loves temporarily. When this happens, it feels like we'll die if we don't have them back, and this mindset allows our ego to take the wheel, so we do things we shouldn't. For example, the ego causes you to text your ex incessantly, to where you ruin any chances of getting back together.

When you really love someone and are sure that they are your soulmate, you should be at peace with letting them go now and then. This can seem like a paradox. On the one hand, you are sure that you both belong together. On the other, you are willing to let them go whenever, as often as you must. When you achieve this delicate balance, they will have no choice but to come back, if for no other reason than the security and confidence in your love that you exude.

To Receive Love, Be Love. Take advantage of the law of attraction, which says what you put out is what you get back. Like attracts like. If you are loving, you will attract loving people. This is Karma in action.

To be clear, this isn't about you being nice now and then. That would be insincere. Your decision to be loving should be born of a desire to truly love, to do better than you have when it comes to your relationships. It's not even about trying to fix your Karma. It's choosing to be light in a world full of darkness. It's truly good to be, day after day, showing kindness in the little things, doing all you do from a place of love. This is genuine compassion.

When you are truly compassionate, you understand that the cashier at the counter didn't mean to sound rude but might just be having a terrible day. You know that the person rudely honking to overtake you is probably struggling with something, and even if they aren't, you understand there is a reason they're that way, and they are no less deserving of love. Everyone you meet, every relationship you have, harks back to your love life. If you are nasty and mean to people every time, and you wonder why you are single or why your relationships don't last, this is something to think about. It's common sense, but now and then, we could use a reminder. So, when you wake up in the morning, make a point of asking yourself, "How can I be compassionate today?" Then move through your day looking for chances to be the love you seek.

Stop Trying So Hard. The rewards of Karma are contingent on faith. In other words, you cannot create good Karma while worrying about the result of your actions. Your worrying over whether you've scored enough cosmic brownie points will negate the good Karma you might have had because you've been fearful that you are not doing enough. This implies you are only good because you think you stand to gain something. Love should be unconditional.

Whether you believe in Karma, it comes for us all. However, when it comes to building positive Karma, you must let go and trust that everything will work out justly. Let go and focus on giving love, not expecting anything in return. Unconditional love is a lot easier than most people think. The secret is to release all fear and worry. Allow those feelings to melt away. Have faith instead, and you will receive the rewards in this life and subsequent ones.

Chapter 4: Don't Let Venus Hurt You

The Dark Side of Venus

For the most part, people only think of satisfaction, pleasure, and love when they think of Venus. However, this planet can have terrible effects on us if we don't watch it. So, we have to be aware of Venus's dark side so that we aren't blindsided by the stuff we need to fix in love and relationships.

Venus is all about hedonism, sensuality, togetherness, and emotions. However, this planet rules over perversion, prostitution, betrayal, and gluttony. To really understand the dark essence of Venus, we should look at the planet closely.

Again, Venus is the solar system's warmest planet. The best way to describe its atmosphere is to say it's hot as hell, covered with sulfuric acid clouds which never allow sunlight to reach its surface. The clouds don't let us see what's on the planet, either. If you could visit Venus, you would feel the same amount of pressure as being 900 meters deep in the ocean. Its temperature is mostly always 460 degrees Celsius, and its surface is nothing but a dry desert with more volcanic activity than any other planet in our solar system. From Earth, the planet looks bright, its light serving as inspiration for many.

When Venus is well placed on your chart, you experience wonderful effects. You live a life full of luxury. You receive a lot of support, especially from women. Your personality draws many to you, and when you get married (or if you are already), you have a fantastic go of things, as the same success that you experience in other aspects of life plays out in your love life as well. You also never have to worry about any issues with your urinary and reproductive health.

However, when Venus is negatively placed, the native has a personality that repels people and is often torn down by women. They perform terribly in their career and find wealth elusive. They don't know the meaning of luxury and have a hard time in their relationships. If they get married somehow, it will be a rough, bumpy, and often short ride. They also have to deal with health issues, explicitly affecting their reproductive and urinary organs.

The Lesson to Learn

Venus was married, but her sexual appetite was so voracious that she couldn't be satisfied by just one person. She had lovers, male and female, and she didn't hold back or shy away from being with them. Yet, she was terribly unhappy in her relationship with her husband, Vulcan. Not only that, but her many dalliances inevitably meant she would be caught one day and would have to answer for her wrongdoings. Vulcan, the god of the kiln and metallurgy, had created a net made of very fine material that couldn't be detected. He draped this net on their marital bed and waited. Eventually, Mars and Venus were ensnared in this net, and then they were mocked by the gods whom Vulcan had invited to ridicule them.

When we allow ourselves to overindulge and give in to our hedonist tendencies too much and too often, we invite trouble into our lives, not just in love but in other affairs. You can tell the sort of effect Venus has on the person who constantly chases highs, stuffs their face with food even though they're full, and sleeps around even though the experience always leaves them empty. When we don't watch out for this hedonistic behavior, we become trapped by the repercussions of our actions, just like with Vulcan's net. The things that should bring us joy and pleasure (or

Venus' and Vulcan's marital bed) become the very things that shackle us and bring us down, to the point of shame.

When we chase the pleasures of life with no concern for the people around us, what happens is we start to destroy the fabric of love that connects us to them. We become arrogant when anyone reaches out to help us or show us where we're going wrong. Nothing and no one is beyond being sacrificed for the sake of feeling pleasure - which is very fleeting. Venus is beautiful and alluring, but you must be wise about how this planet can affect you, so you do not allow its charms to become your downfall.

You've probably wondered what it was about Venus that led her to look for love in all the wrong places. She was one of the most beautiful goddesses and could have had anyone she pleased, yet no one was enough. It's easy to judge, but this is a metaphor for how we mortals do the very same thing. We go seeking love in all the wrong places. We seek toxic people or toxic habits just so we can feel like we're worthy, when the whole time, the love we seek lies within us. So, it's when we realize that we are worthy, we can break free from our addictions to toxic people, toxic circumstances, and the toxic thoughts we allow to run through our heads on a loop.

Lucifer Morningstar...AKA Venus?

You know the story behind why Lucifer was cast down from heaven. If you don't know, it was basically because of his arrogance. He was the most beautiful of the angels and the lord of music. He was the "bright morning star," yet he lost his place. This was because he loved himself to the point of sheer pride, and this pride became the anchor around his neck that dragged him down to hell, according to the Bible. He got jealous, and he figured since he was so stunning, he deserved to be on god's throne. He also didn't get what all the fuss was about god's creations: Humans. So, he sought to overthrow him, but that didn't work out well for him or those who sided with him. This is what most people know about Lucifer. He's the Prince of Darkness, or Beelzebub, in Christian and Jewish traditions. The lord of hell is also known as Shaytan or Iblis in Islamic traditions.

You'll also find Lucifer in Greek mythology. His name is originally Latin for "light-bringer," and in Greek, this translates to "Phosphorous" or "Heosphoros." Both words originally come from the Hebraic *Helel*, which means "the bright one" or "the shining one."

After the sun and the moon, Venus is the third brightest celestial body that can be seen with the naked eye. Ancient Sumerians called her Inana, Acadians as Ishtar, and Hindu astronomists as Saint Shukra. You can only see this planet twice a day: At sunrise and sunset. For this reason, they called her both the morning star (Tiomoutiri) and evening star (Ouiaiti) in ancient Egypt. In ancient Greece, the morning star was Hesophorys or Phosphorus, while the evening star was called Hesperus. Rome as well understood that they were one and the same planet, but they continued to use both names, calling the morning star Lucifer and the evening star as Hesperus.

So why is Lucifer thought of as the devil? This is a misinterpretation. The word *Lucifer* pops up once in the Bible in the book of Isaiah, in the twelfth verse of the fourteenth chapter. It reads, "How are thou fallen from heaven. Oh, Lucifer, son of the morning. How art thou cast down to the ground, which thou who didst weaken the nations." *Helel*, the Hebrew word, only came up once in the original text. *Hele Ben-Shahar* is an honorific title that means "Son of the morning," which was a title given to the Babylonian king in those times. Back then, kings were thought of as stars, so verse wasn't speaking of Satan but of the Babylonian king who oppressed the people of Israel.

Helel (Venus) tried to climb over the walls to get into the Northern city of the Gods. He did so because he wanted to be king of all heaven, but then he was driven out of the city by the sun. So, the Biblical verse only likened the Babylonian king to Helel. Lucifer was never a horrible, evil being but the morning star, Venus. We have Christian writers, Augustine of Hippo and Tertullian, to thank for misinterpreting the word Lucifer as the Devil or Satan. It also didn't help that Dante Alighieri's The Divine Comedy and John Milton's Paradise Lost made this misinterpretation more widely accepted.

Lucifer and Venus are the same beings. As the morning star, Venus is the embodiment of self-love. Like the evening star, she is about selfless love. When she disappears, she is being transformed, dying to be reborn. This teaches us we can and should find a balance between self-love and selfless love to express both healthily.

If we swing too far toward selfless love, we risk becoming resentful and angry, even in our "selflessness." This is no longer *love*. What it is, is an odd kind of pride. Maybe you know someone who says, "I'm always doing stuff for people, but no one ever asks how I'm doing." If you tell them to quit, they don't. They just keep on complaining and keep on being "selfless" because deep down, they're proud of being the giver and never the receiver. It's all for their ego.

However, swinging too much toward the side of self-love can be problematic. You can and should love yourself, but when you do so to the point of neglecting others, you become arrogant. You walk over others' feelings. If it isn't about you, it's none of your business. As a result, you lose your compassion, your humanity, and ultimately, your soul. Excessive self-love that leads to pushing people away is often a sign that something's amiss deep down. You are trying too hard to compensate for something, and rather than admit you aren't perfect, you continue to force the point that you are, no matter whose feelings get hurt in the process. You need not be a particle physicist to know how terrible this will bode for your relationships, both present and in lives to come. The thing about Venus is that her energy is honest, and her strength lies in her vulnerability. So, love yourself, but be at ease with vulnerability. Admit you are not perfect and love others while understanding they have the same vulnerabilities you do.

Negative Effects of Venus in Each House

The First House: This person is selfish and arrogant. They think they are better than everyone and love to revel in self-praise to where no one else exists, and they only look out for number one.

If this is your placement, decide that you will be deliberate about checking in with others. Make a point of caring about how someone else's day went. You can help them feel better by doing little acts of kindness. For example, try praising someone else for a change and enjoy how they light up when you do that. You just might find yourself positively addicted to finding the good in everyone and letting them know it.

The Second House: This person spends money on the most irrelevant things. They also tend to expect a thing from others and are constantly disappointed.

Be conscious of your spending habits. An excellent question to ask yourself before you click the buy button or head to the counter is, "Do I really need this?" Don't be in a hurry to answer. Also, make a list of your priorities to know what you need to get. This way, you'll never find yourself in a tight spot because you don't have money left for the essentials.

Lastly, you should learn that sometimes people don't do as they promise, and it's not out of malice. Of course, you can ask for help, and you can look forward to someone giving you what they promised, but in the end, you should be deliberate about finding ways to provide yourself with what you want or make things happen in your own little way.

The Third House: With Venus here, one might enjoy mind games a little too much. They will flatter their way to whatever they want. However, this constant flattery makes them lose other people's trust, as it's obvious they aren't genuine and shouldn't be believed.

The next time you flatter someone, check in with how you feel. That insincerity is clearly communicated to them, no matter how slick you think you are being. If they don't consciously acknowledge it the first few times, they will eventually. Decide that you will value honesty tempered with tact above all else. Understand that if someone wants to help you with something, they will anyway. You need not schmooze them with lies. Also, if they don't want to help, that's fine. No one owes you, and you don't owe anyone either.

The Fourth House: With this Venus placement, you are likely to experience betrayal from the people you are most comfortable and familiar with. The best way to deal with this is to know that people hurt people, sometimes accidentally, other times on purpose. Whichever the case may be, you are the only one who can decide to hold yourself captive to their terrible deeds. So be quick about forgiving, and don't let a few rotten eggs convince you that all of humanity is completely worthless. This sort of thinking is no way to live.

The Fifth House: The native of this placement experiences a lot of turbulence in their relationships. They love the thrill of dating many people. However, they want nothing more than to have people be attracted to them, which causes instability in their relationships.

You can still appreciate all kinds of people without becoming romantically linked to them. Also, if you look closely, you'll see that your partner has many aspects to them that you may have never noticed before because you didn't take the time to look at them closely. Finally, you should know that everyone has different tastes, and you won't always be someone's cup of kombucha. That's okay, and it says nothing about whether you are desirable or worthy of love. (Hint: You are worthy.)

The Sixth House: When Venus is in the sixth house, there is a severe lack of confidence in choosing what you should do with yourself, career-wise. You might find that your mind constantly flutters from one choice to the next. In extreme cases, natives with this placement might simply give up on what they want to do with themselves in life.

If you can't work out what to do, make a list of the things that excite you. Look through that list and ask yourself which of those things are available for you to do now. Work your way through the list, and you'll see where your heart belongs. Give things time, rather than hopping around like a housefly around a fruit bowl. You might surprise yourself with what you settle on. Or you might discover that you are a "multi-potentialite," meaning you are good at several things. Don't listen to that silly saying, "Jack of all trades, master of none." It's true, but not for everyone.

The Seventh House: The terrible effect of Venus in this house is that it causes one to be incredibly egotistical. They might have issues holding down a reliable job because of their behavior. There is no stability with them when it comes to working.

Take a moment to discover what drives you to be all about yourself. See how you can channel that love for yourself to others. Take stock of how your egotistical behavior has affected you negatively. If you still have a few friends hanging around, sit with them and ask them to tell you the truth about yourself and how you can be a better person. Resist the urge to butt in and defend yourself as they tell you. Truly listen. Check in with yourself to discover if and how what they're saying is true. Thank them, and truly resolve to implement their advice.

As for work, find something that matters to you and see how you can make that pay you. When it matters, it will hardly feel like work as it gives you joy, and you could just go on and on. With time, you will find that you've become a much more dependable, stable professional, which will work wonders for your career.

The Eighth House: In the eighth house, Venus causes a lot of negative mental chatter. When you are overcome by excessive internal monologue, you might deal with major setbacks and problems in life. Also, the natives of this placement are often very interested in paranormal studies and supernatural matters. While this is a good thing, with the negative influence from Venus, this can easily translate to paranoia and mental health issues.

Just because the thoughts zip through your head doesn't mean they are true. It doesn't mean you must own them. Your mind is a tool. Use it constructively by giving it what to think about. Give it a mental diet of uplifting, focused thought, and watch your life transform. You'll find that even in the face of problems, you have the strength within you to handle all things. You always have. Finally, don't allow what you learn about supernatural matters to overwhelm you completely. Take what you find helpful and discard the rest.

The Ninth House: When you have Venus in the ninth house, you obsess over wanting the perfect relationship. You have an unmistakable idea of what you want love to look and feel like, and when your relationship doesn't match that standard, things get very rocky. Often, you move from one relationship to the next, seeking your impossible ideals.

Perfection doesn't exist. The road to despair and depression is paved with the search for perfect ideals. Learn to find the good in your relationship. Learn to work through the issues you have with your relationship with your partner as a team. You will find that the relationship still won't be perfect with time and effort, but it will be a lot sweeter and enrich your souls in beautiful ways.

The Tenth House: With Venus in the tenth house, the possibility of being betrayed by one's nearest and dearest are very high. Also, there is a chance that they will experience a terrible monetary loss at least once in their life.

When betrayal comes, you and you alone can determine how to handle it. When you hold your head up high, smile and nod, and refuse to be bogged down, then you will have demonstrated true strength of character. Those who betrayed you will have instant regrets about doing so, and some might even seek to amend things and can become lifelong, trusted allies if you want that.

The Eleventh House: Bad health affects the native of this Venus placement. The chances are that their father also experienced the same health issues. Also, there is a possibility that they will experience terrible loss in terms of finances because they listen to the wrong people, whether friends or colleagues.

Be mindful of your habits. Treat your body with love and respect. Feed your mind with good thoughts as well, and your body will reap the benefits of that. When you want to enter a deal, be sure to do your homework. If something sounds too good to be true, then do some digging. Even when it sounds like a real and solid deal, you should still understand the risks of what you are getting into. That way, you are better prepared for any challenges and could even avoid taking too hard a hit.

The Twelfth House: In this house, the marriage fails. The man with this placement struggles because he doesn't have much of a sex drive, so there is no satisfaction in the bedroom department for his partner. Also, natives of this placement are very secretive and tend to bottle up their emotions.

You can try meditation, healthy living, and natural remedies to boost your libido. Semen retention is equally powerful as well, as you build up sexual energy, which your partner will appreciate when you unleash it. Also, it's okay to let others in on your feelings. Be glad if someone makes you feel like an idiot for sharing because you now know not to share with that person. However, people are inherently good for the most part, and we all work through the same emotional turmoil in one way or another. So, stop bottling it all up. There is nothing secret about your secret. We all are going through the same things.

Chapter 5: What Venus Says about You – Part I

We've talked about houses briefly earlier, but now it's time to get into the meat of the matter. We're going over how Venus influences you depending on the house it's in on your natal chart. Before we start, I want to clarify that you shouldn't make decisions based on this information alone. The effects Venus has on your life can be affected by the placement of other planets on your chart. Also, the purpose of astrology isn't to tell you that your life is doomed and there is nothing you can do to fix it. It's to show you what you need to pay attention to, so you can be more fulfilled. In other words, there is no such thing as a fixed destiny. With that out of the way, let's begin with the houses.

Venus in the First House

This house is all about the ego and the self. It is ruled by Mars and correlates to Aries. When you are a native of Venus in the first house, you have a charm like none other. Your magnetism is strong and undeniable. You are attractive, and you know it - and so does everyone else. You have a confident swagger about you, an elusive quality that draws people in when you walk into the room. And when you walk out? Like the best of perfumes, you leave them wanting more as a little of your magic lingers, and they struggle to hold on to it.

You also attract people who are charismatic like you. You are very comfortable around others, and that fact is one of the many things about you that makes others feel the warm fuzzies in their tummies. You have no problem creating instantaneous bonds. People in this placement are usually seen as open books.

As Venus rules the first house, it represents all things about joy, pleasure, and love. So, since you are inclined to be the very best at all times in all ways, these three things aren't an exception. You know how to enjoy yourself, and you are at peace with doing so.

You draw the most passionate people to you. Your zest for life makes you want to experience the best of its pleasures in bigger and better ways. You appreciate the big things and the small things, as they all add to our excitement. Because of your charm, many people want to associate with you. You are a party person and the center of attention. You enjoy being in a new relationship because you love the warmth that comes with new beginnings. Nothing thrills you more than the excitement of new love.

What to Look Out For

You want a partner who is there for a long time, not just a good time. You might love short relationships and dates, but eventually, those will get old for you. You have it in you to be loyal and committed, so you want to settle with someone who's got long-term goals.

Sure, many adventures are calling your name and many experiences asking you to live them, but you need to slow down a little, so you don't jump into things you aren't ready to handle. You might also notice that you are not the best at making a fixed decision. To fix this, you must become more confident in yourself and your abilities. There is no competition out there and no one to beat, except the person in the mirror who tells you that you are not good enough. Finally, you need to learn to be more patient with yourself and others. This is the key to happiness, especially with your Venus placement. So slow down, take it easy, and channel your energy and attention toward finding the best partner for you, someone who will be there in sunshine and rain.

Venus in the Second House

This is the house of material possessions and values, except land and real estate. Ruled by Venus herself and connected to Taurus, this house teaches you how to help yourself when you are in need. It teaches you the importance of putting yourself first for a change. This house is a source of income that makes it possible for you to handle the affairs of the first one. It's the house of Taurus, which is the epitome of all forms of wealth.

The second house is about what you eat, where you go, and what you spend money on. This house shows you your luck when it comes to money. Your earning power is more than the average person's. To work harmoniously with the second house, be willing to spend a little more on something good for you or even cheat on your diet - while making sure not to go overboard so you can still take care of the essentials.

Now, Venus in this house is all about wealth, possessions, and financial security. As a native of this house with Venus in it, you adore everything about expensive cars and homes, accessories, clothing, and food. You are very fine with spending your money because you know you can afford to. You know the importance of money when it comes to socializing and experiencing a richer world.

You are well-to-do and live a comfortable life, especially if Venus is in an earth sign like Capricorn, Taurus, or Virgo. You value art, jewelry, and the fine things in life. You are hedonism personified, which can be a good thing on the one hand, and on the other, can be problematic if you are too self-indulgent.

Chances are you have a career in the beauty industry, arts, and entertainment, interior design, fashion, or any profession requiring you to have a good sense of aesthetics and tons of creativity. If you don't already work in these fields, consider a career change.

You always have good luck with finances, and making money is easy for you. No one gets how the material world works better than you do, and yet, for all your materialism, you are down-to-earth and practical, especially if you are an Earth sign.

What to Look Out For

When Venus expresses herself negatively in this house, you find you spend way too much money, to where it's an issue. Financial success isn't about how much you spend but how much you keep (and grow). You might find you spend too much in a bid to seem affluent, but the more you focus on your image, the more you will be ensnared in Vulcan's net of despair and shame. Sometimes, you might go to the extreme of material gain, where you become stingy.

With matters of the heart, you must take it slow. Things may feel fantastic and heady with the new person you are dating, but you must take it easy. Get to know who they really are before you decide to swap rings and recite vows in front of an old-robed guy. The good news is when you do find your match, your love lasts.

According to Venus on your natal chart, you are attracted to affluent, genuine, and beautiful people. You desire security and stability in your relationship. You love to be loved, and you delight in a partner tangible in how they express their affections towards you.

Venus in the Third House

This house governs thought and communication as Mercury rules it. Its zodiac sign is Gemini. When Venus is in this house, you have a deep appreciation for intelligent, stirring conversations.

You love languages as well, and it shows when you travel and meet with people from other cultures besides your own. You love to get into lively discussions and heated debates, which you often win because you deeply enjoy mind games. Also, you love it when you meet someone who challenges you mentally.

Venus is all about sensuality and love, and the things that bring you the most joy in life. In this house, that means constantly interacting with others, exchanging ideas and thoughts. You love a large circle because there is a lot on your mind you want to share, and you also want to explore everyone's thoughts. So, the more, the better.

If you are going to remain engaged in any activity or remain with someone, they need to be smart because your mind needs constant stimulation. You need to find people who share the same proclivities you do and enjoy attention just like you do. Make it a goal to create a balanced relationship with someone, with equal give and take on both sides. You want someone who can connect with you intellectually and make you laugh, too. You love to flirt as well, which is not weird for you since this house is about communication and Venus is about love.

You are the epitome of wisdom, refined in every way. You usually know what to say and when and how to say it. Expressing yourself is no problem at all. You are infinitely curious about everything. Diplomacy is your wheelhouse, and you could never be accused of having terrible social skills. You'd make an excellent writer or teacher, as this placement means you have a knack for literature. You are an artistic, creative person, and you most likely enjoy good poetry as well.

The third house is also about learning. Venus, in this placement, loves to learn. You'll find you never stop educating yourself. You genuinely believe you are a lifelong student, and chances are you have books for days in your home. You are also gifted with dexterity, which means you can use your hands quite well. Consider working with your hands or taking a class to learn a skill that requires dexterous hands. You will find a lot of luck through communication, writing, and your immediate environment.

No one is better at handling chaos than you - and sometimes, you are the creator of said chaos. Ironically, you absolutely abhor conflict. You don't have issues seeing where someone else is coming from, and this is a skill that serves you well in negotiations. You are exceptional when it comes to settling arguments. You can use this skill to your advantage for getting what you want while remaining charming and kind.

You probably had terrific rapport with your siblings as a kid, and if your Venus isn't afflicted, then this will be a lifelong relationship. Your childhood was a good one, too. You might be popular where you live. Neighbors love you, and your acquaintances think fondly of you.

What to Look Out For

You can be a bit of a busybody and a gossip sometimes, and this is part of why you have issues making and keeping close friends or building more depth and strength in your relationships. You are the sort of person who has a thousand and one acquaintances but a grand total of maybe five friends that have somehow remained with you over the years.

Sometimes, you are drawn to people and circumstances that are fun, but in the end, they aren't any good for you. It would be wise if you didn't engage to begin with, so you don't have to worry about any nasty repercussions later. Adventures are nice and all, but you would benefit from having someone at home waiting for you to return. This someone should also be willing to take off with you at a moment's notice now and then to do something new and fun.

If you want better relationships, you need to slow down and know who you are dealing with first. Don't just assume at first blush that everyone you meet must be a unicorn that farts glitters and rainbows. Instead, allow them time and space to show you the sort of person they really are. Just because they're sharing so much about themselves and giving your mind a lot to chew on doesn't mean they are a good fit for you, as a friend or a partner.

Venus in the Fourth House

This house belongs to the Moon and Cancer. This placement implies that you were born to a supporting, loving family in a beautiful home. This is the house of home and family, and with Venus ruling, it makes sense that you were born under such wonderful circumstances. Family matters to you. You are conservative, and your values stem back to your roots.

The fourth house is ruled by the Moon and connected to Cancer. It tells you all you need to know about your family life, from the sort of home you were raised in all the way to the one you create as an adult. It shows your ancestry, roots, and karmic heritage and governs all land and real estate matters.

Your family life is full of harmony and love, so you are full of good cheer and optimism. You find it necessary to be in a warm, loving home so you can always be your best. This placement shows you will raise a wonderful family of your own, and you will relate well to each member. You will be the one who quickly makes all conflict disappear.

You are very affectionate and fiercely loyal to the family you are from and the one you raise as a grown-up. Your parents were very loving and supportive, and you love them just as much in turn. Also, your entire family is financially successful. You love learning about your ancestry, and traditional values hold great significance for you. Your family instilled values in you growing up, and so you do your best to live by them. You raise your kids to also take on those values.

You have a lot of luck with matters of land ownership and real estate. When you seek answers, you find them in your past. Consider a profession in archeology, history, or ethnology, as you'd do well in these fields.

You probably do a lot to make your home look beautiful. You are amazing at interior design, and you know the perfect home decor to use to give your place a welcoming warmth. You are passionate about creating a safe and comfy place for you and those you love. You are a homebody, and it's no surprise.

You are drawn to those who are conservative and respect traditions. You don't want instant romance. You want something that lasts forever. For this reason, natives with this placement tend to marry much later in life. Emotions matter a lot to you, and you want to know you can feel safe with the person you are in a relationship with. You are charming and tend to attract partners to you rather than go after them yourself. Family matters to you and is non-negotiable.

What to Look Out For

You might find yourself suffering from domestic issues or problems with your spouse, friends, or mother. However, things can work out well if you become more aware of your behavior and how it leads to undesirable outcomes. Also, you tend to be egotistical, which might make you lose the very moral values you hold so dear.

When things get tough, channel the love you feed for family towards repairing broken relationships. Also, take advantage of your open nature to connect with your loved ones and see how you can do better or right by them.

Chapter 6: What Venus Says about You - Part II

Venus in the Fifth House

If you are looking for the perfect partner, go for someone who has Venus in the fifth house. They are often driven to make the relationship succeed and make sure that they and their significant other are pleased. Ruled by Leo and connected to the Sun, the natives of this placement are some of the most fun people you could ever meet. They love people who are charming and are put off by vulgarity.

They have a fondness for the arts and can be artistic themselves. If this is your placement, you seek a loyal lover. You are not interested in short dalliances. You want love for a lifetime. You are affectionate, caring, sweet, and would never even dream of cheating on your significant other. You'd make a fantastic parent because you know how to have fun, and you enjoy spending time with kids because you are also young at heart and haven't lost your sense of play.

You are very romantic and a real live wire. You are a social butterfly who's fun to be with. You love life passionately, and you extend that love to your friends, interests, and hobbies as well. You inspire people positively wherever you go. You are the popular one in the bunch, and you also have a flair for drama, especially when you know all eyes are on you.

You'd love nothing more than to be able to show off your lover to your colleagues and friends. You also love it when your partner is proud of you and shows it as well. When they don't express their love for you enough, you feel depressed and lonely. Your first experience with romance must have been at quite a young age, and when you felt that heady rush of love, you knew you wanted nothing more than to feel that passion repeatedly because that's what makes you tick.

You love so much that you always want to be *in it*. The good thing is, you are not just in love with being in love; you are always one hundred percent head over heels in love with whoever is with you at any given moment. You enjoy the feeling of having crushes, as it makes you feel young.

At your core, you are very sensual. You want to experience every pleasure. You want to see the beautiful places and people in the world. You want the best of wine and the best of music. You also want the best when it comes to lovemaking, and you could never be accused of not knowing what to do in bed. You are the ultimate flirt, and you love the feeling of touch. You also know how to communicate intense passion with just a simple touch.

What to Look Out For

If this is your placement, realize that you tend to grow dependent. Overindulgence in life's pleasures is something you want to look out for. Also, you can be difficult to please because you won't settle for less. This can be a good thing, but it can also be terrible when you don't acknowledge that not everyone's a mind reader, and it's hard for others to do things exactly as you'd prefer.

Be very careful with financial matters, like investing and gambling. Never risk more than you can afford to lose, and always accept the risk of whatever you are getting into before you begin a business venture. Also, be proactive about finding ways to mitigate your risk.

Be mindful of your need to be loved and admired, as that can easily give you a big head or make you desperate for attention and praise. You feel insecure when no one is feeding your ego. So, understand that even when no recognition and attention are coming your way, you are still a wonderful, whole person. You should remain confident in who you are when you are with others and when you are alone.

You might also be promiscuous, much like Venus, getting involved in several romantic relationships simultaneously. Somehow, you can love each partner with the same intensity and for different reasons. However, if you are polyamorous, own up to that and make sure your partners understand that about you, so they don't feel hurt when they discover they're not the only one. Even in your polyamory, you still can channel all your love towards the right partner for you.

Venus in the Sixth House

This is the house of work and health, ruled by Mercury, connected to Virgo. It shows you your attitude towards work and how disciplined you are. It reveals if you are a slave to routine or a disorganized person, and it also shows you your tendencies with your health and diet.

When you are a native of this house, you are conscious about your health, love your work, and are always on a quest for self-improvement. Venus in this house means you value your routines, and you also love fitness and health. Thanks to the harmony Venus brings, you have a passion for taking care of yourself and getting better at the things you do. You get a lot of satisfaction from your work and knowing your body is in good condition. Whatever your zodiac sign is, Venus softens it so you experience the sixth house in the most pleasurable way for you.

You are the sort to be proactive about your finances and health so you can be at peace. You love feeling great and looking great. You are so in tune with your body that you know what it needs at every turn. You know when you'd need to have some water or take a nap, and you let nothing else get in the way of what your body asks for. You intend to live a long, full, healthy life, and chances are you will.

You are a team player, and the best kind, too. You are very considerate of other's feelings and needs, and you are conscientious in all you do. Whenever you disagree with others, you always find a way to meet them halfway so that everyone's happy. You are very service-oriented, and you go the extra mile with your thoughtful gestures, which come with no strings attached. For you, the ultimate gratification is knowing you've done your work the way you should and that it's a very well-finished product you've put out there.

You are the kind of person who's constantly seeking ways to help others. You enjoy being of service. You are patient, kind, and personable and will even put on a happy disposition to make others feel at ease even if you don't feel so hot at the moment. You will go to great lengths to make others happy.

When it comes to working, you love what you do, and you are easy to work with. You create harmony for your clients, customers, and colleagues alike. But while you make a point of doing the best you can, you also don't take yourself too seriously, choosing to keep your positive outlook and patience even when things are complicated.

What to Look Out For

One thing to be aware of is your love for health and fitness can sometimes lead you to bouts of hypochondria. Resist the urge to have Google or WebMD misdiagnose you with a condition you don't have. Your desire for a flawless body can lead you to go to extreme lengths, too, so be mindful of putting a lot of pressure on yourself to fit some lofty ideal you have of the human physique. Often, natives of this house eventually come to a place of self-acceptance, choosing to be alright with the way they are.

You also tend to be judgmental of others' flaws. It's not because you mean to be malicious, but simply because you can't help but notice them. You offer advice to others, even when you weren't asked, and this comes off as intrusive and critical, even if you mean well. Don't offer advice if you weren't asked for it.

Your desire to please and appease people might turn out to be a bad thing if you do so at the expense of yourself. However, sometimes, you must put your foot down and put yourself first. Be more assertive. Each time you choose to assert yourself, you'll get more comfortable doing so, and you can find the perfect balance between helping others and having boundaries.

Venus in the Seventh House

The seventh house is ruled by Venus and connected to Libra. It's the house of relationships and marriage. Also called the house of partnerships, it shows you the sort of partners you go for (in love and in business) and your tendencies in love. Most of us are drawn to natives of this house, and for a good reason: Venus is the goddess of love, and Libra is a light, air sign that shows us how not to take things too seriously.

When you have Venus in this house, you probably will have good luck in relationships and a happy marriage when you are ready to settle down. If Venus isn't afflicted, then you will have a charming and attractive spouse who does well for themselves financially. This placement also shows that you are at your best when you are in a relationship. You don't like being alone for any reason.

Natives of this house value commitment in their relationships. The house is also in charge of public associations. It illustrates whether you enjoy working behind the scenes or don't mind a more public function.

You have a great capacity for love. This, in addition to your charm, captures people's hearts. You create harmony and balance in your relationships, and you are even better at that when relating one-on-one with people. Your close friends matter a lot to you, and they will verify that fact. There is an intense intimacy (not necessarily sexual) when it comes to your relationships and friendships. All emotional bonds matter to your heart. You love it when there is a balance in giving and taking as well.

Since the public adores you, you would do well in any job that requires you to work with them. You would also be an excellent counselor or a lawyer, as the seventh house endows you with a lot of luck in legal issues. You are a negotiation expert, able to see things through other's eyes and win them over to your side. You are the best at keeping the peace and finding solutions that work for all parties in a disagreement.

This house is the best one for Venus to be in when it comes to business partnerships. When your natal chart offers this planet harmonious aspects, you will gain a lot from working with the right partners. You do your best work when someone works with you and gives you the support you need to keep pushing.

What to Look Out For

You might only ever feel loved and worthy of love when you are with someone. It's difficult for you to learn to be happy being by yourself. You are constantly chasing love so that you can feel like you are complete. This weakness is even worse when Venus is in an uncomfortable sign, like Scorpio or Virgo, or when she is afflicted.

You want nothing more than to be seen as worthy and beautiful by someone else before you see yourself that way. The trouble is this is yet another manifestation of Vulcan's net, as you become utterly dependent on others. If you don't watch out, you become an addict with relationships as your drug of choice.

Another thing is that your constant need to be cooperative, while a good thing, can be trouble. You might find you don't stand up for yourself at all, allowing your partner to walk all over you, whether that's in business or love.

Understand that you have all the love you seek within you. You don't need someone else to complete you, for you are perfect as you are. If it helps, see yourself through the eyes of another, and begin to fall in love with yourself. Make a point of enjoying your own company, taking yourself out, and treating yourself right. This way, regardless of whether you are paired off with someone or all on your own, you won't feel incomplete or unhappy because you know that you are all you need to feel whole.

When you are in love with yourself, you find it easier to stand up for yourself. You won't stand by and watch someone try to take advantage of your easy-going, cooperative nature. Instead, you will call them out and have no trouble kicking them to the curb when you notice that they're nothing but poison to you.

Venus in the Eighth House

The eighth house is the house of death and rebirth. It also represents your joint assets with your partner. Ruled by Pluto and connected to Scorpio, it shows your relationships with your in-laws. Finally, this is the house of mystery, secrets, occult knowledge, secret societies, and mining. It's all about intense, deep transformations, being in charge of all things hidden, like taboos and your subconscious too.

When Venus is in the eighth house, you are fascinated by things that are hidden. You also can't help being secretive and passionate. You stand to gain a lot from others in life, having a lot of luck with other people's money and pooled resources. Odds are you gain a lot of financial abundance through marriage or legacy.

Scorpio is a mysterious, emotional, passionate water sign, one that is very investigative and resourceful. Any planet placed in this house would also be affected by these same qualities. In addition, you have a magnetic power to you, full of charisma and secrets. Everywhere you go, you ooze mystery, and this makes it very hard to resist your charms.

Just as you are mysterious, you are drawn to mystery yourself, having a high affinity for things that are beyond logic. While others shy away from matters like death and the afterlife, you find them fascinating. You are interested in these phenomena, and so you love horror movies and detective shows and books.

You spend a lot of time pondering the occult and hidden things. This makes you a good fit for a job as a psychologist or a detective. You would also do well working in spirituality fields because you are drawn to matters of the spirit, and they give you great joy in life.

Your Venus placement makes the opposite sex want you intensely. When your Venus is in Scorpio, you are very attractive. You are the most powerful magnet to the human heart. This doesn't automatically mean you will find true joy in your relationships.

Your relationships help you with your spiritual growth, especially when they come to an end. They also leave you a lot richer than when you started out, for some reason. Also, you are most likely going to live a long life and die a peaceful death.

What to Look Out For

You can get so used to getting good things that you become self-indulgent and even entitled. So, now and then, try to be aware of just how much you are indulging in things you shouldn't and how you could channel that energy to things that would serve you best.

Since the eighth house is a hidden one with many planets, you don't quite get emotions, and on top of that, you don't know how to be whole on your own. However, when you learn to fall in love with the mystery of you, you will become the strongest you've ever been on your own, and that happiness that used to elude you in relationships will now fill your life and your subsequent partnerships going forward. So, where having this house placement often means you won't have a long-lasting marriage, that will change for you.

You are very emotional, and you want nothing more than to share all of you with your soulmate, holding back nothing. You are hungry for intimacy. The trouble with this is this desire can consume you, causing you to become possessive or jealous to the point of doing things you might regret. Remind yourself there could never be another like you and that you are a beautiful soul very deserving of the love and passion you seek. Remind yourself that while you may be able to get the intimacy you want from someone else, you can connect with your true self and find all the love you want and more within you.

You are very passionate, and as a result, you get into a lot of love affairs. You are the quintessential femme fatale or homme fatale, and you tend to have a lot of drama in your life. You might find yourself in a relationship with the wrong person for you, maybe because you felt the need to save or help them, as inspired by Venus. However, it's not your place to help others sort through their problems or change, especially when they aren't even willing to.

Chapter 7: What Venus Says about You - Part III

Venus in the Ninth House

The ninth house is the house of wisdom and travel and is ruled by Jupiter, connected to Sagittarius. The natives of this house often have relationships with foreigners with a much different experience and view of life. Venus represents the concept of relatedness and what you deem beautiful. So, when this planet is in the ninth house, it causes you to connect more with your divinity and set things up to have a broader view of life (in this case, through your partner's eyes). Also, since it is in charge of your beliefs and truths, it causes you to connect with other religions, philosophies, and other interpretations of life than you are used to. This opens you up to a world of infinite possibilities.

You have a pleasant disposition to learning. You are the one person who loved their college years. Teachers loved you as well, and you loved them in turn, recognizing the value they imparted to you. You are also very popular in school and are drawn to those who enjoy learning just like you do.

You'll do well in research, translation, academics, law, or publishing. You have partners who share your desire for exploration and adventure. You love going on deep dives into matters of the mind and are always up for a trip to the weirdest places.

You seek your values in other traditions and cultures, so you don't find your relationships fulfilling if there is no growth. This is why you meet your lovers in spiritual places, places of learning, or on long journeys away from home. As a result, your relationships often feel like you are discovering yourself, and you find that there are always physical and mental adventures with endless possibilities.

You desire partners that are stimulating and present a challenge. You love it when they have the same philosophies on life as you do while offering you a different perspective you'd never have considered. You enjoy gaining new knowledge, as this adds to your value system. You appreciate distant lands and different cultures more than others, and sometimes you get the sense that you are more native to a country other than yours.

When you grow in awareness, you enjoy life. This is your pleasure and where you find your happiness. You have a moral code you always live by, drawn to spiritual and religious ideals. You can see the beauty in the unusual and the foreign, and so you make a superb mediator and diplomat. You do well while studying abroad and connecting people of different cultures to one another. Even in business, you tend to have foreign partners and business interests. Thanks to Venus, you travel in style to the most luxurious places, very dissatisfied with your own environment.

What to Look Out For

You are not a fan of sitting still since there is so much in the world that you need to explore and experience. Unfortunately, this means you have trouble developing roots or genuinely connecting with people because of always being on the move. Thankfully, we live in an age where you can always stay in touch through social media or video calls, so you would do well to maintain the friendships you find during your travels.

You find it easy to fall in love and often do so too fast because you don't need too many facts before deciding on your love interests. You have a much more different definition of love from others in that you are not overly attached. You let go of others if you find they restrict your choices or lifestyle. You might benefit from learning to compromise occasionally.

You don't mean to lead people on, but you do because you don't put as much emotion into your actions or words as others think you do. You might do something that you don't think of as a big deal, but then to the other person, it's significant. Be mindful of killing someone else's romantic desires and dreams by your callous attitude towards sex and love.

You can be erratic, moving from lover to lover, seeking the proverbial greener grass. Instead, you should let all your partners know that your relationship isn't exclusive and make sure they know where they stand regarding your commitment level and emotional investment. This will make it easier for everyone involved.

Venus in the Tenth House

The tenth house is the house of career and reputation. The tenth house is connected to Capricorn and ruled by Saturn. Capricorn is one of the more serious signs, which is all about hard work and continues to grind even when everyone has gone home for the night. This is the classic high-achiever. This house shows your public persona as well as your work life. Those with a powerful tenth house have the best work ethic and are more ambitious than others. This makes them very successful.

With Venus in this house, you are all about your goals and ambitions. So, you are always successful in any field you are in. You value your professional life, and Venus helps you by bringing you people that will propel you to greater heights in your career. This house also shows that one of your parents has given or will give you a leg up to get you higher on the professional ladder.

You don't take no for an answer, as you are always bullish on whatever you've set your heart on. Nothing matters more to you than being the very best at what you do. You have no limits in your mind about the heights you can attain, and you keep the long term in full view, taking very calculated steps to get you where you've envisioned.

You know your beauty is an asset to achieving your dreams, and your grace also paves the way for success. Venus gives you its energy, empowering you in all you do. Your smile is an effective weapon that no one can stand against. Venus brings you harmony and luck on your natal chart, and this is part of why you achieve the most amazing things in your career.

You'd make a great diplomat, and you would do well working with the public. You are charming, polite, and have excellent manners. Your kindness endears you to one and all, making you very popular and loved. You are also famous - or at least you will be if you aren't already. Everyone in your hometown knows who you are, and they think of you in a good way. You are gifted with artistic talents and have an eye for aesthetics. You are attractive, beautiful, and always well dressed. Your bosses favor you and do what they can to help you get ahead in life.

With love, you aren't the sort to fall head over heels for someone. You think your way into love, choosing your lover with your mind, not your heart. You think carefully about whether a prospective lover will work well with you or not.

You are drawn to people in power, those who have achieved the same success you chase. However, you don't just sell your soul to the highest, most powerful bidder. It matters to you that these people are also kind and honorable. This is the same expectation you have of your partner. You want someone responsible and who you can rely on at any time. This means you are conservative, and you value tradition a lot. Chances are you'll meet your lover through work. While you enjoy climbing the social and professional ladder, you like to earn your position. You don't want it handed to you when you've done nothing to deserve it, in your opinion.

What to Look Out For

You care about how you look in the public eye. For this reason, you would rather follow the trends than set your own. This is a problem when you find that you are losing yourself and not doing what your heart truly desires because you want to keep everyone else happy. Understand that you must feed your soul as well, and this means that sometimes, you must color outside the lines, regardless of what everyone else thinks.

Allow yourself to use your heart – not just your mind – when choosing someone. There is no reason this choice should be an either-or thing, where you either think or feel your way into it. When you incorporate your heart in decisions surrounding love, you will find your love life is a lot more rewarding than when you simply choose a partner based on your thoughts about their adequacy.

Venus in the Eleventh House

This house is ruled by Uranus and connected to Aquarius. It's the house of friendships, acquaintances, and humanitarianism. You are a social creature, always loved in the groups you are a part of. You might have even met your partner through one of the organizations or groups that matter to you. You love to volunteer and help others in need.

Your life is all about helping and being helped. In this house, you learn about all the resources you are not yet aware of that will be instrumental to achieving your goals. The help you need comes through your friends, network, and other members of the organizations you belong to.

Being an air house, the eleventh house is about socializing and communicating as well. You love being around others, making new friends, and being part of things you think are more significant than just you or your life. You'll also find you have many friends with this exact Venus placement, and they can give you a boost in your private and professional lives. You always have someone ready to show you a new opportunity for fun or business and who can help you get started with or involved in a new venture.

This is a good house for Venus to be in when it comes to finances, as it shows you what you will receive and how much you will make through your career. You have no shortage of interests, but the things you love the most are joint projects where you work with others. Therefore, you often sign up for so many things and join every society and organization that resonates with you.

Your circle of friends is quite extensive, which is no surprise seeing as you are adept at socializing and others find you attractive and seek you out without you moving a muscle.

You have so many thoughts and ideas swimming around in your head, and they're smart, for the most part. You love to think about how things are made or done and how you can do those things more efficiently. When you connect with like-minded people, you have a blast!

Volunteering matters to you, not just because of the good you do, but because this is the primary way you meet lovely people who are also interested in making the world better, however possible. You are a humanitarian at heart. This placement makes you one of the more tolerant and open-minded people out there. You are no traditionalist as you continue to evolve with the times.

You think of your lover as your friend. It's not just about romance for you, and that's a good thing because friendship is the foundation of long-lasting relationships. You and your lover have the same visions and goals for life. Your intelligence is what probably drew them to you and draws others to you as well. As far as you are concerned, it is crucial to connect with your lover on a mental level as well, so you go for someone who shares your vision.

If you are still searching for your soulmate, then you should become more active with volunteering, charity work, social activities, fundraisers, and things of that nature. Also, spend more time with your friends. For all you know, you might be looking right at your soulmate, and you don't know it yet. Usually, people with this placement become romantically involved with a friend or a mutual friend. Therefore, you should get out more if you are tired of being single.

What to Look Out For

You belong to the house of ideals, where Venus blesses you with many of them - sometimes a little more than you can handle. Since there aren't many Earth signs on your birth chart, this means you might lose touch with the real world every now and again. It would be wise of you to schedule your time, as there are only so many hours in a day. Don't take on more than you can chew. Handle the causes nearest to your heart and prioritize them so you don't feel like you've bitten off more than you can chew.

Also, you are always giving so much of yourself. This is admirable, and you might not even have any complaints about that, but take some time to replenish your energy, so you have more to give. Self-love is key.

Venus in the Twelfth House

Ruled by Neptune and associated with Pisces, the twelfth house oversees healing and spirituality. The planets in this house aren't easy to access, and you might sense that you are missing their energies in your life. Having Venus in this house implies issues with self-worth. The natives of this placement have a hard time valuing themselves and can't connect with others as deeply as they'd like. They don't get the love they desire and tend to fall for those unwilling or unable to love them, often finding themselves in secret relationships.

A twelfth house is a foggy place that doesn't fit in with our everyday life. It depicts the aspects of you that are hidden and unknown. It's the house of confinement, seclusion, and isolation; think jails, hospitals, or monasteries. This house is also tied to faraway countries on the ocean's other side.

It possesses a strange duality because, on the one hand, it could lead to divine inspiration, but on the other hand, it could lead to a bad case of maladaptive daydreams. Thus, this house is associated with hidden enemies, inspiration, addictions, sleep, dreams, overseas, hidden places, unconditional love, the ocean, maritime issues, and spirituality.

Pisces exalts Venus, and while the only planet that does the best here is Jupiter, the goddess of love does offer you some protection as well. You are compassionate and kind. When Venus isn't too afflicted, you do your best to help everyone, especially those who need it or who are suffering. In turn, when you feel like all is lost, life helps you out as well.

You might often be overwhelmed by the feeling of just wanting to quit, and it is usually at this point that help comes your way through some higher force, just as those with Jupiter in the twelfth house receive divine intervention in times like these. You are always protected.

You are shy and sensitive. Being introverted, you need your space and lots of me-time. You have strong intuition and sensitivity, but you need to have your solitude for you to let these qualities work for your good. So, turn your back on the world now and then. In these solitary moments, focus on yourself and your connection to the divine spark in you.

You have artistic skills and are inspired easily by mysterious Neptune. Art allows you to express yourself, recharge, and destress at the same time. You would rather create your art on your own with no disturbance or interruptions, as you can't stand it when your flow is broken. You are full of emotions, but for the most part, you hide them from others, or you repress them.

What to Look Out For

For some reason, you keep falling for people who cannot date you in public, either because they're married or because your differences in social standing would be a hindrance or an issue with them. You may have experienced this so often that you've simply chosen to stop letting them know how you feel.

You might even be married or in a relationship when you fall for someone else. You fight with yourself on the inside, wanting so badly to be with this other person but not wanting to cheat on your partner and hurt them. But we don't get to pick and choose the emotions we feel. You might find it best to be open about your feelings to both parties and let the chips fall where they may.

Your love life causes you so much grief, and you've experienced great pain and heartbreak at least once in your life. For some reason, Venus causes people in the twelfth house to fall for emotionally unstable people. Your partner has also experienced great pain and suffering, and not surprisingly, you attracted them. This is the sort of person who is always drawn to you because they can sense you want to help them. However, remember that before you can help anyone, they must first be willing to help themselves and put in some effort.

You have some terrible habits which you keep secret. They make you feel good, but you must know where to draw the line. Don't allow self-indulgence to go overboard and trap you in a state of dependence and addiction. Whether it's drugs or sweets that you have when no one is looking, be mindful and make a conscious decision to say "No thank you" when the urge comes up to indulge.

The reason you have this secret habit is that you repress your desire to be loved. Realize that love is a human need. It's natural, and try as you might, you won't be able to get rid of it. It must express itself in some way. So rather than allow that to happen through self-indulgence, dare to express your desires. Decide that no matter how your loved one reacts, you won't let it get to you. You can love someone without their permission, and you can still love yourself and maintain your dignity in the process.

Chapter 8: Venus and Your Partner

Synastry Defined

Your birth chart shows you how compatible you are with your partner, where you both excel as a couple, and the struggles you will need to overcome in love (and business, even). Synastry is the process of learning about your relationship compatibility with others through the stars and planets on your chart. It can be incredibly illuminating what you learn from this practice and very helpful too.

Everyone has their unique natal chart, mapping out where the heavenly bodies were placed at the moment of their birth. When you breathe your first breath, the planets imprint their energies on you, and these energies depend not just on their location in the sky but where they are relative to one another. We all have ten planets and luminaries, so possible combinations are abundant with them all. That's why you could be a Virgo, for example, and not entirely identify with the generic descriptions most blogs or books assign the sign. You have to consider your chart as a whole. The same applies to synastry. You must view your partner's *entire* chart and then work out the interplay between their planets and luminaries and yours as well.

Synastry goes beyond the usual Sun sign compatibility study with its too-broad strokes. There is some value in finding out how well Leo and Taurus would fit together, but there is so much more that comes to play when working out compatibility between two people.

Why do we fall for the people we do? Sometimes the reason makes complete sense. Other times, you find yourself with someone you'd never in a million years have thought would be your partner. Either way, once Cupid has shot his arrow, there is no use resisting. Our seemingly irrational choices in love will make sense when we turn to the art of synastry, where Venus plays a critical role.

To work out how a relationship is playing or will play out, you only need to look at each person's chart to see how they both handle matters of the heart, noting the differences and similarities. Then, you need to work out if the love planet makes an aspect to the other person's planets, angles, or luminaries. When Venus's aspects point at planets to one person's chart from the other's, the other person is romanticized and idealized. The partner who has the contacted planet comes to have high expectations of Venus.

Synastry involves overlaying the natal charts of you and your partner and then seeing where your planets fall within astrology's twelve signs. Also, the housing system matters in interpreting your synastry correctly. For instance, if one of you has three planets in Gemini, they will be in a specific house compared to the other person's chart. Say you have three planets in Scorpio which land in your partner's eleventh house, then this implies that each of the themes of your planets will play out in the capacity of that house and what it stands for. For example, where Venus represents love, beauty, and romantic attraction, placed in your partner's eleventh house, it will lead to you both becoming close friends if there is romance in the picture. Similarly, if your partner has Jupiter in Scorpio, which lands in the twelfth house on your chart, there is a deep subconscious and psychic bond between you. You may even dream of each other before you meet, and you must have known each other very well in a past life.

Since there are various themes in each synastry chart, some relationships will play out like a fairy tale, while others will feel like a lot of work. This means that not all relationships are meant for you. However, you will gain a deeper understanding of the themes that will pop up again and again in your relationship as you dive deeper into your synastry. However, please don't judge people based on what their synastry reading with you shows. Relationships don't just happen; they take work, so don't go looking for the ideal when you can take what you have and make it beautiful. Also, remember that the stars do not set your destiny in stone. The same idea applies to synastry.

Venus in Your Partner's House

The First House: As friends or lovers, you share a lot in common. You make your partner feel confident and attractive to you. They feel like they have found their ideal match if you both are attracted to each other. The attraction is intense. You love the way they act, dress, and speak. You are inspired by them, viewing them as the very height of attraction.

Your partner, being a native of the first house, feels like a million bucks whenever you are around. Be careful, though, because you don't want to find out that you are only attracted to them for their looks or mannerisms, and you don't want them to feel that way, or you will lose them.

The Second House: Venus here isn't great for romantic relationships, as this planet influences you to only think about what you stand to "gain" from the relationship. This causes your partner to be suspicious of your true motives, and it could also make them think you see them as an object to be owned since this house oversees material possessions.

The Venus person can teach the other to be reasonable and practical with their finances. Since the sensual Taurus rules this house, there is room for physical attraction which can become deeper. It's just not the best place for Venus to be in when it comes to romance. However, if you both value financial wellbeing, and your partner is comfortable taking care of you in terms of material things, this can work out fine and last a lifetime.

The Third House: With this synastry overlay, you are both at ease communicating with each other. You speak with respect and sympathy at the forefront of your mind. The person in this house stimulates the Venusian's mind and feels that their ideas and thoughts are appreciated. You share the same tastes in art and are the couple that loves to write each other cute little love notes.

The trouble with this position is that the person in this house or both parties may have trouble speaking their truth or get into arguments if they think their partner will not respond positively. This causes superficiality in the relationship. Also, there is that constant feeling that there are things that haven't been addressed. You must both learn to speak your mind, even if it will cause some turmoil at first. Since you both love each other, you will find a way to work it out.

The Fourth House: This is an excellent place for Venus, who sees the house person as a great mate and the perfect candidate for starting a family. They feel whole together. The house person may not be a homebody, but they will enjoy spending time with their partner alone in their bubble. The Venusian might find that their partner reminds them of a female family member to which they are close.

While the Venus person may not usually care much for family, they desire to be a part of one with the fourth house. They also feel connected to the other party's family, which further drives their desire to create one with the same love and happiness they witness. The house person desires nothing more than to enjoy spending time with you and become a homemaker.

Sometimes the Venusian will have trouble opening up, and the house person will feel this. The former acts so secretively not because they want to be difficult, but likely because they had a terrible childhood and didn't have the best home environment. For this reason, they find it hard to just take words and actions at face value and trust that there is no other shoe waiting to drop. However, with time and patience, the Venusian can learn to open up about their feelings, and the relationship will become even richer for it.

The Fifth House: The love here is just like a fairy tale. Venus sees the house person as beauty personified and is mesmerized by them. The Venus person wants to have their babies, even if they're not the world's most attractive person, because they can see what's special about their soul. If this is you and your partner, you love spending time with each other, and it's never a dull moment. Also, your partner loves to hold your attention too. However, you both need to know you might over-indulge in life's pleasures to the point where you forget your responsibilities.

The Sixth House: This is a good one for the long haul. The person in this house appreciates all that the Venusian does for them each day. The Venusian, in turn, simply loves to help and be of service in any way that will make life easier for them. It's easier for these two to love each other than for other matches. You share the same passions when it comes to routines, and you both care about exercise and health. You might even work at the same job. You help each other to get rid of your bad habits without being critical or nagging.

The person in this house feels like they are exceptional, thanks to Venus. Since Leo rules the 5th house, and it's a fixed sign, the intense good feelings that both partners share will most likely last for as long as they live. The house person just needs to make sure they're not taking the Venusian's undying devotion and attention for granted and not taking advantage of it either. In other words, they need to allow the Venusians their own time and space with the people and things that matter to them, too.

The Seventh House: Communication is smooth between you two. When troubles arise, the Venus person knows how to set the house person at ease, and the house person loves that about them. You balance out your strengths and weaknesses nicely.

Your personalities are an excellent match, and the same goes for your mannerisms. When one of you is tired, the other is there to pick up the slack. There is a chance the person in this house doesn't have the same level of attraction that the Venusian has for them. When this is the case, the latter feels like they're always in the other's space and will tend to back off or shut down completely. However, when you are both in love, things work out harmoniously. The odds look good for you both, but look at the rest of your synastry chart to see how the other aspects and placements can affect the way you relate with each other.

The Eighth House: The romance is deep and intense here, and the same goes for sexual attraction. You find it easy to talk about taboo subjects, like death, sex, the occult, and more. You share your secrets, and nothing shared between you two will make it out of your bubble. This house is one of the joint resources, and the Venusian has a lot to bring to the table. You are both great at creating wealth that lasts a lifetime together, and you have no qualms pooling your resources.

If you had to describe this placement, it would be all-consuming, intense, and complex. It demands attention, but the trick is knowing how much of your focus to give it. Your shared experiences will be intense. This isn't for everyone since some people just want light and fun relationships. Still, the depth of this connection you both share will be advantageous and profoundly transformational. This placement shows obsession, so you want to remember that if you are a love addict.

The Ninth House: You both feel an affinity with each other regarding your outlook and philosophies. Venus is the teacher, counselor, or advisor to the house person. You both might share the same religion or cultural background, and even when you don't, you are both heavily invested in learning what makes the other person tick.

The Venusian inspires the ninth house person to learn more and travel, bringing you both together. You and your partner should travel more and learn about other cultures and philosophies besides those you are already familiar with. There is less of that eighth house possessiveness in this placement, so Sagittarians and air signs will do well here. The relationship is one where freedom and lightheartedness abound. Both partners often find themselves helping out, volunteering, and joining humanitarian causes.

The Tenth House: Work comes before play in this relationship, so each partner does their best to support the other's professional goals and even develop a working relationship. The Venusian sees the occupant of this house as someone who can help them get ahead in life. The latter allows the former by giving them a sense of boundlessness, encouraging them to be more imaginative and creative, which leads to success in their career.

Both parties love public attention and love to capture it together. However, you need to remember that material possessions are only a part of what makes true happiness and not the whole picture. Life should be about being better than yesterday and not about comparing yourself to or competing with others.

The Eleventh House: This is a perfect aspect because nothing matters more to Venus and the native of this house than friendship. You both share a large circle of friends and are part of organizations and groups that matter to you. There is a lot of lightness, joking, and fun. Your friendship strengthens your love and vice versa.

In a group, it's not hard to see the love you have for each other, and you are both very entertaining and lively. The person in this house can help the Venusian expand their social circle and grow their network so they have more people who can help them when needed in one way or another.

You both enjoy public displays of affection and sharing your hopes and dreams with each other. Communication happens seamlessly with you two, and when there is the occasional hiccup, you both work it out because your default mode is to seek to understand the other person and to be understood as well. However, you should both be wary of giving in to jealousy and toxicity because it's a huge turnoff.

The Twelfth House: The outcome of this relationship depends on whether you are both mature, confident, and comfortable with yourselves. It might take time, but the Venusian will eventually come to understand the other person's tendencies and shortcomings. If they have the other person's best interests in mind, then things will work out well for both.

Venus will help this house person overcome their phobias, secrets, and all the things they hide from the public, but only if the other person is ready and willing to address all these issues. Many people run away from relationships like this as it would break down their walls, demolish what doesn't serve them, and build them back up to be better and stronger. It's not a sexy process, so it's understandable why people in this house take off running when Venus comes around.

The connection here is subconscious and deep. Sadly, there can be issues with trust, as the house person believes the Venusian is playing tricks when that isn't the case. However, their ability to understand each other is unrivaled by other pairings. This relationship will force you to go deep within yourself and become a better person.

Chapter 9: When Venus Meets Other Planets

Venus Synastry Introspects

Now we're going to talk about how Venus manifests when she is in contact with other planets. Every planet has its own unique energy, and so when they come together, these energies combine in unique ways that express themselves differently than when they are solo. Remember that the effects of each planet will be a lot stronger when they show up in the houses they rule over or interact with.

Venus-Sun: There is harmony here as both partners share common interests. The Venusian makes the Sun person feel more loving and beautiful, while the former thinks the latter is intriguing and charming. They both share a mutual attraction that isn't as sexual or insistent as other introspects like Venus-Pluto or Venus-Mars. Contentment is the keyword for this duo. Other aspects to them might cause some difficulty, like the quincunx, square, and opposition. The Venus native has a value system at loggerheads with the Sun native's perspective on life. They vacillate between over-indulging each other one minute and frustrating each other the next.

Venus-Moon: These aspects are put together to smooth out the creases caused by their more troubling aspects in love. This doesn't mean they don't have their trials and disagreements, but there is usually a feeling of compatibility and harmony. The attraction here is less about sexuality and more about a comfortable familiarity they share. They both need to create a home together and love to spend a lot of time with each other. Physical presence is almost non-negotiable with these two. Even when they're not really talking, they love to know the other is just in the other room or somewhere nearby because they are close by. They're tender and caring with each other. When there is a problem, the Moon person may think the Venus person plays too much at the cost of their emotions. On the other hand, when the Moon person has issues they need to resolve, the Venus person often chooses to turn on the charm and smooth things over instead of confronting the problems head-on. These problems that Venus decides to gloss over can ruin the integrity and emotional commitment of the relationship.

Venus-Mercury: Mercury is the closest planet to the sun and the god of travel, trade, and communications. In Roman mythology, he is a messenger who learns important news before anyone else of supreme authority. He is also in charge of leading the dead to the underworld. In one way or another, Mercury is always close to the mystery. He possesses the most astonishing mental abilities. He also has the most valuable contacts and a knack for reaping the material reward in all circumstances.

Mercury's intellect – combined with Venus's sensuality – is an interesting mix. This couple loves pleasurable activities they can share. This relationship involves a lot of talk. Their more challenging aspects with the quincunx, square, and opposition indicate that they do have misunderstandings that can ruin their flow. Sometimes one person might complain that the other talks are a wee bit much. Still, they both strongly desire to communicate with each other, that it's almost like they're both chomping at the bit to grab the mic.

With Venus-Mercury conjunction, there is a synthesis of intellect, a desire for love, peace, and harmony. This couple enjoys art and music and has a talent for both. Venus blesses the other person with coquetry, while Mercury influences Venus with passion and eloquence.

The Venus-Mercury sextile is full of charm. The partners here love to go to conferences and events where people communicate and share knowledge. There is productivity here and success in trade and making new, valuable friends and acquaintances.

Venus-Mercury trine encourages flirtation and romance, laziness, pleasure-seeking, and noisy parties. The couple has excellent skills with acting and oration and a desire to make everything around them beautiful.

With Venus-Mercury square and opposition, things aren't so great. The former is a sign of instability and a lack of consistency, which causes the couple to get into situations they will eventually regret. The latter is shows oversensitivity and nervousness, causing a desire to be unnecessarily eccentric and take on risks they shouldn't.

Venus-Venus: The trine, sextile, and conjunction show clear compatibility with each other, both in their relationship styles and values. They are comfortable with each other. While they may have different ways of expressing their affection and love because of the sextile and trine, they are enough of a match to share a bond and different enough to keep things dynamic. They can be romantic without feeling like their love style is too passive or aggressive for the other or too impersonal or intimate. The shared quincunx leads to a primarily stimulating, sometimes frustrating attraction. The frustration comes from the difference in styles that can exist (even with a Venus-Venus inter aspect), making both parties feel underappreciated. It would help this duo to look past the difference in love languages and see right through to the heart.

Venus-Mars: The red planet is the god of war, known for its tenacity, courage, and fearlessness. This god is consistently achieving goals and defending his borders and interests. But, in a terrible mood, he wreaks great destruction.

Much like the original Venus and Mars, romance and sexual magnetism are here, with the latter being very insistent. The attraction bit is not as competitive or insistent as their hard aspects, as it is pleasant and smooth. There is some friction with the quincunx, square, and opposition.

With time, the sexual energy can grow quite disruptive if both parties do not keep it in check. This couple finds that things get hot and heavy in the bedroom after an argument. They may not know it, but their arguments are actually rooted in sex.

To fix their conflict, the couples may give up their egos, let down their guards, and get intimate with each other, so they have less reason to argue. This happens because the square has intense physical attraction and sexual tension that doesn't show up for what it is and is often mischanneled. The Venusian is easily offended and hurt by the Martian. Sometimes the former enjoys the latter's direct approach. Other times, not so much.

Venus-Mars conjunction endows the couple with sensitivity, charisma, and a desire to be loved. The duo is intense and passionate, but their emotions are short-lived. They have high sexuality and a hot temper.

As for the Venus-Mars sextile, they aren't as flippant as the previous couple. Their love is durable, faithful, unshakable. They love all living creatures, are optimistic, and choose to be merciful in all their dealings.

The Venus-Mars trine couple is very romantic, creative and loves to go on adventures. They have an easy go of making money but aren't the best at saving it. However, they are a self-reliant couple, and their love is usually the talk of the town.

When the pairing is a Venus-Mars square, there is extravagance, capriciousness, and idleness. The couple's sexuality is unbridled and uncontrolled, leading to cheating, promiscuity, and indulgence in base instincts, using alcohol, drugs, and eating unhealthy food.

The Venus-Mars opposition couple tends to experience sadness and loss because of their imprudence. They have issues with contracting venereal diseases and lose a lot of money because they spend recklessly. They experience a lot of quarreling in their relationship and in relating with others as well. With these two lovers, jealousy, aggression, and violence reign supreme.

Venus-Jupiter: Jupiter is our solar system's largest planet, named after the Roman god of lightning and thunder, which the planet experiences a lot. Jupiter is a wise, generous god who always makes sure everyone gets their just deserts, spiritually and materially.

Venus-Jupiter conjunction demonstrates itself as generosity. There are benefits to be had with this pairing. The couple enjoys generosity, prosperity, and paradoxically can be lazy, proving prosperity isn't down to hard work. Each person pulls the attention of the opposite sex. Together, they enjoy a happy relationship that lasts long and can lead to marriage. They're friendly and hospitable to each other, have a great sense of style and an evolved taste when it comes to art.

Venus-Jupiter sextile offers support from people with power and influence, gifts from fate, and a life full of luxury and entertainment. The couple has no issue communicating with each other, finding a lot of common ground. They find success, especially when they connect with their spiritual side and focus on the common good.

Venus-Jupiter trine is the couple that invests in making the home and body beautiful. Chances are they're into fashion, design, and styling. There is material success here, and they do well in relating with their families. They both come together to make sure they are successful in their finances and all their affairs.

Venus-Jupiter square and the opposition aren't so lucky. With the square, the couple engages in dangerous adventures and can experience financial losses. There is infidelity and deception in this relationship. As they neglect health matters, they develop issues with their bodies. They can also be quite vain and excessively gullible, making a mockery of them and their union. As for the opposition, there is a lot of debt to contend with, as they take loans to keep up appearances. They also get into the worst investments. Lies and hypocrisy are the order of the day, and the relationships here often fail because of financial issues.

With the more positive aspects, this couple is helpful in their relationship. Many aspects flow between both planets, creating smooth sailing for these two. Forgiveness is the main theme, making it easy to sustain their warmth and get over minor snafus. They both can rise above being petty, with a genuine desire to make each other happy. They are both givers and enjoy sharing, which makes up for the more challenging aspects that both share. People notice how they enjoy each other and seek to be a part of that. Sometimes though, both be a little too optimistic and must face reality now and then.

Venus-Saturn: Saturn is the god of time who was cast down from his throne in a terrible way. The myth has it that he ate his kids because he was afraid they would overthrow him, which wound up happening anyway. Saturn is cautious, incredulous, diligent in work, and enjoys solitude. This planet isn't one for the terrible quality of work, idleness, or noisy parties and get-togethers. It's the planet that helps you focus, organize your priorities, create a good plan, and then execute accordingly.

Venus-Saturn conjunction promotes loyalty and reliability in a relationship, but the couple is restrained when it comes to romantic feelings. Instead, it drives the sense of duty and eagerness to work, to look at things rationally and practically.

A Venus-Saturn sextile indicates success owing to working long and hard. It's about self-sacrifice for others and makes it all too easy to understand others and feel where they're coming from. It encourages good relationships between parents and kids. This aspect influences this couple to save, care and do their best for the other person to foster balance and peace.

Venus-Saturn trine is about volunteer work, charity, and helping those in need. The couple influenced by this aspect is a lot more rational, focused, and diligent about their endeavors and relationships. They create savings, budget their money wisely, and make sound investments that pay off.

Venus-Saturn square suffers from misunderstandings and breakdowns in communication. There is no satisfaction in life for them. Often, there is a cloud of pessimism above this duo. They want solitude and lean toward asceticism. There are also issues with shyness, indecisiveness, and disappointment.

Venus-Saturn opposition causes the couple to face fears and internal anxiety. They suffer from losses, and there is hardly any love here. At best, they experience apathy towards one another and have a terrible habit of making a big deal of minor home issues. There is a huge chance that one or both partners will take on more responsibilities than they can handle, and this will lead to resentment.

As for the positive introspects, they might struggle, but they will take their relationship to greater heights when they put in the work to understand each other. They love to be with each other. Their sexual relationship starts fine, but with time sex becomes sporadic, stunted, and predictable. There is no more spontaneity in the relationship caused by their daily power struggles.

The Venus person feels like the Saturn person restricts and oppresses them and feels like they're constantly being nagged and criticized. The Saturn person feels a strong, unhealthy desire to limit and control the Venus person. Still, there is some stability and steadiness in their affection and love for each other, tinged with some self-consciousness and reservedness about their romantic and sexual desires and emotional expression.

Venus-Uranus: Uranus is an eccentric blue, creative and original, much like the god of the same name. Uranus had all kinds of kids: Nymphs, giants, cyclops, revenge goddesses; you name it. Uranus is a God who can either reveal your genius or drive you mad.

Venus-Uranus conjunction is an inspiring aspect that gives many original ideas, causes our fantasies to awaken, and moves us to seek freedom. The couple with this aspect is spontaneous and unpredictable. It's very easy for them to confuse some other emotion for love. There can be a lot of drama and romance here.

Venus-Uranus sextile leads to a deep and rapid establishment of romance, which can lead to marriage out of nowhere. Charm and attractiveness are the main elements here. The couple desires nothing more than to be beacons of beauty in society. They are lucky in love, incredible flirts, and know-how to charge a place with emotions.

Venus-Uranus trine is excellent for selling innovative inventions and ideas, as well as mediation and management. Chances are the couple work in art or entertainment as artists, writers, or musicians. They are optimists and have fascinating conversations. They also have spontaneous adventures and are generally successful.

With the square aspect, there is infantilism, impulsiveness, and a tendency to do things on a whim. There is too much negative drama, and there can be quick marriages and even quicker divorces. Also, this couple struggles with a mountain of unfinished projects. The opposition aspects cause inconsistency and carelessness. Expect this relationship to be plagued by mood swings and conflicting feelings. Everything is fast-paced here, so nothing is stable.

With the positive aspects, this is a combination full of thrills and excitement. Sounds great, but the trouble is that they might be plagued by a sense of dissatisfaction with each other. This satisfaction isn't in the bedroom, as things can get very explosive, but these partners quickly grow restless, and there is always an unsettling feeling that lingers between them both. This is because one person (usually Venus) feels loving and romantic, while the other (Uranus) can be very distant. Their relationship can also be erratic, but oddly, they love it that way, as things are never dull and offbeat enough to keep them interested.

Venus-Neptune: Neptune shares the same traits as Uranus in terms of fantasy, but where Uranus moves toward eccentricity and rebellion, Neptune is about feeling others and getting in touch with invisible, subtle worlds. The planet encourages this person to develop their intuition and draw everyone around them toward the mystical. It causes increased awareness of energies. Neptune is the god of the oceans and seas, and like water, he is receptive and spiritual.

Venus-Neptune conjunction encourages romance, dreams, and a detachment from reality. It fosters healing too. This relationship will be full of mystical, somehow, and both partners are likely to be spiritual. However, it's easy for them to be vulnerable and suggestible, more than most.

Venus-Neptune sextile involves using intuition and prophetic dreams to resolve all issues. The couple will experience success with teaching kids, social projects, and rendering services to others. In addition, this sextile encourages platonic love, making a new and unusual relationship that remains intriguing throughout.

Venus-Neptune trine fosters business success, especially in the fields of art, education, and event planning. The couple can expect many wonderful surprises, profit-yielding offers, and deals that work out wonderfully.

Venus-Neptune square causes a struggle between emotions and thoughts. There are temptations to be overcome, issues with sex, and neuroticism. It's a little too easy to fall into gambling, drugs, and alcohol, to where they lead to one's destruction.

Finally, Venus-Neptune opposition can amplify distrust in the relationship, which ultimately shoves one or both parties to betrayal. There is no discipline here at all. Also, there is a propensity to seek quick and easy cash, which often leaves the pairing broker than they started. Expect disappointment, fanaticism, and mental illness.

When Venus-Neptune aspects are positive, the relationship continues to evolve as it plays out in different ways over time. Initially, the relationship is consuming in a good way. There is a connection between both souls. Then reality begins to hit, and things don't look as lovely as they once did. They can overcome their disappointment if they allow the relationship more time to develop, which will allow their emotions to come full circle. When this happens, they realize that while the reason they loved the other person never existed outside of their head, they do can love the other for their true self. If they don't allow time and put in the work to make things right, these introspects will experience bitterness and disappointment.

Venus-Pluto: Pluto is known as the dwarf planet, cold and dark. It's the smallest in our solar system but by no means insignificant in astrology, as it is named after the god of the Dead, which the ancient Romans found frightening. Till now, Pluto intimidates one and all, as it offers twists of fate so radical when we come under its influence. Its orbit is unusual, too. Sometimes, it's closer to the sun than Neptune is. Other times, it moves to the furthest extreme of our solar system. So, you could call this the god or planet of extremes.

Venus-Pluto's conjunction involves loyalty, depth in emotions, and a desire to fight for one's values. In addition, there is intense sexual desire and equally intense emotions. Finally, there is the need to possess a passion for growth and general insatiability. The couple here can expect success in their finances and will find ways to channel their passion and enthusiasm in creative ways to boost their bottom line.

Venus-Pluto sextile encourages creation rather than consumption. It is about inventiveness, organizational capacity, and oratory. Venus-Pluto trine is about your ability to control your subconscious mind and transmute negative thoughts and emotions into positives. It's about being disciplined with emotions and getting rid of all feelings and connections that do not serve you. This couple will have beautiful experiences and the most unusual adventures which will please them. Their relationship is strong, and their love is so powerful that it builds itself back up if anything manages to tear at it.

The Venus-Pluto square is rife with immorality, jealousy, violence, lust, poverty, excuses, a refusal to take responsibility, and constant blame. Expect fatigue, exhaustion, and disease. As for the opposition, there will be problems in the relationship because the couple gives in to aggression. They don't keep their emotions in check, preferring to start drama.

With the more positive aspects, there is magnetic, intense attraction. This relationship is built to last and very significant. The love between these two transforms everyone. For things to work, there must be a physical presence. When they're apart, jealousy rears its ugly head. The problematic aspects show up as an intense rollercoaster of emotions, with swings from bitter opposition to extreme love and support.

Venus-Chiron: This combination is a potent one. The love has a healing quality to it, thanks to Chiron. The love they share for each other can soothe and heal the wounds from past relationships. They feel an intense need to be together, to create a home, and live out their lives with one another for as long as they have. Warmth and joy are abundant here. Challenging aspects cause irrationality in their reactions to one another. However, this is a response to the past trauma which they've brought into this relationship. When this couple chooses to be aware of the struggles each one had to endure in the past, it becomes easy to talk and work through the problems, helping them see that their fears are no longer valid in the present.

Chapter 10: How to Strengthen Your Venus

Venus equals beauty. Having her positive energy shining through you and in all aspects of your life allows you to appreciate beauty not just physically but also in every other way. It also allows others to enjoy your beautiful soul, which lends you natural charisma and magnetism.

Those with a strong Venus are passionate about luxury, the arts, and creativity. They have no shortcomings when it comes to physical attractiveness and charm. Also, they tend to have wealth and riches.

When you possess a strong, positive Venus, you have a good life. You don't have to struggle through business, love, or anything really, as the goddess will bless you with beauty, riches, grandeur, and favor. Usually, those who have a positive Venus find that they're settled in life from 22 to 24, in all aspects. Having a strong Venus gives you a great body, a desire to be spiritual, confident, a great life partner, and sexual magnetism. Your creativity levels will be through the roof, and your artistic side will come through. The money would never be an issue for you because you'll have abundance and know how to keep – and grow it!

As you know, Venus, along with other planets, may not necessarily work out great, depending on other factors on your natal chart. For instance, Venus in conjunction with Mercury or Mars might mean you won't have a great family life, or you'll get one but only in your old age.

Where Venus would ordinarily give you a lot of love, laughter, and friends, you might have to deal with the inability to love yourself passionately. You might also struggle with skin issues and reproductive diseases and find it hard to get along with your lover. You might also find that you are always sleepy during the day, have way too much sexual energy that disrupts your life, and makes you think about cheating on your partner.

Don't despair, though. There are ways to strengthen your Venus so you can live your life to the fullest with this planet's positive energies on your side.

Strengthening Your Venus

Vedic astrology offers interesting and effective ways for you to amplify the positive effects of Venus in your life while getting rid of the negative. Let's look at some things you can do to make this happen.

Dress up in the right colors. Wear bright white clothes or pink in any shade. Venus favors these colors, and their vibrations attract good luck, favor, wealth, and love into your life.

Give your spouse or partner respect. Even if things aren't working out so well between you right now, make a point of respecting them. Not sure how that would play out? Just think about whether you'd appreciate them doing to you what you are about to them. Think about the golden rule here and treat them the way you'd love to be treated. Don't overthink about how they're responding to this because that's not the point. You are doing this in honor of your Venus, and with time things will begin to correct themselves. Your partner will adjust their attitude, or the right person for you will come your way, and there will be a seamless transition to the next relationship.

Give gifts and sweets to widowed women and little girls. Venus cares strongly about them. The planet's energy is expressed in the playfulness and lightheartedness of little girls and in the wisdom of the widowed women who have known what it is to love, beloved, and not be loved enough or in the right way. As you give them the gifts, understand that you honor Venus in them, and in turn, Venus will honor you by granting you her favors.

Choose to be good, always. Do the right, loving thing in every situation. Decide that no matter how anyone else is being, you will act and think from a place of love to yourself, to them, and to everyone else you meet. Then, as you choose to give out love, more love will find you.

Worship Lakshmi. Lakshmi is the goddess of wealth, an aspect of Venus. You can research this goddess and see what items you can keep around your home or wear that would keep her in your mind. Wear hot pink, red, gold, green, white, or purple. Chant the mantra *Shrim* (pronounced Shreem) first thing in the morning and last thing at night, 108 times. You can also do heart chakra meditations. On Fridays, you can fast in her honor. Keep roses and lotuses around your home, and use fragrances like jasmine, rose, sandalwood, and of course, lotus. If you are going to set up an altar, put one for Vishnu as well because Lakshmi won't stick around if he's not there.

Indian Goddess Lakshmi

Fast on Fridays. I've mentioned this before, but it bears repeating as a point on its own. Whether romantic or financial, if you have a goal, decide that your Fridays will be fasting days in honor of Venus. When you fast, you cause her to release her blessings on your life in torrents. Fasting is an excellent demonstration of submission to Venus, and it cleans you out inside and out, spiritually and physically. It gives you the willpower you need to accomplish the impossible. It is often a great way to appease any planet if you fast on the day that corresponds to that planet.

Make donations. According to Vedic astrology, the best way to get rid of Venus' malefic effects is to donate. Therefore, you can donate food, silver, perfumes or donate to a cause for women or little girls. Specifically, you can donate curd, sugar, camphor, and ghee if you can find them. If not, simply donating funds to honor Venus will suffice.

Chant mantras. Other than the Shreem mantra, you can chant the Venus Beej Mantra: *Aum Dream Drum Sah Shukraya Namah.* Do this 108 times. You can use prayer beads to help you keep track of your chant. If you prefer, you can also chant *O Shum Shukraya* 108 times each day.

Wear Venusian ornaments. Silver, white topaz, opal, and diamonds will strengthen your Venus.

Dress up and improve your personal hygiene. Venus is a planet of beauty, and she loves everything attractive. So, look your best as well. Take care of yourself, dress better, and clean up. Bathing twice a day should be mandatory. Look good even if you are not leaving the house. These are the things that will draw the positives of Venus to you.

Get organized. Look around you right now. What does your home look like? If it's a mess, that won't do. You can strengthen Venus by keeping your space aesthetically organized, so start putting things back where they belong and clean up your space. Then, when you get the time and money, decorate your home to look welcoming and beautiful. When your space is vibrant, clean, and organized, you encourage positive Venus energy to flow around you and to you.

Resist the urge to criticize. Do you always have complaints? If you are the kind of person who sees the bad before the good, then this is something you need to work on. Venus isn't a big fan of criticism or nagging. Start with that, and she'll take a hike and take her gifts along with her. So, you need to work on your mind. Train yourself to look for the good in everything and everyone. Even that one coworker you despise probably has one good or nice quality about them. Maybe it's sparkling white teeth, or beautiful eyes, or that one shirt they have that makes them look good. When you genuinely seek to find the good in everything, you will. Not only that, but you will also start to see more and more reasons to be appreciative, and Venus will bless you with more to be thankful for as well.

Avoid unnecessary conflict. It's going to happen that you disagree with someone. We're human, and this is unavoidable. However, if you habitually clash with people, this is counterproductive to strengthening your Venus. Being that problematic person will cause your inner beauty to fade, and you won't have peace in your life. So do your best to continually find ways to meet the other person halfway so that you are both happy. If they choose not to be agreeable, no matter how hard you try, master the fine art of walking away.

Get creative. When was the last time you invented something or wrote a poem? When did you last make up a song or a story? Or paint some art? When was the last time you played just for the sake of playing, just to enjoy the process of creating? If you don't remember, then it's time to change that. Move away from the monotony of life. Dedicate time every day to something creative that will allow you to explore all your imaginative power. Even if all you can do is a daydream, do that. Allow yourself that creative playtime, and Venus will manifest stronger in a positive way in your life.

Don't take things from others for free. This is very important, especially when it comes to things you could easily get yourself. When you do this, you are putting out the energy that says you can't afford those things or that you don't have enough. As a result, your life will reflect that you don't have enough money to handle those things. You will become dependent and begin to make decisions that do not serve you.

Don't wear clothes twice without washing them. When you repeat your clothes, this can draw negative energy to you. So always make sure you wash them before you put them on again.

Keep something square and silver in your purse or wallet. This attracts the wealth of Venus and keeps out all stagnant negative energy that would horribly deplete your finances if you are not careful.

Seek your mother's blessings before you leave home. If your mother has passed or is estranged, you can seek the blessings of whoever else you consider a worthy parental figure. Better yet, you can choose to take a few minutes to seek Venus' blessings before you head out, trusting that she has heard you and granted them to you.

Self-Love

Some people think that self-love is the same as vanity, conceit, and selfishness, but that's not what it is. It's the same as having high self-esteem. It's the ultimate way to strengthen your Venus. As a matter of fact, if you look at several of the items I mentioned in the previous section, they're all about loving yourself, which means thinking of yourself favorably and treating yourself the same way you would someone you love.

Before you can be a complete, whole person who is able to love others, you need to be in touch with the world of feelings within you. This means you must come to know your strengths and weaknesses and choose to love yourself despite your imperfections. When you can accept yourself, warts and all, then others will also love you for who you are. Beyond that, you will find you there can love others and establish harmonious relationships with them.

People equate love with caring about someone other than yourself or putting their needs ahead of yours. This isn't the way love is supposed to be. There must be balance in matters of the heart. Only when you love yourself can you love others because it's through loving yourself, you understand that others need to feel that same love you have found within you. Self-love will show you that there is no reason to go chasing love outside of yourself. It's already all in your soul if you are willing to peek inside it.

Now, balance is essential. Some people take self-love too far, as I've already mentioned, demonstrating it as arrogance. At that point, that's no longer self-love. It's a desire to hide one's flaws and insecurities because they feel pain looking at them. You can distinguish between an arrogant person and a self-loving one. The former says, "I have no flaws. Therefore, I am lovable." The latter says, "I am flawed, but I love myself just the same." There is different energy there.

Loving Others

Just as you love yourself, channel that love toward others and experience the good Venus can bring to your life. However, there is also a risk here, as mentioned before, where you begin to chase others, begging and demanding that they love you because you don't understand that the love you seek you must first give to yourself.

Seeking love outside of you will lead to heartbreak and sadness. It will inevitably lead you to addiction. You can't live this way because it's not sustainable. If you only love those who love you, what happens if or when they stop? If you only feel love when you take drugs and alcohol, what happens when your dealer moves to another state, or the liquor store shuts down? You leave yourself vulnerable, and not in a good way. So, learn to get the love you seek from within you. Strengthening your Venus will help tremendously with that.

If you make your love conditional by basing it on how the other person treats you or responds to your acts of kindness, then you aren't truly loving, and chances are you still have work to do to understand self-love. When you genuinely love others, you do so from a place of power. You do so with reckless abandon, knowing you don't need them to give you back that love because you have it in abundance. When this is how you love - not requiring or demanding to be loved in turn and not caring if you are - then ironically, you draw more love unto yourself.

Conclusion

A funny thing about being in healthy, loving relationships is that somehow, it acts as a magnet, pulling in good things from all other aspects of your life. People fall in love, and during that same period your business or health improve. This is no coincidence. This is Venus at work, and you should put yourself in place to receive her blessings in your life, too.

The journey to a more vigorous, more positive Venus may seem very daunting. You may feel like your relationship is past saving, or your character is beyond redemption. However, this isn't true. You only need to decide right here, and now that you are going to make the changes, you must.

Do not demand perfection of yourself in this process because you won't get it. No one does, no matter how much they "have it together." Perfection doesn't exist, so don't make your goal about chasing unicorns!

There is also no reason to compare yourself with others or to use them as yardsticks. Again, we're all going through something. One person might have things figured out in one department, but then they could be struggling in another department that you've got flowing well for you. So, the comparison is pointless and will only kill your joy.

You deserve love, and more than that, to be loved the way you want. The more you show yourself this truth, the easier it will get each day. You will find the strength to say no to further toxicity, whether from people, situations, or habits. You don't have to get there today, but you can take one small step daily. In a matter of time, you'll look back and be amazed at how far you've made it.

There are so many who have radically transformed their love lives by working with Venusian energies consciously. All these people are no different from you. There is no reason you can't have your own testimony to share. Don't let your fears and doubts hold you back from trying to do better with yourself. Your partner will thank you for it, and your potential will manifest.

While you may have come to the end of this book, let this be the start of a new chapter in your life. Let it be one where you are committed to loving yourself in every way, every day. This doesn't mean that you'll do nothing about your flaws and give yourself a free pass. On the contrary, you will discover that you are very committed to working on your weaknesses and being a better person because of your newfound self-love. When you demonstrate this level of care and commitment to you, you teach others exactly how to treat you, and this is how you draw the love you seek. Self-love is Venus' ultimate lesson for us all.

Part 7: Jupiter in Astrology

The Ultimate Guide to the Planet of Luck, Fortune, and Opportunity

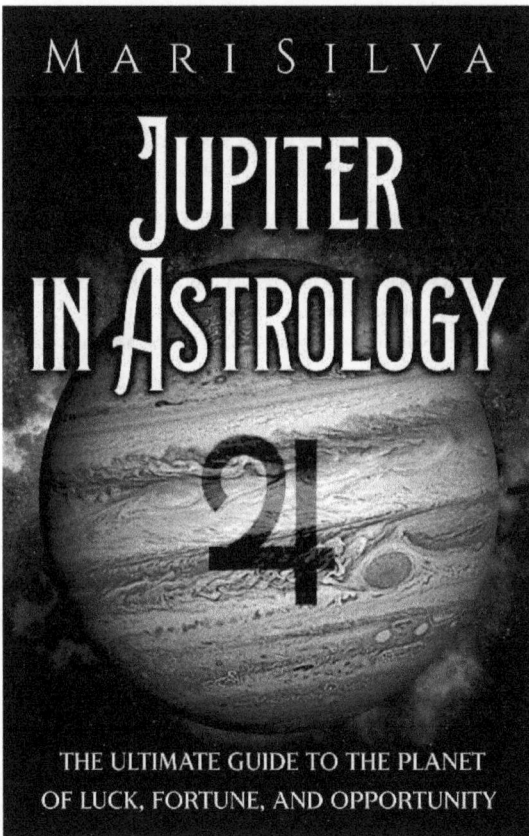

MARI SILVA

JUPITER IN ASTROLOGY

THE ULTIMATE GUIDE TO THE PLANET
OF LUCK, FORTUNE, AND OPPORTUNITY

Introduction

As the biggest planet in the solar system, Jupiter possesses a mystical vibe and boasts spectacular features. The planet's powerful gravity field acts as a shield to protect the Earth from space debris and meteors, which is why it is deemed the *world's protector*. The clouds surrounding Jupiter get their hues from ammonia crystals, which are also their main components. Due to the massive amount of gas it holds, Jupiter is called a "gas giant" along with Saturn.

Along with the astronomical domain, the planet is also an integral part of the astrological and spiritual realms. Jupiter rules Pisces and Sagittarius and resides in one zodiac sign for around a year, completing one round in approximately 12 years. It influences its natives to be more optimistic, look on the bright side, and be grateful for their blessings. Jupiter holds the power to attract wealth and prosperity, even when it is in a weak position. However, if malefic planets surround it, Jupiter may also cause destruction to its natives' lives.

Jupiter is the planet of luck, prosperity, and opportunity. It is truly called the "thinking-person" planet. This gigantic planet is our mind's guardian and rules spiritual learning. It can help us rediscover our authentic selves and mold our ideologies. A healthy Jupiter can also help you find answers in the spiritual realm or guide you throughout your journey. Seek this planet's help to combat adversities and assess your values. If you've been feeling like you are reaching the edge or have been pessimistic lately, Jupiter can pull you out of your misery. This benevolent celestial body brings good fortune, especially to those who've been poverty-stricken or who have been in a slump for years.

Due to its might and vigor, Jupiter was named after the Roman Sky God. Zeus, in Greek mythology and Brihaspati in Hindu mythology, also share similar attributes with Jupiter, thereby making him a primordial deity in all cultures. Vedic astrology also dignifies Jupiter and believes in the power and influence of the planet in its grounded state. Several strategies and "kriyas" are deployed to please Brihaspati or Guru and harness the planet's magic to bring good luck. This is also why astrologers mark Jupiter's position in a person's horoscope and use it to determine their fate.

In a way, Jupiter influences our attitude and life philosophy. Its position in each house will determine your professional and financial status. For example, Jupiter in the second house will influence the native to overeat or overspend. If you let it, Jupiter will act as your guru and help you combat every adversity. In the end, you have to search for true happiness and prosperity in your home and heart instead of seeking it in the external world. If you learn the right way to manifest this planet's energy, it will assist you at every step. From picking your college to finding your inner calling, Jupiter will act as a tool to raise your consciousness and help you make the right decision.

In this book, you will learn everything about Jupiter and realize its positive influence on a native's life. Whether you are a beginner who wants to start exploring the astrological realm or an experienced enthusiast who wants to dig deeper and discover every detail about planets in astrology, this book will help you. The chapters are easy to read and provide detailed insight into the mythological, spiritual, and astrological realms of Jupiter. You will learn about Jupiter's influence in various cultures, its key traits, unhealthy states, negative implications, and its conjunction with all zodiac signs and planets. Lastly, you will also tap into some effective ways and strategies to manifest Jupiter's positive influence in your life.

If you are intrigued and want to know more about Jupiter's role in astrology, then this is the book for you.

Chapter 1: Jupiter: The King of the Gods

Known as the god of justice and the skies, Jupiter has been deemed the main god in all mythologies. He ruled over the heavens and the Earth and governed all living beings. Jupiter's might, vigor, and huge size were the main values that inspired the planet's name. This chapter will discuss Jupiter as a God and as a planet to draw parallels between both domains and help readers understand its significance in astrology.

Jupiter as a Planet

With a diameter of 88,846 miles, Jupiter is considered the mightiest planet due to its huge size and powerful demeanor. The planet's average distance from the Earth is approximately 444 million miles; from the Sun, its distance is 466 million miles. Due to the huge distance from the Sun, the planet takes around 11.86 years to complete one revolution. With the Sun as the center, Jupiter is the 5th distant planet with 11 moons. An average of 9 hours and 55 minutes are spent for one rotation. With a geocentric motion of 00°04'59" per day, Jupiter displays a surface temperature of around -148°C.

Ganymede, Io, Callisto, and Europa are some of the well-known natural satellites of Jupiter, among a total of 63 bodies. Jupiter is primarily made of gases with certain liquid constituents. Due to its huge size, Jupiter can be easily spotted in the sky when correctly located. The extreme pressures and temperatures on and around Jupiter make it an unconducive planet on which to live. Jupiter's rings are believed to be comprised of dust particles and interplanetary meteoroids formed due to the constant collisions of smaller celestial bodies around the giant planet. Due to the Sun's position, only a part of Jupiter's rings is visible from Earth.

The Mythological Role of Jupiter

Jupiter was one of the most important gods in several mythologies. He was known by different names in Greek, Roman, Hindu, Egyptian, and several other mythologies. In particular, Jupiter was recognized as the main god in Roman and Greek mythologies. Around 117 CE, when the Roman Empire was at its peak, the Romans followed a polytheistic religious system, where they worshipped multiple gods at once. While most gods were believed to be associated with Roman roots, some of them were borrowed or inspired by other cultures.

Among all cultures, Romans were particularly fascinated by the Greek gods, which is also why many gods share similar names in both cultures. Romans called Jupiter the god of the sky, and Greeks called him "Zeus." Hindu mythology also placed great emphasis on the Jupiter god, who was called *Guru* or *Brihaspati* in Sanskrit.

Jupiter in Roman Mythology

For ancient Romans, Jupiter was considered the king of the gods and was named *Jove*. He ruled the sky and represented thunder. Brother to Ceres and Pluto, Jupiter overthrew Saturn's rule and became the prime deity. Saturn was married to Ops, the Earth goddess. When Saturn was in command, he killed his children in fear of losing his throne to them. He was cursed to be overthrown by one of his children, which is why Saturn killed Pluto, Vesta, Juno, Ceres, and Neptune one by one as soon as they were born. When Jupiter was born, Ops secretly transferred him to Crete, thereby saving his life. Saturn received a stone in exchange and believed that Jupiter was dead.

As fate decided, Jupiter was destined to rule the sky and take his father's throne. Jupiter was also thirsty for the throne as his main goal was to avenge his siblings' deaths. As Jupiter grew strong and mighty, he was capable of fighting the powerful Saturn. In one attempt, he forced Saturn to spit out all the children he swallowed. When the siblings reunited, they joined forces with Jupiter to overthrow Saturn. The army grew as the Hundred-handed Giants and Cyclops joined them. Saturn, along with the Titans, formed another powerful group to fight Jupiter's army.

After a long battle, Jupiter finally won and sent the Titans to Tartarus, where they were imprisoned for life. When Jupiter was ready to rule the other gods, he established a system with the help of his brothers to divide the universe. With this in place, the gods assumed that the universe would be supervised with scrutiny, and all living beings would likely thrive in harmony. While Neptune took over the seas and Pluto was put in charge of the underworld, Jupiter became the god of the heavens. Collectively, they ruled over the entire universe to ensure peace and harmony.

Jupiter in Roman mythology was the equivalent of Zeus in Greek myths, who was the god of the gods and the ruler of the sky. This is why the prevalence of Zeus can be found in Roman art and Latin literature, where the Greek god was named "Iuppiter" (after "Jupiter"). Pluto and

Neptune, Jupiter's siblings in Roman mythology, were Hades and Poseidon, respectively, in Greek mythology. Poseidon ruled the seas, and Hades was in charge of the underworld. Diespiter, the main god of the ancient Italic group, was also considered to be Jupiter's equivalent as he was the ruler of daylight.

Jupiter's sister, Ceres, was the goddess of fertility and growth. Vesta, Jupiter's second sister, was the goddess of the home. Juno, also Jupiter's wife, was the goddess of marriage, maternity, tranquility, and family. The Roman goddess, Juno, was the equivalent of the Greek goddess, Hera, as both represented maternity and growth and were married to the sky god. Jupiter and Juno gave birth to the god of war, Mars, and played a significant role in Rome's establishment. The couple also gave birth to a daughter, Bellona, who also represented war. Other children included Juventus, the goddess of youth, and Vulcan, the god of fire.

According to some tales, Jupiter was unfaithful to Juno and birthed other children with multiple partners. He met Maia, the goddess of fertility, and gave birth to Mercury, the god of commerce and messages. He also gave birth to Venus, the goddess of love and beauty, with Dione. Jupiter's daughter, Minerva, was born after he raped Metis.

The name "Jupiter" may have multiple connotations. Since the ancient Latin alphabet did not recognize the letter "J," the name Iuppiter directly derivates the original moniker. The word "dyeu" is derived from Proto Indo-European roots, which is also speculated to be the base of Zeus's name. It roughly translates to "day," "sky," or "shining object," which represents the sky and daytime. The word pater means "father" in Latin. In a way, the names "Diespiter" (for the Italics), "Dyaus pitar" (in Sanskrit), and "Zeus Pater" (for the Greeks) stem from the same words, which roughly mean "The Sky God." These inferences declared that Jupiter was indeed the archetypal primary god in many mythologies at the same time.

When Jupiter took over the throne, he only took command of the skies and heavens instead of being an active member of battle. He supervised his army and provided weapons. He often sat on his throne with his staff and a royal scepter. Jupiter's bearing was, in turn, fed by the sacrifices made by the Romans. The worshippers believed that their Mediterranean empire flourished only because of Jupiter's noble and powerful rule. Many religious officials (augurs) traced the path of birds and eagles to derive auspicious timings and decode omens. They believed that Jupiter influenced the eagles' paths, which is why they deciphered the birds' movements in the hope of finding auspicious and inauspicious traces.

The Sky God was also a significant part of "the Capitoline Triad," a trio that included his daughter Minerva and his partner, Juno. Jupiter was well-regarded and respected by the Romans. They built a temple in his honor in Rome's famous Capitol Hill. At one point, Jupiter succeeded above all gods and was the most important deity of the time. Worshippers sought Jupiter's blessings before entering a battle as his mercy was supposed to bring victory. Jupiter's rule and significance massively grew. At one point, the Roman state formalized Jupiter's worship for a lifetime and even imposed it on some people.

Ancient Roman worshippers illustrated Jove with a thunderbolt and an eagle as his symbol. An oak tree symbolized Jupiter. Over time, the eagle was adopted as the Roman army's common symbol due to this precedence. Some even embossed this symbol on coins, thereby signifying the stance of Jupiter in Roman mythology. Many devotees built temples in the name of Jupiter and sacrificed their lives as a tribute to the Sky God. Many scholars also devised a religious calendar significant to Jupiter. The Roman calendar identified several public holidays and festivities in the name of Jupiter. Several festivals related to wine and viniculture were devoted to Jupiter when the season's first grapes were cut.

Jupiter in Hindu Mythology

Vedic astrology draws parallels between the nine planets and their mythological figures, thereby relating each planet to a presiding deity. Jupiter is called "Brihaspati" or "Guru" in Hindu mythology. He is the reader of minds, teacher of the gods, Lord of Speech, beloved of the gods, and the Lord of Power. While some scriptures claim Brihaspati to be the incarnation of Lord Brahma, others deem Jupiter to be the manifestation of Lord Vishnu and Ganesha. A popular anecdote tells the story of Guru being sired from the sky with seven rays and seven faces. He was a devotee of Lord Shiva and worshipped the god for thousands of years until he was given the title "the Guru of Gods."

According to Vedic scriptures, this Hindu god was perceived as a symbol of fire and sage. Brahma's son, Angiras, gave birth to eight sons with Shraddha, one of whom was Brihaspati. He stayed with his father during his prime years and learned a lot from Angiras. One day, he decided to leave his house and gain spiritual knowledge from the external world. He got engrossed in deep meditation for centuries. Over time, the demigods recognized his penances and made Brihaspati their guru. He became the primary advisor and guided the gods through the demonic moves of the Asuras (the Devils or Demons).

According to a tale, Bhrigu (Venus), the Devil's teacher, embarked on a journey to seek blessings from Lord Shiva. His main intention was to become powerful and insightful to destroy the gods and take their place. When Indra, the King of Gods, recognized Bhrigu's intentions, he quickly sent Jayanti (his daughter) to retrieve the information. Jayanti lived with Venus for a couple of years and pretended to be his disciple. One day, when Lord Shiva finally blessed Bhrigu, Jayanti offered Bhrigu to be his wife. Bhrigu agreed on the condition that they could be married only for ten years, and they'd have to live away from the devils.

Brihaspati took this golden opportunity to disguise himself as Bhrigu and planned to live with the devils for ten years in the hope of purifying their hearts and transforming their evil intentions. Eventually, Brihaspati succeeded in eradicating greed, lust, and hatred from the hearts of the Asuras. After ten years, when Bhrigu returned home to the Devils, the Asuras failed to recognize their real teacher. After a while, they declared that Brihaspati was their real teacher, and they preferred him over Bhrigu. This made Venus extremely angry, and he stormed away, cursing them. After a while, Brihaspati transformed into his real avatar and decided to return to heaven.

When the Asuras realized that they would be left alone and without guidance, they immediately sought forgiveness from Bhrigu and pleaded with him to return. Even though Bhrigu gave in and agreed, his curse was still effective, which made the Asuras extremely weak and incapable of fighting the gods. Jupiter's wisdom and divine power made him the "Devguru" in Vedic astrology. He was also associated with the Dakshinamurthy god. His knowledge held the ability to expel negative forces and darkness around him. This is also why Hindus avidly worship Brihaspati even today.

Another popular tale tells the story of Brihaspati and Two Brahmins. The two often went to their king to beg alms. The king lived with his seven wives in a huge palace. However, the

Brahmins were often sent back by the wives, and they returned home empty-handed. Since the Jupiter God was believed to be a Brahmin, too, he was furious at the king's and his wives' behavior. He cursed the king and his kingdom, which steadily deteriorated into poverty. The youngest of the seven wives realized the ill effects of rejecting the Brahmins and realized her mistake. Even though the others still refused to give alms, the youngest wife fed the Brahmins and sought their advice to fight their adversity.

The Brahmins suggested that the only way to please Brihaspati was to fast all day and feed all the Brahmins in their area. The youngest wife took the advice and held a fast all day. Meanwhile, she prepared food for every Brahmin in her area and fed them. Slowly, the king's family got back on their feet and were blessed with wealth. As the other wives realized the influence of Brihaspati, they also fasted at regular intervals and gave alms to every Brahmin who visited their palace.

The Brahmins also spread some other beliefs and traditions among the common people. If a wife expected her husband's safe return from a foreign land, she had to keep two hand-molded human figures behind her door. To combat poverty, the Brahmins suggested molding the figures on a box. According to another tradition, a king looking for his successor needed to hang a garland on a female elephant's tusk. The male who was later garlanded by the elephant was announced as the next king.

In Southern India, devotees revere Jupiter as "Dhakshinamurthy." Dakshin means *south*, and Murthy (or "Murthy") translates to *stone*. Even today, a dedicated stone idol is recognized as the Jupiter god in India, and people refer to their god as "Narayan." People believe that worshipping Brihaspati can give them strength and power to defeat their enemies. Astrologers suggest chanting the mantras, "Om graam greem graum sah brihasptaye bamah," "Aum hreem kleem hoom brihaspataye namah," and "Om graam greem graum sah gurve namah" to please Brihaspati.

Vedic astrologers believe in the power of chanting the Gayatri Mantra, especially when paired with the mantras of Brihaspati. They suggest meditating and reciting these Gayatri mantras of Brihaspati or Guru:

> • "Vrusha Dhwajaaya Vidhmahe, Gruni Hasthaaya Dheemahi, Thanno Guruh Prachodayat"

> • "Aum Guru Devaya Vidmahe, Parabrahmane Dheemahi, Tanno Guruh Prachodayat"

> • "Om Suraachaarya Vidmahe, Surasreshtaya dheemahi, Tanno Guruh prachodayat"

Chanting these mantras 108 times using a 108-Rudraksha Bead Rosary can bring inner peace and help you manifest Jupiter's positive energy. If you are experiencing the planet's malefic effects, astrologers suggest organizing a "Puja" or an auspicious offering using yellow flowers to please Brihaspati.

Jupiter in the Astrological Domain

Vedic astrology defines Jupiter as an auspicious planet that tends to bring luck, prosperity, and wisdom to the natives. They are also blessed with abundant wealth, spirituality, generosity, and high-quality education. The planet is not only the biggest among all nine planets, but it also has the largest influence on people. If the native holds a strong Jupiter in their horoscope, they will soon be blessed with children and success. This is also why Jupiter is known as the "significator of wealth and children." Jupiter signifies masculine energy and favors the male gender. The planet establishes a deep connection with children and infants.

Since Jupiter takes around 12 years to orbit around the Earth, the natives can benefit from growth and self-reflection. They will likely be blessed with a life-changing opportunity during Jupiter's auspicious transitioning phase in a specific house. For example, when it moves through the 4th house, you may buy a big house or move to another country. If Jupiter passes through the 5th house, you may soon experience childbirth or become a grandparent. Jupiter takes around 1 year to transit from one zodiac sign to another. This makes a total of 11 to 12 years as Jupiter completes one round through all the 12 zodiac signs.

Vedic astrology connects the color yellow and gold to Jupiter. The planet represents the abdomen as the main body part and governs the 4th day of the week, Thursday. Since he is called Guru in Hindu mythology, Thursday is also called "Guruvaar." Jupiter rules the northeastern direction and rules the pre-winter or fall season, called "Hemant" in Vedic etymology. The planet represents Yellow Sapphire as its gemstone and gold as the main metal. Citrine and Topaz are two other substitute gemstones. In a healthy state, Jupiter promotes understanding, opportunities, wealth, enthusiasm, growth, and expansion. On the other hand, an unhealthy Jupiter can exude negativity, indulgence, bigotry, smugness, and extravagance.

Jupiter is exalted when it sits in the Cancer zodiac sign, which can be extremely beneficial for the native. By contrast, the planet debilitates the native when in conjunction with Capricorn, which can be inauspicious for the native. Jupiter is closely associated with the zodiac signs Pisces and Sagittarius. During its strong state, it can bring success to the native's professional life. They will likely perform better as a public representative and excel in their career. If the native is thinking of starting a business, this is the right time as they will steadily climb the ladder to success. However, if the planet conjuncts with certain malefic celestial bodies like Mars, Rahu, or Saturn, the native may suffer a financial loss or a breakup. This inauspicious conjunction also creates Guru Chandal yoga, which reduces Jupiter's power.

If Jupiter stays afflicted for a long time, the native may also be poverty-stricken. On the other hand, an auspicious Jupiter can bring the natives close to social welfare and make them good teachers. They are often proven to be great mentors, leaders, managers, social workers, and priests. According to the Vimshottari Dasha system, Jupiter can stay in a person's life for 16 years. The person may suffer from the planet's benefic or malefic effects during this period, depending on Jupiter's position and transiting phase.

Chapter 2: Jupiter's Luck

Jupiter is a lucky planet because it speeds through the zodiac in a shorter time than any other planet. This means that Jupiter's influence will have more effect on one sign for a given amount of time than any other planet at that position. Since astrology is based on cycles, throughout one complete orbit around the sun, the cycle of Jupiter will have its effect in each sign of the zodiac. In this chapter, we will discuss the symbolism of Jupiter, its exaltation in Cancer, what kind of luck readers can expect if they have Jupiter placed in their natal chart, and how they can harness this energy to elevate themselves further.

The sign that Jupiter is transiting while a person is born will affect the interpretation of that particular birth chart, and thus, its influence on their good fortune or lack thereof can be assessed. When discussing luck, the house where Jupiter is placed can indicate what areas of a person's life can expect expansion and success. The house that Jupiter rules will also be affected either positively or negatively, depending on the aspects it receives from other planets.

Jupiter is considered lucky in Vedic astrology because its natural course is to expand. The Vedic astrological perspective is that Jupiter's natural state is expanding; therefore, anything it touches will expand similarly. Therefore, when Jupiter is placed in a sign, an auspicious or malefic influence is assumed. This influence may not be considered positive in Western astrology, but there are other ways to look at Jupiter's luck. Western astrology looks at the sign where Jupiter resides as a marker of what is being affected by luck associated with Jupiter. In this way, it acts similarly to Vedic astrology because Jupiter's influence will be present only if the sign itself indicates a similar kind of energy.

Jupiter's Astrological Role

In western astrology, Jupiter is considered the planet of good luck and fortune. It rules over churches, philosophy, ethics, morality, and all that is big. The expansive nature of Jupiter makes anything it comes in contact with very valuable and influential in some way. In this sense, one could say that everything affected by Jupiter's natural energy is "lucky." This planet is associated with abundance, prosperity, and good fortune. Even its element, which is a fire in western astrology, speaks to how expansive it is. Everything on the earth that is burnt by fire expands.

Symbolism of Jupiter

Jupiter is considered to have a masculine polarity. Its element is fire, and it is placed in the sign of Sagittarius, which also has a fiery nature because of its association with this element. The planet rules over prosperity, good fortune, expansion, travel, religious matters, higher learning, judgment, ethics/morality, and writing.

In western astrology, the glyph for Jupiter is made up of two circles that are connected by a cross, or an oblique line, which goes through the center of each circle. One circle represents "expansion" while the other means "goodness." One can consider this to mean that whatever it touches is encompassed by both qualities.

In Vedic astrology, the glyph for Jupiter is a downward triangle with its point facing inward. It has three line segments attached to it that all have lines going away from the deity. The symbolism of this is that whatever Jupiter touches will be affected by its element and, therefore, will expand in some way while losing some quality as it does so.

Why Is Jupiter Considered Lucky?

Jupiter is considered lucky because it has a very strong positive energy attached to it. It also has qualities that allow it to expand into something without losing essential elements. These are mainly the qualities of fertility and creativity that can be amplified by being in Cancer, Jupiter's exaltation sign.

Luck is a very subjective topic, and when it comes to Jupiter's influence, one can only tell what they will personally get from it. There are always many factors that play into the situation, and each should be taken into consideration. Luck is not an all-or-nothing situation but rather something that needs to be nurtured.

Exaltation of Jupiter

Jupiter is exalted in the sign of Cancer, a water sign. The exaltation means that it will be at its best when placed here because of the element associated with Cancer and Jupiter. The expansionary energy of Jupiter finds a natural balance in this sign because water can expand infinitely without losing any quality. Its positive qualities can be amplified, while its malefic qualities are minimized.

Jupiter in Cancer is also considered lucky because water is a symbol of fertility. In addition, anything existing in the sign of Cancer has a very strong connection to the principle form of creation - reproduction. The symbolism here is that whatever house Jupiter occupies will be very prone to experiencing good fortune, creativity, and fertility. In the house it rules over, Jupiter will ensure that these positive energies are present.

It is also symbolically significant that Jupiter rules over the 10th house in a natal chart, representing one's profession. As this is a professional planet, it makes sense that its natural state of expansion will always benefit anyone who devotes themselves to their career. Therefore, if you have Jupiter placed in your tenth house, you are very likely to have success in your career, especially if it is the profession of your choice because you will benefit from Jupiter's luck and expansionary energy.

Exalted Jupiter and Luck

Typically, if a planet is being affected by transit, then anything that planet rules will be especially lucky for you during this period. For example, when Jupiter is in Sagittarius, it can make your dreams come true because the first house is about all areas of your being. Because of how universal this is, a positive transit means that the houses in your chart ruled by them will be amplified. If you have a lucky planet transiting through your 10th house of career or status, this is said to show that you will experience success and fame during that time.

If Jupiter is being affected by a good transit while it rules your natal 10th house, then there is no way you will not have a boost in luck and success. Since Jupiter's most important role is as a carrier of life force, it can benefit your profession because a healthy body at work results in excellent performance, bringing more money and increasing your status.

If you are trying to climb the social ladder, then this transit is said to help. If you are trying to get a promotion or even a new job altogether, then Jupiter's luck will have your back. Some people experience the famous "lucky break" during this time which propels them up the career ladder faster than they thought possible.

However, if you have a malefic planet transiting through your 10th house, it will entail obstacles and challenges. If the ruler of your 10th house is retrograde or combust, then this could also bring bad luck to your career goals and ambitions.

Jupiter's Effects When Transiting through Its Own House

When Jupiter transits through its sign Taurus or Aquarius, depending on whether it is night or daytime, it is considered extremely lucky, and anyone who has that transiting planet in their chart will experience an increase in luck. Other positive things people experience during this transit: good health, happiness, fertility, creativity, intellectual growth, philosophy, religion, travel (especially by air), and all other forms of expansion. Those with Taurus or Aquarius as their rising sign, moon sign, and/or first house will especially benefit from this transit.

Transiting Jupiter's Effects When It Enters a New House

When Jupiter enters a new sign of the zodiac, it is considered extremely lucky; whatever planet transits through this area of your birth chart will be very beneficial for you. This is because Jupiter represents luck and expansion, both of which will be very positive in whatever area of your life the transiting planet is entering.

For example, if you have the sun sign Sagittarius and Jupiter enter Capricorn on the 28th of January, the day that Jupiter entered Capricorn this year, then all things associated with the sun sign Sagittarius will be very lucky for you during this time. The expansion and luck that Jupiter brings are amplified if it rules over one of your houses because, in Vedic astrology, a planet ruling over its own house is said to function at its full potential. This means that whatever area of life is ruled by Sagittarius will be extremely lucky for you during this time.

Jupiter's Return

Whatever planet transited this area of your birth chart and ruled over one of your houses will be very beneficial for you during this time because its return is said to function at its full potential. In Vedic and Western astrology, this is considered extremely lucky when Jupiter returns to the sign it was in when you were born. The return is considered even luckier if that planet rules over your first house because, in Vedic astrology, a planet ruling over its own house is said to function at its *full potential.* This means that whatever area of life is ruled by Sagittarius will be extremely lucky for you during this time.

Jupiter as an Agent of Expansion

It is believed that Jupiter expands whatever area it's transiting, which includes people's lives. This planet is said to show where relationships are heading or expanding, and if you have a good relationship, it can be made stronger during this transit. If Jupiter rules your 7th house of open enemies, on the other hand, this means that your friends will become more distant because of relationship struggles.

If Jupiter rules your 7th house of open enemies, it indicates you need to be more mindful of your present relationships and make sure they are not headed in the wrong direction. If you have no real friends during this time, then it is said that acquaintances will become distant, which is the result of relationship struggles.

Jupiter's Effects on People with Different Birth Charts

In a natal chart, Jupiter's effects are going to depend on how it functions. The houses of the birth chart that it occupies and rules over will determine what area of your life is most affected by this planet.

Number of Houses Ruled: The more houses that Jupiter rules in your natal chart, the more luck you are said to have in your life. The reason is that in Vedic astrology, a planet ruling over its own house is said to function at its full potential. This means that whatever area of your life is ruled by Sagittarius will be extremely lucky for you during this time.

Planetary Sign: If Jupiter is in a fire sign, it will be very beneficial for you because Jupiter brings luck, success, and expansion to the areas of your life ruled by Aries and Leo. If Jupiter is in an earth sign, then it will bring success in money matters.

Jupiter's Modern Ruler: If Jupiter falls in the first house of your natal chart, then you will be very lucky in life because Jupiter is the modern ruler of your first house. Thus, whatever planets fall in your first house (or transit through it) will also be extremely lucky for you during this time.

Exaltation: If Jupiter is in its exaltation sign of Cancer, then it will be very lucky for you.

How to Benefit from Jupiter's Lucky Return

To benefit from this transit, you need to understand how the planets work. For example, if you have Saturn in your birth chart and it is transiting through an area of your birth chart that Jupiter rules, then whatever area of life is ruled by Sagittarius will be very lucky for you during this time. So, T any investment made under this transit will be successful.

Jupiter is said to have the effect of bringing success in whatever it transits through, and therefore if you have Jupiter's natal sign (Libra) or exaltation sign (Cancer) rising then, you will benefit most from this transit because Jupiter rules those signs respectively. You can benefit from this transit by using your Sagittarian qualities to your advantage. For example, you can pursue a cause or idea that you believe in because Jupiter is luckiest when it's used with its *natural tendencies.*

Doing Good Deeds and Charity

If you are able, give money to charity or donate time and/or skills to a good cause because Jupiter will magnify the effect or results of these actions. This would be a perfect time to give back; it'll bring you luck and happiness.

In both Western and Vedic astrology, good deeds and charity are said to be rewarded by Jupiter because, in Vedic astrology, a planet ruling over its own house is said to function at its full potential. So, anything that you spend money, time, or any other resource on will bring you success during this transit.

Doing Meditation or Fasting

If you are able, do some form of meditation or fasting during this transit because doing things like this brings peace and clarity in whatever you are trying to accomplish. If you do some sort of spiritual practice (like meditation or fasting) during this time, you will benefit most from this transit because Jupiter rules those signs.

Doing Yoga or Pilates

If you are able, do some yoga or pilates during this transit because it will bring expansion to all of the houses involved in your natal chart, and since Jupiter rules Sagittarius, which is a fire sign, it will help to bring success to whichever planet is transiting through that house.

How to Know If You're Lucky during This Transit

Not everyone is born under a Jupiter transit, so if you can make the most of this transit, then it will seem like you're very lucky during this time. The best way to know for sure is by looking at your birth chart and understanding which planets are being affected. For example, if Jupiter is transiting through the first house of your natal chart, then that means you will be very lucky during this time. By understanding how planetary transits work, you can make full use of this transit and feel like your whole life is a lucky streak.

If you want to know if this transit will be lucky for you, look at your natal chart and see which house Jupiter rules. Also, look at which house Saturn currently rules because any area of life ruled by Saturn (such as your profession or long-term goals) will be luckiest for you during this time. If Jupiter is transiting through your 12th house of spirituality, then that means you can progress spiritually in ways that expand your mind and bring you peace. If Saturn is transiting through your 7th house of relationships, then that means any relationship you engage in during this time will be very solid.

Suppose Jupiter is transiting through a house filled with planets like Mars, Mercury, and Uranus. If you are experiencing success in all areas of life being affected by this transit, then it is said that your faith and confidence will increase. In that case, those areas of your life will become exceptionally lucky for you because it combines the luckiness of Jupiter with the other powerful planets. Your lucky streak will bring a lot of happiness to your life during this time.

Financial Luck

Success will happen in areas like money and career if you can make the most of your resources during this transit. If you want to feel successful during this time, look at your natal chart and see what houses Jupiter rules because doing those activities or using those resources during this transit is said to bring success.

If you have debts that need to be paid, it is said that Jupiter will help you to pay those debts because of how powerful it is. This good fortune will not go unnoticed. Success in money matters and other highly valued resources can be yours if you can make the most of this transit.

If you have goals you want to accomplish, this transit will help make those dreams come true because of how lucky this combination of planets is. Having Jupiter in Sagittarius will bring success to your "spiritual life," and the first house rules all areas of your being, so if things like peace and happiness are important to you, then make the most of this transit because that is precisely what will happen.

During this period, every area of your life will be affected by luck and good fortune, but it is believed that the areas ruled by Jupiter in your natal chart are where you will benefit most. If you do something to engage with these areas, not only will you feel as if every day is filled with luck, but success in those areas will also be yours.

In this chapter, we discussed the general luck that Jupiter transits bring to a person's life. We also talked about how lucky areas of your life are affected and what you can do to make the most of it. Jupiter transits are the most fortunate times in a person's life regarding encounters, relationships, opportunities, and luck. In Hindu astrology, Jupiter is considered the lucky planet because of its influence on exaltation and its ability to expand areas of life ruled by it. It is also exalted in Cancer, which symbolizes luck because this sign rules resources. Anyone with this arrangement will have an easy time acquiring those resources. Vedic wisdom believes that having Jupiter in Sagittarius or Pisces during a person's Saturn return is the best possible combination of luck because it can result in success and opportunities being brought to their lives.

Chapter 3: Do You Feel Lucky?

Most of us consider luck to be a major part of most people's lives. However, while luck is often considered a reason behind some of our significant life events, most people don't think about luck otherwise.

What Is Luck?

Before you can understand luck in detail, it's essential to define the concept of "luck."

The dictionary definition of luck is "a force that brings good fortune or adversity" or "the events or circumstances that operate for or against an individual." It is, essentially, the explanation we give to the chance that any given event will result in a positive (or negative, in the case of bad luck) experience.

In general, "luck" as a concept can be broken down into three components:

- Luck is either good or bad.

- The luck we experience is a result of chance.

- "Luck" as a concept applies to a sentient being. This means that only a sentient being can experience luck – a book, for example, cannot be unlucky in and of itself. It is only considered unlucky if it causes bad events to happen to a person.

The idea of luck has also been expressed using the terms "good fortune" (in the case of good luck), "speed" (used during the Middle Ages to mean good fortune, prosperity, and abundance), and "chance" (most often used when playing a game).

Luck in Mythology

Luck plays a major role in the religion and mythology of several cultures. These include:

Tyche in Greek Mythology

Tyche was the goddess of fortune and prosperity and was the daughter of Aphrodite (goddess of love) and either Hermes (the messenger god) or Zeus (the king of the gods and god of the sky and thunder).

Unlike modern conceptions of luck, Tyche did not rule over the fortune of individual people. Rather, she was considered to hold dominion over the fortune of cities as a whole, playing a part in how a city's destiny unfolded.

Her major centers of worship were Itanos in Crete and Alexandria in Egypt. Alexandria was also home to the Tychaeon, the temple of Tyche. Scholars note that the years following the death of Alexander the Great – and the infighting between his generals for control over his kingdom – led to an increase in Tyche's worship, as people ascribed the political turbulence to her influence.

Fortuna in Roman Mythology

Fortuna is the Roman version of Tyche and is considered the personification of the concept of luck. She is also considered the goddess of fate and chance.

Fortuna could bring either good or bad luck and was a representation of life's capriciousness. She was usually depicted as either veiled or blindfolded, and the blindfolded depiction of Fortuna is still referenced in the modern Italian phrase "la fortuna è cieca" or "luck is blind."

Like Tyche, Fortuna was thought to be the daughter of Jupiter, the Roman equivalent to Zeus. Her earliest temples were located right outside Rome, on the banks of the Tiber. Other major centers of worship included:

- Forum Boarium

- Praeneste (home to what was considered to be the most magnificent of Roman Fortuna temples)

Additionally, dedications to Fortuna have been discovered across the breadth of the ancient Roman Empire.

Fortuna remained a part of popular imagination even after the worship of the ancient Roman gods declined, and Christianity became the major religion. Her cult was popularized by author Boethius and was referenced throughout the Middle Ages and the Renaissance, including major works such as Dante's Inferno and Machiavelli's The Prince.

Seven Lucky Gods in Japanese Mythology

In Japanese Mythology, luck is the domain of a grouping of seven gods. The six main deities are:

- Ebisu (god of prosperity and wealth in business)

- Daikokuten (god of commerce and prosperity. He can also take female form and is then known as Daikokunyo)

- Bishamonten (god of fortune in war and battles)

- Benzaiten (the only "permanent" goddess among the seven, goddess of financial fortune, talent, and beauty)

- Jurōjin (the human incarnation of the southern pole star and the god of longevity and the elderly)

- Hotei (god of fortune and guardian of children. Also considered the god of prosperity.)

Additionally, there is a seventh deity in the grouping, which differs depending on tradition. Most traditions hold that this seventh deity is one of either Kichijōten (god of wisdom, luck, and longevity, and thought to be the reincarnation of Husan-wu, a Taoist god) or Fukurokuju (goddess of beauty, happiness, and fertility).

How People View Luck

There are several ways in which people view luck, including:

- **As a Lack of Control:** Luck is completely beyond a person's control and includes events that happen by chance. This perception of luck can be divided into three types:

  - constitutional luck (luck based on factors that cannot be changed, such as genetics)

  - circumstantial luck (covering situations like accidents, both positive and negative)

  - ignorance luck (luck that is only identified after the event passes, rather than during it happening).

- **Spiritually:** This belief holds that it is possible to change or influence luck through spiritual or religious means or performing certain rituals. Traditional African religions, for example, may employ the use of voodoo and hoodoo to influence luck, while Ancient Mesoamerican religions incorporated human sacrifice as a way to influence luck.

- **Self-Fulfilling Prophecy:** Some believe that luck can be influenced by positive thinking. Depending on a person's view of their own luck, their response to events changes, which can, in turn, change the result of that event. For example, if a person believes they are unlucky, they may be anxious or nervous during a job interview because they expect to fail. This nervousness, rather than bad luck, can result in a rejection attributed to further bad luck. In this way, luck is not only a self-fulfilling prophecy but also circular.

However, this is just one way of looking at luck. Another perspective on luck breaks it down into three "faces," each making up a different facet of luck. Under this theory, luck can be broken into:

- **Superstitious Luck:** The belief that you can influence your luck (or the luck of others) by performing – or avoiding – certain tasks. For example, some people believe that walking under a ladder is unlucky, leading people to avoid doing so. On the flip side, you can also find certain talismans or objects that bring luck to the bearer. For example, a four-leafed clover is an Irish and Celtic symbol of good luck that has spread across the world, to the point where people often search for four-leafed clovers before an important event in their lives.

- **Retrospective Luck:** This involves attributing past experiences to luck after the event has already happened. One example would be stepping back to the sidewalk instead of crossing the road, only to have a car speed past the next second. While you may not think of your action as being particularly relevant while you stepped back, you will likely attribute your escape to luck once the event has happened.

- **Future Luck:** This face is relatively similar to the self-fulfilling perspective discussed above. It notes that believing in your own luck can create further luck in the future. For example, you'll be more willing to apply for a job you aren't fully qualified for because you believe in your own luck. If you then get the job, your belief in being lucky will be reinforced, and you'll act similarly in the future, while a person who believed they were unlucky (or simply didn't believe in luck at all) may not have applied to the job in the first place. Additionally, it notes that lucky people can transform bad luck into good luck, a thought similar to the saying, "when life gives you lemons, make lemonade." It essentially means that a person who believes in their luck will be able to see the opportunity hiding behind an event that others may see as bad luck and be demotivated by.

Luck in Religion

Apart from mythology, luck is also referenced explicitly in many religions still practiced today. These include:

Lakshmi and Ganesha in Hindu Mythology

Hindu myth and religion references two major deities who rule over good fortune: Ganesha and Lakshmi.

Ganesha is considered to be the remover of obstacles and the god of auspicious beginnings. He is one of the most popular deities in Hinduism and is the elephant-headed son of Parvati (goddess of love and fertility) and Shiva (god of destruction, time, and dance).

As a non-sectarian deity, he is worshipped in several ways. He is invoked before the traditional dance and music performances in South India and is associated with several festivals, including:

- Ganesh Chaturthi (the major festival associated with Ganesha, a ten-day celebration that usually takes place in late August or early September)

- Ganesh Jayanti (a festival celebrating the birth of Ganesha)

Lakshmi is one of the principal goddesses of the Hindu pantheon. Alongside fortune, she is also the goddess of wealth, power, beauty, and prosperity. She is the wife of Vishnu (god of preservation, karma, protection, and restoration) and is part of the Tridevi (or triad) of Hindu goddesses alongside Parvati and Saraswati.

Like Ganesha, Lakshmi is worshipped by Hindus around the world. Major temples dedicated to her include:

- Mahalakshmi Temple, Kolhapur

- Mookambika Temple, Kollur

- Lakshmi Temple, Khajuraho

- Golden Temple, Sripuram

- Chottanikkara Temple, Chottanikkara

Additionally, she is also worshipped during Diwali, the festival of lights and one of the most important festivals in Hinduism, and during Sharad Purnima (a harvest festival).

Buddhism

Buddhism does not believe in the concept of luck (or fate and chance). Instead, according to Gautama Buddha, founder of Buddhism, every event that happens has a cause.

This cause can either be material or spiritual. The reason for this teaching is due to the central precept of karma in Buddhism. According to the principle of karma, there is an interplay of cause and effect that takes place.

Essentially, the intent and the actions of a person influence their future. This influence is not merely limited to your current life and instead continues past your death. Thus, good intentions and actions result in happier rebirths, while bad intentions and actions result in worse rebirths.

Per this principle, every event that has happened to you has been caused by your actions. No greater force affects the way that events unfold, nor are events simply a balance of probabilities.

However, it should be noted that, in practice, belief in luck is still prevalent among followers of Buddhism. For example, in many Buddhist countries such as Thailand, Buddhists wear amulets blessed by monks as a way to attract luck and protect them against harm.

Hinduism

While Hinduism reveres Ganesha and Lakshmi as deities of luck, another tradition holds that luck is a relatively unimportant part of a person's life. Unlike Buddhism, Hinduism does not eschew luck altogether. Instead, it places greater importance on the concept of Puruṣārtha.

Puruṣārtha literally translates to "object of human pursuit" and refers to the goals that a person should aim for. It covers dharma (righteousness), artha (prosperity), kama (pleasure or love), and moksha (that is, liberation, spirituality).

Per the Bhagavad Gita, the holiest of Hindu scriptures, being conscious of one's Puruṣārtha results in a positive movement of the Daivam or the Cosmic Wheel of Action.

The Cosmic Wheel of Action keeps stock of a person's past and present actions and helps determine how a person's life unfolds.

Thus, similar to Buddhism, in this version of Hinduism, each event taking place in a person's life is the result of the way their actions affect the Cosmic Wheel of Action.

Christianity and Judaism

While Christianity and Judaism both believe in luck and chance, they note that these forces are completely under God's sovereignty. Not even actions as small as the roll of a dice escape His control.

Therefore, there is no true random chance – every action is a result of God's will.

God's will may be passive or active. While His active will is often noticeable by the people it affects, His passive will may not be. His passive will involves Him allowing actions to happen and events to unfold as they will, rather than Him directly causing something to happen.

Thus, while luck and chance exist, they are not truly random and can always be attributed to God.

Islam

In Islam, the idea of luck is mentioned in the Quran as "a force that brings good fortune or adversity." That said, like in Christianity and Judaism, luck is not truly random.

Instead, actions are determined by Allah, and they are predestined based on a person's actions in the past. As Islam believes in predestination, luck is not truly "luck" and merely represents one's predestined fate.

In Islam, believing in luck and related concepts is forbidden, as it is purely within the realm of Allah, and wearing lucky charms and amulets is expressly prohibited.

While the concept of the "evil eye" and evil eye charms is popularly thought to be Islamic in origin, it is, in fact, a representation of an older belief. The evil eye dates back to at least the 8th century BC and may be associated with the Eye of Horus.

Types of Luck

There are considered to be four major types, or classifications, of luck. These are:

- **Blind Luck:** The type of luck which is purely random and is not a result of individual actions. If a person is at the right place, at the right time, and performs the right action, they will get good luck. An example of this is winning a scratch-card lottery – the victory was pure blind luck, as none of your actions would influence the result.

- **Luck in Motion**: This type of luck is a result of the action. It holds that by performing an action, you will stumble into a related piece of luck. For example, if you are a writer, posting your work online means that you are likely to experience luck in motion, perhaps by stumbling into a literary agent who reads your work and wants to help you get published. This luck holds that a person must take action to be lucky and pushes people to act.

- **Luck Recognized:** With this type of luck, something lucky happens in a person's life because they can recognize the opportunity in front of them. The recognition is usually a result of knowledge and experience, even if it is not a conscious recognition. For example, if you are a long-term financial investor who invested in Bitcoin early, you would have "gotten lucky" because you were able to identify an opportunity where no one else could.

- **Luck as Directed Motion**: Something lucky happens because you take purposeful action towards it. Where Luck in Motion resulted in luck due to random motion, Luck as Directed Motion requires you to take purposeful action based on your knowledge and perspective. For example, a popular online artist may believe a large commission is simply a lucky break. However, it is, in fact, Luck as Directed Motion because it would never have taken place had the person not spent their time building their social media presence, so the luck happened as a consequence of an action

Are People Born Lucky?

One of the biggest questions that many people have about luck is a rather simple one – are people born lucky?

After all, there has to be a reason why some people are luckier than others, right?

The challenge in answering this question lies in another simple question: what do you classify as *luck*?

We know the literal definition of luck, as well as what people, myths, and religions have thought it to be. However, the fact is, every person has their own definition of luck.

Some people may think of themselves as being lucky if they have the basic necessities in their life – that is, shelter, food, entertainment, and enough money to live within their means. On the other hand, other people may only think of themselves as lucky when they are wealthy and can fulfill their needs, wants, and desires. Finally, others may think of luck in non-material terms, considering themselves lucky in terms of the people they have in their lives and the experiences they have had.

As discussed above, one of the many understandings of luck is the self-fulfilling prophecy – the luck that one makes by believing in their own luck. Thus, it is possible to "make" yourself lucky – but how do you do that?

There are four principles you can follow to maximize your luck. These are:

- Maximize your chances (opportunities) by building strong interpersonal networks, being open to new experiences, and having a relatively relaxed approach to life.

- Listen to your lucky hunches, and take steps according to your gut instincts and intuition. These "hunches" are often borne of personal experience and knowledge and can help you take advantage of all that life has to offer you.

- Expect good fortune in the future as this will encourage you to keep trying to achieve your goals, even when the chance for success seems minor. This can help you ensure positive and successful interpersonal interactions.

- Turn your bad luck into good by looking for the silver lining and not dwelling on the reasons behind your bad luck. Additionally, take the steps that are necessary to prevent future bad luck.

Ultimately, people's understanding of their luck differs depending on their perspectives. It is impossible not to *ever* experience bad luck in your life. However, depending on your actions, it may be possible to understand how lucky you are – and make changes that lead to more good luck instead of bad luck.

Chapter 4: A Challenged Jupiter

If you are reading this book, you are most likely a strong believer in the effects that the planets and their placements can have on us. Planets and their location in the zodiac can give us a great insight into our future perspectives. This is not to say that they affect the entire scenario or course of our lives. If a planet is well-placed in your Horoscope, then the outcomes will be positive. Similarly, bad or weak Horoscope placements suggest negative results.

Vedic Astrology explains that benefic planets are well-positioned in one's birth chart. Meanwhile, planets that aren't well-placed are known to be malefic. Over and above, each planet is also characterized by its nature. Some planets are inherently good, while others are typically negative. This distinction is determined by whether they help or harm the affected areas or the aspects of our lives for which they're responsible. So, how each planet affects us depends on both its placement and nature. Both benefic and malefic planets can go against their nature, depending on the astrological signs or zodiac locations they house. For instance, planets in the 6th, 8th, and 12th houses, known as the malefic or Dusthana houses, can negatively affect people. The Dusthana houses are among the most stressful locations on the birth chart.

When benefic planets become in charge of a quadrant, they generate evil outcomes. On the other hand, malefics that own quadrants result in good things. Planets – regardless of their nature – own over the 1st, 4th, 7th, or 10th houses, 5th and 9th houses, or the 3rd, 6th, and 11th houses. Evil planets become more malefic, usually hitting the pinnacle of their power in the 10th house. Also, the beneficial planets become worse at the 10th house, and they're not as bad at the 7th house, then they become slightly better at the 4th, and so on.

Thus, good planets, such as Jupiter and Venus, become rather adverse when they own quadrants. For example, they can inflict or signify some type of death to the affected individual when they inhabit the 2nd or 7th houses. The Moon is usually less Malefic than Mercury, which is less unfortunate than Jupiter and Venus.

Jupiter is among the most benefic planets, according to Vedic Astrology. Strong house placement is linked to positive impact. However, weak placement in any of the houses can spiral some negative effects.

Jupiter, as you are aware, is normally associated with good fortune, wealth, and abundance. It reflects those propensities when the affected person is ethical, kind, forgiving, and generally good and why Jupiter is also called *Guru*. It's a representation of graceful individuals, elderly qualities, great respect, and fine business. Jupiter symbolizes knowledge, education, teachers, and learning capacities. When Jupiter occupies an unfavorable house, like the 6th, 8th, or 12th, the native may experience multiple challenges in these areas. Businesses, marriages, and health problems or physical maintenance, such as looking after their hair, may be affected.

Those who suffer from Jupiter's negative effects may experience pessimistic thoughts, possibly resulting in less-than-ideal and bleak behavior. Natives of a weak Jupiter placement may have to deal with depression.

In this chapter, we will discuss the possible negative effects of Jupiter in each of the houses. We will also explore how Jupiter is especially weakened or debilitated in Capricorn. Although it is such a bright and promising planet, you will understand why Jupiter can become so unlucky. You will gain insight into how this celestial body behaves when it's challenged. Luckily, if you think you have a weak Jupiter placement in your birth chart, we are here to tell you how you can turn your luck around.

General Negative Impact

Jupiter is associated with a wide array of aspects of life, such as the principles of healing, expansion, growth, miracles, good fortune, and prosperity. Jupiter also governs the law, wealth, higher education, great businesses, knowledge, religion, wealth, and long-distance travel. The problem is that with an unfortunate Jupiter placement in the zodiac, any of these vital aspects, if not several, would be impacted. While this means that having this benefic placement in your birth chart can be exciting and rewarding, it also means that a bad placement can be quite detrimental.

A result of a negative Jupiter energy may result in delayed and problematic marriages. People with this placement may also struggle with personality changes. They may also be overruled and influenced by others and their opinions. Natives of Jupiter in Capricorn are very pessimistic and may have a cynical approach to life. They may feel constantly depressed. Their cold and demotivated nature may also keep them from exploring resources and retaining knowledge.

Weak Jupiter in Each House

As we mentioned above, good planets can turn unlucky when they are placed weakly in any of the houses. They also turn especially malicious when they occupy certain houses, like the Dusthana houses, for instance.

1st House

Jupiter is generally positive when it occupies the 1st house. However, when it's weak in its placement, it can cause its native to hurt those around them unknowingly. Not only may this hurt the individual's reputation or cause others to dislike them, but it can also trigger a wide array of problems. People who unintentionally inflict pain on others may find themselves involved in minor mishaps and major issues at several points during their lives – explaining why they have to be very careful in all their relationships. They should also properly calculate any decision they're about to make.

2nd House

Natives with a 2nd house Jupiter placement are typically blessed. However, as you know, a weak house placement can result in a negative impact. A weak Jupiter in the 2nd house can make its native highly dependent on comfortable living. The individual may think that they need to lead a lavish lifestyle to survive. This obsession may cause them to go down the wrong path to generate more money. Natives with a Jupiter 2nd house placement may also have stomach or gut health issues.

3rd House

3rd house Jupiter placements make for intellectual individuals. While it is a generally good house placement for Jupiter, it may sometimes cause the natives to feel a little lost. People with Jupiter 3rd house placements may feel as though they are being pulled in countless opposing directions simultaneously. This is because they are very keen on learning all about everything, causing them to feel stressed.

4th House

While Jupiter in the 4th house becomes a malefic planet, it may sometimes pose promising potential. 4th house Jupiter placements result in largely pessimistic natives. These individuals may have disruptive relationships with their mothers and life partners. They tend to be sensitive, which leaves their decision-making abilities in bad shape.

5th House

Jupiter in the 5th house makes for wonderful natives. However, they may be a little ego-eccentric. Since they are very creative individuals, a weak placement may result in memory issues. Their affected memory capacity or power may cause them to face difficulties in the area of study.

6th House

Natives with Jupiter in the 6th house are very determined and hard-working. These traits may result in a build-up of tension, negatively impacting their mental health. These individuals are deeply affected by even the slightest criticism. Natives of the 6th house Jupiter may be hostile to anyone who speaks negatively of their work.

7th House

Individuals with 7th house Jupiter placements are typically gifted with multiple pleasures and joys. On the downside, they may find themselves caught up in an affair with another person. In some cases, this will end in separation. The breakup may perhaps result from the native's inability to express feelings of fondness and sympathy toward their partner.

8th House

Those who have their Jupiter occupying the 8th house may sometimes be intellectual and knowledgeable. Unfortunately, this placement is generally malefic, getting in the way of the native's relationships. They are generally reserved in their communications with others, which often causes them to be misunderstood.

9th House

Jupiter's 9th house placements are auspicious, increasing their chances of finding success. However, a weak placement may result in highly attached individuals. This attachment, however, is directed toward friends rather than family. This may stir up family issues since they tend to travel out and about frequently with friends.

10th House

10th house Jupiter placements, as we mentioned above, are very malefic. While it may sometimes signal professional success, the natives may be very egotistic, disrupting their social life and causing them to have fewer friends.

11th House

An 11th house Jupiter placement is the exact opposite of Jupiter occupying the 10th house. Jupiter in the 11th house suggests abundance, joy, wealth, and health. Natives also have good relationships with almost everyone. The disadvantage here may be that all these relationships may result in difficulties with time management.

12th House

A Jupiter placement in the 12th house is a highly unfavorable one. Jupiter in Capricorn (or the 12th house) are always debilitated. We'll discuss this in more depth in the following section. When Jupiter is strong in this house, the native may be generous and interested in areas of spirituality. However, it also signals business and financial loss and differences of opinion with the native's father.

Jupiter Debilitated in Capricorn

Jupiter is debilitated in Capricorn because its placement in the 12th house prevents it from maintaining its positive qualities. Jupiter in the 12th house struggles to be caring, positive, and gentle. This is why natives of this position may be hard-working, pessimistic, and rigid individuals.

Besides, Capricorns, or at least the more grounded ones, are naturally more inclined toward law and order. They are not interested in spirituality, exploration, religion, higher wisdom, and similar areas. This is another prominent reason why Jupiter is debilitated in Capricorn and fails to perform its function in that area of the zodiac effectively.

When Jupiter falls in this sign, it creates an unfavorable celestial body combination. This paves the way for damaged Jupiter and Capricorn characteristics, though this combination's negative implications can be canceled. Neecha Bhanga Raja Yoga, a very powerful combination often signaling abundance, can do just that.

Pessimistic Natives

Since Jupiter is a naturally optimistic planet, its debilitated Capricorn placement results in pessimism. The affected individuals may be unable to see anything but the negative aspects of each situation. They always expect the worst.

Since Jupiter is also closely linked to faith and spirituality, these individuals often believe that the evil aspects of life are stronger than the good ones. This belief can be detrimental because we can find peace of mind knowing that righteousness always finds its way. Since they are pessimists with bad faith, they become obsessed with the idea that the bad side always wins. This obsession causes them to adopt unhealthy, immoral, and evil tactics to get what they want. Some cases, however, have slightly better outcomes.

Fearing the evil side of others may disrupt the native's progress, causing them to lose confidence in their abilities, preventing them from taking any action forward. They become stagnant, unable to fulfill their goals or aspirations.

If Saturn gets involved, this debilitation may be canceled, taking some of the horrible outcomes away. While the individuals remain pessimistic, they can generally maintain their composure when bad events take place. They become cold, stable, and calm. Since they don't keep their expectations high, they rarely ever get disappointed. This all helps them overcome challenges easily.

The weak placement, therefore, doesn't mean that the affected individuals can't be successful. Although they are cold at times, their tactful approach allows them to minimize risks. They are well-prepared with resources and knowledge, which paves the way for opportunities of a different kind.

Lack of Gratitude

Since Jupiter is also associated with gratitude, Jupiter in Capricorn signifies a lack of gratitude and thankfulness. Those affected tend to take everything for granted. Being unaware or appreciative of what you have, opportunities unwittingly begin to slip away, leaving the natives with fewer financial and spiritual options.

It should be noted that a lack of gratitude tends to repel all the good things in one's life. When you don't appreciate what you have, you spend less energy, time and focus on giving back and maintaining it. Whether the good things lie within a family, opportunities, friendships, or valuables, these are all things that need attention. Gratitude attracts more goodness because you receive the opportunity to build something stronger out of what you already have.

If Saturn is involved, the natives of the placement may just be able to make up for the lost opportunities through hard work and discipline.

Lost Spirituality

Jupiter is known as the planet of spirituality, indicating that an unlucky placement may result in a lost spiritual compass. Some natives may not even believe in higher powers, divinity, or any other spiritual principle. They may not believe in the concept of punishment for sins and bad deeds and reward for good deeds.

Even those who are aware that higher powers and good and bad exist still choose to reject them. They prefer following terrestrial rules and laws instead, possibly sprouting from the fact that Capricorn is an Earth sign. These individuals may also struggle to follow abstract guidance with no solid laws present.

The worst outcome of this placement may result in someone who not only rejects the idea of spiritual guidance but also purposefully walks down the sinful road. This is what happens when a lack of gratitude is combined with lost spirituality. The outcome is a rigid individual with a brittle heart and emotions. They simply become blind in terms of morals and the truth. Since what is forbidden is desired, sins may become too attractive to the point where righteousness, ethics, and morals can be easily left behind. Profits, success, gains, and desires are then further repelled, all in return for momentary joy and pleasure.

If Saturn is in the picture, natives are righteously directed, rectifying debilitated Jupiter. Since Saturn is associated with karma, natives are motivated to avoid bad deeds and sins to escape punishment.

Social Effects

The lack of gratitude also makes those with Jupiter in Capricorn unable to perform favors without expecting anything in return. This means that they won't show kindness or help others without getting something out of it. This behavior and mindset affect their ability to build and maintain social relationships.

Natives also tend to be rather formal or utterly casual in their interactions. Their professional, reserved approach repulses generous, genuine individuals. This way, these individuals push any pure relationships based on love and care out of their lives. They, in turn, attract harmful individuals or those with similar mindsets. All their relationships become motivated by advantage and interest.

We are a product of our social environment. If you surround yourself with good people, you will be successful. If your friends are kind, you will be kind. Similarly, when your behavior drives all the good people away, you attract people with the similar "what's in it for me?" mindset.

This is why a Saturn placement helps the affected individual surround themselves with good people. This way, they'll become better individuals themselves. Saturn also gives the natives some humanistic characteristics, allowing them to show respect and earn it back. Their reserved approach, when used correctly, helps them thrive in environments where a level of professionalism is required.

Financial Issues

A Jupiter in Capricorn suggests that its natives may be unable to obtain and maintain financial wealth. Since Jupiter is linked to prosperity and wealth, a weakened placement means abundance can't be provided.

The affected individuals may struggle to generate profits and savings, resulting from the individual's heightened greed. The constant desire for more material wealth causes them to partake in unethical money-making activities. This behavior is additionally reinforced due to their lost spirituality and lack of spiritual guidance, attracting more misfortune.

With Saturn involved, the financial struggles may become opportunities for profit and gains. It encourages the natives to learn from their previous mistakes and experiences to avoid making similar mistakes. They essentially become stronger and wiser. Since Saturn is associated with the sense of responsibility, its placement reinforces a sense of maturity and responsibility within the native, allowing them to become more successful.

Remedies

Fortunately, having a bad astrological placement doesn't mean that you should give up. While you can't change your birth date or how the stars are mapped out in your birth chart, there are a few things you can do to alleviate the results of an inauspicious Jupiter placement. From gemstones to pujas, your options are endless.

You can make a paste of sandalwood and turmeric and apply it to your forehead. You can wear yellow, or preferably gold, jewelry to strengthen Jupiter's benefic power. You can also wear yellow frequently. If accessible, every day for 8 days before you begin something new, offer turmeric to a temple. Feed cows jaggery and fast on Thursdays to strengthen your Jupiter placement. If it doesn't contradict your faith, you may worship Lord Vishnu. If you do so, make sure to sing Vishnu Sahasranamam. You can also chant Guru Mantra 108 or 28 times a day. On every Purnima, Satyanarayan Katha while fasting. You can wear a topaz ring on your index finger. However, make sure that you wear it first on a Thursday. Another powerful remedy would also be putting butter oil on Shivlinga.

If you already have a strong Jupiter placement, never try to make it stronger; doing so could result in horrific adverse results. If you want, you can aim to achieve balance instead.

Jupiter is among the strongest planets in astrology. While it is generally a very benefic planet, characterized by its abundance and positive outcomes, a bad Jupiter zodiac placement can be destructive. This is especially true for Jupiter in the 12th house, as Jupiter debilitates in Capricorn. Luckily, if you have an unfavorable Jupiter placement, there are a few things that you can do to help remedy the situation.

Chapter 5: Finding Your Luck Part 1

Jupiter is the largest planet in the solar system, and it is made of hydrogen. It does not have a solid surface, and it derived its name from the Roman god. Jupiter affects the 1st, 2nd, 3rd, and 4th signs of the zodiac, namely Aries, Gemini, Taurus, and Cancer. This chapter discusses the effects of Jupiter when aligned with other signs of the zodiac. It talks about the positives as well as the negatives that can be a result of this alignment.

Jupiter in Aries or First House

Your personality is shaped in a big way by a planet that is in its first house. In other words, Jupiter will make you happy, and never underestimate your luck with Jupiter in Aries or in the first house. Aries means action, so it is vital to take some physical risks to increase your chances of achieving your aspirations. You need to act on your instincts; you will realize that you can never go wrong when trying something challenging.

While others shy from the competition, a Jupiter Aries soul thrives on it, allowing you to test your skills against others. If you want to gain insight into Jupiter in Aries, you should view Aries as a sign that tilts forward, thereby heralding new things. Jupiter usually brings about a burst of enthusiasm when it is in Aries. In other words, it helps you walk confidently in life, and your head will be leading as ruled by Aries.

When people walk, their body language will reflect their confidence as they appear to be optimistic in whatever they are doing. When Jupiter is in the first house, it means you are ready for everything that comes your way. The chances are high that you will take great risks when aiming to attain positive results from whatever course of action you decide to take. While risk-taking is good, there is a danger that you may start something more terrible than you can imagine when you leap before looking.

Jupiter as a Confidence Booster

However, when you take a risk, you should expect the outcome to go either way. With Jupiter in Aries, you feel optimistic when you start something new. If you are in a leadership position, you are ready to get busy and going. If you are used to starting things the same way, nothing will be new, and you will be confident that you will achieve your desired goals. For instance, if you are an educator, you come across new faces in every class, but you are ready to deliver.

Specific factors within the astrological make-up are what keeps you going. Some people may run out of steam, but compared to the rest of the planets, you become committed to completing what you have started. In other words, Jupiter is a confidence booster, and it compels you to complete your projects. Discipline is a critical element that must prevail in whatever you do if you want to attain your goals.

Additionally, Jupiter makes you feel that you are on the right path, and you thrive when you discover your inner self. Aries is the sign of warriors, and you are most likely to thrive when you are involved in physical competition. However, when you are in a remote place, things may be tough for you. Many people are invigorated by bustling places. You can experience several things in a single day. Travelling can help you test yourself.

Jupiter in the First House (or Aries) means that you create a first impression among the people you meet. Aries is a sign that requires self-reflection if you are selfish or bossy. It will take a lot of confidence to make different things happen. Since Aries is the first sign of the zodiac, you have a gift of acting and taking creative risks. You can encourage others to be active when they observe you in action.

You will become a cheerleader for other people when you see them going through challenging times. However, if your current setup does not challenge you, you will likely pick fights and become argumentative. You need to look for new experiences to avoid this danger.

Jupiter in Taurus

Of all the planets, Jupiter is believed to be the luckiest. It represents optimism, growth, expansion, and fortune. The planet is about expanding our minds as well as wealth. When Jupiter aligns with Taurus, a unique combination is created. While Jupiter is ready to expand, Taurus is there to slow things to a desirable pace and make them realistic. While Taurus denotes patience, you do not necessarily need to be discouraged by the slow pace of different activities. If you use the alignment of Jupiter and Taurus well, you can turn your dreams into attainable goals.

What It Means When Jupiter Is in Taurus

Spirituality is part of our everyday lives, but it is easily lost due to many reasons. Jupiter symbolizes wisdom and encourages deep thinking, whereas Taurus is the most unmoving sign of the zodiac. When the two come together, we realize that we already have the answers we always seek. However, we get the opportunity to eliminate distractions and apply the wisdom that is often lying dormant in our minds.

If you have a long-term goal, Jupiter in Taurus presents the opportunity to make a positive movement toward its attainment. During this time, we are energized to take practical measures to work toward achieving dreams that we have always wanted. You also get the chance to check different things on your priority list one by one until you get the desired result of something you are working toward.

When you are working toward achieving your goal, Jupiter provides the desire for growth, while Taurus offers patience. Combining these two forces will drive us to trust the process where we can reach a tangible and clear level of success. When Jupiter is in Taurus, life can be prosperous. Jupiter represents fortune and good luck, while Taurus symbolizes wealth and money. This cosmic relationship can bring about handsome financial rewards. When Jupiter is in Taurus, this is a good period when you can look into your financial situation and find some growth opportunities.

Taurus is a sign that often enjoys good things and rarely gets the opportunity to say no. It is your responsibility to be careful about your impulses and become patient during the transition period. Jupiter is concerned about new opportunities, idealism, and forward-thinking. When Jupiter moves backward during the retrograde cycle, we get the pulse to slow down and ask where we are heading. During this same period, we find ourselves considering and re-evaluating whether we are working on appropriate things.

Negative Things to Check

We also tend to ask if we are moving in the right direction and check if we have the resources to achieve what we want. This is the time to consider if the results will bring happiness and fulfillment. While these are tough and negative questions, it is imperative to get the answers. You need to pause and refine your plans to be able to build a sustainable path before you decide to forge ahead. Taking big risks can be detrimental if you belong to Jupiter in Taurus. All you need to do is create a concrete goal in your mind and take your time to achieve them. Patience and determination are necessary to achieve success in your endeavor.

With goodwill on your side, you have financial luck and are constantly analyzing your situation and checking for opportunities to make more money. If you are generous, you will realize that good fortune will also come back your way. You should surround yourself with the things that you desire to have in your life. The following are traits of Jupiter in Taurus:

- Determined
- Sensual
- Charitable
- Realistic
- Patient
- Sensible
- Stable
- Materialistic

With these traits, you are destined to reach greater heights and attain your desired goals.

Jupiter in Gemini

If you have Jupiter in Gemini, it has a great impact on love, career, luck, and others. Your personality is reflected by the following positive keywords: social, creative, knowledgeable, fast-paced, and stimulating.

Knowledgeable

Gemini loves mental stimulation and encourages knowledge development. Jupiter in Gemini can be irrational, so they tend to rely on social skills to bring back their luck.

Creative

Creativity is related to knowledge expansion, and it helps us look for better ways to achieve whatever we want. When used properly, creativity can help you reach dizzy heights in whatever you want.

Witty

With Jupiter in Gemini, everything is focused on good fortune, travel, and values. If you have Jupiter in Gemini, you can use your wit to maintain a positive attitude. This positivity helps you attract a lot of opportunities in your life.

Social

Gemini needs other individuals to live as social creatures, and this will always ground them to reality. You need to exercise patience with your Jupiter in Gemini spouse. It usually takes time to acknowledge other people's positions. However, once you grab their attention, they are willing to transfer their happiness to you.

Jupiter in Gemini: Positive Traits

When you are Jupiter in Gemini, you are always looking for ways to identify new opportunities and gain more knowledge. This type of search opens new possibilities for you, and traveling helps you gain exposure to opportunities that can offer better rewards in your life. The Jupiter in Gemini also loves to interact with different people, which helps them get out of many difficult situations. They are also knowledgeable about different topics.

Jupiter in Gemini: Negative Traits

The negative keywords associated with Jupiter in Gemini are irrational, critical, overburdened, and harsh. Therefore, the natal chart indicates that the individuals belonging to this category must choose specific risks carefully. In most cases, they feel that they should take every challenge but end up being overburdened with a lot of work. As a result, they become flighty when they are overwhelmed by several tasks.

The Jupiter in Gemini rarely capitulates when they are in an argument with others. They are critical, and their sharp tongue often lands them in trouble. However, they slow down at times to focus on other people. The challenge is that they spend little time on others which can make their loved ones feel neglected.

As you can see, Jupiter in Gemini is interested in spreading information to other members of society. These people always have interesting stories to share in developing their wisdom. This will help them to have good friends and families. Wherever they go, they will find themselves expanding their horizons and exploring new things.

Jupiter in Cancer

Jupiter exhibits its maximum potential when it is in Cancer. When Jupiter is aligned with Cancer on the natal chart, it offers good protection, fortune, and prosperity. It is a social planet that influences all generations of people. The influence of Jupiter should be viewed in the house of the natal chart about other planets.

People born with Jupiter in Cancer exhibit specific characteristics they possess and are discussed in detail in this section. For instance, the chances of reaping the rewards are high, and the planet also ensures financial stability, which is everyone's aspiration. People will have no financial challenges when this planet is positioned well.

Jupiter in Cancer: Men

Strong bonds with their families characterize Males with Jupiter in Cancer, and they also love to spend time with them. These people love to see others happy, especially the ones they care a lot about. The other thing is that the men are happy about their traditions, and they identify with them. When it comes to helping others, they feel happy to render free services. Interestingly, many men who belong to this group like to join the hotel and catering industry, offering food preparation services for other people. In most cases, the guys work from home, getting financial security in whatever they do.

Jupiter in Cancer: Woman

The women belonging to this group are attentive, and they bond well with their families and their loved ones. They love to spend time with their families and loved ones. Females in this group can work well with family members in ventures started by their ancestors and are proud of their roots. These ladies are excellent cooks, and they do what they love most when it comes to preparing different dishes. As a result, they often choose careers in the restaurant and hotel industries where they can do what they love without any hindrances.

Another thing about women in this category is that they do not like to waste money. They are economical and also concerned about generating positive results in whatever they are doing. They get substantial revenue in their business. More importantly, the women are generous, and they love other people. They believe in sharing with others to get inner satisfaction.

Good Traits

The people in the Jupiter of Cancer are helpful, generous, and want to help others achieve their desired goals. These individuals have outgoing personalities, and they often want to pursue their careers in restaurants and hotels where they serve other people food and beverages. Some individuals in this group are in real estate, and they believe in working to gain financial independence. When they venture into these areas, they come across excellent opportunities that offer them handsome financial rewards. In most cases, they like to invest in family businesses to assert their allegiances to their roots.

Individuals who belong to Jupiter in Cancer are optimistic, and they believe in working hard and saving money to enjoy their desired goals. By paying attention to different people, they learn many things that can help them improve their businesses. They also prefer to live in big homes where they share everything with their loved ones. Home is a critical element for the people in this group since they derive mental stability and comfort from living with others. They do not hesitate to help other people in need where possible.

Bad Traits

Jupiter in Cancer is often viewed in a positive light, and it does not reflect bad traits. However, the bad placement of Jupiter on someone's natal chart can lead to financial misfortune. You can also struggle to attain your financial goals. Individuals who wrongly place themselves where they do not belong often experience limited financial fortunes and opportunities.

General Information

As you have observed from the detailed description of Jupiter in Cancer, individuals like to venture into the tourism, hospitality, and recreation industries. These industries allow them to interact with different people to fulfill their personalities. For instance, working in taverns, bars, and restaurants can be satisfying to individuals with outgoing personalities. These individuals are also nurturing, and they want to see others prosper in their lives.

As the largest planet, Jupiter spends a year in each zodiac sign. It influences generations that are born within that period of the year. When different signs of the zodiac are aligned with Jupiter, different traits and relationships are often portrayed. Many people often find inspiration from these traits, and they guide them through different situations.

Chapter 6: Finding Your Luck Part 2

This chapter discusses the effect of Jupiter in Leo, Virgo, Libra, and Scorpio signs. It also highlights the positives that come from these relationships, as well as any potential negatives. As you go through this chapter, you will gain insight into personality traits symbolized by these signs.

Jupiter in Leo

If you are Jupiter in Leo in the natal chart, you will get a lot of attention due to your commitment to getting brighter, bigger, and courageous. When you desire to achieve something, you want to make everyone know your intention, hence the attention you draw. In short, Jupiter in Leo represents people who are joyful, generous, and proud.

How Jupiter in Leo Impacts Personality

The people with Jupiter in Leo have sensitive egos, and they often express them openly for everyone to see. These people are outgoing and charismatic, and they tend to attract many people since they are highly opinionated. When they talk, many individuals will be interested in listening to what they have to say. This is not usually possible with other people who seem to be reserved. However, these Jupiter Leos need to be wise and persuasive if they want everyone to appreciate them.

Jupiter represents generosity, while Leo symbolizes confidence. Therefore, it is not surprising that individuals born with Jupiter in Leo are proud, and they do not easily believe that they may be mistaken. When they start to influence other people, they grow through leveraging their confidence and strength. They can gain confidence by pretending to know what they are doing. These people gain confidence depending on the attention they get. They are likely to make good teachers and politicians due to the desire to grab other people's attention.

Charisma

Jupiter Leos are charismatic, and they always wish to use their creativity to prove their capability in different things. They want to celebrate their ideas while convincing others to tow their line of reasoning. Jupiter offers a lot of hope which makes the Leos capable of appealing to the emotional interests of many people. They are also proud of their successes which they want to share with others. A high position in society means a lot to their egos.

Jupiter in Leo Men

The Jupiter in Leo males want to be in control and lead others. However, they respect the opinions of others in a group. Leos are confident and optimistic in whatever they do. They are determined to achieve goals that will make everyone happy. Men with Jupiter in Leo are rational, practical, and calm in whatever they do. If you want to win their favor, you only need to praise them for their exceptional leadership qualities. When they are appreciated, they will set high standards for everyone.

Jupiter in Leo Women

The main aspect about Jupiter Leo women is that they are often stubborn, and they do not want to learn from others. They are overconfident and arrogant at times and end up losing focus on essential things in life. However, she makes a loyal mother, although she's shy about her feminist tendencies. Jupiter will keep her determined to succeed, and she prioritizes her family and work.

Positives

The Jupiter Leos do everything wholeheartedly to ensure they attain the desired results. When you commit yourself to something, the chances are high that you will achieve your goals. Additionally, these persons are affectionate and loyal to their loved ones. They are always ready to stand by the individuals they love most. These people are also generous, and they often pay attention to others at the expense of their own needs. They spend a lot of energy and effort to make others happy.

Optimism is another critical element that motivates these individuals to be kindhearted and willing to help others. Their principles are based on a strong work ethic and integrity that help them to attract love. They will succeed in anything because they are interested in getting the best out of their goodwill. Due to their creativity, careers in the entertainment industry are most appropriate. They will shine in drama and show off their status and express themselves how they want.

Negatives

Individuals belonging to Jupiter in Leo often have a fragile ego, and they may not accept criticism. As a result, they end up being susceptible to moodiness which can affect their relationships with others. When one is moody, the element of objectivity is often lost, and it may be difficult for such people to learn from others. Additionally, appreciating other people can also be problematic when one is self-centered. These individuals can also become dangerous and fierce if someone tries to betray them.

Jupiter in Virgo

When Jupiter is in Virgo, different things happen, affecting an individual's personality in many ways. While Jupiter wants to make noise, Virgo prefers to be humble. As a result, Jupiter in Virgo is a moment when we must focus on paying attention to our jobs and doing something right. There is no need to seek approval from other people in what you are doing. Instead, you should aim to achieve your goals. Their faith is more practical when Jupiter is in Virgo. Productivity and efficiency are areas that are likely to expand during this transitional period.

Positives

Jupiter helps us be idealistic, energized, and forward-thinking, but we are often forced to pause and take our time when the big planet is in retrograde. This is the time you should do some introspection. You also get the opportunity to self-reflect to see if you are doing good things to others since it is the right thing to do. Doing positive things to other people makes you feel satisfied and happy.

Another positive aspect about Virgo is that it helps us seek more details and increases our intelligence and sharpness. When you face a particular situation, you try to look for critical information that will help you overcome the problem. Jupiter also increases our optimism about the different things we are doing to increase the chances of obtaining our goals. We gain an understanding of how various things function during this transition.

Negatives

It may be harder to focus when Jupiter is in Virgo, and this can impact performance. The challenge is that we often find ourselves being driven in different directions, impacting our commitment to attaining goals. Jupiter will be concerned about goal attainment, but Virgo can resist it, making it challenging to create a balance towards goal achievement. The other issue is that the individuals can be judgmental.

Traits of People Born With Jupiter in Virgo

If you are born with Jupiter in Virgo, you belong to a group of nurturing people who are also caregivers. You will find joy in helping others and taking care of the needy. Many people will appreciate your help, and they view your valuable assistance as a favor. However, this is also a gift if you can go out of your way just to help others. Few people can do that, so you must view yourself as blessed.

Naturally, you are a hard worker who is self-reliant and also interested in staying balanced. Jupiter's desire for growth and Virgo's demand for details will keep your mind active and drive productivity. In whatever you are doing, you certainly need some form of mental stimulation to keep you going. This mental stimulation can be beneficial to you and other people in your life, but you should remember that it can also be exhausting. Remember that overworking can be stressful, so you need to be smart to achieve the best goals in your specific field.

Another crucial aspect that you should know is that competition isn't everything. Most people born when Jupiter was in Virgo are motivated by the desire to achieve their set goals and help others in different ways. Many people get their energy from the belief that what goes around comes around. In other words, they believe in happy returns in whatever they are doing.

Another important element about your traits is that you view yourself as perfect, and you often wonder why other individuals fail to imitate you. You may be judgmental, but it is vital to be open-minded when dealing with others. A more carefree attitude will make you happier.

The following are the traits of people who were born when Jupiter was in Virgo:

- Intelligent
- Rational
- Perfectionist
- Cautious
- Attention to detail
- Critical
- Discerning

When you are in this category, you possess the power to overcome different challenges in life.

Jupiter in Libra

Libra is the only sign represented by scales and something that does not symbolize a living creature. However, this does not necessarily mean that all people born when Jupiter was in Libra lack heart. You favor fairness, you are the most objective, and you also possess the power to open up to new relationships. You feel satisfied by doing something to your community to help other people.

Positives of Jupiter in Libra: Women

When Jupiter is in Libra, women are more energized, and they are interested in strengthening their relationships with other people regardless of where they come from. Your desire to empathize with others grows during this period, allowing you to be closer to the people you love. You are highly motivated to provide new ideas to other people, and you find fulfillment in ensuring that fairness prevails.

Another important thing that you can freely discuss with your loved ones is the inequalities in your relationships. You can also benefit from airing your views without fear or favor since this is your time to be objective in a relationship. You should also use this opportunity to take necessary measures that can help you reach your destination.

Jupiter in Libra Men

The males with Jupiter in Libra are concerned about ensuring that everyone feels equal, including women at home and in the workplace. Some men develop strong ties to women to the extent of being labeled feminists. Jupiter makes these men generous, and they are also interested in fairness. Mutual trust is the basis for the growth and development of a perfect relationship. It is important for the parties concerned to show gratitude for the favor portrayed by the Libras.

Traits that Determine Love in Jupiter and Libra

Jupiter and Libra will guide you in love toward getting a faithful partner. Jupiter acts as the largest planet of vision, while Libra weighs the advantages and disadvantages in a relationship. When Jupiter is in Libra, you will realize that you will be open to new relationships that work in your favor. In addition, you also get the power to terminate bad relationships that have been working against you.

Another element is that you will get the power to move on with your life when Jupiter gives you strength. You are reminded of the positives surrounding you and your real identity. You also get the assurance that you have an inner strength that you may not be aware of. You can use this strength to your advantage and be empathetic when dealing with other people. You feel the suffering of other people and show a strong desire to help.

Men who were born when Jupiter was in Libra want to make sure that everyone feels that they are equal. They can go out of their way to ensure that the people around them feel comfortable. Males belonging to this category are also fair and objective. You seek to understand the situation first before you jump to conclusions. Jupiter in Libra shows that an individual is fair, reliable, and honest. You have someone to lean on if they are closer to you.

Jupiter in Scorpio

Jupiter in Scorpio says different things about astrology and the personality traits of people born during this period. Even though Scorpio is dark and forceful energy, it represents bright energy if Jupiter is in Scorpio. When you combine these two, they produce a powerful magician who can solve complex issues. In astrology, Jupiter is viewed as a social planet that spends about 12 months in each zodiac sign. As a result, many interpretations are assigned to the events and circumstances during that specific year. Therefore, Jupiter returns to Scorpio after 12 years, and the world is believed to go into a protective mode.

Pluto rules when Jupiter is in Scorpio, and different experiences are interpreted through the narrative of self-interest and self-preservation. If you are born during this period, you are likely to be more protective than most people. When Jupiter is in Scorpio in the natal chart, it means the individuals born during this season are intense, decisive, and have willpower and commitment. They also have the emotional strength and always try to get to the bottom of the situation.

People who are born when Jupiter is in Scorpio believe that character is more crucial than status. As a result, they strive to build a strong character that defines their personality rather than focusing on elements based on social status. These individuals are risk-takers, and they are interested in accomplishing challenging goals. As risk-taker, they're not afraid of undertaking challenging tasks since they believe in perseverance and hard work.

The other important element about people born when Jupiter is in Scorpio is that they are diligent problem solvers. They are willing to solve different challenges, and they also like to help people realize their goals. When faced with a problem, they utilize all the opportunities available to get a solution. As a result, they can earn or gain enormous wealth since they are self-reliant and resilient. Achieving your goals can be difficult if you lack the commitment to whatever you are doing.

The people born when Jupiter was in Scorpio also have a keen interest in the metaphysical and occult. These often have a connection with the spiritual world, where matters of life and death are often dealt with in detail. The individuals involved are interested in researching different things related to taboos, mysteries, evil, and other hidden things. As you have observed, these people are interested in solving even challenging life puzzles. If you belong to this category, you are interested in exploring the subconscious to find meaning in issues that are often viewed as complex. The quest to solve problems and find answers to hidden aspects of life drives many people in this group to dedicate their time to conducting research.

Jupiter in Scorpio and Luck

Jupiter in Scorpio represents good luck in different financial situations, and you can also make lucky guesses. You are likely to be well respected in a particular area ruled by Scorpio in the natal chart. The individuals involved use their knowledge, inner strength, and courage to prosper. These are the basic tenets to achieve your desired goals in life.

Negative Traits

Those born when Jupiter was in Scorpio can be excessively possessive, obsessive, secretive, and self-protective. The other negative aspect is that Jupiter in Scorpio can lead to elements of high risk-taking or gambling. Some individuals can even develop toxic personalities that affect not only themselves but others.

Positive Traits

Jupiter wants you to be happy and thrive in whatever you do, while Scorpio is concerned about ensuring that you become stronger to survive. While Jupiter and Scorpio appear like an odd combination, they can create potent energy that provides the people with Scorpio with the power to thrive, survive, and be happy.

As you can observe, Jupiter is the largest planet, and it spends 12 months on each sign in the natal chart. Various interpretations of events that happen in the real world are often attached to different interpretations. In this chapter, you have learned different aspects about Jupiter when it is in various signs.

Chapter 7: Finding Your Luck Part 3

As Jupiter moves through all the planets, they are personified, as you will have observed in the previous chapters. This chapter discusses the effect of Jupiter on the signs that involve Sagittarius, Capricorn, Aquarius, and Pisces. It also talks of positives and potential negatives likely to happen when Jupiter goes through these signs in the natal chart.

Jupiter in Sagittarius

When you were born with Jupiter in Sagittarius, your life is full of love, and you are destined to meet loving people as you travel across the globe. While traveling and mingling with people from various cultural backgrounds, you will build strong relationships with them. You will be more interested in building friendships with different people and understanding their culture, making you a sociable human being.

Personality Traits

If you were born with Jupiter in Sagittarius, you are curious to know different things. You are mainly interested in religion, philosophy, and spirituality. The concepts of spirituality and religion are usually controversial since they interpret various things in different ways. In other words, people who belong to different religions have different world views of the same thing. While people attach different connotations to the same thing, and if your sign on the natal chart is Sagittarius, you tend to be inquisitive. You try to get answers to various things instead of blindly accepting everything.

Because of their curious attitudes, persons born in Sagittarius are entrepreneurs with great ideas and visions. These individuals are visionaries who are willing to take serious leaps in their lives to pursue better-paying opportunities. While you can be a visionary, the chances are high that you can experience some challenges in becoming a project manager. You need to slow down and evaluate the situation to make informed decisions.

Positives

People who belong to the Sagittarius sign possess faith and positive energy that drive them to work hard until they attain their desired goals. The Sagittarians boast of traits that help them overcome different situations they can encounter in their lives. These individuals are not scared of facing challenges. Nothing is free; you have to work hard. This is true of people born with Jupiter in Sagittarius. Self-confidence is a powerful trait that you should possess if you want to achieve all your goals in life.

Negatives

While the people born with Jupiter in Sagittarius are visionaries and entrepreneurs, they are overconfident at times. As a result, they fail to differentiate a gamble from a calculated risk. As a result, they end up failing to attain the desired goals.

If you decide to start a business, overconfidence can be detrimental at times if you fail to understand the implications involved in what you are doing. Another issue is that overconfident people often believe in their views and no one else's. This is dangerous since the stance you take can compromise the outcome of the project you are working on.

Undermining teamwork is suicidal since it may be difficult to achieve all your goals without help from other people. Many people only learn that teamwork is vital after a few tough lessons, especially when undertaking a large project. Your positive energy will also contribute to the team's performance. It is essential to learn that self-centeredness is not a good thing when working with other people. Sharing ideas and knowledge can go a long way in encouraging collective decisions.

However, besides these negatives, the movement of Jupiter into Sagittarius is great news for everyone. Jupiter symbolizes positive growth and bravery. The universe will ultimately reward you for your fearlessness. You need to embrace your courage to achieve whatever you desire in life. You may also experience *eureka moments* in your life as you discover many things that can foster a positive romantic life. You are also likely to experience radical changes like new job prospects and other life-altering moments. Great works will lead to major milestones. In short, Jupiter encourages life-changing development and growth.

Jupiter in Capricorn

The people born with Jupiter in Capricorn are high achievers, and their achievements determine their happiness. Nothing will stop you until you get to the top whenever you choose to raise the bar higher. You need a clear structure and vision that will guide you to overcome challenging scenarios that you may encounter. You may enjoy working independently, but you will also realize that collective action is vital if you aim to achieve a mutual goal. While you may be hesitant to pursue other things, you will understand that failure can be a game-changer in your life. It helps you devise new strategies that can help you achieve long-term growth.

Personality

The value system of the people born with Jupiter in Capricorn is based on hard work and self-determination. Of all the zodiac signs, Jupiter in Capricorn is probably the most disciplined. Jupiter brings good fortune to people who put effort into different things, and they are often rewarded for their integrity and honesty. Through discipline and dedication, you are bound to realize your goals since nothing can stop you.

Jupiter in Capricorn is systematic, and it is also used to assess ideology and values. These were developed over time and represent good fortune and luck to different people. Another crucial element about the Capricorn sign is that it offers calculated decisions that provide people with wisdom and experience. The chances of obtaining positive results will be high if you follow tried and tested methods to pursue your project.

Positive Traits

Jupiter in Capricorn offers endless career opportunities that help you climb the corporate ladder in any job you hold. Capricorn stars bring you fortune and luck in your job. Stability and optimism are other traits that define Capricorn in Jupiter people. When you are stable and optimistic, you believe that the sky's the limit and everything is possible. This belief system motivates you to aim for higher things in life. As long as you believe that everything is possible, you can realize all the goals that you have set.

Patience and endurance are other positive traits of Jupiter in Capricorn people. While many people expect quick results in different things they do, it is not always the case. If you lack patience, you may not be able to achieve the goals you set. Excellent things do not come easily in life since you need to endure the trials and tribulations you are likely to encounter. When the going gets tough, you should never look back if you want to reach your destination. The symbol for Capricorn is a mountain goat that presses on no matter how bad the terrain is or how harsh the conditions are. They endure anything that comes their way.

Capricorn people are diplomatic, and they approach different issues with caution and diligence. They first get vital information that helps them to navigate different situations. The tenacity of these individuals is what keeps them successful. They are cautious when dealing with new opportunities. While they can lose out on bigger rewards by avoiding bigger risks, the good thing is that they rarely fail.

Negative Traits

The notable weakness of Jupiter in Capricorn is their quest for more power. The Jupiter in Capricorn people want status, and they want to control different things and other people. They believe they are better than others, and this is the primary source of their selfishness. The bad part about selfish behavior is that it drives these individuals astray, and they may fail to achieve their goals. Jupiter with Capricorn also consists of corrupt, demanding, and greedy people. They are more concerned about their ends, and they prioritize material possessions over pertinent issues in life.

Uncontrolled greed often leads to competition that can end up taking away strong ethics. To maintain logical minds, there is a need to create a fine balance that also helps maintain their fortunes. However, Jupiter in Capricorn people stand out because they can plan for the future and have exceptional knowledge about different things.

Jupiter in Aquarius

The Aquarius sign in the zodiac says a lot about people who were born during this period. As Jupiter transits through Aquarius, it allows us to look outside the confines of individual life to view the entire world. It encourages people to think outside the box and helps us realize that each person is important in life. Everyone has an important role in life since we constitute a small fraction of the greater community.

Personality Traits Jupiter in Aquarius People

When Jupiter is in Aquarius, different things that define our personalities happen. This sign is based on idealism which helps people see what is wrong in the world around them and develop innovative and unique methods to change things. Aquarius in Jupiter gives us the ability to do things differently to create an ideal future. It is easier for us to consider other people's needs in society, regions, nations, and the world at large.

Jupiter in Aquarius provides optimism for the future regardless of how bad things may appear at the present moment. The ideas and solutions we have can help us create a better tomorrow. This will help us see opportunities instead of limitations and differences. Additionally, Jupiter in

Aquarius helps us to connect easily with other people who share the same vision as we do. It becomes easier to join forces to implement the changes that should be made to improve our lives.

Jupiter encourages learning, and it allows us to acquire knowledge from others. By listening to other people, we learn different things about the world around us. Respect for other people's opinions is critical to promoting the exchange of knowledge. When you exchange your ideas with other people, you will gain insight into different things. This also helps you treat other people with respect if you find someone willing to listen to your views.

Therefore, if you were born with Jupiter in Aquarius, you have the freedom to do as you wish. You stand out as an intelligent person who is also an innovator, and you use your creative mind to appeal to the emotional interests of many people. Aquarius people are also persuasive when they communicate with others. If you belong to this group, you can think outside the box, and others do not believe in the existence of such a thing. This gives you the autonomy to fully control your destiny.

However, you need to realize the significance of numbers or teamwork. If you are aligned with people who share the same views as you, you are likely to pull your ideas together to achieve greater things. You will be focused on the bigger picture due to your mental prowess. The other characteristic of these people is that they fight for other individuals' rights. As a compassionate person, you feel that humanity should not suffer when you are there. Every person has the right to be heard and not oppressed by anyone.

Positive Traits of Jupiter in Aquarius

People born when Jupiter was in Aquarius are regarded as intelligent, and they can collaborate with others to solve different problems. These individuals are idealistic, broad-minded, and progressive at the same time. Great minds are liberated and think independently; these traits help them be more focused on specific issues in life. Another positive element is that Jupiter in Aquarius people are inclusive, and they can also work well with different people.

Negative Traits

The main challenge with Jupiter in Aquarius people is that they have a strong desire to be right all the time. As a result, there is a high probability that they may be intolerant to other people if they have differing viewpoints. It is vital to remember that we need to look further than our personal preferences. We need to ensure the well-being of other people since we belong to one broad category commonly referred to as humanity. Individualism can distract other people from focusing on pertinent issues in life.

Jupiter in Pisces Personality Traits

Pisces is the final sign out of twelve in the Zodiac. The most notable trait about Jupiter in Pisces people is that they display the most maturity out of all the signs. A watery fish symbolizes this sign. Meditation plays a crucial role in helping people understand matters of the spirit and their conscience. You appreciate the good things about yourself when you spend more time meditating. However, you also love other people and are willing to listen to their concerns.

Jupiter encourages people to keep a positive attitude to find fulfillment and love in whatever they are doing. You should not suffer in isolation or affect other people with your harsh words.

Instead, you are born with unique qualities of open-mindedness. This will help you find lasting love as a result of your exceptional reasoning.

The following are the popular facts concerning Jupiter in Pisces:

1. Jupiter in Pisces encourages individuals to have positive attitudes toward their lives. If you are always negative about different things in life, you may fail to achieve your desired goals. Instead, optimism encourages you to pursue whatever dream comes your way and execute your plans without fear. You will gain self-confidence if you believe that you can achieve whatever you want in life.

2. You tend to be open-minded and approach different things in your life with objectivity. You are willing to explore and discover new things in life and generate knowledge to help you and others.

3. Another personality trait of Jupiter Pisces people is that some do not want to conform to society and do not believe in stereotypes of women. They have free spirits and believe in their views, and do the things they feel are good.

4. Men are not easy to read, and some of them are regarded as challenging. They keep their cards guarded and take time to reflect on the best way to approach life. However, this does not necessarily mean that they are hiding something.

5. The combination of Jupiter in Pisces comprises people who often like to ask tough questions. The aim is not to stir any trouble but to probe answers that provide clear meanings to different things. Pisces in Jupiter can be a game-changer in life since it helps many people discover new knowledge.

Pisces in Jupiter in love sets the stage for lasting love in your life. If you listen to Jupiter, you will find love in your life and feel fulfilled when you show affection to your loved ones. Never lose hope in your life since everything will be alright at some point. The partners who understand what you want in life are the best love prospects in your life. When you ask for privacy, any person who may want to force matters is not the right person for you.

Whatever your religious upbringing or cultural background, nothing can break you down. The hope you get from Jupiter in Pisces will keep you alive and strong to fulfill all your aspirations. However, your worst elements in love are the partners who shun your quest for universal truth in different things. You should find a person who can always stand by and also respects your instincts. Overall, Jupiter in Pisces brings hope, and you need not fear the unseen.

This chapter highlighted the meanings often attached to people who belong to different signs of the zodiac. Depending on your sign, many things can be attached to your personality, and some of them might be true.

Chapter 8: Jupiter and Your Partner

Jupiter is generally referred to as the ruler of happiness. Jupiter is associated with optimism, luck, tolerance, and justice. However, that's not all. Jupiter also rules over your overall worldview and life philosophy. When it comes to love, Jupiter can have a significant effect on your relationship. Whether you will have a harmonious marriage or get along with your partner depends on the placement of Jupiter in your partner's house.

Similarly, your Jupiter can also affect your partner. Jupiter can have a powerful effect on your marriage, even more than Venus. Jupiter can even determine whether you will get along with the other person or not. If your Jupiter's are compatible, you may be able to lead a harmonious partnership and vice versa. If your Jupiter's get along, then even after you've had a clash with your partner, you will be able to make up for it at the end of the day. But, if your Jupiter's do not get along, then no matter how much you try, you will never be able to make it work.

Let's find out how the placement of Jupiter in your partner's house can affect your relationship.

Jupiter in the First House

If your partner's Jupiter is located in your partner's first house, then they are probably prone to sudden outbursts of enthusiasm. People with Jupiter in their first house are the optimistic ones in life who always have their heads up high and are ready for anything that life throws their way. If you like to travel and have a deep love for adventure, you probably have Jupiter in Aries. As a person with Jupiter in your first house, you feel your best at the beginning of things. You're the torchbearers of revolutions. You're at your best when you're challenged; you love living on the edge! We all have positive and negative traits. You might want to look at your partner's traits to understand them better and make sense of how to balance things when it gets difficult.

Positive Traits

- With Jupiter in your first house, you radiate confidence. You tend to leave a lasting first impression on people because of this trait.

- You're the go-getter, the Initiator of things.

- You're a natural leader with the ability to act quickly in difficult situations

- You're the courageous one who can be bold and take creative risks

- Good at handling emergencies

Negative Traits

- As a leader and someone so passionate about their work, you can come off as bossy or even selfish

- You have a strong sense of self, but this can cause you trouble. As you have a firm belief in your decisions and capabilities, it can make you argumentative and may lead to heated arguments.

- Being a hard-working risk taker, you can easily burn out. It is important to take a break and explore the wild.

Jupiter in the Second House

If money just seems to flow easily to you then, Jupiter might be in your second house. You have an accurate judgment when it comes to dealing with financial matters. Jupiter in the second house enhances your income. With Jupiter in your second house, you will have lifelong financial stability. You will make all the right money moves.

Additionally, you will also have an influential personality. You will be the life and soul of the party, with hundreds of contacts. No matter where you go, you're able to make friends easily. You will be successful in terms of money, power, and social life. You will succeed in these areas of life without much effort. You'll have it so good that it would leave people wondering how you do it! Like any other sign, you have some positive and some negative aspects. Let's take a look at them to help you understand you or your partner better.

Positive Traits

- Money comes easily to you
- You're successful and have all the power, money, and friends
- You're a good leader and an authority figure
- Amazing at analyzing financial matters and handling money
- Generous when it comes to giving to others

Negative Traits

- You can over-indulge in comforts and luxuries
- People of this Jupiter placement tend to be materialistic
- May have to deal with health issues

Jupiter in Third House

If your Jupiter is located in the third house, you're probably charming, open-minded, and talkative. People cannot seem to get enough of you, which may cause you to lead very busy social lives. You're the socialites of society. You have a love for sharing ideas and giving advice. Everyone comes to you for advice because you're just that good at communication and giving advice. You're the happy-go-lucky sort of person who is always optimistic and happy. You also do not like to show your feelings when sad to keep others happy. As a socialite, you may probably get to hear a lot of gossip. You need to use any information you receive wisely, or it can get you into trouble and strained relationships with others. You can speak and write better than other people do. You have a stunning business sense and know what moves to make! Let's take a look at the positive and negative effects of your Jupiter.

Positive Traits

- You're the optimistic type that can light up any room you enter

- You're always happy, and your happiness is contagious

- You're great at giving advice.

- You're remarkable at communication. It is easy for you to share your perspective and understand where the other person is coming from.

- You are practical and pragmatic

- Good business sense

Negative Traits

- You may repress your feelings to make others happy

- As a talkative person, you may end up saying things you shouldn't have said

- You might be a bit materialistic, and you may probably do worldly things. It may even make you seem selfish.

- If not kept in check, you can be conceited

Jupiter in the Fourth House

The placement of Jupiter in your fourth house can make you come off as charming, and you tend to attract like-minded people in your life. If you have Jupiter in your fourth house, then you're really lucky. It is possible that no matter what you do, things just tend to go in your favor. It is very likely (because of your amazing luck) that you attained wealth at a very early age. You are the generous type with a great love for your friends and family. You are the determined type who knows what you want, and you probably always get it. You're likely very good-looking, and you attract people like magnets. Your adoration for your parents and family is like no other. You like to shower them with presents and have deep respect for them. You have a liking for prosperity and happiness and will do anything to get it. As a partner, you long to make a beautiful, happy, and loving home. If you or your partner has Jupiter in this house, then having a happy home is extremely important to both of you. Let's have a look at the positive and negative traits of this Jupiter.

Positive Traits

- You're extremely generous and have a deep love for your family

- Making your house members happy is your priority

- You're a successful individual with a liking for money

- You tend to be spiritual, and that makes you inclined toward careers like astrology

- You're a good listener and peacekeeper

Negative Traits

- People of this Jupiter can be manipulative to get things their way.

- You can be over-emotional and sensitive, especially when it comes to familial relationships

- You do not like change and can sometimes seem inflexible

Jupiter in the Fifth House

If your Jupiter belongs to the fifth house, then you're probably a free-spirited creative soul who craves authenticity. You're always eager to get more from life and have a liking for love, friends, and sex. You're the brave type who is open-minded and loves to share your opinions about life with others. So much so that it can even overwhelm the people around you. If you're an inhabitant of this Jupiter, then you may have more than one partner. You enjoy variety, and it may remain so until you commit to someone or get married. You are probably interested in law and order. If you pursue a career in law, then you will probably succeed. You get along with children easily, and they may find a friend in you. Let's take a look at how this Jupiter affects your negative and positive traits.

Positive Traits

- You're an open-minded individual who can talk about anything
- You crave authenticity and are free-spirited
- Children love you and may look up to you
- You're humorous, and that's what people love about you
- You're amazing at art and love to create what makes you happy

Negative Traits

- You are pessimistic when it comes to life, and your pessimism can become an obstacle for you
- You tend to scrutinize a lot, and your speculation may cause you to lose precious time and opportunities
- You tend to become vain
- You tend to procrastinate when it comes to creating art

Jupiter in Sixth House

If you have Jupiter in the sixth house, you are probably an intelligent person who has a great love for knowledge. You're a kind-hearted soul who loves to help others and at the same time inspire them to be their best selves. You may have never had trouble finding jobs because of your intellect. You are also popular among colleagues because of your kind heart and soul. Because of your kind nature and peaceful personality, you may not have many enemies. You tend to get along with everyone pretty well and bring harmony with you wherever you go. You have a deep desire for work, and you center your life upon work.

Moreover, you derive your sense of self and gratification from your work, making you more work-oriented. Your love for your job makes you attract money and also makes you a great colleague. You have the power to make stressful situations better by cracking a joke or two and making light of situations. Let's take a look at the positive and negative traits of this Jupiter and see how they affect you or your partner.

Positive Traits

- You're good at what you do, and that's what makes you a favorite among your colleagues

- You have a positive attitude towards others.

- You tend to see the best in people and inspire them to improve

- You believe in treating everyone with respect, which makes you a great human being to be around

- You can make light of difficult situations

Negative Traits

- You're not good at taking criticism; you take it to heart even when it's coming from a good place.

- You see the good in everyone, but it causes you to be naive.

- You are controlling and may dismiss someone for not liking what you like

- Your high standards can cause you to expect a lot from others and yourself

Jupiter in the Seventh House

If you have Jupiter in the seventh house, you're probably a very generous person and are also more successful than your parents. You're an extremely fortunate person, and you always get it your way no matter what you get into. Your charm can turn anyone into a fan. With Jupiter in your seventh house, you may be living in a place far from home and have a lover from a completely different culture and heritage. You may have met the love of your life as people with this Jupiter tend to have a very happy married life. As a good negotiator, you can bring people together and turn enemies into friends. Let's see what positive and negative traits to expect in yourself or your partner with this Jupiter.

Positive Traits

- You're an extremely generous person and believe in sharing your success with other people

- You are a successful and lucky individual

- You tend to have a happy and blissful married life

- Your charming and harmonious personality can attract anyone!

Negative Traits

- People of this Jupiter may have issues with fidelity

- You may have trouble showing affection and sympathy to your partner

Jupiter in the Eighth House

If you have Jupiter in the Eighth House, you possess an analytical personality that likes to strategize everything before diving into things headfirst. You're the kind of person who seeks pleasure in solving mysteries and complex puzzles that seem impossible to solve. You like to dissect and interrogate things until you get to the root cause of it. You're also a friendly person who likes to inspire people to seek pleasure in all walks of life. Your Jupiter is located in the eighth house, which means you will have an expansive sex life. So, that's an aspect you'll likely enjoy. You're also a very loyal friend. Let's see what positive and negative traits to expect in yourself or your partner with this Jupiter.

Positive Traits

- You're great at analyzing complex situations and solving them
- You're a great and loyal friend
- You are likely to be rich and successful
- You have a positive attitude and can heal quickly from emotional problems

Negative Traits

- You may have issues with fidelity
- May be unable to have a connection with people
- May repress your problems

Jupiter in the Ninth

If you possess Jupiter in the ninth house, then you're probably the wisest person in your circle. You like to stay relaxed and not worry about things that don't matter. You need to express yourself and be your true unapologetic self. You're an adventurer and like to travel and learn about everything you come across. You have great luck, and you believe in genuinely enjoying life. If your partner has their Jupiter in the ninth house, they probably like to seek knowledge wherever they go. People with this Jupiter like to get educated at all ages and times. Their love for knowledge sets them apart from the lot. Let's take a look at the positive and negative traits of people with this Jupiter.

Positive Traits

- You have a deep love for knowledge, and you're a wise individual.
- You love adventures
- You inspire others to reach their true potential
- Extremely generous and giving

Negative Traits

- You tend to leave your friends and family behind due to your love of adventure
- Due to your curious nature, you may develop an interest in gossip
- You procrastinate a lot

Jupiter in the Tenth House

Having Jupiter in the tenth house makes you an extremely lucky individual. People with this placement tend to have great luck when it comes to careers. However, they can become too relaxed, which can cost them their jobs. You're probably a friendly, charming, and pleasant individual who likes to be free as a bird. Comfort makes you feel amazing. You probably have a deep love and adoration for your parents and the people who raised you. Let's take a look at the positive and negative traits of your or your partner's Jupiter.

Positive Traits

- You have a wonderful reputation among people
- You're hardworking and recognized for it
- You're friendly and charming
- You're honest and talented

Negative Traits

- You may need to be more accommodative
- You should not test your limits when it comes to luck
- You may come off as self-centered or boastful

Jupiter in the Eleventh House

People with their Jupiter in the Eleventh house are happy people who love to work with others. You like to have relaxed and flexible relations with others and go with the flow. You're an innovative person who has a great love for knowledge. People with this Jupiter tend to have fewer children and may not have many children. You reap success by helping others and opting for careers that revolve around helping others. If you or your partner have this Jupiter, you should know that people with Jupiter in the Eleventh house usually have an extremely successful married life. Let's look at the positive and negative traits of this Jupiter.

Positive Traits

- You're a team player and love to collaborate with others
- You like to create flexible situations for others
- You're a relaxed and easy-going person
- You have a great love for knowledge

Negative Traits

- May become too dependent on luck
- May become lazy when it comes to getting things done
- You may become manipulative at your worst

Jupiter in the Twelfth House

If you have Jupiter in the twelfth house, then you're probably the kind of person who does not let any obstacle stop them from reaching their goals. You are at your best when you're meditating or isolated. You are also a naturally relaxed individual who does not let the problems of life stress you out. You're also an extremely intuitive and compassionate person who enjoys good fortune. You love to learn about how the human mind works. You get excited by the mysteries of life. You're the dreamer who believes that remarkable things are supposed to happen to you. Let's take a look at the positive and negative traits of your or your partner's Jupiter.

Positive Traits

- You're a relaxed and flexible individual
- You're an extremely generous and compassionate human being
- You don't let the difficulties of life get to you
- You're intuitive and have a strong spiritual side

Negative Traits

- People with this Jupiter may have big egos
- May have trouble keeping secrets
- You may become distracted and unpredictable
- You tend to be cynical about things

In conclusion, the positive aspects of Jupiter in each house outweighs its negative effects. Jupiter has an expansive effect on the areas of life which are affected by it. It is important to know if your partner's Jupiter complements yours so you can have a harmonious and happy relationship. Understanding your partner's Jupiter placement can be healthy for your relationship.

Chapter 9: Jupiter in Conjunction

In astrology, Jupiter is talked about quite a bit in conjunction with other planets because the effects of Jupiter are so expansive. Its energy allows us to expand our vision and gives us hope, which is why it's an important planet in synastry (making comparisons between people's charts). When Jupiter conjuncts another planet, there will be a lot of energy surrounding that area of the horoscope, and because it is expansive, there will be a lot of growth.

However, these planets don't only show where we expand; they also show areas of our lives where we set up boundaries and feel safe. Where Jupiter's influence is felt strongly in the chart, those parts of our lives are open, and where the conjunction lies is where we set up those boundaries.

We also have to remember that when planets are near each other in the sky, they influence each other, so these aspects and their effects are not always straightforward. The combination with Jupiter will always be similar because of their expansive nature, but how it shows up in your chart has the potential to be different for everyone.

Regarding transits, conjunctions will last a month or two, depending on how close the planets are to each other in the sky and how long it takes for them to move into the orb. They can feel like they go by faster because of their short duration, but while they're happening, there's usually some significant event or change related to the area of life influenced by the planet being conjunct Jupiter.

What Is a Conjunction?

A conjunction is when two or more planets are in almost the same position in the sky. They form a line with each other and make connections to other planets, points, and houses within a horoscope.

When Jupiter turns direct at the end of October, it will be involved in its fourth exact conjunction with Saturn since 2013 and their exact third one since September of this year. We're now seeing the third part of their cycle, which started in 2013. To understand this conjunction and what it means for us as individuals and as a society, we'll take a look at each aspect's previous transits and see how they worked out and what happened during them.

As always, this is only one perspective among many. Understanding these aspects and their previous transits can help to give us a deeper understanding of what we may be going through or what will happen in the future when they come around again. It's important to remember that this is not destiny, there are other factors involved that change how these transits work out for us, and we can always make changes in how we're living our lives.

The Great Conjunction

The Great Conjunction was the last conjunction of Saturn and Jupiter at the end of Sagittarius's third decan, which occurred just after World War II ended. This period and this aspect have been associated with upheaval and change. There were two other Great Conjunctions, one at the beginning of the Age of Pisces and one in Aquarius. However, just following WWII was the most recent. Because it was between two mutable signs, it was a time when there was a lot of free movement within society and people having their spiritual awakenings and wanting to join groups of like-minded people. It was a time when society had no boundaries, and the majority were searching for spirituality within themselves while others were looking for it in other places.

Right now, we are in conjunction between Saturn and Jupiter; this period is known as *The Great Conjunction* because it has been happening for hundreds of years, and each one has had an incredible effect on the world in some way. The chart of this conjunction shows that it is time for us to look at how we're setting ourselves up for the future, and hopefully, this chapter will help you do just that!

The Great Conjunction of 1489: This was when Uranus was in Aries and Neptune was in Taurus. Mars was in Cancer, and Jupiter was in Gemini. The world was on the brink of change as Columbus sailed west to find a new trade route to India, Vasco de Gama sailed around Africa's tip and up the east coast of Asia, and Djenghi discovered Timbuktu. This Great Conjunction established our current society by setting up the rules of how trades, travel, and religion work.

The Great Conjunction of 1689: At this time, Uranus was in Gemini, and Neptune was in Cancer. Mars was in Libra, and Jupiter was in Scorpio. This was when Napoleon created the Code Napoleon that still influences our legal system today. Newton's Law of Universal Gravitation was developed, and Kepler discovered that planets orbit the sun in ellipses. This Great Conjunction brought us a massive change to how we see our world through science and is also where we set up new ideas of justice and equality.

The Great Conjunction of 1821: At this time, Uranus was in Cancer, and Neptune was in Leo. Mars was in Scorpio, and Jupiter was in Sagittarius. This was when workers started to demand more rights and people became involved with Spiritualism, Theosophy, and the occult. The industrial revolution had finally reached its peak, so it was also a time of change from old ways of thinking to new ones on a more materialistic level.

The Great Conjunction of 1929: At this time, Uranus was in Leo, and Neptune was in Virgo. Mars was in Sagittarius, and Jupiter was in Capricorn. This is a time when people were rethinking how political systems should work with the revolutions that happened worldwide. People also became involved with urban living and consumerism. It's a Great Conjunction where we set up the world as it is today through our social systems and how we live our lives.

Now: This Great Conjunction started in 2020, with Mars moving into Aquarius and Jupiter entering Pisces on January 15th-16th (depending on your time zone). The Sun is also in Aquarius for a total solar eclipse. Uranus will soon leave Aquarius and enter Pisces, bringing more change into our world. This great conjunction will go on until 2026, and during this time, the shifts of power are going to happen so fast that it may be hard for most people to keep up. The energy of the Great Conjunction is pushing us toward awakening to our truth and souls; this phenomenon is reflected in the recent revolutions that forced many corrupt leaders out of power.

The effects of conjunction in transit are very similar to when they take place within your birth chart because transits work according to where planets are located in your natal chart. Most planets will not change signs when they are in conjunction with another planet, which will be true during any transit.

The thing to learn from this is that The Great Conjunction sets up the foundation for whatever is to come. Many boundaries society has established are being broken down at this time, and it's a time when we can reinvent ourselves to have a better future. This is your opportunity to get in touch with your soul so that you can set up your future to be better than ever. Things are changing rapidly, so try your best to ride the waves of change rather than be sucked under them.

Jupiter's Conjunction with Planets

Jupiter is a planet that encourages growth and expansion, which means it naturally converges with the energies of other planets. When two planets align in one area of the sky, it's called a conjunction. It doesn't matter if they are both visible at once and not, as conjunctions occur when their orbits line up no matter where they are in the sky. When Jupiter and another planet are in conjunction, that area of life is influenced by both planets to create a new influence on how you see the world and interact with it. The effects of conjunction can be seen both in the natal chart and when it is actually happening within your lifetime.

Jupiter Conjunct the Sun

When conjunction occurs between Jupiter and the Sun, it brings good fortune if nothing disrupts it. This fortune can manifest as money, success, and happiness. You might receive an award or recognition for something you've worked hard on. If Jupiter is making a hard aspect to the Sun, it can slow down this process because it causes Pluto-like delays. In transit, this conjunction will make you feel good about yourself. If you were born around this time, you're likely to be a happy and optimistic person who enjoys life. Jupiter in conjunction with the Sun in the natal chart brings out your best qualities and highest ideals.

Jupiter Conjunct Mercury

When Jupiter and Mercury are together, this influence can make you feel like you're on top of the world. It brings an abundance of intellectual knowledge and money, and it helps with memory and practical skills. If you were born around this time, you're likely to be a smart person with a love for learning. You also find it easy to hold your own in conversations on any subject, and you know what to say at the right time to make other people like you as well. During transit, you will find it easy to achieve your goals through communication, such as writing or speaking. If you are born with Jupiter and Mercury together, people may look up to you for your wisdom and intelligence. In the natal chart, this combination can make it easier for you to think and become a leader in some way critically.

Jupiter Conjunct Venus

Jupiter's conjunction with the romance planet Venus brings out the best in your relationships. It makes people more sociable and friendly, where they can make new friends or meet a potential romantic partner! In transit, this is a great time to go on social outings or to sign up for events that interest you. For those born around this time, you feel attraction more easily than others, and you are often the one who leaves an impression on other people for better or worse. In the natal chart, this combination can bring out your creativity in ways that attract attention from other people.

Jupiter Conjunct Mars

This conjunction usually makes people more confident and willing to take risks. It's like having a guardian angel looking over you that wants the best for you, even if it means making mistakes along the way. During transit, this is a good time to start working on something where you need to take action quickly without thinking too much about it. For those who were born around this time, your natural bravery helps you get ahead in life. In the natal chart, this combination can make you more competitive than you usually are and help with physical activity and sports. However, it can also cause you to speak out when you shouldn't and get in a lot of trouble as a result!

Jupiter Conjunct Saturn

When Jupiter comes together with Saturn, there is an emphasis on taking life seriously and applying yourself. If something is required to be done, you work hard until it's finished, no matter how long it takes. This influence can make you more responsible about your money, and other people depend on you for advice or help. In transit, this combination brings delays and obstacles that are annoying but also give a chance for you to take a break and get your bearings. For those born around this time, you are likely to have discipline, which will help you achieve great things in life. In the natal chart, Jupiter conjunct Saturn can make it easier for you to get through difficult times by making use of what you've learned before.

Jupiter Conjunct Uranus

When Jupiter meets the planet of spiritual awakenings and radical change, it gives a lot of positive energy. This influence can make you feel more optimistic about life in general, and others may see you as someone who wants to help them reach their potential too. During transit, this combination brings sudden opportunities that would be hard for you to miss. It's important to take advantage of them while they're there! For those who were born around this time, you are likely to have unconventional interests and ideas that may surprise others at first. In the natal chart, this combination makes it easier for you to become more aware of your inner voice, which holds all kinds of wisdom from your subconscious mind.

Jupiter Conjunct Neptune

When Jupiter comes together with Neptune, it brings an optimistic outlook on life that makes you feel more connected to the world around you. You can see the bigger picture and become more spiritual or philosophical. During transit, this influence connects you with others who share similar ideas and also encourages artistic expression. Sometimes it can also make you more gullible than usual so be careful not to accept things at face value. For those born around this time, you are likely to have a lot of ideas and are compassionate to others! In the natal chart, this combination makes it easier for you to have dreams or visions that give important insights into your life and what it means.

Jupiter Conjunct Pluto

This is a strong influence that gives people the confidence to get through obstacles in their lives that seem too hard to tackle. You feel like you can achieve anything with enough effort, even if the situation seems hopeless at first. In transit, this combination brings opportunities where something that was once hidden now becomes plain to see. For those born around this time, you likely have the power to accomplish whatever goals you set for yourself! In the natal chart, this combination gives a strong sense of purpose and direction in life, which can help you get through difficulties with ease without being too concerned about them.

Jupiter Conjunct the North Node

When Jupiter comes together with the North Node in your chart, it represents an important opportunity for growth and expansion that you might have been waiting for. You are likely to encounter positive people with whom you share similar aspirations, and this influence makes it easier for you to learn new things too. During transit, this combination brings many favorable opportunities that can help you get ahead in life. If you were born around this time, your life path will likely be one of growth and learning, which is a wonderful thing! In the natal chart, this combination brings the strength of purpose to accomplish your goals by helping you find the right way to go about them.

Jupiter Conjunct the South Node

When Jupiter comes together with the South Node in your chart, it represents an important opportunity for growth and expansion that you might have been waiting for. You are likely to encounter negative people who will test your patience and make you wonder what they're after, but this influence also makes it easier for you to learn from such experiences. During transit, this combination can give your insight into your previous mistakes and help you avoid repeating them. If you were born around this time, your life path is likely one of growth and learning, which is wonderful! In the natal chart, this combination brings the strength of purpose to accomplish your goals by helping you find the right way to go about them.

Jupiter Conjunct the Midheaven

This combination brings optimism and good fortune to your life, often bringing sudden changes that can give you opportunities to get ahead more easily than usual. It can also encourage you to take risks that turn out to be fruitful too, which is why it's sometimes called the "winning" aspect. During transit, this influence gives you the chance to experience something new while also encouraging you to embark on an adventure of some kind! If you were born around this time, your life path would likely be one of growth and learning, which is a wonderful thing! In the natal chart, this combination brings the strength of purpose to accomplish your goals by helping you find the right way to go about them.

Jupiter Conjunct the Ascendant

When Jupiter comes together with the Ascendant in your chart, it brings optimism and good fortune into your life, encouraging you to enjoy yourself within reason. It also encourages growth in personal relationships; this influence may bring positive changes to the people around you. During transit, this influence can help you make a good first impression on others so that they feel comfortable trusting and supporting you in return. If you were born around this time, your life path will likely be one of growth and learning, which is a wonderful thing! In the natal chart, this combination brings the strength of purpose to accomplish your goals by helping you find the right way to go about them.

This chapter discussed the conjunction of Jupiter with other planets as well as what it means. It also talks about The Great Conjunctions that have shaped our current society. The planet

Jupiter also influences society and reflects a symbolic Great Conjunction. It is the planet of luck, growth, and expansion. Jupiter brings optimism and good fortune to the chart. It conjuncts, encourages growth in personal relationships during transit, and has a strong will to accomplish one's goals in the natal chart. Those born around these times likely have a path of growth and learning.

We also discussed the conjunction of Jupiter with other planets in the natal chart. It brings optimism and good fortune to your life, often bringing sudden changes that can give you opportunities to get ahead more easily than usual. During transit, this influence gives you the chance to experience something new while also encouraging you to embark on an adventure of some kind! The conjunction with the South Node, Midheaven, and Ascendant encourages optimism and good fortune in your life and helps you make a good first impression on others. These combinations bring optimism and good fortune, the chance to experience something new and embark on an adventure, and can make one's first impression a good one.

Chapter 10: How to Strengthen Your Jupiter

There are various ways to strengthen your Jupiter to bring in wealth and abundance. These remedies can help you avoid hurdles, obstacles, and difficult life circumstances.

If Jupiter is placed in a weak location in your natal chart, this can cause adverse situations. It might make you choose the wrong path in life, or you may not be able to have wealth and children. You could suffer from a deficiency in your confidence, concentration, and faith. You might be pessimistic and devoid of spiritual wealth, or you might lack knowledge.

It could also cause health issues such as obesity, inflammation, diabetes, and problems with the liver, hips, stomach, and feet.

Many who have a weak Jupiter may notice that they have two personalities, frequently pretending they are someone they are not. People may not like to eat the food you cook.

The better your Jupiter, the more knowledge you will have. With this knowledge comes wisdom and truth.

A weak Jupiter means that you are missing a pillar of support from the divine.

These solutions work in two different ways. The first is that it strengthens the weak planet. The other way is that it protects the planet.

Jupiter can cause more serious issues if it is weak in a house in your birth chart.

- **1st House** - Your self-confidence can plummet, and you may suffer from negative thought patterns

- **2nd House** - You may suffer in your mind over problems with the paternal property. If the dispute reaches a courthouse, your weak Jupiter could mean that you lose the case.

- **3rd House** - You may have problems with your siblings

- **4th House** - You may go through severe problems. Your mother may have serious health issues. You could suffer from bad anxiety and mental health issues.

- **5th House** - Even if you are intelligent, you will have problems concentrating. You will find it hard to study and succeed in your professional life.

- **6th House** - You could have a lot more enemies than friends.

- **7th House** - Your marriage may be delayed, which can lead to all kinds of problems

- **8th House** - Your health may be bad, and your relations with your in-laws might suffer

- **9th House** - You could be inclined towards bad deeds, leading you on a path of bad karma

- **10th House** - You could have issues with your business and having stability in your work life

- **11th House** - Despite how much you love them, your relationship with your brothers may get worse

- **12th House** - Even if you make money, you may never be able to save it

Those with positive Jupiter exhibit traits such as having a good body with a great personality. They may have great relationships with wonderful people. Their skin will be good, and when other people meet them, they are left with a great feeling.

They may enjoy eating fried or roasted foods, which can cause health problems. However, their liver and stomach will be fine due to Jupiter's positive influence.

When you begin to strengthen your Jupiter, many of the problems above can be avoided or overcome.

Remedies

• Saffron

For breakfast, you should try and have something with saffron in it, or have a little saffron before eating anything else in the morning.

Every day after a bath, apply a dot of saffron tilak to your forehead and navel.

• Peepal Tree

Beginning on a Thursday, offer water, yellow pulses, and a yellow sweet to the tree's roots. Do this every day. This will make your Jupiter strong to attract wealth and money.

Wearing the roots of the banana or peepal tree is also beneficial. It should be worn on your right arm on a Thursday.

• Charity

Yellow is closely associated with Thursday. Every Thursday, you should donate yellow pulses which have been wrapped in yellow cloth, yellow sweet, yellow flowers, banana, jaggery, turmeric, and holy books to a temple.

All of these articles are related to Jupiter, which is why they should be donated.

Giving yellow sweets and pulses to a sage is also helpful.

Donating stationary or other school items to a school or too young children is beneficial as it is believed to make Lord Jupiter happy.

• Offer Pulses to a horse

For seven Thursdays, offer yellow pulses. Once the seven Thursdays are over, give these to a horse.

• Chanting Mantras

Chanting Vedic Guru mantras can help to prevent the problems a weak Jupiter position can give you.

After chanting mantras, wearing a Pukhraj stone on your finger is said to bring Lord Jupiter's blessings.

- **Turmeric**

You should keep five chunks of turmeric inside a yellow cloth. Keep this on you as much as possible.

Add turmeric to water to make it into a paste; apply this to your forehead. Often you will feel calm, and you will sense divine protection around you once you have applied it.

When taking a shower, add some turmeric. This herb holds many important proteins and can help remove negativity.

Keep a glass of water in the room where you do sadhana. Add a pinch of turmeric to the water. You can also play some mantras over the water and then sprinkle them around the home, helping remove negativity in the environment.

- **Selfless Work**

You should carry out volunteer work or selflessly help others. Anyone who needs help, whether in your circle of friends or family or someone far away, should be helped if you have the means, time, and resources. This will help strengthen your Jupiter.

You should try and help blind or disabled individuals.

- **Wear Yellow**

Try to wear yellow jewelry or clothing every day. Gold is great for jewelry.

You should wear something yellow on your forehead like a cap, scarf or turban. This helps to mitigate the planet's negative influence.

- **Fast on Thursdays**

It is best to avoid consuming any salt to get the most benefit. This works for both men and women but works exceptionally well for women. It helps to deal with issues a woman could be facing due to her weak Jupiter, such as a delay in marriage.

- **Meditate**

If you find that gurus have been unable to help you or that you have been cheated, practice meditation as much as you can – one of the best remedies for a weak Jupiter.

- **Bananas**

Giving out bananas to young children and sages, specifically on a Thursday, is said to make Lord Jupiter give you wealth and health.

- **Respect**

Jupiter represents a learned individual. This is why it is so important to ensure you show and maintain your respect towards elders, teachers, and gurus.

Look after them, serve them, and seek blessings from them.

- **Gemstone**

It is recommended to wear yellow sapphire or yellow topaz as a ring or as a necklace. When wearing it as a ring or necklace, the bottom part of the stone should be touching the skin.

This will help improve your career, business, marriage, and love.

- **Psychological Remedies**

Jupiter represents the teacher. By learning to manifest this planet's attributes within you, you can improve your relationship with the planet. Begin practicing integrity in whatever you do; avoid lying, and remain curious.

Cultivate humility within and use every situation as a lesson in this journey of life.

- **Food**

According to Ayurveda, the planet Jupiter shows Kapha. When the planet is weak, this can cause an imbalance of Kapha in the body.

Kapha increases strength, regulates the mind, and protects tissue.

There are some things you can do to mitigate the effects of a weak Jupiter on your health.

Ensure you drink enough water and have lots of fruit. Prioritize movement and ensure you move your body regularly. Consider walking, running, swimming, or yoga.

Ensure you stay warm, as Kapha dosha can make you sensitive to the cold.

Have honey and ginger tea often. Have enough bitter flavors in your diet. Don't have a lot of sweet or salty foods.

Massage your body with warm sesame oil.

Follow these guidelines and see how your health physically and mentally changes. Do all of these, especially if you notice that your physical health is not the best. You must keep a close eye on your health to assess when you need to make a change.

- **Color**

You may have noticed that several remedies for a weak Jupiter are related to the yellow color. This is because yellow is the color of Jupiter. Colors are used as a way to balance energy.

The chakras in the body are all associated with different colors, just as the planets are. When there is an imbalance in that color, this can create problems with the associated chakra and the planet.

Color therapy is a way to bring back the balance, so you should follow these guidelines of wearing more yellow and offering yellow items.

If Jupiter is in a weak position, it is important to follow these remedies to improve your life and remove obstacles. Even if you don't feel like you have suffered such a negative impact because you have achieved a certain level of success or wealth, it can come crashing down very soon.

To prevent this from happening, you must ensure your planets are strong and balanced.

Conclusion

Congratulations on making it this far! You have successfully gained insight into Jupiter's role as a powerful influence to attract luck, wealth, and prosperity. Most people are unaware of Jupiter's strength and demeanor. If you are one of them, this book will remind you about the planet's versatility.

Let's recap what we've learned so far. We began by talking about Jupiter's role in various mythologies. Jupiter was the most powerful deity in Roman culture. He shared attributes with Zeus in Greek mythology and Brihaspati (Guru) in Hindu mythologies. Jupiter was the god of the sky and heaven and governed the livelihood of all living beings. According to Roman myth, Jupiter fought Saturn to take his throne. In Hindu mythology, Brihaspati is considered a knowledgeable teacher who can guide his pupils in the right direction. Vedic astrology places a strong emphasis on Brihaspati's power. Astrologers suggest following several tricks and strategies to please Guru and attract good luck.

We covered Jupiter's astrological role and the luck it brings. It is so lucky and powerful that Jupiter has been named the "benefic planet." While it brings luck in almost every area of your life, Jupiter is known to attract luck in three specific ways; success, money, and love. Jupiter shows you the right path and helps you mark successful spots that will likely increase your wealth and attract fame. The house and zodiac sign it is located in also show Jupiter's influence on your life. Along with money and success, Jupiter also brings you close to a partner of your choice, which results in successful love life.

A challenged Jupiter can pose a threat to the natives' lives and bring bad luck. Jupiter stays exalted in Cancer and debilitated in Capricorn. Since Jupiter and the Moon get along, the former also aligns with Cancer (the sign representing intuition and emotions). Jupiter uses its wisdom and philosophical approach to align with Cancer's secure and intuitive energy, forming a strong union. By contrast, Jupiter does not match Capricorn's energy. Since this zodiac sign believes in social hierarchies and power, Jupiter fails to align its humanitarian and philosophical take with Capricorn. This planet is all about diverting to social causes and selfless mobility, which is quite the opposite of what a Capricorn believes in.

Jupiter's nature rapidly changes when placed in different zodiac signs. The planet portrays different signs in each zodiac sign. It can be detrimental to Virgo and Gemini, whereas it can act as an abode for Sagittarius.

Lastly, we talked about harnessing Jupiter's energy by strengthening its position in your horoscope. If you want to attract love, money, and success in your life, implement certain tips that put Jupiter in your favor. For example, Vedic astrologers suggest offering your prayers to Brihaspati every Thursday. You can also try having food infused with saffron in the morning. Some other methods include wearing yellow, chanting certain powerful mantras while meditating, wearing the roots of the Peepal tree on your hand, indulging in social work, or donating to charity. Some of these tips can also improve your physical and mental health.

With this, you can also combat all hurdles and obstacles stopping you from achieving your goals. With the power to attract success and beat shortcomings, Jupiter is truly the mightiest planet and the "God of the Gods."

Happy manifesting! If you think that this book has helped you in any way, suggest it to your loved ones so they can discover this undervalued but powerful astrological subject. Whether they are curious about astrology and planets in general or want to harness Jupiter's energy to attract good luck, this book will help them too.

Part 8: Neptune in Astrology

The Ultimate Guide to the Planet of Spirituality and Mysticism along with Its Impact on Psychic Abilities, the Third Eye Chakra, and Divine Creativity

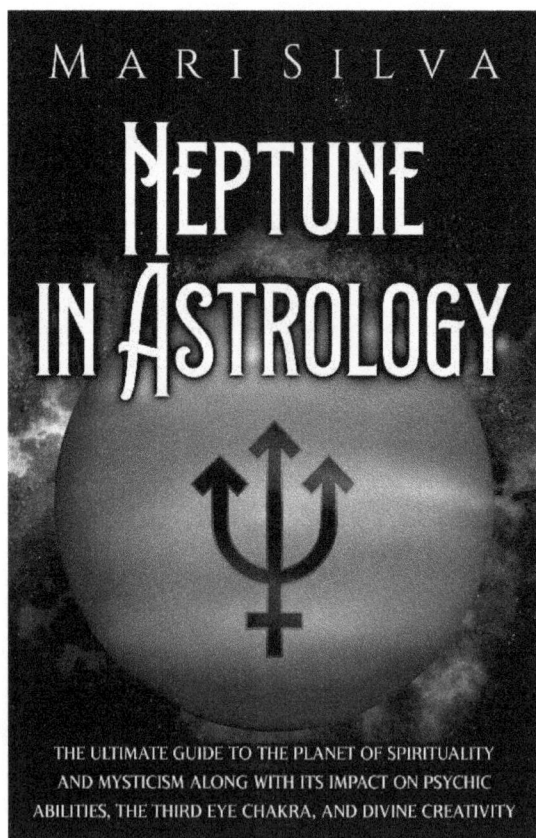

Introduction

Neptune is one of the solar system's biggest gas giants, orbiting the Sun at a distance of 2.8 billion miles. It is one of the most beautiful and mysterious planets owing to its icy demeanor and magnificent hue. Neptune is also the ruler of both the spiritual and esoteric realms. Dreams, delusions, fantasies, and other invisible aspects of one's subconscious mind are governed by Neptune. Have you ever attempted to create a vision board? If you answered yes, you must be aware of the Law of Attraction and how it can help you achieve your dreams and desires. These desires are referred to as "Neptunian vibes."

Neptune, the planet of inspiration, embodies spirituality and beauty. It strengthens your intuition, influences your dreams, and stimulates your creative impulses. It aids in the cleansing, purification, and refinement of your energies. Neptune instills sympathy in us and characterizes the vibrations that exist under the surface. It opposes coarseness and increases self-awareness. It motivates people to explore their artistic and creative sides. Neptune's energy and frequency are tuned into all artistic disciplines, including photography, music, dance, film, poetry, and painting. This is also why it symbolizes emotional subtlety and inspires people to make sacrifices for noble deeds.

According to Roman mythology, Neptune is the ruler of the sea – the god governing ice, rain, and other water bodies. He also represents beverages and liquids of all kinds. Neptune is associated with drugs, both good and bad. Good drugs make you healthy, whereas bad drugs make you suffer. The celestial body is commonly known as the "Planet of Mist" due to its watery and liquidly demeanor. It represents distinct characteristics and inspires one to break the monotony. It helps you escape your mundane life and pushes you into a heavenly state. It also tells you that you can achieve your goals and break down barriers.

Neptune also emphasizes some negative traits, which include a clouded perception and complications. If you are not self-aware, you can easily deceive yourself. The planet rules the zodiac sign Pisces and will stay in it for around fourteen to fifteen years. Due to this long span, several generations are affected during the entire course. Despite being associated with the invisible realm, Neptune is a powerful force that can make or break your fate. Due to its strong gravitational pull, Pisceans are believed to possess a magnetic personality and pull others towards them. If placed in the wrong house or a negative position, the native can get into a state of confusion or stir up drama in their everyday life.

The planet takes 165 years to complete one orbit around the Sun due to its faraway position and huge orbital radius. When integrated with the Virgo archetype, Neptune can help the native to heal. The planet is also deeply connected with the Third Eye chakra, located at the pineal gland. To manifest Neptune's energy, you must "learn to activate the Third Eye and maintain its balance with other chakras." Learning some effective ways to awaken Neptune's dormant psychic powers can also help in the healing process.

This book covers everything about Neptune in the astrological and mythological realms. The chapters are categorized into different behavioral patterns and astrological references related to Neptune and its mystical power. You will learn about Neptune's role in mythology, its ruling sign, significance in Vedic and Western astrology, the planet's journey, and effects through various houses in different birth charts, its relationship with other planets, the Neptunian archetype, the planet's connection with the third eye chakra, and Neptune's psychic ability. Ultimately, all the chapters will walk you through Neptune's identity and characteristics to help you unravel its true potential.

If you are intrigued, read on to find out more about Neptune's role in astrology.

Chapter 1: Neptune - The God of the Sea

To understand the spiritual importance of the planet Neptune, you must understand how the planet has been viewed through history. The final planet in our solar system was named after the Roman god of the sea, but there's much more to it than meets the eye.

Neptune in Hindu Mythology and Astrology

In Hindu astrology, the planet Neptune is associated with the god Varuna.

Though Varuna was initially a god of the sky, he is best-known in his later incarnation as the Vedic god of the seas and oceans.

Varuna traveled and roamed on Makara, a legendary sea-creature that is approximately associated with a crocodile. The Makara is a guardian of gateways and thresholds, and Varuna similarly represents a gateway between the human and the divine.

According to some myths, he was the son of Kashyapa, one of the seven ancient sages, rather than a child of any other deity. Furthermore, in the Vedas, he is referred to as the patron deity of physicians and provides them with remedies to help treat humanity.

Varuna interacts directly with Rama, the epic's hero, promising not to interfere when the bridge to Lanka is built in some versions of the Hindu epic Ramayana. In this version, he is one of the rare deities that appear directly to human heroes.

Along with being the god of the oceans, Varuna is also said to be the guardian of the West. In the early Upanishads, he is also dependent on the "fire of the soul," a reference to the role that the planet he is associated with (Neptune) plays in affecting human spirituality.

Finally, he is also said to be the guardian of moral law, one who plays the role of judge. In this role, he is often associated with Mitra, and in his role as Mitra-Varuna rules over human oaths and how humans interact with and relate to each other.

Neptune in Roman Mythology

As mentioned, Varuna is not the only deity associated with the planet Neptune. The planet is also named after the Roman god of the sea, the counterpart of the Greek Poseidon.

Like Varuna, Neptune was also a god of the oceans. However, his rule over water was not limited to the oceans, and he also had mastery over freshwater. Like Poseidon, he was also the god of earthquakes due to his temperamental nature and was also the progenitor of horses.

Neptune was a sibling to five other major Roman deities – Jupiter, king of the gods; Juno, his wife and goddess of marriage; Pluto, god of the underworld; Ceres, goddess of agriculture; and Vesta, goddess of the hearth, home, and family.

The six divine siblings were the children of Saturn and Ops (Roman counterparts to Cronus and Rhea).

According to mythology, Saturn swallowed each of his children whole after their birth, as he was terrified of being superseded by one of his children – including Neptune, who, along with his siblings, spent his early years trapped in his father's stomach.

His mother, Ops, grief-stricken at the loss of her children, tricked Saturn into swallowing a rock instead of the youngest of the siblings, Jupiter. Jupiter would grow up to trick his father into regurgitating the stone – and with it, his siblings.

Following their freedom, the siblings turned on their father, waging war for control of the heavens. Following their victory, three of the brothers divided the world into spheres of control. To Jupiter, he gave the skies and kingship over all gods. To Pluto – he gave the rule of the underworld, and to Neptune, the seas and oceans of the world.

Neptune was a volatile and emotional god. With his wife Salacia, he was the father of Triton, Rhodes, and Benthesicyme. He also fathered many heroes through affairs with mortals and deities alike, including Orion and Atlas, the mythic king of Atlantis.

He was also an angry god, which is reflected in the ways that seas and oceans often experience storms. His temper is said to be the reason for both storms in the seas and earthquakes on land, and it was believed that this nature had to be appeased before ancient sailors could set out on a journey.

According to Ovid, storms sent by Neptune shaped the world as we know it today. He caused floods that shaped the valleys through which the waters flowed and drowned the world in its entirety. Only when there was only one man and one woman left alive did he allow his son, Triton, to signal the waters to recede. After the floodwaters receded, the shape of the land left behind was as we know it today.

Neptune was one of the most important deities in ancient Rome. He was worshipped during the Neptunalia, held during the height of the summer, and was one of only four gods to whom a bull could be sacrificed (alongside Apollo, Mars, and Jupiter). He even had one major temple dedicated to him in Rome, which stood near the Circus Flaminius.

Neptune and Water

As is obvious from the planet's associations with Varuna and the god Neptune/Poseidon, Neptune is intrinsically linked to water. Superficially, the reason for this link seems clear. For one, the planet was named after a god of the oceans. Additionally, when most people think of the planet, they visualize it as blue, which can be seen as another link to water.

However, this linkage also reveals the deep spiritual meaning of the way the planet affects people. Water is associated with unexplored depths, hidden wisdom, creativity, and spirituality in many traditions.

One of water's major symbolic links is with the idea of purity and fertility. Water is seen as the source of life, and many creation myths involve the first deities emerging from primordial waters. Indeed, water deities are often counted among the oldest in many pantheons, including Egyptian (Nu, Tefnut), Greek/Roman (Pontus, Thalassa), Mesopotamian (Abzu, Tiamat, Nammu), and Hindu (Varuna).

Furthermore, water is often linked to the Mother Goddess, including Kali, the pre-Vedic Great Mother. The symbol for water, a circle with a horizontal line, is often seen as symbolic of a womb, from which all life begins.

Both the ancient Egyptians and Native Americans considered water to be intrinsically symbolic of life.

For the ancient Egyptians, it was a link to the river Nile that was crucial to the continued prosperity of Egyptian civilization. Without the annual floods, there would be no crops and no food.

For Native Americans and other peoples of North America, water was often a valuable and rare commodity, especially among those living in the more arid regions. Thus, water was seen as a life-giving force and played an important role in many creation myths.

Water Creation Myths

In the earliest Sumerian creation myth, Nammu was the primordial sea goddess. It was she who gave birth to both heaven and earth, and she was known as the "Lady of the Beginning," who was also the source of life.

Later Mesopotamian creation myths involved a union between Tiamat, the goddess of the sea, and Abzu, the god of fresh water. It was from this union between the waters that all the gods of Babylon were born.

Following a war between the gods, Tiamat was killed, and her body cleaved into many pieces that formed the different aspects of the universe.

- Her ribs became the vault of heaven and earth
- Her eyes were the sources of the Tigris and Euphrates, the key rivers that allowed Mesopotamian civilization to flourish
- Her tail became the Milky Way

Thus, Tiamat and the waters she represented literally became the source of all life in the universe.

In Egyptian mythology, Nu was considered the personification of the primordial waters from which all life arose. Nu was made up of both the masculine and feminine in the form of Nun and Naunet and was closely associated with several water deities, including:

- **Mut,** a mother goddess who was said to have given birth to the world and who was the wife of the sun god Amun-Ra
- **Naunet,** the feminine aspect of Nu
- **Neith,** a goddess who was said to have woven the universe into being, using the primordial waters. Her many roles included being the goddess of mothers, childbirth, rivers, and water, and she was also the one who governed the way the universe functioned.
- **Hapi,** a god associated with the annual flooding of the Nile. The flooding of the Nile was crucial for the growth of Egyptian crops, and in years when the flooding was low or absent, there would almost certainly be a drought and food shortages. Though male, Hapi was depicted as being androgynous in appearance. He was known as "the Primeval One" and was shown in art with long hair, breasts, and a false beard.

In Greek and Roman cosmology, the world's creation was at the hands of the earth mother goddess, Gaia. However, besides being mother and grandmother to the gods, she was also mother to Pontus, the primordial sea god.

Pontus was husband to Thalassa, his feminine counterpart and the primeval goddess of the sea. The two would become parents to the Greek storm giants and the fish that populated the sea. Some myths also hold Thalassa to have been the mother of the love goddess Aphrodite, as she was born of the sea after the severed member of Ouranos (the personification of the sky and husband of Gaia) was thrown into the sea.

In Japanese creation myth, the primordial waters play a crucial role in the creation of the world. The creator deities are Izanagi and his sister-wife Izanami. The two of them were the eighth set of deities born after the creation of the world.

In those times, the Earth was a watery, shapeless chaos. The two deities used a jeweled spear to swirl the waters, resulting in the creation of various landmasses, including the islands that make up the Japanese archipelago. They were also parents to many deities that made up a good portion of the Japanese pantheon.

Other Symbolisms of Water

At the same time, water is a transitional substance –a property well known by the ancient Greeks, who understood the constant metamorphosis represented in water's ability to easily cycle from liquid to solid to gas.

In the Taoist tradition, water is a symbol of wisdom. In its liquid form, water moves in the path of least resistance. It molds itself to fit the container in which it is held without struggle – a symbol of higher wisdom, to which the Taoists believe all must aspire.

Water is also a source of constant mystery. Much of the deep oceans remain unexplored by humans, and many water creatures still hold mysteries that scientists have not yet uncovered.

Though the planet Neptune is named after a male deity, its waters are innately linked to womanhood and the divine feminine. This combination can be seen in pearls, the bounty of the ocean. A pearl is symbolic of the union between the feminine (water) and the masculine (fire). In some Greek and Roman myths, Poseidon/Neptune inherited rule over the oceans and the seas only through his marriage to Amphitrite/Salacia, who was said to be the personification of the sea. This arrangement was one of the reasons that the Poseidon of Greek mythology had no dominion over freshwater the way Neptune did in Roman mythology.

Water is symbolic of the unseen influences that act on human beings, represented by intuition, dreams, and psychic perception. We cannot see into the depths of the seas and oceans, but we always know that something is lurking underneath. Similarly, while we may not be able to understand the source of intuition very well, we know that there is much more to our emotions than meets the eye. Water reminds us to take the time to explore these emotions and learn to understand ourselves and others better.

Additionally, water serves as a reminder to embrace change and to be flexible. In the same way as water takes on the form of the container in which it is held, so too must we learn to adapt. Likewise, water can also carve out paths through mountains to reach its destination – a reminder that while we may find ourselves going with the flow, it isn't the same as being meek, submissive, and accepting of situations that we know will cause us harm.

Finally, water is a symbol of life and healing. It has, for centuries, been viewed as a source of cleansing and renewal, a cause of healing for even the most serious of ailments. Just like water clears away the mud and grime from a person's body, so too can it clear away the dirt on a person's heart and mind, allowing them to have better clarity of vision and understanding of their place in the world.

The Glyph of the Planet

Another important consideration to keep in mind when trying to understand the power and influence the planet Neptune holds over people is the glyph denoting the planet.

The symbol for the planet Neptune is an artistic representation of the trident. The trident was the three-pronged weapon of both Poseidon and Triton. The lower half of the trident resembles a cross.

The trident is also similar in shape to the *trishula* - a divine weapon of the gods Shiva and Durga in Hinduism. The three points of the weapon represent several trinities, depending on the source and religious tradition. These include:

- •Spiritual, psychic, and relative
- •Clarity, knowledge, and wisdom
- •Heaven, mind, and earth
- •Practice, understanding, and wisdom
- •Soul, passion, and embodied-soul
- •Prayer, manifestation, and sublime
- •Creation, order, and destruction

As discussed above, these are all markers of the influence that the planet Neptune holds over humans. Neptune is the planet that rules over illusion, confusion, inspiration, and dreams. It is also linked to the waters of creation, destruction, and purification.

Neptune also rules over the star sign Pisces in astronomy, a sign that is aligned with the attributes mentioned above (namely, intuition, dreams, and psychic ability).

Similarly, the three prongs of the trident in the Neptune symbol also represent trinities, namely:

- •Body, life, and death
- •Past, present, and future
- •Mind, body, and spirit

Neptune was said to have transformed during his time in his father Saturn's stomach, where he understood the mysteries of the world. Thus, his dominion over waters fits, as water is symbolic of deeper emotions and dreams - and it is this relationship represented by his trident.

The cross at the lower part of the glyph represents matter, while the crescent represents the soul. Thus, the soul is symbolically crucified on the cross or crucified in the matter.

It is like the shepherd's crook, which is considered a religious symbol in both Druidism and Christianity.

Other interpretations and symbolic meanings of the glyph of the planet Neptune include dreams, the occult, imagination, esotericism, magic, intuition, invention, psychic ability, and perception. Neptune is the planet of constant contemplation and of uncovering hidden meanings. The cross in the glyph serves as a grounding element, reminding people to keep themselves grounded in physical reality even as they explore the spiritual.

Neptune is also said to rule the pineal gland, which emphasizes the symbolism of the glyph. Like the glyph, the pineal gland also represents psychic abilities, including higher awareness, an understanding of divinity, and visions. This gland is of particular interest to occult and esoteric practitioners because of its link to these phenomena.

Additionally, the link of the glyph to emotions and magic links the glyphs to the water that Neptune represents. Just as water is symbolic of the unknown abilities that we all have, the glyph also represents the ability to understand these abilities through water magic better.

As mentioned above, the trident was the weapon of the male sea gods Poseidon/Neptune and his son Triton. In Hinduism, it is most closely linked to the destruction god Shiva.

However, in many other (and often older) stories, the trident is linked more to goddesses than gods. As mentioned previously, in Hinduism, the trishula is also wielded by Durga, the principal aspect of the Hindu mother goddess and the goddess of preservation (the opposite of Shiva).

Older Greco-Roman stories hold that the original wielder of the trident was Amphitrite/Salacia, and it was only through his marriage to her that Poseidon/Neptune gained dominion over the oceans – and the right to wield the trident that gives him this control. In these stories, Amphitrite/Salacia is not merely a goddess of the sea - rather, she is its personification and much stronger than her husband.

Thus, the trident is also linked to feminine energy, similar to how water is linked to the mother goddess and the divine feminine. It serves as a reminder of the masculine and feminine energies that mix deep within you (similar to how the trident is held by both male and female deities) and reminds us to stay balanced even as these energies combine.

Like the planet Neptune in myth, the gods representing the planet (including Neptune and Varuna), and the many symbols of both the waters associated with Neptune and the glyph represent the planet, Neptune represents an awakening of the spirit.

It is a symbol of developing self-awareness, the dissolution of the boundaries between the spirit and the self. It represents an urge to transcend and become something greater than you currently are and is an uplifting and transformative force. It can inspire visionary ideas, religious devotion, creativity, and compassion.

However, the influence of Neptune is not always positive. At its worst, its influence can result in a loss of the sense of self and can trigger self-destructive behavior. It can be regressive and lead to escapism, madness, and addiction.

To learn more about how the influence of Neptune affects your life, continue reading this book.

Chapter 2: The Astrological Role of Neptune

This planet represents psychic receptivity, inspiration, intuition, dreams, illusion, and confusion. Neptune manifests an individual's dreams into reality. Since dreams strengthen your imagination power, they are also an integral part of any creative process. When artists or architects get an idea in their dreams, they often wake up and doodle their idea in the middle of the night. Later, they build on this idea, which turns out to be a creative venture. They often claim that these ideas were "life-changing" or "out of the box." However, they must control their thoughts and try to manifest only positive outcomes.

Astrological Role of Neptune

If Neptune is associated with Venus, the individual can be highly creative and has the potential to become an artist. This combination also symbolizes sensitivity and generosity. The individuals are compassionate, kind, and philanthropic. When it comes to personal relationships, they are more giving and do not expect much in return. They are loyal and can make sacrifices for their loved ones. When Venus and Neptune align, the natives can easily portray their creative abilities and can appreciate the creativity around them. They love to decipher art and read poetry. When someone offers kindness, they are easily touched, which makes them more sentimental than others.

The concept of life and death seems like an illusion. The frequency and energy particles around us govern our existence. In a way, Neptune represents this energy, which follows us from birth to death. Depending on Neptune's position in the house of your birth chart, you may experience confusion or disappointment. In extreme cases, the planet may also create an illusion and push the person into a state of trance or hypnosis. The individuals are often driven to fashion, television, movies, theatre, and any other form of artistic and glamorous disciplines. However, some are mostly drawn to the outer glamor and fail to recognize the inner struggles; this symbolizes the state of confusion represented by the planet. If the planet is in a favorable position in the individual's horoscope, they may be blessed with fantastical writing ideas. Neptunian individuals possess the potential to become acclaimed fantasy writers as well.

Neptune's aggressive side can make an individual irrational and put them in a state of despair. Dreams can steadily turn into fantasies and push the person into a downward spiral. If they fail to change their habits, the person's daydreams can turn into nightmares over time. Doubt and deceit may become a regular part of their life. Neptune's negative connotation does not necessarily indicate misfortune. However, it can mean that the person may constantly worry or feel stressed, leading to the buildup of negative thoughts. An extremely negative Neptune means that the individual may be subjected to deception, alcohol addiction, or drug abuse.

When the person reaches their materialistic age, the effects of Neptune seem invisible. Stellium is the point where Neptune forms a tight connection with other planets. When it meets benefic planets, the individuals may be blessed with concentrated intuitive power and higher caliber than their competitors. Some may even have psychic powers. On the other hand, Neptune's conjunction with malefic planets can result in chaos and doubt.

Neptune and Its Zodiac Sign, Pisces

Individuals born between mid-February and mid-March fall under Pisces. The zodiac sign is associated with water and is symbolized by a pair of fish. The natives are generous, kind, empathetic, and emotional. They often put their emotions ahead of their practical thoughts and actions. Neptune is Pisces's ruling planet, and both share several traits. Compared to other water signs, individuals born under Pisces are more grounded and agreeable. They are laidback and portray strong emotions. Due to their empathetic nature, they are willing to sacrifice a lot for the people around them and often go beyond their limits to help others. They are artistic and extremely creative. On the flipside, Pisces can be overly trusting and moody.

Neptune rules Pisces, and both collectively represent understanding, depth, and perspective. Pisces thinks emotionally and puts thoughts over logic when connecting with others. They are empathetic and spiritual, just like Neptune. Both Pisces and Neptune symbolize fluidity and the serenity of water. Neptune's presence in Pisces blesses individuals with a unique perspective. They observe their surroundings from a different point of view and get more visual clarity. As their emotions and spiritual energy align, they gain the strength to walk through the fog and the ability to see ahead clearly.

When both types of energies come together, a person will undergo collective progress and become more self-aware. They start valuing the little things, and the symbiosis shines like gold. When Neptune passes through Pisces, the planet inspires individuals to explore their inner thoughts and emotional intelligence. Consider this a sign of spiritual awareness. The rising energy compels them to take a new course and connect with their sacred feelings. Both Pisces and Neptune feel mystical, which is why they are intricately connected to spirituality and sacredness. Once the individual gets a creative idea and wants to showcase it to the world, this collaboration helps them take the right approach.

When Neptune retrogrades in this zodiac sign, the person may start overthinking or overreacting over tiny matters. They may often shut themselves from others. However, the natives get the chance to explore their deepest and darkest corners, which can help in self-acceptance. The light shines upon the native but in an inward direction. They also get to identify their darkest fears, which can help the individual combat and replace them with positive feelings. Their mundane realities and holiest hopes are also revealed over time. When these individuals finally connect with their inner self, they no longer must rely on others or the outer world.

They begin to experience inner peace and feel complete, valuing themselves and others around them. This inner unity integrates with their outer personality and becomes a part of their whole. If Neptune is positioned in Pisces's natal chart, the native possesses the ability to decipher their dreams and strengthen their imagination power. They can also easily distinguish between dreams and reality, giving them an uncanny ability to control their imagination. If they want, they can also manifest their dreams into reality.

For example, if the person thinks about or misses someone, they may have the opportunity to meet them during the day. Similarly, if they crave ice cream, they may walk by an ice cream shop or receive ice cream from someone within the next few hours.

Astrologers recommend using Neptune's energy to manifest positive dreams. However, since the planet also affects the native's negative imaginations, you must be careful. Since worrying and feeling anxious can lead to the manifestation of your negative thoughts, you should learn to combat stress and focus more on positive outcomes. Know that your power lies within your thoughts. Turn your habit of daydreaming in your favor.

Neptune in Vedic Astrology

In Vedic astrology, Neptune is defined as the planet of dreams, confusion, illusion, and inspiration. A person's imaginative power majorly delves into Neptune's energy, position, and current form.

According to Vedic astrology, the best profession and disciplines for these natives can be fishing, cloud seeding, pharmacy, psychology, shoemaking, fortune-telling, anesthesiology, swimming, asylum head, and acting. Since most of these professions are related to art, creativity, mind, or spirituality, Neptune favors the individuals in these areas. The planet also rules the nervous system, mind, and pineal gland. An afflicted Neptune can result in depression, anxiety, or other mental health issues. Since Neptune rules the mind, the way you think and feel can directly impact your mental health. Effective treatment options include hypnotic therapy along with spiritual monitoring. In extreme cases, afflicted Neptune can also affect eyesight and cause foot-related problems.

In Western astrology, Neptune is the planet that represents inspiration, imagination, idealism, deception, inspiration, addiction, and fear. Neptune can be found in the 12th house in Western astrology, which is a sign of isolation, reflection, and withdrawal. This can be related to Neptune's connection with dreams and creativity. Since the planet is in the sign of Pisces, it is associated with spirituality and mysticism. This tie with spirituality can result in religious beliefs which affect how a person interprets reality.

In both Vedic and Western astrology, Neptune rules magic, wizards/witches, illusions, hallucinations, and the realm of possibilities. It is also connected to creativity (Vedic), as well as subconscious, psychic abilities, and mystery (Western).

Neptune in an Exalted Form

As explained, Neptune is very involved with conscious energy, intuition, creativity, dreams, and illusions. As an exalted planet in the sign of Cancer, Neptune brings a higher level of spiritual consciousness. Individuals with strong Neptunian influences are extremely sensitive to their inner selves. They can use this ability for good or for bad when Neptune is in an exalted position. They may be exceptionally gifted and capable of conveying messages on a spiritual or artistic level. Some people devote their lives to assisting others in difficult situations. Some people come across as impostors because they do not use their abilities for good and can become self-absorbed, elitist, and/or overly emotional.

Neptune – in an exalted sign – has times when the person can move forward with their spirituality and intuition. They are very creative with their ideas and use vivid imagination.

Neptune brings mercurial, impressionable attitudes, making it difficult to build a solid base for a strong personality. It is quite easy for a Neptune native to slip into a habit of the mind and become a victim of addiction. When Neptune is in an exalted position, the person feels exceptionally motivated and spends time alone to meditate and regenerate.

With Neptune in an exalted position, the person needs to keep their ego under control. It will be easy to become sidetracked into gazing into the world of illusions and fantasies instead of remaining dedicated to the real world. Neptune in an exalted position gives the person a very strong imagination, which they can use for positive or bad intent. A person with a well-aspected Neptune can use their ability for good, and they may be seen as a very caring and compassionate member of society. If the person has bad intentions, they can become self-absorbed, egotistical, and even delusional to the point of convincing themselves that their illusions are real.

Neptune in an Exalted Form When Square or Opposing a Natal Planet

When Neptune is in an exalted position, but it squares or opposes a natal planet, the person must be extremely careful with focusing their energies on any activity. They must be careful not to become addicted to the idea of being able to communicate with spirits or have visions into other worlds. Neptune in this position represents a time of confusion and deception where the person may try to convince themselves and others that they have special powers. These are dangerous times when the person can become obsessed with their spiritual abilities and lose touch with reality.

Neptune in an Exalted Form When Sextile or Trine a Natal Planet

When Neptune is in an exalted position but sextiles (or trines) a natal planet, the person will be blessed with a very fluid consciousness and intuition. They will have strong spiritual influences that allow them to be inspired with artistic creativity. The person can positively use their gifts to benefit themselves and the people in their lives. They will see a strong flow of ideas in an artistic or spiritual form that they can use to make money.

Neptune in Detriment Form

Neptune in detriment form brings with it a very vulnerable and sensitive personality. The person may appear as though they are out of touch or become unaware of what is going on around them. They may be very dreamy, artistic, and idealistic, making it difficult for them to remain in touch with reality. They may become very withdrawn and lose themselves in their imagination. Neptune in detriment form is a sign that the person has trouble making decisions. They may let their emotions get in the way of making important choices. Neptune in a bad position can radiate an extremely deceptive vibe, making it difficult for others to comprehend them.

People with Neptune in a detriment form feel overwhelmed by the world around them and try to escape into a world of illusions and fantasies. They may become very lost in their inner world and neglect the real world around them. They may be very shy, withdrawn individuals who are sensitive to the point of being easily hurt. They may be very impractical and disorganized, making it difficult to complete their daily tasks and responsibilities.

In a detriment form in the chart, Neptune represents an individual who is easy to deceive and manipulate – which may happen when Neptune is placed in Virgo. Neptune in this sign can indicate that the individual is very creative but also very ungrounded. They may be very sensitive, shy, and introverted. They should try to avoid the tendency of escaping into their little world as this will only limit them in the real world. Neptune in Virgo may give the person a strong love of nature and animals. They should try to avoid falling into a pattern of self-deception as this could lead them into a life that is completely out of touch with reality.

Neptune in Detriment Form When Square or Opposing a Natal Planet

When Neptune is in detriment form and square or opposing a natal planet, the person needs to find a balance between their emotional and intellectual needs. They should not let the tendency of escaping into their inner world prevent them from working in the real world. If they can find a balance between their emotional and intellectual needs, they may feel emotionally balanced and achieve their life goals. If they cannot find a balance, they may become very emotionally unstable, which could lead them to become lost in their imagination.

Neptune in Detriment Form When Sextile or Trine a Natal Planet

This placement represents an individual who is compassionate and caring. When Neptune is in detriment form and sextile or trine a natal planet, the person may be sensitive to their surroundings. They may use their imagination in a positive way which can bring them great creativity. Their imagination may inspire them to become very artistic. The individual may have a strong interest in spirituality and religion, leading them into a very spiritual profession. If the person can handle the tendency of becoming lost in their imagination, they may become very intuitive and see beyond what is seen on the surface.

Neptune in a Debilitated Form

When Neptune is in a debilitating form, it can bring deception, confusion, and chaos. The person may not be able to determine how to handle the world around them. Sometimes they may turn to drugs and alcohol as a way of escaping reality. They may be very ungrounded and may be unable to maintain a work or study routine. They may have a very cloudy personality which makes it difficult for others to understand them. They should try to engage themselves in activities that will help them focus their energy and become more practical. If they cannot balance their emotions and intellectual needs, they may become very confused regarding their abilities.

Neptune represents the ability to be creative and inspired. When placed in Capricorn, a debilitated form of Neptune, it can make the person feel very uninspired and may not be able to complete tasks. This placement may also indicate that the individual is easily deceived and should be careful of those around them.

Neptune in a Debilitated Form When Square or Opposing a Natal Planet

When Neptune is in a debilitating form and square or opposing a natal planet, it can indicate that the person may have trouble determining how to handle their emotions. They may not be able to define what they are feeling or how to express their feelings. The individual may feel very confused regarding who they are and what they want. They should try to engage themselves in activities that will help them focus their energy and become more practical. If this is not possible, they may be more of a daydreamer who prefers to escape into their own world.

Neptune in a Debilitated Form When Sextile or Trine a Natal Planet

When Neptune is in a debilitating form and sextile or trine a natal planet, the person may be very affected by their emotions. They should find an activity that engages them and helps to release their emotions healthily. This placement is good for artistic work and may indicate that the individual will have a very active imagination. They may be very intuitive and sensitive to their surroundings. If the person can handle their emotions, they will have a strong intuition to lead them into creative professions or hobbies.

As with other planets in astrology, the position of Neptune is somewhat subjective since it depends on how the individual perceives reality. One person may see Neptune as something they can use to expand their imagination, while another may see it as something that takes away their ability to maintain a solid grip on reality. One person may be able to deal with their emotions far better than the other person who sees Neptune as a planet that makes them feel confused and lost. This chapter discussed the effects of Neptune when it is in its natural position, when it is debilitated, and what happens when it squares or opposes another planet.

The role of Neptune is to help the person find a balance between the spiritual and mundane worlds. It guides them in finding their inner-self and the meaning of life. The person must try not to fall into a pattern of self-deception as they can become very lost in their world and lose sight of reality. They should try to remain grounded and not totally forget about the real world as they explore the spiritual world. If they can positively use their imagination, they may evolve into very compassionate and loving individuals who give of themselves for the sake of others. They may become self-absorbed and delusional if they use their imagination negatively.

Chapter 3: Neptune through the Houses I

This chapter discusses Neptune's journey and its effects through the houses in the birth chart. The first part explains how each house represents different aspects of our lives. The next section highlights what the planet brings when it is located in the first (the self), second (material possessions), third (communication), and fourth (the home) house. The chapter will also focus on both negative and positive outcomes and recommend ways to avoid undesirable results.

Neptune in the Houses

The position of Neptune in the zodiac has a great influence on the personality of the people born during the 13 years when Neptune is in one sign. Neptune in different houses also provides inspirational and mystical influences that are experienced by each generation. As illustrated below, Neptune in the house shows where people often seek the ideal or deceive themselves.

•With **Neptune in the First House** in the natal chart, this means you are compassionate, mystical, and have musical ability. You are aware of your immediate environment either consciously or unconsciously. However, you may not be able to realize your shortcomings. Solving conflicts can be challenging as you seek to become an independent person. You can end up deceiving yourself if you fail to transform the conflict into positive energy.

•With **Neptune in the Second House,** you may be blind to your financial blunders, or you can use your intuition to make money. You may also love get-rich-quick schemes, and this may be your major weakness. Creating a comfortable relationship with material things will be difficult for you. You need to make a realistic decision about how you spend your money.

•If **Neptune is in the Third House,** you are an artist and use your intuitive mindset into creativity. If you are a filmmaker or poet, you can use your creativity to reach your goals. However, the challenge you are likely to face is to integrate your imagination and communication.

•With **Neptune in the Fourth House** in the natal chart, you can have unrealistic expectations from family, and you do not want to take responsibility or believe that you are an adult. There may also be some misunderstandings with your family. It is essential to maintain a distance and remain sober when dealing with family matters.

•If **Neptune is in the Fifth House,** you are disillusioned by romance and children. While you are capable of artistic expression, you may not be aware of your talents. On the positive, you are a romantic person, unlike others. Do not pursue ill-conceived ideas.

•With **Neptune in the Sixth House,** you have a deep interest in intuitive matters, and Neptune helps you accept psychic energies. Positive people and a good diet matter in your life. You are probably overwhelmed by activities, and the challenge of organizing your day can be real. Take note of your body's reactions and interpret them realistically.

•If **Neptune is in the Seventh House,** issues like marriages and partnerships are either psychic or spiritual. These unions are likely to disappoint and may emanate from the fact that you did not have a realistic image of your partner in the first place. Apart from these shortcomings, you are still capable of attaining selfless love.

•With **Neptune in the Eighth House**, you can harness psychic energy to reach greater heights. You have a deep interest in matters of spirituality, and your partners may deceive you. Instead of instilling fear, death may arouse you.

•When **Neptune is in the Ninth House**, you have a deep interest in spiritualism and mysticism. While you are obsessed with spiritual issues, you must take time to plan things.

•If **Neptune is in the Tenth House**, you can gain recognition for a unique achievement, often happening to artists like poets, musicians, and others. Creative work plays a great role in your life. You may have great ideas, but everything may seem trivial. You can mesmerize different people with your great ideas and imagination. The tenth house is often associated with the father, who may not always be available.

•With **Neptune in the Eleventh House**, you can find great inspiration from friends and associates. You were born to connect with all living beings, and you are full of love. You are also involved in charity work and helping others. However, you may have problems judging your goals. Never give up responsibility and choose your friends wisely.

•If **Neptune is in the Twelfth House,** you have deep spiritual compassion and are likely to succeed in different facets of metaphysics. You may wish to return to the womb, and the material world can be challenging for you. Dimensions can open up to you, and they may be unattainable to others. Avoid drugs.

Neptune in the First House (The Self)

If you have Neptune in the first house, you carry the whirlpools of this planet with you. When Neptune is in this position, it represents identity, physical body, personal outlook, and approach to life. The individuals with Neptune in this position are often thin-skinned, far-away, dreamy, and mysterious. It adds a stormy, sensitive, and magnetic reflection to their being.

They can also respond perceptively to different things around them since they have a unique gift of picking the emotional tone existing in the atmosphere. Neptune can absorb all experiences in the atmosphere, and it is changeable. It can also lead to prophetic premonitions that are not easy to interpret.

Negative Traits of Neptune in the First House

The challenge with people with Neptune in the first house is that they are not clear about what they want in life. As a result, they may find themselves drifting without a specific direction. When trying to establish some sense of self-determination, the individuals often find the lines blurred. They also experience problems in functioning properly in the world. The first house rules the physical aspect of the self or person, leading to unexplained tiredness. Confusing illness can also occur. Neptune often leads to escapism, and the individuals within this placement may find themselves drawn to alcohol and drugs. Some people often see alcohol and drug abuse as a means to escape the challenges of life.

Positive Aspects about Neptune in the First House

When dreamy lenses are used to view life, they can possess some form of magical realism. It offers artistic, musical, and imaginative opportunities that place individuals with Neptune in different aspects of creative expressions. With Neptune, you will find yourself reflecting unconsciously on other people's needs. However, such projections without physical contact can be dangerous, leading to the creation of weak boundaries. However, the main aspect is that a person with Neptune can be a channel of longings, ideas, and dreams. In some cases, the dreams may come true.

Another aspect about Neptune in the first house is that it outlines the circumstances surrounding one's birth. The person may feel as if they have no choice but the will of their mother. That element of struggle at birth is absent since the mothers are often drugged and are unconscious. Therefore, the birth process will not be very difficult, and it happens as if it is under the water. The individuals involved will later deal with reality in life with the same passivity as in birth.

How to Avoid Undesirable Outcomes

Neptune in the house does not emphasize one-on-one relationships. Relationships can exist in the form of victim and savior situations. Neptune comprises addictive tendencies, and it can lead the individuals to be emotionally manipulative and display a high propensity to fuse with others. Neptune will also display compassion that helps other people to be attracted by healing and counseling roles. Elements like sympathy, empathy and the ability to get into someone's feelings will create a connection. When the qualities are used properly, they will show compassion for everyone.

Neptune in the Second House (Material Possessions)

People with Neptune in the second house in their birth chart are unfortunately presented in a bad light. These individuals tend to be extravagant, and they have issues with their wealth and possessions. As a result, they often find their lives revolving around debt repayment. They lack financial judgment, and this means that they should get other individuals to handle their accounting.

These individuals should not trust their ideas since they might be unrealistic. However, some of them can pursue interesting careers in life. They pay too much attention to what intuition tells them instead of following logic, leading to the challenge of managing wealth. They believe that one day, wealth will come to them and that they will become very rich. As a result, they struggle to make a decent living. Therefore, they should revise their attitude toward money.

When Neptune is in the second house, the people with this placement often feel that they are rich regardless of their material possessions. While this optimistic view towards wealth is good, they should change their approach to life since their money is often spent on valueless things. At times they are very generous, and their money and other possessions quickly disappear. Neptune in the second makes the individuals confused and impractical concerning financial practices.

While dreams of becoming wealthy are good, they are in no way beneficial since *they do not make any difference.* These individuals are also easy to trick once promised of schemes that can make them rich in a short period. The problem of quick earnings often affects many people. A lot of people tend to be swayed by promises of tremendous wealth and other unproven opportunities. These people may not see reality concerning their money. It is also vital for these individuals to learn to say no if asked for financial help. If Neptune is in this house, it reveals the areas where most people become unhappy in their lives due to their attitudes.

The Good and Bad Components

The good thing about people with Neptune in the second house is that they are full of ideas. They also have great taste. Many people believe in themselves, and this helps them gain some sense of self-fulfillment. With clear objectives, these individuals can work diligently to attain their dreams. To pursue happiness, these people should not overly rely on what others say about them.

On a different note, these individuals must not rely too much on intuition when pursuing business. Believing in dreams is not always the best way to run a business. Living in a world of dreams may not offer positive results. They should try to be pragmatic to overcome some of the challenges they encounter.

Neptune in the Third House (Communication)

The ocean inspires people with Neptune in the third house, and they have sensitive minds. The minds of such people have no boundaries, and they do not know where their words can take them to. Neptune consists of rich and deep imagination that assists in dealing with perceptions and new ideas. Neptune's placement is capable of picking what other individuals are thinking. Those people who belong to this placement of Neptune do not learn through traditional ways. Lack of attention to their surroundings can be a big problem.

Negative Traits of Neptune in the Third House

The third house is responsible for ruling the daily facets of life. However, Neptune represents a gullible mind that often forgets mundane tasks and is often absent. Other factors like evasiveness and resistance to speaking honestly are also common. The problem is that these individuals are afraid of becoming victims of untruths and misinterpretations.

The problem, in some instances, can be attributed to underlying emotional and mental problems. Impaired hearing and vision, as well as neurological disorders, can cause severe effects. Hard and often cold facts do not appeal to these individuals. The subject must have an interesting theme. Otherwise, it will not stick in their minds for long. Neptune works best in the artistic world like music, photography, painting, novels, and poems. Neptune tends to think in pictures, which is why art is inspirational to many of its natives.

If you belong to Neptune in the third house, it is hard for you to absorb dry and cold facts as you have a talent for visualization. You are dreamy and perceptive, which makes you think deeply. However, you might miss some vital details, and sticking to schedules might be challenging. Communication, attending to errands, and other essential daily activities can be difficult for you. You may also miss or often be late for important appointments.

Apart from these likely downsides, you can imaginatively and creatively express yourself. You possess great charm, but you can cause misunderstandings since you are not always definite in what you say. Learning might not appeal to your interests since it is not creative.

Neptune in the Fourth House (The Home)

The fourth house is commonly known as the home of the family. If you belong to Neptune in the fourth house, your personality traits are characterized by excess. Your emotional state often leads you to view different things in extremes, and Neptune does not help or change anything.

Personality Traits of Neptune in the Fourth House

As you have observed, your emotional state will make you view different things from extreme angles. In most cases, you feel people are trampling on you. To avoid this, you feel you want to be alone. However, neither of these two might be correct at times. At times, pessimism tends to affect many people to the extent of viewing themselves as losers. Neptune represents spirituality, intuition, and idealism. Neptune has intuition and idealism. People with Neptune in the fourth house are highly intuitive; if this is you, you can understand different things using your instincts without applying conscious reasoning.

You can tell or read different situations to find out if anything is wrong. You often display a passion for lending a helping hand to someone who might appear to be in deep pain. Additionally, you are always ready to listen to your loved ones so that you can help them.

Positive Traits of Neptune in the Fourth House

You desire to be the host with Neptune in the fourth house. You aim to create a perfect, comfortable, and lovely home where most people you know may want to hang around. Home is best for you, and it is the most important component in your life. You want to preserve your home as part of your family tradition, where it is passed through generations. You can also view your past from another perspective and remember certain things from another angle.

You need to slow down and allow others to take stock of you. Additionally, take some time to reflect on yourself to forget about external problems. You can achieve this by relaxing and stopping worrying about what is going on with other individuals. However, remember to avoid being carried away by your daydreams since this can cause more harm to your personality. Some people end up seeing their dreams as reality, and there is a danger of getting carried away. You need to be yourself, and you will realize that people will love you for your thoughtfulness, making you feel good if you interact with people who genuinely want to help.

Negative Traits for Neptune in the Fourth House

With Neptune in the fourth house in the birth chart, you are caring and thoughtful. You prioritize other people's needs. However, this is mainly influenced by your desire for a close family. This might be something that you lacked as a child, or you now have different perceptions as you are older. You will want to become a nurturing parent, but at times you fail to understand certain things. You want to become a role model, but life will not always go the way you want. Uncertainty is the major setback in your endeavor.

Chapter 4: Neptune through the Houses II

Houses represent some part of your life or overall life experience. Many people look into houses to gain insight into their experiences concerning certain areas of life. This chapter highlights Neptune's journey in different houses in the birth chart. It examines what will happen when Neptune is located in the fifth (creativity), sixth (routines), seventh (partnerships), and eighth (transformation) houses. It also shows the good and the bad effects Neptune might bring and recommends ways to deal with the negative effects.

Neptune in the Fifth House (Creativity)

The people born with Neptune in the Fifth House in the natal chart have creative components and artistic talent. Neptune quickly falls in love, and their creative minds will get into contact with objects around them. If you belong to this placement, you can prove your prowess in poetry, music, acting, and visual arts. Children born to such individuals are sensitive, possess creative talents, and are intuitive. However, the procreation of children often takes place under mysterious conditions. Some people cannot remember what transpired when their children were procreated.

Traits of Neptune in the Fifth House

The following are some of the positive traits that characterize people born with Neptune in the Fifth House. Neptune represents the capability to love, and dating is religious. Everything associated with love has some religious connotations.

Once you win the love you want, sex becomes smooth, and it liberates you. Sexual relationships occur smoothly and gently with your partner. Sex acts as an inspiration in whatever you do. Neptune allows you to utilize your imagination in everything concerning love.

People with Neptune in the fifth house have a unique understanding of other people, and they have the rare gift of being able to explain different things. Both children and adults will listen to such people. The educators can solve various issues related to love affairs.

Some people who experience intimate problems can refuse to let go and try other methods. Education can play a major role in salvaging relationships that are on the verge of collapse. For instance, moral development and understanding of the opposite sex can be a source of fortune. Neptune is great for musicians, actors, and other artists. They can idealize the people they love and show great care and intimacy.

Fantasies do not usually represent reality, which is one reason why they are shrouded in secrecy. Neptune represents positive elements and resonates with good traits. The presence of Neptune provides the first child with the dreamer's character. The child will be very creative and likely to become an artist. Neptune will create secrecy around the native children concerning their sexual affairs.

Neptune in the fifth house can be victimized, but the native is ready to accept and suffer together with the person they are in love with. Most people with challenges concerning their sexual lives are attracted to individuals with Neptune in the fifth house. This placement often leads to the creation of victim/savior types of relationships.

Negative Traits

Fear of rejection is the major factor that impacts many people born with Neptune in the fifth house. Once a person is rejected, they will feel some form of ideological dismay and deep concern. As a result, other people will end up deliberately displaying asexuality to protect themselves from unwanted attention. Other people can end up being tricksters to portray a different image or misrepresent reality to their lovers to preserve love.

Addressing Negative Traits

The fear of rejection in love does not bode well with different people since they feel inferior or bad about themselves. However, rejection is common, and there are genuine reasons for that. Therefore, to overcome the fear of being rejected, you need to believe in yourself and accept the things you cannot change to avoid unnecessary heartbreaks. You should know that love and relationships are not automatic. You should not expect anything when you decide to date someone.

You need to take certain steps that will help ensure that your love does not deprive another person of happiness – a major concern in different relationships. It is essential to create a fine balance in a relationship to ensure that it is not one-sided. There should be mutual understanding in a relationship. Learn to respect your partner to enjoy a lasting union.

Neptune in the Sixth House (Routines)

Neptune in the Sixth House is associated with the routines and habits of the individuals. The house is related to work and other factors like processes, challenges, struggles, and all the temptations that come with it. This placement also relates to the native's professional life, particularly relations with coworkers, working environment, work, and life balance. The sixth house is also the House of Health since most things are centered on health-related issues. The following are the traits that characterize this house.

Positives of Neptune in the Sixth House

The Sixth House's central themes are service, health, and work. The house is primarily concerned with the native's health or well-being and their attitude toward maintaining it. The sixth field prioritizes a link between work and good health since they go hand in hand. The house emphasizes dietary habits since they help us deal with different challenges that can happen in life. Individuals must stay healthy in these relations to function normally. Fitness and health are top on the priority list, and they lead to the creation of a harmonious life.

Negatives

With Neptune in the Sixth House, many people are often distracted from their businesses and daily obligations. This planet is dreamy, and it does not favor a planned routine. It is also imaginative and primarily concerned about setting the soul free. Some people with this placement of Neptune in the Sixth House find it perfect and in sync with the natal chart. They can function well without a well-planned and established routine. Their routine is rather not to have anything organized. Individuals will never forget their intuition and rituals when it comes to health, work, and diet.

The natives can be flexible but without losing their sense of duty and responsibility. They can combine these two components for their benefit and the benefit of others. When things do not look favorably on the chart, they can turn things the other way round. As a result, the natives can end up avoiding their duties and become unreliable and forgetful. This will lead to the creation of a chaotic situation.

Another negative aspect about Neptune in the Sixth House is that it is often associated with troubles at work, skepticism, shame, and trickery. Such types of inconvenience are common in the workplace, and they often affect how you relate to your core workers. Ultimately, enmity and trickery at work can affect your performance.

Alternative Path to Address Issues

The natives with the placement of Neptune in the Sixth House often lose a sense of limits regarding the aspect of serving or supporting others. They want to assist others, and this is a good gesture. While this is a positive thing to do, it can be costly. Such people can end up being manipulated or exploited, and, in some instances, they cannot resist it. The other aspect is that the native can end up being too dependent on other people. As a result, they end up feeling helpless, confused, useless, and weak when there is no one to lean on.

To avoid such a scenario, natives in this placement should know that too much of anything is always dangerous. They should avoid being too generous or over-dependent on other people. Moderation is critical if you want to achieve your desired goals and objectives. The individuals with Neptune in the Sixth House can build their world where they can create a balance between real-life duties and work. The alternative fields of interest they can pursue does include medicine – helping. natives to combine their inner spirituality with mental and physical health with their work, thus fulfilling their intuitions.

Neptune in the Seventh House (Partnerships)

With Neptune in the Seventh House of the natal chart, individuals tend to move toward the themes of idealization, merging, sacrifice, elevation, and inspiration. Deception, addiction, confusion, and victimhood are also other elements peculiar to this house. The mix of things creates what can be affectionately known as "open enemies." Neptune has a close link with the invisible. The subconscious element becomes part of the mix. These are the operational things that cannot be seen with a naked eye.

Positive Traits

The position of Neptune in the seventh house suggests that relationships are determined by the storehouse individuals have of Neptunian qualities. Elements like a sense of unity, unconditional love, and acceptance, and the ability to inspire others to reach greater heights in their lives help build a strong bond in their relationships. The dynamics found in this placement play a critical role in shaping the native's relationships with others. Strong unions are built on their willingness to help other people realize their goals.

Negative Traits

Neptune is associated with the invisible. The individuals in this placement can collude with partners to make subconscious and secret agreements that may not be in their best interest. Unconditional love and acceptance are good, but they may lead people astray. For instance, you should ask yourself what you will benefit from showing such great love to others. If you carefully look at it, you will end up giving more than you benefit from in a relationship. As a result, the partnership can end up working against you. A true relationship should be mutually beneficial.

At times, there may be clandestine contracts that can lead partners to suspend many elements in their lives which they may feel are negative. They will do this to sustain intoxicating relationships on the understanding that the two parties will not confront each other in the relationship. This selfless agreement may not be binding in the long run. It is based on the appeasement of the other party, which can lead to anger. The other party or both can begin to believe they have been tricked or lied to.

This happens when the parties realize that their relationship has not yielded the expected results. The idealizers will only see what they want to see and often have limited knowledge of the person involved. They will only realize that the selective perceptions they hold are an illusion based on their imagination. They are obsessed with the perfected ideal rather than the real person.

Extreme idealizers often refuse to view anything from another perspective except their own ideal, believing that they are giving unconditional love.

The problem is that the person who is often flattered that they are being given unconditional love will, over time, feel some form of discomfort developing. They will realize that they are not fully appreciated for who they truly are but are being treated in the way the idealizer prefers. In other words, the notion of unconditional love is not sustainable in the long run since the other party can have other views.

How to Address Negativity

Neptune in the seventh house is often associated with disdain and negativity. Individuals need to understand that the self-inflicted suffering that emanates from these partnerships does not make them more spiritual than others. Before exhibiting this type of behavior, ask what you will get out of the relationship instead of sacrificing your commitment over nothing. The partnership may not be worth it if it offers mistreatment and unhappiness.

The other challenge faced by many people is to make a distinction between something ideal and something concrete. It is vital for individuals to fully understand the difference between the two. Over idealization does not help a lot since it can be viewed as self-deception. One needs to accept reality and see relationships as they are and nothing else. Idealizing other people can only bring disappointment at the end of the day when the other party realizes that they have not benefited from the union as they expected.

Neptune in the Eighth House (Transformation)

The presence of Neptune in the Eighth House indicates death. The native should be wary of the issues that involve life and death. They may fall into lethargy or trances, and they should have instructions about what to do in the case of apparent death to avoid being buried alive. Natives should alert their friends and relatives about their circumstances or write a paper that a stranger can read. Death can be caused by different factors like mental shock or any kind of disaster.

Positive Traits

The native's view of death may be original, and they are based on some interesting theories pertaining to this topic. Their mind may tell them to dwell on the subject, or they may have a great fascination about it. The subject is ever-present in their mind, and they also have some form of addiction to spiritualism. People born with Neptune in the Eighth House should be careful to avoid drugs that can impact their consciousness. When you are in this placement of Neptune, your intuition can tell you different things that are likely to cause death. Drugs and alcohol are some of the elements that you must avoid.

Negative Traits

As you have observed, the eighth house is commonly known as the goods of the dead. The native must be prepared for different forms of disappointment that may arise because of loss. While the natives can benefit from the legacies, they are likely to be at the mercy of the executors. However, the issue does not apply to the case involving inheritance; it can be somewhat confusing for you to understand, so take the necessary steps to understand it fully.

The eighth house also indicates the goods of the other partner in business. Individuals born with Neptune in the Eighth House must expect some form of vagueness, deception, and disappointment. It will be a big blunder for natives to marry for financial gain. If they attempt it, they will certainly not obtain it. You can lose property after marriage. If you intend to enter a business partnership, you should regard the capital of the other partner with doubt. You must not base your business on promises that may fail to materialize.

How to Address Negative Issues

Natives must be careful when it comes to making their will. As a native, make sure that your will has no loopholes that can cause disputes upon your death. Make sure the will is in safe hands or choose proper executors. You can ignore shared resources and be extra careful when dealing with money. It is vital to pay attention to avoid problems that are likely to arise because of your high degree of trust. To solve some of the problems related to financial issues, it is a good idea to enlist the services of a professional advisor like an accountant.

It is also crucial to avoid alcohol in situations that involve sex so you can follow your desired will. You are likely to be passionate when it comes to sexual matters. You can suddenly realize that your desire has disappeared before you fulfill it. If you are celibate, you can invoke religious reasons.

Houses describe various aspects of your life experiences when Neptune passes through them. As you have observed in this chapter, there are different connotations associated with each house in the natal chart.

Chapter 5: Neptune through the Houses III

This chapter examines the movement of Neptune through the last four houses of the natal chart that include the ninth (travel), tenth (public image), eleventh (humanitarianism), and twelfth (the subconscious) houses. The positive and negative elements will be discussed for each house and recommendations given for dealing with the potential of negative outcomes.

Neptune in the Ninth House (Travel)

The placement of Neptune in the Ninth House can reflect someone who is a visionary since they are in connection with their higher self. If you believe in negativity concerning this placement, it can lead you to illusions. The ninth house in the natal chart shows your travels or journeys that are represented at the physical and mental levels. It is primarily concerned with growth, and the search for meaning is pivotal in your life.

Personality Traits

Individuals with the placement of Neptune in the Ninth House are curious about discovering their purpose of existence. In all their journeys, there will be an element of seeking the truth involved. As a result, such people rarely stop learning to fulfill their quest to gain knowledge about different aspects of their lives. The ninth house also indicates that spirituality is an important component of your inner self.

The ninth house supports individual growth on different levels. The planets that belong to the ninth house suggest that the people born within the same period are interested in learning various things about the world around them. Natives also believe that constant learning is an effective method of bettering themselves or improving their knowledge about different things surrounding them. Education is a key component to individuals within this placement. Their position in the birth chart is a testimony that they love learning.

Your personality and philosophy consist of religious elements, and you view life as part of something bigger. Life connects you with the divine, and you often think about different elements that shape life. You often think beyond reality to seek divine answers to the questions you may have. Many questions are answered through religion which also guides many people's lives.

Positives of Neptune in Ninth House

Neptune in the ninth house, individuals are very religious – and they learn several things through religion. This placement allows them to develop strong morals and ethics that help them live in harmony with others. Through traveling, you will learn a lot of things, particularly the cultures of other countries. Travel is also an effective component of creative inspiration that shapes your life. You will learn to be open-minded from the philosophies and religions you encounter in your journeys in foreign lands.

Negative Traits of Neptune in Ninth House

As mentioned, Neptune in the ninth house is crucial for aspects like spirituality and religion. A close relationship with the divine is the key to this placement. While strong faith is a positive aspect of life, it can sometimes impact people in negative ways. As you can observe, many people with Neptune in the Ninth House are overly religious, and they believe that the divine overrides everything. However, this may not always be true since there are certain realities that we must face.

Instead of believing in verifiable scientific data, people with strong connections with the divine may see things differently or have different views. This leads to disillusionment and deception, where some people fail to comprehend the truth about many things. Overly religious people are gullible, and most of them can be influenced easily. As a result, the chances are high that you can easily fall prey to individuals who have bad intentions. Neptune tends to cover things in front of you with fog, and you will end up failing to see clearly.

How to Address Negative Elements about Neptune in the Ninth House

You should be careful and try to watch the illusion of Neptune that can affect your rational thinking. If you are over religious, there is a danger of becoming too optimistic, and you tend to see the situation in a better light than it is. Neptune, at times, is detached from reality. It views everything as benevolent and good. Other ninth house people have a strong intuition that helps them connect with the world. However, you need to realize that your truth is a perfect way of gaining new knowledge. You have a right to think differently, even outside the spiritual realm.

Neptune in the Tenth House (Public Image)

Neptune in the Tenth House is characterized by problems to the natives who belong to this placement. It shows that the individuals involved will face many financial challenges in their lives. These financial problems are likely to emanate from deception from other people concerning monetary issues. The issue here is that tenth house people are highly intuitive and tend to believe in their imagination.

The problem with some individuals of this group is that they strongly believe in their intuition more than anything else. As a result, these persons are likely to make poor decisions based on their intuitions. However, facing reality at times can go a long way toward helping the affected people overcome some of the forces that affect their finances. When dealing with financial issues, you need to apply objectivity and rational thinking instead of believing in unseen powers hoping they will offer you the desired results.

Another trait of people with Neptune in the Tenth House is that they are likely to be involved in the advertising and publicity worlds. In some ways, other natives may find their professions linked to reformatories, prisons, institutions, and oil. However, the native may encounter some challenges concerning trade fluctuations, impacting their financial situation, as indicated earlier.

Negative Traits

The financial challenges often encountered by the tenth house people can be attributed to different factors. Instead of solely relying on intuition, you should know that you can achieve professional success if you pursue a few secret endeavors. The problem with sharing all your plans with everyone is that other people can deceive you, and you fail to achieve your desired goals. Therefore, too much believing in other people can be your big letdown. However, if you act professionally, you are likely to be rewarded.

Another negative element concerns afflicted Neptune, which often leads to the absence of practical ideas. Lack of pragmatism often drives many people to their downfall and ultimate disgrace. You should try to come up with practical ideas before you begin your project. The good thing about practical ideas is that they bring tangible results, and you can evaluate them and make necessary changes. This makes it different from believing in divine power when undertaking a project that should produce observable output.

Positive Traits

Not every element of Neptune in the Tenth House is associated with problems, as highlighted above. For instance, when Neptune is retrograde, there are chances of great creativity that can be enjoyed by the people who belong to this placement. If natives work where inspiration and vision are required, they are likely to use their creativity to achieve the desired results. Many people are inspired by the desire to see their visions come to fruition and help solve different problems.

If you are a visionary, you learn the significance of being impersonal. You will realize that it is not critical after all to identify with social position or status. You will become a role model who is committed to achieving success in different social issues. You will be driven by the desire to see your vision come true. Additionally, imagination and intuition will play a critical role in guiding your professional career. You also get the opportunity to learn the essential basics of life. You will be more interested in the mystic and creative professions.

How to Address the Negative Elements

It is vital to believe in yourself and try to brainstorm different ideas that can lead to success. You must not see yourself as a failure or incapable of achieving your goals. More importantly, the natives in this placement should be careful and avoid being influenced by other people's judgment. You must believe in yourself and have self-confidence in whatever you do. You will realize that you can achieve your desired goals without any influence from other people.

Neptune in the Eleventh House (Humanitarianism)

The eleventh house symbolizes peer relationships and friendships. This placement for people with Neptune in their natal chart represents critical life lessons concerning boundaries. True friendship usually takes place between two peers on a mutual basis where they treat each other as equals. The one-sided friendship is likely to be unsatisfying to both parties in the long run. No one should yield excessive power or influence in a true friendship.

Fortunately, for the people in the eleventh house natal chart, Neptune represents compassion and willingness to serve a friend in need that, in most cases, is unfortunate. We all go through difficult times that social or economic crises may cause at some point in time. Therefore, the desire to pitch in and help your friend experiencing hardship is a wonderful thing you can do to uplift their spirits.

Positive Traits

A true friend always tries to give back regardless of their current situation. When your colleague is down due to poor health, and you give a helping hand, they will always try to give back at some point in time. The good thing about true friendship is that it is reciprocal. Instead of just waiting to receive from other people, you also must do something good for your friends. You may not give back the same things you received, but anything you do out of love will be well appreciated. True friendship is not about showing off material wealth but an appreciation of the union.

Another benefit of true friendship is that it helps build a strong bond between the people involved. You can learn a lot of things from someone who cares about your welfare. If you are in a relationship that allows you to exchange ideas and everything with the other party freely, you can enjoy social security. You will always have someone to lean on during difficult times.

Negative Traits

While true friendship is about helping each other, Neptune in the eleventh house represents people who are always helping others. As a result, the friendship can end up becoming a bit parasitical because other people are always looking for someone to pull them out of trouble. Individuals moving on a destructive path need help, but the situation can end up disappointing others. Some relationships will ultimately turn sour if the other party is always looking for assistance. If you feel the friendship is straining you, you need to check where it went sour.

You may also realize that co-dependent relationships, especially in situations involving destructive behavior, can be harmful. When you find yourself stuck in a draining relationship, it may not be doing any good to you or the other party involved. You cannot always be available to solve other people's problems. You should know your limits and give your friend enough room to put their house in order. If you are ever-present, you may be setting an imbalance unknowingly, which will impact your friendship in the long run. You must know the boundaries that exist in your friendship.

It is recommended that you seek new friends that you can connect with through mutual respect. You should use self-introspection and understand your habits since they can contribute to the imbalances in friendship. Look at your history of friendships and understand where you went wrong. If you realize that you may have contributed to the collapse of your previous friendships, make sure you do not repeat the same mistakes. More importantly, you must respect other people's privacy.

Neptune in the Twelfth House (The Subconscious)

Neptune in the Twelfth House is also known as the subconscious since it affects the subconscious mind. At times it can cause fears that emanate from the problems that you experienced in the past. Fear of the unknown is a great challenge for many people since it impacts different aspects of their social lives. The main issue here is that people will tend to focus on the wrong things in life.

Negative Aspects

It may not be easy for individuals to overcome the challenges they face in their daily life if their mind continues to dwell in the past. These people usually rely on the spiritual world for guidance in whatever they do. As a result, materialistic success is not highly prioritized by individuals who are mainly concerned about negative things that affect their lives. Negativity is retrogressive in life, and you will realize that you cannot succeed if you always believe that you are incapable of attaining your desired goals.

Afflicted Neptune also causes subconscious distortions in life where people are diverted from reality. Some people will end up focusing on misdirected fantasies to evade the reality of life, which can be harsh at times. Life comprises several challenges, and things may not always go the way you want. Instead of running away from the truth, it is essential to find a way to overcome the challenges you encounter.

Positive Traits

Neptune in the Twelfth House people have great empathy toward mentally or physically handicapped people. They are willing to assist others despite the challenges they may be facing in their lives. On a positive note, it is good to offer a helping hand to someone in need regardless of your situation or status. You can get inner satisfaction that helps you forget your own challenges if you help others. Neptune in the twelfth house also states that individuals should also try to focus on their souls. Whenever you soul search, you are likely to realize the areas where you go wrong to take corrective measures.

Recommendations

Fear impacts the subconscious mind and, ultimately, the well-being of the person involved. To overcome this challenge, there are different measures you can take. Find a cool place where you can relax and breathe deeply while you clear your mind of the obstacles that disturb your focus. Meditation can go a long way toward helping you focus your energy on the positive aspects of life. Meditation is also good for your mental health to help you avoid focusing on things that do not add value to your life.

You should also learn to draw inspiration from accepting reality in your life. You cannot change certain things, and in some instances, you only need the commitment to make a difference. Therefore, it is vital to be rational when you deal with different things that affect the mind. Spiritual inclination and intuition can provide you with guidance on what you want to achieve. However, some people miss the plot when they overly rely on their intuition more as a way of escaping the realities of life. If you want to achieve the best in life, you should be objective.

On average, Neptune spends at least 14 years in each house on the natal chart. The effects of Neptune in different houses apply to different countries, cities, and organizations. The houses in Neptune have different connotations depending on their position on the natal chart. As you will have observed, there are both positive and negative traits brought about by Neptune as it passes through each house.

Chapter 6: Relationship with Other Planets

This chapter covers what happens when Neptune aspects other planets. It explains what happens when Neptune is in sextile, conjunction, square, trine, or opposition with other planets within the solar system. It also highlights the hard and soft aspects of different planets. In this chapter, you will also learn the meaning of interactions between Neptune and each planet.

Understanding Neptune

Neptune planet consists of mysteries and illusions that have a strong influence on different generations. The power of the planet also manifests in imagination and fantasy. Neptune moves slowly across the zodiac and spends almost 14 years in each sign. When this planet was discovered, it brought about an interest in spiritualism. When featured in any zodiac sign, Neptune is spiritual, idealistic, healing, selfless, and connected to the unseen. When a conjunction is formed between Neptune and another planet, the planet will gain the above qualities from the combination.

Neptune/Mercury Aspects

Mercury has the name of the god of trade and travel, and it symbolizes communication skills, a keen mind, and the capability to profit. A person with strong intellectual capabilities can benefit from useful acquaintances from Mercury. As a result, the Neptune/Mercury pair provides keen intellect, curiosity, and good powers of perfection and logic.

Favorable Aspects of Mercury

Mercury-Neptune Conjunction - This conjunction impacts the interest of almost everything supernatural. This combination is dreamy and romantic, which makes it defenseless against aspects like destiny's unexpected tests. Cruel deception or insidiousness can trap people at times.

Mercury-Neptune Sextile - Favorable to all creative creatures, particularly people who understand philosophy and religion.

Mercury-Neptune Trine - Provides excellent imagination, and this aspect is ideal for mystical novel writers and science fiction writers. At times, however, people can avoid reality and withdraw from the public.

Unfavorable Aspects of Mercury

Mercury-Neptune Square - This aspect can push you to make mistakes even though you want to use your brain. You often forget crucial points and end up not knowing how you can make rational decisions. The people who belong to this category love art which includes music, poetry, and mysticism.

Mercury-Neptune Opposition - It shows that individuals involved lack clear relationships and insight. Furthermore, they are likely to fall prey to deception and should learn to protect secrets. They are fascinated by unlimited and uncontrollable fantasies.

Neptune/Venus Aspects

The Venus/Neptune combination provides respect for balance and financial acumen, social skills, aesthetics, and comfort. Venus comes from the goddess of inspiration, love, and beauty.

Favorable Aspects of Venus

Venus-Neptune Conjunction - Neptune can idealize the image of other individuals. It increases emotional response, which means that it becomes easier to be disappointed when you are in a close relationship.

Venus-Neptune Sextile - People live in harmony, are pleasant, and gracious. If these individuals organize an event or exhibition, the chances of success will be high. These individuals often experience positive surprises in their lives.

Venus-Neptune Trine - Provides great talent in art, and the individuals involved can write extraordinary novels. They also enjoy dating under mysterious circumstances.

Unfavorable Aspects of Venus

Venus-Neptune Square - Can bring problems related to the understanding of love and its manifestations. You are likely to experience excessive sensitivity or laziness. Prudence is required when you handle relationships and finances.

Venus-Neptune Opposition - Likely to create a distorted world view due to reliance on illusions. Idleness and the love of pleasure often contribute to drug and alcohol abuse. Neptune can also lead to the concealment of personal life facts, but they can be forcibly detected.

Neptune/Mars Aspects

This pair brings confidence, initiative, and assertiveness. In astrology, Mars is renowned for providing people with energy in different aspects of life.

Favorable Aspects of Mars

Mars-Neptune Conjunction - Reflects a constant improvement of a person since they have great potential. The individual pays attention to religion and spiritual initiation. Many people in this category love to dance and have excellent flexibility.

Mars-Neptune Sextile - Promotes the development of skills like acting that can help different people in life. The individuals concerned have life strategies, calculating personalities, and they can control emotions without causing harm.

Mars-Neptune Trine - This combination makes people sensitive and receptive. Inspiration can positively affect others, and love of good things takes center stage.

Unfavorable Aspects of Mars

Mars-Neptune Square - You will experience strange and incomprehensible desires that are not usually compatible with your life. If you suppress these desires, you are likely to develop irritation and nervousness. If you do not suppress these desires, elements like debauchery and drug abuse are likely to appear.

Mars-Neptune Opposition - The control of your subconscious aspirations is likely to be weakened. Things that contribute to different problems in your married life, like drugs and alcohol, should be avoided.

Neptune/Jupiter Aspects

The conjunction of Jupiter/Neptune is characterized by generosity, optimism, and some respect for cultural diversity and higher learning. Jupiter is responsible for handling the social ties of man, and it provides a feeling of fullness.

Favorable Aspects of Jupiter

Jupiter-Neptune Conjunction can make your appearance unusual, but there is a chance of getting a big profit. For instance, you can get a high-paying job, but your relationship with other people will not always be good.

Jupiter-Neptune Sextile - While you can analyze different things, some individuals can feel lonely and likely to be victims of frequent depression. The creative potential is often wasted, and some individuals may visit a monastery to search for the meaning of life.

Jupiter-Neptune Trine - Reflects an interest in spiritualism and mystical inclinations. The desire for ideas, imagination, demonstrations, music, and art is apparent among the people who belong to this category. Your sense of reality is usually distorted by the endless twisting of subtle complications in life.

Unfavorable Aspects of Jupiter

Jupiter-Neptune Square - The desire for mystical gatherings and travel is common. However, there is an element of laziness present that can lead to excess weight, change in appearance, and an increase in body fluids. Natives often have a problem assessing their position in life.

Jupiter-Neptune Opposition provides a propensity for mysticism, and the notion of faith is likely to be distorted. People can sympathize, help, but they cannot judge. You need to be wary of destructive behavior like drug, alcohol, and substance abuse.

Neptune/Saturn Aspects

The pair of Saturn/Neptune provides self-discipline, resolve, and organization. Regardless of its position in the horoscope, Saturn is among the brightest of planets. You need to check the position of Saturn if you want to gain insight into factors that lead other people to overestimate their lives.

Favorable Aspects of Saturn

Saturn-Neptune Conjunction - Deals with mysticism and contemplation of events that can stimulate constant interest. This will help you to get a view into the future using your knowledge of the past.

Saturn-Neptune Sextile leads to idealism. Some people have big requirements and responsibilities, which means that they have high expectations of others. Imagination and discipline are used for practical purposes.

Saturn-Neptune Trine helps increase your thought process and provides the chance to meet several global issues. Human motives and behavior are well understood by different kinds of people, and there are also influential members in different groups. These individuals are charismatic, and they stand out from the rest.

Unfavorable Aspects of Saturn

Saturn-Neptune Square - This often leads to the development of conflicts with the standards that are generally accepted in society. It represents betrayal and meanness, which can trigger issues with law enforcement representatives. There is likely to be a feeling among other people that the power structures are not protecting the citizens.

Saturn-Neptune Opposition - External life circumstances can shake the stability of life in general, and, in some instances, people may not adequately assess themselves. They cannot see the inconsistencies and contradictions in their actions. Natives can work, but they often lack patience, discipline, and a competent approach to business.

Neptune/Uranus Aspects

The pair of Uranus and Neptune provides progressive insight, originality, and a willingness to experiment with new things. The attachment to material things often deters many people from becoming free. According to Neptune, there is a need for radical change, such as abandoning the desire for financial stability.

Favorable Aspects of Uranus

Uranus-Neptune Conjunction - Our desire for change is awakened by this combination. However, you need to take care of yourself and the environment. This aspect deals with creative potential based on sensitivity and identity.

Uranus-Neptune Sextile makes individuals idealize almost everything, and creativity is manifested by their fantasies. Photography, design, and publishing are the most suitable professions.

Uranus-Neptune Trine - It arouses the interest of occults and mysticism, especially among the twentieth generation. Intuition and clairvoyance are likely to shape the behavior of these people in many ways.

Unfavorable Aspects with Uranus

Uranus-Neptune Square - Your peace of mind is likely to be disturbed because of your grumbling and uncompromising attitude. You are likely to experience difficulties in practicing meditation and studying.

Uranus-Neptune Opposition - You need to make an informed decision when you answer critical questions about stressful situations. Conflict with intuition is likely to be possible.

Neptune/Pluto Aspects

The pairing provides objectivity and the ability to transform their surroundings into better conditions. Pluto symbolizes mass catastrophes and wars and consists of nuclear energy.

Favorable Aspects of Pluto

Neptune-Pluto Conjunction - The pair helps you to understand the hidden meanings of various things in life. It is often associated with political issues that affect society or the entire country. People usually seek to include other individuals in their faith.

Neptune-Pluto Sextile impacts the generation and encourages spiritual development. Additionally, it promotes creativity and other supernatural possibilities.

Neptune-Pluto Trine - This occult lasts longer and leads people to follow intuition, trust clairvoyance, and mystical tendencies.

Unfavorable Aspects of Pluto

Neptune-Pluto Square can overstrain your intellectual and mental capabilities. The perceptions of the world and the desire to control often influence the behaviors of many people.

Neptune-Pluto Opposition - The desire for power and subcontract instincts often contradict. The problems of religion and social attention that exist in this sphere are unavoidable.

Neptune/Sun Aspects

The stressful and harmonious aspects significantly lead to an increase in imagination. The stressful aspects present the negative elements of Neptune, which means you should be careful of issues like substance abuse. If people play with your sympathy, you may end up becoming a victim. You may always be saving people, or you will get into a situation where you want the same people to save you. You are okay with any of the options above since you can always perform some charitable work that will keep Neptune happy.

Neptune/Moon Aspects

The Moon is viewed as a representation of emotions and instincts. Neptune plays a significant role in refining anything that it touches. Therefore, when Neptune and the Moon form an aspect, you are likely to experience refined receptors that are sensitive compared to others. This combination provides intuitive connections, responsiveness, and profound sensitivity. Imagination and talent are regarded as a talent that helps you accomplish your goals. Additionally, Moon and Neptune people can visualize the right picture in their minds. This will help them to perform better in different disciplines.

Hard vs. Soft Aspects of Neptune with Different Planets

Neptune is a planet of idealization, insight, and inspiration. It operates mysterious implications and suggestions that are often sensed or felt rather than being seen. It uses extra senses apart from the ordinary five we know in extending its reception. Neptune is a spiritual force, and it can be viewed negatively when it is combined with situations that require rational or physical materials. Planets aspecting Neptune will be refined and softened. The following are the hard and soft aspects of the relationship between Neptune and other planets.

Aspects of the Moon and Neptune

Hard Aspects

The natives often project their confusion into the world, and there are often subconscious forces in relationships that are not understood by many. The native will absorb the atmosphere around them, but they will still find some difficulties adjusting emotionally to the situation they feel has led them astray. Despite many false starts, the native remains committed to feeling better. This will eventually lead to a more robust and realistic view of emotional inspirations.

Soft Aspects

The natives can offer their emotions away if they are ready for an inspirational opportunity. The native will not attract misunderstandings about their emotional idealism. The soft approach does not provide the emotions but just ensures that your feelings are inspirational. Other people are not aware that they have strong ties with their families.

Aspects of Mercury and Neptune

Hard Aspects

The native will resort to some phony jargon, but that does not fool anyone except themselves. The native must try to eliminate vagueness by following their unique style. However, they will learn to combine all the inspirational effort offered by Neptune. This will help them think inspirationally.

Soft Aspects

The native may wander in ways that cannot be easily understood or followed by others. They are inclined to certain worldly attitudes and are not likely to change the situation because of the gratification they already get. The circumstances do not force the native to come to terms with the real side of Neptune.

Aspects of Neptune and the Sun

Hard Aspects

Neptune consists of inspiration, idealization, extrasensory, and extended vision that become strong when they are in a hard angle. There should be an element of ideals and nature, and the native is supposed to incorporate the two. At times, the native must stand up for their ideals, spiritual values, and inspiration. They should advocate positive idealism and overcome negative reactions.

Soft Aspects

The native is emphatic, and their intuition creates domestic and financial opportunities that can promote advancement. The native is not forced to present themselves inspirationally. However, they may dramatize things and end up exaggerating or distorting events.

Aspects of Neptune and Mars

Hard Aspects

The natives are often rational except in situations that involve Neptune and Mars. Their subconscious desires are not controlled by discipline, and their energies are diffused to an unreal motivation. The native often acts unnaturally, and issues like sexual deviation could be a cause for concern. However, they cannot ignore this pattern which will force them to place their passions on a spiritual plane. The native can experience mental illnesses due to suppressed desires.

Soft Aspects

The native will see it fit to take an indirect route of expression at the expense of a direct one. They find this option easy since there would be hard angles. Another important aspect is that the native is good at art as a way of expressing themselves. They also look for the best in other people but also find it challenging to maintain their standards at the same time. The native may need to retreat from the everyday world to recharge.

Aspects of Venus and Neptune

Hard Aspects

The subconscious forces strongly influence the Native's affections and emotions. They have distorted perceptions, and they end up succumbing to their wishful thinking. They also encounter problems in adjusting to their affectionate nature. The native will gradually become mature to align themselves with finer details in life that suit different situations. The native must overcome their great sense of insecurity to make informed decisions.

Soft Aspects

The native is sensitive, imaginative, and they are highly romantic. They also have a sixth sense that attracts people who may be looking for moral support. The natives have talent in arts, music, and poetry. They also seek affectionate things that will inspire them to obtain self-fulfillment. The soft angle is inspirational since it is different from the often hard and routine work.

Aspects of Neptune and Saturn

Hard Aspects

The pair involves two parties that share very little in common. Saturn involves firm foundations, sound attitudes, careful measurements, properly laid plans, practical objectives, and sound attitudes. The native has a challenge of combining the two to make sound inspirational principles, introduce hope, and redesign practical solutions that are less oppressive and adaptable. The native should adopt realistic ideals. On the other hand, Neptune suggests that the borders should be dissolved, measurements disregarded, espousing spiritual values instead of material values, and prioritizing inspiration instead of practical considerations as a guide.

Soft Aspects

The native does not face any conflict between practical and ideal. They view these two concepts as interchangeable, which sets them apart from others. The native can lose people around them who may cause a rift between the practicality and ideals they are working for. In this case, the native has strategic talents that can help them discover hidden secrets.

Aspects of Neptune and Uranus

Hard Aspects

Whenever the native tries to allow themselves inspirational spirit flights, they often feel isolated due to the uniqueness of the settings they encounter. The uncontrollable factors seem to be major obstacles that affect natives when they try to pursue the matter, even if they are getting closer. The sense of inspiration is overshadowed, but the native must believe the authority of their insights to overcome the hurdles. They should not be confused by other people's insights that may not be on the same wavelength as their desires. These people may end up turning to drugs and alcohol to escape the bedeviling situation.

Soft Aspects

On a positive note, the native is sensitive, intuitive, kind, and their spiritual faculties are highly developed. They can also appeal greatly to the masses, and they can join associations that teach yoga, astrology, and other subjects meant to raise spiritual awareness among different people. The native will find it exciting to entertain a variety of propositions.

Aspects of Jupiter and Neptune

Hard Aspects

Jupiter states that the code must be established first, and these often affect the natives in their bid to follow their divine inspiration. The native will be forced to adjust their idealism. Another aspect is that the native is compassionate, and they often experience a feeling of mystical or religious tendencies. The native often experiences some difficulties in adjusting their senses of inspiration and the same sensitivity patterns that have been followed by people who previously faced the same challenge.

Soft Aspects

The native's awareness of the rules already laid down by religious orders will make them easily follow the trail. This can create a limited spiritual intensity that lacks originality. The native must avoid substances like alcohol, drugs, and overeating which can affect their welfare.

Aspects of Neptune and Pluto

Hard Aspects

The native is different from other peers, and they are likely to be involved in religious, racial, and social conflicts. The urge for power and subconscious desires can lead to tension that can affect relationships between the natives and other people. The native will find it difficult to reconcile with people living in spiritual darkness.

Soft Aspects

The native is likely to identify their spirituality with the unfortunate people who may be lost or trapped somehow. Their interest is to share their burdens instead of focusing on doing something about the situation.

Neptune forms different relationships with all planets. As you have seen above, many elements influence the types of friendships created when Neptune pairs with different planets of the zodiac.

Chapter 7: The Neptunian Archetype

The Neptunian archetype is connected to deep self-exploration, a thirst for transcendence, intuition, creativity, and connection with the divine. Thus, having this archetype makes one fascinated by spirituality and mysticism or live their lives according to those principles. The Neptunian archetype functions mostly on a subconscious level, which means that its presence is revealed through dreams, imagination, and intuition. This chapter will clearly define the Neptunian archetype, explain how it implies the presence of these traits, and end with a small test to help the reader find out if they are Neptunians.

What Is an Archetype?

Before we start explaining what exactly this means, let's cover some basic information about the term "archetype." This word is defined as an original model from which all things of the same kind are copied or upon which they are based. Archetypes are patterns of behaviors, thoughts, and feelings that are common to humanity. They influence our daily behavior without us having conscious awareness about them. These patterns can be seen as themes important to all human experiences. For example, an archetype related to home is the Castle.

It represents safety and comfort, having ties to childhood. We all have an archetype that relates to blood relations because they are linked with our biological needs and safety, among other things. An archetype is also associated with the past, present, and future because every culture seems to have them. The Mother archetype can be found in all her representations in all cultures and periods. It is possible to find the Warrior archetype, too, because of his importance to our history and evolution as a species. These are only some of the many archetypes that exist, and we all possess at least a few of them within our subconscious minds.

The Origin of Archetypes

Archetypal structures are believed to have their origin outside the realm of consciousness. This is to say that our minds do not create them. Instead, archetypes are thought to have an external source of origin, reflecting the nature of archetypal images, which are sometimes described as gifts of nature. Archetypal patterns and images, such as the anima and animus, present themselves in dreams and visions or through symbols.

When we consider the source of their origin, it seems that they are present in the collective subconscious – displaying the theoretical construct developed by Carl Jung to explain human behavior. Its structure is mostly made of subconscious layers. These serve as storage for the memories, behaviors, and emotions that every human has in common with others. In other words, it is the part of our brain that contains all possible experiences from birth onwards.

The Neptunian Archetype

Neptune is the archetype of universal love, spiritual truth, psychic receptivity, and imagination. This archetype is closely connected to the divine, especially in a Neptunian's willingness for union with God or the universe. Neptunians are known to have great intuition, as well as a thirst for transcendence. They also need deep self-exploration and work with creative activities to achieve this goal. They can find their true passion through creative activities. They are also optimists who refuse to settle for less than their heart truly desires.

What Does It Mean for One to Be a Neptunian?

The archetype of Neptune offers a variety of lessons and qualities. In general, those who possess this archetype can find their true calling in creative activities. They are born to explore the deeper meaning of life, which is why they need self-discovery and introspection. Neptunians are also seekers of spiritual truth who look for divine experiences and revelations. Those with this archetype can awaken their psychic potential, which leads to enhanced creativity. Neptunians can have prophetic dreams, out-of-body experiences, and other types of extrasensory perceptions.

Neptunians are also extremely subjective and can be quite impressionable. They tend to get attached or involved with things quickly, making them feel attached to certain people, places, and things. At the same time, Neptunians are extremely sensitive beings who often have a hard time asserting themselves. They are very receptive to the energies of others, so their energy levels can decrease if they spend too much time with negative people. Neptunians also have a strong need for other people in their lives, especially if Neptunians can't express themselves because they can become insecure and even depressed.

Neptunians are known to have great imaginations. They can easily visualize things in their mind with little information, which often leads to heightened creativity. They can also become very good at visualization, which allows them to create their realities. Neptunians are very helpful, so they always seek to help others whenever possible. This archetype is also very romantic, as Neptunians love to fall in love with the idea of love, helping them become very good at encouraging others and bringing out the best in them.

At the same time, Neptunians can sometimes idealize their love interests or romantic partners. This outlook can make it difficult for Neptunians to find people with similar mindsets, which is why they often end up attracting the wrong types of people. Neptunians are also very intuitive, making them prone to depression when their intuition leads them to a negative conclusion. This influences Neptunians to seek guidance from others, as they often don't trust their intuition.

Neptunians are known for their sharp intuition, making it easy to judge another person's intentions. They are also very creative individuals who can see beauty in everything, which allows them to create works of art that can touch the hearts of millions. Neptunians are sensitive souls, so they also have a deep need for harmony within their lives. They refuse to settle for less than what makes them happy, which is why they often attract people with a lot of dreams and romantic ideas.

Examining the Neptunian Archetype

This archetype makes it difficult for Neptunians to understand themselves in a variety of different ways. At their most basic level, Neptunians are known for their need for self-exploration and deep introspection. They can feel as if they are lost and incomplete, which encourages them to seek out their true calling and path in life. Neptunians are also extremely impressionable beings, which means they can develop their intuition and psychic abilities without even realizing it.

Neptunians are primarily concerned with the mystery surrounding life, the universe, and everything else in between. They find it difficult to express themselves in a simple manner, which is why they often try to share their ideas and concepts through art. Neptunians are extreme romantics who love the idea of love and the idea of having a significant other. They can spend countless hours imagining what it would be like to have someone else by their side, making it difficult for these individuals to find true love.

Neptunians are also very helpful and have a deep need to help others and make the world a better place. They can become disillusioned when they notice that their efforts aren't making a difference in society, which is why Neptunians are more prone to depression. This is also why they can sometimes feel incomplete as if there's something wrong with the world and the people in it. Neptunians often try to pinpoint this problem by digging deep within themselves, which can eventually positively impact their interactions with society.

Neptunians are very spiritual individuals who spend far too much time focusing on the superficial aspects of life. They have a deep need to understand what defines reality, which means that Neptunians must spend a lot of time reflecting on their own experiences. Neptunians often have very mystical personalities, which is why they can't help but feel drawn to the unknown. These individuals are also concerned with uncovering ancient secrets and truths, making them feel like they don't belong in this present-day world.

Generally, Neptuniansare also unattached to material things, which means that they are usually very generous people. It can be difficult for Neptunians to recognize that other people have loved ones and families, so they are often very distant from their friends and family. Neptunians can easily go days without talking to anyone, which can cause them to feel lonely and misunderstood.

The final trait that all Neptunians share is their ability to tune into the cosmic vibrations of the universe effortlessly. This allows them to find inspiration in seemingly random events, which is why Neptunians are some of the most creative individuals on the planet. They have a strong intuition that allows them to foresee certain events long before they happen.

Divine Creativity

Divine Creativity is the idea that humans are born with a deep need to express themselves through art. It is believed that all of us have a divine calling and purpose, which is why we must spend a lot of time trying to uncover our true path in life. Neptunians are the best example of people who have such a need, which is why they are so selective about the kind of work they do.

Neptunians are primarily concerned with art, which means that they are constantly finding new ways to express themselves. It is common for Neptunians to treat their work as a form of communication, which is why they are never fully satisfied with their creations. They are constantly looking for ways to improve their work, which is why they are always trying to evolve their craft. This process can be very difficult for them because it often involves exposing themselves to the world, which can cause them to feel vulnerable.

Neptunians are extremely creative individuals who have a knack for artistic expression. They can be very picky when it comes to their work, which is why Neptunians are always looking for new ways to express themselves. They are constantly trying to challenge themselves, which can cause Neptunians to feel as if they are stagnating in life. It is also common for Neptunians to use their creativity to try and understand the world around them, which is why they are often very spiritual people.

While Neptunians are constantly trying to improve their craft, they can also be very objective about their work. Neptunians tend to be more concerned with the symbolism behind their creations rather than how aesthetically pleasing they are. They view art as a form of communication, which is why Neptunians try to stay true to their inner voice when they are creating something. Neptunians don't want to explore new artistic ventures if they feel as if the journey is shallow, which is why they tend to stick with the things that make them happy.

How Neptune Plays a Fundamental Role in Unlocking Divine Creativity

Neptune is the planet that governs creativity, which means that Neptunians are naturally drawn to the arts. Natives are very emotional individuals who tend to be very enraptured by their feelings. It can be difficult for them to understand the feelings of other people, which is why they are often detached from friends and family. These people spend a lot of time in isolation, which is why they are constantly trying to find ways to improve themselves.

Neptunians have a strong intuition that allows them to connect with the cosmos, which is why they are often very creative. They can spend days alone in their room just thinking about ways to express themselves. They also have a natural ability to make the impossible possible, which is why they sometimes surprise people with their abilities. These individuals are always trying to push the boundaries, which is why Neptunians are often seen as rebels.

Neptune governs creativity because it governs imagination. This means that natives are very open-minded people who believe that anything is possible. They refuse to be boxed in, which is why they can be very spontaneous. Neptunians are always looking for new ways to explore the world, which is why they tend to have a lot of hobbies and interests. It is common for them to feel as if they don't belong in this world, which is why they can be very spiritual individuals.

Divine Creativity in Mythology

Neptune was the Roman god of water and sea, which means that he governed the ocean. It is common for individuals to use their creativity to try to understand the world, which is why many of them become artists. It is also common for Neptunians to use their creativity to immerse themselves in the ocean. That's the reason why they are often very connected to their emotions.

Neptune was also the god of earthquakes, which means that the natives can be very connected to their emotions. These individuals tend to have a strong intuition that allows them to connect with the universe. Neptunians are frequently chaotic because they have a difficult time managing their feelings. It is common for these individuals to be drawn to the ocean because it represents the unconscious, making them constantly try to make sense of their inner world.

Neptunians are often depicted as dreamy individuals who are constantly trying to escape from reality. That's the reason why many Neptunians feel as if they don't belong here. Neptunians are often very independent people who prefer to work alone. They don't like to be restrained or told what they can and cannot do. That's the reason why many of them are rebels. They have a hard time taking orders, especially when they feel as if their creativity is being stifled.

To get a better idea of how Neptune influences the world, consider the works of Sir Isaac Newton and Sir William Herschel. Newton was a physics genius who used his prodigious mind to revolutionize our understanding of the world. Through his work, he established laws that govern physical motion, which he published in his iconic work "Philosophiae Naturalis Principia Mathematica." Herschel was one of the first individuals to map out the cosmos fully. He was a pioneer of astronomy who discovered Uranus, which he originally named George's Star after the king.

How To Determine If You're a Neptunian

It is important to know that some individuals are simply more creative than others. If you think that you're a Neptunian but aren't particularly creative, it is likely that you're simply not using your creativity. It is important to challenge yourself every day and think about different ways that you can express yourself. Find something that you're passionate about and work it to the bone, which will allow you to unlock your creative potential. To figure out if you're a Neptune person, think about your creative abilities.

Are You Creative?

If you're very creative, then it is likely that Neptune is influencing your life. Neptunians are constantly using their imagination to try and understand the world. They are dreamers who constantly feel as if they don't belong in this world. If you're a Neptunian, you'll likely be drawn to the ocean because it represents your subconscious. To get a better idea of how Neptune influences your life, think about your dreams.

Are You Dreamy?

Neptunians are always looking for new ways to express their creativity, which is why they're constantly dreaming about the future. These individuals are always trying to escape from reality and connect with their inner world. That's the reason why Neptunians are drawn to the ocean. If you're a Neptunian, you'll likely be able to remember your dreams at night because they will often connect with your emotions.

Are You Very Emotional?

Neptunians are very connected to their emotions, which is why they have a hard time controlling them. These dreamers are especially sensitive to the feelings of others and will often feel hurt if they don't receive the love that they need. Neptunians are often unpredictable, which makes them fascinating to other people. If you feel as if you don't fit in with this world, then it is likely that Neptune is influencing your life.

Do You Feel like You Don't Belong Here?

Neptunians are constantly trying to transcend their reality so that they can be one with the universe. They have very powerful intuitions that help them learn about the world. These individuals are also capable of extreme creativity. They are often very poetic with their words and are incredible artists. It is very hard for natives to survive in this world, which is why many of them go through a lot of pain. If you're a Neptunian, you'll likely feel like an alien at times.

Do You Feel Alienated?

Neptunians are often very spiritual people who always feel as if they don't belong in this world. They are constantly trying to better themselves and live up to their full potential. Neptunians are impressionable and romantic individuals who will often feel as if they've found their soulmate at first sight. If you think that you're a Neptunian, ask yourself if you feel like your soul-mate is out there.

Neptunian Personality Quiz

Do you:

- Always feel as if you don't belong? 5 Points
- Have a hard time controlling your emotions? 5 Points
- Feel as if you're a dreamer? 5 Points
- Often feel as if your soul-mate is out there somewhere? 5 Points
- Feel connected to your emotions? 5 Points
- Often feel alone when surrounded by people? 5 Points
- Have an extremely vivid imagination? 5 Points
- Often try to escape from reality? 5 Points
- Have a deep connection with the universe? 5 Points
- Think about the future often? 5 Points

If you scored:

40-50 points: You're definitely a Neptunian!

30-40 points: You're likely a Neptunian.

20-30 points: You may be a Neptunian.

0-20 points: You're probably not a Neptunian.

This archetypal chapter covered the archetype of Neptune and its different manifestations in your life. Neptune plays a fundamental role in understanding what the divine is. That's why this archetype has an extremely powerful connection with God or the universe. Neptunians are always trying to transcend their reality to understand the true meaning of life, which is why they are often confused when they finish this life. If your life has been influenced by Neptune, then this chapter may have shown you what influences your inner world.

To be a Neptunian means to have a deep connection with your emotions and an obsession with creativity. If you feel as if these words describe you, then it is very likely that your archetype is Neptune! At the end of this chapter, you will have found a quiz to help you determine whether Neptune is influencing your life. If you scored 30 points or more, Neptune is likely influencing your life.

Chapter 8: Healing Your Neptune

A heavily aspected Neptune can bring a lot of problems in the native's life. If the planet dominates a person's birth chart, they will likely indulge in alcohol and drugs, procrastination, daydreaming, and self-sacrificing, etc. One of the most effective ways to encourage the healing process and reduce the impact of a negative or heavy-sided Neptune is by integrating Virgo archetype activities. You should also follow certain things and let go of certain beliefs to further reduce the effects of an affiliated Neptune.

Integrating Virgo Archetype Activities

Virgos think practically and do not let their emotions win over their thoughts and beliefs. By integrating the Virgo archetype activities in your life, you can bring logic, purification, and awareness towards health in your life. As a Neptunian, if you are feeling diffused, vague, or have a stinging emotional pain in your heart, your Neptune may be emitting low or negative vibes. Since you may lack discipline during this phase, certain activities can help you get back on track and bring some consistency to your life. Your plowing and grounding power will also be enhanced by incorporating certain activities into your lifestyle, which will help with your progress.

Journaling

Journaling is the best way to release stress and raise self-awareness. Due to an afflicted Neptune, you may not be able to identify your goals or may experience brain fog. You need to identify your areas of dominance and jot them down in your journal. Since it also helps you prepare an action plan, you can envision your dreams turning into reality. Basically, you need to tap into your subconscious mind and put your inner thoughts and feelings on paper.

Meditation

Since Neptune helps you connect with your consciousness and raise self-awareness, you should meditate every day to get in touch with your Source. This will help you decipher your true purpose and your calling. Meditation is a skill that needs to be developed over time. Meditate for 10 to 15 minutes, twice a day, to see results. Find a quiet room and sit comfortably with your legs folded. Place your hands on your knees and join the tip of your thumb with your index finger to form a circle. Relax your shoulders and close your eyes. Take deep breaths and concentrate on your breathing pattern. If you find yourself getting distracted by your thoughts, bring your attention back to your breathing pattern. Play some calming music to release stress.

Exercise More

Virgos are extremely health-conscious and focus on their physical fitness. Neptunians have to indulge in more physical activities as it raises awareness about their body and helps build a new habit. Go for a walk outdoors in nature or exercise at home every day. Experts recommend learning martial arts and practicing it every day. Exercising every day will help enhance your physical and mental fitness, which is highly recommended for Neptunians.

Practice Kindness

Help people in need and try to be kinder. Everyone is going through something, and your specific act of kindness can make their day. However, do not go out of your way to show random acts of kindness (we will talk more about this in the next section). Kindness and generosity are good for your mental and emotional health. It also releases stress and boosts your immune health.

While being kind to others is important, it is necessary to be kind to yourself too. Think positively and practice self-love. Reach out to yourself and others.

Develop your Skills

If you're good at something, develop that skill. When you are completely confident, teach it to others and offer it to the universe. It does not necessarily have to be a tangible or educational skill. It can be about teaching gratefulness, being compassionate, or learning to love yourself. Many people are going through the exact process and may need help to overcome their adversities. By teaching them your skill, you are not only helping them but also yourself.

What You Should Not Do

Act like a Victim

Nobody is a victim. Everyone is subjected to hardships and injustice all the time. However, this does not automatically make everyone a victim. Everyday mishaps like spilling coffee on your shirt, not being able to start your car, or not getting enough praise for your work instantly churn the overthinking wheel and push you into a conundrum. If you often feel that the universe is acting against you, you may develop a victim mentality. Feeling like a victim all the time can destroy your relationships, career, and even your mental health. Neptunians should instead feel more comfortable and confident for their creative juices to flow.

The idea is to feel grateful to combat your growing victim mentality. We use our physical strength, mental ability, and spiritual motivation to co-create everything and exist symbiotically. Everyone has a role to play in creation. Once you start recognizing your role and significance in the process, you will realize your potential and stop acting like a victim. Whether it is the creation of the cosmos or existing in someone's life, you are a part of the bigger picture, and you matter. All the parts of creation, which can be pleasant, unpleasant, relevant, and irrelevant, engulf you in the process. With this, you will feel grateful and more in sync with your true self.

Rescue Everyone All the Time

Being the savior for everyone can diminish your self-worth and raise the expectations of others around you. Do you always feel the need to make others happy during their dark phase? Are you always the only one looking out for your loved ones and making sure they are happy all the time? Are you the only one who picks up a fallen bird on the curbside and tries to rescue it? If yes, you need to stop rescuing everyone all the time. Whether it is a minor situation or a major crisis, you are probably always on high alert and ready to rescue.

At times, even if people do not ask for help, you may be compelled to rescue them, which can feel abusive or crossing a border. Giving unsolicited advice to someone out of concern is also one of the unhealthy traits of trying to rescue people. You may have assumed that you are playing the martyr role and pulling people out of a rut, whereas in reality, you are pushing people away. Over time, this can also result in an unstable relationship and raises the chances of losing your friends and family. So, stop trying to rescue humanity all the time, especially when it is not in your hands.

Substance Abuse

Apart from drug and alcohol abuse, you should also consider treating and eradicating your addiction to other toxins. Since Neptune's influence often projects a hypersensitizing effect, it is easy to fall into the trap of alcohol, drugs, and other toxic substances that can ruin your life in the long run. This is often the case with individuals who experience the conjunction of Neptune and the Moon or the Sun. Furthermore, the natives with a rising Pisces, or conjunction with the Ascendant, can also easily find themselves becoming a victim. Unluckily, the person can also become more sensitive to all kinds of toxins and harm their body.

Letting these vices affect your body is like leaving your home's doors and windows open while you are away. In a way, you're inviting trouble in your sacred sanctum. Treat your body like your home. Understand the ill effects of toxins and substance abuse and eradicate these vices at the earliest time possible. If it feels difficult, seek help. Ask your loved ones to encourage you, talk to your doctor, and try to find inspiration around you. A little patience and determination can go a long way. Limit your alcohol intake and keep away from drugs. Over time, you will also be able to connect to your soul as the veil between your physical and spiritual existence is lifted.

Do Tasks Out of Guilt

Don't simply hop on to tasks out of guilt. This will eventually lead to unsatisfactory results and unhappiness. Despite giving your best performance and being on track, you may still feel unsatisfied. In this state, you are more focused on your guilt and are unable to see the positive parts of your process and results. In a way, this can turn into a negative behavioral trait where you always focus on finishing up tasks out of guilt. This diminishes your creativity and can result in a creative block over time, which is something Neptunians can't afford.

This toxic cycle of feeling guilty for not doing things and then doing them out of guilt is labeled "productivity guilt." Instead of being harsh on yourself, find ways to complete tasks with a fresh mind. Make a to-do list, redesign your schedule, and work smartly. At times, wasting time can also help you to unwind and destress, which is the key to a more creative approach. In the end, you will get the hang of the process and build the ability to reframe your creative process and approach. Lastly, remember that confronting guilt can be excruciating but extremely necessary.

Always Give and Never Receive

Even though giving is a positive trait, you need to understand its limitations. Going above and beyond your circumstances to give to people will result in chaos and dissolution. People will start expecting more and will fail to recognize the importance of giving in return. In the long run, you may also be taken for granted. In a way, the trait of giving can develop from the need to feel superior or to boost one's ego. Are you giving love and materials to others just to feel better about yourself? What are your exact motives behind giving? Do you want to be recognized as a giver in your social group? Or are you doing it out of guilt for receiving more love and possessions than others?

Figure out why you feel the need to give to people. It can be due to the need to feel validated or being praised for your selfless acts. At the same time, know if you are expecting anything in return. If you are raising your expectations with this deed, your Neptune may be shadowing your personality. In the end, it often leads to disappointment. Instead of beating yourself up for receiving and not being given anything in return, feel grateful for having such people and blessings in your life.

Things to Do Instead

Keep Healthy Boundaries

Neptunians often fail to recognize their limits and boundaries, especially when dealing with people. Everyone likes to have their own space, which Neptunians should acknowledge. Since it is difficult for them to realize the starting and ending points, Neptunians should be more careful when comforting or dealing with their loved ones. Failing to do so can result in broken relationships or distancing due to intrusion. It can be difficult for Neptunians to keep healthy boundaries unless their loved ones confront them about the intrusion. Maintaining healthy boundaries and giving personal space is the key to building flourishing relationships.

When they are in the right state of mind, Neptunians can successfully work on self-reflection, which can help them establish clear boundaries. This is important in every domain of their life (personal, professional, and social). This will also help you develop emotional intelligence and mental well-being. Furthermore, learn to recognize trigger points. Not everyone will confront you about your intrusive nature. Explore your thoughts and comprehend how they align with your loved one's mindset. Since this process can be overwhelming, start small and take it one step at a time. Staying alone can help too. When you are by yourself, you understand the importance of isolation and being alone with your own thoughts, which can help you create healthy boundaries.

Learn to Say "No"

Neptunians are unable to say no due to the fear of losing their loved ones or letting them down. At times, they will go out of their way to meet others' expectations. Natives with a strong Neptune fail to cultivate discernment in fear of being drowned in others' eyes. Some even chase the feeling of validation. They want to show up for others, which puts them in the limelight. The first step to learning to say no is to realize your main objective. Do you want to please people? Or do you feel the need to help others out of pity?

At times, saying no is important for your emotional and mental health as well. Developing healthy beliefs when denying requests is the second step toward learning to say no. Note that you are not rejecting the person by saying no. When you agree to a plan with a flicker of doubt in your mind, you are actually saying no to another important prospect. Most of the time, the other person will likely understand your situation instead of taking it negatively. Neptunians need to learn to voice their opinions, too – and find the right way to say "no" is an integral part of the process.

Detoxification

You need deep cleansing and detoxification to get rid of harmful substances, chemicals, and toxins. Detoxification helps improve your physical, mental, and spiritual health. Since Neptune represents higher energy and expression, you need to get rid of the obstacles blocking your pathway, and detoxification is the right approach. This also helps clear out irrelevant or harmful illusions that can be detrimental to your progress. You need a complete mind-body-soul detox to start on a fresh page and get closer to your goals. With a clear mind and soul, Neptunians can tune into their creative side and make real progress.

To detoxify your body, you must eat a nutrient-rich diet and add more fruits and vegetables to your meals. Drinking a lot of water helps a lot. It flushes out harmful toxins from the body and gets rid of free radicals that can otherwise result in health issues. For mental detoxification, take regular breaks and rest. Do what you like and get rid of social media for a day. Lastly, attract positivity by being happy and grateful. This will help with spiritual detoxification. Go for a walk every day for 30 to 45 minutes to get some exercise and fresh air.

Learn to Surrender

Surrender and let go. Let the divine order take care of your worries and put things in place. Worrying about things that are out of your control will increase stress and block your growth path. Neptunians need a clear mind and soul to release their creative juices. However, constantly worrying about things out of your control can drain your energy and likely result in emotional trauma over time. Remember, by surrendering, you are not being irresponsible or quitting. You are simply letting the universe set the order and getting off the painful bandwagon that forces you to participate in life against your will.

When you surrender, you accept yourself, which includes all your imperfections, pain, limitations, and disappointments. You accept all your negative parts along with the positive traits, which makes you humbler. Note that surrendering or letting go is an act of control. You need to figure out how and when to let go of some things, which will prepare you to act at the earliest. What is standing in your way? Why are you unable to let go? Take time to comprehend the situation and take it one step at a time. The idea is to explore your conscious mind and be comfortable when expressing your feelings.

Question More Often

When Neptune shadows one's horoscope, the native is often unable to see clearly and gets trapped in their own illusions. They may often fail to see and understand their surroundings, which can impact their personal and professional lives. The world we see and perceive through our senses may not be the actual reality. Since everyone has a different perception, their idea of reality may greatly vary too. Being curious and asking questions about everything can help you grow and take a step toward personal and professional development. What you may be seeing is distorted reality. Things aren't always the way you analyze them or assume them to be.

Abide by the quote, "Assume nothing and question everything." It is also time to question your inner devil's advocate and comprehend your progress. Questioning everything also helps enhance your decision-making skills, which can result in spiritual growth. From ideas to thoughts and decisions to information, question everything. Do not be afraid to ask questions for fear of being judged. It is time to reinvent the wheel and change your thought process, which is only possible by bringing your inner critic out.

By incorporating these additions and changes into your lifestyle, you can take complete control over your physical, mental, emotional, and spiritual health. You become more empathetic and can relate to your environment and consciousness, which can ultimately help in healing your Neptune.

Chapter 9: The Ruler of the Third Eye

Neptune is associated with the Third eye chakra because it rules the subconscious realm of reality beyond physical sight. In this chapter, we look at Neptune and its connection to the third eye.

Neptune's symbolism is often confused or misinterpreted with other planets, including Pluto, Uranus, and Saturn. Neptune's ruling element is water, and Pluto's ruling element is also water. Saturn's ruling element is earth, while Uranus's ruling element is air. Neptune rules the oceans, and when referring to the chakras, the third eye chakra contains the element of water. Neptune has a very fluid and changing personality as well as physical appearance. In astrology, it is considered the most distant planet from Earth. It is also known as a "higher octave" of Mercury, and its ruling element is air, which is associated with the element of Uranus.

The Connection between Neptune and the Third Eye Chakra

The third eye chakra contains many abilities such as insight, intuition, and psychic ability. And as mentioned, Neptune is connected with this chakra because it rules the subconscious realm of reality. This ability is known as "astral projection" and allows a person to travel beyond their physical body. Neptune rules over the invisible world, and astral projection is considered an invisible ability that contains supernatural powers. The third eye chakra is located within the forehead and is often associated with the color indigo.

The Chakra System

The chakra system is a form of energy within the body that brings forth many abilities. The Hindu religion believes that there are seven main chakras within the body, which are located throughout the human body. Each chakra has a different purpose, and these centers are associated with many abilities such as clairvoyance, psychic dreams, and telepathy. The seven chakras are as follows:

Root Chakra: Located at the base of the spine. This center contains bodily energy and is associated with instincts, survival, and desire.

Sacral Chakra: Located in the lower abdomen below the navel. This center is associated with emotions, pleasure, relationships, and sexuality.

Solar Plexus Chakra: Located in the stomach and contains personal power and ego.

Heart Chakra: Located in the center of the chest and associated with feelings, love, compassion, and unity.

Throat Chakra: Located in the throat and contains spiritual wisdom, truthfulness, and self-expression.

Third Eye Chakra: Located in the center of the forehead and is associated with psychic abilities such as insight, intuition, and spiritual wisdom.

Crown Chakra: Located on the top of the head and known as the "unity chakra" because it is associated with unity.

Location of the Third Eye Chakra

The third eye chakra is located in the pineal gland, also known as the "third eye," because it is associated with psychic ability. The third eye is also associated with the sixth chakra in the Hindu religion, which includes the crown chakra within its seven main centers. The third eye is the center of clairvoyance, and this means being able to see things that are not visible at that precise time in reality. Many people have heard of auras, which are invisible to the naked eye. Many people claim that they have the ability to see a person's aura, and this is associated with clairvoyance.

The third eye chakra is located in the center of the forehead, which makes it one of the main chakras to focus on during meditation. By meditating, a person can relax their mind to bring forth various abilities, including insight and intuition. The chakra system is associated with many supernatural abilities because it brings about psychic powers. Meditation on the third eye will bring about these powers, and Neptune is known as the planet of the mind and several other things that are associated with it.

Neptune in Astrology: The Ruler of the Third Eye

Neptune is known as the planet of spirituality, which means that Neptune is associated with anything that is connected to the mind and body. Neptune is connected with anything that has to do with psychic abilities, which include telepathy and clairvoyance. Neptune is also connected to spiritual enlightenment, which will lead to the opening of the individual's third eye. Neptune is often associated with dreams and will bring about psychic dreams. Neptune is also associated with the universe, which brings about another connection to telepathy.

Consequently, Neptune rules over the sixth chakra or the third eye. The third eye occurs in many religions and is a main part of the chakra system. When an individual meditates, they will want to focus more on the third eye because it will lead to psychic powers that include insight and intuition.

Neptune's Similarities to the Third Eye Chakra

Since Neptune rules over the third eye chakra, there are many similarities between Neptune and this specific chakra. The third eye is located on the forehead, which is where many people feel that Neptune rules over because it is in the same location. Neptune is associated with dreams and psychic abilities, which are both connected to the third eye chakra.

Neptune has the power to impact the third eye with its energy, which is also known as Neptunian energy. This form of energy will help an individual meditate and will bring about psychic abilities.

How Neptunian Energy Can Impact the Third Eye Chakra

Neptune's energy has the ability to impact the third eye with its energy, which will then impact several chakras. An individual needs to meditate on Neptune so that they can bring forth this energy. Meditation is a process where an individual will focus their mind and body so that they can relax and unleash the natural power of the third eye.

When an individual meditates for a long period, they will be able to focus on all seven chakras. The third eye, as explained, is related to psychic abilities and insight, which will bring about the ability to see things that are not in reality. When an individual meditates on the third eye, they will be able to balance out their chakras and find inner peace.

Neptune is known as the planet of spiritual enlightenment and connects to anything related to this topic. Psychic abilities are often associated with Neptune, which includes premonition and perception. Meditation focused on Neptune will help an individual focus their mind and open up the third eye chakra, which will then bring psychic abilities to the forefront.

Neptune rules over anything that has to do with spirituality, which will bring forth psychic abilities. Meditation to Neptune will help bring about psychic dreams and access to the universe. When an individual meditates, they must focus on the third eye so that they can connect with Neptune. When an individual brings out Neptunian energy during meditation, it will lead to insight and intuition.

Neptune brings forth psychic dreams, which align with the third eye. Neptune also brings forth spirituality, which is associated with the third eye. Neptune rules over anything that has to do with spirituality and connects to psychic dreams, insight, and intuition. Meditation to Neptune will connect with the third eye chakra so that an individual can meditate more on this specific chakra. Neptune's energy can help individuals meditate and will bring about intuition, which is connected to the third eye.

Importance of the Third Eye's Alignment

For the third eye to benefit from Neptune, it must be aligned. The lower five chakras need to be in balance, which will lead to spiritual enlightenment. The third eye is the last chakra that must align with Neptune before an individual can reach spiritual enlightenment through Neptune's energy. Once the lower five chakras are in balance, an individual will be able to realize this enlightenment because the third eye will be able to benefit from Neptune.

The lower five chakras are the part of the body where communication is sent, acting as a link between the physical and spiritual world. Once these chakras are in balance, the individual will be able to realize spiritual enlightenment. Neptune's energy will bring about spiritual enlightenment, which will align with the third eye chakra. An individual needs to meditate on Neptune so that they will be able to balance out their chakras. An individual will only realize spiritual enlightenment if the third eye is in alignment with Neptune's energy, which is why it is important for an individual to meditate on Neptune.

The third eye chakra must align with Neptune before spiritual enlightenment can be realized. Psychic abilities are associated with Neptune, which will help the third eye become aligned and bring forth spiritual enlightenment. When an individual brings forth Neptunian energy during meditation, it will help balance out the lower five chakras. When these lower five chakras are in balance, the third eye will be in alignment with Neptune's energy, which will lead to spiritual enlightenment.

Neptune helps an individual meditate on psychic abilities. Neptune's energy can help individuals to meditate and will encourage intuition, which is connected to the third eye. Neptune rules over anything that has to do with spirituality and connects to psychic dreams, insight, and intuition. For this reason, Neptune's energy will connect with the third eye chakra so that an individual can meditate more on this specific chakra.

How to Balance the Chakras to Bring About Spiritual Enlightenment

Each of the seven chakras in the body is responsible for a different part of human existence. These seven different chakras obtain energy in different ways. One way is through the seven main planets, Earth, Sun, Mercury, Moon, Venus, Mars, and Jupiter. While these planets are the main source of energy, there are other sources such as the Moon's North and South Node, asteroids, meteors, and comets.

The chakras of the body obtain energy from planets and celestial bodies. When these seven chakras obtain the right level of energy, an individual can achieve spiritual enlightenment. Spiritual enlightenment is when an individual sees beyond the physical world and realizes that there are other dimensions on Earth. This realization comes from a balance of chakras, which is why it is important to have balanced chakras so that the third eye can obtain energy from Neptune.

Many different practices are needed when it comes to achieving spiritual enlightenment. Some of these practices include meditation, visualization, chakra chanting, yoga postures, and breathing exercises. All these practices will help bring about spiritual enlightenment, but proper breathing techniques will help align the lower five chakras with the third eye.

Meditation

Even though we already talked about meditation earlier, we will dig a little deeper to emphasize its importance. Meditation is one practice that will help bring about spiritual enlightenment. Meditation is a way to balance the chakras and helps align the lower five chakras with the third eye. It also helps to relax the body and increases the body's capacity to hold more oxygen. Meditation helps an individual connect with themselves and realize that they are not just a physical being.

Meditation helps individuals relax and become at one with their thoughts, which will allow the individual to see beyond the physical world. One can meditate on the third eye chakra to help balance it with Neptune's energy. This will allow an individual to see past the physical world and into other dimensions. Once this realization has been achieved, spiritual enlightenment can follow.

Visualization

Visualization is another practice that will help bring about spiritual enlightenment. Visualization helps individuals to focus on the lower five chakras and connect with the third eye. Meditation and visualization go together with each other, so practicing both exercises will bring benefits to the individual. The best way to visualize is to know exactly what an individual wants out of life.

Visualization helps a person focus on the goal at hand and go after it. Another benefit of visualization is that it will help an individual focus on their dreams and goals, which can lead to spiritual enlightenment. When an individual is in a relaxed state, they can visualize their dreams, hopes, and goals; if they can do this, then spiritual enlightenment will follow.

The individual should visualize themselves being happy and content with their life. Visualizing can be done anywhere and at any time, but the individual must make sure that they are in a relaxed state while doing this. All the individual has to do is close their eyes, focus on breathing deeply, and visualize themselves achieving everything they want in life.

Chakra Chanting

Chakra chanting is a practice that helps to align the lower five chakras with the third eye. The most powerful time to chant a mantra is just before going to sleep. This is because an individual has just finished a stressful day and is about to go into a deep sleep. Chanting will help relax the individual before they go to sleep.

A mantra is a word or phrase that has a special meaning for an individual. The individual should chant their personal mantra to help align their chakras. A word or phrase that will work for an individual is "I am." The individual can chant this phrase repeatedly before they go to bed. When it is time for the individual to fall asleep, they should repeat this phrase one final time. By doing this, they are helping their third eye align with the rest of their chakras. The individual can do this every night to help bring about spiritual enlightenment.

Breathing Techniques

Breathing techniques are another practice that helps to align the lower five chakras with the third eye. Breathing exercises help an individual relax and bring more oxygen into their body. This will help an individual relax the muscles throughout the entire body, which will allow for spiritual enlightenment to become a possibility. The individual should take slow, deep breaths before attempting the breathing exercise. The person should also take some deep breathes and then exhale slowly. They should then place their hands on their stomach and breathe in through their nostrils and out through their mouth.

The individual should keep doing this until they feel relaxed and can breathe easily without any tension in the muscles throughout their entire body. Breathing exercises help karma and can help them to achieve spiritual enlightenment if the individual practices them every day. The best time to do this is in the morning when you wake up, but breathing exercises can be done any time of the day. As long as you are relaxed while doing them, spiritual enlightenment can be achieved.

Diet

A great way to balance the chakras and help bring about spiritual enlightenment is by eating certain foods. There are foods that help with each chakra, and by eating them, the individual will be helping to bring about spiritual enlightenment. Fruit and vegetables contain important vitamins and minerals that help to bring about spiritual enlightenment.

You should eat lots of yellow and orange-colored fruit and vegetables since these are the ones that help bring about spiritual enlightenment. These fruit and vegetables are bananas, carrots, oranges, grapefruit, sweet potatoes, and corn. Every time you eat any of these foods, you are bringing more spiritual enlightenment into your life.

You shouldn't eat too many fruits and vegetables that are green because these will conflict with the chakras. These include green grapes, cucumbers, and broccoli. Even though these foods have a lot of vitamins and minerals, they won't help you reach spiritual enlightenment as much as yellow and orange-colored fruit and vegetables will. The best way for you to eat fruit and vegetables is to choose them by their natural colors. For example, instead of eating purple grapes, an individual should eat carrots or grapefruit. These foods have the same number of vitamins and minerals, but they will help to align the chakras.

Aligning the Chakras with Other Practices

There are other practices that you can do to align the chakras and bring about spiritual enlightenment. The best way for you to meditate is on a comfortable chair or on the floor. You should look straight ahead and think about your breathing until you feel relaxed. This will bring about stress relief and allow you to go into a meditative state.

You should keep your eyes closed when you inhale and exhale. If your eyes are open, you may see colors, lights, or different images that will take you out of your meditative state. When you feel relaxed, you should focus on your third eye chakra. The best way to do this is by trying to see an image of the chakra inside your mind.

You should see a bright, blue-colored circle near the center of your forehead. You may or may not be able to see the circle right away, but if you keep practicing, this will come. Once you can see the circle, you should put all your focus on it. You should meditate like this for 10 to 20 minutes every day.

Once you start meditating regularly, spiritual enlightenment will bring about positive results into your life. You may feel happier and healthier than you have ever felt before. Spiritual enlightenment is something that cannot be explained to you, but once you feel it for yourself, there is no going back.

The third eye (or the sixth chakra) is one of the seven energy points that run along the spine. This chakra helps to bring about spiritual enlightenment and enhance your ability to have visions.

When working, the third eye chakra will help you become more intuitive and feel as though you are a part of something bigger than yourself. This chapter discussed the connection between the third eye chakra and Neptune, which is where the planet's energy comes from. It also shed light on how you can align your chakras with other practices, so you can attempt to reach spiritual enlightenment.

Chapter 10: Neptune and Psychic Abilities

As you know, the planet Neptune is a gas giant that is considered one of the four outer planets in our solar system and intricately connected to our psychic abilities. It has immense power over us through its influence on our dreams, imagination, and spirituality. Neptune rules the invisible world, which includes such things as supernatural abilities, psychic senses, and spiritual connection. Neptune's presence in your birth chart means that you will likely be blessed with strong psychic powers.

Neptune's Impact on Psychic Abilities Based on Houses

Neptune rules over psychic abilities such as telepathy, which is the ability to communicate with others through mental means. Neptune also holds influence over other supernatural abilities, such as clairvoyance, where a person has the power to see events that are not visible in the present time. Neptune is also connected with psychic dreams, which often give insight into the future of a person.

Here is how Neptune impacts a person's psychic abilities based on their houses and the planet's state of conjunction or position.

Psychic Abilities in the First House

The native is blessed with amazing clairvoyant and precognizant abilities. They can enable their senses to find out more about a person's feelings, experiences, and future. They are free to explore new dimensions beyond reality. However, exaggerated use of their senses can lead to subconscious travel, which can be dangerous. This type of experience is also connected to astral projection, which helps the native become more empathetic. A debilitated Neptune can result in psychic attacks, which is why they need to be more careful.

Psychic Abilities in the Second House

A strongly aspected Neptune makes the native more intuitive. They can easily find out answers just by looking deep inside. They are also quite imaginative and creative. When they tap into their subconscious mind, they may get vivid dreams that represent their purpose and goals in life. If they take them seriously, they can also transform their talent into a skill. The native's intuitive hunches lead them in the right direction.

Psychic Abilities in the Third House

A properly-placed Neptune in the third house blesses the native with intuitive powers. They can easily reach other planes that are typically invisible or inaccessible to normal people. By engaging their senses, they can emit and receive information from other dimensions and planes. One of the strongest psychic abilities they possess is telepathy. They can tap into others' subconscious minds and align with their frequency to create a telepathic effect.

Psychic Abilities in the Seventh House

The natives are highly empathetic. They are strong, artistic, and idealistic. Instead of focusing on acquiring information, they gather incoming information and enable their minds to retrieve as much data as possible. Compared to other houses, the seventh house with a strong Neptune means indicates strong imagination and visualization powers. With practice, consistency, and experience, they may also be able to read minds. Most natives are blessed with clairvoyant abilities as well. The native should be careful when dealing with their partners and sustaining relationships.

Psychic Abilities in the Eight House

The native is open to receiving energy from different planes and dimensions. However, if they do not receive anything, they can cause harm to their loved ones and peers. They welcome astral beings and spirits. They may become more involved in spiritual theories like life after death and reincarnation. They may also dig deeper to know more about spiritual realms and internal healing.

Psychic Abilities in the Ninth House

The natives can see the future in the form of visions and illustrations in their minds. Some possess strong psychic abilities from birth, whereas other natives need to develop their skills over time. They are attracted to philosophy and mystical theories. They can be reverent and idealistic. Subjects like immortality and spiritual thinking are of great interest to the natives. At times, they get prophetic dreams that can change a person's life.

Psychic Abilities in the Twelfth House

If Neptune is strong in the twelfth house, the native can successfully bridge the gap between their unconscious and conscious mind. With practice and concentration, they can recall their past lives in the form of recurring memories. Since not all are aware of this experience, they ignore their ability to decipher their memories. The natives develop an interest in the occult, psychic studies, and spirituality as they grow up.

Uranus Sextile Neptune

The natives can easily unravel their psychic abilities and keep them activated with a little practice and concentration. They experience altered states of spirituality and consciousness. It is extremely easy for natives to reach another dimension and use their psychic abilities. However, they must be aware of their powers and abilities. In most cases, they use their power for the betterment of humankind in general.

Mercury Opposite Neptune

If these two planets stand opposite to each other in your natal chart, you will likely see images, develop visions, or indulge in fantasy. With some practice, you can see others' auras and learn more about their fate. On the flip side, you may not be able to see or read the images visible to others, and therefore, miss obvious hints, which can impact your psychic abilities.

Mercury Trine Neptune

You are curious about your psychic abilities and relevant subjects like metaphysics, other dimensions, and telepathy. Any subject defying rational observation is the least of your concerns. You may keep learning about the other domains as you get the time and happily teach them to others as well. You may be blessed with creative skills like creative writing and art.

Mercury Sextile Neptune

You are a diehard fiction and fantasy fan. Your ideas are original, and you are blessed with strong intuitive powers. Your special talent is reading and writing poetry. You can not only decode the aspects in the intangible dimension but also speak and write about them. Among all psychic abilities, clairvoyance is your strongest weapon.

Mercury Conjunct Neptune

Your psychic abilities and intuitive powers are so strong that you can, at times, get confused between your true perceptions and these illusions. Your idealistic and mystical bend does not allow you to concentrate on mundane tasks. You are always inclined towards psychic and metaphysical subjects and spend more time learning about them.

Moon Sextile Neptune

You like people who are kind, compassionate, peaceful, sensitive, and artistically inclined with your thoughts and emotions. With your psychic power, you can easily connect with others, which strengthens your ability and helps you establish valuable connections and personal relationships. Typically, natives are connected with the females in their lives, which include their sisters, mothers, and close female friends.

Sun Quincunx Neptune

Your psychic powers may overpower your true personality, which is why you must be careful when using your strengths for your benefit. Your hypersensitivity to your surroundings can turn into a creativity block and challenge your true abilities. It is necessary to distinguish between your perception and illusion. You can be highly affected by dissonance, ugliness, or pollutants.

Ways to Awaken Dormant Psychic Powers

We all are blessed with psychic powers. However, we must learn how to awaken and activate them, which is possible only by implementing certain mental and spiritual activities into our lifestyle. The idea is to exercise the inactive and dormant psychic abilities lying within that can transform your life. The more you practice and train, the stronger your psychic abilities get. Just like you need to train for physical endurance or any other skill, you also need to practice training your psychic abilities. Here are some effective ways to do it.

Take Care of Your Physical and Mental Health

When you take care of your physical and mental health, you also develop your emotional and spiritual fitness. Over time, you will also notice an improvement in your psychic abilities.

Physical Health: Focus on what you eat and prepare a balanced diet. The food you eat defines your health in the long run. Make sure that your meals are nutrient-rich and fulfill your daily nutrition count. At the same time, focus on physical activities. Get your daily dose of exercise or physical activity to keep yourself fit. It can be a simple cardio exercise like walking or running or an intense sport. Get proper sleep and drink more water to keep yourself physically fit.

Mental Health: Meditation helps to relax the mind, which brings forth the true powers of psychic abilities. Neptune is associated with deep meditation, which gives insight into the third eye chakra's psychic abilities. Other ways to develop mental fitness include aromatherapy, visualization practices, journaling, de-stressing, and taking frequent breaks.

Learn to See Auras

Auras are the energies surrounding bodies. Every person has an aura, but it is invisible to the naked eye. Auras are made of frequencies and vibrations that align with the person's vibes. Basically, they are the electromagnetic field that takes the shape of a person's silhouette. They can be positive, negative, or neutral and represent their color accordingly. Your aura represents your energy and your soul's plight, which is why it can change from time to time. While some are born with the instinct of seeing and deciphering auras from birth, others need to develop this skill.

Individuals interested in this art often get involved in the healing process and pursue psychic abilities as a full-time position. With patience, time, and a lot of practice, you can successfully start seeing auras and decipher the associated hues. Learning to see auras can also help cleanse your chakras and balance them. Since chakras need to be activated to start the internal healing process, practicing aura-reading can help to a great extent.

Learn to read different colors and hues when practicing this skill. If the aura looks black or grey, the person may be disturbed or likely possess negative energy. On the other hand, a white aura represents peace, calmness, and a well-balanced personality. A person's aura is depicted by seven levels that are shaped like the body's silhouette and can be visualized in concentric shells. The seven levels, which also represent the seven chakras, can be deciphered through different colors. Certain aura-reading practices include developing your peripheral vision, engaging your senses, and boosting concentration.

Prepare a Dream Journal

A dream journal acts as a gateway to open your senses and reach your subconscious. When you make a dream journal, you are compelled to recognize your goals and write them down, which brings you a step closer to your real purpose. This is specifically more effective if you are unaware of your goals and confused about what you want to do in life. Your dreams can be related to your relationships, career, or self-improvement. Writing your dreams in your dream journal can also help clear your mind and release stress. With this, you can create an action plan and visualize your dreams coming true.

Your true purpose and creative experiences are intricately weaved into your spiritual callings, which are manifested as your dream. They make your creative potential and survival function more attainable. The most effective way to manifest your dreams into reality is by remembering and writing them down as soon as you wake up. Human memory does not always hold on to the exact version of dreams. They are changed and manipulated over time, which is why recording them at the earliest is crucial. Even though there is no specific way to keep a dream journal, you can follow a few steps to reap maximum benefits.

Start by setting an intention. Realize the importance of having dreams and goals. They need your complete attention and time. Before you go to bed, repeat the phrase, "I will remember and record my dreams tonight." Try to maintain different versions of dreams journals to find out what works the best. For instance, some people prefer doodling or illustrating their dreams. On the other hand, some prefer recording their dreams on voice notes and then translating them to find out their true purpose.

Implement the Art of Psychometry

Psychometry is the art of sensing a person's or object's energy through touch. Since a person's possessions absorb the owner's vibrations and energy, touching them can help you decipher their energy. You can sense the person's energy in the form of colors, images, smells, emotions, tastes, and sounds. You get a vivid sense of their frequency, which can help you form a strong impression of the person's personality. Irrespective of the nature, size, color, and texture of the object, a psychic can easily decipher its energy by holding it in their hand.

By developing the skill of "scrying," you can "see" images and colors that are ordinarily invisible. A psychic with extraordinary skills and abilities can detect a person's past, present, and future and roughly outline their fate. In some cases, they can also tell a person's experiences based on the possessions they owned during a specific period in their life. Even though everyone can feel someone else's energy up to a certain point, you need to practice enhancing your psychometric power.

Follow these steps to uplift your psychometric power:

• Find a quiet spot where you can concentrate. Sit with your legs folded and meditate for a few minutes to clear your mind.

• Once you feel calmer, keep your eyes closed and ask your partner or friend to place one of their belongings into your hands. You should not know anything about the object.

- Hold the object and feel it from every angle. Concentrate on the recurring images in your mind. What do you see? What kind of sensations do you feel? Do you feel any emotions? What are your thoughts?

- If you do not feel anything, do not force it. Simply focus on receiving the energy or information. You can take the next step of interpreting it later.

- Do not discard any thoughts or images if they feel useless or insignificant. They may seem useless to you but can be important to the owner.

- Trust your senses and guides. With concentration, dedication, and practice, you will slowly develop the skill.

Psychometry reminds us that every person possesses and emits different energies.

Take Assistance from Psychic Tools

These tools help strengthen your psychic abilities and make you more aware of the energies around you. Your hands and body act as your primary psychic tools. However, you can also take help from certain objects that are believed to recognize and align spiritual energies, which can make your reading stronger. Psychic enthusiasts often lean on these tools to do accurate readings and improve their psychic skills.

Pendulums: This tool is made of a crystal or a stone hung onto a cord or chain. If you are in doubt, you simply hold the pendulum in one hand, ask your question, and let the tool answer for you. You can decipher the answer by following the pendulum's swaying direction. It is believed that the practitioner's energy and intuition direct the pendulum's motion and act as a guide.

Tarot Cards: These cards also represent the practitioner's intuition and help decipher their true intention. Tarot cards are commonly used by psychics to determine a person's fate or emotions. Typically, the practitioner asks a question to the person, who then draws a card. A deck of Tarot cards is divided into Major Arcana and Minor Arcana cards, collectively making a total of 78 cards.

Dowsing Rods: These rods also align according to the energy and vibrations to which they are exposed. Dowsing rods point in specific directions during practice, which helps the psychic find the right direction. In essence, the person holding the dowsing rods usually knows the answer deep down but is unable to decode it. With the help of dowsing rods, they can dig deeper and use their intuition.

Along with these practices, you can also try taking psychic lessons and read more about interacting with your intuition to gain better results. A person's psychic abilities allow them to peek into another realm that can be beneficial to their growth and that can attract positivity. Everyone has psychic abilities, which, when used on an ongoing basis, can prepare them for the future. Note that regular practice is necessary for you to enhance your psychic skills and make it a daily part of your routine. This will guide you in the right direction and help you make better decisions in the future.

Conclusion

Congratulations on making it this far! You are now aware of Neptune's astrological and mythological role and ready to manifest the mystic planet's energy in your life. We hope this book helped resolve your curiosity about Neptune's effects on expanding awareness and deciphering psychic phenomena.

Let's recall what we've learned so far. Neptune's spiritual and astrological roles are extremely versatile and help you become more aware of your creative side. The planet controls our desires and aspirations. It rules our fantasies and pushes us into oblivion. Depending on its position and nature, it can make or break your fate. It also tunes you with cosmic consciousness and helps you see beyond the "normal" intellect. If Neptune doesn't rule in your favor, it can bring confusion and chaos to your life. You may end up daydreaming too much, which can also result in procrastination and negatively impact your work.

Neptune is the God of Sea in Roman mythology and Varuna in Hindu mythology. He governs all water bodies and acts as a bridge between humans and the divine. Poseidon, the Greek god, was swallowed by his father, Saturn. Jupiter, the God of Heaven, and Pluto, the God of the Underworld, are Neptune's siblings. The trinity represents intellectual, subconscious, and conscious realms. The Hindu personification of Neptune is Varuna, the god of divine authority and the sky. The trident or Trishul is a significant part of Hindu mythology, with the three pongs representing Neptunian energy. The cross on this trident symbol represents psychic intention.

Neptune is exalted in Cancer and debilitated in Capricorn. Neptune's conjunction with other planets can determine the native's fate. For example, the planet's positive conjunction with Mercury can spark supernatural interest in the native. By contrast, negative Mercury-Neptune conjunction means that the person can easily make silly mistakes and lack insight. Furthermore, Neptune's association with Venus can enhance the native's emotional response. However, an unfavorable outcome can mean that the person may possess a distorted view of their surroundings. Likewise, Neptune forms a favorable and unfavorable association with all the planets, which can impact the native's life.

Neptune behaves differently in every house and impacts the native's journey throughout their life.

- The first house represents the self
- The second house represents material possessions
- The third house represents communication
- The fourth house represents the home
- The fifth house represents creativity
- The sixth house represents routines
- The seventh house represents partnerships
- The eighth house represents transformation
- The ninth house represents travel
- The tenth house represents a public image
- The eleventh house represents humanitarianism
- The twelfth house represents the subconscious

Depending on Neptune's position, the native may suffer negative consequences or a positive outcome.

The planet rules the Third Eye chakra, which defines intuition, imagination, psychic ability, and creativity. A person with an active or open third eye gets insightful ideas and often relies on their "dreams." Their subconscious mind brims with ideas that can make a difference. The chakra, in its open state, invites thoughts and messages that drive the person's imagination. This is exactly what Neptune strives for. If the Third Eye chakra is blocked, the person may face a creative block or experience a slump. Despite being presented with a concrete solution or an image of the concept, these individuals may still feel confused or fail to grasp the exact idea. Such are the negative repercussions imposed by a Neptune at an unfavorable position.

If you think that this book has helped you gain a deeper insight into Neptune's role in astrology, pass on the knowledge to your loved ones and encourage them to get their copy too. Even if they are unfamiliar with Neptune's role in astrology or are only dabbling in the subject, this book will assist readers in manifesting the planet's positive energy. Good luck!

Part 9: The Moon in Astrology

The Ultimate Guide to Moon Magic, Lunar Phases, and What Your Zodiac Sign Says About You

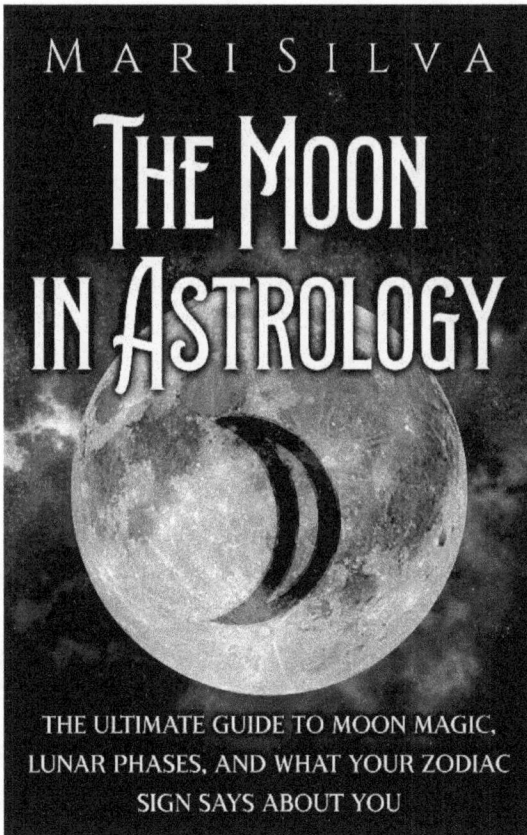

MARI SILVA

THE MOON IN ASTROLOGY

THE ULTIMATE GUIDE TO MOON MAGIC, LUNAR PHASES, AND WHAT YOUR ZODIAC SIGN SAYS ABOUT YOU

Introduction

Despite having reached and walked on it, humankind is still fascinated by the amazing celestial body of the Moon. Ever since the dawn of cognizance, the Moon has been a subject of interest and curiosity. While the relative movement and position of the celestial body can determine the natural forces on the Earth, the Moon's power also describes a person's emotions and consciousness. It enables people to find their true purpose, live in harmony with others, and evoke the emotions needed to lead a peaceful life. The celestial body rotates close to Earth and illuminates the surface to strike a balance between utter darkness and brightness.

Despite being smaller than other planets, the power and the gravitational pull of the Moon have stirred interest and curiosity for ages. Past and present-day astronomers use a geocentric approach to decipher natal charts, with the Sun and Moon being significant parts of the readings. The Moon lacks atmosphere, which makes it susceptible to hard rocks, meteor attacks, and an accumulation of debris. However, it can keep its surface free and devoid of wind which keeps its surface intact and prevents significant changes. One can draw this comparison with a person's soul and outer influences. In a way, the Moon symbolizes the need to remold your soul and emotions to avoid exposure to outer chaos.

In astrology, the Moon is a feminine symbol, with the Sun being its counterpart. Collectively, they are vital to the existence of all living creatures, and they monitor and control the natural forces on Earth. Being the feminine entity, the Moon governs our inner child and teaches it to feel safer and more secure in life. She symbolizes fertility, repressed memories, and intuition. A person's astrological chart carries the Moon sign based on the body's position and movement. Since the Moon moves at a fast pace, a few hours can drastically affect a person's fate and bring significant differences in birth charts.

In essence, the Moon covers the entire zodiac wheel in just a month's time, which also characterizes our present-day calendar. The Moon's rapid movement imposes the need to read and pinpoint the exact time of a person's birth. While your Sun sign determines your outer personality and life in general, your Moon sign represents your impulses and emotions. They signify the need to control your emotions and unlock your inner awareness to achieve more stability in life.

If you have been struggling to cope with your emotions lately, consider deciphering your emotions and intuition. By learning more about your Moon sign and its position in your natal chart, you can have better control of your life. This book will elucidate on the spiritual and mythological effects of the Moon and explain its role in your astrological chart. You will learn about the lunar phases and nodes to understand various Moon signs in depth. Furthermore, you will also learn the right way to tap into this celestial body's energy to reap maximum benefits and get your life back on track.

Whether you are seeking knowledge of the Moon signs and the body's significance in your birth chart or are simply curious about astrology and its distinct faces, this book will help you by providing all the information you need. It is easy to read and understand, which ideally makes it a perfect guide for beginners just taking their first steps into astrology. Upon grasping the concept of the Moon sign in its entirety, you will successfully prevent your inner child from repeating the same mistakes, and you can channel your emotions in the right direction.

If you are intrigued and want to learn more about the Moon's role in astrology, then this is the right book for you.

Chapter 1: The Moon as a Goddess

Primarily perceived as a celestial body prompting the solar system's behavior and controlling the tides, the Moon has also been considered a cultural, mythological, and spiritual symbol for centuries. Certain characteristics like immortality, femininity, enlightenment, and eternity are closely associated with it. In the past, the Moon was worshiped as a holy element, and the deity was believed to be a goddess representing fertility and growth. The mythological ties and spiritual affinity with the Moon are associated with the beliefs formed in the past.

Mythological and Spiritual Aspects of the Moon

Being the graceful goddess of luminescence and fertility, the Moon has been perceived as a deity for many years and carries mythological and spiritual connotations in many religions. This celestial body that moves in circles and controls lunar cycles also governs the cycle and rhythm of time. Ancient scholars examined the movement and position of the Moon to track time and determine the fate of newborn babies. While some religions and cultures follow the Sun's path to design their calendars and follow their beliefs in chronological order, others still monitor the lunar cycle to date.

The Moon has also invoked the curiosity of traditional and modern astronomers and astrologers, which is why the celestial body is an important part of natal charts. The Moon's brightness and luminescent nature give mortals hope. The radiance is symbolized as awareness and enlightenment that influences people to seek truth and find their true purpose. The Moon, the Sun, and the stars are manifestations of wisdom and worldly knowledge. They speak to you and deliver musings that not all can decipher. However, if you understand the nature of the Prophets and Luminaries (the archetypes of the celestial bodies), you can achieve divinity and righteousness.

The Moon and the Sun thrive in harmony. Just like they create an even balance between day and night, dark and light, and yin and yang, fasting and prayer, they can develop synergy and induce spiritual growth. The Sun is the Moon's patron. Without its light, the Moon fails to shine brightly and spread brightness on Earth.

Typically, a lunar cycle is counted as a 29.5-day loop, aligning with a woman's menstrual cycle. The words "moon" and "menstruation" share linguistic roots. This, in turn, helped women across many civilizations to keep track of their menstrual cycles.

The Moon's Significance across Civilizations

The Moon has intrigued several civilizations from the dawn of time. Many ancient scholars and poets were fascinated by the peculiar nature of this celestial body and often drew parallels between the Moon Goddess or God and their counterparts. The body's bizarre and fascinating glow led ancient philosophers and scholars to discover its supernatural implications. Every culture and civilization shaped its own version of the Moon deity. While the Greeks called their Moon Goddess Selene, the Egyptians addressed their Lunar God as Thoth. Similarly, other cultures and religions drew implications of their own beliefs and illustrated distinct versions of the Lunar God and Goddess, who stem from similar convictions.

The Moon was considered a noble, natural body that supervised the welfare of mere mortals. On the flip side, some accounts portrayed the Moon as a darker force that led to negative behavior in humans. Whenever a full moon was spotted, the association between criminal acts and lunacy was put forward as being caused by this natural phenomenon. Some storytellers even formulated the idea of werewolves that became more active during full moon nights, thereby causing harm and spreading havoc. These negative implications linked to the Moon were a significant part of European cultures and civilizations. The prominence of lunar eclipses and bad omens further connotes the dark side of some versions of the Moon.

Some Western cultures also spread the story of a man's face on the Moon, which has become a popular tale narrated in schools to this day. While some ancient researchers claimed that the Moon had a perfectly round and smooth surface, others argued that the body possessed a dark and rocky surface.

Lunar Deities across Various Cultures

The Moon Goddess was perceived in different forms across various cultures and religions. While some versions shared similar attributes, others were quite distinct.

Luna in Roman Mythology

Luna is the sister of Sol, the Sun God, and is deemed his female counterpart. Even though they represent the distinct characteristics of day and night, they thrive in harmony and are pretty significant in Roman mythology. Luna was one of the prime goddesses in the "diva triformis" (the three goddesses), a trinity that included Hecate and Proserpina. Collectively, they represent childhood, motherhood, womanhood, old age, and marriage. While some records state that Luna was called Juno and Diana, others address them as the Moon Goddesses. Luna's image is associated with a crescent moon and a chariot. Her main illustration represents Luna standing while riding the chariot.

She often rides the chariot to cross the sky, moving across the horizon that symbolizes the completion of a night and the start of a new day. Luna symbolizes agriculture and fertility as farmers needed protection from moonlight and dark nights to encourage healthy crop growth. This symbolism makes Luna a primordial fertility goddess, and she plays a significant part in Varro's list of essential deities. Luna was widely worshipped by the Romans, who made dedicated altars and temples for the goddess. Her main temple was set atop the Aventine Hill, which was later destroyed by a fire.

Despite being inferior to other gods, Luna was still popular among her devotees and enjoyed the sacrifices and offerings made for her. Some even compare her to the Greek Moon Goddess, Selene, and deem them the same. Ancient Romans claimed Luna to be Selene's Romanized version and started worshipping her. However, unlike Selene, Luna supposedly shares many attributes with the Romans, which made her stand out and become well-respected. Luna's two-yoke chariot is called "Biga," associated with horses or other animals that act as the main carriers. Some illustrations portray her with two oxen pulling the chariot.

Selene in Greek Mythology

Selene, the Titan Goddess, was one of the most important deities of the ancient Greeks and is still known as the Moon Goddess. Ancient poets and scholars exemplified her as a beautiful version of the moon, after which she became a recurring figure in Greek mythology. She is illustrated as a chariot rider with winged steeds and a crescent-shaped crown on her head. Some records depict her wearing a shining cloak while riding a horse. She was the daughter of Theia (Euryphessa) and Hyperion (The Titan Light God) and the lover of Endymion (the shepherd prince).

Zeus was pleased with Endymion and blessed him with eternal youth. Some stories claim Pan and Zeus to be Selene's lovers. The God Sun, Helios was Selene's sibling, and the brother-sister duo was worshipped as the sun and the moon, respectively. They worked in harmony and audited the movements of the celestial bodies to govern day and nighttime. Ancient Greeks regarded both figures as significant deities as they brought balance to their lives and always monitored the well-being of humans. According to a myth, Selene and Endymion birthed fifty daughters who represented the fifty forms of lunar months. Collectively, the daughters were called the "Menai."

Other records claim that Helios and Selene were, in fact, lovers and gave birth to the four-season goddesses, the Horai. The stories that claim that Zeus and Selene were lovers explain the birth of Dionysus, who represented theater and wine. Selene is known to travel across the sky on her chariot with her white horses. As she travels, she leaves a trail of silvery light that provides enough light to the living beings on Earth. At the same time, she keeps an eye on them and looks after their sleep.

Chang'e in Chinese Mythology

The East Asian version of the Moon Goddess, Chang'e, is a significant part of Chinese folklore and appears in many accounts. The deity's tale is associated with betrayal and sacrifice. Chang is the goddess's actual name, and the suffix "e" refers to a young and beautiful woman. Older stories address the Moon Goddess as Heng'e. However, it is believed that the ruler, Lui Heng disliked the idea of sharing his name with anyone, which is why they referred to the goddess as Chang'e. Despite the name change, the worshippers were devoted to the goddess and made several sacrifices in her name.

She was believed to be a young, beautiful girl working under the Jade Emperor at his palace in heaven. Chang'e resided with fairies and immortals in the palace and lived a peaceful life. However, her peace was disturbed since the day she broke an expensive and unique porcelain jar. She was banished from the Empire and sent to Earth to live with other mortal beings. Only by contributing to a noble service or valuable cause on Earth could she be allowed to return to heaven. As she began living with a low-income family, Hou Yi, a young hunter, befriended Chang'e, and they started spending a lot of time together, and they eventually grew fond of each other. According to a popular legend, Hou Yi saved Earth from the blaring heat spread by ten suns as he shot down 9 of them.

As a token of admiration, Emperor Lao gifted him an elixir of immortality that Chang'e ended up drinking. She ran towards the moon and floated in the sky to keep a distance from her husband, Hou Yi. However, he chased her and tried to stop her from fleeing by shooting arrows towards the moon. He missed his shot, and Chang'e disappeared into the sky. To date, she is associated with the Moon Goddess, and the couple symbolizes yin and yang.

While the female Lunar deities are well-known across various religions and cultures, the male Lunar figures are also a significant part of the mythological lore. Even though some male deities barely possess lunar aspects, they are still significant to their cultures due to their symbolization.

Chandra in Hindu Mythology

Chandra, or "Chandrasekhar," is the alleged eighth incarnation of Lord Shiva, who was a vital part of the Hindu Trinity- Brahma, Vishnu, and Mahesh. He is represented with long, luscious locks on his head and a half-crescent moon depicting his name. His name translates to "as bright as the moon," which portrays his beautiful image on his marriage day. In essence, Chandrasekhar is known to be Lord Shiva's most beautiful incarnation or version to date, where he shines and glows. Chandra literally means *Moon* and symbolizes emotions, senses, and wisdom. Faithful devotees often receive blessings in the form of a healthy and disease-free life.

Chandra possesses the nectar of the Gods, also known as Soma, and uses it to grow plants and put life into vegetation. He also controls the water waves and tides in deep seas and oceans, making him the legislator of nourishment and fertility. In the past, Indian women were encouraged to fast on Mondays to please the Moon God and find a suitable partner. This tradition still exists in some parts of India.

He thrives in the northwest direction and represents the Cancer constellation. According to a myth, Chandra was born from Arth Rishi's tears of joy. The Moon God in Hindu mythology is portrayed as a slim and tall deity with kind eyes and polite speech. His aura is infectious, and his demeanor makes one seek inner peace. He holds a lotus in one hand and is driven around in a chariot pulled by ten horses.

Sin in Mesopotamian Mythology

Sin, or Nanna, is a lunar deity of the ancient Mesopotamian or Sumerian people. Even though the Moon God was primarily worshipped in the city of Ur, devotion to him spread across the rest of the region after he was considered a significant deity. Today, you can still find several temples spread across the region, supposedly dedicated to the Moon God. Sin represents a bull and is deeply associated with cattle.

Just like the distinct phases of a menstrual cycle in a woman's body, the different versions of the moon during a cycle signify the deity's association with fertility. Enlil, the Sky God, fell in love with Ninlil, the Goddess of grain, and they gave birth to Sin. The Moon God's influence on the Mesopotamian people grew, and they started designing their calendars based on the moon's direction and the lunar cycle.

While Sin was illustrated as a half-moon, Nanna was portrayed as the new or full moon. The deity's symbol, the bull, was also associated with the moon's crescent shape. Nanna wears a crown resembling a moon disk and is called "Lord of the Diadem." Nanna is extremely wise and helps those who are confused or are seeking knowledge. Priests, mortals, and other gods also visited Nanna to gain advice. Sin is a part of the holy triad of the ancient Mesopotamian religion, which comprises Ishtar (Venus), Shamash (Sun), and Sin.

Thoth in Egyptian Mythology

Thoth was essentially associated with the Ibis bird of wisdom, as he possessed immense knowledge and wisdom on several topics. Ra, the Sun God, was always fascinated by Thoth's wisdom and appointed him as his personal advisor. His knowledge and personal attributes were often compared to the Greek God, Hermes. Thoth was a significant deity in ancient Egypt, especially in agriculture and astronomy. Some myths claim the Moon God to be Set and Horus's son who was conceived during battle. Other myths tell of Thoth's peculiar birth event where he appeared from Set's forehead.

The Moon God has several depictions and is illustrated in various lights in Egyptian mythology. Other accounts claim that the god is Ra's son and that he fathered Thoth from his lips. Ra was the Moon God's only parent, which is why he was labeled as "the god without a mother." The story behind Thoth's existence and predominance is associated with his symbolization of the Ibis. It says that Thoth was, in fact, the Ibis, and he created life on Earth by laying a cosmic egg.

Thoth has three wives who are also significant to ancient Egyptian religion. While the goddess of balance and truth, Ma'at, is Thoth's principal wife, some even claim Seshat (the Goddess of Books and Writing) and Nehmetawy (The Goddess of Safety and Protection) to be his dominant partners. Thoth symbolized a crescent moon and played a vital role as the Moon God in the past. He is also closely associated with a specter, stylus, scales, and a papyrus scroll.

The Moon's Spiritual Importance in Today's Time

Over time, as humans got more curious and delved deeper into scientific research and studies, their perception of the Moon steadily shifted from a mystical power to a dry wasteland. However, certain cultures still believe that the position and relevance of the Moon determine their fate. Ancient beliefs – merged with present-day astrological readings – have spurred modern spiritual denotation of this celestial body. Since it takes around a month to form a new moon, the modern way of following time shows implications from the past. Today, one can hardly deny that the Moon's energy and synergy are sending messages and vibrations that possess the power to manipulate our thoughts, emotions, and feelings. In fact, these manifestations can also affect the people around us.

The changes in tides and oceans are caused by the Moon's gravitational pull, especially during the Full and New Moon day. One can say that a person's body, which is mainly made up of water, is also controlled by the Moon's movement. Humans tend to feel more emotional or experience a surge in their emotions on prime days, which are specifically apparent on a Full Moon.

In a way, the Moon's movement and phases also affect the Earth's frequency and magnetic field due to salty water in oceans and fluctuating water levels. These changes affect not only our brain's cognitive capacity but also our sleep and brain wave performance. As you can see, the Moon's mystical power can lead to significant changes in our body, mind, and soul. Specific modern-day techniques are being implemented to manifest positive changes in humans during different phases of the Moon. For instance, certain self-care strategies can help a person feel more at ease on a New Moon.

While the Sun defines our outer personality and extroverted nature, the Moon signifies unconscious thoughts and beliefs, which can be effectively remolded for better outcomes. If you learn the right way to unlock the mystical nature of the Moon, you will be blessed with abundance and creativity.

Its Role in Modern Witchcraft and Wicca

Modern witchcraft and Wicca magic are still being practiced in some regions, and the Moon is the central element of every reading.

A Lunar cycle is completed over the course of around 27 days. The different phases of the Moon, including the waxing and waning, are studied to attract positivity. Specific rituals are performed to access the Moon's spiritual energy and harness its power.

If you are successful, you can easily reach your goals. While the Moon's waxing phase is used to attract positivity, the Moon's waning phase is used to send negativity or any unwanted object out of your life. The Full Moon phase is the most fruitful event of all phases, and it is marked as the "harvest" season.

Not all magicians and witches prefer to work on Dark Moon days as it may have negative repercussions. On a positive note, one can perform magic on a Dark Moon day to rewind, refresh, and bring closure to complete the circle.

Chapter 2: The Moon in Astrology

The mythological and spiritual implications of the Moon lead to its significance and relevance in the world of astrology. It impacts the emotional and spiritual well-being of every individual in one way or another. While several Western cultures perform their astrological readings using the Sun signs, Hindu culture designs their natal charts based on individual Moon signs. In the past, Hindus based their birth dates according to the Moon's position and relevant signs. The birth date was marked as the day when the sign overlapped with Moon's entrance. However, after the British established their base in India, people celebrated their birthdays based on the calendar dates.

The Moon's Astrological Significance

When a person is born, their natal chart includes the Moon's position and behavior to determine their fate. Lagna, or the ascendant in the horoscope, is a respected and influential house. The involvement of the Moon in this house makes it the Chandra Lagna, which is used to determine *a person's fate* when they are born. The Moon influences the Cancer sign and is associated with other planets in a clockwise direction.

It takes around 324 days to orbit around all zodiac signs, thereby becoming a part of each sign for several days (around 27 days) throughout the year. The Moon governs the fourth sign and Cancer's fourth house. You can study the astrological implications of this celestial body by examining its conjunction with other planets, day of the week, color, body parts, emotions and values, constellations, emotional health, and professions.

Day and Color

In astrology, the Moon is associated with Monday and the color white. Some claim that the word "Monday" was derived from "Moon."

The shadowy and emotional demeanor of the Moon resembles the first day of the week, which often feels intuitive and moody. At times, taking the first step can feel quite challenging. Like the New Moon (the first phase of a lunar cycle), Mondays can feel overwhelming. However, as the days pass, you get comfortable with the flow. This allocation of the week's first day can be dated back to the Babylonians' time when ancient scholars divided a lunar cycle into four quarters. The implication is that the first day was linked to the Moon's first phase of birth. As mentioned, Hindu women fasted on Mondays to please Chandra and attract suitable partners for marriage.

Since the Moon's surface is white and bright, this hue is quite significant to the planet. The cosmic rays, energy fields, and the Moon's aura are represented by white. This hue is made from the seven colors of the spectrum, thereby making it the purest shade of all. It motivates people to gather inspiration from their surroundings and take the spiritual path. In the past, devotees dedicated white flowers and objects to the Moon. Typically, white jasmines, lotuses, and lilies were associated with the Moon Goddess. Objects like white sandalwood, curd, milk, and rice flour were also considered sacred. However, astrologers refrain from using too much white as it can reverse the positive effects.

Other Planets

The Moon is friendly with Jupiter and Mars as all three thrive in harmony. When these planets align together, the person may be blessed with immense luck or mental peace. Astrologers consider this association to be optimistic. On the other hand, it fails to create a healthy connection with Saturn, Ketu, and Rahu. Furthermore, it keeps a safe distance from Mercury as both share a neutral relationship that is neither imperial nor hideous. However, if Mercury starts dominating the Moon, the person is susceptible to neurological disorders. Even though the Moon is neutral and tries to be fair to all, its union with other planets determines the body's status. If the other planet is regressive, it can negatively affect your mental and emotional health.

Despite sharing a strong bond with the Sun, the correlation does not bring much to the table. Collectively, they represent confidence and ambition. The Venus-Moon pair symbolizes love and romantic relationships. If this combination is prominent in your astrological chart, consider taking a creative profession like music production or fashion design, as you will likely succeed in your career. If the Moon's pertinence is strong with Rahu or Ketu, you can suffer from financial loss or mental health issues. A steady balance between these two planets can mean liberation or enlightenment.

Emotions and Values

The Moon is peaceful and calm by nature and inspires others to seek solitude by regaining consciousness and self-awareness. It symbolizes emotions, imaginative power, the importance of being or having a mother, mental stability, prosperity, wisdom, peace of mind, and trading. It is feminine by nature and thrives at a low temperature. The Moon can be very fruitful or extremely negative depending on the position and phase. A well-placed planet depicts a healthy relationship with your parents, especially your mother, and a supportive family. You are blessed with a healthy mind and emotional availability. You have immense wealth and a big house where you are at peace and able to live comfortably.

The Full Moon, which also stands at the highest order of a lunar cycle, brings joy to one's life, and it is regarded as beneficial. On the other hand, the New Moon, which is basically non-existent, is perceived as malefic. If the Full Moon overlaps with your zodiac sign, you will likely gain wisdom or be blessed with creativity. In essence, the Moon represents every feminine aspect of living beings and the universe. Beauty, happiness, eyesight, well-being, mind, and memory are some of the other attributes presented by this orbiting energy.

Constellations

The planet is associated with the Sravana, Hasta, and Rohini constellations (also known as "Nakshatra"). As the Moon orbits the Earth and takes around 27 days to complete a cycle, it also covers the 27 Nakshatras or Lunar Mansions during this period. Typically, the Moon enters, stays, and exits one Nakshatra every day. Your Moon Nakshatra significantly influences your self-awareness and consciousness, which is why you should learn more about your constellation. Other constellations that blend well with the Moon's energy include Vishaka, Punarvasu, and Purva Bhadrapad. In other constellations like Uttra Khad, Kritika, Ashlekha, Uttara Phalguni, Revati, and Jyestha, the amalgamation results in neutral to favorable outcomes.

Every lunar mansion is supervised by one planet – each distinct in both nature and characteristics. As the Moon enters different mansions every day, your birthday will be marked based on its position. This mansion or constellation will be marked as your Moon Nakshatra. While the Moon's energy is solely powerful, its symbiosis with respective Nakshatras makes it even more authoritative. By successfully deciphering your Moon Nakshatra, you can unravel your life's purpose and hidden intricacies, which will attract success and emotional well-being – the right path towards self-discovery and fighting inner conflicts.

Gemstone

It represents the gemstone, pearl, which is also white. A pearl enhances a woman's physical appearance and makes her look more beautiful, which is also a symbolism portrayed by the Moon. Furthermore, a pearl represents depth and awareness, which also aligns with the Moon's values. It is believed that a person who wears a real pearl daily can attract fame and appreciation over time. In some cases, wearing this gemstone can also alleviate certain physical health symptoms related to cough, cold, bronchitis, throat issues, hysteria, eye diseases, typhoid, varicose veins, tumors, and intestinal disorders, among many others.

You can either place a pearl near your bedside or wear it as a pendant or a ring. Astrologers suggest wearing a pearl weighing between 1200 to 1400 mg. You can also pick a pearl with more weight. If you are wearing it as a ring, put it on your dominant hand's little finger so that it makes contact with your skin. Hindu astrologers suggest dipping the pearl in holy water for 10 to 15 minutes before wearing it. To achieve more favorable outcomes, wait for the next Monday to arrive before you put it on your finger. When wearing it, chant the mantra, "OM CHANDRAYA NAMAH." Use a soft brush and soapy water to clean the pearl from time to time, as accumulated dust can reduce its positive effects.

The Moon also symbolizes the hare. While some of the stories associated a hare with the Moon, the significance can be drawn from the steadiness of this animal. Just like a hare jumps and leaps around at a fast pace, the Moon also moves faster than other planets. Vedic lore depicts the Moon as a rabbit because it steadily leaps and hops from one place to another without resting at one spot for long.

Metal

It represents metal and silver. While some may argue that the bright, silvery illumination is the basic correlation of this metal with the celestial body, astrologers claim that the purifying properties of silver align with the Moon's cleansing nature. When you think of moonlight over a silent lake, you can imagine a clear, silver palette shining over the water surface. It looks like liquid silver with mysterious properties. It helps release stress and encourages you to explore the beauty of nature, much like the Moon itself. Metal is related to sensuality, femininity, and connectivity. Silver also exemplifies the properties of minerals and gemstones attached to it, thereby making the effects even more potent.

Body Parts

The Moon firmly signifies motherhood and fertility. Certain body parts like the heart, eyes, bodily fluids, and lungs are also associated with it. In essence, it also governs women's breasts and lactation during childbirth. Vedic astrology believes that the Moon rules a person's left eye and nostril. If the Moon enters an unfavorable mansion or transits into a hostile state, you may likely face issues around any of these body parts. While minor cases include sleeplessness and fatigue, some may suffer from adverse health conditions like asthma.

Emotional, Mental, and Physical Health

If the celestial body is placed in a weak position, the person will likely suffer from respiratory issues, cardiac problems, weak eyesight, cold, or depression. On the other hand, a well-placed planet portrays better physical and mental health along with strong imagination and intelligence. If the Moon rules in your favor, you can implement certain effective strategies like meditation to combat physical problems and enhance your mental power.

Profession

The Moon supports professions like fishing, water trading, sailing, pearl trading, gynecology, or dairy farming. Since the Moon represents motherhood, gynecology can be a rewarding profession for ambitious people.

The Moon and Its Ruler, Cancer

While the Sun rules the Leo sign, the Moon looks over those under the sign of Cancer. Since it is a Water sign, Cancer dominates a person's spiritual and emotional side. When combined with the lunar attributes, individuals born under this zodiac sign possess strong emotions and are more attuned to their feelings. They are self-aware and can empathize with others. The lunar waxing and waning nature emphasize the recurring changes and cyclical patterns associated with the Moon. When compared to Cancer's attributes, people may likely display cyclical behavior too.

While your own emotions govern your condition, your mood may also change or become influenced by the distinct energies around you. At times, these situations can make it more difficult to accept changes and adapt to new environments, affecting you emotionally and mentally. You must develop skills to take control of your life and emotions. If you are successful, you will likely have optimum emotional balance. In some cases, the Moon may inspire you to take a more traditional approach and be deeply involved with your family and loved ones. If you are experiencing similar nurturing or protective feelings, remember to give space to your loved ones while you take care of them.

While Scorpio debilitates the Moon and reduces its positive impact, Taurus elevates the celestial body and promotes better outcomes.

The Moon and Scorpio

While the association of the Moon with this zodiac sign is already grim, the former's position and affiliation with an ominous planet can negatively impact a person's fate. This cooperation is often perceived as a bad omen by astrologers. In this case, the Moon is extremely weak and can also be destructive in some cases. As mentioned, if this version of the planet aligns with Saturn, Ketu, or Rahu, it can result in severe mental issues like forgetfulness, obsessive-compulsive disorder, poor decision-making skills, migraine, or depression.

The Moon and Taurus

Unlike Scorpio that debilitates the Moon, the Tarusu supports and enhances it. Since this zodiac sign works well with the Moon, it empowers a person's fate when they are born. This version of the white celestial body is extremely powerful. The person is blessed with immense creativity and a strong mind. They possess impressive imaginary skills as well. Furthermore, the Moon's power is also tested according to the house it is placed in. If it is placed in Kendra with the 7th house, it makes one of the most powerful versions of the Moon.

How to Strengthen a Debilitated Moon

Fortunately, you can implement certain tips to strengthen a debilitated moon and turn the results in your favor.

Donate Wisely

Individuals with a weak Moon should refrain from accepting silver in any form. Whether it's a reward or a donation, do not accept silver. However, you can demand silver in the form of jewelry from your mother and wear it as a chain. Some other objects significant to the Moon are milk, white flowers, and crystals. It is believed that donating milk can also bring a positive change.

On the other hand, you can donate silver to those in need. Since real silver can be pretty expensive, astrologers suggest donating a single silver thread as it is more affordable. Donations shouldn't be announced to the world. Keep it to yourself and just accept the gratitude from the ones receiving it. Do not feel proud or egoistic when donating something and try to forget it. Note that the Moon supports humility and modesty. It is important to stay grounded.

Try Visualization Techniques

Certain visualization techniques are not only useful for your mental peace and spiritual growth, but they also strengthen your Moon's position. In essence, they activate your Third Eye or Ajna chakra that deliberately flushes out negativity from your system. This, in turn, helps make room for positive thoughts and manifests better outcomes. Performing visualization techniques also helps you channel your emotions and attract happiness. The idea is to think of a positive outcome and believe that you have already achieved your goal; while it may seem useless, it works.

Basically, by thinking that you have overcome your current problem, you manifest the Moon's and the universe's energies to experience it in real life. Since it can be challenging to concentrate and visualize your outcomes, practice meditation to improve concentration. Along with performing visualization techniques, you can also practice breathing techniques like Anulom-Vilom and Diaphragmatic Breathing.

Wear the Moon's Gemstone and Metal

As mentioned earlier, wearing an authentic white pearl can strengthen a debilitated moon and help you stay attuned to the Moon's energy. To further strengthen its power, pair the pearl with a silver necklace or a ring. Since silver represents the Moon and possesses purifying properties, this combination can help cleanse your emotions and soul. You can also get a necklace made with real silver and a white pearl as its pendant. Remember that the necklace or ring should always stay in contact with your skin.

You can also get an auspicious showpiece made of real silver and place it on your mantle or bedside. Keep it clean and dust-free to unravel its maximum power. Some other objects you can keep in your house to strengthen your Moon include peacock feathers, small plants, and silver "supari." The plants should face north if you can, fast on Mondays, and eat healthy during the rest of the week.

Conduct a "Shanti Kriya"

This kriya or ritual is based on psychic energy and enables the forces to divert the Moon's positive energy in your favor. It involves a holy ritual with tantras and meditation exercises. The priest or astrologer performs the kriya chants, a series of powerful mantras to induce positive vibrations and make the ritual more successful. While taking help from an astrologer can help you achieve better results, you can also learn some mantras and chant them on Mondays while performing the kriyas. For instance, the Prarthana mantra, Avahan mantra, and Chintan or Chandra Dhyan mantra are used to ward off negative energies and bring more positivity.

You can make a few minor changes in your daily life like wearing white clothes, eating white foods like rice, coconut, and kheer, meditating and chanting mantras on Mondays, and using crystals for internal healing. Note that these rituals and actions can take some time to show a positive outcome. You must be patient and believe in the process.

Some of these techniques and rituals will also be discussed and elaborated on in the last chapter, which considers some effective ways to strengthen a weak Moon.

Even though the Moon sign is not as popular as the Sun sign, it is still considered an important celestial body in Vedic astrology. The Moon is now considered to be the most powerful and important natural body in this domain.

Note that the accuracy of the Moon's position and orbiting energy must be calculated with precision. An inexperienced astrologer may draw inaccurate results, thereby damaging your birth chart. It is crucial to find a wise and experienced astrologer who can perform meticulous calculations and make an accurate birth chart. They will also advise you on the right way to combat stress or other mental health issues based on your condition by computing the Moon's position and its association with other planets.

Chapter 3: Your Moon Signs I

Your moon sign is directly related to your emotional energy. It indicates your personality and innate reactions, and it highlights what you need to feel more secure. Your moon sign shines a light on your emotional state and intuition.

Aries Moon Sign

Aries is a cardinal fire sign; when you are born with the moon in Aries, there is likely a very strong need for independence. You are also likely to be very assertive. You will feel your best when you are dealing with things that are exciting and challenging. These challenging experiences bring you immense joy. New experiences allow you to bring out your innovative side.

Characteristic Traits

Aries often indicates emotional independence. You might find that you put in your time, effort, and energy, expecting the same in return. You are, however, quick to forgive but are easily hurt. You will often find yourself chasing freedom and alone time. Although you give to others, this need for solitude is important for you to recalibrate and get a sense of your own self. Feeling pressured or controlled by others dampens your spirits and your innate need for independence.

A cardinal sign is a front-runner in the zodiac signs. They are go-getters, dynamic, and incredibly powerful. As a cardinal sign, there is often a need and deep desire to act. You may find that you like to get things going, and you don't take a back seat. You always try to move things forward and set them in motion.

Strengths

You are very likely a straight-talker, and you don't feel the need to hide your feelings or thoughts with niceties. Instead, you prefer to be upfront, and you tend to deal with things directly and clearly. You have this warrior-like sense that allows you to deal with hardships efficiently. Because of that, you may find that you often expect others to do the same.

You are often able to intuitively draw on the internal resources you need in a time of need. Often, when you have a goal in mind, you can speed toward it completely focused. You can easily remove all distractions that keep you from your goal. Your moon in Aries gives you the necessary focus and internal resources needed to thrive. Because you move quickly and focus, others are easily left behind when you concentrate on what you want.

Aries moons tend to be extroverted and love attention from others. Your emotional reactions may be big displays that capture the attention of others. If you are happy, your happiness is displayed loud and proud. If you cry, you tend to cry your eyes out. You express your emotions in an incredibly intense way. People may want to get to know you because of the way you present yourself.

Weaknesses

A weakness of this placement is that you might find yourself making decisions based on your first instinctive feelings. You find yourself rushing in, and this leads to errors of judgment. To avoid this, you should learn how other people feel and think and make your decisions accordingly. Don't feel the need to ignore your instincts, but instead, use this alongside a good understanding of the situation in front of you to make the best possible decision.

Another weakness you could exhibit is impatience. You may want everything to come easily, and you expect others to move as quickly as you do, leading to constantly getting annoyed – or even outbursts of anger. To deal with this and to avoid getting irritated by how slow something is progressing, be realistic. Realize that not everything can happen with the snap of a finger. It takes time for goals to actualize and become a reality.

Taurus Moon Sign

Those who have their moon in Taurus are often calm, mellow, and grounded. The moon and Taurus go hand in hand, and this is an easy and relaxed fit. You are grounded in your body, as opposed to being so consumed by the thoughts in your head. In this modern world, it is hard to find people who are grounded. The rush of our lifestyles has meant that many have retreated to the safety of their minds, limiting them from enjoying the wonder and joy of everyday life. It may mean that they make mistakes and live in a place of fear, and are consumed with meaningless thoughts.

Characteristic Traits

With the moon in Taurus, you are much better equipped to handle the world around you calmly. You may notice that you deal with things at a slower pace compared to others because you have the advantage of being grounded in the present. You love to focus on the small joys of life.

Strengths

Taurus is a fixed sign that means you can easily put all your energy into one thing and complete it well. Pair that with your innately grounded nature, and you may find that you can make great strides in your hobbies. The moon in Taurus will actually help you find your hobbies and discover your talents easily.

Your patient nature gives you the necessary time and energy to allow you to immerse yourself in whatever you want or need. You find yourself craving stability more than anything. You may seek situations and partners that allow you to feel complete comfort, security, and stability.

However, a drawback to this desire for stability is that it may make you rigid and unwilling to change. If you are unaware that you have innate patience, a need for stability, and being grounded, it can easily turn into laziness.

Weaknesses

Because you are so attached to your routines and habits, you may hesitate to make big moves or changes that improve or add benefit to your life. You could miss out on important opportunities by deliberating rather than taking action. It is best to become aware of your tendencies and know how you act or think during important phases of your life to combat this. The more aware you become, the easier it will be for you to make a change.

Start taking action. Some fear may arise because it is not in your nature to make decisions quickly. You need to push through that fear. Feel it, process it, and overcome it. Allow yourself to think and reflect and then, once you have all the facts, allow yourself to make a choice that could lead to change.

Often, you may fear change and consider it to be a bad thing. You can easily become stubborn, which, in turn, leads to stagnation in life. Choose instead to make new and bold choices. Get used to overcoming the fear and choose to do something anyway.

Gemini Moon Sign

The air sign of Gemini in your moon may mean that you have an innate thirst for knowledge. You have a deep desire to understand and know as much as you can about the world around you. You are very likely a curious individual with an incredibly active mind.

Characteristic Traits

The underpinning theme of this sign is communication. You may love sharing information and knowledge with others. You could be a very chatty person with a lot to say. You may also have friends from all walks of life and the ability to move around and fit in with all kinds of people. Sharing ideas, information, and knowledge spark joy, allowing you to be friends with different types of people. You feel like you are being true to yourself the most when you are engaged in learning new things.

Strengths

Your mind is often active and constantly taking in and processing information from the world around you, sometimes leading to you feeling overwhelmed – but you may like how often and how fast your mind works.

Gemini is a mutable sign, and there is a need for new stimulation and change. You could find yourself becoming quickly and easily engrossed in new things. Becoming bored easily may be one of your habits, but you are adaptable and a great multi-tasker. Taking on multiple projects and doing several tasks at once often comes naturally to you.

Often, you don't feel the need to study or learn much about something to feel like you know it. You may only need a glimpse to be satisfied. Just like how you can jump from group to group, you can easily jump between ideas, concepts, and facts.

You need to develop the skill of discretion as this will help you avoid getting yourself into any sticky situations.

Your inquisitive nature helps you connect with others. You can easily speak to people about their problems and issues, finding out what makes them tick. You don't care much for their deep emotional problems but rather the oddities of their life issues or circumstances.

Once you have someone figured out, you may feel the need to move on to the next person, no longer interested in what this particular person has to say. It feels as if you have satisfied your need for information, and your desire to get to know other people is genuine. Don't mistake it for anything else. You only think of moving on to the next person because you want to know more people.

The moon is associated with nurturing, and you may find that you can easily make others feel good about themselves with what you have to say. You can nurture others with your words, and you make them feel better.

You may be known for your humor and ability to entertain. It is often easy for you to keep things fun and entertaining. Gemini moons tend to use humor to avoid or release feelings of tension. Do you often find yourself making jokes about things that are emotionally difficult? You find this easier than most and like to use humor to distract yourself and others. Compared to more emotional moon signs, the Gemini moon is more detached, making them seem superficial.

You can easily tread on the surface of situations, with an uncanny ability to keep things light and easy if they start to get a little dark.

Weaknesses

A problem you may run into is that it could be hard for you to feel your emotions. Instead, you find it easier to objectify your experiences and categorize them in a way that detaches you from having to feel anything.

You tend to avoid any deep emotional situations and stick to the rational side of things. You may use logic to deal with a situation as opposed to feeling your emotions. The problem with this is that you may begin to suppress your emotions over long periods, which can cause problems for you in the long run. Your emotions may blow up over minor things, and you may struggle to regulate your emotions.

Begin to tune into your emotions and use them to assess how you truly feel about a situation instead of just relying on your logic. Tuning into this may help you make better decisions based on a more informed understanding of yourself.

Your love for both words and numbers means that you may enjoy the hustle and bustle of trade or retail. Gadgets, tech, and new innovations may excite you.

Cancer Moon Sign

Cancer moons are at home, as the moon rules Cancer. Cancer is a cardinal sign, which means you very likely have a deep desire to take action. Especially when it comes to others, you may feel responsible for both the physical and emotional well-being of others.

Characteristic Traits

You may have a deep need to nurture, and connect with others, especially with your loved ones. Your emotional health often stems from the relationships you have developed with your family. There is an innate desire to support, protect, and nurture.

As the moon rules Cancer, this strengthens the emotional, empathetic, and intuitive aspects. You may find yourself being strongly influenced by your emotions and mood that constantly fluctuates and the moods of others around you.

Strengths

Consider the moon, which is cyclical in nature. Just as the moon wanes and waxes, you, too, are a cyclical being. Your emotions wax and wane just like the moon. Logic and rationality take a backseat for cancer moons. Instead, internal cycles and instincts often take over.

As you learn to get in touch with this natural rhythm, this internal sense of self can be used positively. The more in touch you are, the more you will understand yourself and what you need in each moment. You will be able to follow your internal compass and make decisions and choices that accurately reflect how you feel.

You will thrive and feel your best when you abide by these internal cycles. Because your emotions are ever-changing, it is best if you respect their ebb and flow and avoid sticking to a rigid routine. Allow yourself flexibility, and don't feel bad if you cannot stick to a strict schedule or are not as productive as you want to be every day. It would be better for you to follow your internal wishes, as this is a great signpost to how you should spend your energy that day. Use this to guide you and as a way to see how much more energy you have and how much you can get done.

One way to use this emotional energy in the right way is to take complete accountability for just how sensitive and emotional you are. Perhaps people have told you in a negative manner that you are too emotional or sensitive. Get rid of this shame and allow yourself to celebrate the fact that you are this way. It provides you with gifts that others do not innately have.

Weaknesses

A weakness of being so emotional or sensitive is that you may find yourself significantly affected by the emotional state of other people around you. Their emotions may affect yours, and you may end up carrying around other people's emotions as well as yours. If this is you, learn to differentiate between your emotions and those of others. Take some time to reflect and find the root of the emotion. If it does not belong to you, permit yourself to let it float away. It is easier said than done but, with practice, you will find that you can release yourself from the burden of other people's emotions and maybe even your own.

Cancer moons may find that they are impressionable and often soak up other people's feelings or opinions and make them their own. Because you are so intuitive, you can easily tune into others and how they are feeling at any given moment and then take on both their emotional burdens and attitudes. Become aware of this when you are around others, question the things you think and feel, and ask yourself if it is truly what you think and or if you may have picked it up from somewhere else.

Your emotional sensitivity is like a superpower, but it can cause you to stress out if you do not use it properly. To make the most of it, you must ensure you stay grounded. Stay centered and connected to your body. You can do this through daily meditation, exercise, spending some time alone, or anything that makes you feel relaxed and in control.

Learning to regulate your emotions will provide you with a healthy way to manage your mood. The more it fluctuates, the harder it will be to act and feel in a way that is authentic to yourself. Learn to stay grounded, relaxed, and in the moment. In this way, you can effortlessly process your emotions and learn to discern between which emotions are yours and which are not.

Chapter 4: Your Moon Signs II

The moon's position in the sky affects a person's mood and behavior. It can also influence things like health, appearance, and creativity. The moon is constantly changing its position in the sky, which means that people are always going through different phases of life. The Zodiac signs are divided by their corresponding moon signs to represent these phases of life. Each one has its unique personality traits as well as strengths and weaknesses that you should know about. This chapter will teach you everything there is to know about the Moon Signs Leo, Virgo, Libra, and Scorpio, so you'll never be caught off guard again!

Leo Moon Sign

The Leo moon sign is ruled by the Sun and has a fixed element of Fire. People born under this sign can be passionate about their interests, but they tend to become obsessive. When they get into something, nothing can stop them from doing it right. However, the problem is that few people have the energy and willpower to go through with their plans when they make up their minds; perhaps this isn't something negative, though, because Leos are just very passionate people! They don't worry too much about what happens in life, but they just live it! If you're hanging out with a Leo moon, you must know their characteristics, strengths, and weaknesses.

Characteristic Traits

People with a Leo moon sign are cheerful, friendly, and confident. They enjoy life to the fullest at all times. Often feeling superior to others, they will expect praise for everything they do. If you're working on a project with them, you can expect a completed job well done. They can show true love in the most spectacular way possible, so if they fall for you, it's usually for good. They are self-centered and can be controlling, but they do it with good intentions. They can work up the courage to be vulnerable. People with a Leo moon sign are warm-hearted and generous, especially when they're around the ones that they love. They enjoy comforts of all sorts, so they'll make sure everything is perfect before doing anything else.

Strengths

Leo moon signs have a big heart, which allows them to do anything they put their mind to. They're strong-willed, confident, and creative. They're not afraid to overcome obstacles to get the job done. Their courageous nature can help them to overcome the fear of failure.

They are also very determined and can inspire others to be ambitious and determined as well. If one thing is worth it to them, they won't stop until that thing is completed. Leos are very passionate about life, and it can make them seem like a powerhouse at times. They're often the center of attention wherever they go because they know how to take control of a situation.

Weaknesses

The one flaw with this sign is their need for praise. They don't like to share the spotlight with anyone else, and they can sometimes be very insensitive towards others. If they're not getting enough attention, they may attempt to get it by doing something drastic. They also get angered quite easily, which can lead them to be impatient and inflexible. They have a hard time listening to the opinions of others, so it could cause issues if you're trying to reason with someone who has a Leo moon sign. While they are quite confident, they also tend to be jealous. If you're a Leo, you should always work on being more open-minded and flexible when it comes to interpersonal relationships. You can also try to curb your jealousy and have more confidence in yourself. It will help you become much more likable!

Leos are ruled by the Sun, so they need to be pampered and appreciated. They can do anything if they're motivated enough, but sometimes that motivation isn't there due to a lack of appreciation. If you want a Leo moon sign to do something for you, make sure that it's worth their while. They need to be appreciated for what they do for others, but they also need to know beforehand what's at stake. If you want them to stick around, make sure that they know you're not just taking advantage of their eagerness.

Virgo Moon Sign

The Virgo moon sign is very reliable and practical. They are excellent at helping others get organized, and they have an eye for details. They like working on small projects that require attention to detail, such as puzzles or intricate drawings. People born under this sign naturally love doing things for other people, so you can expect them to be good friends.

You can also expect them to be good conversationalists. Virgo moon signs are very interested in learning new things, and they love to discuss their thoughts with others. If you have something interesting that you want to share, you should look into telling a person born under this sign because the odds are that they will listen intently. They also love to have fun, so you can be sure that they will love any of your jokes and stories.

Characteristic Traits

The Virgo moon sign has many wonderful traits. They are very honest, and they are willing to listen to constructive criticism. These people also love to read, and you can expect them to learn more and more throughout their lives. You can never say that a person born under the Virgo sign doesn't have an eye for detail because they catch every little detail in life. They are very intuitive, and they will always try to help others when they can. If you are trying to organize a group of volunteers, someone with the Virgo moon sign would be an excellent choice. They also enjoy assisting in the community and giving back in any way they can.

People born under the Virgo moon sign are excellent problem solvers. They love to fix things, and they will give you their full attention when you need them most. You can expect these people to help you feel better if you are going through a rough patch in your life or if you have made a mistake. These people also possess many strengths that make them an excellent choice when it comes to jobs. They will always follow the rules and be on time regardless of how much pressure they are under at any given moment.

Strengths

The strengths of the Virgo moon sign include their practical nature, sense of responsibility, and their ability to work with others. If you have a task that requires someone who can follow orders well and work in groups, then this is the person for the job. These people may seem cold and distant on the surface, but they are very sensitive and intelligent deep down, though they may choose not to exhibit that feeling. If you need help organizing your life, this is also a sign that will *be happy to assist you*!

When dealing with a person born under this sign, you should make sure to give them lots of attention when they need it and praise them for getting things done at work or school. Although these people enjoy helping others out, they are also very focused on their goals. To get the most out of them, you should avoid distracting them from their work when they are in the zone. You will be glad that you gave them attention at the end though because they always finish the job quickly and masterfully.

Weaknesses

The weaknesses of the Virgo moon sign include being too critical and lacking a sense of humor sometimes. These people can be challenging to handle when frustrated or upset, so it's best not to upset them in the first place if possible. Also, if you tell one of these people your life story, then don't be surprised if they go into detail about how they would have improved it. They may seem to overanalyze everything. You can expect them to spend more time thinking about what is going on in their lives than actually doing something about it.

People born under this sign love getting involved with lots of different kinds of activities. However, they always feel like there is not enough time for themselves. These people want to get things done right away because they hate putting things off, but unfortunately, this causes them extra stress because they try hard to keep up with everything. To overcome these weaknesses, try to relax and do things at your own pace. You will accomplish more if you are less critical of yourself and others.

It's also important that you learn to laugh sometimes. If anyone knows how to lighten up a situation and find humor in anything, then it's the Virgo moon sign. People born under this sign need people around them to feel like life is worth living. They love being with friends or family just as much as they enjoy helping out in the community! Just remember that they can be very sensitive despite their harsh sense of humor, so it's best not to take them too seriously most of the time.

Libra Moon Sign

The Libra moon sign is ruled by Venus and has an even element of Air. People born under this sign are very indecisive, making it difficult for them to make up their minds about anything. They like having things just the way they are so that they can have a harmonious environment around them. When they aren't working toward perfection, they easily become restless. This need for perfection can cause them to be hard on themselves when things don't go exactly how they planned. The only way that they'll overcome this is if someone encourages them. Being flexible will bring more opportunities to them in the long run. Otherwise, they'll continue on the same self-destructive path until something extreme happens to change their mindsets.

Characteristic Traits

People with a Libra moon sign make great diplomats because they know how to please others. They're always in tune with their surroundings, so they can easily get along with many different kinds of people. On the one hand, this could mean that they'll be able to talk to anyone about anything but, on the other hand, it could also mean that they never say what's really on their minds. This hesitancy is mostly due to fear of rejection or disapproval from others. Their indecisiveness makes it difficult to speak up when something goes wrong or when things need to be fixed.

They're very patient and tolerant in almost all situations. If you try giving them a task or goal with an unknown outcome, you should expect them to take as long as they need to complete it. They're easily bored and have a hard time focusing on one thing at a time, which is why being with other people can be quite difficult for them if they can't find something that interests them. If you want things done now, you'll need to give them some extra incentive or encouragement to get it finished.

Strengths

Libra moon signs are charming and sympathetic, which makes them very likable. They try to do everything peacefully and fairly. They have a propensity for helping others, especially when they can see that there's something wrong with them. Libras believe that all people deserve respect regardless of who they are or what they look like. They are also good mediators because they can sit back and take points from both sides of a situation to create a solution.

They're usually among the first people who try to make peace with others when there's a conflict between two groups. Libras have strong communication skills, which include listening as well as speaking. They like having a harmonious environment around them and can be very helpful if you need them for something.

Weaknesses

This moon sign tends to stray away from goals in favor of pleasure. They believe that everyone is entitled to it, which may cause them to slack off on their work or personal obligations. This attitude leads to procrastination and a lack of self-discipline, as well as poor decision-making in general. They also like being around people who are going through problems because it allows them to fix things, even if they didn't necessarily cause the problem in the first place. If you're a Libra moon sign, you need to work on your discipline. You also need to start accepting responsibility for what you do, even if other people are involved. It will help you a lot in the long run, and it will give you more self-confidence!

Scorpio Moon Sign

People with a Scorpio moon sign are determined, resourceful, and strong-willed. They have an uncanny ability to know what others are hiding from them, making it difficult for them to trust others. This ability is mostly because they're very secretive and private about their own lives. They like being in control of their destiny and don't like being told what to do.

Scorpios are very passionate people who find it difficult to express their emotions verbally. They're very intense in every aspect of their lives, and when they're focused on something, they pay their full attention to it and put all of their energy into it. They prefer things to be a certain way, making them stubborn when defending their opinions. Scorpio moon sign people tend to have a magnetic personality that draws people to them. Even those that aren't overly friendly are very sociable.

Characteristic Traits

Scorpio people are the most complex of all moon signs. They have a great deal of passion, and they express their creativity through intense emotions or physical actions. Scorpio is ruled by Mars, which gives strength to bold actions, determination, courage, and fighting spirits. Those born under this sign are resourceful and have an uncanny ability to uncover secrets.

Scorpios are born investigators. They like knowing the truth and getting to the bottom of things, making them incredibly good at detective work and other professions involving solving cryptic clues. They're very passionate people who experience life on a deep level. While they may not always show it, they have strong feelings about everything that crosses their path.

Strengths

Those born with a Scorpio moon are passionate and intense. They possess incredible strength of character, which makes them capable of going to great lengths to achieve their goals. While they may hide it well, those born under this sign have an incredibly magnetic personality that draws people to them. Although they tend to be private about certain things in life, they're not afraid to get involved in events that affect them.

Scorpios tend to be very good at getting people to open up to them because they possess the ability to tap into people's secrets. Those born under this sign are good at reading people, and they have an impressive ability to uncover mysteries.

People with a Scorpio moon sign tend to be very resourceful, as they can get out of tough situations using their quick thinking and intelligence. They're also quite resourceful at home, as they have a knack for making things with their hands. They're not afraid to take chances in life.

Weaknesses

Scorpio moon sign people tend to be very secretive and private about the personal details of their lives. It's difficult for them to become close friends with others because they don't like being told what to do. Most Scorpios have a deep, dark sense of humor. They like to play pranks on others and enjoy playing practical jokes. The biggest challenge for Scorpio moon sign people is that they often can't stand being around other people with a high opinion of themselves. To overcome these weak points and make the best of their personality, it's helpful for Scorpio moon sign people to surround themselves with other people. It's also helpful to gain the approval of others. These weaknesses can make it very difficult for Scorpio moon sign people to achieve their goals. However, if they can overcome them, they can accomplish almost anything.

This chapter discusses the following four moon signs: Leo, Virgo, Libra, and Scorpio. Leo Moons are passionate people that love to feel appreciated for their efforts. They enjoy being in a leadership position and often volunteer or help out in the community. Virgo Moons like to fix things, and they will give you their full attention when you need them the most. These people possess many strengths that make them excellent choices for jobs: practical nature, sense of responsibility, and ability to work with others. Libra Moons are very social and like to be in a group and be involved in many different activities. They always feel like there is not enough time for themselves. Scorpio Moons are intense, passionate people who enjoy helping others in the community. They are very intuitive.

Chapter 5: Your Moon Signs III

This chapter will cover the third part of moon signs; the Sagittarius, Capricorn, Aquarius, and Pisces Zodiacs. These four zodiacs all have great characteristics that they bring to the world. However, depending on your moon sign, you may not possess these traits immediately. The traits could take a while to develop. There are always good and bad things about every trait of any zodiac. You need to know your traits, but you shouldn't be afraid of them. It is all about learning how to use your traits wisely and positively.

Sagittarius Moon Sign

Sagittarians are energetic and optimistic. They love outdoor activities such as hiking, horseback riding, or any other sport that involves being with nature. Sagittarians tend to be blunt sometimes, but they also speak the truth. This candidness makes people trust them even more because they don't sugarcoat anything. Sagittarians can be hurtful when in an argument, but only because they don't know how to keep their anger in check. They are generally friendly toward everyone around them, and they always seem to have a friend nearby when it's needed the most. They also enjoy good trust and honesty between people. They are never afraid to show their emotions to anyone because it keeps them grounded – and it also means that they are very friendly toward others.

Sagittarians tend not to be as blunt in their conversations, but they can still be straightforward, just like any of the other signs. Their bluntness depends on who they're talking to and what kind of relationship the two share. One major thing about Sagittarius is that many of them want independence from everyone and everything around them but sometimes possess an addictive personality toward certain things. For example, some Sagittarians will obsess over fitness or food, while others will become addicted to less healthy things such as drugs or alcohol. This sort of obsession doesn't mean they are bad people, but it can be challenging to stay on the correct path. It's important to understand that a Sagittarius needs balance in everything that comes into their lives.

Characteristic Traits

Sagittarius is a fire zodiac sign, which means that they are motivated and hardworking. Sagittarius possesses an inquisitive mindset. They are constantly wondering about what's going on in the world around them. However, keeping their minds busy when being curious is not an option. Sagittarians need to keep themselves occupied with other things.

As far as careers go, Sagittarians may be interested in careers that involve travel, such as a flight attendant or something similar. They may also pursue careers that require a lot of thinking and hard work but are still fun. Their minds are always wandering, so Sagittarians have very high expectations of themselves and others around them.

In relationships, they tend to focus on their independence more than anything else. However, this doesn't mean they don't want a relationship because it's the opposite! If they get into a committed relationship with someone and have more than just physical attraction, it means the person has earned their trust completely. They will forever be there whenever needed, even if neither of them shares the same feelings at that moment in time.

Strengths

Sagittarians will possess abilities that can take them far in life. They are intelligent and extremely hardworking. They won't let anything hold them back from reaching their goals, and they are willing to work as hard as they need to if something is worth it. A Sagittarius also has a personality that allows them to trust others very easily. This means you should be able to trust every Sagittarius you meet because they will never betray your trust in any kind of way.

The energy level possessed by a Sagittarius is very high, making this zodiac sign extraverted. They are always looking to socialize with more people, and they don't care what the situation is. They can make friends in almost any kind of environment, whether it's a party or any other kind of social gathering. Sagittarians also have minds that allow them to be curious all the time, and they will learn something new every day without trying too hard.

Weaknesses

A Sagittarius definitely has weaknesses. They tend to develop addictions to things like food or drugs but try to hide this from others while secretly pursuing them. To avoid these problems, a Sagittarius should make sure to maintain a healthy relationship with everyone around them so there won't ever be any mistrust or unwanted problems.

Advice: Try to stay as positive as possible. Remember that patience is a virtue and will help you greatly! Understand the difference between friendliness and rudeness. Don't let your bluntness hurt anyone's feelings because everyone makes mistakes. So don't make the mistake of being too harsh on them. Be calm and rational during arguments or when you are expressing your emotions. Find peace in everything around you by staying as balanced as you can! Share your thoughts more often about certain topics, so you get to know others better without being rude or offensive!

Capricorn Moon Sign

It's a cardinal sign, which means that Capricorns are motivated and hardworking. They will also have a curious mindset. Capricorn tends to be very ambitious in whatever they do, even if it just involves relaxing. They pay attention to everything because of how curious they can get about things that don't matter to others. They think highly of themselves and what they've done in life so far.

In relationships, they tend to focus on individuality more than anything else. However, they are also very loyal to the people that they are with. They tend to keep their feelings hidden from those they care about, but once you get them out of that shell, you can have a long and happy relationship with them.

Capricorns have great leadership qualities and can take charge if need be, even if they aren't in any sort of position to control anyone else. They may become leaders by taking charge of themselves or others depending on the situation. They may even become followers if they see someone else is better equipped to lead.

Characteristic Traits

Capricorns are generally strong and ambitious. They tend to be hard workers, but they also have a higher chance of developing stress in their life. Stress isn't always bad, though, because Capricorns seem to work better under pressure, leading to success in the end if they let themselves get stressed over certain situations in their life.

They like to take care of things, and they normally do things that need immediate attention right away. Sometimes this can hold them back from doing other things with their free time because they are so used to taking care of important things first instead of putting them off or never dealing with them.

They are also very independent people. They usually do their own thing and get on with what they want to do without letting anyone else influence them or their decisions. If someone tried to stop them while working toward something, it could cause a small uproar between the Capricorn and that person because of how much pride they have in themselves and how much they want to accomplish that others couldn't do before them.

Strengths

Capricorns are generally great with money. They are also very ambitious and hardworking, which may help them in their lives by giving them the motivation needed to do whatever they set their minds to and accomplish everything they need on time. These types of characteristics are great for work and school.

Capricorns have a sense of humor, but it is usually dark or sarcastic. They don't always use their sense of humor, but when they do, you will realize that Capricorns have more life experience than it might seem. They also have a good sense of what will happen in the future, but they may be too focused on the goals so that they could miss out on opportunities that could have made them more successful had they noticed them earlier.

Weaknesses

Capricorns tend to stress themselves out a lot over how long things take to accomplish, making them lose focus on what they need to get done and become distracted by something else due to their abundant curiosity. They also tend to not share with those around them because of their independence, which leads to others misunderstanding them and even hating them simply because they do not know the true person behind the mask.

Advice: Don't hold grudges against anyone. If you do, you'll never find happiness in a relationship or with yourself. Learn from your mistakes and try not to make the same ones again. And if you can't seem to get over someone, learn to live without them so that you don't ruin your future by focusing on something that happened in the past.

Aquarius Moon Sign

Those born with the Aquarius moon sign are usually described by their family and friends as independent, rebellious, original, unique, creative, compromising to a certain extent but mostly single-minded. They like to find new experiences and surroundings since they love variety. Their world is subjective of their moods which can be erratic at times. They may prefer some emotional distance between themselves and the rest of the world. However, all these traits make up an interesting character that never fails to fascinate those around them.

The tendency of this moon sign is toward humanism in all things from philosophy to art to politics. This sign loves change for change's sake, so they sometimes cause upheavals without thinking about the consequences.

Aquarius moon signs are idealistic, but they can be cold and inflexible. There is a tendency to be aloof in their dealings with others, as they tend not to reveal their inner thoughts and feelings easily. They have an easy time with people who share the same life perspective and approach, but otherwise, they may lead a lonely life. They may also isolate themselves from the world, feeling that everything and everyone is against them. However, if given enough attention and love, these individuals make good friends with those who know how to handle them.

Characteristic Traits

The sign Aquarius is ruled by Uranus, which gives us the typical traits of an Aquarian personality. The qualities that you display the most are originality and rebelliousness. You have a strong sense of individuality even if you belong to a group. You may be somewhat unemotional while engaging with people, but you make up for it with your witty comments and sarcastic remarks amongst close friends or family members. You can be quite detached from other people's emotions but sensitive to their needs. However, due to this characteristic, you may appear cold toward some people, and they may feel that they are not important enough for you to invest time in them.

Strengths

Aquarians can be objective and detached from their own emotions. This gives them a lot of strength, especially in life-threatening situations, as they can make decisions without having any emotional baggage associated with it. These individuals also have a strong sense of individuality and the need for freedom, allowing them to break away from powerful norms even if doing so ruffles some feathers. Due to this nature, they can easily climb up the corporate ladder or become successful entrepreneurs.

Weaknesses

The Aquarian moon zodiac sign has many weaknesses due to being emotionally detached from other people or things around them. Since these people decide everything by themselves, they may not get what they want at times because others disagree with their ideas. They can also be judgmental toward others which makes them appear cold and unemotional. People with an Aquarius moon sign are also known for being so tactless in most situations that they would never think about the implications of their actions first before actually doing them.

The Fixed Air element associated with this sign can keep an Aquarius calm under pressure. Still, suppose there is a lot of emotional baggage attached to the situation. In that case, these individuals will feel disconcerted and may react irrationally or aggressively because of their inability to control their emotions.

Advice: You should try to avoid any sudden changes or movements in your life because this may have repercussions on your emotional well-being and will also trigger impulsive actions. The best way for you to handle these situations is by thinking through them before actually doing anything else, as it would help you remain calm under pressure. You need to break away from the herd and do what's right for you. Otherwise, you are too much of a conformist at heart, but you enjoy life so much more when you go against conventions once in a while *just for the sake of doing so.*

Pisces Moon Sign

Pisces is the twelfth and last sign of the zodiac, and it can be difficult to find an accurate description of how these individuals behave. Pisceans are known as dreamy and imaginative people who ignore practicalities in favor of helping others or just lazily floating through life. However, what most people don't know about this sign is that every Pisces hides a very determined and hardworking personality, doing whatever they want without being told to do so.

Characteristic Traits

A water element governs the sign Pisces, and that makes them detached from reality at times. These individuals tend to enjoy the company of other people but may appear aloof or emotionally detached. They also have a strong sense of imagination, allowing them to see things in a subjective way rather than from an objective viewpoint. Pisces moon sign individuals are quite sensitive and caring toward others without getting too emotionally attached.

Strengths

Despite their relaxed nature, you can rely on Pisceans when it comes to taking care of themselves because they would always do whatever it takes to ensure that they're physically healthy before anything else. That applies to the people around them as well. This quality makes them so charming as companions since they will never let you down – even if they cannot spend much time with you. Since they care for your physical well-being, you can trust them with your personal matters as well.

Weaknesses

Pisces Moon sign individuals are known for their egotism and overindulgence in fantasies which eventually drains them of all energy, leaving them vulnerable to any emotional triggers and prone to breakdowns. Their sensitivity also makes it difficult for them to maintain relationships since they tend to see things from an unrealistic point of view. Pisceans often let their emotions dictate their actions rather than being guided by logic and reason. This may lead to irrational behavior on your part, especially when you become too attached to someone or something, which could lead you to do reckless things.

Advice: Pisces need to eliminate the habit of ignoring practicality so that they can do whatever they think is right. It may end up being so wrong that you'll regret not listening to the advice of the people close to you. Pisceans need to grow up and take responsibility for their actions rather than run away from them or just ignore them altogether. You should learn how to live your own life by accepting a certain amount of risk so that you won't be bogged down by regret at a later time.

This chapter has given you a brief introduction to the zodiac signs of Sagittarius, Capricorn, Aquarius, and Pisces. Sagittarians are active, adventurous, and love to travel. They have a great sense of humor with an optimistic outlook on life. Capricorns like being in charge, so they work hard for the things they want in life. Aquarians bring balance because their main goal is peace of mind. Pisces are sensitive, intuitive, and emotional creatures who need lots of attention from others!

Chapter 6: The Lunar South Node: Your Past Life

If you've been into Astrology for a while now, you probably already know that since the moment you were born, the stars in the sky are aligned in a certain way that reflects your life's purpose. Your personal birth or natal chart is mapped out from the first breath you take. Many believers in Astrology use this unique configuration to provide a lifetime of learning. Birth charts and South Node signs can help you unlock several possibilities, identify your potential growth, and provide you with clues as to your destiny or purpose. They also help draw attention to the areas in our lives where we cling to our habits too much. According to Astrology, these habits (the ones we do automatically without even thinking about them) are considered Karma or South Node habits. In this chapter, we take a closer look at the South Node signs of the moon and how these particular positions affect your Karma and past life.

What Is the Lunar South Node in Astrology?

Each person possesses special traits that have been embedded within their personality from the moment they were born. We are all born with inner weaknesses and strengths that we hold on to, whether we do it consciously or subconsciously. In Astrology, these qualities are believed to follow us from our past lives, and they eventually become part of us. Your South Node signs represent the people you were before you came into this current life. However, the qualities associated with these signs are the ones you're meant to leave behind to achieve personal fulfillment. We are all meant to become someone different in this life, even if we are used to certain habits that are difficult to let go of.

Your birth chart includes two important aspects, the South and North nodes, which are connected even though they're opposite nodes that drive opposite behaviors and personality traits. These nodes are not planets. They are two opposing intersection points made up of the moon's orbit and the ecliptic plane on your birth date. Both points are referred to as lunar nodes. The South node describes the person or qualities you should leave behind, while the North node represents the person you should try to become and the qualities you should work on gaining. Without working on dropping your negative traits, you may never feel fulfilled or achieve personal growth in your life.

The South Node in Each Sign

The entire Astrology culture is built on the belief in reincarnation and Karma. According to Astrology, our past lives are supposed to help us become better equipped for the challenges of each life we live. Your South node sign is different from your main astrological sign. Instead, it represents the qualities of the sign that you should try to avoid. We continue to come back as bodies on Earth, and as long as that keeps happening, we will always face new challenges. Let's get into more detail about what each sign represents as a South node and how you should work on yourself to come closer to the qualities of your North node.

The South Node in Aries

If your South node in Aries indicates that you lacked perspective and were selfish about your needs in your past life, you have always loved to be the center of attention and have subconsciously overlooked other people's needs. It has always felt natural to you to act ruthlessly. Aggression is your default coping mechanism. However, you're also unstoppable when it comes to getting what you really want. What you need to do in this life is to overcome your increased passion, commit to your partnerships, and cooperate more with others. You should work on achieving more inner peace rather than chasing the dream of being the best. Aries tend to be impulsive, and they rush into quick decisions, which is something you need to work on! Sometimes, you may need to listen more and acknowledge that other people may have different points of view.

The South Node in Taurus

Taurus South node indicates a past materialistic life. You've been surrounded by everything you want, from security to luxurious earthly treasures that helped you survive for too long. This fortunate standing in life gives you many materialistic traits. You seek wealth and other tangible treasures. You may also naturally feel that you're responsible for everyone around you. Well, it's time to let go. It's not your responsibility to take care of those around you to the point of ignoring your mental health. It's also time to start searching for spiritual gratification (and overcome your fear of the unknown). Instead of chasing earthly leisure, you should be looking for a deeper journey. Focus on your spiritual instincts and let them guide you instead of depending on the practicality of your earthly possessions. It's all about embracing the non-material side of your personality.

The South Node in Gemini

You've lived a dishonest past life, and you could always get yourself out of the toughest situations with your words. You always refuse to be held accountable for any situation, even if you caused it. In this life, you should focus on speaking more truthfully instead of engaging in time-wasting drama. Focus on being more productive and stay away from your two-faced nature that influences your decisions. Only make room for one personality to take over and use it to increase your productivity. You should also be taking more risks and looking at the world differently. It's not as dark a place as you think, so get out there, travel, and see the world. You can miss many opportunities by staying in your comfort zone, so the goal is to be more productive and take more risks.

The South Node in Cancer

You have a codependent personality that prioritizes the needs of other people around you over your personal needs. You're too focused on receiving affection from those around you, and you lack self-reliance. However, it's time for you to be more comfortable staying alone. Stop letting your fear of being left alone keep you from going after your dreams. It's also time to stop seeking affection from others and to focus on yourself at all times. Start listening to your head more, in the same way you'd let your heart have a say in every decision. Sometimes, it's okay to be selfish and put your own needs first, so stop wasting your energy on people around you and engage in more self-care activities. Your purpose is to love yourself and shift your attention to self-development to feel fulfilled in this life.

The South Node in Leo

You've suffered in the past when no one was there to see your sacrifices. So, now it's time to focus on moving on rather than taking things personally all the time. You should understand that everyone else around you has their problems, and nobody has time to deal with your conflicts. You tend to overestimate your power all the time, but it's time to let go of the past and become more down-to-earth. You should also overcome your obsession with attention and vanity, instead, show affection to those around you and pay more attention to their needs. Don't let your past define you, and be more open to change. It's not always necessary to be in the spotlight or be the best at what you do. The more open-minded you become, the fewer problems you will have in your relationships.

The South Node in Virgo

The past lives of a South node Virgo lacked mystery and were obsessed with control. You tend to overanalyze everything around you, even the beautiful things, until they start to look ugly. You investigate even the smallest details and continue to look for a straightforward answer. In this life, you need to embrace other forms of healing and art, such as using your imagination and writing poetry. You don't have to be in control all the time. It's only making you anxious, so let go. You can find peace and serenity in mystery. You can pursue something deeper in life if you switch your attention from yourself. That's all a Virgo needs to mature and to let go of their past lives.

The South Node in Libra

You have a long past of letting your friends steal your thunder, and you tend to give up the spotlight so that you can avoid conflict. This time you should go after your dreams and let your name be known. You always ignore your personal needs to achieve peace, but you need to be more selfish and draw attention to your opinions. Even if it causes controversy or leads to conflict, the most important thing is to speak up and let your opinions be known. You can't survive in the shadow of others, and maintaining your relationships is not more important than your comfort. While most Librans try to avoid it, a conflict is not the worst thing in the world. So be more courageous in expressing yourself and make your opinions known.

The South Node in Scorpio

You need to stop being so possessive and manipulative all the time. Your past life's power was to use temptation to get others to do what you wanted. You're also so reliant on their kindness that it's hard for you to let go and provide for yourself. You need to leave those qualities behind in this life and start depending more upon yourself for emotional support. Build your foundation and create your own ways as others will follow when you focus on yourself and achieve success. Unlike many other South node signs, a Scorpio must focus on tangible things rather than getting too caught up in what they can't control. You can't control everything and everyone, so shift your attention to what you *can* change.

The South Node in Sagittarius

Sagittarius South nodes express their philosophies loudly and base their problem-solving decisions on unrealistic and fanciful ideas. However, they always seem to lack focus on the matter at hand. To feel more fulfilled in this life, you need to ground yourself or settle somewhere. You need to give yourself time to focus fully on the objective truth instead of chasing esoteric theories or ideas. Understand that the adventures you engage in are only a coping mechanism to avoid certain areas in your life. Most of the time, you're running away from yourself, trying to find an escape from people who are distant from you or places that are far away. Unfortunately, this comes with great sacrifices, and you'll eventually lose it if you don't pay attention to what you have. Get closer to your roots, stop taking or indulging, and start exchanging equally with other people around you.

The South Node in Capricorn

Your past life has taught you that success and wealth bring happiness and inner peace. Now, these two qualities have burned you out so much that you're left alone with an empty heart. You're isolated, and the only thing you know by nature is overworking yourself. However, it can be a toxic trait sometimes if you start believing that you're superior to others. You also mute your intuition and neglect the relationships in your life, but it's time to change that. Listen more to your intuition and value your partnerships and relationships. Sometimes, you need to realize that the people you love are more important than your success. Make that clear and express your affection. Surrounding yourself with your wealth is only going to push people away. Always choose love over materialism.

The South Node in Aquarius

Aquarius South nodes are known to be relaxed but supportive when you need them. This is only at their own expense. If your South node sign is Aquarius, you need to stop hiding your feelings. You think that showing emotions will make you look weak or alienate your peers, but this is not true. Even if it's true, who cares? Understand that your emotions matter and that you need to listen to your heart more often. Avoiding the discomfort of others will only cause you to bottle up your feelings and overlook things that really matter to you. Your needs are more important than the satisfaction of your community, so make sure you express them clearly. You've already been taking care of everyone's feelings for too long. In this life, it's all about listening to your true self and getting you what you need.

The South Node in Pisces

If your South Node is Pisces, it indicates that you may have been a passive person who watched their life go downhill without really doing anything about it. You keep thinking that there's nothing that can help you take control of your fate. Focus on reality. Stand up for your opinions, and don't let others abuse or use you like you always do. Stop playing the role of the victim and start taking action when it comes to the problems in your life. Your goal is to become more concerned with objectivity and look away from your irrational theories and thoughts.

Deciphering the Karmic Signature

If we let our karma or South Node qualities take over, we will lead a life of stagnation and never find our true purpose for this life. This is why it's important to understand our karmic signature, which refers to the meaning behind our South Node signs. Many books and articles mention numerous techniques that we can apply to understand the cosmic position of our South Nodes and how this affects our karma. Some of the most dominant studies illustrated a very helpful technique using Pablo Picasso's Gemini South Node.

Picasso's South Node is located at 10 degrees of the Curiosity sign, Gemini, which lies in the 11th house of groups according to the birth chart of lunar nodes. According to the chart, his rebellion was classified in the 5th house of love affairs, shown in his countless number of women and partners. His karma was falling for peer pressure and trying to belong. Let's use Picasso's birth chart to get into more detail about interpreting the karmic signature.

Assess the Qualities of the Planet that Rules the South Node Sign

The science of Astrology and planets is very interesting to people who are into human psychology. It's compelling to read about how the planets that express each sign represent a spectrum of human behavior and personality types. For example, in Picasso's case, the ruler planet of his south node sign is Mercury, representing curious types of people. Some other signs may have more than one planetary ruler. For example, Aquarius has Saturn, the Hermit type, and Uranus, the Rebel type.

Identify the House Position of the South Node and Establish the Biographical Content

This part of the analysis is where we acknowledge our long-term goals and make connections to get closer to them. In Picasso's example, and as previously mentioned, his SN is located in the 11th house of groups. Here, Picasso's karma was the inability to break the restrictions of the group and their judgments toward him. In other examples, the South Node can be located in the house of pleasure or fun. This type's karma can be related to the inability to entertain oneself or find joy in individuality.

Look for Ways to Attain the Goals of the South Node Sign

There is always a goal for each Astrological sign. These signs represent your values and priorities. They always guide you to a certain extent, which is believed to be supported by the movement of planets. If we take Picasso's example, his South Node was in the Gemini region. This type thrives on new information and uses a young person's curiosity to get what they want. They always seem edgy and bubbly, but their goal is to focus on themselves and become more productive. Read more into the goals of your SN sign and figure out if they align with your life purposes.

Connect the South Node Ruler with Its Position

Even though Gemini SNs are curious, the group hinders their desire to search or understand everything around them. The ruler of Picasso's SN was Mercury which lies in the 4th house family, implying a tendency to follow external influences. Now, both houses on the chart, the SN's house, and the ruling planet's house, suggest that Picasso's personality was highly overwhelmed by the crowd.

Look into the Planetary Ruler's Sign

On the birth chart of lunar nodes, you can determine the signs of the planet that rules your South Node sign. This lets you tap into even more knowledge around how your type behaves and perceives life. Picasso's ruler planet, Mercury, was in the Scorpio sign area, and this translates to the type that always stretches into unprecedented new models. It shows a fascination or obsession with taboos.

Put Everything Together

If we look at Picasso's lunar positions and house groups, we can see many contradictions between them. However, the point is to determine your life purpose and understand your karma before it has a chance to take over your destiny. Gather all the information you come up with after studying your birth chart and SN, and ask yourself whether there is anything else left unresolved. Is there a dream or person you're longing for that was never there before? Assess your SN qualities and be open to getting closer to your North Node qualities to feel more fulfilled in life.

Our lunar South and North nodes determine a lot about how we are supposed to live our lives. These signs always hint at something. They guide you to your true fate and help you overcome the qualities of your past lives – an important reason to learn about all your South node classifications. Focus on approaching your North node goals and qualities to become better equipped to deal with the upcoming challenges.

Chapter 7: The Lunar North Node: Your Life Purpose

The North Node shows us the things and experiences we must go through to develop and grow spiritually. We are unique human beings with our unique paths in life, and our North Node helps clarify the path.

The North Node shows us where we can grow or expand and gives us the ability to integrate important life lessons. It may feel good or stifling to think that your North Node clarifies your purpose or destiny. Perhaps you don't want to feel like destiny is in place, and you would prefer to choose your own. But your North Node is not forcing you along any particular path. Instead, it shows you where you would feel the most fulfilled and aligned. Each of us has a destiny or purpose in this life, and being aware of your North Node and your unique purpose makes things just a little easier for you.

What Is the Lunar North Node in Astrology?

When reading about your North Node, you may not resonate with it. However, this does not mean it is inaccurate. Your North Node merely shows you where you can expand, evolve, and grow. It does not mean this is how you are already. It just points to your innate skills and characteristics. Due to conditioning and life events, many of us lose touch with our inner selves. We feel like strangers to ourselves, and our authentic nature is pushed down.

Learning about your North Node may feel a little bit like learning about a stranger, but it illustrates to you what your soul needs. Don't be afraid to leave your comfort zone, and let these new qualities and attitudes take form in your life. It may feel awkward or unnatural at first, but give it some time. Try it on for size, and see how you can slowly begin to adjust your approach and thoughts to align with your North Node.

Your North Node is essentially your roadmap to success, and it certainly won't look like anyone else's or resemble the standard view of success. Permit yourself to shed these societal standards to give yourself the highest chance in life.

The North Node in Each Sign

As explained in the previous chapter, the whole Astrology belief system is built upon Karma and how humans go through their many lives. We are reincarnated in different forms of lives each time, and our South node represents our karma or the qualities we should try to avoid. Oppositely, your North Node is the sign you should try to become closer to, and therefore, you'll have a fixed opposite North node to your South one. Let's take a look at how this looks and what the North node represents in each sign.

Aries

When the North Node is in Aries, the south is in libra. Remember, the North and South Nodes, just like the directions, are directly opposite each other. Together they form the nodal axis. If you know what one node is, you will automatically know the other.

If your North Node is in Aries, you might find that you would do best to balance looking after yourself with looking after others. You should be focused on yourself by healing, evolving, and growing in a way that allows you to flourish. Move away from feelings and attitudes of dependency on others. You could easily form codependent patterns with others. Instead, learn to detach. Begin to do things for yourself, learn who you really are and what you truly want.

The more authentic you become, the more fulfilled you will feel. Ignore the things that lead you toward attachment, external opinions, thoughts, and feelings. Go inwards and seek internal validation. It will help you develop the independence you need to walk the path of your destiny more easily.

Your life should revolve around bringing your passionate ideas to fruition. You are a warrior in your lifetime, so stay on this path. You will often find yourself being a pioneer on a path toward love and justice.

Learn to live alone, to be by yourself, for yourself.

Taurus

With your North Node in Taurus, it is important to let go of the needs of others. Discover yourself, and begin to develop self-reliance. You must start to establish deep self-worth within yourself. Nothing and no one outside of you can provide you with that. The more you look for it anywhere else, you move further away from your path.

To walk the path of purpose, you need to be able to give yourself what you need without relying on others.

Your sign appreciates beauty, pleasure, and love. You need to learn what you truly value, as this will help you manifest the beautiful things you want in your life. Don't self-sabotage by feeling unworthy. Instead, know that you are truly worth everything you desire and more. Allow yourself to receive from the goodness of the universe.

Gemini

The Gemini North Node is on this planet to connect to others. You can relate and communicate with others easily. The wisdom that you have stored inside of you is ready to be shared. You love to share information and exchange ideas and knowledge. Use this to help you determine where your natural talents lie.

You may feel the urge to share with others through writing, speaking, reporting, teaching, marketing, or even just having a conversation. You may become a writer, a poet, a teacher, or someone that strikes up conversation wherever you go. This ability to communicate and share ideas will help you walk the path of your destiny, giving you clarity and fulfillment.

You will often find that you can sit with others and discuss opposing ideas without feeling the need to force your ideas. You can easily see both sides of the coin and weigh up either side, giving you the ability to learn and share knowledge, ideas, and wisdom objectively. You are not always swayed by emotions or unconscious bias, and this will help you make decisions rationally and objectively.

Cancer

The Cancer North Node might feel like they struggle to balance their family and career. Part of your life purpose is to build a healthy family experience and home. These mean a lot to you and add to your feelings of happiness and stability.

You need to create a nurturing and safe space for yourself and your family, helping you along your path. It is okay to be vulnerable, to let go of rigidity and expectations. Perfection should be left behind so you can truly step into your authentic and aligned self.

It may be hard for you to achieve your desires when you are holding so tightly onto them. Instead, let go a little, and witness how much easier it is. It's okay to let go of seriousness, and you may find that your life falls into a natural flow.

Leo

The Leo North Node is very likely to be comfortable being the extroverted, open, and social fire sign. You may be affectionate and incredibly vibrant and bold. The spotlight was made for you, so don't be afraid to step into it when you need to. When someone opens up the space for you to take a central role, take it as your right.

Get used to making big moves without fear, opening up entirely new paths for you. Your open and affectionate nature invites people in and makes you someone that can easily relate to others. You can make tons of new friends and create a large network thanks to your natural ability to be vibrant and inviting. Use this to help you walk your life path.

Know that you are always being invited to take up space. It is your birthright, and you are here to express yourself. Step into the magic of who you are, and continue to make choices that leave you feeling empowered. The more empowered and creative you feel, the closer you become to your destiny.

Virgo

The North Node Virgo may find a lot of satisfaction from being practical and detail orientated. Your life may become a little easier by developing a healthy routine and a set of rules around your daily life. This doesn't mean you turn into a type A, but establishing rules and routines will help you significantly.

Setting clear and defined goals helps you achieve your destiny. The clarity and purpose of your life will manifest when you set out to achieve it in a practical and organized manner. Of course, you shouldn't abandon all emotions or feelings. Instead, your intuition should be finely balanced with logic and intellect in every part of your life, helping you make the right choices.

Setting boundaries with both yourself and others is important. You become empowered through being focused and organized. Acting in this way gives you the confidence and energy you need to achieve your goals.

The North Node Virgo is a healer. Part of your destiny on this planet is to heal. You may find yourself serving others and being devoted to healing. You are here to find the meaning of unconditional love.

Libra

The North Node Libra should focus on being kind and just - the attitude with which you face life. Competition should be avoided, and instead, you should dedicate yourself to forming meaningful bonds with others. It is important that you are sensitive to others and what they feel and desire.

You are on this planet to learn about relationships, commitments, and partnerships. If you find yourself with a past littered with relationship or commitment issues, this allows you to learn the lessons necessary to evolve into who you are meant to be. Don't view these experiences negatively but, instead, view them for what they truly are, a lesson to learn to reach your true self.

You are here to learn how to have a relationship with someone without developing codependency or abandoning yourself. You must find the balance between yourself and others.

You have innate leadership skills and often pride yourself on your independence. It would be best if you learned to become diplomatic when you communicate. Libra is associated with justice, and with your North Node Libra, this may indicate being on a path to create justice for yourself or others.

Scorpio

The Scorpio North Node is here to bring forward the energies of passion and freedom. In this lifetime, you are here to release attachments and feel truly free. You must work through any attachment issues and deal with any fears related to feeling controlled. The two may appear hand in hand in some circumstances, and this only occurs for you to achieve transcendence even faster.

Your soul has this deep desire to change, evolve, and grow. Listen to this call, and don't allow yourself to get sucked in by other people and eternal attachments. Your life is a journey of continuous release that will lead you to your most authentic self.

It would help if you learned to deal with life fearlessly, and any crisis or sudden change that occurs should be dealt with head-on. You must get comfortable with transforming and shedding old identities and beliefs. This opens you up to beautiful mystical experiences.

Sagittarius

The Sagittarius North Node is here to escape their comfort zone. You need to get away from home and seek out expansive experiences all around the world. The wisdom you need may lie in any corner of the Earth. You are here to live a big life, inspiring others with your actions and vision. Freedom is often your main priority, so allow it to guide you.

The vision you have and the actions you take to achieve it inspire those around you. You are here to make big moves, so fight any fear. Perhaps previous conditioning or other aspects of your life hold you back from living your life in an intended way. Know that you are here to truly inspire others, and the more aligned you become, the easier it is for you to do that.

Don't rely too much on logic, and instead, use your intuition to guide you, as this will help you make the best decisions and choices. Choosing to be more logical and rational may mean coming across big, exciting opportunities. Tune into your intuition to master your reality and bring forward the experiences that help you along on your journey to your destiny.

Capricorn

The Capricorn North Node is here to help you develop into a strong and independent character. You need to take radical responsibility for your actions to take complete control of your life. The more accountability you take, the more aligned you become. Realize life is not happening to you. Instead, it is happening for you. The things that occur around you are happening because of you. You must be able to adjust your behavior, energy, attitudes, and thoughts so that you can manifest the things you truly want.

If you don't assume a certain level of accountability, you may find that the things that manifest into your life are happening based on negative beliefs that you chose to ignore. Be brave enough to face the mistakes and habits that keep you from blossoming into your true self.

Alongside this sense of responsibility, balance it out with sensitivity. You are a leader, and you can achieve great things. Capricorn is a hardworking sign, and you are here to own these leadership abilities and show others how to make great strides just as you have. Own this part of you and shed any shame surrounding these leadership desires. This is your destiny and your birthright.

To reach the emotional and financial status you want, define your goals practically and maturely. Let go of any external attachments to see your goals and desires come to fruition. Attachments may hold you back from prospering into the person you have the potential to become.

Aquarius

The Aquarius North Node is here to help you to be carefree and liberated. It would help if you had time to be alone, savor solitude, and rid yourself of the desire to need validation from others. You may even find yourself being validated, but the things you want are often only a distraction, so detach yourself from these feelings and go inwards. This is where you will find greater fulfillment.

You are here to be innovative and authentic to yourself. You can aid in creating a world where others can also step into their own authenticity. The innovative aspects of this placement help you make the world better and freer for others.

In relationships, you must shed fears for your partner to be themselves instead of what you want them to be. Every person is equal and has the right to be treated in a just manner. Use this to help direct your relationships with others.

The Aquarius North Nodes are humanitarians, and the more you focus on making a difference, the more fulfilled you will feel. Embrace your eccentric attitudes and unique self, as doing this wholeheartedly will help give others the confidence and power to do the same.

You will find that you thrive in a community and when working with a team, although you should always ensure you remain calm, collected, and able to consider other people in any situation. Allow your humanitarian instincts to guide you as you chase your goals.

Pisces

The Pisces North Nodes are here to move with the flow of life and to let go of any tight grip on routine or rules. You should heal feelings of guilt and trust that there is a larger plan in place. The more you allow yourself to relax with the flow of life, the more aligned you will become with your destiny. Allow yourself to relax, and you will see that the doors of destiny open up with ease.

Your intuition is important, and you should begin to develop sensitivities to be in touch with it. It is intuition that will help guide you to make the right choices and decisions.

Self-love is key here, and developing this allows you to trust the greater plan in place. It will help you make choices from a place of ease and fulfillment. This self-love also helps you treat others with compassion and respect.

It may be odd when you don't feel like your North Node accurately represents you. This is normal because your North Node is more of a map to your success. Allow yourself to feel the gap between who you are now and who you can be, and use it to give you the boost to make the necessary changes.

You don't need to change all at once. Begin slowly, and start to add one new attitude or line of thinking to your life. Try it on for size, and see how it feels to be that person. If it feels too odd, take it down a notch until it feels more comfortable, and then slowly increase the feeling until you naturally become that individual.

This process should be one of enjoyment, so allow yourself to know that it is always for your own good. It does not always have to be a struggle but instead, choose to adjust and add these changes to your life slowly. You might resonate with some aspects of your North Node, but not with all the others.

The North Node is a roadmap to your success, but the road map is littered with lessons – which is how you come into your success. The quicker you can transcend your circumstances and issues, the quicker you achieve success. Dive deep into your North Node and witness the transformation ahead of you.

Chapter 8: The Moon with Other Planets

The relationship of the Moon with other planets is quite intricate. Ancient Vedic astrologers deemed the Moon to be the queen or ruler of the nine imperial planets. As the lunar cycle passes and enters a new phase every 2 to 3 days, it also shifts its position in relevance to other planets. While the Moon develops a strong relationship with some planets, it simply touches the roots of other celestial bodies. This chapter covers the Moon's distinct effects as a sole body and in conjunction with each planet. Along with this, we will also draw parallels between the Moon's behavior during the conjunction in the natal chart and the transit phase.

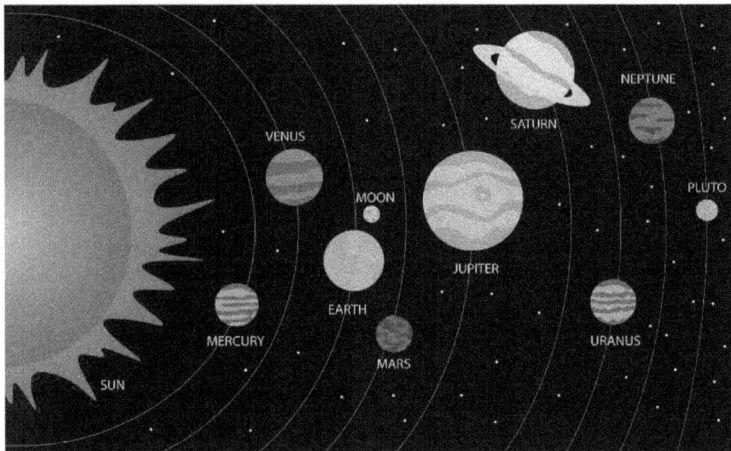

The Conjunction of the Moon with Other Planets

When the Moon is entering a different phase and shifts its position, it is known to be in "transit." It can affect its conjunction with other planets and manipulate their qualities too. As the name suggests, the Moon in transit is constantly shifting or moving. When we talk about the correlation of transits in natal charts, we are actually looking at the Moon's position and movement in relevance to a specific planet at a given moment. The natal and transit elements of natives can heavily influence their characteristics and personality.

Moon and Mercury

Mercury symbolizes the nervous system and the mind. When the planet affiliates with the Moon, representing the soul and mind, the conjunction results in an adaptable and wise disposition. Collectively, the celestial bodies influence an emotionally stable and conscious environment. People with this conjunction on their natal charts can express their emotions and feelings with ease. Their ability to express their feelings with ease also helps them make honest friends. This conjunct in the Transit phase can result in heightened sensitivity and emotional vulnerability. The native can also experience more mood swings now and then.

Born under the Moon-Mercury conjunction, you will likely be blessed with creativity, wisdom, and oratory skills. However, the native often lacks the ability to focus, resulting in poor decision-making skills, leading to instability in their personal and professional lives. Despite lacking mindfulness skills, the native can still fulfill difficult tasks due to their sharp mind. They need to boost their concentration levels and sharpen their attention. Failing to do so can lead to negative repercussions and the development of vices like alcohol abuse, addiction to gambling, or cheating. In some cases, the person can also develop such habits due to being pushed into a downward spiral, affecting their personal life and career.

If they fail to pull themselves up, they will likely become cheats, criminals, or fraudsters. Their charming personality may fool others into believing them. Even if they have bad intentions, others may refuse to believe it due to their attractive demeanor. If the conjunction affiliates with atrocious malefic, the person can turn into a nasty criminal.

Moon and Venus

Venus represents air and symbolizes feminine energy – just like the Moon – creating a kind, gentle, and loving personality, which helps the native form strong relationships. Everyone gets along with the native when the conjunct occurs in the natal chart. The person possesses great imagination powers and can maintain harmonious personal and professional relationships. Due to this, they also have a huge network and a healthy social life. Since they are quite outgoing and extroverted by nature, the natives are often concerned about their looks and pay extra attention to grooming. They focus on their style and hardly step out without getting ready.

Due to their emotional availability, the person can have a happy and loving family. They are loyal to their spouse and deeply care about their children. They have a keen eye for art and a love of gathering exotic objects. Individuals with a well-balanced Moon-Venus conjunction are known to be talented gardeners and indulge in landscaping. They also love animals and are often found adopting pets. Their love and care for their loved ones are reciprocated, inspiring the native to build more lasting bonds.

This affiliation can bring issues in the individual's married life if they get overly sensitive during the transit state. In general, they are more relaxed in this state and prefer to hang out with their loved ones. Since the person is likely to be more popular in their social group, they also attract sexual relationships and energy. When buying artistic or designer objects, they value their worth and do not mind spending more money on valuable items. They believe in self-care routines and often pamper themselves by shopping, visiting spas, or getting a haircut.

Moon and Rahu

The Moon needs to be in the waxing or complete phase during the conjunction with Rahu to get better results. If it is in the waning phase, it can become weaker during transit. The native possesses exemplary imaginative powers, which can also lead to increased sensitivity and the development of psychic abilities. In extreme cases, they will likely start overthinking and get influenced by their surroundings. They will seek validation from others and fall victim to unhealthy environments and toxicity. The natives can also attract toxic people if they become vulnerable. To avoid this, they should choose their environment and friends with care and precision. If you fail to monitor Rahu, it can turn monstrous and push you into a deep well of desires. Over time, the demonic energy will also instigate you into copying others.

This conjunction can be dangerous and results in the development of mental health illnesses like obsessive-compulsive disorder or depression. Typically, children are easily influenced by this conjunction. If parents fail to monitor their behavior, they may develop vices and bad habits. Over time, it can be difficult to pull them out. It is necessary to bring positive influences into their lives to keep Rahu from overshadowing the Moon's power. Whether it's your natal chart or the transit phase, Rahu's dominance can majorly impact your life. Keep away from overindulgence and enjoy things in moderation.

Moon and Ketu

While this conjunction is majorly perceived as a negative affiliation, certain aspects favor the combination of Moon and Ketu. In general, Ketu possesses feminine energy and is believed to be a "sannyasin." She travels from one point to another in search of alms and begs to make a living. The body intersects Earth's orbit and descends from the Moon's tip. She resembles a serpent due to the shape of her body and is illustrated as a headless figure. The native with this conjunction in their natal chart will likely develop mental health issues. Some may even suffer from an inferiority complex or excessive jealousy. They are easily humiliated in public and are unable to accept criticism. The affiliation of the Moon with Ketu is not as healthy as other partnerships. The native lives in their own world with a frantic imagination.

While some develop mental health issues, others are susceptible to phobias. They are indecisive by nature and are rarely influenced by the positive energies or auras around them. Since the negative repercussions are only visible after a person reaches a certain age, treating the shortcomings is not an option. Astrologers suggest performing Ketu Dosha and Chandra Dosha, which are two remedies to cure the consequences. Ketu is intricately connected to past lives and spiritual energy. It can push a person into complete isolation. Getting back from that can be quite challenging, often leading to depression and eating disorders.

Moon and Mars

This pairing is quite strong and blesses the native with qualities like dynamism, prosperity, and generosity. They have good physical and mental health and rarely fall sick. If a person's natal chart depicts this affiliation, they are likely more courageous and stronger. If you are one of them, look within yourself and get in touch with your emotions, as this act can help you fight for the betterment of your family. In a way, it is also related to personal growth. However, during the native's bad days, they can easily get irritated and be more confused, especially when dealing with their emotions. This behavior is usually found in the natal charts with the Moon in transit. If you feel more irritated or agitated lately, it is time to take a step back and relax. However, if this behavior is not controlled, you can end up making bad decisions that can also affect your loved ones.

If the planets meet in an evil Nakshatra or house, the combination can transform the native's noble thoughts into dark actions. If necessary action is not taken, they can turn evil and lose direction. They may show signs of irritability, impatience, and clumsiness. Over time, they may also develop vices like alcohol abuse, womanizing, gambling, and drug abuse. This affiliation in an unfavorable house is considered worse for females as it indicates the death of a close relative.

Moon and Jupiter

Just as the conjunction of the Moon with Mars is considered to be overall favorable, the affiliation of the former with Jupiter is deemed to be noble too. The native is blessed with great physical health and loyal friends and family. They also possess creative skills and attract wealth by legal means. They are loyal to their profession and believe in hard-earned money. However, if the conjunction is afflicted, the native may suffer from a major financial loss. It can either be in the form of car accidents or a big business loss.

In some cases, the native will weigh finances over reputation and choose the latter. For them, reputation and respect stand at a higher position than financial status. If this continues over a long period, they may also loosen ties with their spouse and children.

In general, healthy conjunction keeps people more positive and encourages them to see the good in people and all circumstances. This enhances their charisma and brings them closer to others. They are admired by their friends and family too. Due to this optimistic nature, they attract positivity and can manifest favorable outcomes. This is also the case with the Moon in transit mode. The native is content with their life and prefers to stay happy. Their good mood is infectious and can brighten other people's days. When starting a new project, they are often careful with setting intentions –another reason to gain favorable outcomes.

Moon and Saturn

This conjunction is another acknowledged affiliation that makes a person honest and clever from birth. It is called "Janma Shani Erashtaka" and is highly influential in Vedic astrology. The native who survives this phase can attract fame and wealth as they grow up. However, the native's natal chart reading can sometimes read guilt and sadness as their main qualities –particularly when the partnership is affiliated. In worst cases, they may also attract mean and abusive caretakers, which can aggravate the situation. They may struggle to find people who appreciate or value them. The need for validation and attention can hinder their emotional security. If a child fails to develop coping mechanisms to attract attention, they may fail to cope with their emotions as an adult. They may either isolate themselves or feel shy.

During the transit phase, the native may feel more distant from others, including their loved ones. Since maintaining relationships is a major task for the native, the established distance can worsen and weaken their bond. In the end, their hardship will be dictated by the inability to express emotions or feelings of rejection. Typically, women feel more prone to emotional hardships due to guilt and emotional unavailability. The native should be more open with their loved ones and work on their communication skills to overcome these issues. Failing to do so can lead to anxiety or depression.

Moon and Uranus

This pairing symbolizes uncertainty, contradiction, chaos, and unpredictability. The native experiences constant shifts in mood, which can increase irritability. They are impulsive and fail to make rational decisions which, in turn, can also affect their decision-making skills. Even though they are not fully prepared to experience change, they are always seeking variation in different domains of their life. This affiliation inspires you to see beyond the common boundaries and widen your horizons. Uranus with the Moon can easily trigger your feelings and generate conflicts. You may not only be at war with your inner self, but you may also try to unconsciously sabotage your relationships. Your behavior and personality may not align at times, which can intensify the conflict. Even though Uranus is progressive by nature and inspires the native to develop a similar attitude, the conjunction can create a conflicting pattern.

While Uranus helps the natives focus on logical and intellectual subjects, the Moon's energy can confuse and divert them towards thinking about their emotions. In most cases, they may also make emotional decisions over rational choices. This results in the conflict between the heart and the mind, which is one of the most difficult situations one faces in their life. Unfortunately, this situation gets worse if necessary steps are not taken to lighten the effects of this conjunction. The native needs a loving and emotionally stable family or loved ones to balance their emotions.

Moon and Neptune

Neptune symbolizes emotional sensitivity. Since the Moon also represents emotions, this conjunction is primarily related to one's emotional health. The native is open to all kinds of influences, which makes them more vulnerable. Your mind invites every kind of feeling, thought, emotion, slur, and suspicion. While this can provide immense knowledge up to a certain point, the inability to filter this information can lead to overthinking and emotional instability. If someone raises their voice or becomes mean, you may not be able to handle it. Over time, you may feel more isolated and prefer staying alone instead of listening to unwanted criticism. Learning some effective ways to shun negative comments and keep rejections from affecting your self-esteem is necessary. If you are born under this conjunction, you may find yourself hanging out with only a handful of people.

It is necessary to keep toxicity out of your life while learning to handle negativity. If you stay isolated for a prolonged period, you can successfully cope with negative environments or toxic people. In a way, you will rarely engage with them, which will completely eradicate the toxicity. During the Moon's transit mode, you may experience heightened confusion or brain fog, and that can impact important decisions. Every insignificant comment or argument may turn into a scandal if you allow it. Be cautious and try not to be vulnerable.

Moon and Pluto

Much like other conjunctions, this association between the Moon and Pluto also indicates an intense emotional connection. Whether you feel happy, sad, angry, or scared, all your emotions will be intensified. You feel emotions intensely and with a heavy heart. Depending on the situation, this can make you feel more grateful or push you into a downward spiral of negative emotions. You can combat this by making necessary changes to your thought process and behavioral patterns. If the issue is related to control or power, you can analyze your condition and visualize the outcome. If you hold more control or power, will the situation or issue affect you in any way? Since you have a stronghold of your feelings and emotions, use this power to turn situations in your favor.

With further improvement, you can heighten your money-making skills and polish your creative abilities to gain recognition. Once you see improvements in some areas, you may also notice a spike in your sexuality. With Pluto in place, there is no middle ground. The native may either portray obsessive-compulsive habits, control their partner, or fall victim to superiority. A proper balance needs to be established to live a long, healthy, and fulfilling life.

Moon and the Sun

One of the most powerful combinations of all, the Sun-Moon conjunction helps one feel at peace. The native has better control of their life and can exude neutral emotions that work in everyone's favor. However, they can get so diplomatic at times that it can be annoying. This can also impact their mental health. Even though the Moon and the Sun share a strong bond and thrive in harmony, their distinct energies can create an imbalance in the native's life. While the Moon is calm and emotional, the Sun is energetic and fiery. Certain zodiac signs like Aries, Leo, and Cancer support this union and make the native more confident and emotionally stable. However, as mentioned, they need to work on their diplomatic nature before it gets ingrained into their attitude.

In these cases, they may also come across as rude and arrogant, even if they don't mean to be. With the help of beneficial celestial bodies, you can deepen your knowledge and gain useful philosophical insights that can likely transform your life. On the other hand, joining hands with malefic bodies can push you into the trap of carnal desires and permanent arrogance. The idea is to become more self-aware and make an internal promise to transform your habits. Analyze whether or not your actions align with your thoughts. If not, set the right intentions and create a plan. More importantly, distinguish between your wants and needs.

Since many reliable online sources allow you to check your Moon's position with respective planets, you can easily find out more about your personality. You can also use this information to gain more consciousness and become more self-aware. If the process seems ambiguous, you can get help from a wise and experienced astrologer to illustrate minute intricacies in your natal chart. Deciphering different pairings and the union of the Moon with each planet is a great way to know yourself better and make a positive impact. Since your personality and well-being can majorly affect your loved ones, too, studying your natal chart and deciphering the Moon's location in transit can be a major step toward self-improvement and self-reflection.

Chapter 9: Lunar Phases

A lunar cycle typically consists of eight phases that can be harnessed to explore the Moon's true potential and, in turn, give you the ability to live your life to its fullest. Like a seed germinates and blooms into a flower, the Moon grows into its full form, dies, and then regenerates, marking one whole cycle. Every phase of the Moon personifies different values and innate qualities that inspire a person to regain balance and live in harmony. All eight phases are so distinct that they are visible to the naked eye. In fact, if you learn about them in detail, you can look at the sky and point out the phase that the celestial body is currently in.

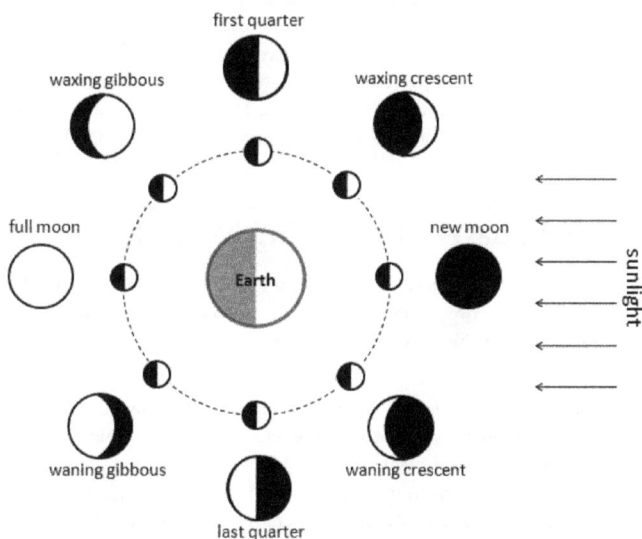

When you cannot see the Moon in a clear night sky, it may be because the moon is in its first phase. As each phase passes, the Moon enters another zodiac sign with an approximate angle of 45 degrees on the longitudinal scale. This adds up to a total of 360 degrees with eight signs on the zodiac wheel. With each phase lasting up to 3.5 days, one lunar cycle takes approximately one month to complete. While some phases gain light as they grow, others lose it, determining their respective characteristics.

First Phase- The New Moon

This phase defines the beginning of a lunar cycle where the Moon is completely invisible due to the Sun's placement. In turn, the Moon does not illuminate the Earth's face, which is why the sky appears dark. The Moon and the Sun are aligned with the Earth's face, which provides the illusion of the Moon being dark or lost in the sky. According to astrologers, both celestial bodies form a symbiosis or thrive in conjunction.

Manifestations: Just like the lunar cycle begins and motivates the Moon to grow, you should also consider setting new goals and intentions to reach closer to your goals. You can either write down your goals and break them into smaller milestones or prepare a vision board to clear your mind. Since the cycle starts on day 1 of the month, you have 29 days to accomplish your intentions. You should not only focus on starting afresh or turning over a new leaf but also on regaining your power or strength to take necessary actions. Decipher this sign to reboot your life and reinstate your energy from the Moon's power. Ideally, this phase represents birth and the steady growth phase that follows as a person grows up.

Typically, a person born in this phase possesses childlike traits. They are full of life, enthusiastic, and ready to take charge. Just like a seed is implanted underground and gets optimum nutrition to burst out and bloom into a flower, this phase encourages you to unleash your true potential and start a new project. Note that over-enthusiasm can often ruin the process, thereby affecting the outcome. It is necessary to comprehend the practical concerns while listening to your gut to achieve favorable outcomes. Stay courageous and shun the peers who put you down. Gather your energy and focus on one thing instead of scattering yourself in multiple places.

Consider this phase a new beginning and an inspiration to promote growth in your personal and professional life. Whether you are having trouble sustaining your relationships or facing work issues, chart out your concerns and set intentions to combat your shortcomings. While vision boards and goal-setting approaches are some effective techniques to set your intentions, you should also focus on chanting positive affirmations every day to see better results. Discard all negative thoughts and make room for positive notions. Let go of the past and learn from your mistakes. If you have held a desire in your heart and mind for a while, consider this as a sign to put it into action.

Second Phase- The Waxing Moon (Crescent)

In its second phase, the Moon appears in a crescent shape due to the Sun's slight movement. However, since the Sun still covers a major part of the Moon, the latter appears as a thin silver lining. The waxing moon signifies building energy and the buried seed that is slowly gaining strength to sprout.

Manifestations: Just like the Moon slowly powers up to retain its shape, you should also work on your inner strength and qualities to boost self-confidence and reach your goals. Other qualities like self-assurance, self-esteem, and compassion should also be polished. Take time to plan out your actions and take inspiration from the crescent moon to move ahead. You can set your own pace and take one step at a time. The idea is to keep moving irrespective of the speed or the pace you pick. Since you have already set your intentions during the first phase, it is time to take the first step by gaining inspiration from the crescent moon. Those born under the second phase of the Moon know that there is more to life and that new adventures await ahead.

Third Phase- The First Quarter (Waxing)

The third Phase (or "waxing") is when the Moon appears sliced in half due to the Sun's coverage. It can take up to one week for the Moon to reach the third phase and display its face in half. Since the Moon completes one-fourth of a lunar cycle, this phase is also known as the First Quarter. At this point, the Moon is in waxing mode.

Manifestations: This phase asks a person to take a break and reflect on their intentions. It emphasizes the importance of pausing and reveling in your life. Take a look at your plans and comprehend whether or not you are going in the right direction. This will keep you from making irreversible mistakes and avoid adverse repercussions. This phase also signifies action and the need to pull yourself from external resistances. While pausing and reflecting on your intentions is necessary, knowing the right way to move ahead is important too. If you are sure about your path, you must put yourself in full gear and take charge.

At this point, the buried seed has sprouted and made its way above ground to turn into a small sapling. Even though it is not fully grown yet, the sapling is absorbing the Sun's energy for optimum growth. However, it needs the will and courage to sustain itself regardless of external forces until it grows into a strong tree that bare hands cannot uproot. Similarly, a person born under this phase is confident, passionate, and willing to take risks. However, they must combat all the challenges and hardships coming their way. They must be quick on their feet and motivated. Since these people have a lot of courage and determination, they often carve their path by taking action under any circumstances.

Fourth Phase- The Waxing Gibbous Moon

The fourth phase reveals a major part of the Moon's surface and is just one step away from transforming into a Full Moon. This phase illuminates the sky and the Earth's surface and is also visible during the daytime. The Sun covers only one-fourth of the Moon.

Manifestations: This phase declares that you are just one step away from fulfilling your goal. You just need a little push and some commitment to achieve what you set out to do. However, you must also be mindful and pay attention to the tiniest details to avoid losing track of time. At the same time, focus on honing your skills to create an edge over your competitors. This phase also keeps you aware and asks you to look back and redesign your action plan if it seems bleak. This is the step where you have to take your goals extremely seriously and put in your best effort to achieve them.

The sapling starts bearing buds at this point, and you can notice tiny fruits ready to sprout. Just like the plant is preparing itself to bear fruits until they are ready to be picked, you also have to take care of your actions and emotions until you reach your final destination. You need proper organization and planning skills to ease the burden. It is also necessary to acknowledge your thoughts and emotions to judge your current condition and lead a peaceful life while getting closer to your ambition.

People born under this phase are naturally curious. In essence, they want to know more about themselves and their life's purpose. If they feel they lack in some way, they instantly seek personal development and find ways to express themselves. While self-analysis is a part of their daily lives, they also watch others around them and acknowledge their usefulness. Since they constantly need motivation, they will likely keep away from people who fail to inspire them.

Fifth Phase- The Full Moon

At this point, the Moon and the Sun stand in opposite directions, leading to portraying a full version of the Moon and allowing it to shine brightly, sending as much light as possible to Earth's surface. The Full Moon symbolizes the completion of a cycle and the urge to start a new chapter. By tapping into this overflowing energy, you can strengthen your intentions and find solutions to your problems.

Manifestations: Even though both celestial bodies are at opposite ends, a person may find it difficult to strike a balance due to the elevated tension. You may feel overwhelmed because of the deluge of emotions. On the bright side, look at the Full Moon as an opportunity to shine bright and reveal your true inner self. If you are successful, you may even find your inner calling. To tap into the Full Moon's true side, you can resort to several tricks and rituals such as crystal healing, meditations, and spell chanting. Be wary of overflowing emotions as they can ruin the entire process and invalidate all your hard work.

The seed you sowed during the first phase has completely bloomed and is bearing fruits at this point. It is ready to be fully expressed and to allow its fruits to be harvested. Just like the Sun and the Moon stand staring at each other in awe, individuals influenced by this phase often seek partners who admire them. Typically, these people are blessed with fulfilled lives and thrive in peace. The Full Moon implies the need and desire of having a loving partner who completes the seeker. Before they find their spouse or soulmate, these people will learn about harmonious engagement in their personal and professional lives. They are blessed to experience varied and interesting adventures throughout their journey.

Sixth Phase- The Waning Gibbous Moon (Disseminating)

The Moon is partially covered by the Sun to the right side during this phase, which forms a mirror image of the Waxing Moon. This form of the body is known as the Waning Gibbous Moon and portrays diminishing powers. The Sun partly creates a shadow on the Moon, slowly heading towards its last quarter version.

Manifestations: This is the step where you take a break again and reflect on your journey. Comprehend your path and acknowledge how far you have come. This is the time to review and assess your progress. If you still feel like changing certain things to accomplish your goals with ease, take a step back and reiterate your plan. At the same time, you should feel grateful to have come this far. All the hard work and time invested is paying off. Take a moment to thank your loved ones and the people who helped you during this journey. Even if you haven't accomplished all your intentions so far, you may still see one of your small goals being fulfilled. At this point, you wish to give back the wisdom and possessions you acquired to date.

Individuals born under this phase are naturally enthusiastic and know how to enjoy their lives regardless of circumstances. The flowers and fruit on the plant are fading at this point. The seeds are falling on the ground and ready to be buried again. The term "disseminating" refers to falling off and giving back. Just like the tree returns the seeds to the Earth to restart the cycle, you should also give away love, laughter, and wisdom to people around you. As well as this, individuals capable of succeeding will find an easier path to accomplish their goals.

Seventh Phase- The Third Quarter (Last Quarter or Waning)

This phase of the Moon is the mirror image of the First Quarter, covered in half by the Sun's shadow. The Moon shines on the left side as opposed to the right side during the First Quarter. It is reaching the last phase of fading away from the night sky.

Manifestations: If you are holding back your emotions or being held back due to some form of negativity, it is time to let go of your gloomy thoughts. Believe in yourself and know your worth. Negative thoughts, along with any kind of fear or self-limiting beliefs, should be discarded. While it is easier said than done, giving up is not an option at this stage. You can seek professional help or lean on your loved ones to combat fear and negative emotions. If you are holding onto the feelings or possessions that are not serving you in any positive way, release them and cleanse your system.

Forgive those who hurt you and begin to seek solitude. Leave your emotional baggage behind before moving forward. Work on your anger and do not regret following your dream. Move ahead with a light heart and mind. The tree you planted is losing its leaves and colors. It has entered the fall season and is embracing the change. People representing this phase constantly reanalyze their situation and redesign old patterns to achieve a better outcome.

Eight Phase- The Dark Moon (Balsamic)

The Sun is dominant over the Moon and covers a major part of its surface at this point. You can only see a thin crescent-shaped illuminating body during this last phase. The Moon is about to fade and give way to the invisible New Moon.

Manifestations: You may or may not have reached your goal or fulfilled your intentions. Irrespective of the outcome, you should reflect on your journey and examine your condition. It is the moment to take pride in yourself and pat yourself on the shoulder. Remember that you cannot control everything, and you are just in the right place. Even if you haven't fulfilled your goals, consider your past mistakes and work out the steps to change. Get inspired and motivate others too. Surrendering to the universe's power will give you peace and propel your actions.

Let fate drive your vehicle and get excited for the new beginnings as you enter a new life cycle. Even though this cycle represents death, it is still an invitation for rebirth or regeneration. The tree you planted is completely dead now but is preparing itself for spring. The fallen seeds are hibernating inside the ground and preparing themselves for the next cycle to begin. You may find it easier to leave others behind and accept your circumstances if born under this phase. You believe in completion and reinstating a new journey. You prefer to spend time alone rather than being with the wrong people.

The next phase is the New Moon, where it completely disappears and marks the beginning of a new cycle. In essence, a lunar cycle is a natural example of a cycle representing birth, death, and regeneration. While the new moon refers to the beginning of a life cycle and setting relevant intentions, the full moon depicts completion, death, or an ending.

It is believed that following the Moon's phases and inculcating relevant values can truly change a person's life. In a way, the Moon gives us signs and wisdom to manifest positive changes to our routines and helps us to become more self-aware. Pay attention to each phase and decipher the innate tone each element carries. Compare your zodiac sign with the phase you were born in to comprehend your emotions and intuition. By digging deeper, you may also find your true purpose or calling in life. To find your birth phase, compare your Sun and Moon signs and count the difference in their placements. The number you get is the Moon phase you were born in.

Chapter 10: Harness the Magic of the Moon

Moon magic and tantras have been a significant part of astrology for ages. The Moon has impacted the gravitational pull and the movement of tides and has acted as a guide for farmers and hunters to grow their crops based on the best seasonal and climatic conditions. However, the Moon has not always been in favor of all living creatures on Earth. While some are blessed with the Moon's valediction, others need to harness the body's power and energy to get better outcomes. While Moon magic was more relevant to ancient scholars and magicians, you can still practice some routines at home too.

Why Are Spells and Rituals Important for the Moon?

As you learned, the spiritual and mythological importance of the Moon can be unraveled by performing certain spells and following some effective methods to please the celestial body. Moon magic and rituals were an integral part of Chinese, Egyptian, and Indian culture in the past. They were considered sacred and pivotal ways to recharge and carry out normal day-to-day activities. Since some cultures still follow lunar calendars and cycles to mark time and dates, channeling the Moon's energy to validate your feelings can be a vital step towards self-improvement.

Every phase of a lunar cycle helps you develop in different areas. For instance, while some seek a productivity boost through spells and rituals, others need insights into inner contemplation and self-care. In a way, the rituals are a screen to absorb in self-reflection and take charge of your personal and professional life. Moon rituals, in particular, send an invite to feel silent and peaceful on the inside. To combat growing despair and challenges, you need to plant some intentions within your mind and follow the lunar phases. This will also make you more committed and provide a definite path to follow with immense focus and perseverance.

Routines and Rituals for Each Moon Phase

Even though we learned about the moon phases of a lunar cycle in the previous chapter, we will recall them here to understand the best ritual or routine to please the Moon at each step. Here are some effective routines and rituals you should perform during each moon phase to harness the magical power of the Moon and feel at peace.

First Phase- New Moon

Your Focus: The first step is to set intentions. Just as the Moon is ready to be born and start its journey, you need to set your goals and illustrate your journey. What do you want to achieve in life? What are the areas you want to improve? Do you see yourself at a specific place after a few years?

Ritual: Since this phase aligns with the idea of stepping into new beginnings, you need a routine that can help with goal-setting and deciphering your thoughts. Journaling is an effective way to clear your mind and begin to design your goals. It also paves a path for introspection and provides the assurance of leading the path.

How to Perform: Buy a bullet journal or make your diary with paper scraps to write your daily thoughts and clarify your vision. To set your goals, you must first learn to read your mind. Are there any areas of your life currently bothering you? Write them down. It could be your career, personal relationships, or even a new project you meant to begin. Chart them out and visualize your goals.

Now, write "New Moon Intentions" on the first blank page along with the date. You can also add pictures or doodles to recognize your concerns or desires. You must practice this routine every day for at least 15 to 30 minutes for effective results. When writing in your journal, create a sacred or clutter-free space to get clearer thoughts. Light a candle and take deep breaths to feel at ease. Set five core intentions and jot them down in bullet points on paper when you are ready to start. Use the present tense and address your intentions in the first person to believe that they are already in action. Read and repeat your intentions out loud and visualize them in real life while closing your eyes.

Second Phase- Waxing Crescent Moon

Your Focus: During this phase, the Moon starts showing itself in the sky, which indicates that it is time to take action. At this point, you should have an action plan ready to start following it. Even if it is a small step, start moving ahead to fulfill your intentions. While leaping is vital to achieving success, you should also learn how to nurture your ideas and heighten your self-esteem.

Ritual: You can take help from some powerful spells or mantras to grow your career or strengthen your personal relationships. Reflect on the intentions you set during the Moon's first phase and cast spells based on the area of improvement. When casting the spells, it is necessary to visualize and think that you have already achieved your goal.

How to Perform: Let's say that your main intention is to find a new job and excel in your career. You can resort to a spell that is further narrowed down and specifically based on your professional goal. For example, if you are looking for a new job, you can cast a spell related to "Demeter & Ceres." On the other hand, casting a Wiccan bath spell will help you have a successful interview. You can alter your spells based on your intentions. If your goal is to find a partner, you have to cast a different set of spells using the same method.

Third Phase- First Quarter

Your Focus: This is the stage when you take action and implement the plan with full force. However, you need clarity to ensure that you are moving in the right direction. Get attuned with your body's natural movement and your thought process. When both are in harmony, you can achieve all your goals.

Ritual: This can be fulfilled by performing a set of breathing exercises specifically meant for the First Quarter phase of a lunar cycle. You can also perform meditation and synchronize your emotions with your actions.

How to Perform: Find a quiet space where you can peacefully perform meditation. Sit cross-legged and play calming music. Close your eyes and clear your mind. If any thought crosses your mind, shift your focus to your breathing pattern. Take deep breaths and keep your focus intact. Perform a breathing exercise called "kumbhaka," where you inhale and hold the same amount of breath but let out double the amount. Since it can take some time to master breathing techniques and meditation, you must be patient.

Fourth Phase- Waxing Gibbous

Your Focus: The Moon is steadily growing and is ready to transform into a Full Moon version. It acts as a fuel to recharge and inspires you to keep expanding and growing. You are putting your maximum effort toward fulfilling your intentions. If you are feeling tired or demotivated, take inspiration from the Waxing Gibbous Moon.

Ritual: Known as the "Intuitive Oracle," this ritual is based on referring to a deck of oracle cards to nurture your actions. Ideally, oracle cards are used to read and interpret your perspective on specific steps you are currently undertaking. Some even use a set to enhance self-awareness and become more intuitive.

How to Perform: When choosing a set of oracle cards, focus on the theme and your intuition. Pick the card that calls out to you. You can also collect several decks and use one based on your current circumstances or mood. Before you shuffle the cards, take a deep breath and clear your mind. Recall your intentions while you are shuffling the cards. Lay them on a flat surface and spread them out evenly.

Now, use your left hand and hover it over the cards at a steady pace. Pause at the card that pulls and draws you in the most. Once you feel this pull, draw two random cards and place them upside down. The first card will declare your main intention, and the second card will validate your action. If you are not on the right path, it is time to change your course.

At the same time, take a pause and analyze your plan again. Make the necessary changes before moving ahead. You must be at the top of your game by this stage, as it will determine whether or not you will achieve favorable outcomes. This ritual will also help you overcome hurdles, combat shortcomings, and nurture new thoughts and ideas.

Fifth Phase- Full Moon

Your Focus: At this point, the Moon grows into a full circle and marks completion. It refers to a phase where you are seeking abundance or have undergone a complete transformation. Practice gratefulness, thank yourself, and acknowledge your journey. Plan around your Full Moon days to perform cleansing and purifying rituals.

Ritual: You need to let go of negativity by writing down all the things bothering you and burning the piece of paper. Watch the paper burn and visualize your negative thoughts vanishing into the flames. You can also take a Moon bath to integrate the celestial body's energy with water. This ritual provokes feelings and unlocks emotional intelligence, which is ideal during the Full Moon phase. With this, you can also decipher the Moon's musings and comprehend the emotions it is trying to evoke.

How to Perform: To prepare your bath, mix 1/4 cup of Himalayan pink salt with 1/2 cup of Epsom salt. Next, you need an essential oil to act as a carrier. You can use lavender, frankincense, jasmine, chamomile, or sweet almond essential oil. Add 2 to 3 drops to the salt mixture. To enhance the mixture's effect, add a few flower petals for an invigorating effect. It is time to prepare your bathtub. Fill it with water and add the salt and essential oil mixture. Dim the lights and light scented candles for a relaxing effect.

When taking a bath, let the water touch your skin and take deep breaths to get into a meditative state. Feel your physical presence and let go of all worries. Remember, this is the time to feel grateful for your existence and your body. As you become more mindful when taking a bath, you will also feel more connected to your mind and soul. At the same time, recall your intentions and start visualizing them. Whether you are looking for a compatible partner or finding a new career choice, imagine yourself in a positive light while letting the water cleanse your soul and mind. Believe that you are destined to achieve positive outcomes.

Once you have finished taking a bath, let the water drain along with your negative thoughts. You are not done yet. After your bath, rub some body oil all over your arms, legs, stomach, chest, back, and neck. To make this routine more effective, play calming music, light incense sticks, or create an ambiance that will heighten your senses. Irrespective of your gender, this routine will help you unravel your feminine side and explore your sexual energy, one of a human being's purest and most vulnerable sides.

You can also take this time to charge your crystals and energize them using the Moon's full power. Place your crystals at a dry and dust-free spot under the moonlight for 48 hours. The best spot is your windowsill, as you can keep an eye on your crystals while they are recharging. Even though you can keep your crystals for just a few hours, astrologers suggest leaving them for at least two nights to soak up maximum cosmic energy.

Sixth Phase- Waning Gibbous

Your Focus: As the Moon starts to fade slowly due to the Sun's coverage over its surface, you should take a step back and reflect on your journey too. The work you have done so far should be validated and appreciated.

Ritual: You can use the Moon's energy (which is still high until it reaches the next phase) to charge any liquid and make "Moon water." People usually use drinking water to make this sacred potion. You can either drink it, apply it to your body, or spray it around your house to get the most out of the Moon's energy. Some even incorporate it into their beauty routine.

How to Perform: To make Moon water, you need one cup of distilled water and a glass jar or bottle. Pour the water into the jar and place it under the moonlight for two days. Make sure to set and recall your intentions when following this ritual. For an enhanced effect, write your intentions down and place the piece of paper near the glass jar. Add your Moon water to your beverages, sip it directly from the bottle, or use it in your skincare routine after mixing it with a few drops of essential oil. When using it, repeat and visualize your intentions.

Seventh Phase- Third Quarter

Your Focus: This is the stage where you let go of the bothersome thoughts and combat stagnation. Just like the First Quarter Moon inspired you to start a new project or relationship, the Third Quarter Moon asks you to let go of the things that didn't work out.

Ritual: At this stage, you can perform exercises related to movement. It could be yoga, dance, or any other movement form inspired by the Moon's flow.

How to Perform: The Moon dance is a popular ritual that many cultures have followed for centuries. Even though it is typically performed on a New Moon or Full Moon day, some prefer to dance during other lunar phases. While some simply move around chanting Moon mantras, others gather in a big circle and perform the Moon dance. "Lightning walking" is another movement exercise where you walk around with heavy feet. This act resembles stomping but feels like a lightning strike. This helps your body release all stagnant energy and gives you fresh power to move to the next phase without any regrets. Any kind of movement will release accumulated negative energy and make room for a more positive aura.

Eight Phase- Waning Crescent Moon

Your Focus: Just like the Sun covers a major part of the Moon's surface to achieve completion, you should also reflect on your journey and analyze your mistakes to learn from them. This is the time to take a pause and contemplate how far you have come. Even if you haven't achieved success or are far away from your goals, you can restart the journey after taking a brief pause. If it seems overwhelming, note that it is okay to surrender. You can withdraw and relax.

Ritual: A clean and clutter-free environment will help you think clearly and bring you peace. The ritual is called "clutter cleanse," where you discard all the unnecessary items in your living space and make your life more pleasant.

How to Perform: Start by making a list of all the unwanted items and possessions in your home. While experts suggest focusing on just one space that you often use to work or sleep in, you can gradually declutter your entire home and feel more energized. Collect and sort all the objects based on their size, nature, and usefulness. If you haven't used a particular item for over a year, discard it. Do not hoard unnecessary stuff. In a way, this will also improve your decision-making skills, which are necessary to develop a clear mind. You can either sell the items or donate them to people in need.

By doing this, you are creating a sacred space for your body and mind. Over time, you will also notice a boost in your confidence and energy levels. Decluttering your living space is not just useful for your mind and soul, but it also reduces the effort you need to put into cleaning. It also enhances your home's aesthetic appeal and makes the spaces look bigger. Your sacred sanctuary is now ready. You can light candles, introduce a pleasant fragrance, or play music to make the spaces more peaceful. Use this new space to meditate every day.

Note that these rituals and routines will take some time to show positive results. Keep performing them over and over again, and you will soon see their benefits as a few cycles pass. Until then, believe in your intentions and focus on your actions.

Conclusion

Before you started reading this book, you may have had a different perspective on the relevance and existence of the Moon in the solar system. While some are aware of this natural body's importance in the world of astrology, others do not regard its prevalence as much as they should. Whether you are a pagan who wants to dig deeper into the astrological realm or a beginner simply dipping their toes in this, implementing the things in this book can help you mold the next chapter of your life. You can go back and refer to the practical guide that teaches the right way to perform magic and rituals to impact a positive change.

Let's cite the notions we've learned so far. The Moon has been perceived as a goddess for centuries and still holds significant implications in various cultures. Even though the illustration and depiction of the Lunar gods are different in all mythologies, the collective attributes depict the Moon Goddess as a dominant force symbolizing fertility and femininity. In the past, devotees made several sacrifices to please the deity, who, in turn, blessed them with wisdom and fertility.

Analyzing your moon sign does not only help you summon your emotions, but it also strengthens your relationship with the important women in your life. The Moon primarily rules over the Cancer zodiac sign and is related to womanhood, fertility, and security signs. The Moon signs govern different emotions and sides of every individual. For instance, while the Capricorn is ambitious and willing to work harder due to the weaker Moon sign, the Taurus glorifies the orbiting energy.

By knowing your place, time, and date of birth, you can easily determine your Moon sign and connect it to your zodiac sign. While some signs can freely express their thoughts and are emotionally available for their partners, others are more reserved and prefer to stay isolated. Furthermore, the Lunar South Node (Ketu) and North Node (Rahu) define the imperfect characteristics possessed by each individual, which are either excessively developed or stand below the usual standard, respectively. Since both nodes stand opposite each other, they depict karmic imbalance. The correlation of the Moon with other planets is quite versatile. While it thrives in harmony with some planets, the natural body creates negative conjunction (contrasts) with other celestial bodies.

The Lunar phases can also be studied to understand the natural cyclical events that can, in a way, govern your life and help you decipher your feelings. As the cycle of life begins from birth, the first phase marks the beginning of any process. As the Moon portrays different forms with each passing phase, it inspires you to set intentions, move ahead, reflect on your mistakes, and inspire others. In a way, it marks the birth and death of any process while signifying the importance of regeneration or rebirth. Every process that ends has a new beginning.

The right way to manifest the Moon's true energy is by performing effective rituals and magic. You can either chant positive affirmations, use crystals, or perform a moon bath to stay attuned with its energy. Recall the other robust ways to perform moon magic discussed in the last chapter.

That's the power of the Moon. You can simply bask under the powerful illumination and feel energized or read the Moon's placement to manifest positive change in your life and find your true self. Now that you have acquired complete knowledge about the Moon's role in astrology, take the leap and use the orbiting body's power to reap maximum benefits. Use this book as an inspiration to change your life and motivate others around you.

Good luck embodying the relevance of "la luna" and "know thyself"!

Part 10: The Sun in Astrology

The Ultimate Guide to the Giver of Life, Its Role in Vedic Astrology, and Sun Sign

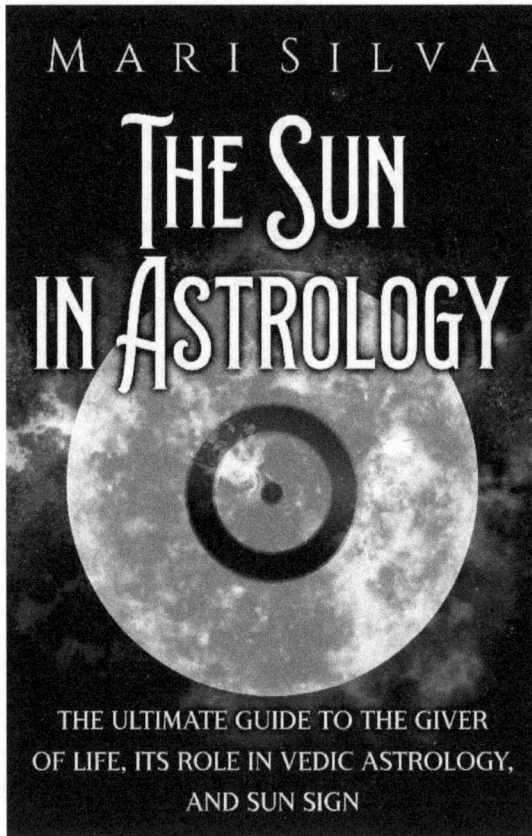

Introduction

The brightest star we can observe, the Sun, is a stationary celestial body that governs the planets in our solar system. Despite being cold and hot, the Sun gives life to humans, and survival without it is simply impossible. This massive illuminating source of life is a projection of humans to the outer world. It is every soul's identity and a navigating channel that helps one find the right direction. While it remains stationary and governs other bodies that orbit around it, the Sun also propels influential energy to help us become more confident and build the courage to fight adversities. This energy is one of the many reasons why the Sun is significant in the realm of astrology.

All bodies and energies revolve around the Sun. Whereas the Sun represents masculine energy, the Moon portrays a feminine role. The Sun's energy influences all the male figures in a family (father, son, husband, and brother). The ruler of the solar system also represents higher power, royalty, and vitality. It influences people to maintain their health and stay mentally and spiritually fit.

The importance of the Sun and its energy has been glorified for centuries. While some worshipped the Sun for its mighty demeanor, others held it as a subject of interest and curiosity. Ancient scholars and analytical learners even studied this celestial body's path of motion to draw birth charts and determine a person's fate and characteristics upon birth. What's more, the Sun's position and movement have also been codified to devise a calendrical system based on solar cycles to tell time. The first calendar was designed centuries ago, tracing the path of solar and lunar cycles to calculate time and accurately determine hours, days, weeks, and years. The Gregorian calendar, the modern calendar we all use, is inspired by ancient solar calendars.

Many scholars even drew parallels between the Sun's energy and humans' health, which was also the diverging point of Vedic astrology. It was believed that the Sun's affliction could help doctors diagnose physical health problems, most of which were related to the heart. Over time, the body's energy manifested into the life of humans by amalgamating it with yoga. For centuries, Surya Namaskars have been some of the most effective yoga practices to help treat a person's mental and spiritual health. The poses and asanas were directly linked to the body's chakras, which helped the healing process.

Today, the Sun is still perceived as one's identity. People consider reading their sun signs and determining their characteristics or fate to predict their near future. The Sun represents Leo due to its fiery and strong nature, but it also has strong connections with several other zodiac signs. By tapping into the Sun's energy, you can revitalize your mind and body and become more self-aware. If you can successfully achieve this, it means you have to be blessed with a creative, fulfilling, and conscious mind.

We've only scratched the surface of some of these interesting topics about the Sun and its astrological significance. These will be elaborated on further throughout this book. Every chapter is categorized based on the Sun's distinct roles in astrology and as the giver of life. In this book, you will learn about the Sun as seen by different cultures and during different periods, branches of astrology, and its significance in various civilizations. You will also discover how the Sun has been used as a timekeeping tool since time immemorial, its relationship with zodiac signs, as well as effective ways to harness its energy and manifest the positive changes in your life.

Read on to explore the significance of the Sun in astrology and its role in all other aspects of our lives.

Chapter 1: Sun as the Giver of Life

Apart from being an astronomical body that provides us with the light and warmth necessary to sustain all life on Earth, the Sun has also played a major role in how human religion and spirituality have evolved over the centuries. Nearly all major ancient religions worshipped the Sun or a solar deity associated with the Sun.

These deities were often marked as uniquely powerful, and – like the Egyptian solar deity, Ra – were usually either the head of their pantheon or considered main leaders in it. Some ancient belief systems took the concept of solar deities one step further into actual sun worship, including the short-lived Atomism that dominated ancient Egypt in the 14th century B.C.

The Importance of the Sun in Ancient Civilizations

Just as the Moon is considered an aspect of the sacred feminine element in many ancient religions, the Sun is considered the sacred masculine element. The Sun was essential to the ancient way of life, and many civilizations deemed it the most powerful element in the world so that their lives were designed to make as much use of the Sun's energies as possible.

The ancient Egyptians designed their homes to store the Sun's heat in the walls so that their homes would stay warm at night. The sun's heat was especially crucial, seeing as desert nights can become very cool, very fast.

The Greeks, Romans, Native Americans, and ancient Chinese used similar techniques when building their homes. In fact, Socrates taught classes on building and architecture to make the best use of the Sun's life-giving heat. The Greeks built buildings with windows facing south to ensure they got the most of the Sun's heat and insulated their north walls (which received the least heat).

The Romans used similar techniques when building their baths, with many baths featuring southern walls made entirely of windows to ensure they got the most solar energy possible. The Anasazi used their knowledge of how the Sun worked to provide their homes with heat during winters and shade in the summer. The homes in Mesa Verde show just how well Native Americans leveraged solar principles to build communities.

Prehistoric Chinese homes would often only open to the south of the structure. This positioning kept the cold north winds out and allowed them to take advantage of as much of the Sun's heat as possible.

Ultimately, the Sun's importance was undeniably linked to its ability to generate, nurture, and sustain life across time and cultures. It was so important that cultures built structures to track its movements, including the pyramids, standing stones, and other earthworks. It's no surprise that these structures are also often seen as spiritually important. After all, the Sun's nourishment of life also included nourishment of the spiritual and mental aspects of life.

The Spiritual Importance of the Sun across Civilizations

As mentioned, the Sun was often the masculine counterpart to the Moon. Most solar deities were male, which reinforced their importance in the ancient world.

The Sun is the planetary force that bestows life and light upon the Earth; it was often regarded as all-seeing. It was linked to justice, enlightenment, illumination, and wisdom. Apollo, the best-known of the Greek solar deities, was also the god of prophecy, the truth, and divine justice.

Given these traits – justice, knowledge, power, and wisdom – the Sun and sun gods were often associated with divine kingship. Countless kings and rulers claimed to be direct descendants of the Sun, which helped them consolidate and ensure their power, and many solar deities were associated with the Supreme Deity of a given pantheon.

For example, in Egyptian mythology, Ra is the dominant of all the gods. He is the king of gods and is considered the creator and nourisher of the Earth. Similarly, in India, the sun god Surya was an all-seeing god who expelled darkness and disease from the world.

In later Roman history, solar worship took prominence, and nearly all deities worshipped during the period (including ones as distinct as Mithras and Christ) were ascribed solar qualities. The Romans celebrated the feast of Sol Invictus (the "Unconquered Sun") each year on December 25th, and this festival would later be co-opted as Christmas.

In the Americas, solar deities were just as prominent. The Plains Indians of North America celebrated the Sun Dance, one of their most important religious ceremonies, while pre-Columbian civilizations in Mexico and Peru involved sun worship, with the Sun playing an important role in both religions and rituals. Peruvian rulers were considered to be incarnations of Inti, the God of the Sun.

While the Aztecs practiced human sacrifice in honor of the sun deities Huitzilopochtli and Tezcatlipoca, the Japanese sun goddess Amaterasu was considered one of the leaders of the Japanese pantheon. She was also the tutelary deity of the Japanese imperial family, and the Japanese state uses solar symbolism as part of its national symbolism until this day.

As demonstrated by Amaterasu, not all solar deities and Sun gods were male. The Sun was a nourisher and giver of life, similar to the role women played and continue to play among humans. Because of this, several female solar deities, including female deities who were not necessarily Sun goddesses but were closely linked to the solar deities of their pantheon.

For instance, in ancient Egyptian religion, the sun disk (a symbol of the Sun) was carried not only by the solar deity Ra but also by numerous female deities associated with him, including:

- **Sekhmet,** the lion-headed daughter of Ra
- **Wadjet,** one of the patron goddesses to the king and the tutelary goddess of Lower Egypt
- **Hathor/Hesat,** the sky goddess who was one of the Eyes of Ra, and acted as either Ra's consort or mother
- **Isis,** one of the best-known Egyptian goddesses, was considered the divine mother of the pharaoh (the Egyptian pharaoh was linked to Horus, Isis's divine son with her consort Osiris). She was also the goddess of magic and wisdom, which were abilities she received in return for curing Ra of snake venom, and both of which are traditionally linked to solar deities.

Sekhmet

Other ancient religions that boast female solar deities include several Native American tribes, including the Cherokee (who worship Unelanuhi), Inuit (who venerate Malina), and Miwok (whose solar deity is Heklooas).

The solar deity in Germanic mythology is often female, while the Moon deity is male. In Old High German myth, the solar deity is the goddess Sunna, while the goddess Sól (also named Sunna and Frau Sonne) is the deity who pulls the Sun through the sky on her chariot. Likewise, the Aboriginal people of Australia generally regard the Sun as female, with solar deities including Bila, worshipped by the Adnyamathanha.

Solar Deities across Civilizations

While solar deities shared common characteristics, their treatment, mythologies, and worship differed across cultures. Some of the best-known solar deities include:

Helios and Apollo in Greek Mythology

Greek mythology featured two prominent solar deities: Helios and Apollo. Of the two, Helios was the older and was considered the personification of the Sun, rather than just a deity who ruled it; same case with Apollo.

While Apollo was a son of Zeus, Helios was a deity from the generation before the gods and was one of the Titans. Helios was the son of the Titans Hyperion and Theia. He was -technically – cousin to the eldest gods (Zeus, Hera, Poseidon, Demeter, Hades, and Hestia), as well as brother to Selene and Eos, the personifications of the Moon and the Dawn.

Helios

While Helios and his siblings were relatively minor gods in Classical Greece, his worship became more prominent toward late antiquity. He was made the central deity of Roman Emperor Julian's religious cult in the 4th century A.D.

However, it should be noted that despite his relatively minor status, the ancient Greeks were still well aware of the importance he held as a solar deity. He features numerous mythological tales, including ones as well known as the abduction of Persephone and the story of Heracles.

Helios was often linked to other Greek deities, including Apollo and Zeus, the king of the gods. Some authors, including Hesiod, directly reference Helios as being "Zeus's eye," while an Orphic saying links Zeus, Hades, and Helios (in his form as Helios-Dionysus) with joint sovereignty. He was also linked to Cronus, father of the eldest gods and known as Saturn in ancient Rome.

Another prominent reference to Helios comes in the form of the Greek Magical Papyri. These are a collection of magic spells, hymns, and rituals used between the 2nd century BC and the 5th century AD. In them, Helios is considered the source and creator of life. He is given far broader powers than in traditional Greek myth and is revered as the lord of the heavens and the cosmos and the god of the sea.

In this collection of papyri, Helios was also said to take the form of 12 hours, each representing an hour of the day. This representation links him directly to the zodiac. He is also sometimes assimilated with the Roman god Mithras and is combined into Helios-Mithras. In this role, he is said to have revealed the secrets of immortality to the author of the text. He is also often linked with the Egyptian god Ra due to his journey on a sun boat and his actions in "restraining the serpent" (usually linked to Ra's eternal battle against Apep/Apophis).

Other links in the papyri include one to the Hebrew god Yahweh. He is the Agathodaimon, "the god of gods," linked to the Egyptian Horus in his role as Horus Harpocrates. Helios is often referred to as Iao, a name derived from Yahweh, and shares many of his epithets.

Apollo, on the other hand, is a different deity altogether. One tale that explains his link to the Sun despite the existence of Helios in the Greek pantheon comes through the tale of Phaeton, one of the sons of Helios.

When Helios allowed his son to drive his solar chariot, he could not control the vehicle, resulting in the devastation of the Earth. In response, Zeus killed the boy with a lightning bolt to save humanity and other life on Earth. In his grief, Helios refused to take up his duties as the driver of the sun chariot, leaving Apollo to replace him in this role.

Apollo is a manifold god with authority over domains such as archery, poetry, music and dance, healing, and disease. He is also the deity of the Sun and the light, and he holds dominion over prophecy, the truth, and the revelation of mysteries.

In his role as the sun god, Apollo was endowed with numerous designations. These include Phobos ("bright"), Helius ("sun"), Aegletes ("light of the sun"), Lyceus ("light," an epithet also associated with Leto, mother of Apollo and his twin Artemis), Sol ("sun" in Latin), and Phanaeus ("giving or bringing light"). As the god of prophecy, he was also referred to as Coelispex (a combination of the Latin words for "sky" and "to look at").

Apollo's worship was not limited to the ancient Greeks, though. He was one of the few gods that remained relatively similar for the Romans, keeping both his name and his function (the other deity to do so was Gaia/Gaea, the personification of the Earth and one of the Greek primordial deities).

Following the growth and expansion of the Roman Empire, Apollo's worship spread across the Roman kingdom and was particularly prominent among the Celts. Like with the Greeks and Romans, he was primarily seen as a sun god and a god of healing. His epithets by the Celts include Apollo Atepomarus ("the great horseman" – in the Celtic world, horses were linked to the Sun), Apollo Belenus "bright, brilliant," a manifestation of his role as god of healing and of the Sun), Apollo Grannus (a spring god of healing), and Apollo Virotutis ("benefactor of mankind").

Apollo was one of the few gods to have multiple cult sites, his first being at Delos (his birthplace in myth) and Delphi (where he slew the monster Python, and home to Pythia, also known as the Oracle of Delphi.

Delphi, this oracle, was the major Greek oracle referenced multiple times in Greek myth). There were also multiple well-known temples in honor of Apollo throughout the Greek and Roman worlds, including ones at:

- Thebes
- Eretria
- Thermon
- Syracuse (Sicily)
- Delphi
- Hamaxitus
- Apollonia Pontica
- Pompeii
- Rome

Shamash in Mesopotamian Mythology

Also known as Utu, Shamash was an ancient Mesopotamian sun god. He was also the god of justice, morality, and truth. Along with his father Sin (God of the Moon) and his twin sister Inanna (also known as Ishtar, the Goddess of the planet Venus, love, beauty, and power, and the Queen of Heaven), he formed an astral triad of deities.

Shamash

As a solar deity, Shamash had dominion over justice and equity. He was revered as the bringer of light, defeater of darkness and evil, and was given the right to judge both gods and men. One legend holds that it was Shamash who gave the Babylonian king Hammurabi his famous code of laws.

Shamash was also considered a bestower of life and light. He was the governor of the entire universe and was one of the only purely heroic figures in Mesopotamian mythology. Due to this, he rarely figured in mythological tales, which instead focused on how gods behave similarly to mortals.

The oldest documents mentioning Shamash (in his role as Utu) were traced back to 3500 BC and also represented some of the first known written Mesopotamian scriptures. He was worshipped for over 3000 years until the fall of Mesopotamian culture.

His main temples were located in Sippar and Larsa, and he was known to be a kind, generous deity. He was considered one of the protectors of the kings of Uruk and played a role in helping Gilgamesh defeat the ogre Huwawa (also known as Humbaba) in the Epic of Gilgamesh. His consort was Aya, who would later be absorbed into the figure of his twin sister, Inanna/Ishtar.

Surya and Savitr in Hindu Mythology

In Hindu mythology, Surya is the chief solar deity and is also known by the names Aditya, Visvasat ("brilliant"), Mitra, and Savitr ("nourisher," though Savitr is also identified as a distinct deity in scriptures such as the Rig Veda).

Surya is first mentioned in one of the oldest surviving Vedic hymns in the Rig Veda, where he is worshipped as the rising Sun and is considered a dispeller of darkness, the deity of all life and one who brings knowledge.

Surya

In the Vedic texts, Surya is the creator of Prakriti or the material universe. He is often part of a trinity of deities, alongside Agni (god of fire) and either Vayu (god of wind) or Indra (god of lightning, thunder, and rains, and the king of the gods). Together, these three deities from the Brahman, a metaphysical concept that symbolizes the eternal truth and the Ultimate Reality in Hindu philosophy.

The figure of Surya was originally several other solar deities, which fused into a single figure. Hence deities like Savitr, Mitra, Aditya, and Pushan are occasionally seen as distinct deities from Surya.

He is also an important figure in Indian astronomy and astrology. In astrology, he is part of the Navagraha, a Hindu zodiac system. He has been one of the primary deities in Hinduism for a significant part of the religion's history. The worship of Surya only declined in the 13th century, likely due to the Muslim conquest of and influence over northern India. He would be replaced in importance by deities like Vishnu and Shiva.

However, numerous Surya temples have survived in the Indian subcontinent, especially in South India. He is still an important deity in this part of the country and remains important to Tamils, who worship him during the harvest festival of Pongal. Other major celebrations linked to Surya include Makar Sankranti, Kumbh Mela, and Chhath Puja.

As mentioned, Savitr is sometimes identified as distinct from Surya, especially in older texts like the Rig Veda. He is symbolic of the Sun before sunrise, while Surya symbolizes the Sun after it has risen. He also represents the life-giving power of the Sun, which is perhaps a reason behind his veneration.

The Rig Veda dedicates 11 hymns to Savitr, and his name is mentioned about 170 times in the text. Of the 11 hymns, Hymn 35 is perhaps the most detailed in its adoration of Savitr and is also known as the "Hymn of Savitr."

Additionally, Savitr is celebrated in the Gayatri Mantra. This hymn is one of the most sacred and best-known in Hinduism and is also among the most powerful. One of the many translations of the hymn into English comes from the Indologist Ralph T.H. Griffith, who translates it as: "*May we attain that excellent glory of Savitr the god: So may He stimulate our prayers.*"

It should be noted that while Savitr stopped being considered an independent deity by the end of the Vedic period and was instead completely subsumed by Surya, he is still worshipped due to these hymns.

In some traditions of modern Hinduism, Savitr is worshipped as Savitri, and the Gayatri Mantra is also known as the Savitri Mantra. In these traditions, this deity is female rather than male, and the understanding of the hymn changes accordingly. Another translation of the hymn comes from the Indian monk and nationalist figure, Swami Vivekananda, who translated it as: "*We meditate on the glory of that Being who has produced this universe; may She enlighten our minds.*"

Lastly, in modern Vedic astrology, the Sun is considered a representative of the soul. Just as solar deities were considered bringers of light, the Sun is the bringer of an inner "solar light" and represents leadership, self-confidence, power, and health in Vedic astrology. Charts that include the Sun in an advantageous position can often indicate that the chart's owner possesses clarity about spiritual matters.

Chapter 2: The Sun as the Timekeeper

As one of the most significant celestial bodies in astronomy and astrology, ancient scholars and locals used the Sun star to tell the time. With the absence of a reliable way to tell the time and carry out daily activities like sleeping, eating, growing crops, and figuring out the seasons, people followed the Sun's path to determine specific points during the day or night. As they realized the importance of marking a solar and lunar cycle to ascertain the day, week, and year, ancient scholars dug deeper and designed their own calendars with specific days and hours to achieve a better sense of time. This innovation allowed commoners to harvest crops based on specific seasons, migrate, and carry out other important activities.

The Concept of Time Based on the Sun's Movement

Many ancient civilizations drafted certain methods to tell time. While some designed tools and devices to locate the Sun's movement, others simply told the time by looking at the placement of other stars and using their instincts.

The Position of the Sun and Stars

Ancient astrologers told the time by locating the position of the Moon, stars, the Sun, and the five planets in the sky. A lunar cycle comprises different phases of the Moon and covers around 30 days of a month. Similarly, the sun's position was determined to denote the "solstice," when the Sun is at the farthest distance and rises or sets across the horizon. At one point, both the sunrise and sunset take place at the closest point, which produces a reverse effect. Over a specific period, this pattern can be traced to form rough circles on the ground and determine the month or year, which is exactly what our ancestors did.

In parallel, some visible stars and constellations were also studied to note the location of the Sun and the Moon. Ancient engineers and architects used this astrological information to design buildings according to the celestial bodies' position and movement. These periods were also considered auspicious or holy, marking when our ancestors carried out important tasks like migrating, trading, and harvesting. The Antikythera mechanism is a device made of wheels and gears believed to be used by ancient scholars to measure eclipses and the Sun's exact position.

Sundial

The first sundials can be dated back to 1500 BC when ancient scholars had designed a tool to tell the time based on the Sun's movement and position. It is known that ancient Egyptians were among the first to craft a sundial to tell the time. Even though the identity of the pioneers is undefined, accounts claim that the Jews, Babylonians, or the Egyptians were the first to use (if not design) this exemplary tool. While the Jews and the Babylonians used a 7-day week system to tell the time, the Romans came up with eight days; the last day is dedicated to buying and selling possessions.

Over time, the Greeks and Romans redesigned the sundial to produce more accurate results. While ancient designs only showed the months of a year, newer modifications divided the sections into specific hours and units. Typically, ancient sundials were designed in four shapes - conical, hemispherical, planar, and cylindrical. The sundial's surface divided the sections into different angles and latitudes, representing specific quadrants or quarters of an hour. Basically, the Sun's shadow on the sundial was the prime time-telling factor. Over time, portable and public sundials also became popular.

Water Clocks

Since sundials could not tell the time during cloudy days or at night, ancient Romans came up with another way to tell the time even when the Sun was not visible. They drew inspiration from sundials and made a water clock with similar calibrations. This device, called the "clepsydra," measured time based on the flow of liquid collected by a vessel. Using this, the outflow and inflow of the liquid were measured to indicate the passage of time based on the bowl's markings. As the water level rose in the bowls, the observer could tell the time thanks to the lines. This design was used in the 5th century with modern pieces using pendulums.

Water clocks gained popularity worldwide through trade, and every region developed its own version of the revolutionary time-telling device. Regions like Persia, India, China, Babylon, and Egypt developed distinct design features that helped the locals tell the time without waiting for the sun to shine. These design elements were further modified over time to get more precise results. For centuries, water clocks remained the most reliable and accurate way of telling time, which is why they were used for over a millennium.

The Development of Calendar Systems around the World

Various calendar systems around the world were developed based on the Sun's position and movement. The solar calendar typically relies on the time it takes the Earth to complete one full rotation around the Sun, which is 365 ¼ days or one year.

Babylonian and Persian Calendars

The Persians have always been curious about the Sun's movement, which led to the design of their calendar using a solar approach. Unlike other cultures that also emphasized the importance of lunisolar and lunar cycles, the Persians and Babylonians only focused on the solar cycle. This focus partly stems from the significance of the folklore "Cyrus the Great" and the holy symbol of the Sun in ancient Persian culture. Ancient Persians devised a calendar based on the movement and observation of the Sun, where one year spanned 360 days. The months were divided based on a lunar cycle, with two to three sections over 30 days.

While no official names were given to the days, every month was designated with the name of a significant festival. To align the seasons with the calendrical system, the Persians added an extra month every six years. Between 650 and 330 BC (the late Achaemenid period), the Empire needed a practical timekeeping system based on ancient Egyptian belief. The most significant days of every month were set aside for the worship of Ahura Mazda, the supreme god of the Zoroastrian religion.

The Egyptian Calendar

Among all cultures and civilizations, the Egyptians were one of the first to devise a calendar based on the Sun's movements and position. According to the Egyptian calendar, one year comprised 365 days, divided into three parts or seasons. Every season spanned approximately 120 days along with an intercalary month. One month comprised 30 days, and four of these months made one season. Collectively, the year was made up of 12 months, which were named after the significant festivals of that time. One month was divided into three "decans," each decan comprising ten days. In the past, royal artisans and merchants enjoyed the last two days of every decan to be off-duty and relax, which is perceived as the modern form of the weekend.

Initially, ancient Egyptians divided one year into 13 months based on the solar cycle. Like the modern calendar, the Egyptian calendrical system had 365 days as one year, unlike the Gregorian system, where one year was 365 ¼ days. This system resulted in the loss of one entire day every four years. Over time, the concept of "Leap Day" was introduced, where an extra day was added to the fourth year to compensate for the loss. However, climatic and natural observations made by experts led to the modern version of the calendar system that is considered the most accurate calendar of all.

The Greek Calendar

Ancient Greek scholars devised different calendar systems based on the understandings and ideals of every region. Among all these, the Athenian calendar is the most popular design to date. The Athenians devised their calendar based on the position of the Moon and the Sun, known as the lunisolar year system. Every 12 lunar cycles in order were regarded as one year, with the No Moon and Full Moon being the start and end of each phase, respectively. Depending on a cycle's duration, one month was considered as either 29 days or 30 days alternately.

In the beginning, the Athenian calendar only had 12 months. Over time, it added a 13th month to the year. The 13 months in order were called Hekatombaion, Metageitnion, Boedromion, Pyanepsion, Maimakterion, Poseidon I, Poseidon II, Gamelion, Anthesterion, Elaphebolion, Munychion, Thargelion, and Skirophorion. Instead of dividing the entire month into weeks, Greeks divided the period of 29/30 days into three parts, with each part comprising ten days. Every month started with a day named "Noumenia" and ended with a day called "the old and the new." Since the Lunar year and Solar year encompassed 354 days, 8 hours, and 365 days, 5 hours, and 48 minutes, respectively, ancient Greek scholars could not align the calendars based on both systems. To solve this problem, they introduced the 13th month, coined the "embolismic month." Although the calendar was not accurate, it was followed for a long time until specific changes were introduced, and the locals began using the Roman calendar for timekeeping.

The Roman Calendar

The ancient Roman calendar stemmed from the Greek timetable with some modifications rooted in Roman beliefs and learnings. Their calendar was first introduced in the 8th century BCE by Rome's first ruler, Romulus. One year was spread across a period of 304 days and ignored the mid-winter period of 61 days. The 304 days were divided into ten months: Martius, Aprilis, Maius, Junius, Quintilis, Sextilis, September, October, November, and December. Over time, as Numa Pompilius took over Rome, he added the missing 61 days and divided them into two months, called January and February.

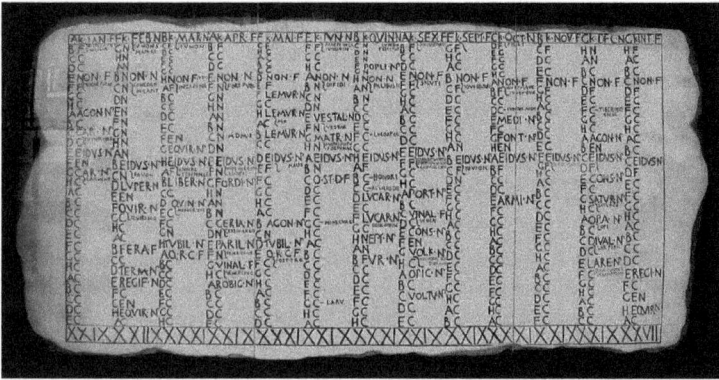

According to Numa, the calendar still failed to adhere to the solar year, which is why he forced the addition of Mercedonus, an extra month in every year. It was added after the 23rd or 24th day of February, thereby pushing the last days of the month even further. In turn, every year ended up having 22 to 23 additional days, which aligned with the concept of a solar year. The Romans were so proud of the timekeeping design that they adorned it on walls and carved its tabular form in stone. The Kalends, the Nones, and the Ides were the three main points of a month, and the days were denoted by names or letters.

The Assyrian Calendar

Compared to other cultures and their calendars, the Assyrian calendar was quite ahead of its time and partly inspired by the Babylonian calendar. It was first recognized in the 1950s, with 4750 BC being the fixed era due to the prominence of the Middle Ubaid period, during which the locals built the first temple at their sacred place, Ashur. Unlike other calendars that mark the beginning of a year around the winter season, the Assyrian calendar starts in the spring. The locals still gather during their New Year's Day and celebrate with food and significant rituals. December 2019 was marked as the Assyrian calendar's 6769th year.

Essentially, if you want to calculate the current Assyrian year, add the number 4750 to the current Gregorian year. This system was used in other parts of the Middle East, such as modern-day Syria, Iraq, Palestine, Lebanon, and Jordan. Every month in this calendar is represented in order by the Month of Happiness, Love, Building, Harvesting, Ripening of Fruits, Sprinkling of Seeds, Giving, Awakening of Buried Seeds, Conceiving, Resting, Flooding, and Evil Spirits. While some months cover 30 days, others can span 29 or 31 days.

Some of these calendar systems vanished with time, yet others were modified and redesigned with modern findings and calculations to devise a precise timekeeping schedule. As you can see, almost every calendar system was designed with similar calculations and holds specks of the modern timekeeping pattern. The calendar we use today was influenced by the past, encompassing many significant learnings based on the movements of the Sun and the Moon.

The Panchanga - Five Limbs of Time

The Panchanga (or the Five Limbs of Time) used in Vedic astrology are significant to Hindu mythology and various cultures. Some astrologers still use the Panchanga system to devise astrological birth charts and determine a person's fate upon birth. The Five Limbs of Time are Tithi (Date), Karan (Half of Tithi), Vaar (Day), Yoga, and Nakshatra (Constellation). Each limb is determined based on every planet's location, movement, and interaction with the Sun and the Moon. Nowadays, astrologers create a tabulated version of each limb to formulate the Panchang and apply it to determine the best days to conduct auspicious celebrations.

Tithi - Date

Every Lunar day in a Hindu calendar is denoted as Tithi. To calculate a Tithi, astrologers observe the Moon's position and alignment with the Sun. When it moves up to 12 degrees to the east, a Tithi is devised. The 15 Tithis in a month are named Pratipada, Dwitiya, Tritiya, Chaturthi, Panchami, Shasthi, Saptami, Ashtami, Navami, Dasami, Ekadasi, Dwadasi, Trayodasi, Chaturdasi, Purnima, and Amavasya (in order). The New Moon or No Moon Day is called Amavasya, which occurs when the Sun and the Moon's longitudes align. These Tithis represent one day each within a fortnight, covering 15 days in a month.

The first Tithi occurs during the Moon's waxing phase and is referred to as the Pratipada Thithi. As the Moon shifts away from the Sun, it positions itself at a 180-degree linear point, marking the Full Moon or Purnima. The length of every Tithi varies due to the Moon and Sun's changing speeds and locations. While some Tithis are calculated as less than 22 hours, others can stretch up to 26 hours.

Karan

The half of a Tithi, a Karan, is calculated when the Moon moves up to 6 degrees from the Sun. It is divided into two categories, Sthira (fixed) and Charan (movable). With this, one month comprises 30 Tithis and 60 Karans. The first seven movable Karans are called Bava, Balava, Kaulava, Taitula, Garija, Vanija, and Visti, and the four fixed Karans are named Sakuna, Chatushpada, Naga, and Kimstughna. As the month passes, each Karan occurs in order and ends with a Tithi.

A person born under a specific Karan will display distinct characteristics throughout their life. Like a Tithi is determined to proceed with an auspicious ceremony, a Karan is also calculated to find the right "Muhurta" or time. While people use Tithis to determine a favorable hour or day, a Karan can help decipher a person's personality. The movable Karans occur almost eight times in a lunar cycle or one month. On the other hand, fixed Karans are constant and are generally considered inauspicious.

Vaar - Day

One Vaar or day is calculated as 24 hours, totaling seven Vaars in a week. Every hour is one Hora. As the sun rises, a Vaar starts and ends with another sunrise. The seven Vaars are named after the ruling planet of each day, namely Sunday, Monday, Tuesday, Wednesday, Thursday, Friday, and Saturday, named after Sun, Mercury (or the Moon in some cases), Venus, Earth, Mars, Jupiter, and Saturn, respectively. In the Hindu calendar, the Vaars are called Ravivaar, Somvaar, Mangalvaar, Budhvaar, Guruvaar, Shukravaar, and Shanivaar.

Since the Sun is located at the center and governs all other planets, the first Vaar of a week starts with Sunday or Ravivaar. This system shows why the first Hora is significant to the Sun. While the Moon, Venus, Jupiter, and Mercury project a mild and kind temperament to their respective Vaars, the Sun, Saturn, and Mars can be harsh and cruel. The former planets allow you to execute auspicious activities, whereas the other planets provide strength and the opportunity to accomplish difficult feats. The 7 Vaars are universal and are used to delimit today's working calendar.

Nakshatra - Constellation

Nakshatras are Lunar constellations that cover the sky's 360-degree spread. With each constellation covering 13.20 degrees, the entire sky totals 27 Nakshatras. In specific order, they are called Ashwini, Bharani, Krittika, Rohini, Mrigasira, Aarudra, Punarvasu, Pushya, Aslesha, Magha, Purva Phalguni, Uttara Phalguni, Hasta, Chitra, Swati, Vishakha, Anuradha, Jyestha, Moola, Poorvashada, Uttarashada, Sravana, Dhanishta, Satabisha, Poorva Bhadrapada, Uttara Bhadrapada, and Revati. Every Nakshatra is housed in four quarters or Padas, which collectively cover 20 minutes and 3 degrees.

Every constellation represents a particular deity, gemstone, color, and Lord or planet. Astrologers study the Padas, Rashis, and Nakshatras to determine the most favorable times for conducting celebrations, moving to a new house, getting married, or starting a business.

Yoga

When the Sun and the Moon separate, their distance is measured over specific periods to determine the Yoga. Formally known as Nithya Yoga, this limb is calculated by adding the Sun and Moon's longitude and dividing it by 13.20. The 27 Yogas identified in Vedic astrology are Vishkambha, Preeti, Ayushman, Saubhagya, Shobhana, Atiganda, Sukarma, Dhriti, Shoola, Ganda, Vriddhi, Dhruva, Vyaghata, Harshana, Vajra, Siddhi, Vyatipata, Variyana, Parigha, Shiva, Siddha, Sadhya, Shubha, Shukla, Brahma, Indra, and Vaidhriti.

Nine of the Yogas are deemed inauspicious, which is when people refrain from celebrations or acquiring new possessions. Among the 18 remaining Yogas, each entity represents a different aspect of life. While some symbolize health and happiness, others stand for growth, success, and splendor. In some versions of Vedic astrology, the Yogas are defined according to the rising and setting time of the Sun, which can affect a person's fate and bring changes to their personality when they are born.

The Five Limbs are not just significant to a person's birth. They also mark auspicious dates for starting a new business, getting married, or harvesting crops during peak season. Some astrologers devise the Panchang so that the person can also be wary of the inauspicious hours or days to avoid any celebration. These include Lagna Pravesh charts, Varjyam, Durmuhurtham, and Rahukalam, which are based on the movement of specific planets and their locations within the active houses.

Chapter 3: Vedic Astrology and the Sun

In Hindu and Vedic astrology, the Sun is the source of livelihood and the main energy of the cosmos. Since it is the essence of living, it is considered the most powerful body of all, especially in Hindu mythology and Vedic astrology. Since Vedic astrologers still devise natal charts based on the Sun's movement, many people hold this unique celestial body in high regard.

The Sun in the Exaltation and Debilitation State According to Vedic Astrology

The position of the Sun in a horoscope varies from person to person, determined by the time of their birth. While some charts display an exalted Sun, others portray a debilitated planet. An exalted Sun is the strongest and exudes a powerful personality. The Sun sits in every zodiac sign for one month. It takes one year for the Sun to complete a full zodiac cycle and transit from one sign to another in different directions. For example, it moves in the northern direction (Uttarayan) when transitioning from Capricorn to Gemini. When moving towards the southern direction (Dakshinayan), it shifts from Cancer to Sagittarius. When it moves from one sign to another, it triggers seasonal changes as well.

Every zodiac sign plays a singular role in the changing seasons and differences in natural phenomena. For instance, while the inhibition of Aquarius and Capricorn by the Sun brings the winter season, Gemini and Taurus bring summer. The Sun's position in each zodiac sign represents the native's sun sign and can be depicted in their natal chart. The Sun can also change houses within a single zodiac sign, which can threaten the native's well-being.

The Sun and Leo

Every zodiac sign conjoins with one solitary planet in its house. In Vedic astrology, the Sun sits in the house of Leo to form a powerful entity. When the native has Leo as their zodiac sign with the Sun in its house, they tend to display strong personality traits and be well-respected in society. They can be stubborn but are quite dynamic and forceful, especially when making important decisions. They will likely be blessed with comfort and easy life. They attract immense wealth and are filled with knowledge. Also, they do not like following orders and prefer to be independent.

The Sun and Aries (Exaltation)

As mentioned, an exalted Sun displays signs of dominance, dynamism, and strength. The natives are powerful, courageous, and possess the ability to become leaders. Aries, the first zodiac sign in the series, exalts the Sun and makes it more powerful. This conjunction can greatly benefit the native. Even though the person does not wish to become the center of attention, they will still be under the spotlight thanks to their exceptional potential and skills.

The Sun and Libra (Debilitation)

Libra weakens the Sun's position and affects the natives' personal and professional lives. They may not be as successful in their careers and will likely lack effective decision-making skills. They are also prone to developing eye or skin problems, some of which are untreatable.

While a debilitated Sun is considered inauspicious, an afflicted Sun is even worse. Natives with an afflicted Sun are often ignored and never get credit for the work they do. Rahu, Ketu,

Saturn, and Mars are the main planets responsible for the malefic effects and weaken a native's horoscope.

The Sun in Different Houses

As mentioned in Vedic astrology, the Sun sits in every zodiac sign's house for one month. In essence, the Sun displays the best results in almost every house. However, it can get slightly weak when entering the 4th and 7th house. The effects are aggravated when the Sun comes in contact with a weak or bad planet. As the Sun moves through the twelve houses, it projects varying effects on the native. While some are blessed with the Sun's benefic effects, others may suffer from its malefic consequences.

1st House

When the Sun is in the 1st house, the native will likely be born early in the morning. They will be tall, lean, and short-haired. Since the Sun's presence is strong in this first house, the native will be independent, strong, and possess great leadership skills. They will be stubborn, refusing to take a "no" for an answer. They will have a healthy heart, strong bones, and great overall physical health. The native is strong-willed and has excellent management skills as well. On the other hand, they may suffer from eye diseases and will probably endure a turbulent childhood.

2nd House

Individuals with the Sun in the 2nd house in their horoscope typically portray a fierce and stubborn nature. They often get into quarrels and debates. They may not be close to their family, and likely won't inherit ancestral property. The natives are directly related to the 8th house, the House of Death – and accounts for why they are blessed with longer lives. Like the first house, the natives in the second house may face adversities during childhood, specifically due to poverty and improper living conditions. These conditions can also stress and weaken them from an early age.

3rd House

As one of the most powerful placements, the Sun in the 3rd house makes for creative, strong, courageous, and confident individuals. They are inseparable from their family and will go to great lengths to protect their loved ones. Achieving wealth, fame, and respect will be some of their major achievements. They are stronger than their enemies and always win. They can communicate well and are fond of traveling. All their adventures and experiences make them wiser and more knowledgeable. In light of this, they must pursue a career in a domain related to publishing, communication, design, or public speaking. The native is at peace and enjoys their life to the fullest.

4th House

People with the Sun in this house are blessed with good memory and intelligence. They are directly related to the 10th house, so they can steadily climb up the ladder and attain higher positions in society. They work hard and believe the fruits of their labor will be visible later in life, which strengthens the core belief of delayed gratification. At some point, the native may face a major financial burden due to the loss of a vehicle, land, or house. Despite achieving success, they will constantly remain anxious due to life uncertainties and difficult childhood.

5th House

The native possesses a sharp mind but is often prone to anger. It can be difficult for them to control their temper. That said, their intelligence and sharp memory help them excel academically. Raj Yoga takes place in this house and is necessary to achieve a meaningful educational background, helping them gain an edge over their competitors. In turn, the native has a higher chance of gaining fame and becoming wealthy. The Sun manifests talent and skills, which also boosts their confidence and productivity. If the native is not careful, they may also develop overconfidence, which can be the starting point of their demise.

6th House

One of the boldest groups of all, the 6th house natives, is fierce, courageous, and physically fit. They are not afraid of their enemies and can easily spot or capture them. This phenomenon is known as "Shatruhanta Yoga," which translates to "conqueror of the enemy." With a steady life force, they can even fight diseases with ease. The Sun in this position can compel them to spend more money, *most of which is unnecessary*. The natives are unable to record their expenditures due to their questionable spending habits. Typically, the natives of the 6th house are good-looking and tend to live a comfortable life.

7th House

When the Sun is in the 7th house, the native is blessed with courage, strength, and a sharp mind. They can overcome adversities and bounce back stronger thanks to their diligence. By contrast, they can exhibit egoistic and stubborn personalities. The repercussions are visible in their marriage as they are unable to balance their personal and professional lives. Jealousy and ego also play a major role in the weakening of their relationships. Natives are often stressed and anxious. They worry about their reputation and cannot stand the idea of being publicly humiliated. A debilitated Sun can also delay the native's marriage.

8th House

The natives in this house are very curious about mystical wisdom and divert their attention toward psychic matters. This curiosity leads many to pursue careers in the occult science of astrology. They can be careless and fight over trivial matters. Natives are often found talking alone or arguing with others. Their minds are unstable, resulting in poor judgment and decision-making. A debilitated Sun can induce heart diseases and stomach-related issues – leading to a shorter lifespan. The native can also be skilled in a medical profession, which can be helpful in the future. They are highly supportive and try to help others as much as they can.

9th House

The natives in this house display signs of confidence, courage, ambition, and diligence. They are supportive and helpful individuals. The Sun's energy is strong in the 9th house, which makes them honest and virtuous. They are inclined toward spiritual energies and practice yoga or breathing exercises to tap into their authentic selves. With their helpful nature, they often partake in volunteering activities and social organizations to benefit the underprivileged. The best professions for natives are in domains such as the law, teaching, and spiritual practice. They love traveling as it feeds their hungry and curious souls.

10th House

Natives in this house want to be the center of attention in every room they step in. They will likely achieve success due to their resilience and courage and will attract fame and wealth. Their work ethic and efficiency make them the star of their workplace and inculcate leadership qualities. These career-oriented natives can become skillful managers and politicians. They want to help others and contribute to society. Many are driven by this instinct, which ultimately becomes their main motto in life. The position of the Sun in the 10th house is one of the most important placements of all due to its versatility.

11th House

The natives support truth and honesty. They are blessed with abundant knowledge and virtue. If the Sun is in an exalted position, the native will likely acquire success and fame at a young age. They respect themselves and others around them. They believe in spirituality and indulge in yoga during their free time, which is also the secret behind their strength, happiness, and exemplary well-being. Stepping into the business world is a great move as they will likely gain success as entrepreneurs. Their sources of income will be steady. However, as they age, they may develop multiple diseases and lose their stamina.

12th House

The Sun's position in the 12th house can make the native irritable, lazy, and easygoing. They often blurt out their opinions without thinking about the consequences. Their main areas of interest include paramedical science, psychic and occult studies. They are directly linked to the 6th house, which can cause harm to their enemies. Despite their friendliness, natives may not share a strong bond with their friends and loved ones. They are often perceived as indifferent and careless. As they age, they may face issues with their income and expenditure and will likely develop eye issues. However, the native will live a peaceful life and ignore all worries.

Significance of the Sun in Vedic Astrology

The Sun represents vitality, health, power, authority, soul, well-being, and ego in Vedic astrology. These concepts and values collectively define a person's soul, displaying both negative and positive traits. This is why the Sun is known as the "Atmakaraka" in Vedic astrology. The body represents our soul in its most authentic manner. Ancient worshippers offered prayers and the Sun God's favorite items during auspicious celebrations and festivals to please him. He was called "Surya Bhagwan" or "Surya Dev," Some of the festivals celebrated in his name were Samba Dashami, Makar Sankranti, and Chhath Puja. Until today, many believers still celebrate these festivals across India to please Surya Bhagwan and manifest his energy.

Nowadays, the Sun God is glorified as the main deity of many temples across India. Some of these famous temples are the Modhera Sun temple in Gujarat and the Konark Sun temple in Odisha. While other cultures view the Sun as a star, Vedic astrology calls it a planet due to its effects and repercussions on humans. In the Hindu religion, astrologers determine the Sun's position to mark its exact location in a person's horoscope. When drawing up their natal birth chart, they also determine the person's future based on the Sun's strength. If the planet is in an ideal position and exhibits strong traits, the person will be blessed with a smooth career and steady relationships. They will also have a firmer say in their personal and professional lives and will likely become leaders.

The Sun in Vimshottari Dasha

While we've already explained the Sun's significance in Vedic astrology in a previous chapter, it's important to know some lesser-known facts about the god's position in Hindu mythology. According to Hindu myths, the Sun God lived in a kingdom called Suryaloka and governed other deities. Despite being strong and powerful, the Sun is easily eclipsed by Rahu and Ketu.

On average, a person lives for 120 years. During this time, their lives are governed by the malefic and benefic effects of the nine planets, known as the "Vimshottari Dasha" or Vimshottari system. The system is further broken down into periods that determine the native's fate. The main phase is called "Mahadasha." When the Sun rules the native's Mahadasha period, they experience a phase called "Surya Mahadasha," a period lasting six years.

Every minute of a person's life is associated with a ruling planet, which helps them determine their next move. During the Sun's presence in the native's Dasha calculations, the celestial body becomes potent and establishes dominance over their life. This helps the native become socially adept and attract wealth. They are blessed with a steady source of income and can climb up the societal ladder with ease. If the Sun is placed in unfavorable houses, it can produce malefic effects such as financial losses, public humiliation, and health conditions.

The Sun as the King and Father of the Cosmic Kingdom

The fact that the Sun is stationary in the solar system while governing other planets that revolve around it showcases its significance in the cosmic kingdom. The Sun's authoritative power and masculine influence help the government or any other higher organization of the kingdom. Although the Sun manifests our soul's energy and is deeply connected to our innermost self, it still inspires us to take action and strengthen our outer shield to reach success and build a name for ourselves.

With this strength, you can overcome all shortcomings and pave the path toward your goals. Other planets respect the Sun's regal status and follow its instructions. It is the natural father of all living creatures and ensures their well-being and vitality. If your horoscope displays a strong Sun in your favor, you may possess exceptional leadership skills, be well-respected in society, and be given a higher role to portray. Individuals with a strong Sun tend to have strong bonds with their father and brother. Moreover, they will likely display signs of maturity, generosity, and dependability, especially toward the opposite gender.

On the other hand, the Sun's weak placement can affect your physical health to a major extent. Ailments like cardiovascular disease, weak eyesight, baldness, weak bones, and poor blood circulation are common with a weak Sun in one's horoscope. People may also experience a deteriorating bond with their father or any other important masculine figure in their life. What's more, natives can also suffer in their professional lives because of low self-esteem or confidence. They can be indecisive, which can affect their projects and stance within an entity. By contrast, a strong placement of the Sun can result in overly exaggerated characteristics like aggression, egoism, and even narcissism.

The Sun's Relation to the Moon in the Zodiac

In essence, the Sun sign represents a person's outer self and personality, whereas the Moon sign symbolizes their soul and inner avatar. Since they collectively represent a person's identity, the two signs are important in the zodiac system. The way both signs combine and thrive in unison determines your presence, character, and well-being. Like the Moon and the Sun co-exist in the universe, they also govern other planets and natives in harmony. However, you can still spot some rare occurrences where the Sun blocks the Moon's light and eclipses it and vice versa.

The relevance of this relationship stems from lunar phases. If both bodies sit in opposite signs, a person born under the Full Moon may be motivated to accomplish their goal or complete important missions. Ideally, both bodies trump every other aspect in our natal charts and are the primary decision-makers of our fates. The Sun governs our life's motion and supervises our progress, while the Moon ensures that we lead a secure and comfortable life. These opposing forces steer our overall well-being.

However, this can also mean that the opposing forces may create an internal conflict and confuse the native. The main interaction between both bodies depends on the varying phases of the Moon and the Sun's position. The relationship is devised in an individual's natal chart during birth. Even a minor change in the waxing or waning phase of the Moon can change a person's life, which makes us all unique and gives everyone their own "soli-lunar signature."

Chapter 4: The Conjunction of the Sun

As everyone knows, astrology allows us to track the relationships and movements between the planets and all other celestial bodies. We then use this information to analyze how these bodies affect our daily lives and our emotions, thoughts, and behaviors. If you've been reading about astrology for quite some time now, chances are you've stumbled across terms such as "square" and "trine" while looking up the description and influence of the planets. These dynamic, fast-changing correspondences are known as "aspects." In astrology, there are five major planetary aspects. They play a significant role in our understanding of how the planets and celestial bodies affect us.

So, what exactly are the aspects? When planets move through the sky in the zodiac wheel, they form angles with each other. Aspects are the description of these angles, and they all mean different things. We know that each planet rules over a specific area of our lives, and we realize that each body has acquired its own distinctive personality over time. However, how they affect us as individuals is determined by their location in the zodiac and their relationships with one another. These relationships, as mentioned, are called aspects. The five major aspects of astrology are conjunction (the topic of this chapter), sextile, opposition, square, and trine. Aspects, in short, are the behavior of the planets when they're present in different signs. It represents how each person takes general action or receives things during that time.

For instance, if two planets in the zodiac wheel are at a 0°, or close to 0°, angle of each other, this would qualify as *conjunction*. If they're at a 60° angle, then it's a sextile. To form a square, they'd have to be at a 90° angle and at 120° to form a trine. If two planets sit directly opposite each other, forming a 180° angle, this would be opposition. Every angle and aspect holds a different meaning. You can take a look at your birth chart to see a visual representation of these degrees.

Some of the five major aspects, like opposition and square, are known as hard aspects. Hard aspects bring along the more unpleasant areas of life, like struggles and challenges. The easy, or sometimes known as soft, aspects are generally positive. They handle the gentler, more favorable areas of life. The sextile and trine are considered easy aspects. A conjunction, however, doesn't belong to one or the other. The planets involved in a conjunction determine its tendency to go in either direction. Still, keep in mind that the involved planets are the real indicators, even with hard and easy aspects. Sometimes, a trine will not be in your favor, while a hard square will provide a helping hand. Expect every planetary Rendezvous to look a little different.

Needless to say, aspects are one of the basic elements of interpretations in astrology. They have the power to change each planetary placement's meaning and influence, which is why you cannot interpret just one planet in a single sign. You must also account for the other energies. Notice if two planets are co-existing harmoniously in conjunction or sitting exasperatingly in a frustrating square. Take Venus as an example. Venus is universally known as the planet of love. There are several positive nuances tied to this planet in general. However, if it's in an unfavorable aspect with Saturn, this may indicate that some difficulties will spiral in your love life.

There are various other aspects that astrologers account for in their interpretations. If you think about it, planets can exist in endless angles, creating infinite aspects. However, grasping a deeper understanding of these five major aspects is a great place to start.

As we hinted above, this chapter delves into conjunctions as an aspect. We won't be exploring just any conjunction, though. We will be exclusively exploring the conjunction of the Sun with the other planets in the same sign. You will begin to understand what makes this a very powerful astrological phenomenon and learn how it affects the various areas of your life.

What Is a Conjunction?

Since a conjunction occurs when two planets align at the same (or nearly the same) location, this aspect describes what happens when the energies of two different points or bodies blend and unite. These two points can be luminary bodies, such as Lilith and Chiron, or planets, like Earth and Jupiter. While they are not planets by definition, the Sun and the Moon do count as well.

From where we see it, points in conjunction appear to move together. They lie within the same zodiac sign, blend their energies, and act and move as one combined force. However, you still need to remember that not all blended energies are harmonious. Being in conjunction doesn't mean that two points are instantly compatible. While some of them, like Venus and the Moon, will cooperate, others like Mars and Neptune will not work together in conjunction. This is because the Moon's focus on feelings and Venus's association with love allows them to work in unison. Meanwhile, Neptune's dreamy and fantastical tendencies disrupt Mars's need for strong competition and action.

Why Does It Matter?

By understanding the locations of the planets on your birth chart, you will gather deeper insight into the universal forces that impact your personality the most. You will also be able to identify all your strongest and weakest points. Finding out which planets or bodies were in conjunction at the time of your birth can help you understand the areas of your life toward which you're most likely to direct your focus and motivation. To help you get a clearer picture, let's say Neptune, whose energy is associated with creativity, and Mercury, which is linked to communication, were both in conjunction at your birth. This would mean that you're skilled at expressing your creative ideas. It also suggests that pursuing a career in science or statistical work would put all your talents to waste.

Solar Conjunct

The celestial bodies that interact with the Sun at the time of our birth impact who we are. Its unmatchable glare makes it impossible for us to observe the planets for a few weeks, as they remain in conjunction with the sun. Harmonious unisons make way for positive changes and events. Meanwhile, the harder gatherings may pose new challenges for you, urging you to overcome several blockages.

Sun and Moon

If the Sun and the Moon were in conjunction during your birth, you might feel like you have emotionally intense and potent willpower. You can express yourself confidently, knowing that you can back and support your arguments with deep-rooted foundations. You have a heightened sense of self, making you a very subjective person; you may find it hard to relate to others or step into their shoes. You are likely a double of the zodiac that the conjunction occurs in. You are typically happy and confident in your abilities with a harmonious sextile or trine. You feel comfortable with who you are, which makes you easy to be around and form relationships with. On the other hand, you may have to deal with inner suffering if you have the challenging opposition and square. Your needs and wants can be conflicting, which makes you easily frustrated, very moody, and restless.

Sun and Mercury

These two celestial points are never more than 28° apart, creating the only conjunction. Your mind is most likely in alignment with your physical self, as Mercury is an avid interpreter for the fundamental solar drives. You probably have a natural inclination for storytelling, communication through art, music, movement (everything non-verbal), gestures, writing, and expressing your views. Since these bodies are so closely orbed, you may have a talkative, energetic personality.

Sun and Venus

Venus generally moves near the Sun, making its only solar aspect conjunction. If Venus accompanies your Sun, others may perceive you as a radiant, friendly individual. If your birth chart shows close conjunction, you may be very skilled at bringing out the beauty in various things, as well as sharing all positive aspects of life with others. You tactfully seek everything that brings you joy, pleasure and is art-related.

Sun and Mars

If this conjunction is present in your birth chart, you are probably a very energetic individual. You are dedicated when it comes to chasing your goals. You like to seize all opportunities on the spot. This conjunction, sextile, and trine show that you like to act in the heat of the moment, which makes you a rather successful person. You like to live on the edge and embrace life with open arms. You're probably over-scheduled, considering that you never say no to anything that comes your way. However, you may be prone to frustration, impulsive outbursts, anger, and rage, with a tense, hostile square. Since it can be hard to keep this intensity under control, you should consider focusing your energy on sports and physical activities.

Sun and Jupiter

If you have this combination in your birth chart, you're probably a lively, flamboyant person. You are innately generous and giving, making you an inspiring figure. You're an optimist at heart who believes in the future and all that it has in store – which can enhance your luck, further increasing your faith in the flow of things. You may also experience abundance in terms of wealth. If you have the opposition or square, you may have overly ambitious thoughts and beliefs. You may think that you can receive all the good things in life without putting in real effort. That said, if you match your innate fine attitude with self-discipline, you will finally defeat your inclination to go with the flow of life.

Sun and Saturn

If your Sun is in conjunction with Saturn, you are probably easily self-motivated. You may carry stress and pressures that only you can relieve by putting in adequate effort (as perceived by you). The trine, sextile, and conjunction of these bodies can help pave the way for you to find a basis for your natural gifts. You're generally a realist who can formulate plans to help you achieve your goals. You are a hard-working individual with high conscientiousness. You tend to set very high-performance standards for yourself, have a strong personality, and are not afraid to take on responsibilities. If you are saddled by opposition, you may feel overly burdened and weighed down. Feelings of failure may never leave you alone. However, this is something you can power through if you work hard and tolerate the frustrations.

Sun and Uranus

People with their Sun in conjunction with Uranus are blessed with an eccentric aura. Conjunction, as well as other harmonies like the sextile and trine, can make them seemingly brilliant. They are risk-takers who insist on following their unique paths. You always stand out, no matter what you choose to do. Your innovative and brilliant ideas can bring groups alive. If you have the less fortunate aspects, keep in mind that you are more likely to experience accidents, partake in high-risk behavior, and suffer from relentlessness and poor judgment.

Sun and Neptune

You are probably a very charming, almost magical individual if your birth chart's harmonies contain the combination of the Sun and Neptune. You consider your imagination one of the real world's forces, making you an artist or a dreamer. You can bring your thoughts to life, which makes you amazing at what you do. You can be very warm and giving, especially to people who seem to have lost their way, making you a memorable person and even the perfect fit for the art of healing. If you have the more challenging squares or opposition, you may end up losing sight of your own way and purpose early on.

Sun and Pluto

The harmonious aspects may impart a sense of presence, awareness, and intensity. You can easily spot out hidden information and find positivity in the things other people typically avoid. You can spiral intense emotions in those around you and have great self-confidence. You believe that people can evolve into new and improved versions of themselves. If this combination is prominent in the harder aspects, you may have an issue with power struggles. You may also feel the need to defend yourself, which can be draining. You will experience phases of destruction before you allow yourself to be renewed.

Planetary Combustion

At different points throughout the year, planets may not be visible in the sky as the Sun falls in front of them, masking them with its blazing energies. This phenomenon is called combustion and is quite a significant event in Vedic astrology. It's also one of the most difficult ones as it destroys the planets' intents and reveals their darker energies. Planetary combustion typically occurs when a planet is 2° to 3° away from the Sun, which makes sense, considering anything that gets too close to the sun ultimately gets burnt.

Vedic astrology assigns a specific distance, in degrees, to each planet. This indicates the distance at which they would combust. If the distance between the Moon and the Sun falls below 12°, the Moon would be combusted. Mars will be combusted if the distance between it and the Sun reaches below 17°. Mercury would be combusted if the distance hits below 14° and would combust at below 12° if it's in retrograde motion. If the distance is below 11°, Jupiter would be combusted. Venus would combust below 10° and under 8° if in retrograde. Finally, Saturn would combust if it hit below 15°.

Keep in mind that ancient texts include a lot of inaccurate information. This is why the majority of modern-day astrologers don't entirely trust these Vedic combustion parameters. According to today's modern research and observations, any planet will start to combust if the distance hits below 10°. If the distance becomes even shorter, at 1°, 3°, or even 5°, the planet would be officially combusted or burned. However, this is a widely controversial topic, considering that planets like Venus and Mercury are always found close to the Sun. Whether Venus and Mercury fall under the entire combustion concept is debatable.

Those two planets can get burned if they wander too close to the sun. However, they are still generally used to its heat. If they are 1° to 4° away, they will get combusted. If any planet in the zodiac becomes combusted by the Sun regardless of its initial qualities, it will lose all of its positive qualities. This means that all benevolent planets will become malicious, and the originally malicious ones will become even more detrimental. This, of course, is the case when no remedial placements are present in the zodiac.

A combusted planet can become entirely negative only if:

- It is weak in Shadbal
- It is present in a debilitated sign
- It is losing its strength in D-9

- It is below Paap Kartari yoga.

Some salvaging factors can allow planets to perform positively in the zodiac, even when they're combusted. These include:

- A combusted planet that's receiving strong benefic elements.
- Some planets, such as Mercury, Jupiter, and Venus, are highly benefic. Their beneficial elements can relieve some of the adversities of combustions.
- A combusted planet that sits in its own sign or in exaltation one in the zodiac.
- The planet can survive and will not strongly impact a certain area of your life.
- A combusted planet that occupies a house where it receives directional strength.
- The benefic planet can receive a sense of relief.
- A combusted planet that's in retrograde.
- Planets in retrograde are generally very powerful.
- A combusted planet that has good divisional chart placements, like D-60 and D-9, and is exalted.

The planet should not be weak in Shadbal for any of these alleviating factors to work.

Auspicious Yogas

According to Vedic astrology, any planet that's placed in an astrology house generates a specific outcome when it's in contact with another planet.

Raj Rajeshwar Yoga

When the Sun is in Pisces, the Raj Rajeshwar Yoga is created. Jupiter and the Moon then exist in their own sign in the natal chart, generating a solid Raj yoga. Anyone with this yoga in their natal chart has a warm and quiet personality, like the Sun and Moon, respectively. These individuals are most likely creative, respectful, and powerful. They may occupy administrative positions.

Bhaskar Yoga

When the Moon is in the 11th house away from Mercury, Mercury is in the 2nd house from the Sun, and Jupiter is in either the 9th or 5th house from the Moon, the Bhaskar Yoga situation is created. This is not a very common sight to see on a natal chart, making whoever possesses this placement an extraordinary individual. Blessed with abundance, love, and various qualities, their character will be prosperous.

Budhaditya Yoga

Because Mercury is near the Sun, it blends with it often. This powerful yoga can halt any malefic intentions of a house in a zodiac. Like Raj Yoga, Budhaditya Yoga makes brave, insightful individuals, earning them the regard and respect of the public. They are also likely to experience financial prosperity.

Vaasi Yoga

Vaasi Yoga is created whenever the Moon is in the 12th house from the Sun. Depending on how close the planets are to the Sun, this yoga can help either manifest through malicious or benefic outcomes. However, it's worth mentioning that its beneficial aspects are a lot less likely to show. In these rare instances, the individual may be sharp-minded, assertive, capable, and knowledgeable. Otherwise, while the person may be blessed with a great memory, they may face countless obstacles and may lack benevolence.

Veshi Yoga

This yoga occurs when any planet, other than the moon, exists in the 2nd house from the Sun. Like Vaasi Yoga, the proximity of the planet indicates whether there are malicious or beneficial outcomes. If a positive planet occupies the house, the individual is likely to have an appealing, attractive character. They are respectful and may hold social or political occupations. Negative placements may result in financial and business-related challenges.

Ultimately, there are various elements to consider when determining how the Sun and the other planets affect our personality. The Sun's various interactions with the different celestial bodies can leave a great impact on our lives. Now you know how the different aspects, conjunctions, and yogas affect you and everyone around you.

Chapter 5: Medical Astrology and the Sun

Medicine and astrology have had a deep-rooted connection for centuries. Ancient medical practitioners in Egypt, China, and India referred to a person's horoscope and located the position of every planet to diagnose underlying issues and ensure proper health for the patient. As the word spread across the globe, Europe joined the bandwagon of medical astrology during the medieval period, specifically around 1450-1700. They took inspiration from Arab medical astrologers and devised their own system to treat patients. In essence, several domains depended on astrology or established a symbiotic relationship to function. The medical domain, in particular, heavily depended on horoscopes, zodiac signs, and planetary movements to diagnose and treat health conditions.

Medical Aspects in Vedic Astrology

Medical astrology is considered a vital branch of Vedic astrology and has proven an effective diagnostic tool to cure diseases. Medical astrology focuses on diagnosing symptoms that lead to diseases and curing them to safeguard a person's life for a longer period. The key was to dig deeper and find the crux of the problem. Upon treating the root cause, the disease could be permanently eradicated, and the person may live a longer life. Any kind of accident or affliction caused by planetary movements may affect the native's health.

A medical astrologer finds the underlying cause of a disease by reading the native's birth chart and locating the Sun's position. Interpreting the birth chart helps them determine the person's strengths, weaknesses, approach towards health, nutritional deficiencies, and the ability to fight certain diseases. Although this process takes time, the results are quite accurate. This analysis also helps the practitioner prepare a diet chart or devise predictive methods to diminish the effects of the disease in question and approach the issue with a holistic mindset. While every planet's affliction indicates a specific disease or an issue in a specific body part, general sickness can mean that the planets are transiting in the houses and zodiac signs.

Remedial astrology is a holistic approach towards healing. It involves the practical approach or science of healing and the study of the planets and their movements in natal charts. The benefits of remedial and medical astrology are gaining traction across the globe. Medical practitioners believe that a person's treatment can be made more effective by treating the soul. Internal healing is the key to a long and healthy life, which is what medical astrology is all about. According to medical astrology, any disease or health issue should be recognized before the symptoms appear, giving the practitioner enough time to understand the problem and treat it at the core.

If the practitioner waits for the signs or symptoms to manifest, the body may be already infected with the disease, making treatment more difficult.

Medical astrologers established links between the planets and their respective organs for better reference. Planets afflict drugs, diseases, and organs, whereas zodiac signs monitor general body parts. This makes astrology a comprehensive system that governs our body and health with multiple entities in action.

This list details the ruling celestial bodies with their concerned body parts:

- **Sun:** Heart
- **Moon:** Ovaries
- **Mercury:** Respiratory System
- **Venus:** Kidneys and Reproductive System
- **Mars:** Arteries, Muscles, Hair, Nails, Teeth, and Reproductive System
- **Jupiter:** Liver
- **Saturn:** Skeleton, Bones, Skin, and Veins
- **Uranus:** Nerves, Brain, and Endocrine System
- **Neptune:** Endocrine System
- **Pluto:** Testes

Similarly, all 12 zodiac signs represent different body parts and organs. If their corresponding planets are afflicted during the conjunction, they can show signs of specific diseases or symptoms of general sickness. And while many scholars saw this association of planets and zodiac signs with organs and body parts as pure dogmas, several cultures have used logic to underpin the innuendos. According to one argument, the planets' physical characteristics can be compared to the relevant body parts to find similarities and prove the validity of the association. For example, the heat and redness emitted by Mars explain its relevance in blood circulation, muscles, and arteries.

Over time, the negative energies of planets were perceived as projections of disease and illness. If a planet failed to sit in the right house or was poorly positioned, the negative manifestation was depicted in the form of a prevalence of a disease, which had to be treated as soon as possible. Typically, a medical astrologer diagnoses a disease by preparing the patient's chart and comparing it with their birth chart. The signs and symptoms were noted to establish an approximate date of the disease's onset. During the process, astrologers found relevance between the disease and the underlying negative energies of the planets.

The Sun's Relation with the Heart

As we know, the Sun represents health and vitality. Every planet represents and governs different body parts. If a planet's position is weak, the native may incur health issues related to the body part in question. The Sun represents the heart, and its affliction can indicate a serious cardiovascular condition. It is a natural Atmakaraka that energizes the body and promotes good health. The huge star is the central governing body of the solar system, just like the heart that pumps and supplies blood to the rest of the body to carry out vital functions. When the Sun is away from the malefic effects of Rahu and Saturn, it indicates good health and overall well-being. This is why the Sun is known as the "Lord of the Heart." Alongside this, the Sun also represents the spinal cord, bone structure, stomach, brain, gallbladder, and eyes.

In parallel, the Sun monitors our digestive system and regulates blood circulation. It ensures that our body gets proper nourishment through the food we eat. Since the heart is responsible for supplying nutrients and oxygen across the body, the Sun's malefic effect can negatively affect the heart, resulting in poor blood circulation.

The Sun's Afflictions in Natal Charts

In Vedic astrology, "affliction" means negative contribution or association. When a planet is afflicted in a natal chart, it may negatively affect the native's life. Note that a weak planet is different from an afflicted planet. When the planet is weak, it can cause minor hindrances or accidents in the native's life. However, if the planet is afflicted, it can cause irreversible damage.

Regardless, both states can be destructive and damaging, which is why the native must be aware of their ruling planet.

An afflicted Sun in a horoscope can result in premature baldness, poor eyesight, cardiovascular diseases, immunodeficiency, bone fractures, neuralgia, improper blood circulation, headaches, and recurring fever. Some natives may also experience anemia, polio, and joint pain. They may get headaches or feel fatigued regularly.

The Sun's position in every house can create distinct effects. For instance, if it is located in the first house, the native can suffer from health issues and poor well-being. If the Sun is placed in the 2nd, 6th, or 7th house, the native may experience problems with their family members. Typically, the following factors can help detect health issues:

- When weaker planets are located in weaker houses. For example, Rahu, Ketu, Mars, Pluto, Uranus, Neptune, and Saturn perform badly in the 12th, 8th, and 6th house
- When bad or negative aspects are projected on any planet like opposition (180°) or square (90°)
- When the Ascendant, Moon, and Sun are collectively afflicted
- When weak planets occupy certain zodiac signs such as Pisces, Scorpio, and Virgo.

It is extremely difficult to detect heart-related issues or cardiac diseases simply by looking at a person's birth chart and physical condition. However, experienced Vedic astrologers can pick points from the patient's Dasha scheme and establish a rough timeline for the illness. The following signs can help point out some unfavorable positions of the Sun in a horoscope, which can be used to detect heart issues.

- When the Sun is positioned in the 12th, 8th, or 6th house
- When the Sun is conjunct with Rahu, Ketu, Saturn, or Mars
- If it is afflicted due to a malefic association caused by the Leo sign
- If the Sun is in a debilitated state
- When the Sun is surrounded by malefic planets (also known as the Paapkartati state)
- When the 5th lord afflicts the Sun

Your astrologer can help you detect whether the Sun is weak or afflicted in your horoscope. You can also decipher the Sun's stance by recognizing certain signs, some of which include:

- Bone-related problems can indicate that the Sun is weak in your horoscope. If afflicted, the issue can turn into something more serious, like osteoporosis, which can be difficult to treat.
- A weak Sun can cause heart problems and or other serious cardiovascular issues. An afflicted Sun can mean recurring heart attacks for the native.
- A weak Sun can also result in physical disorders like blindness or deafness.
- Due to the ill effects of a weak Sun, the native will likely suffer from mental issues, mainly due to clashes and disagreements with their father.
- The native may suffer from poor eyesight or other vision-related issues, including short-sightedness or color blindness.
- Poor blood circulation and related illnesses are also common due to a weak Sun.
- Issues like stress and anxiety can be caused by low confidence, resulting from a weak Sun. This can also affect your professional life and lower your self-esteem.
- If the Sun is weak or afflicted, you may feel tired all the time. You may not be able to complete basic tasks and walk around with a limp. Your body may feel loose, and you may be easily overwhelmed.

Any of these signs can indicate that the Sun in your horoscope is either weak, inauspicious, or afflicted. Nowadays, many people suffer from heart problems and cardiovascular diseases worldwide. This is why medical astrologers suggest focusing on empowering the Sun while taking care of your body with a wholesome diet and regular physical activity.

A Holistic Approach to Better Health

Empowering the Sun and harnessing its energy has become necessary to fight heart-related diseases and maintain overall health. Doctors suggest taking a holistic approach towards building your physical and mental health with a diet and an exercise regimen favorable to the Sun and your body's vitality.

It is believed that certain medicinal plants are associated with a ruling celestial body. In the case of the Sun, plants like eyebright, rosemary, and chamomile are known to induce positive effects thanks to their color and aroma. Ayurveda suggests consuming spicy herbs like black pepper, cayenne, and cinnamon or fiery herbs like cardamom, calamus, bayberry, or saffron to harness solar energy. Practitioners also suggest using certain oils associated with the Sun's power, like eucalyptus, cinnamon, saffron, and camphor. They can be used for cooking or in aromatherapy practices as essential oils.

Other plants like Frankincense, Bergamot, Bay Laurel, Juniper Berry, Neroli, Carrot, Angelica, Motherwort, Rosemary, Ginger, and Mandarin are good for the heart and improving blood circulation. Since some of these plants depend on the Sun's energy and light to grow, they can turn their malefic effects into beneficial ones. Growing these plants in your garden can also help improve your memory and make you more knowledgeable.

In the past, medical practitioners did not understand the chemical composition of medicinal herbs and plants. They referred to the plants' shape, size, and color to determine their potency, a dependency known as the "doctrine of correspondences." According to the practitioners, God had inscribed a pattern and elaborated a system to decipher the effectiveness of each plant. These signs were based on hidden features and textures that helped distinguish the types to treat specific diseases. For example, doctors used red herbs to treat hemorrhages and fevers and yellow flowers for liver problems. Even if the herbs did not do much to treat the issue, they were still incorporated in the treatment.

Still, practitioners realized early on the importance of a good and healthy diet for internal healing. Your doctor can help you prepare a diet plan that will not only be good for your heart and brain but also promote better overall health. Incorporate foods that are good for your heart, like berries, jaggery, almonds, whole grains, beans, walnuts, green leafy vegetables, and other items rich in Omega-3 fatty acids. Needless to say, the food you eat can help cleanse your internal system and fight free radicals, which can otherwise pose a threat to your health.

Vedic astrologers suggest practicing these habits every day to counteract the effects of an afflicted Sun:

- Fast once a week, preferably on Sundays.
- Chant the mantra, "Om hram hreem hroum sah suryaya namah," a few times every day. The native should complete 6,000 chants within 40 days.
- Chant the Gayatri mantra, "Om bhur bhuvah svah, tat savitur varenyam, bhargo devasya dhimahi, dhiyo yo nah prachodayat" a few times a day.
- Donate sugar candy and wheat to the underprivileged once a week, preferably on Sundays.

According to Vedic astrology, some common remedies and healing tips in everyday life include:

- Performing Surya Namaskar twice a day, especially in the morning. This yoga practice is also good for your heart and overall health. It promotes flexibility and boosts concentration.
- Wearing orange or yellow-colored outfits.
- Using "Ek Mukhi Rudraksha" to reduce the Sun's ill effects and attract its positive energy.
- Wearing gold in the form of rings, necklaces, and pendants.
- Incorporating yellow-colored foods in your diet.
- Wearing a ring with a real ruby gemstone. Consult an experienced astrologer before taking this step, as you must wear it on auspicious days. It is also important to focus on the placement and the type of metal you are using.
- Using a copper pot to offer water in the direction of the Sun every morning. This is the best way to start your day on a positive note and absorb those bright, cheerful sun rays that can improve your health. It also helps alleviate stress up to an extent.
- Meditating every day and practicing breathing exercises. Meditation is the best way to calm yourself down and release stress. It clears your mind and provides energy. To attract positive vibrations, chant "Om Suryaya Namaha" 108 times while meditating. If possible, pick a spot outdoors to absorb sun rays in the morning.
- Attaching a Bel tree root to a white thread and wearing it around your neck. This can reduce the negative impact of a malefic Sun. You can also tie a Baelmool root in a pink cloth and place it on your waist or arm. If possible, place the bundle in your pocket early in the morning on a Sunday as the Sun aligns with the Uttarshada, Uttarphalguni, and Kritika Nakshatras.
- Drinking water from a copper glass or bowl.

These remedies will likely reduce the Sun's malefic effects and promote a healthier life. If turned into habits, some of these practices can also encourage self-improvement in relation to your personal and professional life.

How Can Homeotherapy Help?

The health benefits of homeotherapy (like homeopathy) are applied to the spiritual teachings of astrology, giving rise to a discipline called "Astro-homeopathy." The astrological readings can detect underlying conditions in a person, whereas homeotherapy can be used to treat the issue at its core. The idea is to extract every deep-seated problem to ensure that they do not occur again, which is also the main goal of homeotherapy. Although it may take some time, the investment is worthwhile as the results are long-lasting.

Aside from consuming a nutritious diet and following homeotherapy, doctors suggest exercising regularly to keep your heart healthy. Even a 30-minute daily walk can improve your heart health and oxygen flow. Other cardiovascular exercises include running, swimming, playing sports, and aerobics. These exercises also help strengthen your bones and joints as well. Since a weak Sun in your horoscope can also cause joint or bone-related conditions, regular exercise can diminish these ill effects. Consult your doctor or a trained fitness instructor to get a customized exercise plan based on your body type and underlying health issues.

Chapter 6: Sun Signs: Aries to Cancer

In astrology, the Sun represents, among many things, the conscious ego. All the other planets revolve around it, and they reflect the workings of our subconscious mind. Western astrology sun signs are Aries, Taurus, Gemini, Cancer, Leo, Virgo, Libra, Scorpio, Sagittarius, Capricorn, Aquarius, and Pisces. Knowing these twelve signs can help astrologers learn more about a person's personality and the meaning behind their birth chart, which shows the locations of the planets. In this chapter, we set out to explore the Sun signs from Aries to Cancer. You'll get a brief overview of each Sun sign, the element and polarity it belongs to, the characteristics of each sign, the symbols behind them, and the perspective between Western astrology vs. Vedic astrology for each sign.

Aries: The Ram

Aries is a fire sign with the qualities of energy, strength, aggressiveness, spontaneity, courage, and pioneering spirit. People who fall under the Aries Sun sign are creative, confident, and independent. They have great ambitions and goals in life. Putting themselves out there comes naturally for them because they like to be the center of attention.

Aries is ruled by the planet Mars, which symbolizes energy, strength, and power. Aries is a masculine sign, so it's associated with fire like all other masculine signs. The Sun stays in Aries from March 21 to April 19. This sign is also associated with the first house because it comes at the beginning of the Zodiac, symbolizing the start of a new cycle. Aries belongs to the group of signs marking the beginning of a new year. Other signs that fall in this category are Leo, Cancer, Libra, and Capricorn.

Element

Aries belongs to the element of fire, like all masculine signs. Being a fire sign, it prefers action instead of words. These people are very enthusiastic and passionate about their goals. However, they may lose interest quickly if no immediate progress is made toward their said goal. They hate to waste time on tasks that do not involve action or anything productive. They enjoy being in constant movement, always on the move. They are also impulsive because they act immediately without thinking twice about it.

Polarity

Aries is a positive polarity sign, so Aries is usually an upbeat sign that likes to stay active and busy. However, the polarity changes when their energy turns negative because they are quick-tempered and impatient. This makes it difficult for them to work with others who have opposite views and opinions in life.

Symbols

The symbol of Aries is the ram. The ram's head is a very prominent feature since it represents its impulsive and quick-tempered nature. Also, another common visual for this sign is the fire that comes out of its horns or head, showing how generous and warmhearted they are because they bring light and warmth to the people around them.

In Western astrology, the symbol for this planet is a circle with an arrow pointing outwards. The circle represents the Sun and its ability to make things grow. The arrow represents Mars, which rules Aries, symbolizing how these individuals excel at progressing towards their goals and making things happen instead of letting them stagnate.

In Vedic astrology, the planetary symbol for Aries is a ram's head. It also has two arrow-like horns, signifying its ability to produce results quickly and take action immediately without hesitation. The type of energy represented by this sign can be seen through the ram's head because it moves around frantically, looking for new things to do.

Characteristics

The symbolism and·meaning behind Aries make it clear what kind of character they tend to have. They are active, enthusiastic people who are always on the move and looking for new things to keep them busy. They prefer being in movement because it makes them feel alive. If you know someone who has the Aries Sun sign, you'll notice how enthusiastic they are and how much energy they have. Aries is also known to be very confident and independent. They have high ambitions in life, and they are always up and running, trying to make progress towards their goals. However, Aries can sometimes act impulsively because they tend to move with haste. If this becomes a negative aspect for them, it could lead to negative outcomes in life.

Taurus: The Bull

Taurus is associated with the second house in astrology as it follows Aries, making it the second sign of Spring. Taurus is responsible for providing food and shelter to humans. The Sun stays in Taurus for approximately two and a half months in the northern hemisphere, lasting from April 20th to June 21st.

The ruling planet of Taurus is Venus, the goddess of love and beauty. People born under this sign are usually attractive, warmhearted people who appreciate the beauty in life and nature. They have a great appreciation for the finer things and enjoy taking pleasure from them. They can be quite stubborn at times because they will refuse to change their views due to their strong opinions.

Element

Taurus is one of the three earth signs, along with Virgo and Capricorn. Earth signs are naturally caring people who have a great understanding of the depth of life. It also helps that they have an excellent sense of taste because they enjoy eating delicious food whenever possible. They also love to be surrounded by aesthetically pleasing things. Being an earth sign, they love anything physical like art and music. They are creative and sensual. Taurus are very artistic people and possess a love for beauty. They appreciate good food, nice clothes, and beautiful art pieces. Taurus is also known to be patient and reliable because they do not like changing their routine or doing anything spontaneously.

Polarity

In Western astrology, Taurus is considered to be masculine or positive. In Vedic Astrology, Taurus is a feminine sign that has both positive and negative qualities. It can act like a masculine sign in some cases because of its dominance and the way it makes decisions without consulting anybody else. However, it also possesses many feminine traits, such as sensitivity and affection. It is also capable of caring for other people, which makes it a very balanced sign.

Symbols

In Western Astrology, the symbol for Taurus is a bull's head facing to the left, representing how Taurus subjects focus on providing for their family and ensuring that all responsibilities are taken care of as efficiently as possible. The second half of the symbol, which is a man's face looking to his left, represents Taurus's natural polarity. This also shows that they are in tune with other people's emotions and can tell when somebody is upset or sad.

In Vedic astrology, the symbol for Taurus is a bull lying down on its side. It has two sharp horns and a one-pointed hoof. The bull represents Taurus's stability and power while lying down on its side shows how passive it can be in nature.

Characteristics

Taureans are known to be grounded individuals who possess a realistic perspective. You can expect them to be practical and pragmatic about the things they encounter throughout their lives. One might even say that they are overly practical because they cannot just sit back and enjoy the moment. Instead, they analyze things and try to figure out their flaws, no matter how much time or energy it takes them. They need something tangible to enjoy themselves properly, which means a lot of patience is needed by others if somebody wants them to be spontaneous every once in a while.

Taurus natives are also known to be stubborn, which means they do not like it when anybody tries to tell them what to do. They prefer making their own decisions and doing things their way. As long as you let them live their lives how they see fit, you will have no problems with them. Taurus will usually not interfere in other people's business, and they expect the same of others in return. They try to be sensible and reasonable because they know that dealing with people in their daily lives is necessary.

Gemini: The Twins

The third sign of the zodiac is Gemini or The Twins. Those born under this sign are considered quick-witted and very outgoing. They love to talk about anything and everything. They are intelligent and possess a great sense of humor. They can easily adapt to any environment because they love making new friends and meeting new people. Gemini is the only sign with two different personalities, meaning they act differently depending on who they are with. It is also the only sign that has a set of twins represented in its symbol. The Sun stays in Gemini for approximately two and a half months, from May 21 to July 20.

Element

Geminis belong to the element of air, thanks to their intellectual mind and quick-thinking skills when it comes to situations where logic is needed. They are very social people, which is why the element of fire would not suit their personality. Fire needs a lot of energy and excitement to keep going, whereas Gemini thrives on information and communication to make them feel alive.

Polarity

Gemini is considered a masculine and positive sign in Western astrology, while, in Vedic astrology, it is feminine with both positive and negative traits. It is masculine when it comes to how they make decisions and the way they show leadership. They are independent and rational thinkers, which can sometimes cause problems with other people because of their habit of questioning everything. On the other hand, Gemini can sometimes be very emotional. These negative traits stem from the fact that they do not always make decisions based on reason and logic. They tend to let their emotions get the better of them, which is why they can prove unpredictable at times.

Symbols

Gemini's polarity shows up in its symbol as well. The Western astrology version portrays two human figures facing each other, whereas the Vedic version has a human figure facing forward with another human figure facing to the side. This symbolizes Gemini's ability to adapt and adjust easily in any kind of environment. The symbol also showcases how peaceful they are by having both figures hold hands, which signifies friendship.

Characteristics

Geminis can be quite charming as people, but not always sweet and innocent. They can also be very selfish at times, acting out whenever they do not get what they want. That is why those unlucky enough to get close to Geminis should be prepared for anything because they will never know what goes on in their minds or how they will react until they have already done something. They are an unpredictable group who can turn into very dangerous enemies if you happen to get on their bad side.

Cancer: The Crab

One of the most emotional signs of the zodiac, Cancer, is also very intuitive and perceptive about their surroundings. They are deep thinkers and have a habit of analyzing everybody they encounter. This can come off as being judgmental or acting stuck-up because their nature is a little snobby – not because they think they are better than everyone else, but because Cancerians want to know someone's motives before befriending them. They do not take things at face value and look for deeper meanings in anything that people say. Since Cancer believes in staying positive all the time, they will only see the negative side of things if they are extremely upset. The Sun stays in Cancer from approximately June 21 to July 22.

Element

Cancer belongs to the element of water because it is a very emotional and unpredictable sign that can often be hard to read. They can be positive or negative depending on the situation, which means when something bad happens, they tend to overreact. On the other hand, when something good happens, they are ready to celebrate and will be extremely happy about it. Cancer's element also explains their sensitivity towards others since water is a very empathetic element that feels things deeply instead of air, which can detach itself from emotions more easily.

Polarity

Cancer is considered a feminine and positive sign in Western astrology, while in Vedic astrology, it is also feminine with both positive and negative traits. It is masculine when it comes to their strength and desire to protect themselves from anything they consider harmful, such as emotional pain or people who want to hurt them physically. They are excellent at storing up information from the past and using it to protect themselves at the right time. They will try to figure out the other person's motives before they say or do anything because they fear being tricked or taken advantage of.

Symbols

The Crab is considered Cancer's symbol in Western astrology, while the lotus flower represents it in Vedic astrology. The Crab refers to Cancer's desire to protect itself from harm, while the lotus flower signifies life and purity since they have an extremely high pain tolerance. The thorny stem represents their ability to withstand physical pain, while the beautiful flowers symbolize their strong emotions that are on display for all to see.

Characteristics

Trying to figure out how a Cancerian thinks or feels can prove difficult due to their mysterious nature. Not only are they afraid of being tricked or taken advantage of, but they also have a hard time trusting other people with their true feelings. They would rather keep things bottled up inside because it is easier than exposing themselves and dealing with the consequences afterward, such as embarrassing themselves if they do not feel the same way. Although Cancerians are sensitive individuals, they hide their emotions behind a tough exterior armor because they do not want to seem weak in front of others. Ultimately, Cancer is an introverted sign that does not like getting involved with things unless they can gain something from the situation. Their emotions are extremely volatile, and they do not want to show anyone how weak their heart truly is because they fear that people will use it against them.

In this chapter, we have covered the Sun's journey from Aries to Cancer and have explained what each sign means for a particular native. We have considered both Western astrology and Vedic astrology to get a better understanding of the nature of these signs. We discussed Aries, the first sign of the Zodiac, to Cancer, the fourth sign of the Zodiac. We talked about Aries' fire element and how it belongs to a masculine quality because there is no such thing as going too far or being soft. The symbol for Aries is a ram, and its characteristics are leading rather than following impulsiveness and the willingness to fight.

We then discussed Taurus, the second sign of the Zodiac. Its element is Earth, while its polarity is feminine, and it is considered a negative sign in Vedic astrology. The symbol for Taurus is a bull, and its characteristics are persistence, possessiveness, patience, reliability. After that, we talked about Gemini, which belongs to the air element yet also possesses masculine characteristics. Its element is dualistic due to the balance between ideas, thoughts, and communication found within this sign. Gemini's symbol is the twins, and its characteristics are being disorganized, impatient, and superficial. Lastly, we talked about Cancer who belongs to water but is considered negative by Vedic astrology. Its element is emotion, and it has feminine characteristics. Cancer's symbol is the crab, and its characteristics involve inquisitiveness, hiding their emotions, suspicion, and worrying too much.

Chapter 7: Sun Signs: Leo to Scorpio

As we've seen, Sun signs in Astrology represent the personality of an individual. The position and movement of the Sun across the sky at different points throughout their lives give insight into their character traits, how they interact with others, and their level of energy. In this chapter, we will be covering the Sun signs from Leo to Scorpio. You'll discover the elements, characteristics, symbolism, and effects of the Sun's transit in the Leo, Virgo, Libra, and Scorpio signs.

Leo: The Lion

Leo represents strength, pride, nobility, royalty, and leadership. Ruled by the Sun, Leo natives tend to have magnetic personalities and are often imposing in stature. Their personality is characterized by being a natural-born leader who longs for the limelight and enjoys praise from others. The Sun stays in Leo for around two months, from mid-July to mid-September.

Element

Leo, represented by Fire in Western astrology, and heat or energy flow within Vedic Astrology, is associated with the Sun. Fire signs tend to be energetic, warm, lively, and adventurous. They take the initiative and pursue a leadership role in most situations. As they blaze through life, they inspire others to act quickly and are generally good communicators. There is a strong presence with those born under fire signs as their fiery personalities can leave others blown away.

The element of Fire is associated with action, boldness, and passion. Fire signs tend to be confident in their actions and decisions. They are self-motivated people who move quickly once they've settled on doing something. According to Western astrology, Fire tends to have an outgoing, energetic nature associated with extraversion.

Polarity

Leo is a masculine sign in Western astrology, which is why it is associated with the Sun. The Sun represents masculinity and vitality. The priority for men with strong Leo energy is to make their presence known and noticed by others. Men may struggle with feeling prideful or arrogant at times, but they ultimately strive to be recognized as confident and powerful leaders.

Women with strong Leo energy usually come across as warm and confident. They use their charm, charisma, and other people-centric skills to draw others towards them. Their attitude generally says, "The world revolves around me," coupled with a sense of pride or arrogance that can attract or repel those in their lives, depending on how it comes across.

Symbols

The Lion is a common symbol for those with the Sun in Leo. It represents strength, pride, and courage. People with the Sun on Leo present the trait of strength represented by the king of the jungle, who is meant to be powerful. They like being in control and having authority over others. Although they have warm personalities, they can be intimidating with their authoritative presence.

The Lion also represents leadership and royalty. Those born under the Leo sign are natural-born leaders who aim to exercise control in most situations, whether in business or at home. They aren't afraid to take charge when necessary and inspire others through their confidence and self-assuredness.

Characteristics

People with Sun in Leo tend to have magnetic personalities and take pride in their appearance. They enjoy attention from others who can appreciate their confidence, charm, and charisma. Those born under this sign are not always concerned about their emotions or how they come across to others, as long as they receive praise. They like being recognized for their accomplishments and love feeling appreciated by others.

Emotions are not always a priority for those with Sun in Leo as they tend to be more goal-oriented. They want to have their presence known and feel most confident when they're the center of attention or at least know that everyone has good things to say about them. If someone does not admire them or says something negative about them, it can affect their mood and leave them feeling empty until they receive validation again.

Virgo: The Virgin

Virgo rules over earth and is considered feminine in Western astrology. Those with this position of the Sun tend to strive for perfection, both in their looks and actions. They are concerned about how they appear to others and strive to achieve a clean-cut, orderly lifestyle that reflects their attention to detail. The Sun stays in Virgo from August 23 to September 22. People born under this sign tend to be perfectionists with a very critical eye, whose approach can sometimes result in self-criticism. They are natural analysts who want absolute control over their surroundings, leading them to become workaholics or overachievers. Those with strong Virgo energy may struggle with feeling insecure at times but tend to be hard on themselves, compared to others.

Element

Virgo is an earth sign. People born under this sign can seem shy and reserved, but they're very observant when it comes to human nature. These individuals are down-to-earth and practical people who can easily move past their emotions as they tend to be more focused on the physical world. They have a good sense of reality and can clearly see the world despite distractions or anything interfering with their perception. They understand things on a deeper level due to their acute way of thinking, making them good problem-solvers and critical thinkers.

Polarity

Virgo is a feminine sign in Western astrology. Those born under this sign are balanced between their masculine and feminine energies, where they tend to be more nurturing and supportive of others, especially those who are struggling. Despite their strong need for control, Virgos don't take advantage of people's vulnerabilities. If someone is down on their luck, those with this sign are the first to lend a helping hand to help them to pick themselves back up again. People will open up to them because they can relate thanks to their shared experiences.

By contrast, in Vedic Astrology, Virgo is masculine. Those born under this sign are very much concerned about their desires and how to fulfill them. They make decisions based on what they think will benefit them the most, even if it comes at the expense of others. Those with a masculine Virgo Sun may become workaholics to avoid dealing with their emotions.

Symbols

The symbol for Virgo is the Virgin. Those with this zodiac sign may be well-known as hopeless romantics due to their desire for perfection in a partner. They would rather stay single than settle for someone who doesn't have all of their desired qualities, regardless of how amazing they might be otherwise. In Vedic astrology, Virgo's symbol is a woman holding sheaves of corn. In Western astrology, the symbol for Virgo is a young maiden holding an ear of wheat. She is thought to be either Astraea or Ceres due to these associations with the goddesses of virginity and motherhood.

Characteristics

People with this position of the Sun are more compassionate towards others than they are towards themselves. They prefer to look out for others instead of pursuing their own needs and wants. Virgos will often sacrifice what they want to help someone else without expecting anything in return. There may be times when people born under this sign feel taken advantage of, but they will continue to offer help and support, knowing that it's necessary. They may come across as perfectionists because they want everything in their own lives to be perfect. They will often hone themselves down to a fine point to continue moving towards their goal of success and wealth.

Libra: The Scales

Those born with the Sun in Libra tend to be communicators who enjoy having a large social circle. They can become restless when they're alone for too long, so they need to maintain harmony throughout their relationships. The Sun stays in Libra from September 23 to October 22. Libras are easy-going but often have a hidden agenda. They want to maintain balance and peace in their lives at all times, which may prompt them to be passive-aggressive or even manipulative when they feel like things aren't going their way.

Element

Libra is an air sign. Those born under this sign tend to be intellectual, communicative, and social people. They are good at getting things done effectively to achieve their goals without creating any conflict or drama. They tend to be fair-minded and like to see both sides of a story before forming an opinion, which helps them come up with a final verdict that everyone can be happy with. People born under this sign can seem to be indecisive, but they're simply weighing the pros and cons of their choices to make an informed decision.

Polarity

Libra is a feminine sign in Western astrology. Those born under this sign are understanding and supportive of those who are struggling. They have a keen sense of justice which compels them to stand up and speak out when they see someone being mistreated. Even though Libras can be seen as observers, it doesn't mean they aren't passionate about things that matter to them. They prefer to listen rather than speak, making it easier for them to maintain a sense of harmony in their relationships.

In Vedic astrology, Libra is a masculine sign. Those born under this sign are more concerned with getting things done rather than spending time planning and strategizing. They have little patience for indecisiveness and will take the bull by the horns whenever possible. They enjoy being physically active and like to maintain an active lifestyle because they get bored easily.

Symbols

The astrological sign of Libra is the scales, symbolizing justice and fairness, which may be why Libras tend to be aware of their surroundings, especially when it comes to social dynamics. They know when something isn't right with a friend, lover, or colleague and will do what they can to fix it.

In Vedic astrology, the sign of Libra is linked to the serpent, symbolizing resurrection and purity, which gives insight into a Library's tendency to cleanse themselves of negative habits to start afresh. In Western astrology, the sign of Libra is also associated with the phoenix that symbolizes rebirth and renewal.

Characteristics

Librans are known to be gentle, tactful, and agreeable people. They work hard to maintain balance in their lives so they can achieve their goals through non-violent means. Even though Librans may appear to be passive or even reserved at times, this is merely a facade that hides their strong yet hidden willpower. They can be shy at first but won't let that stop them from making their interests known.

Scorpio: The Ruler of the 8th House

Those born with the Sun in Scorpio tend to be emotional people who are very protective of themselves and their loved ones. They will do whatever it takes to take care of those closest to them, leading them to become obsessive or possessive at times. The Sun stays in Scorpio from approximately October 23 – November 22.

Element

Scorpio is a water sign. Those born under this sign are very intuitive individuals who can delve deep into the minds of those around them. People with this position of the Sun know what motivates someone before they even say anything, and it helps them form better and more accurate opinions about people.

Polarity

Scorpio is a feminine sign in Western astrology. Those born under this sign do whatever they can to maintain their independence and freedom by keeping those around them at arm's length. They are very private individuals who guard their emotions fiercely, making it hard for others to approach them, let alone see beyond the surface.

In Vedic astrology, Scorpio is a masculine sign. Those born under this sign are more intensely focused than Libras, which can be off-putting for people who don't understand their motivations. They tend to overreact when they feel threatened and make it difficult for others to get close to them and form any kind of real connection.

Symbols

The astrological symbol for Scorpio is the scorpion which represents sex, death, and rebirth. People with this sign in their astrological chart tend to hold very strong emotions and passions beneath the surface. They spend a lot of time pondering these thoughts but don't often share them with others, which leaves people intrigued by what could be going on in their minds.

In Vedic astrology, Scorpio is linked to the eagle, which symbolizes spiritual wisdom and enlightenment. With this sign, the person will tend to be a deep thinker who spends a lot of time contemplating life and its place within it. They constantly ask themselves why they do certain things and how they can do them better, giving them an eye for detail when analyzing habits and behaviors.

Characteristics

Those born with the Sun in Scorpio tend to be very passionate and intense people who aren't afraid of expressing what they have to say. They can come across as domineering or aggressive, but their actions are typically rooted in a desire to protect themselves and those around them from harm. This sign is thought to correspond closely with magic, which is one reason why these people are often drawn to the occult. People born under this sign aren't afraid to take risks if they feel that taking them will make their life better, even if it means failing miserably at them in the end.

This chapter covered the Sun signs from Leo to Scorpio. It explained elements for each sign, the masculine and feminine characteristics of each sign, symbols for the signs, and the traits of each Sun sign. Starting with Leo, the Sun stays in this sign from July 23 - August 22. This is a fire sign which means those born under it are very energetic people who easily display their emotions. Leo is considered a masculine sign in Western astrology, but it is seen as a feminine one in Vedic astrology. When it is in Leo, the symbol for the Sun is the Lion symbolizing power, royalty, and strength. A person born under this sign will be very proud and often need admiration from others. However, they are equally as capable of giving it.

We then discussed the Sun sign Virgo, a feminine earth sign (females are more common than males) that resides in the Sun sign Virgo from August 23 - September 22. In Western astrology, this sign is considered masculine, and in Vedic astrology, the Sun stays in this sign for two months, meaning both genders are candidates for this Sun sign. The symbol for Virgo is the Virgin with a sheaf of wheat signifying work and harvest. People born under this sign will often be hard workers who never seem to take a break from their tasks because they like to finish what they start. They are down-to-earth and practical people who display their emotions less freely than others.

Next, we talked about Libra, which the Sun resides in from September 23 - October 22. It is considered a masculine sign in Western astrology, while it is considered a feminine Sun sign in Vedic astrology. The symbol for Libra is the scales, symbolizing equality. This is an air sign meaning that those born under it are quite introspective and intellectual people who spend a lot of time contemplating their inner thoughts and feelings rather than expressing them. Those with their Sun in this sign are fair-minded people who like to come up with creative solutions to difficult problems for the benefit of all.

Lastly, after Libra, we discussed Scorpio. This is a water sign, meaning that those born under it are emotional and often secretive people who prefer to keep their thoughts and feelings to themselves. In Western astrology, it is considered a feminine sign, while in Vedic astrology, the Sun stays in this sign for two months so both genders can claim Scorpio as their Sun sign. The symbol for Scorpio is the scorpion which symbolizes sex, death, and rebirth. People with their Sun in this sign are passionate people with a lot of intensity inside, and they can also be very intense lovers.

Chapter 8: Sun Signs: Sagittarius to Pisces

By now, it goes without saying that the Sun is the life of all living things on Earth. And while it won't live forever, its positive effects are felt by all who walk upon and inhabit this planet. The Sun occupies Sagittarius, Capricorn, Aquarius, and Pisces from November 21 until April 18. These four signs are different as they belong to two separate planets, Jupiter and Saturn. In this chapter, you'll discover the elements, characteristics, symbolism, and effects of the Sun's transit in these four signs.

Sagittarius: The Minister and Advisor

Sagittarius is an optimistic, honest, confident, and free-spirited fire sign. Sagittarians are straightforward people with a great sense of humor. They're often blunt in their thoughts but can also be philosophical and frank when it comes to the truth about themselves or others. These people have high principles, and their code of ethics is important to them. They're excellent advisers and messengers thanks to their good judgment, strong intuition, and to have a great sense of direction. A Sagittarius can achieve success in many areas due to their optimism and enthusiasm for life.

Saturn is considered the enemy of the Sun, whereas Jupiter is seen as his minister and advisor. In Sagittarius, which belongs to Jupiter, the Sun represents happiness and optimism. As it travels through this sign, it gives humans a love for adventure and a need for freedom. The positive effects of the Sun when it occupies Sagittarius can help the native feel less inhibited and more willing to take risks. The Sun in Sagittarius allows you to see life as an adventure, learn from your past, focus on the path ahead, and feel great about yourself.

Element

The Sagittarius sign belongs to the element of fire and is ruled by Jupiter. Sagittarians are envied by many for their optimism, honesty, confidence, and great sense of humor, as well as their high principles. The element of fire is positive as it represents warmth and inspiration. According to Vedic astrology, the fire element is associated with both energy and transformation. Fire rules the emotions, so Sagittarians need to remember that they need to take care of themselves emotionally to avoid stress or burning out.

Symbol

The symbol for the Sagittarius sign is the centaur. Centaurs are mythical creatures with the head, arms, and torso of a human and a horse's body, legs, and tail. This creature represented freedom to roam any land since they could run on both lands and in water. The centaur was known to be half-man, half-animal in both its human and horse features. This symbolizes the need for humans to find a balance between their spiritual and animalistic sides. The Sagittarius symbol is a centaur because this sign represents freedom and optimism. The Sagittarian finds a sense of balance through action rather than meditation.

Characteristics

Sagittarians are straightforward and frank when it comes to the truth. They are excellent advisers and messengers as they generally have strong intuition and a great sense of judgment and direction. They're optimistic and enthusiastic about life, which allows them to achieve success in many areas. They tend to be honest with themselves about their feelings and needs, while others can sometimes struggle with this. These people need to remember that they must take care of themselves emotionally to avoid finding themselves in insufferable situations.

Effects

As the Sun travels through the Sagittarius sign, it reminds humans to embrace adventure and preserve their freedom. Sagittarians are more willing to take risks because optimism and enthusiasm are present in their life. The negative effects of the Sun when it occupies Sagittarius can cause the native to be blunt, sometimes offensive, without thinking about how this may affect others.

Capricorn: The Mountain Goat

In Capricorn, which belongs to Saturn, the Sun represents a drive for power, authority, and ambition. When going through this sign, the Sun can cause humans to be obsessed with achieving their goals and destroying anything that gets in their way. When the Sun leaves Sagittarius and enters Capricorn on December 22, those born under these signs will find themselves drawn to power and authority. They will also feel a strong need to prove themselves capable of achieving their goals.

Element

The Capricorn sign belongs to the element of earth and is ruled by Saturn. Capricorns are hardworking, responsible, patient, and trustworthy people with a strong desire for success. They're skilled at using their mind and determination to achieve what they set out to do. The earth element is positive as it represents reliability and strength of will. According to Vedic astrology, the element of earth is associated with both the aforementioned traits and realism. In Western astrology, earth rules over stability and materialism.

Symbol

The Capricorn symbol is a mountain goat because this sign represents both leadership and ambition. Capricorns are hardworking people who constantly seek to improve their lives while staying practical about achieving their goals. The mountain goat is, in fact, an excellent climber and leader. This sign can lead others while standing on top of a mountain peak facing downward toward their subjects. This represents both leadership and ambition and the need for Capricorn natives always to be goal-oriented to succeed.

Characteristics

The Capricorn sign has an emotional depth and is passionate about life. The Sun moving through Capricorn can cause those born under this sign to become more responsible, serious, ambitious, and focused on their goals. This can also affect the way they see themselves, as they may be drawn to a materialistic world with many opportunities to achieve success even at an early age.

Capricorn is a cardinal sign and is the most ambitious of all Earth signs. Being ambitious means that this sign has an unwavering desire to achieve their goals and become successful in life at all costs. The symbol for this sign is the mountain goat, representing a hardworking, responsible person who focuses on setting and achieving their objectives. A Capricorn native has a natural sense of leadership and is very goal-oriented.

Effects

The Sun in Capricorn can cause people to gain better focus while becoming obsessed with achieving their goals. The negative effects of the Sun when it moves through Capricorn are that these natives can become obsessive, controlling, and insensitive towards others. They will work restlessly until they have reached a certain level of success, which explains why this sign tends to be more ambitious than others.

Aquarius: The Water Bearer

In Aquarius, which belongs to Saturn, the Sun represents a desire for knowledge, higher learning, and new ideas. These individuals can teach others and use their minds to advance themselves further to achieve success. When the Sun moves through this sign from December 22 until January 20, it enters the last third of Saturn's territory, which will compel those born under this sign to become more ambitious. Aquarians will find themselves drawn to radically new concepts and ideas, especially when they go against the norm. These people will also feel a strong need to break free from anything that makes them feel trapped or restrained.

Aquarians are considered some of the most unpredictable people in the zodiac because they don't like to follow conventions and rules. They aren't too concerned with what others think of them and would rather trust their emotions. Natives of this sign often have a strong sense of social responsibility and can be very helpful to those around them. They're known for their friendliness, and they tend to think of others before themselves.

Element

In Western astrology, the element of air is associated with both science and philosophy. Air rules over intelligence and memory as well as communication. The water element, on the other hand, represents emotions and intuition. In Vedic astrology, Jupiter (the son of Saturn) rules the element of water. Water rules over intelligence and imagination. The Aquarius symbol is a man pouring water from two pitchers to represent both the thirst for knowledge and the desire to share that knowledge.

Symbol

The Aquarius symbol is the Water Bearer as it represents one who can control life's most powerful forces, including water. The Sun rules over all fiery energy, and fire represents both wisdom and passion. This is why the Sun in Aquarius can push natives to be intelligent, insightful, emotionally sensitive, and introverted. In Vedic astrology, the symbol for Aquarius is the Great One. It represents a desire to achieve greatness or success.

Characteristics

People born under the Aquarius sign are helpful, calm, and friendly. They love to be around others but can also be introverted at times when feeling overwhelmed by their emotions. These natives do not like to stay in one place for too long and prefer exploring new things as often as they can. They're extremely intelligent and like to stay educated on a variety of subjects. Aquarians are also sympathetic and giving, but they can be distant when it comes to relationships.

Aquarius individuals don't like to get involved in things that make them feel overly emotional. They're not overly concerned with their image and the opinions others have about them, meaning they don't let things get to their head. Aquarius natives also hate being controlled, so they don't let money have power over them. These people are highly intelligent and can be excellent teachers. Aquarians are known to be rebellious and can see difficult concepts in a new light. They are also creatives at heart, which means they may have great imaginations and easily develop new ideas.

Aquarius is a fixed sign, meaning these individuals are loyal and stable. Being ruled by Saturn, they tend to be more ambitious than other earth signs and are generally skilled at getting things done even when it seems impossible or unlikely. They enjoy doing things their way and are very independent individuals.

Effects

As the Sun enters Aquarius, those born under this sign will become more introverted and emotionally sensitive while becoming more intelligent, insightful, and analytical. They may also experience bouts of aloofness caused by their natural ability to focus all of their energy on whatever task they are trying to accomplish.

The Sun in this sign can cause one to become dreamy and detached from the rest of the world. These people will often have interests that are considered unusual by others. However, other people's views do not interest them as they're too focused on their projects or goals. These people are also likely to be very committed when it comes to the tasks they set out to accomplish, which can cause them to lose perspective on everything else that's going on around them.

Pisces: The Fish

In Pisces, also belonging to Jupiter, the Sun represents self-sacrifice, altruism, and a deep appreciation for spiritual matters. When traveling through this sign, the Sun can cause humans to have a strong need to put others' needs before their own. When the Sun enters Pisces on February 18, those born under these signs will find themselves drawn to humanitarian endeavors and a need to help others. They will also feel a strong need for spiritual fulfillment and possibly psychic awareness.

Element

The Pisces' element is water, which represents love and emotions. In Vedic astrology, the planet that rules over this sign is Jupiter (the son of Saturn). Water represents intelligence and imagination. Pisces is ruled by Jupiter, the planet that represents expansion. In Western astrology, Jupiter symbolizes good fortune and abundance. Because the water element is expanded by earth and its ruler (Jupiter), Pisces also signifies success.

People born under this sign can be very understanding, caring, loving, intelligent, artistic, and/or musical, depending on other astrological influences in their birth chart. Pisces natives are compassionate with a deep sense of spirituality, which others may or may not understand.

Symbol

According to Greek mythology, the fish was revered as it was considered a symbol of fertility, creation, and life. It was also believed to have been an "unbreakable" animal, explaining its ties to the earth with the world of the waters. The Pisces sign can symbolize a fluid connection between earthly desires and our spiritual self, or it may indicate that one is superior in understanding and communicating their emotions. The fish is a symbol of fertility, and in the zodiac, water flows around the Earth. Jupiter rules Pisces as well as Sagittarius.

Pisces represents our connection between the physical world and the spiritual realm. They may possess psychic or mystical abilities or feel drawn to topics of spiritual or psychic matters. Jupiter also rules Pisces, representing knowledge, expansion, luck, and abundance, indicating that a person with this sign will have an overwhelming sense of compassion for others. They may also be intelligent and full of imagination.

Characteristics

People with this sign will have varied interests, and they feel happy doing several different things. They typically enjoy being around others and love to make new friends. They also like having the freedom to do whatever they choose as far as their life choices. When the Sun is traveling through Pisces, people are likely to want to help others and be more caring than usual. They may engage in humanitarian endeavors and pursue spiritual fulfillment, or they might have heightened psychic awareness. Pisces natives are likely to experience a strong need for emotional intelligence in their choices and life plans.

People born under the sign of Pisces will often have a deep sense of spirituality. Although this sign is ruled by Jupiter, representing good luck and abundance, Pisces can also indicate strong psychic abilities. They may also be very compassionate, and understanding or they could develop these traits with time. This sign also symbolizes a fluid connection between the earthly desire for material gain and the spiritual self.

Effects

When the Sun is in Sagittarius, it represents our desire to expand and grow to better understand the world around us. When the Sun travels through Pisces, people are likely to feel a strong need for spiritual fulfillment or experience psychic awareness. They want to help others and may become more compassionate than usual. However, this sign is ruled by Jupiter, which helps Pisces people develop their imagination and love for exploration. They are often highly intelligent and creative.

In this chapter, you discovered the characteristics of four zodiac signs: Sagittarius, Capricorn, Aquarius, and Pisces. You also learned about these four placements' effects on a native being born under each sign. We also mentioned how the placement of the Sun in any given zodiac sign could affect people who were born under it. Now, you should better understand how these four signs differ, as two of them belong to Jupiter, the minister and advisor of the Sun, and the other two belong to Saturn, the son of the Sun, who is considered its biggest enemy. You learned what one could discover about themselves as the Sun moves from Sagittarius into both signs of Saturn, namely Capricorn and Aquarius, and finally finishes its journey in Jupiter's sign, Pisces. This transition affects a native and what it means in actual life.

Chapter 9: The Sun in Yoga

According to Vedic practitioners, yoga and astrology go hand in hand. Despite being different in terms of practice and actions, both focus on internal cleansing and spiritual healing. In a way, astrology and yoga form a symbiotic relationship. They share many principles like positive energy, chakras, and internal makeup. If applied correctly, both disciplines can become useful tools to combat adversities and feel at peace. Yoga and astrology have thrived for centuries, thanks to the work of many scholars, practitioners, and enthusiasts boasting the merits of each practice. They have successfully stood the test of time and are still used for spiritual cleansing today.

The Sun's Role in Yoga

Among all celestial bodies, the Sun, in particular, is closely associated with yoga and astrology. Yoga can help unravel the true potential and energy of the Sun, which can then be redirected towards internal healing. The Sun helps a person heal and feel alive, which is also one of the main goals of yoga. On cold winter days, the Sun's radiance and warmth feel comforting and uplifting. Similarly, yoga also helps us be at ease and rejuvenates our minds. When we connect with our inner selves, we feel just as warm and connected. In a way, both the Sun and yoga ignite the internal fire and illuminate our lives.

Several ancient Hindu accounts like the Yajurveda, Rigveda, and the Upanishads emphasize the importance of "Agni," the internal fire represented by the Sun. According to Ayurveda, Vedic astrology, and yoga, the Sun embodies sustenance and intelligence. Learning the right way to exude these qualities can truly change one's life, which is where yoga steps in. With consistent practice and deep learning, one can regulate their circadian rhythm and get more attuned to the Sun's vibrations and rhythms.

The Importance of Surya Namaskar

Surya Namaskar, or "Sun Salutation," is the act of worshipping or paying respect to the Sun by performing a set of asanas (postures). Surya translates to "Sun," and Namaskar translates to "salute." This practice is a form of modern Ashtanga yoga and should not be confused with Patanjali's Yoga Sutras. When performing a round of Surya Namaskar, the practitioner honors the Sun and thanks it for providing life and vitality. According to Vedic astrologers, this practice is the best way to honor the giant star's existence and its role in this universe. One round of Surya Namaskar comprises 12 asanas that are divided into two sets (one set comprises six poses, and the other set repeats the same poses in reverse order).

Each of these poses is meant to be performed specifically while maintaining composure and regulating your breathing pattern. Surya Namaskar has multiple benefits. Performing it regularly can help develop your physical strength and flexibility. It also helps release stress and keeps you calm. Astrologers suggest performing Surya Namaskar every day to strengthen the Sun's position in your horoscope and intensify its placement in your natal chart. With this, you can combat the ill effects of a weak or an afflicted Sun and reap more positive outcomes in your life.

Many practitioners have been performing Surya Namaskar for decades and swear by the positive benefits they have reaped. From weight loss to spiritual awakening, the benefits of Surya

Namaskar are plentiful. Even though it takes time to notice positive results, the effects are life-changing and can replenish every form of your being.

The Twelve Steps and the Twelve Zodiac Signs

The twelve steps of Surya Namaskar reflect the twelve zodiac signs or constellations in the sky. Since the Sun follows a dedicated path to cross the sky over a year, it sits with every zodiac sign at some point. We can draw parallels between the chart of the zodiac constellations, and the twelve yoga poses to understand the manifestation of energy in all twelve pairings, one at a time. Let's take a look at each of these twelve Surya Namaskar poses and the right way to perform them, along with their connection to a specific zodiac sign.

Step 1: Pranamasana - Prayer Pose

Stand straight on your mat and bring your feet together. Keep your shoulders relaxed and expand your neck and chest. Take a deep breath, join your palms together, and place them in front of your chest. Exhale and hold this position for a few seconds.

Relation with Zodiac Sign: Aquarius

Planet: Saturn

Mantra: Om Mitraaya Namaha (One who is affectionate).

Step 2: Hastauttanasana - Raised Arms Pose

Take a deep breath and raise your arms above your head such that they almost touch your ears. Stretch your entire body from your feet to your fingers and feel the stretch in your spinal cord. Do not bend backward. Instead, keep your pelvis stretched towards the front.

Relation with Zodiac Sign: Pisces

Planet: Jupiter

Mantra: Om Ravaye Namaha (One who shines).

Step 3: Hasta Padasana - Hand to Foot Pose

Exhale and slowly bend your upper body from the waist until your nose almost touches your knees. Keep your spine straight, exhale, and stretch your arms toward the ground. Keep them straight and beside your feet. Try to touch the floor with your palms. You can slightly bend your knees at this point.

Relation with Zodiac Sign: Aries

Planet: Mars

Mantra: Om Suryaya Namaha (One who generates activity and disperses darkness).

Step 4: Ashwa Sanchalanasana - Equestrian Pose

Inhale and bring your left leg forward while pushing your right leg behind. Stretch it toward the back as much as you can. Place your right knee on the floor and let your palms touch the floor as you did in the previous step. The left foot should be straight and in alignment with both your hands. Look up and stretch your neck. Keep your spine straight.

Relation with Zodiac Sign: Taurus

Planet: Venus

Mantra: Om Bhaanave Namaha (One who shines).

Step 5: Dandasana - Stick Pose

Inhale and slowly push your left leg back while keeping your right leg stretched. With this, your body should form a straight line. Keep your arms straight and your palms touching the floor. Look down.

Relation with Zodiac Sign: Gemini

Planet: Mercury

Mantra: Om Khagaya Namaha (One who moves across the sky).

Step 6: Ashtanga Namaskara - Salute with Eight Points

Slowly straighten your hips to bring your entire body to the floor. Keep your palms on the floor and let your knees touch the floor as well. Once the body is aligned with the ground, raise your hips while keeping your knees on the floor. Slide your body to the front and let your chin and chest touch the floor. Your posterior should be slightly raised. With this pose, you are paying your respects to the Sun with eight points (two feet, two hands, chin, chest, and two knees).

Relation with Zodiac Sign: Cancer

Planet: Moon

Mantra: Om Pooshne Namaha (One who fulfills and provides nourishment).

Step 7: Bhujangasana - Cobra Pose

Straighten your knees and let your hips rest on the floor. Keep your palms on the floor and raise your upper back. Slide to the front and raise your chest. Bend your elbows and push your shoulders at the back. Inhale, look up, and bring your chest to the front. Exhale and push your tummy toward the floor. Tuck your toes and stretch your body as much as you can.

Relation with Zodiac Sign: Leo

Planet: Sun

Mantra: Om Hiranya Garbhaya Namaha (One who is filled with wisdom).

Step 8: Parvatasana - Mountain Pose

Exhale and slowly raise your hip area towards the ceiling while keeping your palms on the floor. Place your head between your arms and look down. Keep your knees and legs straight, and your heels should touch the floor. As you raise your tailbone and hips, your body should make an inverted "V" posture resembling a mountain.

Relation with Zodiac Sign: Virgo

Planet: Mercury

Mantra: Om Mareechaye Namaha (One who gives light).

Step 9: Ashwa Sanchalanasana - Equestrian Pose

Inhale and slowly release your hips to bring them back to the floor. Straighten your legs and let them rest on the floor. Bring your right leg to the front while pushing your left leg behind. Bend your right knee and place your right leg between your hands with your palms touching the floor. Your left knee and toes at the back should touch the floor. Try to push your hips down as much as you can. Look up and stretch your neck. Keep your spine straight.

Relation with Zodiac Sign: Libra

Planet: Venus

Mantra: Om Aadityaaya Namaha (The Divine Mother of the Cosmos, Son of Aditi).

Step 10: Hasta Padasana - Hand to Foot Pose

(This is the same pose you performed in step 3. It is important to perform a correct transition from the last asana to the next pose for effective results.) Raise your hips towards the ceiling and bend your upper body. Bring your feet together. Try to touch your knees with your nose while keeping your legs straight. Keep your arms straight and beside your feet. Try to touch the floor with your palms. You can slightly bend your knees at this point.

Relation with Zodiac Sign: Scorpio

Planet: Mars

Mantra: Om Savitre Namaha (One who takes responsibility for everything).

Step 11: Hastauttanasana - Raised Arms Pose

Slowly roll out your spine to raise your upper body. Inhale and raise your arms as you straighten your back and upper body. Your body should be perpendicular to the ground. Push your hips out and bend backward to stretch your body as much as possible. Your arms should be beside your ears. Stretch your entire body from your feet to your fingers and feel the stretch in your spinal cord.

Relation with Zodiac Sign: Sagittarius

Planet: Jupiter

Mantra: Om Arkaaya Namaha (One who is glorified and praised).

Step 12: Tadasana - Standing Mountain Pose

With this step, you are back to the initial position. Take a deep breath, join your palms together, and place them in front of your chest in a namaste position. Exhale and hold this position for a few seconds. Bring your arms down and loosen your body. Feel the sensations throughout your spine, arms, and legs.

Relation with Zodiac Sign: Capricorn

Planet: Saturn

Mantra: Om Bhaskaraya Namaha (One who spreads cosmic illumination and wisdom).

Spiritual practitioners advise doing Surya Namaskar early in the morning. With practice and consistency, you can increase one round per session. Practice it on an empty stomach to reap maximum health benefits as well. Over time, it will become a habit and a part of your routine.

The poses or asanas governed and shared by two zodiac signs at once are ruled by one planet. For example, poses 1 and 12 are related to Aquarius and Capricorn, respectively. Saturn rules both these signs. Since both poses are also the same, correspondence makes sense. The two asanas that occur just once in one round of Surya Namaskar (poses 6 and 7) are represented by the Moon and the Sun, respectively. Both the celestial bodies are independent and opposites, just like the two poses.

The Sun and Pranayama

The Sun is connected to Pranayama, which means "Purification of Breath." This breathing technique is quite popular among yogis and spiritual practitioners. Surya Bhedana is a Pranayama technique dedicated to the Sun. Surya means "Sun," and "Bhedana" translates to "piercing." This breathing technique is dedicated to the Sun and the Moon and their unison. The left nostril depicts the Moon and its calm energy, whereas the right nostril represents the Sun's activity, action, and heat. Surya Bhedana and Chandra Bhedana are related to the syllables "ha" and "tha," respectively. Collectively, they make the world "hatha," meaning "balance."

Basically, Pranayama is performed by blocking one nostril and letting air in through the other in an alternate manner, regulating your breathing pattern and restoring balance in your body. Surya Bhedana Pranayama enhances your "prana," or body heat, to induce vital force and improve your health. It also helps stimulate your mind and enhance your creativity. By learning the right form and practicing it consistently, you can put your plan into action and reach your goals with ease. Since the right nostril represents this Pranayama, you must breathe in through the right nostril and exhale from the left nostril to energize the Sun factors.

How to Perform Surya Bhedana Pranayama

Follow these steps to learn Pranayama the right way and reap its maximum benefit.

1. Pick a quiet spot and sit on a mat in a comfortable position. Keep your spine straight.
2. If you are seated in a cross-legged position, place the back of your left hand on your left knee, and join the tips of your thumb and index to make a circle.
3. Close your eyes and raise your right hand toward your face. Allow your middle and index finger to touch your forehead.
4. Use your ring finger to close your left nostril and breathe in through your right nostril. Hold your breath and place your thumb on your right nostril to block it. Lift your ring finger and allow the air to escape through your left nostril.
5. Repeat this in an alternate fashion by switching your finger and thumb to block each nostril in every round. Practice this for a few minutes.

This practice is related to the simple Pranayama breathing technique that uses the alternate breathing method. To perform Surya Bhedana Pranayama, breathe in through your right nostril and keep exhaling from the left without switching fingers.

Chakras Related to the Sun

The Sun is related to both the Solar Plexus chakra and the Crown chakra. In a literal sense, chakras translate to "spinning wheels" in Sanskrit. They are the energy centers within a body and are spread across the centerline of the body. Among the seven chakras that govern different body parts, the Solar Plexus (Manipura) and Crown (Sahasrara) chakras are closely associated with the Sun due to their matching frequencies. If you stand under the sunlight for a few minutes, both these chakras will receive energy and get cleansed. In a way, the Sun's energy balances these chakras, which are vital to improving your wellbeing and health.

Solar Plexus Chakra

The third chakra, also known as the "Manipura" chakra, is located at the center of the diaphragm. It governs your body's energy and symbolizes your identity and ego. It represents authenticity, personal freedom, willpower, and motivation. Due to its connection to the digestive system, this chakra is associated with the gut's brain and internal emotions. The color yellow represents this chakra. Like the Sun represents fire and heat, the Solar Plexus chakra is also represented by fire, which is also the chakra's main element. It uses heat and fire to regulate metabolism and maintain physical health.

How to Open the Solar Plexus Chakra

Opening your Solar Plexus chakra and balancing it is important. If left in an inactive state, you may suffer from intestinal or pancreatic problems along with emotional issues. To open or unblock this chakra, you must chant positive affirmations regularly. Practice visualization techniques to attract positivity and fend off negative energies. Another effective way is to perform yoga poses like Ardha Matsyendrasana (Half Spinal Twist), Dhanurasana (Bow Pose), and Paschimottanasana (Classical Forward Bend), which focus on improving your gut health and eliminating toxins from your body. Take a walk under the Sun and absorb morning sun rays for internal cleansing.

Crown Chakra

The Crown chakra is located above the head and acts as the center of wisdom, consciousness, enlightenment, and spiritual energy. An open Crown chakra can align with the universe's frequency and help you gain immense knowledge and creativity. It also establishes a deeper understanding of your surroundings and helps you tap into your spiritual energy. Both the Sun and the Crown chakras are related to masculine energy and divinity. Both are located at higher positions and act as governors. The Crown chakra reminds us that we are a part of the greater good and the universal forces instead of being alive as separate entities. We are an integral part of the cosmos.

How to Open the Crown Chakra

A blocked or closed Crown chakra can induce feelings of dissociation, boredom, general disinterest, and isolation. The person may feel stuck in a routine and detached from their life's purpose. In some cases, they may develop signs of depression or skepticism. To open your Crown chakra, engage in practices like visualization, journaling, and meditation. Certain yoga poses like Sasangasana (Rabbit Stand), Gomukhasana (Cow Face Pose), Ardha Ustrasana (Half Camel Pose), and Sirsasana (Headstand) can also help. More importantly, practice gratitude. Write down three things you are grateful for every day and feel blessed for being alive.

The Sun's Influence in Healing the Soul and the Mind

The Sun's energy and powerful rays can impact your physical health and make you stronger. Absorbing a healthy amount of sun can indeed help strengthen your internal system and rejuvenate certain parts of your body. For example, walking under the sun helps your body to get its daily dose of vitamin D, which regulates cell growth and reduces inflammation. It can also strengthen your bones. While the Sun provides various physical health benefits, it can also heal your mind and soul. People with little to zero sun exposure likely develop mental health issues like depression and moodiness over a prolonged period.

Sun rays also boost serotonin production, which can help you sleep better and improve your bedtime routine. You need quality sleep to function properly and keep your body and mind healthy. Sungazing is a practice followed for centuries and has been revered by ancient scholars for its benefits. This meditation practice allows your body to soak in the Sun's energy and feel recharged. Sungazing is known to be a booster for your soul and spiritual awakening. It promotes relaxation and inner peace, which are required to keep your soul happy.

Chapter 10: Keeping Your Soul Sunny

The Sun is life-giving, a blazing light in the midst of darkness. The Sun is the root of all life, and without it, we would be plunged into darkness. It is thanks to the Sun that you exist; it is the reason you are alive, breathing in the fresh air. The Sun is the reason everyone and everything you love exists.

Every single thing you come across on this earth is filled with energy. Everything embodies the energy of the Sun - the food you eat, the trees you see, and the people in front of you. Every aspect of this earth is alive and organic, brimming with the energy of the star of light. You may have noticed that the moon affects your mood on certain lunar days, such as the full or new moon day. In other words, you will often find that the changes in the moon affect your emotional state. Our minds, bodies, and hearts are all governed by external influence from the universe around us. The surrounding universe affects us because we are an entire universe ourselves. Each of us holds a whole universe within us – the energies of worlds, suns, moons, and stars exist inside us.

Humans are at their prime when they lead their life in tune with the Sun. Our circadian rhythm regulates our sleeping pattern, allowing us to shut down at nighttime and settle in for a restful sleep. Ayurvedic practitioners believe that metabolism is connected to the movement of the Sun, and that's why they advocate lunch as the biggest meal of the day, as the Sun is at its brightest during this time. You may feel tired and sluggish when you eat a lot at night, supposedly because the metabolism is slower when the Sun goes down.

Many engage in sunbathing as a way to receive physical health and spiritual benefits from the Sun. It is believed that this helps regulate the circadian rhythm, produce vitamin D, boost the immune system, and stimulate the pineal gland.

Light after Darkness

In life, we all go through moments of peril and darkness. Moments where it feels like we will never come out from under this blanket of darkness. Whoever we are and whatever we do, it is unlikely we will have escaped this blanket completely. It shows up in our lives seem to haunt or taunt us, to push us down a gloomy hole, one which we can barely scrape ourselves out of.

We live in a world of polarity, where there is darkness but also light. This darkness pushes us to go within, and that signifies it's time for a change. The darkness takes us for fools, but it has come to take us out of suffering.

In the physical world, every day, we witness the rising of the Sun piercing through the darkness of the night. It brings with it a glow, new hope, a fresh new start. The Sun says, come and try again; the doors of hope have arrived. Come and start fresh; the day is yours. This experience occurs within us, too. The light comes to disrupt the darkness, and we find that we must leap on this glimmer of hope! Just as the Sun rises every single day, so shall we. As we choose to mirror life's natural circles, we find ourselves moving back and forth between light and dark.

In those dark moments, we find ourselves cursing our bad luck, wishing we were someone else. But it is these moments that are vital to our growth. It is this darkness that is necessary for us

---

to move fully into the light. It is this cyclical part of life that we must embrace. The sooner we begin to embrace the light, fully, deeply, the sooner we can come out of the darkness.

How to Embrace the Power of the Sun

The power of the Sun can aid your growth and guide your path towards spiritual evolution. Consider the magnitude of this life force. Perhaps in our modern, fast-paced lifestyles, we have become desensitized to just how incredible this star is. But you being here, reading this is your inner-self nudging you back to these primordial life forces. In ancient times, our ancestors understood nature. They understood how potent nature was, and they used it to heal and aid themselves. We, too, can use it in this way, despite all the commotion and rush surrounding us.

It's all about choosing to slow down and listen to our inner calling. *If your inner voice tells you to embrace nature as you have never before, now is the time*. Living in alignment with the Sun will help you become the healthiest and happiest version of yourself. Give it a go!

- Become an early-riser. In yogic traditions, the hours of the morning are said to have a certain spiritual power. This is the ideal time to meditate or practice yoga. 4-6 am is a potent time, helping to increase your mental clarity and positive energy. If you can't fathom waking up this early, try waking up 10-15 minutes earlier every day. This will help you slowly adjust to a different sleeping routine, and you will eventually notice the positive effects of being an early riser. It will help motivate you to continue on this Sun-seeking path.
- In Ayurveda, the Sun is considered the "source of all life." Another step to maintain a connection with the Sun is to honor it. Cultivating a practice of reverence is almost an act of rebellion in an age accustomed to social media likes and external validation. Self-esteem and personalities have been built around these online societies. Turning to the Sun and honoring it brings you back to your true self. Sitting in the Sun in honest gratitude opens your heart, mind, and soul back to the source of all things. You let this light enter and flow through you, healing you physically, emotionally, and spiritually.
- Sit in the Sun every morning, meditating or doing breathwork. Even a few deep breaths will help you build up this practice of presence and reverence. The idea isn't to worship the Sun but rather to allow the light of the Sun to remind us of the light within ourselves.

Each of us has a natural "sunlight" inside us. This light is our guide, our hope, and a source of healing. Connecting with the Sun gives us the power to remember this. This light can easily be snuffed out by the digital age, where we are racing against time to be the best in the eyes of others. It is a rarity to see someone slow down, feel grounded, and choose to reject these new societal norms.

The sunlight gives us this power. Its potency reminds us just how stunning, incredible, and life-giving we are. Each of us represents our own universe with our own Sun. This Sun within us is in our control, and we get to choose when it rises and when it sets. Choose every day to connect with the inner and external Sun. Choose to be light, choose to be sunny.

Healer

The Vedas worship this star of light. They view it as the source of light for the whole world. The light is not considered a material force but rather a power of love, life, and intelligence. The Sun is also not seen as an entity far away from us, but rather that its presence is here on Earth, touching our hearts and filling us with life.

The Sun is not simply seen as a physical star, for it represents the concept of light and consciousness. The Sun is merely a way to showcase these ideas. When deeply understood, the Sun is an internal source of energy. It is a doorway to a higher realm, a realm which we can travel through by harnessing the power of the Sun.

Worshipping the Sun is seen as a path to enlightenment and self-actualization. The Vedics observe a Sun ritual that involves making offerings to fire, connecting them with the powers of the Sun deity. They believe that we are all children of the Sun, existing on this Earth to bring the truth forward. For this reason, the Sun is considered to be at the core of who we are, with every soul being its own spiritual Sun.

The Gayatri mantra is one of the most important Vedic mantras and is often used in yogic practices. It is used to draw in the spiritual essence of the Sun, welcoming it into our mind, body, and heart.

We meditate upon the supreme light of the Divine transforming Sun (Savitri) that he may stimulate our intelligence.

The chanting of this mantra occurs at important points during the day, including sunrise, noon, and sunset. The power behind this does not simply represent the transformational power of the Sun but also the power of the spirits to take us out of the ego's darkness into the infinity of the authentic self.

Many parts of the world and religious texts revere the Sun and honor it, whereas, from a western perspective, the Sun is often feared. It is viewed as cancer-causing and skin-destroying. We are advised to cover up and slather on sunscreen at the smallest hint of sunray. Many believe that the Sun accelerates the aging process and ruins our health by causing skin cancer. Why is it that so many people around the world sunbathe, even worship the Sun, and do not find this to be the case?

We can use the intelligence held within the sunlight as a source of intellect, wisdom, and love. That said, how can we merge this with our current understanding of the Sun as being detrimental to our health? There is plenty of literature on the health benefits of sunlight exposure which make for a greater understanding of how the Sun can benefit us in various ways.

One of the reasons the Sun is viewed as the meaning of life is because it is life-giving. Without it, neither we, nor animals, nor plants would breathe, eat, or grow. In light of this, returning to the Sun as a form of healing can grant us many great benefits. Experiencing this warm, healing light for a few moments in silence is a treasure in this age.

Positive Energy

Do you find yourself struggling to fight your inner demons?

Do you often experience moments of darkness?

Is there a part of you that wants to break free and unshackle itself?

The Sun is your answer, both physically and metaphorically. Begin a daily practice of honoring and spending time by yourself in the Sun. How this looks to you may not be exactly the same as other people practice, but you must make it your own. You may enjoy exposing your bare skin to the sunlight, reading a novel, doing yoga, or simply gazing up toward the Sun for a few minutes. Of course, you should practice safe sun exposure and not spend hours in direct sunlight. Moderate yourself and maintain a good balance so you can reap its physical and spiritual benefits.

The Sun's ability to detox further connects you with yourself, deepening your intuition and cultivating presence. Sunlight can be a potent cure against depression, grief, and misery. Many have found that a dedicated sunbathing practice has helped to cure many a depressive or dark episode.

Viewing yourself as being connected with the Sun will even allow your soul and personality to become sunnier and happier. Have you noticed how your mood changes on a sunny day compared to when it's gloomy? Truly, the Sun does fill you with positive energy! Even on the darker days, though, how do we keep this sunny energy within us? The sunlight inside us cannot always rely on the Sun itself; instead, we must cultivate a way to always be sunny without the Sun's warm and reassuring shine.

Here are a few ways you can implement this sunny mood into your everyday life:

- Practice gratitude. If this is difficult for you, concentrate on everything you are grateful to the Sun for. You'll soon realize the list is longer than you'd expect. From the fresh air you breathe to the food you eat, the Sun should be shown gratitude for these life-giving powers. As time goes on, it will become easier for you to find things about yourself and your life for which you are thankful. This practice begins to rewire your brain for positive thinking and self-fulfillment.

- Prioritize movement. How well does it feel being out in the Sun? That little sweat you break often feels like a detox. To keep your attitude and mood sunny, try and get some exercise every day, which is important for your emotional, physical, and mental health. We store so much stress, emotion, and pain in our bodies that working out can be a phenomenal relief. If you find it hard to go to the gym, begin by stretching at home, go on a jog, or play a follow-along exercise video suitable to your level.

- Cultivate presence. We have mentioned presence several times throughout this chapter, yet it is important to mention it again. Many of the problems we face mentally and emotionally often stem from overthinking. They arise as our minds constantly go in circles, thinking our way into problems. It is difficult for us to stop for a second and ground down into the here and now. How much of our environment do we truly notice and appreciate? Are we really here at all? The more present you can be, the more you realize how nonsensical many of your supposed problems are. The more present you are, the more space you have for joy, bliss, and happiness.

If you find it difficult to practice presence, which can be hard, especially with so many distractions, pointless screen time, and our busy lifestyles, here are some useful tips:

- Take a few moments during the day when you feel your feet on the ground, your legs on the chair, your back against the wall, or anything else that feels relevant in that moment. Notice these body parts – how they press down, how they're grounded. Embrace the sensations without thinking too much.

- Begin a meditative practice. A few minutes each day is a great place to start if you don't have a routine already, as the resistance levels may be high. Start small and slow, then witness your mind and practice grow before you.

- Stop and smell the flowers. Make it a point to start reconnecting with nature. The flowers on your morning commute, the trees that shed and grow leaves, the grass that you tread on every day. Start noticing these small things, and you will soon find it much easier to stay in the present moment.

The Sun has been a symbol of the self, the soul, and life since time immemorial. Sun worshipping has been around for thousands of years, with ancient civilizations devoting a true appreciation and understanding of this life-giving source. The Sun teaches us a valuable lesson, namely that life is for living. That every day we must rise and start anew. That new beginnings are for everyone.

The Sun is the clarity amidst confusion and distractions. In this world of fast-paced, active lifestyles, we face much fogginess. The Sun is the disruptor of not only the fog but the darkness, too.

Finally, the Sun we know teaches us much about our internal Sun. It is by having reverence and appreciation for the external Sun that our internal Sun begins to awaken. Connecting with this Sun helps to give us the motivation and inspiration to move forward in life, to feel true joy, bliss, and presence.

Conclusion

Congratulations for making it this far! Before you began exploring the different versions and roles of the Sun in astrology, as a timekeeper and a healing entity, you might have imagined this celestial body as nothing more than a ball of fire vital to the Earth's existence. As you flipped the pages, you realized that the Sun plays an even bigger role in the astronomical, medical, spiritual, and astrological domains. Now that you've gained insights into the Sun's role as a giver of life and have learned its significance in astrology, you are ready to harness its energy to revitalize your mind.

Let's recap all the insights we've gathered so far. The Sun plays an important role as a **life-giver** and in governing the planets within the solar system. The center of attention and the ruler of the planets, the Sun, has been the main deity in many belief systems that include solar motifs. The Sun God was the main ruler and influencer of the ancient Egyptians, Sumerians, and Indo-European people. Devotees sacrificed their lives and celebrated the Sun God's presence by observing rituals and offering prayers. According to them, pleasing the deity was indispensable as it procured healthy crops and governed the livelihood of all mortal creatures.

The Sun as a timekeeper has been a major subject of interest among scholars, intellectuals, and astrology enthusiasts. They studied the pattern of the Sun's location and movements to tell the time and determine the hours, days, weeks, months, and years. Ancient Greeks and Romans used devices such as sundials and water clocks designed based on the Sun's motion in the sky. The shadows on a sundial's surface formed a set of lines and angles that indicated a particular hour of the day. Water clocks were designed using a set of vessels with markings on the surface that helped the observer calculate the hour.

In Vedic astrology, the Sun is considered one of the most significant celestial bodies alongside the Moon. When a person was born, Vedic astrologers calculated the Sun's position to produce a natal chart, which represented the person's fate, personality, wealth, ambition, power, recognition, health, and fulfillment. The Sun stays in an exalted position when it meets Aries, thereby creating strong conjunction. By contrast, the Sun's debilitated position with Libra can negatively impact the native's life.

The Sun's **conjunction with other planets** is another interesting topic we've tapped into. An afflicted Sun in a horoscope can make the native's life worse. They are not given enough credit for their work and will likely suffer in their personal lives too.

The celestial body has also been a part of **Vedic and medical astrology** for many centuries now. Because it represents the heart, the Sun can help diagnose cardiovascular issues, making treatment easier.

It also represents a person's characteristics and determines their fate based on their sun sign. Lastly, the Sun's energy can be manifested by incorporating it into yoga practices and performing relevant asanas or breathing exercises. Surya Namaskar and Pranayama are two effective practices to harness the Sun's energy and heal your mental and spiritual health. When done correctly, they can also help open the Solar Plexus chakra and Crown chakra to improve your health.

Whether you are simply curious about exploring this new domain or wish to dig deeper in the study of the Sun in astrology, you can go back and refer to the relevant chapters and gain a better insight. If you think this book has helped you in any way, don't hesitate to spread the word and let your loved ones manifest the Sun's positive energy, too. Ask them to grab their copy and learn more about this ruling celestial body and its significance in astrology. Good luck, and happy manifesting!

Here's another book by Mari Silva that you might like

MARI SILVA

ZODIAC SIGNS

The Ultimate Guide to Aries, Taurus, Gemini, Cancer, Leo, Virgo, Libra, Scorpio, Sagittarius, Capricorn, Aquarius, and Pisces

Your Free Gift (only available for a limited time)

Thanks for getting this book! If you want to learn more about various spirituality topics, then join Mari Silva's community and get a free guided meditation MP3 for awakening your third eye. This guided meditation mp3 is designed to open and strengthen ones third eye so you can experience a higher state of consciousness. Simply visit the link below the image to get started.

https://spiritualityspot.com/meditation

References

Planets – Sun. (2017, September 25). Retrieved from Horoscope website: https://www.astrology.com/planets/sun

The Sun in Astrology. (n.d.). Retrieved from Astrograph.com website: https://www.astrograph.com/learning-astrology/sun.php

The Sun in Astrology, the zodiac. (2015, May 8). Retrieved from Cafeastrology.com website: https://cafeastrology.com/sun.html

Ancient solar: How ancient civilizations harnessed the Sun's energy. (n.d.). Retrieved from Cleanchoiceenergy.com website: https://cleanchoiceenergy.com/news/Ancient_Solar

Cartwright, M. (2016). Surya. World History Encyclopedia. Retrieved from https://www.worldhistory.org/Surya/

Mishra, B. K. (2019, October 31). Sun God worshipped across cultures'. Retrieved from Times Of India website: https://timesofindia.indiatimes.com/city/patna/sun-god-worshipped-across-cultures/articleshow/71826105.cms

Team Vidhya Mitra. (2021, March 29). What is Sun in Astrology? What does Sun Represent in Vedic Astrology? Retrieved from Vidhyamitra.com website: https://vidhyamitra.com/sun-in-astrology/

Ancient Egyptian calendar: 1st calendar known to mankind. (2019, September 11). Retrieved from Egypttoday.com website: https://www.egypttoday.com/Article/4/74680/Ancient-Egyptian-calendar-1st-calendar-known-to-mankind

Early Roman Calendar. (n.d.). Retrieved from Webexhibits.org website: http://www.webexhibits.org/calendars/calendar-roman.html

Grattan, K. (2016, May 16). A brief history of telling time. The Conversation. Retrieved from http://theconversation.com/a-brief-history-of-telling-time-55408

Greek calendar. (n.d.). Retrieved from Worldtempus.com website: http://en.worldtempus.com/lexique/greek-calendar-108.html

Rajendran, A. (n.d.). What is Tithi in Hindu Calendar? – How is Thithi Calculated in Panchangam? Retrieved from Hindu-blog.com website: https://www.hindu-blog.com/2010/01/what-is-tithi-in-hindu-calendar-how-is.html

Short Guide on Nakshatras/Stars in Astrology - GaneshaSpeaks. (2017, February 20). Retrieved from Ganeshaspeaks.com website: https://www.ganeshaspeaks.com/astrology/nakshatras-constellations/

Telling the time with the Sun. (n.d.). Retrieved from Org.uk website: https://www.sciencemuseum.org.uk/objects-and-stories/telling-time-sun

The five building blocks of Panchang. (n.d.). Retrieved from Astrosage.com website: http://astrology.astrosage.com/2013/11/the-five-building-blocks-of-panchang.html

astrologerbydefault. (2019, June 24). psychologically astrology. Retrieved from Psychologicallyastrology.com website: https://psychologicallyastrology.com/2019/06/24/sun-mahadasha/

Effects of Sun in different houses. (2019, June 17). Retrieved from Astrotalk.com website: https://astrotalk.com/astrology-blog/effects-of-sun-in-different-houses/

Ghosh, A. P. K. (2020, December 16). Presence of Sun in 12 different houses of horoscope. Retrieved from Bigumbrella.co.in website: https://www.bigumbrella.co.in/presence-of-sun-in-12-different-houses-of-horoscope/

indastro. (n.d.). Sun planet – Sun effects in Astrology – Sun planet Astrology. Retrieved from Indastro.com website: https://www.indastro.com/planets/sun-planet.html

Sun & Moon Combinations: How Well do your Sun & Moon get Along? (n.d.). Retrieved from Southfloridaastrologer.com website: https://www.southfloridaastrologer.com/sun--moon-combinations-how-well-do-your-sun--moon-get-along.html

The connection between the Sun and moon in astrology. (2019, March 13). Retrieved from Askastrology.com website: https://askastrology.com/sun-and-moon-in-astrology/

Auspicious yogas formed by Sun in Vedic Astrology. (2019, December 18). Retrieved from Astrotalk.com website: https://astrotalk.com/astrology-blog/sun-in-vedic-astrology/

Conjunction Aspect meaning in astrology. (2018, January 29). Retrieved from Labyrinthos.co website: https://labyrinthos.co/blogs/astrology-horoscope-zodiac-signs/conjunction-aspect-meaning

Hall, M. (n.d.). Aspects to natal Sun in birth chart. Retrieved from Liveabout.com website: https://www.liveabout.com/sun-aspects-sun-signs-206275

Kahn, N. (2019, January 26). What conjunction, Trine, square, opposition, and sextile mean in astrology & birth charts. Retrieved from Bustle.com website: https://www.bustle.com/life/what-conjunction-trine-square-opposition-sextile-mean-in-astrology-birth-charts-13108526

Rosen, B. (2018, January 7). UNDERSTANDING PLANETARY COMBUSTION AND PLANETS TOO CLOSE TO THE SUN PART 1 - applied Vedic astrology. Retrieved from Appliedvedicastrology.com website: https://www.appliedvedicastrology.com/2018/01/07/understanding-planetary-combustion-planets-close-sun-part-1/

(Soni & View my complete profile, n.d.)

Soni, S., & View my complete profile. (n.d.). Vedic Astrology Research Portal. Retrieved from Blogspot.com website: https://astrologywithsourabh.blogspot.com/2015/05/all-about-planetary-combustion-in-vedic_62.html

Diseases in medical astrology. (2013, October 26). Retrieved from Astrovastutips.com website: https://astrovastutips.com/diseases-in-medical-astrology/

Kaushik, A. (2020, September 1). Nine planets & their associated herbs ! Ayurveda remedies. Retrieved from Astrokaushik.com website: https://astrokaushik.com/nine-planets-their-associated-herbs-ayurveda-remedies/

Medical Astrology - the planet and its related disease. (n.d.). Retrieved from Astrobix.com website: https://astrobix.com/learn/312-medical-astrology-the-planet-and-its-related-disease.html

Medical astrology and astrological medicine. (n.d.). Retrieved from Homeoint.org website: http://www.homeoint.org/morrell/astrology/medical.htm

Signs and remedies of weak Sun in horoscope - Ruby.Org.In. (2017, December 23). Retrieved from Org.in website: https://ruby.org.in/blog/signs-remedies-weak-sun-horoscope/

Vedic Medical Astrology - Medical Astrology - vedicnakshatras.Com. (n.d.). Retrieved from Vedicnakshatras.com website: http://www.vedicnakshatras.com/vedic-medical-astrology.html

View all posts by Dr. Deepak Sharma →. (2015, February 3). Heart attack and Astrology. Retrieved from Astroyantra.com website: https://www.astroyantra.com/heart-attack-astrology/

12 Astrology Signs. (n.d.). Retrieved from Astrology-prophets.com website: https://www.astrology-prophets.com/12-astrology-signs.php

12 Signs & their Significations (Part I). (2015, March 25). Retrieved from Theartofvedicastrology.com website: http://www.theartofvedicastrology.com/?page_id=127

Regan, S. (2020, May 30). Don't relate to your sun sign? It may be different in Vedic astrology. Retrieved from Mindbodygreen.com website: https://www.mindbodygreen.com/articles/how-to-calculate-your-sun-sign-in-vedic-astrology

Zodiac Constellations. (n.d.). Retrieved from Constellation-guide.com website: https://www.constellation-guide.com/constellation-map/zodiac-constellations/

12 Signs & their Significations (Part I). (2015, March 25). Retrieved from Theartofvedicastrology.com website: http://www.theartofvedicastrology.com/?page_id=127

12 Zodiac signs of Vedic Astrology. (2019, August 3). Retrieved from Astroved.com website: https://www.astroved.com/blogs/12-zodiac-signs-vedic-astrology

Dr R Nageswara Rao, vedic indian astrologer from http://www. askastrologer.com. (n.d.). Zodiac or rasi chakra in astrology and meanings of 12 zodiac signs in indian hindu vedic astrology. Retrieved from Askastrologer.com website: https://askastrologer.com/indian-hindu-vedic-astrology-zodiac.html

Hassan, A. D. (2015). Zodiac signs: The banished hero. Outskirts Press.

KellyWriter, A., & 12/07/, Z. (2020, December 7). What is Vedic astrology & how to find your Sun sign. Retrieved from Yourtango.com website: https://www.yourtango.com/2019327900/what-vedic-astrology-horoscope-meaning-each-zodiac-sign

Lesson 1. (2009, October 22). Retrieved from Astrojyoti.com website: https://www.astrojyoti.com/lesson1.htm

Astrologer, D. A. S. K. (n.d.). Zodiac Signs & lord Planets, Rashi Lords Astrology. Retrieved from Astrologer-astrology.com website: https://astrologer-astrology.com/zodiac_lord_indian_vedic_astrology_jyotish.htm

Rashi signs- free Indian astrology, 12 sun sign by name, Hindu zodiac signs. (n.d.). Retrieved from Astrodevam.com website: https://www.astrodevam.com/knowledge-bank/zodiac-sign-rashi.html?

Vallée, G. (2020, March 1). What's your Vedic astrological sign? Retrieved from Birla.ca website: https://birla.ca/en/whats-your-vedic-astrological-sign/

Zodiac signs: Significance of 12 sun signs. (2016, November 25). Retrieved from Ganeshaspeaks.com website: https://www.ganeshaspeaks.com/zodiac-signs/

(N.d.). Retrieved from Vedicfeed.com website: https://vedicfeed.com/traits-of-different-horoscopes-of-hindu-astrology/

Correlation between sun salutation and Vedic astrology. (n.d.-a). Retrieved from Altervista.org website: http://andreasyoga.altervista.org/sun-salutation-astrological-correlation/?doing_wp_cron=1629928290.3482990264892578125000

Correlation between sun salutation and Vedic astrology. (n.d.-b). Retrieved from Altervista.org website: http://andreasyoga.altervista.org/sun-salutation-astrological-correlation/?doing_wp_cron=1629969632.3922810554504394531250

Mahabir, N. (2021, March 17). Surya namaskar: How to do this warming yoga practice to connect to the rhythm and energy of the Sun. CBC News. Retrieved from https://www.cbc.ca/life/wellness/surya-namaskar-how-to-do-this-warming-practice-to-connect-to-the-rhythm-and-energy-of-the-sun-1.5951832

Manipura Chakra: Healing powers of Solar Plexus Chakra. (2020, September 3). Retrieved from Arhantayoga.org website: https://www.arhantayoga.org/blog/manipura-chakra-healing-powers-of-the-solar-plexus-chakra/

Mathur, N. (2020, February 16). Surya Namaskar (Sun salutations) and astrology. Retrieved from Cosmicinsights.net website: https://blog.cosmicinsights.net/surya-namaskar-sun-salutations-and-astrology/

No title. (n.d.). Retrieved from Com.my website: https://astroulagam.com.my/lifestyle/surya-namaskar-decoded-136815

Stokes, V. (2021, July 1). Want to harness the healing power of the Sun? Some say Sun gazing meditation can help. Retrieved from Healthline.com website: https://www.healthline.com/health/mind-body/sun-gazing

thejoywithin. (2019, July 30). How to do Surya bhedana pranayama: Sun piercing breath. Retrieved from Thejoywithin.org website: https://thejoywithin.org/breath-exercises/surya-bhedana-pranayama-sun-piercing-breath

Christopher. (2021, January 16). Sun symbolism (7 meanings in culture & spirituality). Retrieved from Symbolismandmetaphor.com website: https://symbolismandmetaphor.com/sun-symbolism-meanings/

Kelmenson, K. (2017, June 6). The potent power of the Sun. Retrieved from Spiritualityhealth.com website: https://www.spiritualityhealth.com/blogs/the-present-moment/2017/06/06/kalia-kelmenson-potent-power-sun

Sun: The eye of the world - spiritual Import of Religious Festivals. (n.d.). Retrieved from Swami-krishnananda.org website: https://www.swami-krishnananda.org/fest/fest_02.html

The Sun in the puranas and the Vedas. (n.d.). Retrieved from Scribd.com website: https://www.scribd.com/document/85910368/THE-SUN-IN-THE-PURANAS-AND-THE-VEDAS

Mack, L. (2021, January 12). How to understand your moon sign. Retrieved from Thecut.com website: https://www.thecut.com/article/moon-sign-astrology-what-your-moon-sign-means.html

The Moon. (n.d.). Retrieved from Astrology-zodiac-signs.com website: https://www.astrology-zodiac-signs.com/astrology/planets/moon/

A Wiccan Guide to Moon magic – Wicca living. (2017, June 16). Retrieved from Wiccaliving.com website: https://wiccaliving.com/wiccan-full-moon-ritual/

Chang'e – Chinese goddess of the moon. (2021, July 1). Retrieved from Symbolsage.com website: https://symbolsage.com/chinese-goddess-of-the-moon/

Luna - Roman goddess of the moon - symbol sage. (2020, December 2). Retrieved from Symbolsage.com website: https://symbolsage.com/luna-roman-moon-goddess/

MacDougal, C. (2019, December 9). How the Moon affects us. Retrieved from Athrbeauty.com website: https://athrbeauty.com/blogs/goodvibesbeauty/how-the-moon-its-phases-affect-us

Selene – the Greek moon goddess. (2020, December 14). Retrieved from Symbolsage.com website: https://symbolsage.com/selene-greek-moon-goddess/

Sin (mythology). (n.d.). Retrieved from Newworldencyclopedia.org website: https://www.newworldencyclopedia.org/entry/Sin_(mythology)

The legend of Chang E. (n.d.). Retrieved from Moonfestival.org website: http://www.moonfestival.org/the-legend-of-chang-e.html

Thompson, A. (2009, October 5). Our changing view of the moon. Retrieved from Space website: https://www.space.com/7338-changing-view-moon.html

---

Thoth -the Egyptian god of wisdom and writing. (2020, October 20). Retrieved from Symbolsage.com website: https://symbolsage.com/thoth-egyptian-god-of-wisdom/

Who is Chandra the Hindu god? (2013, February 13). Retrieved from Synonym.com website: https://classroom.synonym.com/who-is-chandra-the-hindu-god-12086016.html

Yanka. (n.d.). Chandra or Moon God – born from the ocean of the mind. Retrieved from Sagarworld.com website: https://www.sagarworld.com/ramayan/chandra-or-moon-god-born-from-the-ocean-of-the-mind

astrosharmistha. (2019, September 19). Moon in Vedic Astrology -. Retrieved from Astrosharmistha.com website: http://astrosharmistha.com/blog/moon-in-vedic-astrology/

Bhattacharjee, A. S. (2018, June 18). Moon Remedies Astrology For Weak, Debilitated, Afflicted, combusted state. Retrieved from Astrosanhita.com website: https://astrosanhita.com/remedies-for-weak-debilitated-afflicted-moon-in-astrology/

HeereJawharat.com. (2015, June). Retrieved from Heerejawharat.com website: https://www.heerejawharat.com/gemstones-astrology-significance/white-pearl-astrological-significance.php

Moon Nakshatra: Your Vedic Moon Sign. (2018, July 25). Retrieved from Serenityspaonline.com website: https://serenityspaonline.com/moon-nakshatra-sign/

Prusty, M. (2019, January 23). Role and importance of Moon in Vedic astrology. Retrieved from Astroguruonline.com website: https://www.astroguruonline.com/importance-moon-vedic-astrology/

Rocks, D. (2013, October 25). Moon in Cancer: Characteristics and personality traits. Retrieved from Com.au website: https://www.starslikeyou.com.au/your-astrology-profile/moon-in-cancer/

Speaks, J. (2020, January 29). 10 best home remedies for Moon planet in males & females horoscope. Retrieved from Jupiterspeaks.com website: https://jupiterspeaks.com/general-remedies-problems-related-planet-moon/

Vani, A. (2013, August 5). How to make your Moon stronger - remedies by Pawan Sinha. Retrieved from Astro-vani.com website: https://www.astro-vani.com/blog/make-your-moon-balanced/

Hall, M. (n.d.). What It Means When the Moon is in Taurus. Retrieved from Liveabout.com website: https://www.liveabout.com/when-the-moon-is-in-taurus-207337

Rocks, D. (2013a, October 25). Moon in Cancer: Characteristics and personality traits. Retrieved from Com.au website: https://www.starslikeyou.com.au/your-astrology-profile/moon-in-cancer/

Rocks, D. (2013b, October 25). Moon in Gemini. Retrieved from Com.au website: https://www.starslikeyou.com.au/your-astrology-profile/moon-in-gemini/

Rocks, D. (2013c, October 25). The Moon in Aries: Characteristics and personality traits. Retrieved from Com.au website: https://www.starslikeyou.com.au/your-astrology-profile/the-moon-in-aries/

Libra Moon. (n.d.). Retrieved from Justastrologythings.com website: https://justastrologythings.com/pages/planets/moon/libra.php

Matsumoto, A. (2020, April 2). Moon in Scorpio: Recognize true value and seize it all. Retrieved from Keikopowerwish.com website: https://www.keikopowerwish.com/blog/moon-in-scorpio-recognize-true-value-and-seize-it-all

Moon in Leo: 5 strengths & 5 challenges of the natal Moon in Leo. (n.d.). Retrieved from https://popularastrology.com/leo-moon

Moon in Virgo. (2016, November 29). Retrieved from Ganeshaspeaks.com website: https://www.ganeshaspeaks.com/zodiac-signs/virgo/moon-in-virgo/

What is your Moon sign, and what does it say about you? (2021, May 23). Retrieved from Russh.com website: https://www.russh.com/what-is-your-moon-sign/

Faragher, A. K. (2018, April 23). What your moon sign says about your emotional personality. Retrieved from Allure website: https://www.allure.com/story/zodiac-moon-sign-emotional-personality

jracioppi. (2013, March 11). New Moon in Pisces. Retrieved from Jenniferracioppi.com website: https://jenniferracioppi.com/new-moon-in-pisces/

Moon in Aquarius sign: Meaning, significance and personality traits. (2014, September 17). Retrieved from Sunsigns.org website: https://www.sunsigns.org/moon-in-aquarius/

Moon in Sagittarius. (n.d.). Retrieved from Lunaf.com website: https://lunaf.com/astrology/moon-in-zodiac/sagittarius/

Admin, D. (2019, August 24). Understanding your lunar south node (AKA karma). Retrieved from Dooznyc.com website: https://dooznyc.com/blogs/the-scope/understanding-your-lunar-south-node-aka-karma

Backlund, R. (2018, April 18). This piece of your birth chart reveals the parts of yourself you're meant to leave behind. Retrieved from Elitedaily.com website: https://www.elitedaily.com/p/what-does-your-south-node-mean-in-astrology-what-it-says-about-the-obstacles-youre-meant-to-overcome-8814403

McKinley, E. (2021, February 20). South node astrology and past life karma. Retrieved from Ouiwegirl.com website: https://www.ouiwegirl.com/astrology/2021/2/20/southnodeastrology

AstroTwins. (2013, October 19). North nodes & south nodes: The astrology of your life purpose and past lives. Retrieved from Astrostyle.com website: https://astrostyle.com/learn-astrology/north-south-nodes/

Fosu, K. (2020, November 3). Astrology: An easy guide to understanding the north node in the birth chart. Retrieved from Mystic Minds website: https://medium.com/mystic-minds/astrology-an-easy-guide-to-understanding-the-role-of-the-north-node-in-the-chart-e1f998bb555a

Johnson, E. (n.d.). Understanding your north node. Retrieved from Zennedout.com website: https://zennedout.com/understanding-your-north-node/

Astrolada. (n.d.). Astrolada. Retrieved from Astrolada.com website: https://www.astrolada.com/articles/planets-in-aspects/moon-with-rahu-in-the-horoscope.html

Carter, J. (2020a, January 2). Moon conjunct Mars natal and transit: New initiatives. Retrieved from Horoscopejoy.com website: https://www.horoscopejoy.com/moon-conjunct-mars-natal-and-transit-new-initiatives/

Carter, J. (2020b, January 2). Moon conjunct Uranus natal and transit: Unexpected opportunities. Retrieved from Horoscopejoy.com website: https://www.horoscopejoy.com/moon-conjunct-uranus-natal-and-transit-unexpected-opportunities/

Partridge, J. (2014, May 8). Moon conjunct Saturn natal and transit – Astrology King. Retrieved from Astrologyking.com website: https://astrologyking.com/moon-conjunct-saturn/

Partridge, J. (2015, April 30). Moon conjunct Mercury natal and transit – astrology king. Retrieved from Astrologyking.com website: https://astrologyking.com/moon-conjunct-mercury/

Partridge, J. (2017a, January 29). Moon conjunct Venus natal and transit – astrology king. Retrieved from Astrologyking.com website: https://astrologyking.com/moon-conjunct-venus/

Partridge, J. (2017b, February 28). Moon conjunct Neptune natal and transit – astrology king. Retrieved from Astrologyking.com website: https://astrologyking.com/moon-conjunct-neptune/

Patchirajan, A. (2017, September 19). Moon & Ketu conjuction. Retrieved from Cosmicinsights.net website: https://blog.cosmicinsights.net/moon-ketu-conjuction/

The Transit Moon. (n.d.). Retrieved from Thedarkpixieastrology.com website: http://www.thedarkpixieastrology.com/the-transit-moon.html

Today, C. (2020, May 23). Planetary conjunctions - DWI-graha samyoga: Moon conjunct with other planets. Retrieved from Ceylon Today website: https://ceylontoday.lk/news/planetary-conjunctions-dwi-graha-samyoga-moon-conjunct-with-other-planets

Crawford, C. (2019, October 21). Moon phases and their meanings — the self-care emporium. Retrieved from Theselfcareemporium.com website: https://theselfcareemporium.com/blog/moon-phases-and-their-meanings

Grabarczyk, J. (2019, November 19). Your quick guide to moon phases, their meaning, and how they impact you. Retrieved from Yogiapproved.com website: https://www.yogiapproved.com/life/moon-phases-meanings-impact/

Martin, L., & Backlund, R. (2017, October 4). How to use each phase of the moon to lead A smarter, more creative life. Retrieved from Elitedaily.com website: https://www.elitedaily.com/lifestyle/moon-phases-affects-body-mind

Eaton, A. (2020, April 10). Moon ritual practices for every lunar phase — oui we. Retrieved from Ouiwegirl.com website: https://www.ouiwegirl.com/beauty/2020/4/8/moon-rituals

Garis, M. G. (2021, March 18). How to take a ritual moon bath and bring forth your wildest dreams. Retrieved from Well+Good website: https://www.wellandgood.com/moon-bath-ritual/

How to align with the four phases of the moon. (2020, February 14). Retrieved from Goop.com website: https://goop.com/wellness/spirituality/how-to-align-with-the-moon/

Hurst, K. (2017, March 23). Simple moon rituals for abundance to enhance manifestation. Retrieved from Thelawofattraction.com website: https://www.thelawofattraction.com/manifestation-rituals-phase-moon/

jracioppi. (2018, March 15). Moon rituals: How to manifest with the moon. Retrieved from Jenniferracioppi.com website: https://jenniferracioppi.com/moon-rituals-how-to-manifest-with-the-moon/

Moon Rituals for guiding intentions. (n.d.). Retrieved from Kelleemaize.com website: https://www.kelleemaize.com/post/moon-rituals-for-guiding-intentions

Stokes, V. (2021, July 30). How to make your own moon water: Origins, lore, and DIY ritual. Retrieved from Healthline.com website: https://www.healthline.com/health/moon-water

AstroTwins. (2016, November 8). Planets & Astrology: Neptune. Astrostyle.Com; The AstroTwins. https://astrostyle.com/astrology-planets-neptune/

Neptune - Susan Miller astrology zone. (2016, April 19). Astrologyzone.Com. https://www.astrologyzone.com/learn-astrology/the-planets/neptune/

Neptune, god of the sea, in Astrology/zodiac. (2015, May 8). Cafeastrology.Com. https://cafeastrology.com/neptune.html

Avia. (2018a, February 19). Neptune Symbol. Retrieved from Whats-your-sign.com website: https://www.whats-your-sign.com/neptune-symbol.html

Avia. (2018b, April 15). Symbolism of water. Retrieved from Whats-your-sign.com website: https://www.whats-your-sign.com/symbolism-of-water.html

Carla Huffman, M. F. T. (n.d.). Myths symbols sandplay. Retrieved from Typepad.com website: https://mythsymbolsandplay.typepad.com/my-blog/2017/10/water-symbolism.html

Davidson, J. (2020, June 15). Planet myths: The story behind Neptune. Retrieved from Jessicadavidson.co.uk website: https://jessicadavidson.co.uk/2020/06/15/planet-myths-the-story-behind-neptune/

Moe. (2014, March 27). Symbol of the Trident. Retrieved from Gnosticwarrior.com website: https://gnosticwarrior.com/trident.html

Neptune. (2017, March 14). Retrieved from Greekgodsandgoddesses.net website: https://greekgodsandgoddesses.net/gods/neptune/

Neptune. (n.d.). Retrieved from Mythopedia.com website: https://mythopedia.com/topics/neptune

Solar System Symbols. (n.d.). Retrieved from Nasa.gov website: https://solarsystem.nasa.gov/resources/680/solar-system-symbols

The Editors of Encyclopedia Britannica. (2015). Varuna. In Encyclopedia Britannica.

Tirza Schaefer. (n.d.). Retrieved from Tirzaschaefer.com website: https://www.tirzaschaefer.com/neptune

Astrosharmistha. (2015, December 15). Neptune – Varun in Vedic astrology blog, Mumbai. Astrosharmistha.Com. http://astrosharmistha.com/blog/neptune-varun-in-vedic-astrology/

Indastro. (n.d.). Position of Neptune: Influence in Vedic astrology. Indastro.Com. Retrieved from https://www.indastro.com/astrology-articles/astrological-characteristics-of-neptune-explained-through-vedic-astrology.html

Martinez, M. (2014, July 11). Neptune – meaning and influence in Astrology. Insightfulpsychics.Com. https://www.insightfulpsychics.com/neptune-planets-astrology/

Neptune astrology symbol - characteristics, planet energy, and more. (2018, January 26). Labyrinthos.Co. https://labyrinthos.co/blogs/astrology-horoscope-zodiac-signs/neptune-astrology-symbol-characteristics-planet-energy

Neptune, god of the sea, in Astrology/zodiac. (2015, May 8). Cafeastrology.Com. https://cafeastrology.com/neptune.html

Vedic astrology predictions of last 3 planets - ganeshaspeaks. (2018, April 9). Ganeshaspeaks.Com. https://www.ganeshaspeaks.com/learn-astrology/how-does-vedic-astrology-view-uranus-neptune-and-pluto-planets/

How to read outer planets in Vedic astrology. (2021, June 14). Clickastro.Com. https://www.clickastro.com/blog/outer-planets-in-vedic-astrology/

Ketu & Neptune - in Your Horoscope - Astrozing. (n.d.). Astrozing.Com. Retrieved from https://astrozing.com/ketu-neptune-astrology-vedic-horoscope-solar-system-sun-sign

Neptune Retrograde: Natal, meaning, & more - Astrology.Com. (n.d.). Astrology.Com. Retrieved from https://www.astrology.com/retrograde/neptune-retrograde

Astrologyplace. (2010, August 24). Neptune in the 1st house. Retrieved from Theastrologyplacemembership.com website: https://theastrologyplacemembership.com/2010/08/neptune-in-1st-house/

Denise. (2019, May 4). Neptune in 2nd house: How it defines your personality and life. Retrieved from The horoscope. co website: https://i.thehoroscope.co/neptune-in-2nd-house-how-it-defines-your-personality-and-life/

Neptune in 3rd House. (n.d.). Retrieved from Astrologyk.com website: https://astrologyk.com/zodiac/houses/3/neptune

Neptune in 4th house meaning and significance. (2015, January 20). Retrieved from Sunsigns.org website: https://www.sunsigns.org/neptune-in-fourth-house/

Neptune in the houses. (2017, February 22). Retrieved from Astrologyclub.org website: http://astrologyclub.org/birth-chart-interpretations/neptune-in-the-houses/

Ms, L. S. (2017, February 20). Neptune in the 5th house – Hypnotic Genius of Hopeless Romantic. Retrieved from The-tarot.com website: https://the-tarot.com/neptune-in-the-5th-house/

Neptune in 6th house. (2020, May 30). Retrieved from Dreamastromeanings.com website: https://dreamastromeanings.com/neptune-in-6th-house/

View all posts by Sagittarian Mind ConsultingTM. (2018, February 22). Neptune in the 7th house : "I get high." Retrieved from Wordpress.com website: https://sagmind.wordpress.com/2018/02/22/planetary-portraits-neptune-in-the-7th-house/

Neptune in the eighth house. (n.d.). Retrieved from Astrolibrary.org website: https://astrolibrary.org/books/crowley-34/

Astrology: Neptune in the houses. (n.d.). Retrieved from Trans4mind.com website: https://trans4mind.com/personal_development/astrology/LearningAstrology/housesNeptune.htm

Stargazer. (2020b, August 18). Neptune in ninth house natal meaning in astrology. Retrieved from Advanced-astrology.com website: https://advanced-astrology.com/neptune-in-ninth-house-natal

Neptune in Tenth House in Vedic Astrology. (n.d.). Retrieved from Astrology-prophets.com website: https://www.astrology-prophets.com/Planets_in_Houses/neptune_in_tenth_house.php

Neptune in the 11th house–setting boundaries in friendship. (2009, April 5). Retrieved from Wordpress.com website: https://skywriter.wordpress.com/2009/04/04/friendship-equality-and-the-neptune-in-the-11th-house/

Neptune in the 12th House Meaning, Natal Birth Chart, Neptune Astrology Free Interpretations. (n.d.). Retrieved from Astro-seek.com website: https://horoscopes.astro-seek.com/neptune-in-12th-house-astrology-meaning

Astrogle. (2018, January 31). Transit Neptune through Natal houses. Retrieved from Astrogle.com website: https://www.astrogle.com/astrology/transit-neptune-natal-houses.html

Luna, A. (2018, September 25). Neptune aspects in astrology. Retrieved from Moonorganizer.com website: https://moonorganizer.com/en/neptune-aspects-in-astrology-2/

Niizato, H. (n.d.). Neptune Aspects Archives - Hiroki Niizato Astrology. Retrieved from Hniizato.com website: https://hniizato.com/category/aspects/neptune-aspects/

(N.d.-b). Retrieved from Gotohoroscope.com website: http://www.gotohoroscope.com/planet-aspects-neptune.html

Enchanted Spirit. (n.d.). Conjunctions of Neptune – when the spiritual self merges with another inner self. Enchantedspirit.Org. Retrieved from https://www.enchantedspirit.org/Astrology/Neptune/Conjunctions-Neptune.php

Astrology Neptune aspects - lesson 5.2. (n.d.). Bobmarksastrologer.Com. Retrieved from https://www.bobmarksastrologer.com/aspectsneptune.htm

An introduction to archetypal astrological analysis by Richard tarnas, ph.D. (n.d.). Gaiamind.Org. Retrieved from https://www.gaiamind.org/AstroIntro.html

Creativity, D. (2016, August 25). Divine Creativity. Sarahhall.Com. https://sarahhall.com/divine-creativity/

Gilchrist, N. (2016, March 2). How to know if you're a Neptune person. Sasstrology.Com. https://sasstrology.com/2016/03/how-to-know-if-youre-a-neptune-person.html

How Strong is your Neptune? Here's the Score! (2010, March 28). Wordpress.Com. https://skywriter.wordpress.com/2010/03/28/how-strong-is-your-neptune-here%E2%80%99s-the-score/

Layton, S. (n.d.). The Neptunian Archetype. Astro-Charts.Com. Retrieved from https://astro-charts.com/blog/2017/the-neptunian-archetype/

Pellard, R., Nicola, J.-P., Rouger, J., & Le Bozec, F. (n.d.). The Neptunian: Psychological profile. Astroariana.Com. Retrieved https://www.astroariana.com/The-Neptunian-Psychological.html

Snyder, M. (2016, August 31). The storms & archetype of Neptune. Northatlanticbooks.Com. https://www.northatlanticbooks.com/blog/storms-archetype-neptune/

Who Are The Neptunians? (n.d.). Mysticmedusa.Com.

Beqiri, G. (2018, November 9). Learning to say no: Six methods you can use. Virtualspeech.Com; VirtualSpeech. https://virtualspeech.com/blog/learning-to-say-no

Layton, S. (n.d.). Healing through Neptune and Chiron. Astro-Charts.Com. Retrieved from https://astro-charts.com/blog/2017/healing-through-neptune-and-chiron/

Pawlowski, A. (2019, November 12). Being kind is good for your health: How to practice kindness every day. TODAY. https://www.today.com/series/one-small-thing/being-kind-good-your-health-how-practice-kindness-every-day-t163335

Sweetman, K. (2013, January 30). Healing Neptune Problems. Empoweringastrology.Com. https://empoweringastrology.com/healing-neptune-problems

Topaz, J. (2017, December 12). Difficult Neptune - Sun contacts: You can't heal what you don't reveal. Lookupthestars.Com. https://www.lookupthestars.com/post/difficult-neptune-sun-contacts-you-can-t-heal-what-you-don-t-reveal

Why surrender. (2016, November 3). Goop.Com. https://goop.com/it-en/wellness/mindfulness/why-surrender/

An astrological view of the chakras. (2015, July 7). Kabbalahsociety.Org. https://www.kabbalahsociety.org/wp/an-astrological-view-of-the-chakras/

Estrada, J. (2020, January 4). 5 expert tips for balancing your chakras, according to Ayurveda. Well+Good. https://www.wellandgood.com/chakra-balancing/

Martin, L., & Backlund, R. (2017, October 4). How to use each phase of the moon to lead a smarter, more creative life. Elitedaily.Com; Elite Daily. https://www.elitedaily.com/p/the-8-moon-phases-how-they-affect-your-body-mind-2754760

Neptune Explained. (n.d.). Hoodmystic.Com.

Surtees, K. (2017, April 24). The Eight Moon Phases as personality types. Kellysastrology.Com. https://www.kellysastrology.com/2017/04/24/the-eight-moon-phases-as-personality-types/

10 tips to develop your psychic abilities. (2013, February 4). Prweb.Com. https://www.prweb.com/releases/2013/2/prweb10316846.htm

How to start (and keep) a dream journal. (n.d.). Thecreativeindependent.Com. Retrieved from https://thecreativeindependent.com/guides/how-to-start-and-keep-a-dream-journal/

Page, B. (2019, May 21). 6 simples ways to practice psychometry. Sentinel & Enterprise. https://www.sentinelandenterprise.com/2019/05/21/6-simples-ways-to-practice-psychometry/

Stardust, L. (2020, December 18). What each aura color means, and says about your personality, according to an astrologer. Oprahdaily.Com; Oprah Daily. https://www.oprahdaily.com/life/a35015599/aura-colors-meaning/

Tarot.com Staff. (2020, August 6). Indicators of psychic ability in the birth chart. Tarot.Com; Tarot.com. https://www.tarot.com/astrology/psychic-ability-in-the-birth-chart

Jupiter. (2017, September 25). Retrieved from Horoscope website: https://www.astrology.com/planets/jupiter

Jupiter. (n.d.). Retrieved from Astrology-zodiac-signs.com website: https://www.astrology-zodiac-signs.com/astrology/planets/jupiter/

Kahn, N. (2021, August 3). The astrology of lucky Jupiter explained. Retrieved from Bustle.com website: https://www.bustle.com/life/astrology-lucky-jupiter-meaning-explained

In-Depth. (n.d.). Retrieved from Nasa.gov website: https://solarsystem.nasa.gov/planets/jupiter/in-depth/

Jupiter. (2017, February 22). Retrieved from Greekgodsandgoddesses.net website: https://greekgodsandgoddesses.net/gods/jupiter/

Jupiter god or Brihaspati Mythological katha, spiritual shades, Jupiter Story. (n.d.). Retrieved from Indianastrologyhoroscope.com website: http://www.indianastrologyhoroscope.com/Jupiter_Mythological_Spiritual.html

Jupiter in Vedic Astrology. (n.d.). Retrieved from Astrology-prophets.com website: https://www.astrology-prophets.com/jupiter-in-astrology.php

Jupiter's Twelve Year Cycle. (n.d.). Retrieved from Astrotrends.net website: https://astrotrends.net/world/jupiter-cycle

Prusty, M. (2018, January 8). Significance of Jupiter in Vedic Astrology - Role of Guru in astrology. Retrieved from Astroguruonline.com website: https://www.astroguruonline.com/planet-jupiter-vedic-astrology/

Thinker, F. (n.d.). Significance of Brihaspati (Guru) Hindu God of The Jupiter in Horoscope, Remedies and Guru Mantras. Retrieved from Blogspot.com website: http://hinduismtheopensourcefaith.blogspot.com/2011/02/significance-of-brihaspati-guru-hindu.html

Brownlee, S. (2020, October 24). All about the lucky planet Jupiter. Retrieved from Astrologyanswers.com website: https://astrologyanswers.com/article/3-ways-jupiter-brings-you-good-luck/

Hillenberg, K. (2019, November 26). Embrace your JUPITER: get more MONEY, SUCCESS and LUCK in Business! Retrieved from Bossbabe.com website: https://bossbabe.com/embrace-your-jupiter-get-more-money-success-and-luck-in-business/

indastro. (n.d.). Understand your Jupiter for luck and success in life. Retrieved from Indastro.com website: https://www.indastro.com/astrology-articles/jupiter-bringing-luck-and-success-to-you.html

Learn more about jolly Jupiter – "lady luck" in astrology. (2020, January 1). Retrieved from Starsignstyle.com website: https://starsignstyle.com/jolly-jupiter-in-astrology/

Matsumoto, A. (2020, May 14). Jupiter - planet of expansion and development. Retrieved from Keikopowerwish.com website: https://www.keikopowerwish.com/blog/jupiter-planet-of-expansion-and-development

Prusty, M. (2018, January 8). Significance of Jupiter in Vedic Astrology - Role of Guru in astrology. Retrieved from Astroguruonline.com website: https://www.astroguruonline.com/planet-jupiter-vedic-astrology/

Ward, K. (2020, May 19). Your Jupiter sign is your astrological career coach. Retrieved from Cosmopolitan.com website: https://www.cosmopolitan.com/lifestyle/a32597390/jupiter-sign-meaning/

Carla Huffman, M. F. T. (n.d.). myths symbols sandplay. Retrieved from Typepad.com website: https://mythsymbolsandplay.typepad.com/my-blog/2017/10/fortune-good-luck-deities.html

---

Carson, L. (lazarte). (2018, July 2). Are some people just born lucky? Retrieved from Medium website: https://lindseyruns.medium.com/are-some-of-us-just-born-lucky-d879a545ed38

Definition of LUCK. (n.d.). Retrieved from Merriam-webster.com website: https://www.merriam-webster.com/dictionary/luck

Ranadive, A. (2016, November 12). The four kinds of luck. Retrieved from Medium website: https://medium.com/@ameet/the-four-kinds-of-luck-ea729970d71d

The four faces of luck. (n.d.). Retrieved from Berkeley.edu website: https://www.stat.berkeley.edu/~aldous/Real-World/luck.html

Boldovski, M. (2019, January 7). Jupiter in Capricorn ♑ ★ debilitated. Retrieved from Astrology.community website: https://astrology.community/jupiter-capricorn/

Gupta, S. (2017, July 21). Weak Jupiter in horoscope? Follow these remedies. Retrieved from Times Of India website: https://timesofindia.indiatimes.com/astrology/kundali-dasha-remedies/weak-jupiter-in-horoscope-follow-these-remedies/articleshow/68206107.cms

HeereJawharat.com. (2015, June). Retrieved from Heerejawharat.com website: https://www.heerejawharat.com/astrology/planets-significance/brihaspati-jupitar.php

(Mona, 2020)

Mona. (2020, May 3). Positive and negative effects of Jupiter in 12 houses. Retrieved from Vedicfeed.com website: https://vedicfeed.com/jupiter-effects-in-12-houses/

Hall, M. (n.d.). Jupiter in first house (or Aries). Retrieved from Liveabout.com website: https://www.liveabout.com/jupiter-in-first-house-or-aries-207200

Jupiter in Gemini sign: Meaning, significance, and personality traits. (2014, September 25). Retrieved from Sunsigns.org website: https://www.sunsigns.org/jupiter-in-gemini/

Jupiter in cancer. (2019, March 24). Retrieved from Dreamastromeanings.com website: https://dreamastromeanings.com/jupiter-in-cancer/

Tarot.com Staff. (2017, May 13). Jupiter in Taurus: Tenacious, cautious, pleasure-seeking. Retrieved from Tarot.com website: https://www.tarot.com/astrology/planets/jupiter-in-taurus

Denise. (2018, August 16). Jupiter in Leo: How it affects your luck and personality. Retrieved from Thehoroscope.co website: https://i.thehoroscope.co/jupiter-in-leo-how-it-affects-your-luck-and-personality/

Freeman, K. (2019, March 16). Jupiter in Libra. Retrieved from Trustedpsychicmediums.com website: https://trustedpsychicmediums.com/libra-star-sign/jupiter-in-libra/

Ht, P. L. C. (n.d.-a). What does a Jupiter in Scorpio natal sign mean? Retrieved from Lovetoknow.com website: https://horoscopes.lovetoknow.com/natal-charts-readings/what-does-jupiter-scorpio-natal-sign-mean

Faragher, A. K. (2018, November 16). Jupiter in Sagittarius: What the lucky astrology event means for you. Retrieved from Allure website: https://www.allure.com/story/jupiter-in-sagittarius-meaning-dates

AstroTwins. (2017, November 14). Want to invite good fortune into your life? Learn your Jupiter sign. Retrieved from Astrostyle.com website: https://astrostyle.com/jupiter-signs/

Freeman, K. (2019, March 16). Jupiter in Pisces. Retrieved from Trustedpsychicmediums.com website: https://trustedpsychicmediums.com/pisces-star-sign/jupiter-in-pisces/

Tarot.com Staff. (2014, July 26). Jupiter in Aquarius: Unique, innovative, socially-aware. Retrieved from Tarot.com website: https://www.tarot.com/astrology/planets/jupiter-in-aquarius

D. (2019a, May 4). Jupiter in 3rd House: How It Impacts Your Personality, Luck and Destiny. I.TheHoroscope.Co. https://i.thehoroscope.co/jupiter-in-3rd-house-how-it-impacts-your-personality-luck-and-destiny/

D. (2019b, May 4). Jupiter in 5th House: How It Impacts Your Personality, Luck and Destiny. I.TheHoroscope.Co. https://i.thehoroscope.co/jupiter-in-5th-house-how-it-impacts-your-personality-luck-and-destiny/

D. (2019c, May 4). Jupiter in 6th House: How It Impacts Your Personality, Luck and Destiny. I.TheHoroscope.Co. https://i.thehoroscope.co/jupiter-in-6th-house-how-it-impacts-your-personality-luck-and-destiny/

D. (2019d, May 4). Jupiter in 7th House: How It Impacts Your Personality, Luck and Destiny. I.TheHoroscope.Co. https://i.thehoroscope.co/jupiter-in-7th-house-how-it-impacts-your-personality-luck-and-destiny/

D. (2019e, May 4). Jupiter in 8th House: How It Impacts Your Personality, Luck and Destiny. I.TheHoroscope.Co. https://i.thehoroscope.co/jupiter-in-8th-house-how-it-impacts-your-personality-luck-and-destiny/

D. (2019f, May 4). Jupiter in 9th House: How It Impacts Your Personality, Luck and Destiny. I.TheHoroscope.Co. https://i.thehoroscope.co/jupiter-in-9th-house-how-it-impacts-your-personality-luck-and-destiny/

D. (2019g, May 4). Jupiter in 10th House: How It Impacts Your Personality, Luck and Destiny. I.TheHoroscope.Co. https://i.thehoroscope.co/jupiter-in-10th-house-how-it-impacts-your-personality-luck-and-destiny/

D. (2019h, May 4). Jupiter in 11th House: How It Impacts Your Personality, Luck and Destiny. I.TheHoroscope.Co. https://i.thehoroscope.co/jupiter-in-11th-house-how-it-impacts-your-personality-luck-and-destiny/

D. (2019i, May 4). Jupiter in 12th House: How It Impacts Your Personality, Luck and Destiny. I.TheHoroscope.Co. https://i.thehoroscope.co/jupiter-in-12th-house-how-it-impacts-your-personality-luck-and-destiny/

D. (2019j, May 4). Jupiter in 4th house: How it impacts your personality, luck and Destiny. Thehoroscope.Co. https://i.thehoroscope.co/jupiter-in-4th-house-how-it-impacts-your-personality-luck-and-destiny/

Ganeshaspeaks.com. (2020a, February 18). Jupiter In The 7th House Of Your Horoscope. GaneshaSpeaks. https://www.ganeshaspeaks.com/learn-astrology/planets-houses/jupiter-in-seventh-house/

Ganeshaspeaks.com. (2020b, February 27). Effects of Jupiter in 8th House In Vedic Astrology. GaneshaSpeaks. https://www.ganeshaspeaks.com/learn-astrology/planets-houses/jupiter-in-eighth-house/

Ganeshaspeaks.com. (2020c, February 27). Impact of Jupiter in Ninth House. GaneshaSpeaks. https://www.ganeshaspeaks.com/learn-astrology/planets-houses/jupiter-in-ninth-house/

Ganeshaspeaks.com. (2020d, March 20). Effect of Jupiter in 11th House in Your Chart. GaneshaSpeaks. https://www.ganeshaspeaks.com/learn-astrology/planets-houses/jupiter-in-eleventh-house/

Ganeshaspeaks.com. (2020e, March 23). Importance of Jupiter In The 10th House. GaneshaSpeaks. https://www.ganeshaspeaks.com/learn-astrology/planets-houses/jupiter-in-tenth-house/

Hall, M. (2018, July 21). Your Jupiter Is in the First House (or Aries). LiveAbout. https://www.liveabout.com/jupiter-in-first-house-or-aries-207200

Jupiter in Your 2nd House: Get Rich Easily. (2017, February 9). The Times of India. https://timesofindia.indiatimes.com/astrology/planets-transits/jupiter-in-your-2nd-house/articleshow/68206254.cms

Importance of Jupiter in fourth house - GaneshaSpeaks. (2020, February 11). Ganeshaspeaks.Com. https://www.ganeshaspeaks.com/learn-astrology/planets-houses/jupiter-in-fourth-house/

Importance of Jupiter in the second house - GaneshaSpeaks. (2020, February 5). Ganeshaspeaks.Com. https://www.ganeshaspeaks.com/learn-astrology/planets-houses/jupiter-in-second-house/

Jupiter in relationship astrology: A philosophical love match? (n.d.). Astromatcha.Com. Retrieved from https://www.astromatcha.com/astrology-compatibility-questions/jupiter-in-relationship-astrology-a-philosophical-love-match/

Jupiter in the 6th house of your horoscope - GaneshaSpeaks. (2020, February 12). Ganeshaspeaks.Com. https://www.ganeshaspeaks.com/learn-astrology/planets-houses/jupiter-in-sixth-house/

Stars, O. M. (2018, November 29). Astrology and your planets in love: Jupiter. Beliefnet.Com. https://www.beliefnet.com/columnists/ohmystars/2018/11/astrology-planets-love-jupiter.html

Times Of India. (2017, February 9). Jupiter in your 2nd house: Get Rich Easily. Times Of India. https://timesofindia.indiatimes.com/astrology/planets-transits/jupiter-in-your-2nd-house/articleshow/68206254.cms

Armstrong, M. (n.d.). Historic great conjunction between Jupiter and Saturn this evening. Retrieved from Astronomynow.com website: https://astronomynow.com/2020/12/21/historic-great-conjunction-between-jupiter-and-saturn-this-evening/

Express News Service. (2020, December 21). Jupiter, Saturn to appear as 'double planet' in rare celestial event on December 21. The Indian Express. Retrieved from https://indianexpress.com/article/india/great-conjunction-on-dec-21-jupiter-saturn-to-be-second-closest-7074304/

Keeter, B. (2020). The 'great' conjunction of Jupiter and Saturn. Retrieved from https://www.nasa.gov/feature/the-great-conjunction-of-jupiter-and-saturn

Luna, A. (2018, September 18). Jupiter aspects in astrology. Retrieved from Moonorganizer.com website: https://moonorganizer.com/en/jupiter-aspects-in-astrology/

Planets in synastry: A beginner's guide to relationship astrology. (n.d.). Retrieved from Everydayhealth.com website: https://www.everydayhealth.com/healthy-living/planets-synastry-beginners-guide-relationship-astrology/

Quint, A. (2020, February 6). Great Conjunction 2020: How December 21's astrological event affects you. Retrieved from Allure website: https://www.allure.com/story/great-conjunction-saturn-jupiter-2020

indastro. (n.d.). Astrology Remedies for Jupiter - Lal Kitab Remedies for Jupiter – Vedic Remedies for Jupiter. Retrieved from Indastro.com website: https://www.indastro.com/remedies/remedies-for-jupiter.html

Jupiter Remedies. (n.d.). Retrieved from Astroyogi.com website: https://www.astroyogi.com/remedies/planetary/jupiter

Miraculous Astrological remedies to strengthen your Jupiter. (2020, June 3). Retrieved from Astrotalk.com website: https://astrotalk.com/astrology-blog/miraculous-astrological-remedies-to-strengthen-your-jupiter/

Posts, V. M. (2019, December 5). Jupiter remedy. Retrieved from Home.blog website: https://anandamoyee.home.blog/2019/12/05/jupiter-remedy/

Trivedi, D. Y. (2021, March 7). Different ways to strengthen weak Jupiter in a horoscope ! A Must Read. Retrieved from Eastrohelp.com website: https://www.eastrohelp.com/blog/strengthen-weak-jupiter/

Want to make your Jupiter strong. Follow these remedies. (2018, February 1). Retrieved from Premiumsapphire.com website: https://blog.premiumsapphire.com/make-jupiter-strong

The Harps That Once. . . Sumerian Poetry in Translation. New Haven: Yale University Press, 1987.

"Inanna-Ishtar as Paradox and a Coincidence of Opposites." History of Religions 30 (1991)

Bahrani, Zainab. Women of Babylon: Gender and Representation in Mesopotamia. London: Routledge, 2001.

Black, Jeremy, and Anthony Green. Gods, Demons, and Symbols of Ancient Mesopotamia. Austin: University of Texas Press, 1992.

Foster, Benjamin R., ed. The Epic of Gilgamesh. New York: W. W. Norton, 2001.

Harris, Rivka. Gender and Aging in Mesopotamia: The Gilgamesh Epic and Other Ancient Literature. Norman: University of Oklahoma Press, 2000.

Jacobsen, Thorkild. The Treasures of Darkness: A History of Mesopotamian Religion. New Haven: Yale University Press, 1976.

Leeming, David Adams. Goddess: Myths of the Female Divine. Oxford, UK and New York: Oxford University Press, 1994.

Leick, Gwendolyn. Sex and Eroticism in Mesopotamian Literature. London and New York: Routledge, 1994.

Stone, Merlin. Ancient Mirrors of Womanhood: A Treasury of Goddess and Heroine Lore from Around the World. Boston: Beacon Press, 1979.

Wolkstein, Diane, and Samuel Noah Kramer. Inanna, Queen of Heaven and Earth: Her Stories and Hymns from Sumer. Harper & Row: New York, 1983.

Cartwright, M. (2019). Hermes. World History Encyclopedia. Retrieved from https://www.worldhistory.org/Hermes/

Chapman, C. R. (2021). Mercury. In Encyclopedia Britannica.

Cook, J. (2018, September 11). Hermes the god of commerce - Jonathan cook - medium. Retrieved from Medium website: https://jonathanccook.medium.com/hermes-the-god-of-commerce-29acbf25d567

Geany. (2015, May 28). Mythology of Mercury. Retrieved from Astrologyclub.org website: http://astrologyclub.org/mythology-of-mercury/

intro. (n.d.). Retrieved from Nasa.gov website: https://history.nasa.gov/SP-423/intro.htm

Marduk (god). (n.d.). Retrieved from http://oracc.museum.upenn.edu/amgg/listofdeities/marduk/

Mark, J. J. (2016). Marduk. World History Encyclopedia. Retrieved from https://www.worldhistory.org/Marduk/

Mercury facts. (2019, September 25). Retrieved from Nineplanets.org website: https://nineplanets.org/mercury/

Nabu (god). (n.d.). Retrieved from http://oracc.museum.upenn.edu/amgg/listofdeities/nabu/

Ogles, J. (2016, August 25). 20 Gay Greek Gods. Retrieved from Advocate.com website: https://www.advocate.com/arts-entertainment/2016/8/25/20-gay-greek-gods?pg=6

Solar System Symbols. (n.d.). Retrieved from Nasa.gov website: https://solarsystem.nasa.gov/resources/680/solar-system-symbols/

The divine doublet: Hermes and Odysseus. (2019, April 23). Retrieved from Harvard.edu website: https://kosmossociety.chs.harvard.edu/the-divine-doublet-hermes-and-odysseus/

webvns. (n.d.). The royal art of astrology. Retrieved from Theroyalartofastrology.com website: https://theroyalartofastrology.com/2017/11/14/god-nabu-rules-mercury/

AstroTwins. (2016, November 8). Planets & astrology: Mercury. Retrieved from Astrostyle.com website: https://astrostyle.com/astrology-planets-mercury/

Before you continue to YouTube. (n.d.). Retrieved from Youtu.be website: https://youtu.be/51ocz1ZxRVE

Boldovski, M. (2019, January 4). Mercury in Pisces ♓ ⋆ debilitated. Retrieved from Astrology.community website: https://astrology.community/mercury-pisces/

favorites of Mercury, Lucky metal, color, direction, gemstone. (n.d.). Retrieved from Indianastrologyhoroscope.com website: http://www.indianastrologyhoroscope.com/Mercury_Favorites.html

Hall, M. (n.d.-a). Mercury in Astrology. Retrieved from Liveabout.com website: https://www.liveabout.com/mercury-in-astrology-206363

Hall, M. (n.d.-b). What is Mercury Retrograde, anyways? Retrieved from Liveabout.com website: https://www.liveabout.com/mercury-in-retrograde-206364

Mercury – trade, commerce, and communications - astrology club. (2014, May 15). Retrieved from Astrologyclub.org website: http://astrologyclub.org/mercury-trade-commerce-communications/

Mercury, messenger of the gods, in Astrology/zodiac. (2015, April 19). Retrieved from Cafeastrology.com website: https://cafeastrology.com/mercury.html

Planet Mercury in astrology- positive and negative influence. (2020, May 20). Retrieved from Astrotalk.com website: https://astrotalk.com/astrology-blog/planet-mercury-in-astrology/

Role and importance of Mercury in astrology. (n.d.). Retrieved from Shrivinayakaastrology.com website: http://shrivinayakaastrology.com/Planets/roleofmercury.html

Role of Mercury in a birth chart as per Vedic astrology. (2018, December 11). Retrieved from Lonelyphilosopher.com website: http://www.lonelyphilosopher.com/role-of-mercury-in-a-birth-chart-as-per-vedic-astrology/

12andus. (n.d.). What's your communication style, according to your Mercury sign? Retrieved from 12Andus.com website: https://12andus.com/blog/view/269031/whats-your-communication-style-according-to-your-mercury-sign

Coughlin, S. (2018, January 12). Your communication style, based on your sign. Retrieved from Refinery29.com website: https://www.refinery29.com/en-us/communication-style-mercury-sign-meaning-astrology

Discover Mercury in astrology and your communication style. (2019, January 3). Retrieved from Starsignstyle.com website: https://starsignstyle.com/messenger-mercury-in-astrology/

NunezAuthor, A. T., & 01/14/, Z. (2019, January 14). How you act when you're trying to prove A point, according to your mercury sign. Retrieved from Yourtango.com website: https://www.yourtango.com/2019320711/communcation-styles-mercury-sign-according-zodiac-astrology

---

12andus. (n.d.). What is the best way for you to learn new things, based on your Mercury sign? Retrieved from 12Andus.com website: https://12andus.com/blog/view/250376/what-is-the-best-way-for-you-to-learn-new-things-based-on-your-mercury-sign

Jamie. (2009, June 15). What kind of mercury learner are you? Retrieved from Pandoraastrology.com website: https://www.pandoraastrology.com/what-kind-of-mercury-learner-are-you/

stacyann. (2018, October 11). Your learning style according to astrology. Retrieved from Stacyannforrester.com website: https://stacyannforrester.com/your-learning-style-according-to-astrology/

Horoscope and Astrology - Homepage. (n.d.). Retrieved from Astro.com website: https://www.astro.com/horoscope

Mercury in the houses of natal chart. (2015, April 13). Retrieved from Cafeastrology.com website: https://cafeastrology.com/natal/mercuryinhouses.html

Mercury in the signs: What your Mercury placement means for you. (n.d.). Retrieved from Vice.com website: https://www.vice.com/en/article/8xwx3v/what-does-mercury-in-the-signs-mean-in-my-birth-chart

Mercury rising - mercury in the first house or ascendant. (n.d.). Retrieved from Futurescopes.com website: https://futurescopes.com/astrology/mercury/2475/mercury-rising-mercury-first-house-or-ascendant

Denise. (2019a, May 4). Mercury in 5th house: How it affects your life and personality. Retrieved from Thehoroscope.co website: https://i.thehoroscope.co/mercury-in-5th-house-how-it-affects-your-life-and-personality/

Denise. (2019b, May 4). Mercury in 6th house: How it affects your life and personality. Retrieved from Thehoroscope.co website: https://i.thehoroscope.co/mercury-in-6th-house-how-it-affects-your-life-and-personality/

Denise. (2019c, May 4). Mercury in 7th house: How it affects your life and personality. Retrieved from Thehoroscope.co website: https://i.thehoroscope.co/mercury-in-7th-house-how-it-affects-your-life-and-personality/

Denise. (2019d, May 4). Mercury in 8th house: How it affects your life and personality. Retrieved from Thehoroscope.co website: https://i.thehoroscope.co/mercury-in-8th-house-how-it-affects-your-life-and-personality/

Hall, M. (n.d.). The Fifth House - astrological houses. Retrieved from Liveabout.com website: https://www.liveabout.com/the-fifth-house-astrological-houses-207253

Introducing Astrology. (n.d.). The faculty of astrological studies. Retrieved from Org.uk website: https://astrology.org.uk/wordpress/wp-content/uploads/IntroducingAstrology.pdf

Mercury in 5th house meaning and significance. (2014, November 1). Retrieved from Sunsigns.org website: https://www.sunsigns.org/mercury-in-fifth-house/

Mercury in 6th house meaning and significance. (2014, November 1). Retrieved from Sunsigns.org website: https://www.sunsigns.org/mercury-in-sixth-house/

Mercury in 8th House. (n.d.). Retrieved from Astrologyk.com website: https://astrologyk.com/zodiac/houses/8/mercury

astrologyplace. (2014, February 25). Mercury in the 12th house. Retrieved from Theastrologyplacemembership.com website: https://theastrologyplacemembership.com/2014/02/mercury-in-the-12th-house/

Bhattacharjee, A. S. (2020a, June 10). Mercury in 9th House Love, Career, Marriage, Foreign Travel, finance. Retrieved from Astrosanhita.com website: https://astrosanhita.com/mercury-in-

9th-house-marriage-love-foreign-travel-career-finance-education-health-in-vedic-astrology-horoscope-kundli-ninth-budh-graha/

Bhattacharjee, A. S. (2020b, October 12). Mercury in 11th House Career, Gains-Loss, Marriage, Friends, finance. Retrieved from Astrosanhita.com website: https://astrosanhita.com/mercury-in-11th-house-career-finance-friendship-gains-loss-marriage-love-astrology-horoscope-kundli-budh/

Mercury in 10th house. (2020, April 26). Retrieved from Dreamastromeanings.com website: https://dreamastromeanings.com/mercury-in-10th-house/

Aspects of The planet Mercury - special Mentality characteristic and other sides of your personal horoscope when Mercury in aspect with other planets. (n.d.). Retrieved from Gotohoroscope.com website: http://www.gotohoroscope.com/planet-aspects-mercury.html

Learn the ancient art of deciphering your astrological aspects. (2021, February 25). Retrieved from Com.au website: https://www.wellbeing.com.au/mind-spirit/astrology/your-astrological-aspects.html

Luna, A. (2018, March 17). Mercury aspects with planets - favorable & unfavorable. Retrieved from Moonorganizer.com website: https://moonorganizer.com/en/mercury-aspects-with-other-planets/

Mercury aspects. (2014, December 6). Retrieved from Astromarkt.net website: http://www.astromarkt.net/astrology_to_study-html/aspects-with-mercury-html/

Planetary aspects. (2015, April 25). Retrieved from Cafeastrology.com website: https://cafeastrology.com/natal/planetsaspectsastrology.html

The meaning of the aspects in astrology. (2015, April 15). Retrieved from Cafeastrology.com website: https://cafeastrology.com/articles/aspectsinastrology.html

Egwu Deus Ikechukwu...(Nigerian), Emma, Sadia, & Ify. (n.d.). Mercury retrograde: Dates and effects to anticipate in 2021. Retrieved from Astrofame.com website: https://my.astrofame.com/astrology/article/mercury-retrograde

Mahtani, N. (2020, June 17). The top Mercury retrograde effect each zodiac sign should prepare for. Retrieved from Well+Good website: https://www.wellandgood.com/mercury-retrograde-effects-by-zodiac-sign/

Markarian, T. (2021, January 11). What does Mercury in retrograde mean? Retrieved from Www.rd.com website: https://www.rd.com/article/mercury-in-retrograde/

Register, J. (2021, January 28). Are you ready for the first Mercury Retrograde of 2021? Retrieved from Cosmopolitan website: https://www.cosmopolitan.com/lifestyle/a35352926/mercury-retrograde-january-2021-horoscope-effects/

Walden, L. (2019, March 7). Mercury will be in retrograde 3 times in 2021 – but how will it affect you? Retrieved from Country Living website: https://www.countryliving.com/uk/news/a26746624/how-mercury-being-in-retrograde-affects-you/

Can you explain Mercury's retrograde motion? Do other planets appear to do this also? (2015, October 26). Retrieved from Astronomy.com website: https://astronomy.com/magazine/ask-astro/2015/10/mercurys-retrograde-motion

Jucutan, M. J. (2020, October 9). Mercury in retrograde: When technology and communications go haywire - GadgetMatch. Retrieved from Gadgetmatch.com website: https://www.gadgetmatch.com/mercury-in-retrograde-when-technology-and-communications-go-haywire/

The six stages of mercury retrograde. (2020, March 6). Retrieved from Cosmopolitan.com website: https://www.cosmopolitan.com/lifestyle/a31249314/mercury-retrograde-stages-shadow-period/

Kahn, N. (2021, May 19). How Mercury retrograde spring 2021 will affect your zodiac sign. Retrieved from Bustle.com website: https://www.bustle.com/life/mercury-retrograde-spring-2021-affect-zodiac-signs

Astrology Zone Admin. (2017, March 14). Table of mercury retrograde dates to year 2030 - Susan Miller astrology zone. Retrieved from Astrologyzone.com website: https://www.astrologyzone.com/updated-mercury-retrograde-dates/

Chan, A. (2016, May 2). 6 productivity hacks that will get you through mercury retrograde. Retrieved from Teen Vogue website: https://www.teenvogue.com/story/mercury-retrograde-productivity-hacks

Lewis, N. (2019, November 4). How to fail-proof your travel against Mercury retrograde. Retrieved from Condé Nast Traveller India website: https://www.cntraveller.in/story/astrology-how-to-fail-proof-your-travel-against-mercury-retrograde-2019-date-tips/

Mercury retrograde: Meaning & overview - horoscope.Com. (2019, August 6). Retrieved from Horoscope.com website: https://www.horoscope.com/mercury-retrograde/

TestaAuthor, G., & 01/29/, Z. (2021, January 29). 11 ways mercury retrograde seriously messes with your relationships. Retrieved from Yourtango.com website: https://www.yourtango.com/2018315873/11-mercury-retrograde-effects-your-relationships

7 Ways to Clear Up A Blocked Throat Chakra. (2019, August 6). Retrieved from Caricole.com website: https://caricole.com/7-ways-to-clear-up-a-blocked-throat-chakra/

Allard, S. (2020, August 19). 5 things to know about Vedic astrology. Retrieved from Hinduamerican.org website: https://www.hinduamerican.org/blog/5-things-to-know-about-vedic-astrology

Ancient Astrology Talks. (2020, February 22). Dhan Yoga in Kundali : Different Types And Combinations. Retrieved from Ancientastrologytalks.com website: https://www.ancientastrologytalks.com/dhan-yoga-in-kundali/

annaicenter. (2013, May 17). Saturn and Chakras a Vedic Astrology Perspective. Retrieved from Wordpress.com website: https://annaicenter.wordpress.com/2013/05/17/saturn-and-chakras-a-vedic-astrology-perspective/

Astro, W. (n.d.). Remedy, FreeWill and simple Astrology. Retrieved from Blogspot.com website: https://wantastro.blogspot.com/2014/01/dushtana-house-lord-6th-8th-12th-house-astrology.html

Astrology: The cadent houses: Falling-away. (2013, July 10). Retrieved from Wordpress.com website: https://astrologyandtheastrologicalworld.wordpress.com/2013/07/10/astrology-the-cadent-houses-falling-away/

Bill gates. (2015, October 3). Retrieved from Planetarypositions.com website: https://www.planetarypositions.com/celebrity-astrology/technologist/bill-gates/

Boldovski, M. (2018, December 14). Dharma Trikona ⋆ the 1st, 5th, and 9th houses in Vedic astrology. Retrieved from Astrology.community website: https://astrology.community/dharma-trikona/

Cain, F. (2013, June 10). Ten Interesting Facts About Saturn. Retrieved from Universetoday.com website: https://www.universetoday.com/15418/interesting-facts-about-saturn/

Chakrapani Vedic Astrology Magnificent Saturn. (n.d.). Retrieved from Vedicastrology.com website: http://vedicastrology.com//chakrapani-vedic-astrology-magnificent-saturn.html

Cheery. (2016, January 9). Upachaya houses. Retrieved from Netchanting.com website: https://netchanting.com/what-is-upachaya-houses/

Choi, C. Q. (2019, May 13). Saturn: Facts about the ringed planet. Retrieved from Space.com website: https://www.space.com/48-saturn-the-solar-systems-major-ring-bearer.html

Cochrane, D. (n.d.). BASIC ALPHABET OF ASTROLOGY. Retrieved from Avalonastrology.com website: http://www.avalonastrology.com/agy101cheatsheet.pdf

Dhara, G., & View my complete profile. (n.d.). Gyan Dhara. Retrieved from Blogspot.com website: http://gyandhaara.blogspot.com/2012/01/law-of-karma-runanubandha-parentchild.html

Dharmasiddhant - principles of Hinduism (doctrines of Dharma [righteousness]) - Hindu janajagruti samiti. (2016, November 28). Retrieved from Hindujagruti.org website: https://www.hindujagruti.org/hinduism/hindu-dharma/principles-of-hinduism

Five Dharmic Debts (Rin) of Every Hindu - Have you paid yours ? (2015, January 18). Retrieved from Sanskritimagazine.com website: https://www.sanskritimagazine.com/indian-religions/hinduism/five-dharmic-debts-rin-every-hindu-paid/

Home. (n.d.). Retrieved from Astrosage.com website: https://ascloud.astrosage.com/cloud/home.asp?openloginpopup=1

House calculator. (2019, December 16). Retrieved from Sparkastrology.com website: https://sparkastrology.com/house-calculator/

How to control Saturn: Dr. Vinay bajrangi. (2020, December 5). Retrieved from Outlookindia.com website: https://www.outlookindia.com/website/story/outlook-spotlight-how-to-control-saturn-dr-vinay-bajrangi/366327

Importance of Antardasha in Vedic astrology. (n.d.). Retrieved from Astrobix.com website: https://astrobix.com/astrosight/223-importance-of-antardasha-in-vedic-astrology.html

In astrology, which planet is responsible for focus on studies? - Quora. (n.d.). Retrieved from Quora.com website: https://www.quora.com/In-astrology-which-planet-is-responsible-for-focus-on-studies

In Depth. (n.d.). Retrieved from Nasa.gov website: https://solarsystem.nasa.gov/planets/saturn/in-depth/

Indian astronomy through ages. (n.d.). Retrieved from Infinityfoundation.com website: https://www.infinityfoundation.com/mandala/t_es/t_es_shah_m_astronomy_frameset.htm

Kahn, N. (2018a, October 11). The real difference between your sun, moon, & rising signs. Retrieved from Bustle.com website: https://www.bustle.com/life/a-sun-moon-rising-zodiac-sign-explainer-that-will-help-astrology-make-so-much-more-sense-12222972

Kahn, N. (2018b, October 16). The ultimate guide to the 12 houses in astrology. Retrieved from Bustle.com website: https://www.bustle.com/life/what-are-the-12-houses-of-the-zodiac-your-astrology-birth-chart-includes-a-lot-more-than-just-your-sign-12239259

Karma and Vedic astrology. (2014, May 16). Retrieved from Net.au website: https://vedicastrology.net.au/blog/vedic-articles/karma-and-vedic-astrology/

Kauai's Hindu Monastery. (n.d.). Basics of Hinduism. Retrieved from Himalayanacademy.com website: https://www.himalayanacademy.com/readlearn/basics/karma-reincarnation

Learn how to strengthen your chakras -. (2018, February 21). Retrieved from Com.au website: https://www.wellbeing.com.au/mind-spirit/spirituality/learn-strengthen-chakras-connect-universal-flow.html

Lifestyle, R. T. É. (2018, February 4). Yoga Poses for your Throat Chakra. Retrieved from RTÉ website: https://www.rte.ie/lifestyle/living/2018/0202/937920-yoga-poses-for-your-throat-chakra/

Midha, G. (n.d.). Farfaraway. Retrieved from Farfaraway.co website: https://www.farfaraway.co/blog/basics-of-vedic-astrology

Moksha: Liberation. (n.d.). Retrieved from Iskconeducationalservices.org website: https://iskconeducationalservices.org/HoH/concepts/key-concepts/moksha-liberation/

Mona. (2018, December 16). 5 basic differences between Vedic astrology and western astrology. Retrieved from Vedicfeed.com website: https://vedicfeed.com/differences-between-vedic-astrology-and-western-astrology/

nimmi. (n.d.). Vedic. Retrieved from Findyourfate.com website: https://www.findyourfate.com/indianastro/vedic-astrology/fouraimsoflife.html

No title. (n.d.). Retrieved from Astrotalk.com website: https://astrotalk.com/astrology-blog/houses-in-vedic-astrology

Pant, A. P. U. (2019, October 20). About Jeff Bezos Horoscope. Retrieved from Pavitra Jyotish Kendra website: https://www.pavitrajyotish.com/article/about-jeff-bezos/

Pizer, A. (n.d.). Find your focus for yoga's Standing Forward Bend. Retrieved from Verywellfit.com website: https://www.verywellfit.com/standing-forward-bend-uttanasana-3567133

Popejoy, M. W. (2016). Steve Jobs. Public Voices, 14(1), 175.

Promotional Feature, HT Brand Studio. (2017, December 11). Dr Vinay Bajrangi explains the influence of Saturn on our lives. The Hindustan Times. Retrieved from https://www.hindustantimes.com/brand-stories/dr-vinay-bajrangi-explains-the-influence-of-saturn-on-our-lives/story-c4kikBkAujpKAseAcS8t6L.html

Prusty, M. (2018, October 22). Most important yogas in astrology - auspicious and evil yoga in kundli. Retrieved from Astroguruonline.com website: https://www.astroguruonline.com/important-yogas-vedic-astrology/

Prusty, M. (2019, January 2). Dhan yoga in astrology - powerful wealth yoga in the horoscope. Retrieved from Astroguruonline.com website: https://www.astroguruonline.com/dhan-yoga-astrology/

Rana, N. (2018, February 3). Sasa Yoga- experience the power of Saturn. Retrieved from Thevedichoroscope.com website: https://www.thevedichoroscope.com/2018/02/03/sasa-yoga/

Relationship between chakras in human body , planets & medical astrology. (2019, July 7). Retrieved from Wordpress.com website: https://anilsripathi.wordpress.com/relationship-between-human-body-chakras-planetsmedical-astrology/

Saturn astrology symbol - characteristics, planet energy and more. (2018, January 23). Retrieved from Labyrinthos.co website: https://labyrinthos.co/blogs/astrology-horoscope-zodiac-signs/saturn-astrology-symbol-characteristics-planet-energy

Saturn facts. (2016, June 8). Retrieved from Space-facts.com website: https://space-facts.com/saturn/

Saturn's rings formed in a smash-up less than 100 million years ago. (2019, January 17). New Scientist (1971). Retrieved from https://www.newscientist.com/article/2190893-saturns-rings-formed-in-a-smash-up-less-than-100-million-years-ago/

Shani Graha and its importance in Vedic Astrology. (n.d.). Retrieved from Issuu.com website: https://issuu.com/starstelldotcom/docs/shani_graha_and_its_importance_in_vedic_astrology

Sharma, D. (2021, May 28). Ustrasana (Camel Pose Steps): Facts,How to do, Benefits,Precautions. Retrieved from 7Pranayama.com website: https://7pranayama.com/ustrasana-camel-pose-steps-benefits/

Soni, S., & View my complete profile. (n.d.). Vedic Astrology Research Portal. Retrieved from Blogspot.com website: https://astrologywithsourabh.blogspot.com/2015/10/all-about-business-in-vedic-astrology.html

Taurus, S. I. (2016, March 30). Astrology at work: Richard Nixon. Retrieved from Goodgollyastrology.com website: https://www.goodgollyastrology.com/68-general-astrology-articles-on-gga/968-astrology-at-work-richard-nixon.html

Team Jothishi. (2019, October 5). The trikonas - sets of three triads in the birth chart - jothishi. Retrieved from Jothishi.com website: https://jothishi.com/the-trikonas/

Times Now Digital. (2020, May 9). Here's how you can worship Lord Shani to keep your karma in check. Retrieved from Timesnownews.com website: https://www.timesnownews.com/spiritual/article/here-s-how-you-can-worship-lord-shani-to-keep-your-karma-in-check/589244

View Articles. (2019, January 9). What is the zodiac? Retrieved from Earthsky.org website: https://earthsky.org/astronomy-essentials/what-is-the-zodiac

What is the difference between the sun sign, the moon sign, and the rising sign? - Quora. (n.d.). Retrieved from Quora.com website: https://www.quora.com/What-is-the-difference-between-the-sun-sign-the-moon-sign-and-the-rising-sign

What is the difference between the Tropical and Sidereal Zodiacs. (n.d.). Retrieved from Astro-calendar.com website: https://astro-calendar.com/shtml/Research/tropsidzodiacs2.shtml

What is the significance of Saturn in astrology? - Quora. (n.d.). Retrieved from Quora.com website: https://www.quora.com/What-is-the-significance-of-Saturn-in-astrology

Why do Indian astrologers consider the moon sign instead of the sun sign of a person for horoscope readings? - Quora. (n.d.). Retrieved from Quora.com website: https://www.quora.com/Why-do-Indian-astrologers-consider-the-moon-sign-instead-of-the-sun-sign-of-a-person-for-horoscope-readings

Yoga Bear. (2017, May 7). 5 yoga poses to balance your root chakra. Retrieved from RTÉ website: https://www.rte.ie/lifestyle/living/2017/0504/872450-5-yoga-poses-to-balance-your-root-chakra/

Yogas – Part I. (2015, June 23). Retrieved from Theartofvedicastrology.com website: http://www.theartofvedicastrology.com/?page_id=561

Hall, M. (n.d.). Uranus: The planets in astrology. Retrieved from Liveabout.com website: https://www.liveabout.com/uranus-the-planets-in-astrology-206370

Redd, N. T. (2018, February 28). Who discovered Uranus (and how do you pronounce it)? Retrieved from Space website: https://www.space.com/18704-who-discovered-uranus.html

The planets' relationship with Greek mythology. (2009, June 3). Retrieved from Greekboston.com website: https://www.greekboston.com/culture/mythology/planets/

Uranus. (2017, February 10). Retrieved from Greekgodsandgoddesses.net website: https://greekgodsandgoddesses.net/gods/uranus/

(N.d.-a). Retrieved from Greekmythology.com website: https://www.greekmythology.com/Other_Gods/Uranus/uranus.html

(N.d.-b). Retrieved from Theoi.com website: https://www.theoi.com/articles/how-did-uranus-get-its-name-as-per-greek-mythology/

Newsom, G. H. (1992). Uranus. Geochimica et Cosmochimica Acta, 56(3), 1422–1423.

The Public. (2020, September 26). The Planet Uranus, Uranus Planet Astrology, Uranus in Astrology, Uranus Astrology, Uranus Planet in Astrology, Uranus Planet Astrology Meaning, Uranus and Its Importance to Astrology, What is Uranus Associated With? , Uranus Zodiac Sign, Uranus Element Astrology, Uranus facts - the public. Retrieved from Thepublic.in website: https://www.thepublic.in/english/religion/planets-in-astrology/planet-uranus-planet-astrology-uranus-in-astrology-uranus-astrology-uranus-planet-in-astrology-uranus-planet-astrology-meaning-uranus-importance-to-astrology-usa-uk-canada-india-australia

Uranus, god of the sky, in Astrology/zodiac. (2015, May 8). Retrieved from Cafeastrology.com website: https://cafeastrology.com/uranus.html

Uranus in Astrology. (2018, June 22). Retrieved from Askastrology.com website: https://askastrology.com/astrology/astrology-planets/uranus/

AstroTwins. (2016, November 8). Planets & Astrology: Uranus. Retrieved from Astrostyle.com website: https://astrostyle.com/astrology-planets-uranus/

Dr. R Nageswara Rao, vedic indian astrologer from http://www. askastrologer.com. (n.d.). Astrology Uranus and computer profession, link between Uranus and computer technology-askastrologer.com. Retrieved from Askastrologer.com website: https://askastrologer.com/articles/Uranusandcomputerprofession.html

Gulino, E. (2020, July 17). How Uranus, the planet of rebellion, rules a generation. Retrieved from Refinery29 website: https://www.refinery29.com/en-us/2020/07/9916358/astrology-birth-chart-uranus-signs-meaning

Rahu and Ketu. (2014, May 16). Retrieved from Net.au website: https://vedicastrology.net.au/blog/vedic-articles/rahu-and-ketu/

Roberts, T. (2014, July 11). Uranus – meaning and influence in Astrology. Retrieved from Insightfulpsychics.com website: https://www.insightfulpsychics.com/uranus-planets-astrology/

Uranus in the signs: What your Uranus placement means for you. (n.d.). Retrieved from Vice.com website: https://www.vice.com/en/article/akweyz/what-does-uranus-in-the-signs-mean-in-my-birth-chart

Denise. (2019a, May 4). Uranus in 1st house: How it determines your personality and Destiny. Retrieved from Thehoroscope.co website: https://i.thehoroscope.co/uranus-in-1st-house-how-it-determines-your-personality-and-destiny/

Denise. (2019b, May 4). Uranus in 2nd house: How it determines your personality and Destiny. Retrieved from Thehoroscope.co website: https://i.thehoroscope.co/uranus-in-2nd-house-how-it-determines-your-personality-and-destiny/

Denise. (2019c, May 4). Uranus in 3rd house: How it determines your personality and Destiny. Retrieved from Thehoroscope.co website: https://i.thehoroscope.co/uranus-in-3rd-house-how-it-determines-your-personality-and-destiny/

Stargazer. (2020, July 21). Uranus in fourth house natal in astrology: The black sheep. Retrieved from Advanced-astrology.com website: https://advanced-astrology.com/uranus-in-fourth-house-natal/

6th house in astrology: Planets in the 6th house. (n.d.). Retrieved from Southfloridaastrologer.com website: https://www.southfloridaastrologer.com/6th-house-in-astrology-planets-in-the-6th-house.html

A person who has Uranus and Neptune in the 8th natal house, will he die young? - Quora. (n.d.). Retrieved from Quora.com website: https://www.quora.com/A-person-who-has-Uranus-and-Neptune-in-the-8th-natal-house-will-he-die-young

Uranus in 7th house. (2019, October 9). Retrieved from Futurescopeastrology.com website: https://futurescopeastrology.com/learn-astrology/uranus-in-7th-house/

Astrohealer. (2017, March 9). 10th House Uranus, 11th House Uranus, 12th House Uranus. Retrieved from Astrohealer.com website: https://www.astrohealer.com/desire-to-separate-uranus-in-the-birth-chart-pt-4-houses-10-11-12/

Faragher, A. K. (2018, October 6). The 12 Houses of astrology: Interpreting beyond the zodiac. Retrieved from Allure website: https://www.allure.com/story/12-astrology-houses-meaning

Uranus in the houses of the natal chart. (2015, April 18). Retrieved from Cafeastrology.com website: https://cafeastrology.com/articles/uranusinhouses.html

View all posts by Sagittarian Mind ConsultingTM. (2018, September 22). Uranus in the 9th house: The futuristic philosopher. Retrieved from Wordpress.com website: https://sagmind.wordpress.com/2018/09/22/uranus-in-the-9th-house-the-futuristic-philosopher/

(N.d.-d). Retrieved from Ganeshaspeaks.com website: https://www.ganeshaspeaks.com/predictions/astrology/effects-of-uranus-with-relation-to-other-planets-2937/

(N.d.-c). Retrieved from Astrologi.no website: https://www.astrologi.no/images/stories/gh/Guides/alan%20oken%20uranus.pdf

Nelson, D. (2021, January 20). You can get a rare look at Uranus between Mars & the moon tonight. Retrieved from Thrillist website: https://www.thrillist.com/news/nation/mars-uranus-conjunction-2021

Hall, M. (n.d.). How to Understand Trines. Retrieved from Liveabout.com website: https://www.liveabout.com/defintion-of-trine-206535

Square Aspect Meaning in Astrology. (2018, February 5). Retrieved from Labyrinthos. co website: https://labyrinthos.co/blogs/astrology-horoscope-zodiac-signs/square-aspect-meaning

DeSimone, M. (2019, May 3). The astrology of the midlife crisis. Retrieved from Tarot.com website: https://www.tarot.com/astrology/midlife-crisis

Hall, M. (n.d.). Uranus: The planets in astrology. Retrieved from Liveabout.com website: https://www.liveabout.com/uranus-the-planets-in-astrology-206370

Kathryn. (2020, November 26). Mid-Life Crisis Astrology Transits: How to navigate the big 3. Retrieved from Kathrynhocking.com website: https://kathrynhocking.com/mid-life-crisis-transits-astrology/

Lazić, M. (2020, April 5). Transiting Uranus in aspect to natal planets. Retrieved from Astrodetoks.com website: https://www.astrodetoks.com/transiting-uranus-in-aspect-to-natal-planets/?lang=en

Shaw, M. (2005, April 11). The Uranus Opposition. Retrieved from Llewellyn.com website: https://www.llewellyn.com/journal/article/787

Surtees, K. (2020, January 16). Working With Uranus Transits: Cycles of Change + breakthrough. Retrieved from Kellysastrology.com website: https://www.kellysastrology.com/2020/01/15/working-with-uranus-cycles-of-change-breakthrough/

The Uranus Opposition and the "mid-life crisis" - Human Design collective. (2019, November 6). Retrieved from Humandesigncollective.com website: https://humandesigncollective.com/blog/the-uranus-opposition-and-the-mid-life-crisis/

Transit Uranus. (n.d.). Retrieved from Thedarkpixieastrology.com website: http://www.thedarkpixieastrology.com/transit-uranus.html

Uranus, god of the sky, in Astrology/zodiac. (2015, May 8). Retrieved from Cafeastrology.com website: https://cafeastrology.com/uranus.html

Uranus Opposition: The midlife crisis. (2019, March 5). Retrieved from Foreverconscious.com website: https://foreverconscious.com/uranus-opposition-the-midlife-crisis

Roberts, T. (2014, July 11). Uranus – meaning and influence in Astrology. Retrieved from Insightfulpsychics.com website: https://www.insightfulpsychics.com/uranus-planets-astrology/

Surtees, K. (2020, January 16). Working With Uranus Transits: Cycles of Change + breakthrough. Retrieved from Kellysastrology.com website: https://www.kellysastrology.com/2020/01/15/working-with-uranus-cycles-of-change-breakthrough/

Vishnu. (2012, August 16). 6 life lessons on embracing change and impermanence. Retrieved from Tinybuddha.com website: https://tinybuddha.com/blog/6-life-lessons-on-embracing-change-and-impermanence/

Connelly, A. (2018, November 6). 10 ways you can change the world today. Retrieved from Org.au website: https://www.amnesty.org.au/10-ways-can-change-world-today/

What is Self-Acceptance? 25 Exercises + Definition and Quotes. (2018, July 12). Retrieved from Positivepsychology.com website: https://positivepsychology.com/self-acceptance/

Allemana, Brian. "An Astrological View of Nelson Mandela." Soulrise Astrology. December 7, 2013. https://soulriseastrology.com/2013/12/07/an-astrological-view-of-nelson-mandela/

Anand, Anju. "PLUTO." Astro Surkhiyan. Accessed August 1, 2021. https://astrosurkhiyan.blogspot.com/2014/03/pluto.html

Astrobix. "Astrology Pluto – Pluto Astrology." Accessed August 1, 2021. https://astrobix.com/astrosight/454-astrology-pluto-pluto-astrology.html

Astrology.Com. "Pluto." September 25, 2017. https://www.astrology.com/planets/pluto

Astrology Library. "Pluto in the Houses — Interpretations." November 15, 2009. https://astrolibrary.org/interpretations/pluto-house/

Astrology.TV. "Pluto in your birth chart: A guide to evolution and power." December 18, 2019. https://astrology.tv/evolution-and-power-a-guide-to-pluto-in-your-birth-chart/

Balz, Dan, and Miller, Greg. "America convulses amid a week of protests, but can it change?" The Washington Post. June 6, 2020. https://www.washingtonpost.com/graphics/2020/politics/protests-reckoning/

Banerjee, Nikita. (2015, July 14). "Exploring Pluto and its significance in astrology." The Retrieved from Times Of India. July 14, 2015. https://timesofindia.indiatimes.com/astrology/planets-transits/exploring-pluto-and-its-significance-in-astrology/articleshow/68206865.cms

Blaze-Maximus. (2020, July 1). "Pluto: Core Significations." Astrobymax. July 1, 2021. https://astrobymax.com/blog/pluto-core-significations

Bonotti, Matteo., and Zech, Steven. T. (2021). "The human, economic, social, and political costs of COVID-19." *Recovering Civility during COVID-19*, (March 2021): 1–36. https://doi.org/10.1007/978-981-33-6706-7_1

Bree. "Higher and Lower Pluto – What Does it Mean?" Spiritual Design Astrology. July 14, 2018. https://www.spiritualdesignastrology.com/higher-and-lower-pluto-what-does-it-mean/

Cafe Astrology.com. "Pluto." May 8, 2015. https://cafeastrology.com/pluto.html

Cafe Astrology.com. "Pluto in the Houses." April 13, 2015. https://cafeastrology.com/articles/plutoinhouses.html

Chernoff, Mark. "9 rules for Turning Endings into New Beginnings." Marc and Angel Hack Life. September 28, 2012. https://www.marcandangel.com/2012/09/28/9-rules-for-turning-endings-into-new-beginnings/

Cosmic Occult. "Generational Planets." August 8, 2017. https://www.cosmicoccult.com/generational-planets/

Denise. "Pluto in Scorpio: How It Shapes Your Personality and Life." The Horoscope.co. August 22, 2018. https://i.thehoroscope.co/pluto-in-scorpio-how-it-shapes-your-personality-and-life/

Desai, Dipali. "What Happens When You Embrace Pluto's Symbolism?" Celestial Space. September 17, 2008. https://celestialspace.wordpress.com/2008/09/17/embrace-plutos-symbolism/

The Editors of Encyclopaedia Britannica. "Hades." Encyclopedia Britannica. Accessed August 1, 2021. https://www.britannica.com/editor/The-Editors-of-Encyclopaedia-Britannica/4419

Edrawsoft. "How to create a life map (With examples)." Accessed August 1, 2021. https://www.mindmaster.io/how-to-create-a-life-map-with-examples.html

Elisha, Omri. "Placing the pandemic in time: Astrology and Covid-19." Social Science Research Council. August 13, 2020. https://tif.ssrc.org/2020/08/13/placing-the-pandemic-in-time-astrology-and-covid-19/

Gill, N. S. "Who Was the Roman and Greek God Pluto?" Retrieved from ThoughtCo. May 30, 2019. https://www.thoughtco.com/pluto-111868

Goldsmid, Edmund, Grube, Herman, and Kirchmayer, Georg K. *Un-Natural history, or Myths of Ancient Science; Being a Collection of Curious Tracts on the Basilisk, Unicorn, Phoenix, Behemoth or Leviathan, Dragon, Giant spider, Tarantula, Chameleons, Satyrs, Homines Caudati &c., Now First Tr. From the Latin, and Ed.* Franklin Classics, 2018.

Guinn, Jeff. "Manson: the life and times of Charles Manson." Simon & Schuster: 2003. https://archive.org/details/isbn_9781451645163_0

Hall, Molly. "Pluto's Meaning in Astrology." Liveaboutdotcom. June 11, 2018. https://www.liveabout.com/plutos-meaning-in-astrology-206366

Harness, Dennis M. "Pluto: A Neo-Vedic View." Dennis Harness. June 20, 2020. https://dennisharness.com/articles/pluto-a-neo-vedic-view/

Hickey, Isabel. "Pluto: Our Inner Darkness Before the Dawn." InnerSelf. March 28, 2021. https://innerself.com/content/personal/intuition-awareness/astrology/planets-transits/5583-pluto-our-inner-darkness.html

Impey, Chris. "Conservation of Energy." Teach Astronomy. Accessed August 1, 2021. https://www.teachastronomy.com/textbook/Matter-and-Energy-in-the-Universe/Conservation-of-Energy/

Keiko. "Pluto – Planet of Destruction and Regeneration." July 22, 2020. https://www.keikopowerwish.com/blog/pluto-planet-of-destruction-and-regenerationnbsp

Labyrinthos. "Astrology Planets and their Meanings, Planet symbols, and Cheat Sheet." January 27, 2008. https://labyrinthos.co/blogs/astrology-horoscope-zodiac-signs/astrology-planets-and-their-meanings-planet-symbols-and-cheat-sheet

Labyrinthos. "Pluto Astrology Symbol – Characteristics, Planet Energy and More." January 26, 2018. https://labyrinthos.co/blogs/astrology-horoscope-zodiac-signs/pluto-astrology-symbol-characteristics-planet-energy

Lantz C.Ht., Patricia. "Meaning and Onfluence of Pluto in Astrology." Love to Know. Accessed August 1, 2021. https://horoscopes.lovetoknow.com/about-astrology/meaning-influence-pluto-astrology

The Magi Associates, Inc. "Magi Astrology." Accessed August 1, 2021. https://magiastrology.com/accuratesymbolisms.html

Mentior, Trudi. "What Your Pluto Sign Means — And How To Find Yours." YourTango. January 13, 2021. https://www.yourtango.com/2017306943/whats-your-pluto-sign-how-it-affects-personality-love-life

Myastrologycharts.com. "Pluto in Gemini." Accessed August 1, 2021. https://www.myastrologycharts.com/plutoingemini.php

Myastrologycharts.com. "Pluto in Sagittarius." Accessed August 1, 2021. https://www.myastrologycharts.com/plutoinsagittarius.php

Myth and Astrology. "Shiva's Shakti and Charon." June 7, 2016. https://mythandastrology.wordpress.com/2016/06/07/shivas-shakti-and-charon/

NASA. "All About Pluto." March 9, 2021. https://spaceplace.nasa.gov/ice-dwarf/en/

NASA. "Pluto." Accessed August 1, 2021. https://solarsystem.nasa.gov/planets/dwarf-planets/pluto/overview/

Osborne, Richard. "Collective Unconscious." *Megawords: 200 Terms You Really Need to Know*, (2001): 77–78. http://dx.doi.org/10.4135/9781446221532.n49

Pattanaik, Devdutt. *Shiva: An Introduction*. Mumbai: Vakils Feffer & Simons, 1997.

Penprase, Bryan. *Stars, Supernovae, and their Aftermath*. Lulu, 2011.

Pironti, Pierluigi. "Post-war Welfare Policies (Version 1.1)." In Ute Daniel, Peter, Gatrell, Oliver Janz, Heather Jones, Jennifer Keene, Alan Kramer, and Bill Nasson (Eds.), *International Encyclopedia of the First World War*, (2017). http://dx.doi.org/10.15463/ie1418.10358/1.1

Psychologies. "Exercises to manage new life transitions." October 22, 2017. https://www.psychologies.co.uk/exercises-manage-new-life-transitions

Radford, Tim. "There may be life on Pluto's moon, say Nasa scientists." The Guardian. January 27, 1999. http://www.theguardian.com/uk/1999/jan/27/timradford

Regula, DeTraci. "Fast Facts on Hades." ThoughtCo. March 22, 2019. https://www.thoughtco.com/facts-about-greek-god-hades-1524423

Rocking Baba. "Planetary Transit – How Long Does A Planet Stay In A Sign." November 20, 2015. https://www.rockingbaba.com/blog/index.php/2015/11/30/planetary-transit-how-long-does-a-planet-stay-in-a-sign/

South Florida Astrologer. "Pluto in the Houses..." Accessed August 1, 2021. https://www.southfloridaastrologer.com/pluto-in-the-houses.html

Stardust, Lisa. "Big Pluto energy: How to Embrace the Most Intense Planet in Astrology." Cosmopolitan. January 14, 2021. https://www.cosmopolitan.com/lifestyle/a29993224/pluto-astrology-meaning-significance/

Stardust, Lisa. "When It Comes to Astrology, if Pluto Isn't Your Fave Planet, You're Not Paying Attention." Cosmopolitan. January 13, 2021. https://www.cosmopolitan.com/lifestyle/a29993224/pluto-astrology-meaning-significance/, https://cafeastrology.com/pluto.html

Stargazer. "Pluto in Eighth House Natal Meaning in Astrology. Astrology. September 11, 2021. https://advanced-astrology.com/pluto-in-eighth-house-natal/

Stargazer. "Pluto in Eleventh House Natal Meaning in Astrology." Astrology. September 14, 2020. https://advanced-astrology.com/pluto-in-eleventh-house-natal/

Stargazer. "Pluto in First House Natal Meaning in Astrology." Astrology. August 26, 2020. https://advanced-astrology.com/pluto-in-first-house-natal

Stargazer. "Pluto in Fourth House Natal Meaning in Astrology." Astrology. Septermber 4, 2020. https://advanced-astrology.com/pluto-in-fourth-house-natal-meaning-in-astrology/

Stargazer. "Pluto in Houses in Astrology." Astrology. September 1, 2020. https://advanced-astrology.com/pluto-in-houses/

Stargazer. "Pluto in Ninth House Natal Meaning in Astrology: A Powerful Mind." Astrology. September 12, 2020. https://advanced-astrology.com/pluto-in-ninth-house-natal/

Stargazer. "Pluto in Second House Natal Meaning in Astrology." Astrology. August 30, 2020. https://advanced-astrology.com/pluto-in-second-house-natal/

Stargazer. "Pluto in Tenth House Natal Meaning in Astrology." Astrology. September 13, 2020. https://advanced-astrology.com/pluto-in-tenth-house-natal/

Stargazer. "Pluto in Third House Natal Meaning in Astrology: Knowledge Is Power." Astrology. September 1, 2020. https://advanced-astrology.com/pluto-in-third-house-natal

Stargazer. "Pluto in Twelfth House Natal Meaning in Astrology." Astrology. September 18, 2020. https://advanced-astrology.com/pluto-in-twelfth-house-natal/

Talbert, Tricia. "Five Years after New Horizons' Historic Flyby, Here Are 10 Cool Things We Learned About Pluto." NASA. July 15, 2020. https://www.nasa.gov/feature/five-years-after-new-horizons-historic-flyby-here-are-10-cool-things-we-learned-about-plut-0

Tamplin, Ed. "2020 Astrology — The dawn of a new world." WellBeing. February 5, 2020. https://www.wellbeing.com.au/mind-spirit/astrology/2020-dawn-new-world.html

Tarot.com Staff. "Pluto." (2011, July 11). https://www.tarot.com/astrology/planets/pluto

Tate. "Nine Ways Artists responded to the First World War." Accessed August 1, 2021. https://www.tate.org.uk/whats-on/tate-britain/exhibition/aftermath/nine-ways-artists-responded-first-world-war

Topaz, Julia. (2017, November 18). "Pluto in the 6th house: Mental overheating." Lookupthestars. November 18, 2017. https://www.lookupthestars.com/post/pluto-in-the-6th-house-mental-overheating

United States Holocaust Memorial Museum. "Adolf Hitler and World War I: 1913–1919. Holocaust Encylopedia. Accessed August 1, 2021. https://encyclopedia.ushmm.org/content/en/article/adolf-hitler-and-world-war-i-1913-1919

Writing for self-discovery. "The care and feeding of a Pluto soul." June 14, 2019. https://writingforselfdiscovery.com/2019/06/14/the-care-and-feeding-of-a-pluto-soul

Casement, Patrick J. *Learning from the Patient.* New York: Guilford Press, 1991.

Chopra, Deepak, and Rudolph E. Tanzi. *Super Brain: Unleashing the Explosive Power of Your Mind to Maximize Health, Happiness, and Spiritual Well-Being.* New York: Harmony Publishing, 2012.

Erikson, Erik H. *Childhood and Society.* New York: Norton, 1950.

Frey, William H., and Muriel Langseth. *Crying: The Mystery of Tears.* Winston-Salem: Winston Press, 1985.

Hand Clow, Barbara. *Chiron: Rainbow Bridge between the Inner and Outer Planets.* Saint Paul: Llewellyn Publications, 1994.

Hay, Louise. *The Power is Within You.* Carlsbad: Hay House, 1991.

Jung, C. G. *Memories, Dreams, Reflections.* New York: Pantheon Books, 1963.

Kessler, David. *Finding Meaning: The Sixth Stage of Grief.* New York: Scribner, 2019.

Lakhiani, Vishen. *The Code of the Extraordinary Mind: 10 Unconventional Laws to Redefine Your Life and Succeed On Your Own Terms.* Emmaus: Rodale Books, 2016.

Smith, William, ed. *Dictionary of Greek and Roman Biography and Mythology.* London: Taylor, Walton, and Maberly / John Murray, 1849.

www.ingramcontent.com/pod-product-compliance
Lightning Source LLC
Chambersburg PA
CBHW031934090426
42811CB00002B/177